'The complex interplay between financial innovation, risk and regulation escapes the understanding of narrow disciplinary perspectives. These essays provide a rich and determinedly multi-disciplinary approach that offers new theoretical insights that might also help shape future policy and regulatory reform.'

Andrew Leyshon, *Professor of Economic Geography, University of Nottingham, UK*

'Ertürk and Gabor have assembled an impressive range of top scholars to explore the global regulatory response to the 2008 financial crisis. They do an immense service to the cause of understanding this complicated event, which still casts a spell over our economies and politics.'

Randall Germain, *Professor of Political Science, Carleton University, Canada*

'This impressive cutting edge collection of essays stands out both for its breadth of topics and the multi-disciplinary group of heterodox experts to analyse the transformation of banking institutions. Given that governments had to devote an unprecedented ratio of annual GDP to rescuing banks, this comprehensive compendium is not only timely, but fills an important vacuum in understanding the global paradigm shift in banking since the financial crisis.'

Brigitte Young, *Professor Emeritus of International Political Science, University of Muenster, Germany*

Routledge Companions in Business, Management and Accounting

Routledge Companions in Business, Management and Accounting are prestige reference works providing an overview of a whole subject area or sub-discipline. These books survey the state of the discipline including emerging and cutting edge areas. Providing a comprehensive, up to date, definitive work of reference, Routledge Companions can be cited as an authoritative source on the subject.

A key aspect of these Routledge Companions is their international scope and relevance. Edited by an array of highly regarded scholars, these volumes also benefit from teams of contributors which reflect an international range of perspectives.

Individually, Routledge Companions in Business, Management and Accounting provide an impactful one-stop-shop resource for each theme covered. Collectively, they represent a comprehensive learning and research resource for researchers, postgraduate students and practitioners.

Published titles in this series include:

The Routledge Companion to Critical Management Studies
Edited by Anshuman Prasad, Pushkala Prasad, Albert J. Mills and Jean Helms Mills

The Routledge Handbook of Responsible Investment
Edited by Tessa Hebb, James P. Hawley, Andreas G.F. Hoepner, Agnes Neher and David Wood

The Routledge Handbook to Critical Public Relations
Edited by Jacquie L'Etang, David McKie, Nancy Snow and Jordi Xifra

The Routledge Companion to Consumer Behaviour Analysis
Edited by Gordon R. Foxall

The Routledge Companion to Philosophy in Organization Studies
Edited by Raza Mir, Hugh Willmott and Michelle Greenwood

The Routledge Companion to Network Industries
Edited by Matthias Finger and Christian Jaag

The Routledge Companion to Strategic Risk Management
Edited by Torben J. Andersen

The Routledge Companion to Philanthropy
Edited by Tobias Jung, Susan Phillips and Jenny Harrow

The Routledge Companion to Marketing History
Edited by D.G. Brian Jones and Mark Tadajewski

The Routledge Companion to Reinventing Management Education
Edited by Chris Steyaert, Timon Beyes and Martin Parker

The Routledge Companion to the Professions and Professionalism
Edited by Mike Dent, Ivy Bourgeault, Jean-Louis Denis and Ellen Kuhlmann

The Routledge Companion to Contemporary Brand Management
Edited by Francesca Dall'Olmo Riley, Jaywant Singh and Charles Blankson

The Routledge Companion to Banking Regulation and Reform
Edited by Ismail Ertürk and Daniela Gabor

The Routledge Companion to Banking Regulation and Reform

The Routledge Companion to Banking Regulation and Reform provides a prestigious cutting edge international reference work offering students, researchers and policy makers a comprehensive guide to the paradigm shift in banking studies since the historic financial crisis in 2007. The transformation in banking over the last two decades has not been authoritatively or critically analysed by the mainstream academic literature. This unique collection brings together a multidisciplinary group of leading authorities in the field to analyse and investigate post-crisis regulation and reform. Representing the wide spectrum of non-mainstream economics and finance, topics range widely from financial innovation to misconduct in banking, varieties of Eurozone banking to reforming dysfunctional global banking as well as topical issues such as off-shore financial centres, Libor fixing, corporate governance and the Dodd–Frank Act.

Bringing together an authoritative range of international experts and perspectives, this invaluable body of heterodox research work provides a comprehensive compendium for researchers and academics of banking and finance as well as regulators and policy makers concerned with the global impact of financial institutions.

Ismail Ertürk is Senior Lecturer in Banking at Alliance Manchester Business School, the University of Manchester, UK.

Daniela Gabor is Associate Professor in Economics at the University of the West of England Bristol, UK.

The Routledge Companion to Banking Regulation and Reform

Edited by Ismail Ertürk and Daniela Gabor

LONDON AND NEW YORK

First published 2017
by Routledge
2 Park Square, Milton Park, Abingdon, Oxon OX14 4RN

And by Routledge
711 Third Avenue, New York, NY 10017

Routledge is an imprint of the Taylor & Francis Group, an informa business

© 2017 selection and editorial material, Ismail Ertürk and Daniela Gabor; individual chapters, the contributors

The right of the editor to be identified as the author of the editorial material, and of the authors for their individual chapters, has been asserted in accordance with sections 77 and 78 of the Copyright, Designs and Patents Act 1988.

All rights reserved. No part of this book may be reprinted or reproduced or utilised in any form or by any electronic, mechanical, or other means, now known or hereafter invented, including photocopying and recording, or in any information storage or retrieval system, without permission in writing from the publishers.

Every effort has been made to contact copyright holders for their permission to reprint material in this book. The publishers would be grateful to hear from any copyright holder who is not here acknowledged and will undertake to rectify any errors or omissions in future editions of this book.

Trademark notice: Product or corporate names may be trademarks or registered trademarks, and are used only for identification and explanation without intent to infringe.

British Library Cataloguing in Publication Data
A catalogue record for this book is available from the British Library

Library of Congress Cataloging in Publication Data
Names: Ertürk, Ismail, editor. | Gabor, Daniela, editor.
Title: The Routledge companion to banking regulation and reform/edited by Ismail Ertürk and Daniela Gabor.
Description: Abingdon, Oxon; New York, NY: Routledge, 2017. |
Series: Routledge companions in business, management and accounting
Identifiers: LCCN 2016011588 | ISBN 9780415855938 (hardback) |
ISBN 9780203733462 (ebook)
Subjects: LCSH: Banks and banking–State supervision. | Banks and banking–Government policy. | Banking law. | International finance. | International finance–Law and legislation. | Financial institutions–Law and legislation.
Classification: LCC HG1725.R68 2017 | DDC 332.1–dc23LC record available at https://lccn.loc.gov/2016011588

ISBN: 978-0-415-85593-8 (hbk)
ISBN: 978-0-203-73346-2 (ebk)

Typeset in Bembo
by Sunrise Setting Ltd, Brixham, UK

Contents

List of figures	x
List of tables	xii
List of contributors	xiii
Acknowledgements	xxi

Introduction   1
Ismail Ertürk and Daniela Gabor

PART I
Knowledges of credit risk and bank regulation   7

1 The credit crisis as a problem in the sociology of knowledge   9
   Donald MacKenzie

2 What's in a name? Provident, The People's Bank and the regulation of brand identity   55
   Liz McFall

3 Reflexivity of shadow banking   74
   Benjamin Wilhelm

4 Interrogating the crisis: financial instruments, public policy and corporate governance   84
   Hugh Willmott

PART II
Critical perspectives on financial innovation   109

5 Reconceptualizing financial innovation: frame, conjuncture and bricolage   111
   Ewald Engelen, Ismail Ertürk, Julie Froud, Adam Leaver and Karel Williams

6 Europe's toxic twins: government debt in financialized times   134
   Daniela Gabor and Cornel Ban

Contents

7   Variegated geographies of finance: international financial centres and
    the (re)production of financial working cultures   149
    Sarah Hall

8   The boundaries of finance as zones of conflicts   159
    Sabine Montagne

PART III
**New approaches to banking, risk and central bank
role in the Eurozone**   **173**

9   The new behemoth?: the ECB and the financial supervision reforms
    during the Eurozone crisis   175
    Clément Fontan

10 Varieties of capitalism and banking in the EU   192
    Iain Hardie

11 The financialisation of local governments: evidence from the Italian case   208
    Andrea Lagna

PART IV
Regulation of misconduct in banking   **223**

12 Libor and Euribor: from normal banking practice to manipulation
    to the potential for reform   225
    Daniel Seabra Lopes

13 Hedge funds: past and present   240
    Photis Lysandrou

14 Offshore financial centres and tax evasion in banking   250
    Silke Ötsch and Michaela Schmidt

PART V
Limits of post-crisis bank regulation   **271**

15 Post-crisis bank regulation and financialized bank business models   273
    Ian Crowther and Ismail Ertürk

16 Financial market regulation: still a regime removed from politics?   289
    Nicholas Dorn

17 Prudential regulation in the age of internal models   303
    José Gabilondo

18 Defences against systemic risk: a greater role and responsibility for
    bank lawyers? Judgement-based bank supervision   317
    Joanna Gray and Peter Metzing

19 Shattering Glass–Steagall: the power of financial industries
    to overcome restraints   335
    Paul M. Hirsch, Jo-Ellen Pozner, and Mary Katherine Stimmler

PART VI
Dysfunctional global finance and banking reform   **349**

20 How finance globalized: a tale of two cities   351
    Gary A. Dymski and Annina Kaltenbrunner

21 How the American financial meltdown of 2008 caused
    the global financial crisis   373
    Neil Fligstein and Jacob Habinek

22 Reforming the culture of banking   398
    Grahame Thompson

23 Consumer finance and the social dimension of banks in a global economy   411
    Toni Williams

Index   427

Figures

1.1	Rating grades	13
1.2	An ABS or CDO	19
1.3	Schematic structure of a typical subprime mortgage-backed security	22
1.4	Packaging tranches of subprime mortgage-backed securities into ABS CDOs	31
2.1	Provident shopping guides, 1954; 1934	58
2.2	The Provident system, 1957 shopping guide	59
2.3	Provident points in the 1961 shopping guide reworked as customer values in 1966 shopping guide	65
2.4	1965 Marketing sample	66
5.1	J.P. Morgan's securitization for RBS	120
6.1	Share of customer deposit in total bank funding, June 2010	138
6.2	Share of domestic government debt in total government debt portfolios, selected European banking sectors, June 2010	143
10.1	Bank assets to GDP, selected EU countries, 1980–2011	195
10.2	Loans and advances as a percentage of bank assets, selected EU countries, 2008–12	198
10.3	Holding of financial assets as a percentage of total bank assets, selected EU countries, 2008–12	198
10.4	Customer funding gap, selected EU countries, 2008–12	201
12.1	Generic information about Libor and Euribor, December 2015	229
15.1	Convergence to 15% ROE in pre-crisis banking	277
15.2	Northern Rock's lower capitalization under Basel II	278
15.3	Manipulation of risk valuation models at J.P. Morgan Chase	283
17.1	Bank's financial balance sheet	305
17.2	Regulatory balance sheet – net of intangibles, write offs, debt-funded assets, and liabilities	306
20.1	Assets of largest bank as % of GDP, selected countries: 1989, 1997, 2004, and 2012	355
20.2	Financial exports as % of all exports, 2005–2012: UK, US, Euro Area	355
20.3	Financial exports as % of GDP, 2005–2012: UK, US, Euro Area, Brazil	356
20.4	Financial and Insurance imports as % of GDP, 2005–2012: UK, US, Euro Area, Brazil	356
20.5	High-tech manufacturing exports as % of all exports, 2005–2012: UK, US, Euro area	357
20.6	Domestic credit to private sector as % of GDP, 1995–2012: UK, US, Euro Area	360

20.7	Net loans and leases as percentage of assets, selected large U.S. bank holding companies: 2007–2013	361
20.8	Core Deposits as % of Assets, selected large U.S. bank holding companies: 2007–2013	361
20.9	Derivatives as % assets, selected large U.S. bank holding companies: 2007–2013	362
20.10	(a) Trough-to-peak GDP and Loan Growth, U.S. Commercial Banks, Average annual % change, Five-year time-spans, 1969-1990. (b) Trough-to-peak GDP and Loan Growth, U.S. Commercial Banks, Average annual % change, Five-year time-spans, 1991 to present	364
20.11	(a) Outstanding real-estate-secured loans, at "Big Four" and all other US commercial banks, in trillions of 2005 dollars, 2002–2011. (b) Outstanding commercial and industrial loans at "Big Four" and all other US commercial banks, in trillions of 2010 dollars, 2002–2013. (c) Outstanding loans to individuals at "Big Four" and all other US commercial banks, in trillions of 2005 dollars, 2002–2011	365
21.1	Mortgage related security holdings of four largest investor types	382
21.2	Model of process of bank crises and recession	385

Tables

1.1	CDO evaluator's three-year default probability assumptions versus realized default rate of US subprime mortgage-backed securities issued from 2005 to 2007	34
6.1	Participants in sovereign bond markets (holdings as % of overall volume, 2010)	140
9.1	Macro and micro prudential supervision in Europe	176
12.1	Excel spreadsheet used for internally informing of the Euribor rate values in one Portuguese retail bank	228
12.2	List of the main public consultations on financial benchmarks, in chronological order	231
19.1	Rhetoric dissociating the Glass–Steagall Act from its moral foundations	341
21.1	Foreign countries with the highest amount of MBS/GDP, 2006	383
21.2	Largest sponsors of ABCP conduits with country of origin	384
21.3	List of countries in the analysis, by first year negative change in GDP	386
21.4	Countries that experienced a banking crisis, 2008–09	387
21.5	Summary statistics	389
21.6	Correlation matrix	390
21.7	Logit models of systemic banking crisis	391
21.8	OLS models of 2009 change in GDP	392
23.1	Household debt, total % of net disposable income, 2000–13	414
23.2	The unequal distribution of debt among British households, 2000–06	416

Contributors

Ban, Cornel (University of Boston) Cornel Ban is Assistant Professor of International Relations at Boston University's Frederick S. Pardee School for Global Studies. He specializes in international political economy and has published articles in *Review of International Political Economy*, *Governance*, *Journal of Common Market Studies* and *East European Politics and Societies*. His book *Ruling Ideas: How Global Neoliberalism Goes Local* is forthcoming with Oxford University Press

Crowther, Ian (Alliance Manchester Business School, University of Manchester) Ian Crowther, ACA, LL.M (Lancaster), joined the University of Manchester Business School as a PhD candidate in Business and Management during August 2013. Over a 16-year period, Ian has worked at numerous London-based banking institutions as a Director, specializing in syndicated finance and in particular private equity driven leveraged buy-outs. Ian has also held senior positions in loan origination, portfolio management and secondary trading of primary and distressed situations pre- and post-global financial crisis, as well as sitting on the European Loan Market Association's Legal Documentation and Trade Practices Committee. Through to 2016, Ian will be completing his doctorate on a critique of UK-based banking regulation: heavily influenced by literatures on financialization, and both cultural and political economy.

Dymski, Gary A. (Economics Division, Leeds University Business School, University of Leeds) Gary Dymski holds a BA in Urban Studies from the University of Pennsylvania, an MPA from Syracuse University, and a PhD in Economics from the University of Massachusetts, Amherst. He has been a Research Fellow in Economic Studies at the Brookings Institution, and an Assistant Professor of Economics at the University of Southern California, prior to joining the University of California, Riverside economics faculty in 1991. From 2003 to 2009 Gary served as founding executive director of the University of California Center Sacramento, the University of California's academic public-policy program in California's state capitol. He joined the Leeds University Business School in 2012 as Professor of Applied Economics. Gary has done research on racial and gender discrimination and redlining in credit markets, on ethnic banking in Los Angeles, on financial exclusion, and on financial crises and community economic development. Current research topics include the subprime and Eurozone crises, financial regulation and financialization, and inequality and economic development.

Dorn, Nicholas (Institute of Advanced Legal Studies, London and Erasmus University, Rotterdam) Nicholas Dorn is a sociologist with interests in law, politics and markets. His book *Democracy and Diversity in Financial Market Regulation* was published by Routledge in 2014 and an edited collection, *Controlling Capital: Public and Private Regulation of Financial Markets*, in 2016.

Contributors

He has published on transnational governance, the European Union, public and private policing and economic crime. He has degrees from the universities of London, Middlesex and Kent. He is associated with the Institute of Advanced Legal Studies, London (Associate Fellow) and Erasmus School of Law, Rotterdam (retired professor).

Engelen, Ewald (University of Amsterdam) Ewald Engelen is the Professor of Financial Geography at University of Amsterdam. His research compares the political economy, financial geography and economic sociology, and focuses in particular on international financial centres, offshore finance, shadow banking, the Great Financial Crisis and crisis responses. He has published on these topics in *Environment & Planning A*, *Socio-Economic Review*, *New Political Economy*, *Economy and Society* and other journals and edited volumes. He co-authored *After the Great Complacence* (2011) from Oxford University Press. He appears regularly on Dutch radio and television and writes columns for *De Groene Amsterdammer*, *Het Parool* and *Tros in Bedrijf*.

Ertürk, Ismail (Alliance Manchester Business School, University of Manchester) Ismail Ertürk is Senior Lecturer in Banking at Alliance Manchester Business School, the University of Manchester. His current research interests are central bank unconventional policies after the crisis, banking crisis and reform, cultural economy, creative industries, financial innovation, financialization, and corporate governance. He has published widely in these areas in academic journals including *Economy and Society*, *Review of International Political Economy* and *Journal of Cultural Economy*. He has also collaborated with the contemporary artists Goldin+Senneby in producing critical art work on financial crisis. He co-edited *Financialisation at Work* (2008) from Routledge and co-authored *After the Great Complacence* (2011) from Oxford University Press. He participated in funded research programmes including European Social and Economic Models of Knowledge Economy and Centre for Research into Socio-cultural Change. He regularly comments on economy and banking on television, radio and print media, including BBC, Bloomberg TV, Channel 4, Sky News, *Financial Times*, *The Observer*, *The Telegraph*, and *Washington Post*.

Fligstein, Neil (University of California Berkeley) Neil Fligstein is the Class of 1939 Chancellor's Professor in the Department of Sociology at the University of California. He has made research contributions to the fields of economic sociology, organizational theory, and social stratification. He is the author of seven books including *The Transformation of Corporate Control* (Harvard University Press, 1993), *The Architecture of Markets* (Princeton University Press, 2001), Euroclash (Oxford University Press, 2008), and *A Theory of Fields* (with Doug McAdam, Oxford University Press, 2012). He is currently working on a book about the financial crisis.

Fontan, Clément (Montreal University) Clément Fontan holds a PhD in Political Science from Sciences-Po Grenoble. His thesis dealt with how the ECB extended its political influence and attributions during the Eurozone crisis. His research results are published in well-renowned French academic journals such as *Politique Européenne*, *Gouvernement et Action Publique* and *Pouvoirs*. Now a post-doctoral student at the Centre of Research in Ethics at Montreal University, his research focuses on inequalities generated by central banks and the crises of financial capitalism.

Froud, Julie (Alliance Manchester Business School, The University of Manchester) Julie Froud is Professor of Financial Innovation at Alliance Manchester Business School, The University of Manchester. Current research interests include developing an understanding of financialization as financial innovation, London as a city state and the role of financial and other elites. Recent ongoing work covers rebalancing the economy and rethinking industrial policy for the foundational economy.

Gabilondo, José (Florida International University) Born in Santiago de Cuba, José Gabilondo (A.B. Harvard; J.D. Boalt Hall) teaches banking law, corporate finance, and tax law at the Florida International University, where he served as Associate Dean for Academic Affairs. Before joining academia, he worked at the US Securities and Exchange Commission, the Office of the Comptroller of the Currency, US Department of the Treasury, and the World Bank. He has presented on business structure and financial law at conferences in Cuba on foreign investment and lawyering. Currently, he is writing a book on bank funding and liquidity after Basel III. He is co-author of *Corporate Finance: Debt, Equity, and Derivative Markets and Their Intermediaries* in the American Casebook Series. His recent articles have defended the Fed's post-crisis transformation into a market maker of last resort, examined risk-based capital standards for financial intermediaries, and analysed the leverage and liquidity dynamics of the new credit market.

Gabor, Daniela (University of the West England) Daniela Gabor is Associate Professor in Economics at the University of the West of England, Bristol. She holds a PhD in banking and finance from the University of Stirling (2009). Since then, she has published on central banking in crisis, on the governance of global banks and the IMF, on shadow banking and repo markets. Her latest publications include a co-edited book with Charles Goodhart, Jakob Vestegaard, and Ismail Ertürk entitled *Central Banking at Crossroads* (Anthem Press, 2014), 'Banking on bonds' (*Journal of Common Market Studies*, with Cornel Ban, 2015) and 'A step too far? The European FTT on shadow banking' (*Journal of European Public Policy*, 2015). With Jakob Vestegaard, she leads the INET grant Managing Shadow Money (2015–17), aiming to rethink money in an age of shadow banking. She tweets @DanielaGabor.

Gray, Joanna (Birmingham University) Joanna Gray is Professor of Financial Law and Regulation in the Law School at Birmingham University in the UK having been previously Professor of Financial Regulation at Newcastle Law School, University of Newcastle upon Tyne. She qualified as a lawyer in the City of London Solicitors in 1989, from 1997 to 1998 was a member of the Financial Services Law sub-committee of the Law Society Company Law Committee at a time when major financial regulatory reform was underway. She has taught on MBA and MSc programmes featuring financial regulatory law and has also conducted executive education and CPD activity for City of London law firms, for clients in the banking and finance sectors and for the IMF and Reserve Bank of India. Her published work includes *Implementing Financial Regulation: Theory and Practice* (Wiley Finance, 2006), and she co-edited *Financial Regulation in Crisis: The Role of Law and the Failure of Northern Rock* (Edward Elgar Financial Law Series, 2011) She has written extensively for both academic journals, such as *Journal of Corporate Law Studies* and *Capital Markets Law Journal,* and practitioner facing journals, such as the *Journal of Financial Regulation and Compliance.*

Habinek, Jacob (University of California Berkeley) Jacob Habinek is a graduate student in the Department of Sociology at the University of California. He is interested in organizational theory, the sociology of science, and social networks. His dissertation contains a set of connected papers that analyse how organizations are internally structured as a set of fields and how organizations are always part of larger fields.

Hall, Sarah (University of Nottingham) Sarah Hall is Professor of Economic Geography at the University of Nottingham. She holds degrees from the University of Cambridge and Bristol and previously taught at Loughborough University. Her research examines the geographies of the international financial system and has been supported by funding from the Economic and

Social Research Council, the British Academy, the Leverhulme Trust and the Nuffield Foundation. Research findings have been published in leading social scientific journals including *Journal of Economic Geography*, *Environment and Planning A* and *Transactions of the Institute of British Geographers*. She is currently a British Academy Mid Career Research Fellow, examining the development of London as the leading offshore renminbi centre and the role of the City in the internationalization of Chinese capital markets.

Hardie, Iain (University of Edinburgh) Iain Hardie is a Senior Lecturer in International Relations at the University of Edinburgh, where he completed a PhD in 2007 after an 18 year career in investment banking in London and Hong Kong. He is the author of *Financialization and Government Borrowing Capacity in Emerging Markets* (Palgrave, 2011) and co-editor of *Market-Based Banking and the International Financial Crisis* (Oxford University Press, 2013). His articles have appeared in journals including *World Politics*, *Review of International Political Economy*, *New Political Economy*, *The Sociological Review* and *Organization Studies*.

Hirsch, Paul M. (Kellogg School of Management, Northwestern University) Paul M. Hirsch is the James L. Allen Professor of Strategy & Organization at the Kellogg School of Management at Northwestern University. His recent work has focused on management and policy issues associated with the mortgage meltdown. He co-edited *Markets on Trial* (Emerald, 2010), one of the first volumes of original essays exploring the meltdown's origins and consequences. Professor Hirsch has received the Distinguished Scholar award of the Academy of Management's Organization and Management Theory Division, and served as President of the Western Academy of Management. He was among the first to anticipate and write on widespread changes in the employment relationship stemming from corporate mergers and continuing on through the present. Professor Hirsch received his PhD from the University of Michigan, and has held appointments at Indiana University, University of Chicago, the US Business School in Prague, and Northwestern University. He also has held visiting positions at Stanford University and the University of Arizona.

Kaltenbrunner, Annina (Economics Division, Leeds University Business School, University of Leeds) Annina Kaltenbrunner is Lecturer in the Economics of Globalisation and the International Economy at Leeds University Business School. Her areas of research are development economics, international finance, monetary economics, international political economy, heterodox economics and methodology. She has published on post-Keynesian exchange rate theory, emerging market currency internationalization, financial integration, external vulnerability, and the Eurozone crisis. She is currently working on financialization, currency internationalization and capital flows in emerging economies.

Lagna, Andrea (Loughborough University) Andrea Lagna is a Lecturer at the School of Business and Economics, Loughborough University. His current research explores the relationship between statecraft and financial innovation. He has recently published in *New Political Economy*, *Competition & Change* and in an edited volume on *Financial Cultures and Crisis Dynamics* (Routledge, 2016). You can read his blog at andrealagna.net and follow him on Twitter: @a_lagna.

Leaver, Adam (Alliance Manchester Business School, The University of Manchester) Adam Leaver is a Professor in Financialization and Business Analysis at Manchester Business School and an active researcher at the Centre for Research on Socio-Cultural Change (CRESC). His main interest is in a cultural/political economy approach to the financial services sector, financialization and financial crisis, where he has published three co-authored books and numerous peer-reviewed academic journal articles. His current research involves using social network analysis to understand relationships within the financial services sector, the changing role of central banks in the global economy and the sectoral and regional effects of crisis within the UK economy. He also has an enduring interest in the sociology of pricing in collectors markets. Adam's co-authored CRESC research has been widely cited in the media. It is also impactful: his work on the regional and foundational economy is actively used by local authorities. Adam runs, and is the main contributing writer to, the Manchester Capitalism blogsite: manchestercapitalism.blogspot.co.uk/. He is also Associate Editor of *Competition and Change*.

Lopes, Daniel Seabra (Research Centre in Economic and Organizational Sociology, Lisbon) Daniel Seabra Lopes is a Portuguese anthropologist. He received his PhD in Cultural and Social Anthropology from the Faculty of Social Sciences and Humanities, Universidade Nova de Lisboa in 2007. He presently works as a researcher at the SOCIUS/CSG – Research in Social Sciences and Management, Lisbon School of Economics and Management (ISEG), the University of Lisbon, being also a Visiting Scholar at the University of Edinburgh (Department of Sociology). He has been developing ethnographic research on retail credit, banking and financial supervision since 2008, and publishing in a number of international journals, namely *Economy and Society*, *European Societies*, *Cultural Studies*, *Social Anthropology* and the *Journal of Cultural Economy*. Daniel Seabra Lopes is also Assistant Professor at the Lisbon School of Economics and Management, where he integrates the scientific commission of the PhD programme in Economic and Organizational Sociology.

Lysandrou, Photis (City University London) Photis Lysandrou is Research Professor in the City University Political Economy Research Centre (CITYPERC). His research interests are in the areas of global finance, European political economy and corporate governance. His recent publications include 'Debt intolerance and the 90% debt threshold: two impossibility theorems, economy and society' (*Economy and Society*, December 2013); 'The contribution of wealth concentration to the subprime crisis: a quantitative estimation' (with Thomas Goda) (*Cambridge Journal of Economics*, March 2014); 'The role of shadow bank entities in the financial crisis: a disaggregated view' (with Anastasia Nesvetailova) (*Review of International Political Economy*, February 2015). He is currently working on papers relating to financialization, dollar hegemony and the euro's economic rationale.

MacKenzie, Donald (University of Edinburgh) Donald MacKenzie is a Professor of Sociology at the University of Edinburgh. He is primarily a sociologist and historian of science and technology. His current research is on the sociology of financial markets, and he is researching in particular the development of automated high-frequency trading and of the electronic markets that make it possible, with a special focus on how trading algorithms predict the future. His books include *Inventing Accuracy: A Historical Sociology of Nuclear Missile Guidance* (MIT Press, 1990), *An Engine, Not a Camera: How Financial Models Shape Markets* (MIT Press, 2006), *Do Economists Make Markets? On the Performativity of Economics* (Princeton University Press, 2007; co-edited with Fabian Muniesa and Lucia Siu) and *Material Markets: How Economic Agents are Constructed* (Oxford University Press, 2009). With his colleagues Diane-Laure Arjaliès, Philip Grant, Iain Hardie and Ekaterina Svetlova, he is currently preparing *Chains of Finance: How Investment Management is Shaped* (Oxford University Press).

McFall, Liz (Open University) Liz McFall is Head of Sociology at the Open University in the UK. She is currently researching how the convergences surrounding digital disruption and the

Contributors

current global wave of health care funding reforms are forging new roles for states, markets and marketing as PI of the Wellcome Trust Award Insuring Healthcare in a Digital World. Her book *Devising Consumption: Cultural Economies of Insurance, Credit and Spending* (Routledge, 2014) argues that states and markets were inevitable if uneasy allies in the promotion of public welfare and consumption. Liz is author of *Advertising: A Cultural Economy* (Sage, 2004), co-editor of *Conduct: Sociology and Social Worlds* (Manchester University Press, 2008) and Editor-in-Chief of the *Journal of Cultural Economy*.

Metzing, Peter Peter Metzing is a PhD student at Newcastle University Business School, Newcastle upon Tyne. His thesis deals with the implications and possible frictions for the role of regulating authorities and investors that come with a shift towards macro-prudence in financial regulation. He graduated in 2011 with MSc Finance and Financial Regulation (distinction), Newcastle University. Before, he graduated in 2009 with Diploma in Economics at Ruhr-Universität Bochum, Germany.

Montagne, Sabine (Dauphine, Université Paris) Sabine Montagne joined CNRS (Centre National de la Recherche Scientifique) as Researcher at Paris-Dauphine University in 2004, having work previously for an investment bank in Paris for ten years and for an institute of social and economic studies for six years. She is a graduate from a French national engineering school (Ecoles des Mines Saint-Etienne, 1983). Her PhD dissertation in socio-economics (2003) analysed the impact of law (Trust law, fiduciary duties and the federal statute ERISA) on the politics of American pension investment. She then turned to the difficulties of European institutional investors to really implement long-term investment policies (2006) and was an advisor of the experts panel for the French White Paper 'Financing the ecological transition' (2013). She is currently working on a social history of American finance, focused on coalitions and conflicts about the overlapping, sometimes contradictory, meanings of prudent investing and the reshaping of the capital/labour nexus.

Ötsch, Silke (University of Innsbruck) Dr Silke Ötsch is a freelance researcher in economic sociology. Her research focuses on fiscal sociology, transformation and financialization. She was a post-doc Researcher and Assistant Professor at the Department of Sociology of the University of Innsbruck (Austria) from 2005 to 2015 and has worked for the universities of Liechtenstein, Dresden and Weimar (Germany), and for firms of architects. Ötsch has engaged in taxation, financial and environmental issues for Attac and civil society networks. More information and publications: http://silke-oetsch.net/.

Pozner, Jo-Ellen (Leavey School of Business at Santa Clara University) Jo-Ellen Pozner is a member of the Department of Management in the Leavey School of Business at Santa Clara University. Her research focuses on questions of organizational ethics, corporate governance, social movements and institutional change. She has a particular interest in organizational and financial misconduct, specifically the ways in which misconduct at the organizational level impacts top management and boards of directors at the companies involved. In the area of impression management, she studies organizational and individual legitimacy, and ways in which people and organizations attempt to appear to conform to established institutional norms. She also studies social movements that promoted acceptance of organic food, craft beer, and low-power FM radio. Professor Pozner graduated with a PhD in Management and Organizations from the Kellogg School of Management, Northwestern University, and holds degrees from New York University, Johns Hopkins University, and Georgetown University.

Schmidt, Michaela (Institute for Comprehensive Analysis of the Economy Linz and Arbeiterkammer Salzburg) Michaela Schmidt is an economist and research consultant in the fields of distributional theory and tax policy at the Chamber of Labour in Salzburg (Austria). Her research focuses on wealth distribution and international tax policies. She is currently writing her PhD thesis on tax and regulation havens.

Stimmler, Mary Katherine (Google) Mary Kate Stimmler is a researcher in Google's People and Innovation Lab. Her research focuses on modern employment challenges such as using social technology to encourage employee voice; finding leading indicators of organizational culture change; and the development of successful managers and teams. She graduated with a PhD in Management and Organizational Research from UC Berkeley, where she studied risk and catastrophe, and holds degrees from Columbia University and London School of Economics. Previously, she was a researcher at the University of Chicago and Caltech.

Thompson, Grahame (Open University and Copenhagen Business School) Grahame F. Thompson is Associate Professorial Research Fellow attached to the CAST research program and NordSTEVA at the Department of Political Science, Copenhagen University, Denmark, and Emeritus Professor of Political Economy at the Open University, England. His research interests are in the areas of the political economy of the international system, global constitutionalization, and the consequences of globalization for the continuation of a broadly liberal domestic and international order. His latest books are *The Constitutionalization of the Global Corporate Sphere?* (Oxford University Press, 2012) and *Globalization Revisited* (London, 2015). Currently he is working on issues of financial security associated with algorithmic trading devices.

Wilhelm, Benjamin (Institute for Sociology of the University of Gießen) Benjamin Wilhelm is a Research Associate at the Institute for Sociology of the University of Gießen, Germany. Here he works on socio-politics of transnational financial streams in the context of post-crisis financial regulation. Prior to this he finished a research project at the Max Weber Center for Advanced Cultural and Social Studies in Erfurt, Germany, on civil society engagement in financial regulation. Benjamin wrote his dissertation on the politics of financial governance and how language enables and restricts present perceptions of future political spaces. His most recent publications on shadow banking appear in the *Routledge Handbook for Heterodox Economics* (forthcoming) and 'Financialization and the three utopias of shadow banking', together with Oliver Kessler (*Competition & Change*, 2013).

Williams, Karel (Alliance Manchester Business School, The University of Manchester) Karel Williams is a Professor at Alliance Manchester Business School where he was Director of the ESRC funded Centre for Research on Socio Cultural Change (cresc.ac.uk). The centre pioneered critical work on shareholder value and financialization, and CRESC authors then produced *After the Great Complacence*, a classic study of the post-2008 financial crisis as an elite debacle. More recently Karel has worked with co-authors on the mundane foundational economy. Their latest book is *What a Waste* (Manchester University Press, 2015) on how public sector outsourcing goes wrong and the public interest report 'Where does the money go' (2016) is the first output from a new project on adult care.

Williams, Toni (University of Kent) Toni Williams is a Professor of Law at the University of Kent. She has published in a variety of areas, including racial discrimination in criminal justice, critical law and economics and consumer financial services regulation. Her current research projects concern the regulation of personal finance products, focusing in particular on the local impact and implications of regulatory policies and projects initiated by global and transnational organizations; the role of law in constituting, enabling and framing financial and other inclusionary practices in Europe and Brazil (British Academy funded); and socio-legal analysis of the regulation of bingo as a social, cultural and economic practice in Brazil and transnationally (ESRC funded).

Willmott, Hugh (Cass Business School and Cardiff Business School) Hugh Willmott is Professor of Management at Cass Business School and Research Professor in Organization Studies, Cardiff Business School. He previously held professorial appointments at the UMIST (now Manchester Business School) and the Judge Business School, Cambridge. He co-founded the International Labour Process Conference and the International Critical Management Studies Conference. He currently serves on the board of *Organization Studies* and *Journal of Management Studies*, and he is an Associate Editor of *Academy of Management Review*. Full details can be found on his homepage: https://sites.google.com/site/hughwillmottshomepage.

Acknowledgements

We would like to thank all of the contributors to the companion for their excellent work and support for this project. In addition, we wish to thank Jacqueline Curthoys, Sinead Waldron and Nicola Cupit of Routledge who from the commissioning stage onwards of this book continuously supported and encouraged us, and accepted delays. We would also like to express our special thanks to Ian Crowther, PhD student at Alliance Manchester Business School, who assisted us with diligence at all stages of this book.

Finally the publishers and editors would like to thank the following for permission to reprint their material.

Taylor & Francis Ltd for permission to reprint Engelen, E., Ertürk, I., Leaver, A., Froud, J. and Williams, K. (2010), 'Reconceptualizing financial innovation: Frame, conjuncture and bricolage', *Economy and Society*, 39(1): 33–63.

University Chicago Press for permission to reprint MacKenzie, Donald (2011), 'The credit crisis as a problem in the sociology of knowledge', *American Journal of Sociology*, 116: 1778–841.

Macmillan Publishers Ltd to reprint Gray, J. and Metzing, P. (2013), 'Defining and delivering judgement-based supervision: The interface with the legal system', *Journal of Banking Regulation*, 14(3/4), 228–40.

Introduction

Ismail Ertürk and Daniela Gabor

In 2016, almost a decade after the 2007 banking crisis, banking is still far from being reformed successfully to serve economic growth. Furthermore the regulators are still unsure about how much and what kind of capital can make banks safe. Direct and indirect state subsidies to the private banks continue almost everywhere in core capitalist countries. To top it all in February 2016 Deutsche Bank frightened everyone by bringing back memories of the failed Lehman Brothers when its share price, due to investors' loss of confidence in a post-crisis creative form of capital called CoCos (contingent convertible capital instruments), collapsed by some 40 per cent in just over a month. Over the same period other European and US bank shares suffered similarly at rates unseen since 2008. In the midst of this nervous stock market turmoil Sir John Vickers, the architect of the UK structural reform in banking, which ring-fenced retail banking from the risky investment banking in banking conglomerates, publicly criticised the regulators at the Bank of England for not following his advice in setting higher capital buffers for banks. Another regulator across the Atlantic, Neel Kashkari, President of the Federal Reserve Bank of Minneapolis, who was one of the architects of the US bailout of banks when he was working at the US Treasury at the time, announced that the problem is the size and complexity of banks not the levels of capital calling for radical splitting up of banks into utilities which both the Dodd–Frank Act in the US and the Vickers Report in the UK had ruled out.

This companion is a response to such vital concerns that surfaced in February 2016 – the regulatory and reform responses to the 2007 crisis have not adequately addressed the root causes of the 2007 banking crisis. The 2007 crisis required a multidisciplinary analysis of what went wrong. Although the failure of mainstream economics and finance has been universally acknowledged alternative approaches have not been accommodated intellectually in policy circles and in some academic research. The objective of this companion is to bring together the works of researchers from a wide range of disciplines to reflect on bank regulation and reform. Numerous books including companions and handbooks have been published on financial crisis and regulation and reform since the crisis. However most of these books tend to reflect a specific discipline's reflection on banking crisis and regulation and reform. In this book contributions deploying a wide range of disciplinary analytical and theoretical tools from economic sociology, heterodox economics, social studies of finance, financialisation studies, legal studies, economic geography, cultural economy, anthropology, international political economy, organisation studies, and so on are included. Both established names in their fields with paradigmatic influences and young scholars exploring new theoretical approaches to banking and finance with diverse national backgrounds are represented.

The companion consists of twenty-three contributions that are grouped in six parts. In Part I, 'Knowledges of Credit Risk and Bank Regulation', four different approaches to credit risk practices in financial institutions in the context of the failure and regulation of such risk technologies in the 2007 crisis are presented. MacKenzie's re-printed socio-historic article draws the attention of regulators with mainstream economics backgrounds to the cognitive and organisational structures that they tend not to problematise in credit risk evaluation practices that were behind the disastrously failed credit derivatives known as collateralised debt obligations (CDOs). McFall, too, introduces a socio-historic analysis of credit risk but highlights non-cognitive aspects of an innovative early consumer credit to low income families by Provident Clothing and Supply. Provident's attempt to become a 'People's Bank' did not succeed due to regulators' preference for size in retail banking although its innovative socially driven credit risk management techniques were successful in both making the provider of the subprime credit systemically safe and low income borrowers having access to socially useful credit. The regulators' attention after the crisis focused on un-regulated financial institutions' role in expanding credit to real estate ownership. Wilhelm analyses this reflexive relation between credit practices and regulators by deploying a Bourdieusian perspective and by underlining the democratically suspect homogenising power of regulation. Willmott introduces corporate governance as a regulatory problematic in analysing credit derivatives that caused the financial crisis of 2007. AIG, the insurance company that sold credit default swaps to banks and hence played a key role in mismanagement of credit risk in housing finance, had serious corporate governance failures in managing risk. Willmott analyses shareholder value-driven corporate governance at AIG that favours high returns to shareholders at the expense of stakeholders that in this case included the taxpayers who ended up bailing out AIG and banks.

In Part II, 'Critical Perspectives on Financial Innovation', empirically and historically informed investigations into financial innovation and financialisation provide insight into the systemic fragilities that financial innovation has caused and temporal material and ideological conditions that it is grounded on. Engelen et al.'s reprinted article questions the scientific accounts of financial innovation in other literatures and instead offers an alternative framework, using the anthropologist Lévi-Strauss's concept of bricolage, that explains derivatives as conjectural improvisations by fee income and bonus driven financial intermediaries. The implication for policy is then to understand financial innovation as a product of a financialised capitalism that progresses through conjecturally formed asset bubbles rather than as eternal scientific solutions to risk management. Gabor and Ban discuss the innovation that allows government bonds to be used as collateral in market-based finance. The collateral motive – that is (shadow) banks' demand for government debt to support wholesale funding – is an important driver of financialisation of government bond markets, with broader political-economy implications. Hardie in Part III is a reference that Gabor and Ban cite in developing their concept of market-based finance and banking. Economic geographer Hall focuses on knowledge and learning that shape working cultures in international financial centres where financial innovation happens and the financial system is (re)produced. Hall draws regulators' attention to the systemic risk importance of informal social and cultural norms that education and training create in investment banking. In Part VI Thompson engages with this issue from the banking reform perspective in the light of fines charged to misbehaving banks and proposes a new set of social and cultural norms that should be promoted in investment banking. The last chapter in Part II is by Montagne who takes a critical stance towards the autonomy that finance is granted in the financialisation literature and argues instead, by invoking 'processual' sociology, that the financial fragility is exported from the bordering social sphere of capital–labour nexus in the economy. Montagne's perspective on finance, based on a historical case study of the emergence of the pension fund industry in the US in the trust form that is shaped by social and legal processes, points to, for the debates on regulating and reforming banking, the problematic of the boundary issues in the economy.

Part III, 'New Approaches to Banking, Risk and Central Bank Role in the Eurozone', opens with Fontan's examination of new regulatory powers that the ECB has gained since the 2007 financial crisis. The manner of transformation of the ECB from a light weight Eurozone institution to what Fontan calls a 'behemoth' with huge micro- and macro-prudential powers over such a short period of time does not bear well for sound regulation of banking in the Eurozone because the political foundations of this transformation are weak. Hardie analyses another transformation in the Eurozone – how banking in the Eurozone no longer resembles what the Varieties of Capitalism literature imagined. Market-based versus bank-based dichotomy in understanding capitalism does not explain adequately and accurately how banks perform their intermediary functions in the Eurozone. Based on empirical evidence gathered from analysis of bank balance sheets Hardie argues that the Eurozone banks themselves are under the discipline of pricing signals from financial markets. Hardie's findings have important implications for both comparative political economy studies and for policy in the Eurozone in reforming banking and finance to create economically useful financial intermediation. The last chapter in Part III examines the case study of Italian municipalities' use of interest rate swaps to avoid fiscal austerity measures imposed on them by the central government. Lagna challenges the mainstream understanding of derivatives as risk management instruments by arguing how they are contingent instruments used as weapons for regulatory arbitrage and accounting dissimulation by the Italian municipalities and hence have contributed to the financial fragility in the Eurozone.

In Part IV, 'Regulation of Misconduct in Banking', three prominent cases of misconduct in banking, offshore financial centres, hedge funds and the manipulation of benchmark interbank interest rates, are critically examined. Lopes employs conceptual tools of anthropology and ethnographic methodology to study the post-crisis Libor/Euribor rate manipulation in banking. His findings challenge the logic of regulators in reforming the existing failed self-regulated system that sets these benchmark interest rates. Lopes argues that a new system that aims to enhance facticity of the benchmark rate by linking the rate determination to actual transactions that take place under improved internal governance mechanisms is a product of regulatory thinking that assumes regulation is about clear-cut solutions and straightforward answers. In reality, as the case of Libor manipulation shows, strategic positions taken by a small number of oligopolistic big banking players in financial markets and the contagious spread of financial practices due to the ease of their reproducibility will always allow conditions of manipulation. Lopes invites bank regulators to address the games played in financial markets due to size and nature of financial products. Lysandrou reflects on the games and strategies that hedge funds play in financial markets and why. Although the regulatory response to the 2007 crisis has removed some of the governance and transparency privileges of hedge funds Lysandrou argues that as long as the fundamental dysfunctionalities in capitalism create the conditions – such as financial markets are unable to meet the institutional investors', like pension funds, needs for high yield and income inequality leads to the concentration of wealth in high net worth individuals – there will be demand for morally and socially questionable hedge fund strategies to generate alpha return. The last chapter in Part IV by Ötsch and Schmidt charts the broader unregulated part of global finance – offshore financial centres. Ötsch and Schmidt provide a detailed historical background to the development of offshore financial centres by underlining the complicity of financial and political elites in keeping such centres unregulated for pursuit of economic and political power.

They also argue that offshore is not as portrayed an entity that is disconnected from onshore economy. Offshore is interlinked to onshore because of elite economic and political self-interests. Offshore, then, becomes a problem of democracy in contemporary capitalism and is not just a technical regulatory issue. Like the previous two chapters in this section this last chapter on offshore banking activity articulates non-technical dimensions of regulating misconduct that increasingly calls for a democratic control of banking and finance.

Part V, 'Limits of Post-crisis Bank Regulation', has five contributions that investigate post-crisis regulatory initiatives from different disciplinary perspectives employing the analytical tools of financialisation studies, international political economy, heterodox economics, law and economics and economic sociology. Crowther and Ertürk discuss the major structural reform initiatives in the UK, the US and the Eurozone that aim to de-risk and re-capitalise national and global banking to make it safer. By focusing on three post-crisis case studies of new types of risks at Barclays, J.P. Morgan Chase and the UK retail banking that the post-crisis reform initiatives failed to identify Crowther and Ertürk argue that shareholder value-driven business models at banks are responsible for new forms of risk taking as well as the pre-crisis ones. Their conclusion is that banking reforms can de-risk banks only by radically reforming financialised bank business models. The second chapter by Dorn in Part V frames the post-crisis economics-driven debate and policy on regulation and reform in a historical context of disappearance of democratic control of financial markets everywhere including in the post-crisis Eurozone. According to Dorn the socially destructive failure of markets in finance produced a policy discourse about more or less regulation rather than a discourse and action about politics of financial markets. Gabilondo's chapter in this section discusses the role of internal stress-testing models in post-crisis prudential regulation in the US. As adequacy of capital in the face of adverse market movements has become the key prudential regulatory concern since the introduction of Basel capital adequacy rules in late 1980s regulators have endorsed the use of such models. But these models have failed to predict the kind of adverse market conditions that caused the 2007 crisis. This did not stop bank regulators expanding the use of stress-testing models to assess individual bank's ability to survive worsening economic and financial conditions. Gabilondo provides an insightful evaluation of the use of such models by the regulators since the 2007 crisis. Gray and Metzing complement Gabilondo's interest in the US prudential regulation of the adequacy of capital in banking with their interest in the UK prudential regulation and the post-crisis shift in optimal governance at banking firms. The pre-crisis light-touch approach to regulation by the then regulatory body Financial Services Authority (FSA) was described as risk-driven and risk-responsive. The post-crisis institutional structure in the UK replaced FSA with the three new Bank of England-led institutions – Financial Conduct Authority, Prudential Regulation Authority and Financial Policy Committee – that respond to judgements formed by supervisors about risks posed by the regulated financial institutions and their managers and key staff. This judgement-led supervisory approach, according to Gray and Metzing, will inevitably invite the scrutiny of public law when regulatory judgements are made on the systemic risk of individual banks. The effectiveness of the new judgement-led regulatory regime in the UK is then going to be tested under uncertainties and costs of possible litigation. The final chapter in Part V by Hirsch, Pozner and Stimmler deconstructs the myth that the Glass–Steagal Act could be resurrected in the aftermath of the 2007 financial crisis in the US to break up and regulate the banking conglomerates to serve all their stakeholders rather than just their management and shareholders. By adapting the 'theorisation framework' as a useful tool to understand the processes and dynamics of resistance by agency in the financial services sector and applying it to both Glass–Steagal before its formal demolition and the regulatory initiatives after the 2007 crisis, the authors explain the political power of financial institutions in the US that have uninterrupted revolving door relationship with regulation.

The final section of the book, Part VI, 'Dysfunctional Global Finance and Banking Reform', consists of four chapters that reflect on banking as part of structural transformations in neo-liberal global wholesale and consumer finance, and how reform in banking would entail more than technical fixes and should involve values and social and political choices. Dymski and Kaltenbrunner challenge the views on expansion of global finance that prioritise the technological revolutions in trading and inventions in information technology used by financial firms. Instead they develop a political economy-driven macroeconomic argument where the historic choice of gold-based international monetary system by the hegemonic economic powers – the UK and the US – and the last 30 years' chronic current account deficits financed by capital account surpluses by both countries and especially the US were the material conditions for the inherently unstable globalised finance. Dymski and Kaltenbrunner give empirical and theoretical account of the historical emergence and interconnectedness of megabank/shadow banking-led financial complex in the US and the UK and especially in the financial centres New York and London. They conclude that to reform banking to serve productive economy requires undoing of the interconnected New York–London axis of global financial complex. The second chapter of Part VI by Fligstein and Habinek alsos engages with the interconnectedness of global banks in an empirically rich argument but offers an alternative explanation and theoretical framework than Dymski and Kaltenbrunner for the specific interconnectedness caused by the securitisation of mortgages in the US. They aim to explain why the collapse of the housing market in the US that triggered the 2007 crisis led to the failure of banks in faraway places like Europe. Their findings suggest that it was the converged business models of banks in Europe and the US that was the cause of contagion. This conclusion disagrees with the sociological accounts of crisis that focus on the shared risks in global financial products that resulted from regulatory convergences and economic co-dependencies caused by macroeconomic imbalances. Fligstein and Habinek's account of the interconnectedness of the European and the US banks through investments by the former in the securitised mortgages produced by the latter and the former's funding strategies of such investments is based on Fligstein's theorisation of the sociology of markets. Fligstein and Habinek's findings and arguments shift the debate on reforming global banks from an emphasis on fragilities built around financial instruments like collateralised debt obligations to an emphasis on social structure of financial markets where banks are the key players. The first two chapters in Part VI set the issue of reforming banks against a background of inherently unstable and dysfunctional global finance and the driving dynamics for such instability. The third chapter by Thompson, on the other hand, readjusts the focus of analysis to the post-crisis scandals like Libor fixing, forex manipulation, mis-selling insurance products etc. in global banking and the public and policy debate on culture of banking and the behaviour of individuals within the banking firm. Thompson draws upon the conceptual tools of cultural economy to propose an alternative culture of banking that is built on a new idea of persona of bankers that he describes as 'artisan of finance'. Thompson admits that modern banking cannot de-invent its technological advances where most of the misbehaviour in banking has occurred. But, he argues, a new persona of bankers shaped around ethics of artisanal mode of production could be socially responsive rather than self-interested in managing money in present day financial markets for present day needs. In this sense Thompson reinforces the importance of education and training like Hall in Chapter 7 to create norms in banking that are socially oriented and artisanal in operational terms. In the last chapter of Part VI Williams discusses transnational policy on protection of consumers of financial products in markets that operate along neo-liberal principles. Such reform agenda, Williams argues, tends to target improving consumer literacy but ignores initiatives to change the predatory retail bank behaviour and to reform the relationship between banks and their retail customers by responsibilising the former. Williams questions the transnational policymakers' reform objectives that aim for financial stability through better protection of financial consumers because reform initiatives do not specifically address the exploitative socio-economic relations in consumer-finance markets.

All twenty-three chapters in six parts collectively raise insightful questions that should inform the policy debates for a socially and economically useful banking that still continue almost a decade after the crisis. The range of disciplines represented in this book also lays the foundations for future multidisciplinary research on bank regulation and reform that is theoretically innovative, empirically informed and socially and politically relevant.

Part I
Knowledges of credit risk and bank regulation

1
The credit crisis as a problem in the sociology of knowledge

Donald MacKenzie[1]

This chapter analyzes the role in the credit crisis of the processes by which market participants produce knowledge about financial instruments. Employing documentary sources and 87 predominantly oral history interviews, the chapter presents a historical sociology of the clusters of evaluation practices surrounding ABSs (asset-backed securities, most importantly mortgage-backed securities) and CDOs (collateralized debt obligations). Despite the close structural similarity between ABSs and CDOs, these practices came to differ substantially and became the province (e.g. in the rating agencies) of organizationally separate groups. In consequence, when ABS CDOs (CDOs in which the underlying assets are ABSs) emerged, they were evaluated in two separate stages. This created a fatally attractive arbitrage opportunity, large-scale exploitation of which sidelined previously important gatekeepers (risk-sensitive investors in the lower tranches of mortgage-backed securities) and eventually magnified and concentrated the banking system's calamitous mortgage-related losses.

Introduction

At the heart of the credit crisis that erupted in summer 2007 and culminated in the near collapse of the global banking system in the fall of 2008 were complex, esoteric financial instruments. At the peak of the crisis, in October 2008, the International Monetary Fund (IMF) categorized the estimated $1.4 trillion losses that, were it not for massive international government intervention, would most likely have caused an economic catastrophe on the scale of the Great Depression. More than half the total, $770 billion, was in mortgage-backed securities, asset-backed securities (ABSs) of other kinds, and collateralized debt obligations (CDOs).[2] The largest single category of loss, $290 billion, was in a class of instruments of which many outside the financial sector had simply been unaware prior to the crisis: ABS CDOs, in other words collateralized debt obligations whose underlying assets are tranches of asset-backed securities, most commonly mortgage-backed securities (IMF, 2008, table 1.1, p. 9). Not only were the sums lost on ABS CDOs very large, but (as discussed in this chapter's fifth section) the losses were concentrated at the very core of the global financial system. ABS CDOs also had wider effects. The "assembly lines" via which they were constructed reshaped the underlying market for mortgage-backed securities in ways that facilitated ever looser mortgage underwriting. Those losses and these processes were by no means the only causes of the credit crisis, but to understand it fully we need to understand ABS CDOs, to grasp how they emerged from the world of mortgage-backed securities and the (cognitively quite different and organizationally largely separate) world of CDOs, and above all to develop a sociological analysis of how these complex financial instruments were evaluated by market participants. For example, differences between how market participants evaluated ABSs and evaluated CDOs, and the location of those evaluations in different groups or departments of credit rating agencies and banks, had a double effect. In a situation in which investment behavior was largely governed by credit ratings, they made the construction of ABS CDOs highly profitable. Simultaneously, however, they left the ABS CDO a kind of epistemic orphan, cognitively peripheral to both its parent worlds, ABSs and corporate CDOs.

In its emphasis on evaluation,[3] this chapter contributes to a growing body of work in economic sociology that shows the importance and richness of what Beckert (2009, pp. 253–4) calls "the value problem," in other words "the processes of classification and commensuration with which actors assign value to goods." As Carruthers and Stinchcombe (1999, p. 353) point out, "buyers and sellers" need "to know the commodities they transact in," and the ease with which those commodities are bought and sold is, therefore, "among other things, an issue in the sociology of knowledge."

Carruthers and Stinchcombe focus on a particular set of knowledge-generating arrangements, to be found, for example, in the trading of the shares of large corporations, that one might call the "canonical mechanism." This involves the standardization of the financial claims or other commodities being traded, continuous auctions coordinated either by an exchange or by dealers who act as "market makers,"[4] and wide dissemination of the resultant prices. These arrangements are, as Carruthers and Stinchcombe show, powerful generators of public knowledge, but they are also limited in their scope, even in their primary domain, the financial markets. The ABS and CDO tranches discussed here were not, in general, traded in canonical-mechanism markets. They were usually bought directly from those who had constructed them, who frequently were dealers based at major international banks, and in many cases then simply retained by the purchasers. Secondary trading of them was on a limited scale and was always "over-the-counter" (conducted by direct institution-to-institution negotiation) rather than on an organized exchange. Even in the limited cases in which some of these instruments were made sufficiently standard that canonical-mechanism trading was possible, there was an undercurrent of dissent, touched on in the penultimate section below, about whether the publicly quoted prices of them were fully reliable and legitimate.

In consequence, this is a case in which the analysis of the "social processes behind the constitution of value" (Beckert, 2009, p. 254) needs to look beyond the canonical mechanism. There is a substantial body of work by economic sociologists on these processes, mainly concerning contexts outside the financial markets and often – though not always – goods and services that are "singular" (Karpik, 2010): not straightforwardly commensurable. The situations on which this literature has focused include those in which the legitimacy of a product or of monetary valuation is contested (see, e.g. Zelizer, 1979 on life insurance and Zelizer, 1994 on children); incommensurable forms of evaluation or "orders of worth" contend (Boltanski and Thévenot, 2006; Stark, 2009): perceptions of value interact with aesthetic judgments (e.g. Velthuis 2005; Aspers 2005); the quality of a product is inferred from the status of its producer (e.g. Podolny 1993, 2005; see Aspers 2009); or the value of a commodity to one buyer depends directly on anticipation of its value to other buyers (as in the case of dot.com stocks or houses bought in the anticipation of selling them to others at a higher price).[5]

ABSs and CDOs are not valued for their aesthetic properties, and the moral legitimacy of monetary valuation of them has never been challenged. With those exceptions, however, all the phenomena listed in the previous paragraph can be found in respect to ABSs and CDOs, and I return to two of them in the conclusion. However, the main way in which the evaluation of ABSs, CDOs, and ABS CDOs contributed to the crisis concerns the apparently "technical" core of evaluation. ABSs, CDOs, and ABS CDOs are debt instruments. They normally entitle investors (a) to defined "coupons" (interest payments), set either as a fixed percentage or as a fixed margin or "spread" over a benchmark interest rate such as Libor (London Interbank Offered Rate) and (b) to eventual repayment of principal (their initial capital investment). The monetary worth of an investment in an ABS or CDO is thus the aggregate present value of those future payments. If the payments were entirely certain, the valuation of an ABS or CDO would be a matter simply of arithmetic, but they are not. There are two main risks: default (in other words that the payments are not made or not made in full) and prepayment (i.e. principal is repaid earlier than anticipated, in a situation in which it can be reinvested only at a lower rate of interest). This chapter's focus is on whether and how those risks were taken into account in the evaluation of ABSs, CDOs, and ABS CDOs.

How might "technical" processes of evaluation of this kind be analyzed sociologically? This chapter draws its inspiration from studies of scientific practice. Historians and sociologists have found that practice to be far less uniform than traditional notions of a unitary "scientific method" might suggest (see, e.g. Galison and Stump 1996) and have sought to capture distinctive clusters of practice in notions such as the "local scientific cultures" of Barnes, Bloor, and Henry (1996), the "subcultures" and "competing traditions" of Galison (1997), the "experimental cultures" of Rheinberger (1997), "epistemic cultures" of Knorr Cetina (1999), "epistemological cultures" of Fox Keller (2002), and "evidential cultures" of Collins (2004).

Can similar patterned differences in evaluation practices be found in financial markets?[6] This chapter suggests that they can,[7] using as its main evidence differences between the evaluation of ABSs and of CDOs, which are structurally very similar instruments (indeed sometimes simply lumped together, as, e.g. by McDonald and Robinson, 2009). In evaluation, as in scientific practices, one can find "aggregate patterns and dynamics that are on display in expert practice and that vary in different settings of expertise ... patterns on which various actions converge and which they instantiate and dynamically extend" (Knorr Cetina 1999, pp. 8–9). Let me call these patterns "clusters of evaluation practices." (Following the literature on science and calling them "evaluation cultures" might be taken to imply greater homogeneity and "bounded-offness" of their practitioners than is the case.[8] It could also be taken wrongly as implying a theory of action as based solely on "belief" and "habit" – for which see Camic, 1986 – rather than self-interested, reflexive rational choice. As discussed in the conclusion, belief and habit were present, but by no means exclusively so.)[9]

The research on which this chapter is based, which is outlined at the end of this introduction, supports six postulates about these clusters.[10] First, clusters of evaluation practices are the path-dependent outcomes of historical contingencies.[11] For example, while the evaluation practices surrounding CDOs always had default risk as their primary object, those surrounding mortgage-backed securities were concerned primarily with prepayment. As the following section will show, that latter focus originally arose because of features of the political economy of mortgage lending in the United States that can be traced back to the 1930s. The focus on prepayment remained in place even in the very different circumstances of the past decade: it formed a criterion on which that decade's subprime mortgage-backed securities were judged superior to their prime counterparts. In emphasizing long-lasting effects such as this, I do not want to suggest that evaluation practices never change. They do – change in them is a major focus of this chapter – but the way in which they change is path-dependent: it is easier, for example, to modify an existing practice than to develop an entirely new one.

Second, the more elaborate of evaluation practices give rise to, and are informed by, distinctive ontologies: distinctive presuppositions about the nature and properties of the features and processes of the economic world. Thus the third section of the chapter will show that the evaluation practices surrounding CDOs came to be oriented heavily to one such feature, "credit correlation" (a term that will be explained in that section), which was a notion entirely absent, at least in any explicit form, in the evaluation of ABSs. Like many scientific objects, correlation was neither simply "real" nor simply "fictional" (Knorr Cetina, 1999, pp. 248–52). It was not observable in any straightforward sense: to invoke it was to invoke the unseen. Yet, like the scientific objects analyzed by Daston (2000), it had the potential to become "more real," as specific markets (the tradable credit indices described below) were created in which its effects were more easily traced. Indeed, some of those involved with CDOs came to hold that in those markets correlation was not just real but tradable. For others, though, the frustrating difficulties of measuring correlation indicated that it was a misconception, an artifact of inadequate models.

Third, evaluation practices become organizational routines, and when different practices are pursued in the same organization, they frequently are the province of separate parts of it.[12] For instance, the evaluation of ABSs on the one hand and CDOs on the other typically became the responsibility of different sections of banks, of the specialist "monoline" insurers, and of credit rating agencies. In the case of the rating agencies, for example, both ABSs and CDOs fell within the remit of their structured finance departments, but the latter had separate groups dealing with each. When ABS CDOs (which are CDOs with ABSs nested within them, so to speak) came into being, the decision as to how to evaluate them was thus also a decision about how their evaluation should be mapped onto the organizational structure of rating agencies. All the three main agencies – Moody's, Standard & Poor's (S&P), and Fitch – found the same solution: they relied on the existing ratings, by ABS groups, of the component ABSs, and assigned the analysis of the higher-level structure to CDO groups. Those groups analyzed that structure largely as if it was simply another variant of a CDO, for which existing practices were therefore appropriate, rather than treating an ABS CDO as a radically different instrument that demanded new evaluation techniques.

Fourth, in modern debt markets (in which I include the markets for bonds, tradable loans, and structured instruments such as ABSs and CDOs) evaluation practices regulate actions and become means of governance via the process of credit rating.[13] Ratings (see Figure 1.1) encode rating agencies' conclusions about either the likelihood of default on debt instruments (in the case of S&P and Fitch) or, in the case of Moody's, the expected loss on them (the likelihood of loss multiplied by its severity). For institutional investors such as banks, insurance companies, and pension funds (private individuals were never major participants in the ABS and CDO markets discussed here), ratings frequently become rules. Cantor, ap Gwilym, and Thomas (2007, p. 14) note that in the United States "there are currently over 100 federal laws and 50 regulations incorporating credit ratings," and they report that the purchases of 74 percent of their sample of US investment fund managers (and 78 percent of European managers) were subject to a minimum-rating requirement: if an instrument's rating was below the minimum, they were not allowed to buy it. Especially toward the end of the period discussed here, banking regulation in particular relied heavily on ratings, with banks able to hold much smaller capital reserves in respect to instruments with high ratings, a factor that greatly enhanced the attractiveness of the most senior tranches of the instruments discussed here.

Fifth, evaluation practices crystallized in ratings reduce a difficult problem of evaluation (assessing complex, novel financial instruments that involve potentially uncertain payments stretching years into the future) to a simple one, by establishing a rough equivalence among debt instruments of different kinds and with different particularities. Though some buyers of ABSs

A problem in the sociology of knowledge

	S&P	Moody's
	AAA	Aaa
	AA+	Aa1
	AA	Aa2
	AA–	Aa3
	A+	A1
	A	A2
	A–	A3
Investment	BBB+	Baa1
Grade	BBB	Baa2
	BBB–	Baa3
Speculative	BB+	Ba1
Grade	BB	Ba2
	BB–	Ba3
	B+	B1
	B	B2
	B–	B3
	CCC+	Caa1
	CCC	Caa2
	CCC–	Caa3
	CC	Ca
	C	C
Defaulted	D	

Figure 1.1 Rating grades

Note: Fitch's grades are identical to S&P's, except that Fitch employs a single CCC grade with no + or –.

Sources: www2.standardandpoors.com; www.moodys.com; www.fitchratings.com. All accessed August 20, 2009.

and CDOs had a good understanding of the detail of evaluation practices (such as the Gaussian copula models discussed below), many did not, and the market for these instruments would have been quite limited if participation in the market required that understanding. Ratings "black boxed" these complexities. They permitted the economic value of different ABSs and CDOs to be compared, both with each other and with more familiar, less complex instruments such as corporate bonds, by comparing the "spread" (increment over Libor or other benchmark interest rate) offered by a given instrument to that offered by others with the same rating. In consequence, as one dealer put it, "You knew that if you hit a certain spread for a given rating, that the deal was sold" (quoted in Securities Industry and Financial Markets Association 2008, p. 22). This spreads-ratings nexus was thus a convention in the sense of the French "economics of convention": a way of turning what might otherwise be radical uncertainty into a form of order that – while never unchanging – is stable and predictable enough to permit coordination and rational action, thus solving the wider problem of social order in markets on which Beckert (2009) and others (e.g. White 1981, 2002) focus. A bank producing a novel instrument could anticipate the most important metric (spread for a given rating) by which it would be judged, and – by discovering the spreads offered by the instruments with the same rating that others had recently sold[14] – could know the combinations of ratings and spreads that were needed for the instrument to be "competitive." The detailed design of both ABSs and CDOs was always informed by how they would be evaluated by the rating agencies, in a clear manifestation of what Espeland and Sauder (2007) call "reactivity": the effects of evaluation or ranking on what is being evaluated and ranked.

Sixth, when they bear upon the same instrument, or same risk, evaluation practices that differ permit a specific form of profit-making: arbitrage.[15] At least some of the time, different practices will lead to the same instrument or same risk being valued differently. In consequence, it may be possible to sell the instrument or risk to one market participant while buying it more cheaply from another, with the difference in prices being riskless profit – in other words, arbitrage profit. Many CDOs and nearly all ABS CDOs were constructed in order to perform arbitrage, and this also became increasingly the motivation for constructing ABSs. The evaluation practices employed by the rating agencies had the consequence that assets that had high spreads and that were only modestly creditworthy could be packaged into instruments with high ratings, which could therefore be sold to investors at lower spreads, with the constructor of the instrument capturing most of the difference as arbitrage profit. As an interviewee put it in June 2006:

> The whole [CDO] market is rating-agency-driven at some level.... The game is basically to create ... tranches of portfolios which are A, AA, or AAA-rated and yield significantly more than a correspondingly-rated tranche of a corporate or an asset-backed derivative, commercial mortgage-backed security would yield.... It's just that there are investors who are constrained by ratings ... and that creates value for everyone else and we're in the business of exploiting that.

Arbitrage of this kind is the central connection between the evaluation practices surrounding ABSs and CDOs and the credit crisis. Ratings-governed investors, the ratings-spreads nexus, differences in evaluation practices, and the way those practices mapped on to the organizational structures of rating agencies created arbitrage opportunities that persisted. One such opportunity was created by the separate evaluation of ABSs and CDOs, following different practices and (in the rating agencies) by different groups. ABS CDOs were created primarily to exploit that arbitrage, and the huge scale on which this was done was among the causes of the crisis. By changing the composition of the underlying market for ABSs, ABS CDOs removed previously influential gatekeepers (the traditional buyers of the lower tranches of ABSs: see Adelson and Jacob, 2008b) and, in so doing, very likely helped clear the way for increasingly reckless mortgage lending. ABS CDOs also magnified the resultant mortgage-related losses in the way discussed in the chapter's fifth section, and a specific aspect of them – their large, apparently ultra-safe, but low-spread "super-senior" tranches – fatally concentrated those losses at the heart of the global banking system.

In showing, in this way, the role of the clusters of evaluation practices surrounding ABSs and CDOs in the genesis of the credit crisis, this chapter is intended to complement, not contradict, existing explanations, both those that focus on macroeconomic factors[16] and those offered by the emerging sociological literature on the crisis (to which the single most important contribution is the collection edited by Lounsbury and Hirsch, 2010). Closest in this latter literature to this chapter are the analyses of mortgage securitization and the role of credit rating agencies in Carruthers (2010), Fligstein and Goldstein (2010), Pozner et al. (2010), and Rona-Tas and Hiss (2010), along with the discussion of credit default swaps in Morgan (2010).[17] I share, for example, Fligstein and Goldstein's emphasis on the role played by government in modern US mortgage securitization and their sense – also to be found in other sociological contributions such as Guillén and Suárez and Schneiberg and Bartley (2010) – that an entirely rational-choice, agency-theoretic explanation of the crisis is unsatisfactory. What this chapter adds to this existing work is (a) extensive primary-source analysis of the practices of credit rating and other forms of evaluation; (b) an interpretation of the consequences of those evaluation practices that focuses not on fees-driven rating-agency wrongdoing and other forms of "amoral calculation" (Vaughan 1996) but on the content of those practices, on their mapping onto the organizational structures of the agencies, and on the arbitrage opportunity to which it gave rise;[18] and (c) a focus, almost entirely missing in the existing sociological literature, on ABS CDOs, on the change they brought about in the structure of the ABS market, on the way in which they magnified and concentrated losses on ABSs, and on the crucial interaction between them and credit default swaps.

There are few reliable secondary sources on the history of ABSs and CDOs to draw on: the best are the insightful, archivally based analysis of the modern origins of US mortgage-backed securities in Quinn (2009); Tett's (2009b) lively, interview-based account of the J.P. Morgan credit-derivatives group; and two other interview-based books (Zuckerman, 2009; Lewis 2010) focused mainly on those who successfully bet against mortgage-backed securities. The research reported here has thus involved the construction of a historical narrative largely afresh, drawing on two main sets of primary sources. The first is 87 interviews, mainly in London and New York, with 77 market participants,[19] including 36 who are or were constructors, managers, brokers, or traders of the financial instruments discussed in this chapter; 14 who are "quants" (specialists in quantitative modeling); 16 who are or have been rating-agency employees; and four who are or were market regulators.[20] The interviews took place in two phases, before and after the onset of the credit crisis in the early summer of 2007. The earlier phase, which consisted of 29 interviews, was a pilot study focusing on what I describe below as "corporate CDOs." The 58 more recent interviews cover the full range of instruments discussed here.

The interviews took a loosely oral history form, in which interviewees were led through those parts of their careers in which they had been involved with the financial instruments examined here. Questioning was semi-structured and was designed to elucidate the evolution of the relevant market and the main innovations and forms of evaluation in it (sometimes specific issues were dealt with by follow-up email questions or repeat interviews). No claim of statistical representativeness can be made: there is no list of individuals involved in the ABS or CDO markets that can be sampled, so the sample was constructed by "snowballing" from an initial set of interviewees identified via documentary sources.

Oral history interviewing has notorious pitfalls: interviewees may have fallible memories and may wish to promulgate particular views of episodes in which they were involved, especially in the aftermath of a disaster such as the credit crisis. The sensitivity of the topic adds other difficulties. Several banks, for example, now insist that all contacts with the press (a category that currently includes research of this kind) must be through their communications department, often rendering direct interview access impossible. (Many banks face multiple lawsuits, and their fear may be that interviewing might produce information helpful to hostile litigants.) Occasionally, interviews had to be conducted in the presence of public relations staff. At other times, perhaps to avoid this kind of problem, interviewees would ask me to ring them from my mobile telephone from outside their building or in its lobby. They would then leave the building and I would interview them in a cafe or restaurant. The need for anonymity is therefore even greater than normal. In order to ensure it, I sometimes use phrases such as "a rating agency" or "a bank" rather than naming the organization in question.

These drawbacks and difficulties of interviewing rendered a second source of primary data, contemporaneous documents, equally valuable, both in its own right and as a means of triangulation. These documents included the specialist trade press, such as Credit and Creditflux (and, for more recent years in which the ABS and CDO markets have become much more prominent, also the *Financial Times* and *Wall Street Journal*), and the technical literature on the evaluation of ABSs and CDOs, including textbooks, manuals, and the technical reports in which the credit rating agencies described the procedures and models used to rate these instruments. Of course, such documents also have their limitations as historical evidence (textbooks, e.g. portray idealized versions of evaluation practices), but they are useful nonetheless. For example, Fabozzi, Bhattacharya, and Berliner's 2007 textbook or Adelson's informal "trip reports" after ABS conferences (e.g. Adelson 2006d) are now windows into a lost world, mortgage-backed securities before the disaster that became apparent only a few months after they were written.

Because of the need to reconstruct an often-intricate historical process in which apparently small choices had large, lasting consequences, this chapter is inevitably lengthy. It has six sections. After this introduction comes a section on the historical shaping of the evaluation practices surrounding securitizations of pools of residential mortgages. The third section deals with the original "corporate" CDOs, in which the underlying assets were bonds issued by corporations or loans made to them. The section shows that although they too emerged from the world of securitization, the evaluation practices of the world of "credit derivatives" that they came to inhabit differed radically. The fourth section deals with the somewhat later ABS CDOs (CDOs in which the underlying assets were ABSs, mainly mortgage-backed securities, not corporate debt) and shows how an alluring arbitrage opportunity was created by the way in which they were evaluated, particularly by how this evaluation was mapped onto the organizational structures of the rating agencies. The fifth section examines the contribution of ABS CDOs to the crisis. It discusses how ABS CDOs changed the ABS market and (via their super-senior tranches) concentrated the resultant losses, and how default swaps both magnified the crisis and – via a new canonical-mechanism market, the ABX – rendered it visible. The sixth section is the chapter's conclusion.

Mortgage-backed securities and the emphasis on prepayment risk

Mortgage lending in the United States was shaped for decades by government responses to the effects of the Great Depression on the housing market. The form of mortgage prevalent prior to the 1930s – a 5–10-year variable-interest loan, which did not fully amortize, leaving borrowers needing to make large repayments of principal at its maturity – greatly exacerbated the Depression's effects, and at its peak "nearly 10 percent of homes were in foreclosure" (Green and Wachter, 2005, pp. 94–5). In response, the Roosevelt administration created three organizations that radically changed mortgage lending. The Home Owner's Loan Corporation used funds raised from bond sales to buy mortgages that borrowers could not repay and replaced them with new long-term (20-year maturity) fixed rate loans that amortized in full. The Federal Housing Administration (FHA) insured mortgages of this new form against default (in return for insurance premiums paid by the borrower), thus helping to restart large-scale private mortgage lending. The Federal National Mortgage Association (Fannie Mae), set up in 1938, tried to foster a secondary market in mortgages insured by the FHA, though in practice it itself and the Federal Home Loan Banks were the main purchasers (Snowden, 1995, p. 262).

Deliberate government action thus brought about the dominance of what Green and Wachter (2005) call simply "the American mortgage": its interest rate was fixed, typically at around 5 percent to 6 percent, even over the long term (in 1948, the FHA started to insure 30-year mortgages), thus protecting borrowers from interest-rate rises; and borrowers had the right to prepay (redeem) mortgages at any point, with no penalty. "The American mortgage" helped change the United States "from a nation of urban renters to suburban homeowners" (Green and Wachter, 2005, p. 97). However, it always had drawbacks – it was, for example, often not available to ethnic minorities (see Stuart, 2003) – and providing it became ever more difficult in the 1960s, as the low-interest savings accounts that traditionally had funded it were drained by the growing availability of higher rates elsewhere.

With renewed direct government borrowing to fund mortgage lending rendered unattractive by the Johnson administration's growing budgetary problems (Quinn, 2009), a solution was found in selling to private investors government-backed securities based on pools of mortgages. Fannie Mae was partly privatized. Its remaining federal sections, renamed the Government National Mortgage Association (Ginnie Mae), gave a government guarantee to securities backed by pools of mortgages, starting with Ginnie Mae Pool No. 1, issued in February 1970. In 1971, the newly created Federal Home Loan Mortgage Corporation (Freddie Mac) started to sell securities based on pools of mortgages it had itself purchased; Fannie Mae began to do so in 1981. By 1991, Ginnie Mae had guaranteed, and Freddie Mac and Fannie Mae had issued, a total of just over a trillion dollars of mortgage-backed securities (Carron, 1990; Fabozzi and Modigliani, 1992, pp. 18–24; Carruthers and Stinchcombe, 1999; Tower, 1999).

That securitization (the packaging of income-generating assets into pools and the sale of securities that are claims on that income) began its modern history in the United States as a government program,[21] and that what were securitized were "American mortgages" – fixed-interest loans with no prepayment penalties – had lasting effects on how mortgage-backed securities were evaluated. The three government-sponsored enterprises – Ginnie Mae, Fannie Mae, and Freddie Mac – set quality criteria for the mortgages they would guarantee or buy, thus defining "conforming" or "prime" mortgages. They guaranteed investors in mortgage-backed securities against defaults on the underlying mortgages, and the full credit of the US government was seen as backing the three enterprises, so investors could treat those securities as involving no risk of default. (Only Ginnie Mae guarantees were legal obligations of the federal government, but investors generally took the government implicitly to stand behind Fannie Mae and Freddie Mac as well.)

Prepayment, though, was a quite different matter. Originally, the absence in "the American mortgage" of a prepayment penalty was of no great consequence, since the costs of refinancing were considerable: fees and loan points (up-front interest payments) could amount to 2 percent of the new loan (Ranieri, 1996, p. 43), creating a de facto penalty. However, as competition reduced those costs, the option enjoyed by borrowers to re-finance without penalty when interest rates fell became more valuable and much more frequently exercised. As one interviewee put it to me, if you held a mortgage-backed security yielding 5.5 percent, and you noticed that new securities were offering only 4.5 percent because interest rates had fallen, you could be certain that the mortgages underpinning the security you owned were "all going to prepay," and you would therefore quickly stop enjoying the higher yield. While most bonds rise in price when interest rates fall (because the fixed "coupons" they offer become relatively more valuable), this effect is therefore much attenuated for mortgage-backed securities: as this interviewee told me, their price seldom rises above 110 (i.e. 10 percent more than their "par" or face value).

As Lewis Ranieri, Salomon Brothers' famous trader of mortgage-backed securities, complained, the absence of a prepayment penalty meant that "the mortgage instrument becomes so perfect for the borrower that a large economic benefit is taken away from the other participants, including the long-term investor" (Ranieri, 1996, p. 43). What came into being, therefore, were evaluation practices among investors in mortgage-backed securities that focused not on default but on prepayment risk. (Indeed, the government-sponsored enterprises transformed defaults into prepayments: if a borrower defaulted, the enterprises paid investors in the corresponding pool of mortgages the sum they would have received if the mortgage had been prepaid at that point.)

Assessing the exact extent to which the prepayment option reduces the value of mortgage-backed securities is a notoriously difficult matter (neither interest-rate changes themselves nor their precise effects on prepayment rates are fully predictable), and assessing it was traditionally seen as the crucial skill in evaluating mortgage-backed securities. Prepayment was, for example, the primary risk of these securities that Ranieri and the other Salomon Brothers' traders (described in Lewis's *Liar's Poker*, 1990) were slicing, dicing, buying, and selling, and it was for their excellent grasp of prepayment risk that the Salomon Brothers' modelers who helped form the famous hedge fund Long-Term Capital Management were known. Prepayment "was a dominant issue," an interviewee told me: "It drove everything in what people would think about."

Government-sponsored mortgage securitization had, however, been successful despite the prepayment problem, which made it an attractive model for banks and finance companies seeking new ways of funding their lending. In 1977, the first modern "private label" (not government-sponsored) US mortgage-backed securities were issued by the Bank of America, in collaboration with Salomon – an event that prompted Ranieri to coin the term "securitization" (see Ranieri, 1996, p. 31) – and from 1985 onward banks also began securitizing auto loans, truck loans, equipment leases, and credit-card receivables (Rosenthal and Ocampo, 1988, table B.1). The generic term "ABS" (asset-backed security) came into use to describe the products of these and other securitizations.[22]

These new private-label securitizations typically involved the parent bank or finance company setting up a special-purpose vehicle (such as a trust) that was legally separate from its parent, so that the creditors of the one had no claim on the assets of the other. The vehicle then bought pools of loans from the bank, raising the money to do so by selling securities that were claims on the interest payments and principal repayments on those loans. Since those securities had no government backing, the risk of default on those loans could no longer be ignored entirely. The early government-backed securities (known as "pass-through certificates") offered identical, equal shares of the cash flow from the underlying mortgages, but increasingly what was created in private securitizations was not a single class of pass-through certificates, but two, three, or more classes or "tranches" of claims differentiated by credit risk, as in Figure 1.2. The lowest tranche – the "first-loss piece" – bore the first losses caused by default on the pool of mortgages or other assets underpinning the securitization. In early deals, this tranche was typically retained by the bank or finance company that arranged the securitization; later, first-loss securities were sometimes sold by private arrangement to outside investors – often hedge funds – who received a large spread (increment over Libor or other benchmark interest rate) for taking on the risk of loss.

Only if defaults rose to such a level that losses entirely exhausted the lowest tranche were the investors in the next tranche, which came to be called "mezzanine," at risk. In early securitizations this tranche was also often retained by the parent bank or finance company. It would typically be bigger than the lowest tranche – perhaps as much as eight times as big (Rosenthal and Ocampo, 1988, p. 10) – which meant that losses on it could in aggregate be large. However, because the cushion provided by the lowest tranche made the probability of mezzanine losses modest,

A problem in the sociology of knowledge

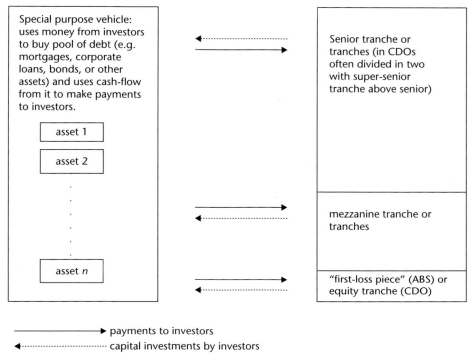

Figure 1.2 An ABS or CDO

Note: Investors in lower tranches receive payments only if funds remain after payments due to investors in more senior tranches are made. In an ABS the assets in the pool are typically mortgages or other consumer debt. In a corporate CDO they are loans made to corporations or bonds issued by them. What is shown is a 'cash CDO': in a 'synthetic CDO' the special purpose vehicle 'sells protection' on the assets via credit default swaps (see the third section of the chapter) rather than buying them.

the bank arranging the securitization could buy insurance against them from the specialist insurers known as "monolines," whose original business had been insuring US municipal bonds. At the top of the hierarchy of tranches was the "senior" tranche, by far the largest, which was always sold to outside investors. With both lower tranches as buffers, the risk of loss on it was seen as very low. Accordingly, only relatively modest "spreads" were thought necessary to compensate for this small risk.

The most prominent of the actors who had to concern themselves with default risk were the rating agencies, whose services had not been needed when securitization was a government program. S&P began to rate securitizations in 1978 and Moody's in 1983.[23] The evaluation practices they employed had three characteristics. First, they were heavily influenced by past episodes of large-scale mortgage defaults. S&P, for example, used the default rates in the United States during the Great Depression as the "stress scenario" for a AAA rating: if a tranche was to be rated AAA, the structure of the security had to protect the tranche from loss even if defaults again rose to Great Depression levels (interview data; Khadem and Parisi, 2007, pp. 546–7). Second, analysis was originally of pools of mortgages, not individual loans. The rating agencies defined the characteristics (such as loan-to-value ratios) of a "benchmark" pool or set of pools and then compared the characteristics of the actual pool of mortgages underlying a mortgage-backed security to the benchmark. Deviations between the two were then translated into set "penalties" (or set "rewards") in the rating processes.[24]

Third, both the rating process and the construction of mortgage-backed securities and other ABSs hinged around the same parameter: the "credit enhancement" or "credit support" level needed for each tranche to achieve the rating that the constructors of the ABS desired. (This level is the total size of the lower tranches, guarantees, reserve funds, and so on that protect a tranche from losses. From the constructor's viewpoint, all these mechanisms are expensive: e.g. if lower tranches are sold to outside investors, the higher spreads required to attract them limit the spread that can be offered on the senior tranche.) For instance, the "penalties" or "rewards" referred to in the previous paragraph took the form of the rating agencies demanding set increases or allowing set decreases in a security's credit support levels to the extent that the pool of mortgages underpinning it was judged riskier or less risky than the benchmark pool. The securities themselves and knowledge of the securities were thus coproduced: credit support levels, the crucial parameters in the design of a tranched security, were determined by the ratings agencies' procedures for evaluating those securities.

From the mid-1990s onward, evaluation techniques based on the analysis of pools were complemented by techniques that did involve estimating the default probabilities of individual mortgages, as least relative to the benchmark of prime lending. The rating agencies developed logistic regression or hazard rate models (S&P's Levels, Moody's Mortgage Metrics, and Fitch's Resilogic), which incorporated characteristics both of the mortgage, such as loan-to-value ratio, and of the borrower, notably his or her FICO score, a measure of creditworthiness developed by Fair, Isaac and Company, originally for forms of consumer credit other than mortgages (see Poon, 2007). The parameters of these models were estimated using large data sets containing both this information and the payment histories of the resultant mortgages, such as those built up since 1991 by the San Francisco-based firm, Loan Performance. The growing use of FICO scores and of models incorporating them both facilitated and was encouraged by increasing volumes of "subprime" lending to people whose impaired credit histories made them ineligible for prime mortgages (Poon, 2009).

From the viewpoint of the quite different evaluation practices that eventually developed around CDOs (discussed in the next section), there remained a striking silence in the evaluation of mortgage-backed securities. There was almost no explicit modeling of statistical dependence among mortgage defaults, in other words no modeling of what CDO specialists came to call "correlation."[25] Defaults were treated mathematically as statistically independent events, with "correlation" handled implicitly. For instance, in the rating of mortgage-backed securities at Standard & Poor's, correlation among defaults induced by macroeconomic variables such as the unemployment rate was handled by continuing to use stress scenarios, even after the regression or hazard-rate models were developed. The latter were used not to estimate absolute default probabilities but to determine the amounts by which the stress-scenario default rates of the benchmark prime pool should be modified for the particular pool being evaluated. (If, for example, the Great Depression-based AAA-stress default rate of the benchmark pool was 10 percent, then the equivalent rate for a pool of subprime, high loan-to-value, low-documentation loans might be 40 percent. In other words, to achieve an AAA rating a tranche based on this pool would have to be able to survive the default of 40 percent of the mortgages in the pool.) So the apparently assumed independence of mortgage defaults was, to quote an interviewee, only "conditional independence": independence conditional on the macroeconomic variables condensed in the historical experiences that had given rise to the stress scenarios.[26]

Another potential source of correlation among mortgage defaults – the vulnerability of a pool of mortgages to local economic conditions – was also handled primarily by organizational procedures rather than mathematical modeling. Geographically concentrated pools were discouraged by applying ratings penalties (again expressed as increases to required credit support levels) to them. With the main mortgage lenders – especially subprime lenders – increasingly operating across the United States, there was no need for them to incur these penalties, and the mortgage pools they presented for rating were typically as diversified as possible geographically. (This unsurprising outcome had significant consequences, as we shall see later, in the evaluation of ABS CDOs.)

With the rating agencies analysing the risk of default, prepayment remained the dominant concern of most investors in mortgage-backed securities. For example, the 2007 textbook on those securities mentioned above in the introduction devoted its section on "valuation and analysis" almost exclusively to prepayment and other matters concerning changes in interest rates, with default scarcely mentioned in that section. As the textbook put it, investors in "senior private label MBS" (in other words, in the upper tranches of private mortgage-backed securities) "typically assume that principal will be returned with 100% certainty.... The driver of performance of these securities is thus not *if*, but *when* principal is paid to the bondholder" (Fabozzi et al., 2007, p. 241; emphases in original).

The "100% certainty" was understandable. The move into subprime was accompanied by considerably increased credit support levels, achieved not just by tranching but by two other safety mechanisms, "excess spread" and "overcollateralization."[27] The resultant typical structure of a subprime ABS is shown in Figure 1.3. As is shown there, around four-fifths of a typical subprime ABS was rated AAA, the same rating as enjoyed by the sovereign bonds of the United States and other leading nations. Although it was universally understood that the default rate on the underlying subprime mortgages would be much higher than on prime, it would have taken what seemed an unimaginably high default rate to eat through all the excess spread, all the overcollateralization, and all the lower tranches to reach the AAA tranches.

Indeed, in practice excess spread and overcollateralization were in general sufficient to protect even the lowest of the investment-grade tranches (the "mezzanine" tranches, usually rated BBB), even when a mild recession caused the delinquency rate on subprime mortgages to double in six months in 2000 and remain high for the next two years (Sanders, 2008, p. 256, chart 2). Although there were some defaults (Ertürk and Gillis, 2005), they were concentrated mainly in a limited number of troubled deals and left the majority of investors unscathed. In retrospect, it is clear that historical contingency played a part in muting the losses in this episode, the first experience of recession since subprime mortgage lending had reached a large scale. House prices continued to rise during it, giving some homeowners the option of selling rather than being foreclosed on and, in particular, limiting lenders' losses if foreclosure did take place (Calomiris, 2009). Indeed, ABS defaults of all kinds (not just of mortgage-backed securities) had been rare until that recession hit. A February 2001 Moody's report noted that "we often hear that no ABS security has ever defaulted" (Harris, 2001, p. 13). While not entirely consistent with the detailed default data in Ertürk and Gillis (2005), the belief is indicative of widespread conviction in the safety of ABSs.

With default still not a major concern of most investors in subprime mortgage-backed securities, the latter offered an advantage compared to prime securities in terms of the traditional evaluation focus, prepayment. Although prepayment rates on subprime were usually higher than on prime mortgages, they were less sensitive to interest-rate changes, thus reducing what was from the investor's viewpoint the traditional main drawback of mortgage-backed securities. As lenders moved into subprime they were able to weaken the entrenched features of "the American mortgage." Floating-rate loans became much more common, as did prepayment penalties, especially penalties for prepaying during the increasingly common period of relatively low – but

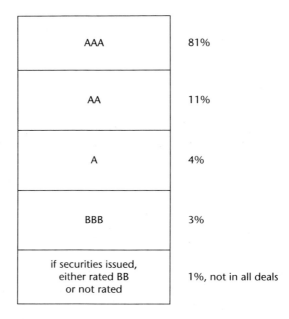

Figure 1.3 Schematic structure of a typical subprime mortgage-backed security

Note: The overall size of the tranches is not shown to scale. The lowest tranche was often replaced by overcollateralization (see note 27 for the meaning of this and of "excess spread"), but if first-loss securities were issued they were generally either unrated or rated BB.

Source: Based on Lucas (2007).

still, in absolute terms, quite high – "teaser" rates (Bhardwaj and Sengupta 2008). In consequence, as a chapter in another textbook put it, "the average lives of the residential [subprime] ABS are likely to be more stable for a given change in interest rates than the average lives of securities created from conforming [i.e. prime] loans" (McElravey, 2006, p. 371). "No income verification" loans were particularly prized from the viewpoint of prepayment: "The capital markets pay a premium" for them, reported Adelson (2006c, p. 14), "because such loans display slower prepayments (and despite the fact that the loans have greater credit risk)."

It would, however, be misleading to suggest that no investors in subprime mortgage-backed securities were concerned with default. While those who bought the higher tranches did largely set it aside, those who bought the lowest externally sold tranches (usually the "mezzanine" tranches, typically with a rating of around BBB, close to the bottom of investment grade) frequently performed their own evaluations of default risk, and they were in quite a powerful position. Those tranches were "historically harder to sell," an interviewee told me, but they usually had to be sold. While the constructor of an ABS might be prepared if necessary to keep the very lowest tranche, retaining the larger mezzanine tranches as well was unattractive. Many deals would simply not have been viable from their constructors' viewpoint if no buyers for those tranches could be found, because those constructors would have needed too much capital of their own (many subprime lenders were quite thinly capitalized).

When constructing a subprime ABS, therefore, those arranging it would often "try to place the BBBs first," secure in the knowledge that the AAA tranches could easily be sold "to people who don't want to think," as another interviewee put it. Mezzanine buyers were often sophisticated: they were "willing to spend the time to understand the collateral and the structure." Some, for example, had developed their own models of mortgage default rather than relying by proxy on the rating agencies' models. These buyers could, and not infrequently did, demand to see the "loan tapes" (the electronic records of the underlying mortgages), which the buyers of higher tranches almost never did, and they had to be allowed a reasonable time (even as late as 2001–03, as much as a week, one such buyer told me) to analyse the contents of the tapes. If they didn't approve of what they found – for instance, over-large pockets of particularly risky mortgages hidden beneath the aggregate data in the offering documents – they might say "I don't like the collateral" and demand that the mortgage pool be changed before they would buy securities based on it.

All that was soon to change utterly. However, before we can understand fully why it did so we need to follow an apparent historical detour. At the end of the 1980s, the securitization of mortgages and other forms of consumer debt was joined by the securitization of corporate debt. On the face of it, it was a small change: the structures of the new instruments, CDOs, were initially almost identical to those of ABSs. Around them, however, a quite different cluster of evaluation practices was to develop.

Corporate CDOs and the emphasis on "correlation"

CDOs were originally a simple extension of the techniques employed in the "private label" securitization of mortgages and other forms of consumer debt. Firms constructing CDOs again set up special-purpose legal vehicles and used the capital raised by the sale of securities to investors to buy pools of corporate debt: at first, bonds issued by corporations but soon also loans made to them. The securities sold by CDOs were tranched in a way similar to a private-label mortgage-backed security (see Figure 1.2).

CDOs began in the exciting but risky fringes of the late-1980s bond market, which traded "junk" (speculative-grade) bonds, typically those issued by corporate raiders as a means of funding their takeover bids. Although they differed in structure from most later deals,[28] what appear to be the first CDOs were issued in 1987 by the San Diego-based Imperial Savings Association, in conjunction with the investment bank Drexel, Burnham, Lambert, whose heavy involvement in the junk-bond market was famously led by Michael Milken. Sharply increased junk-bond default rates, the February 1990 bankruptcy of Drexel, and the imprisonment of Milken for securities violations temporarily returned junk bonds to the margins of finance. However, from 1996 on, CDOs started being used on a large scale by banks to shed credit risk from their portfolios of loans to corporations and to reduce the capital reserves that regulators insisted they hold in respect to that lending. In November 1996, the United Kingdom's National Westminster Bank completed a $5 billion securitization of its loan book known as Rose Funding (previous CDOs had typically been a tenth of that size or smaller). In 1997, further large CDOs were created by, among others, Swiss Bank, NationsBank, Bank of Tokyo/Mitsubishi, Credit Suisse, ABN Amro, Rabobank, J.P. Morgan, and Sumitomo (First Union Securities, Inc. 2000).

Success in selling these huge "balance-sheet CDOs" revealed that they were profitable in their own right, quite apart from their effects on the loan books and capital reserves of their parent banks: investors would buy their tranches at spreads that were sufficiently low that the aggregate flow of cash to those investors was less than the income generated by the loans in the CDO's pool, so generating an arbitrage: a risk-free profit. Balance-sheet CDOs were therefore quickly joined by what insiders explicitly called "arbitrage CDOs," which would buy corporate bonds or loans on the open market and capture this arbitrage.

As described above, the political economy of US mortgage lending led to evaluation practices focused primarily on prepayment. The latter was a peripheral concern in the evaluation of CDOs (with no equivalent of government action on behalf of mortgagors, prepayment of corporate loans was generally either prohibited or subject to stringent penalties), and default was always the focus, with the rating agencies playing an essential role right from the start. In the early balance-sheet CDOs, banks often did not let investors know the names of the corporations whose loans had been packaged and sold, fearing loss of those corporations' business if they discovered that their bankers had publicly divested themselves of exposure to them. In that situation, investors had little but ratings to go on.

Rating agencies were told the composition of a CDO's pool, and – at least in the United States – the corporate debts that formed the pool would typically already have been rated. By the early 1990s the rating agencies had accumulated data sets of corporate defaults from which what they called the "idealized" default rates corresponding to a particular rating could be inferred. (For example, Moody's early 1990s estimate of the 10-year default rate of companies rated AAA was 1.0 percent; for BAA companies, it was 4.4 percent. See Lucas et al., 1991, p. 6.) These databases could also be used to estimate recovery rates: the typical extent to which the loss following default was less than total. For example, Hourican (1990, p. 338) noted that "studies indicate that defaulted bonds trade at an average price of 40 percent of par [face value] one month after default."

Default probabilities and recovery rates thus seemed knowable. But how could they be combined to estimate the probability of different levels of loss in a CDO's pool? If corporate defaults were statistically independent events, then those probabilities could be calculated using only elementary probability theory.[29] However, it was also clear that the assumption of statistical independence was untenable:

> For example, among companies rated Ba at the beginning of 1974, 6.1% defaulted over the next 10 years, compared with 21.2% over the 10-year period beginning in 1981. The magnitude of variations in these default rates suggest the presence of correlation, meaning that if one company defaults, there is a greater likelihood that others will default.
>
> (Lucas et al., 1991, p. 2)

As with mortgages, some of this correlation would be common exposure to the same macroeconomic conditions. With no publicly available model of correlated corporate defaults to draw on in the late 1980s and early 1990s, the rating agencies initially handled that issue using a "conditional independence" approach closely analogous to that used in rating mortgage-backed securities. In evaluating CDOs, both S&P and Moody's again "stressed" historically average corporate default probabilities by greater amounts for higher targeted ratings and then used those stressed probabilities in a calculation that assumed defaults to be independent events. The additional correlation that would come from poorly diversified pools of assets (e.g. loans heavily concentrated in a particular industry) was again handled procedurally, just as it had been for mortgages. Thus S&P "notched" (reduced by one or more ratings grades) the ratings of all the debt instruments in any industrial sector that formed more than 8 percent of a CDO's pool (interview data; Standard & Poor's, n.d., p. 36).[30]

These relatively simple ways of evaluating CDOs, in which correlation was not modeled explicitly but handled procedurally, changed more quickly than their counterparts for mortgage-backed securities and in quite a different direction. The impetus for change was external to the rating agencies: the growing influence within banking of derivatives, notably options and interest-rate swaps.[31] By the 1980s, professional traders of these derivatives did not simply evaluate them by following set procedures akin to those then used by the rating agencies but employed explicit, sophisticated mathematical or economic models, many based on the eventually Nobel Prize-winning Black–Scholes–Merton option model (Black and Scholes, 1973; Merton, 1973). These models had an impact on the evaluation practices surrounding mortgage-backed securities – since prepayment is an option, one can apply option theory to calculate by how much it reduces a security's value, and the Salomon team were known for their skill in this – but they brought about a far more radical change in the evaluation of CDOs.

Black, Scholes, and Merton had also applied their options work to modeling the value of a corporation's debt.[32] Oldrich Vasicek (a Czech-born probability theorist who had worked at Wells Fargo, where Black and Scholes were consultants) then showed how this approach could be extended to value a large, homogeneous, highly granular portfolio of corporate loans (Vasicek, 1991). Vasicek's model was commercially confidential, but a more general computerized simulation version of it was incorporated into CreditMetrics, a system for measuring credit risk developed by J.P. Morgan. The bank, which was a particularly active proponent of the credit default swaps discussed below, made both CreditMetrics itself and a detailed description of it (Gupton, Finger, and Bhatia, 1997) available to other market participants, because (as an interviewee involved told me) it wanted to promote the market for these swaps by giving other banks a way of measuring how they could use them to reduce credit risk. In these "Gaussian copula" models, correlation – previously handled procedurally and almost entirely implicitly – was modeled explicitly.[33]

The creators of the big "balance-sheet" deals that made CDOs mainstream were typically not in banks' securitization or junk bond departments but in their derivatives teams, especially those specializing in interest-rate swaps. In consequence, despite the similarity in structure of ABSs and CDOs, the creators of the new wave of the latter thought of them not as securitizations but as "credit derivatives," a term that first came into use in the early 1990s at Bankers Trust (see Sanford, 1993, p. 239), a bank that was prominent in developing new derivatives to disaggregate and make tradable the different aspects of what an interviewee then employed there called the "bucket of risks" involved in lending. Sometimes the derivatives teams discovered only accidentally that others in a different department of the same bank had long experience of similar structures:

> One of the salespeople in Bank of America was in our Chicago office [in 1997], getting a cup of coffee, showing it [a planned CDO-like instrument] to a colleague. The guy behind [an ABS specialist] leans over and says, "that's a really neat idea." He's been doing that for years ... securitizing ... putting diversified pools of assets into a vehicle and tranching off the risk.

By the mid-1990s, the derivatives teams already inhabited a world in which sophisticated mathematical models were central, and they were quick to adopt Gaussian copula models of CDOs (interview data; Tett, 2009b). That then made purely procedural ratings techniques such as notching begin to seem outdated: as one interviewee employed at a rating agency in this period told me, notching was "not a proper correlation method." All three main agencies largely switched to evaluating CDOs using Gaussian-copula software systems: S&P with its November 2001 CDO Evaluator, Fitch with its July 2003 Vector, and Moody's with its May 2004 CDOROM.[34]

By making credit correlation explicit for the first time, these and other copula models raised the issue of how to measure it. It was a crucial issue: the assumption of low levels of correlation was at the very core of the rationale for CDOs, especially arbitrage CDOs. They depended on being able to take a diversified pool of corporate bonds or loans with relatively modest ratings (and the high spreads that went with those ratings) and package them into a structure that would have large tranches with higher ratings. Those tranches could then be sold at lower spreads, and the difference could be pocketed as arbitrage profits. Low correlation was what made the high ratings justifiable and the arbitrage feasible, in effect making relevant the analogy with coins tossed independently. (One coin can easily turn up tails; twenty independently tossed coins are most unlikely to.) If the correlations among them were low, a large portfolio of corporate bonds or loans was most unlikely to suffer the large number of defaults that would endanger a CDO's AAA tranche, even if each of those individual bonds or loans was rated BBB or even BB.

In the way Gaussian copula models were formulated in the late 1990s at banks such as J.P. Morgan, which had overtaken Bankers Trust as the leading player in the credit derivatives market (Tett, 2009b), the correlation between two corporations was the correlation between the changing market values of their assets. However, this market value is not directly observable (it can diverge radically from the "book" value of those assets on a corporation's balance sheet). So, as a former J.P. Morgan trader told me, they – and also others in banks using Gaussian copula models – simply took the readily measurable correlation of two corporations' stock prices as a proxy for their unobservable asset-value correlations, even if doing so had, as one textbook put it, "no theoretical justification" (Chaplin, 2005, p. 260).

With the exception of Fitch, which adopted a modified version of this way of estimating correlation, the rating agencies took other approaches more deeply rooted in their organizational practices. When Moody's started using Gaussian copula models, its modelers used either estimates based on the judgments of experienced ratings staff or values implied by patterns in the records of their actions in downgrading or upgrading corporations (Fu et al., 2004).[35] When Standard & Poor's was designing its new Gaussian copula system, CDO Evaluator, released in November 2001, it did seek econometrically to estimate the correlation values that would yield the degree of clustering of corporate defaults that had historically been encountered (Parisi, 2004, p. 2). However, the limited number of cases in its default database as it stood then made that estimation hard (only with version 3.0 of Evaluator released in December 2005, when the default database was much larger, did S&P fully embrace these estimates), so consistency with previous organizational practice was also a criterion that shaped the original choice of correlation parameters. In line with the "conditional independence" approach used prior to the Gaussian copula, the correlation between firms in different industries in the original version of Evaluator was set at zero (Bergman, 2001), with dependence on common macroeconomic conditions captured by continuing to "stress" default probabilities, raising them most if a AAA rating was sought. The choice in that original version of 0.3 for the correlation between corporations in the same industry similarly reflected previous practice, an interviewee told me. The value 0.3 was chosen "partly to maintain consistency with the previous notching scheme": when applied to similar asset pools it tended to generate similar results, that is, similar ratings and credit support levels.

Although no one at the time could have foreseen it, this apparently small, technical decision in late 2001 (the choice of an intra-industry correlation of 0.3) was pivotal to the chain of events that I will turn to in the next section. First, though, other ways in which the arrival of derivatives specialists transformed securitization need to be considered. They brought with them a new instrument originally developed in the early 1990s at Bankers Trust (Tett, 2009b, p. 24): the credit default swap. It is a bilateral contract in which one party, the "protection buyer," pays regular premiums to the other party for "protection" against default by a third party (Ford Motor Company, for instance) on bonds issued by it and/or loans made to it. Should Ford default, the protection buyer has the right to deliver Ford's bonds or loans to the protection seller and receive their full face value. The protection buyer does not need to hold Ford's bonds or loans: it can simply purchase them at the point at which they have to be delivered (following default they will be trading at a fraction of their face value).

As the former Bank of America credit derivatives specialist put it to me, credit default swaps gave him and his colleagues a capacity the ABS world of the sarcastic coffee-queue interlocutor quoted above did not have, for all its much longer experience of securitization: "what he couldn't do ... was synthetically transfer" credit risk. Swaps made "synthetic" CDOs possible. Instead of the special-purpose legal vehicle having to buy loans or bonds for its asset pool, it could simply sell protection on them via credit default swaps, using the premiums it received from the swaps to pay the investors in the CDO. Those investors faced a broadly similar pattern of risks and returns (again, e.g. investors in the lowest tranche were first to lose their capital, in this case if one or more of the swaps was triggered by default on the bonds and/or loan it covered), but a synthetic CDO was quicker and easier to construct than a cash CDO, as the CDOs involving the actual purchase of assets were called. Credit default swaps also made single-tranche CDOs possible. Such a CDO does not involve a separate legal vehicle: it is simply a bilateral contract between an external investor and a dealer (typically a credit-derivatives trading desk at a major bank), in which the investor earns regular fees by selling the dealer protection on a particular tranche of losses on a mutually agreed pool of corporate bonds and/or loans. Introduced around 2001, by 2003 single-tranche deals dominated the corporate CDO market (Reoch, 2003, p. 8). Because they too were synthetic (the corporate loans or bonds in question served simply as a reference pool, a way of defining the deal; they didn't have to be bought), single-tranche CDOs could be set up almost immediately: "single-tranche technology is all over in a week," said the above interviewee. "You dream up the portfolio on a Monday, structure on the Wednesday, Thursday, and Friday."

Single-tranche CDOs greatly increased the salience of "correlation." Even once it has been completed, a single-tranche CDO leaves a dealer with a position that needs to be hedged. (The dealer has bought protection, and thus the hedges will consist predominantly of sales of protection. Since these are income generating, they earn the dealer the money to pay the investor and earn a profit from the deal.) This hedging was not a simple task, because the fluctuating value of a tranche reflects not just changes in the perceived individual creditworthiness of the corporations in the CDO's reference pool but also changing beliefs about the likely clustering of defaults – in other words, about "correlation." To help them hedge the latter, in 2003–04 the main credit-derivatives dealers set up markets in tranched, tradable credit "indices," which they could use to trade correlation. (That realist phrasing is deliberate: "correlation" was increasingly talked about, for example, in the trade press, not as a parameter of a model but as a real phenomenon with real implications.) Such an index resembles a standardized synthetic CDO – in most cases with a fixed list of 125 corporations each making up 0.8 percent of its reference pool – and protection can be bought or sold on either the index as a whole or on standard tranches of it. The indices (which quickly became liquid, high-volume markets) provided a new way of estimating correlation. A Gaussian copula or similar model could be applied "backwards" to infer the correlation levels consistent with the prices of protection on index tranches. (For example, if the cost of protection on higher tranches has increased, but the cost of buying protection via credit default swaps on the individual corporations making up the index is unchanged, it can be inferred that participants' estimates of correlation have increased, or indeed, if one wants to be fully realist, "correlation itself" has increased.)

Along with broadly canonical-mechanism markets in credit default swaps that had also emerged (see, e.g. Rule, 2001), the tranched index markets were the foundation of a wider epistemic change that seemed well under way at the time of the first interviews for this research, in 2006–07. The models used by the rating agencies to evaluate CDOs and ABSs such as mortgage-backed securities were explicitly backward-looking: their parameters were mainly either crystallizations of previous organizational practices or estimated using data from recent or (in the case of the Great Depression) distant historical experience. The new canonical-mechanism markets freed CDO modeling from these organizational and statistical traces of the past: for example, both correlation and default probability could be inferred from today's market prices, not past experience.[36]

The change sharpened already-existing differences between the evaluation practices surrounding ABSs and CDOs, but it was never complete: among the rating agencies, only Moody's made much use of this approach, and even there it was only as a complement to more traditional techniques. It did, however, seem a harbinger of the eventual complete integration of CDOs into the full cognitive world of modern derivatives modeling. The "quants" who populated that world – who often had PhDs in mathematics, physics, or engineering – could seem very alien to ABS specialists who prided themselves on understanding the everyday material and legal realities of lending. As one of the latter complained to me, those quants had "never gone out to collect any money," whether "with lawsuit or baseball bat." In consequence, they "didn't have to be very intimate with the underlying," in other words with the debts that ultimately underpinned the instruments whose prices they modeled: they "could treat it as an abstraction." For a brief moment, nonetheless, it seemed as if the future might be theirs.

The evaluation of ABS CDOs and the arbitrage opportunity it created

However, alongside the world of corporate CDOs, with its increasingly sophisticated products and models, another world of CDOs had developed: CDOs in which the underlying assets were tranches of ABSs, residential mortgage-backed securities in particular. Viewed from the corporate CDO world I have just described, ABS CDOs could seem laggards: a "very boring part" of the market, as one interviewee put it, in which profit came only from "originating transactions; it didn't come from risk-taking, it didn't come from like good credit assessment. It was purely, you know, in structuring fees." The main industry body, the International Swaps and Derivatives Association, standardized the terms of credit default swaps on ABSs only in June and December 2005 (Damouni 2005), six years later than it had done so for their corporate equivalents. The single-tranche CDOs that reshaped the corporate CDO world were relatively rare in the world of ABSs. A set of tradable ABS indices (the ABX) was launched only in January 2006, and a tranched ABS index (TABX) only in February 2007. As innovations of this kind, originating in corporate CDOs, were replicated for ABS CDOs, the latter nevertheless would catch up, an interviewee told me in January 2007: "The asset-backed arena . . . is going to ape, I think, the corporate. . . . [The] ABS market will get there in half the time it took the corporate market." Before that could happen, however, ABS CDOs, that "boring part" of the market, were to be at the core of the greatest financial crisis for the best part of a century.

ABS CDOs emerged in the second half of the 1990s, though they formed only a small market (of the 283 CDOs issued in 1997–9, only eight were ABS CDOs; Newman *et al.*, 2008, p. 34, exhibit 1), and originally had structures quite different from those of the decade to come.[37] What is to my knowledge the first with that structure was issued in 1999 by a team at Prudential Securities involving Chris Ricciardi, who was later to help make Merrill Lynch into a giant-scale constructor of ABS CDOs. The team found themselves at a disadvantage in corporate CDOs, because Prudential had little involvement in the forms of corporate lending then popular as asset pools. However, as Ricciardi told the trade magazine *Credit*, "Once you have CDOs, people ask, 'what else can I do with CDOs?'" (Fahmy, 2005). Prudential had a large ABS business, and Ricciardi noticed that some classes of ABS – such as the subordinate tranches of ABSs whose pools were second-lien mortgages – offered higher spreads than equivalently rated corporate debt. So the arbitrage that could be achieved by packaging corporate debt into a CDO could be done even more profitably with ABSs.

The attractiveness of ABS CDOs similar to the Prudential deal was greatly enhanced by the 2000–02 downturn, which led to defaults and bankruptcies (e.g. of overambitious telecoms providers) that caused substantial losses to investors in the lower tranches of many corporate CDOs. In that context, the excellent performance record of mortgage-backed securities made them seem an attractive substitute for corporate debt. In a single year, ABS CDO issuance more than doubled (to in excess of $20 billion in 2001) and the ABS share of the CDO market roughly tripled (Hu, 2007), and issuance continued to grow sharply thereafter: in 2006 alone, ABS CDOs totaling $307.7 billion were issued.[38] While the pools of the early ABS CDOs often contained ABSs from a wide variety of sectors – such as securitizations of aircraft and equipment leases, auto loans, and credit-card receivables (Roy and McDermott, 2007) – several of those sectors also suffered badly in the downturn (Adelson, 2003; Perraudin and van Landschoot, 2004). Accordingly, ABS CDOs increasingly replicated Prudential's design. By 2004, it was common for three-quarters or more of the pool to consist of subprime mortgage-backed securities (Whetten and Adelson, 2005, p. 2).

By the end of the 1990s, CDOs had largely split off organizationally from the world of securitization and ABSs from which they had sprung: they were the province of different teams or even different departments of banks. There were therefore often fierce battles over which team or department should have responsibility for the new and highly profitable ABS CDOs. An interviewee at one leading investment bank, for example, described how there had previously been a clear division of labor between its Structured Transactions team, which handled corporate CDOs, and its Securitized Products Group, which had responsibility for ABSs. The influential head of the latter told the former that they "can't do that [ABS CDOs] without us," and eventually a compromise was reached to conduct the activity jointly with a "50:50 split on revenue."

The arbitrage that was the basis of the profitability of ABS CDOs depended entirely on the ratings of their tranches, and by the late 1990s the rating agencies also had evolved a division of labor, at least in their large head offices in New York (analysts were sometimes less specialized in smaller offices such as those in London). Unlike in the banks, though, there seems to have been little conflict over who should have responsibility for rating ABS CDOs: in all three agencies, CDO teams took on the new ABS CDOs, using the ratings of the underlying mortgage-backed securities or other ABSs that their ABS colleagues had already produced. That organizational division of labor mirrored the existing division for corporate CDOs, in which the CDO teams reused ratings of the underlying corporate debt produced by their colleagues in the department that rated corporate bonds. (Such conflict as did take place seems mainly to have concerned ABS CDOs in which the underlying ABSs had not been rated by the agency in question, but only by others. At least one Moody's analyst took the view that it was improper to rate an ABS CDO under these circumstances.[39] In general, though, it was regarded as acceptable when rating an ABS CDO to use another agency's ratings of the ABSs, at least so long as one "notched" them – i.e. slightly reduced these ratings – if the other agency could be viewed as less rigorous.)

Mapping the evaluation of ABS CDOs onto the organizational structure of rating agencies in this way had the additional advantage of minimizing the additional work that needed to be done. By in effect treating ABSs as if they were corporate bonds or loans, existing CDO models could be used with little or no modification. Of the three necessary sets of parameters, the first two – the default probabilities of the ABSs in a CDO's pool and their recovery rates in the event of default – could again be estimated relatively easily: the former from ABSs' ratings, with corrections increasingly made for the growing evidence that ABSs were less likely to default than corporate bonds with the same rating (see, e.g. Roy and McDermott, 2007); and the latter from data on the limited number of ABS defaults that had taken place (Ertürk and Gillis, 2005; Tung, Hu, and Cantor, 2006). Again, though, correlation posed the rating agencies the most challenging problems. (Recall that if correlation is high it is impossible to form large highly rated tranches from a pool of assets with only modest ratings.) All three of the routes, discussed in the previous section, by which knowledge of corporate credit correlation was generated were largely blocked when it came to ABS correlation. First, there was no full equivalent of corporations' stock prices to use, because ABSs did not trade in a canonical-mechanism market. Second, the very advantage of ABSs – the rarity of ABS defaults – made extracting a reliable correlation estimate by analysis of the clustering of defaults even harder than in the corporate case. Third, until February 2007 (at which point the TABX index touched on in the next section was introduced) there was no tranched ABS index market from which beliefs about correlation could be inferred.

That left essentially two choices: either estimating correlations from the performance record of ABSs as crystallized in an agency's own previous actions in upgrading or downgrading ABS tranches (these ratings transitions are more plentiful than defaults, thus easing the estimation problem) or directly employing human judgment. Moody's used baseline estimates based on ratings transitions, with judgmental additions (Toutain *et al.*, 2005). Fitch's correlation estimates were based on "expert assumptions" (Zelter, 2003, slide 5; see also Gill *et al.*, 2004, p. 10). Standard & Poor's attempted to estimate ABS correlation econometrically, and my sources conflict on the success of the effort. Parisi (2004, p. 2) suggests that correlations were estimated in this way, while an interviewee reports: "We did try to estimate ABS correlations, but the data was too limited to derive reliable/stable estimates, given the relative stability of ratings, paucity of defaults and the number of different asset classes with different dynamics resulting from different transaction structures and underlying assets." According to this interviewee, consistency with previous practice again played a role, in particular in the choice of the same correlation, 0.3, between ABSs in the same sector (i.e. same type of lending) as was used for corporations in the same industry.

Moody's estimates of the correlation between ABSs in the same sector (such as subprime mortgages) were also around 0.3.[40] Fitch's explicitly judgment-based ABS correlations were higher than S&P's and Moody's: Whetten and Adelson (2005, p. 2) report the use at Fitch of intrasectoral ABS correlations in the range 0.3 to 0.55, and 0.55 seems to have been the figure used for subprime residential mortgage-backed securities. However, for reasons to do with how Fitch implemented its Gaussian copula model, its 0.55 may not in practice have been more onerous in its effects on ratings than S&P's 0.3.[41] In addition, Fitch was in relative terms an increasingly marginal player. S&P and Moody's each rated between 85 percent and 95 percent of all CDOs (ABS and CDO investors typically expect instruments to have ratings from at least two agencies), while Fitch's share of CDO ratings slipped from around 65 percent before 2004 to around 15 percent in 2006–07 (Barnett-Hart, 2009, p. 18, figure 8). In consequence, the rating of ABS CDOs was in practice done by assuming a correlation of 0.3 (in the case of S&P) or close to 0.3 (in the case of Moody's) between ABSs from the same sector, such as subprime residential mortgages.

It was a consequential assumption. A correlation of 0.3 or thereabouts made it possible not just to package the higher tranches of subprime or similar mortgage ABSs into "high-grade ABS CDOs" but also to package their mezzanine tranches into "mezzanine ABS CDOs." As shown in Figure 1.4, the AAA tranches of the latter would be smaller in aggregate than in high-grade ABS

A problem in the sociology of knowledge

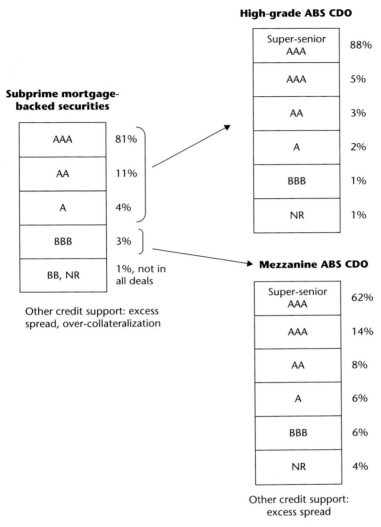

Figure 1.4 Packaging tranches of subprime mortgage-backed securities into ABS CDOs
Note: Tranche sizes not shown to scale. 'NR' means 'not rated.'
Source: Modified from Lucas (2007).

CDOs, and some use of excess spread (see note 27) would normally be needed to achieve the requisite level of credit support. Nevertheless, to be able to take BBB raw materials and fashion a product that was mainly AAA was an enticing arbitrage opportunity, and it was one that was pursued with great vigor in the years immediately prior to the crisis.

The arbitrage was a result that was possible only because of the assumption of relatively modest correlation: one interviewee told me that assuming 0.5, rather than 0.3, would have undermined the arbitrage, leaving mezzanine ABS CDOs economically unviable. Given that – and given the dependence of rating agencies on fees earned from the issuers of securities, and the possibility of those issuers "ratings shopping" (choosing the agencies that offer the more favorable

31

ratings) – should we interpret the choice of a correlation of 0.3 or thereabouts as strategic behavior guided by anticipated fee income?

Consider, for example, S&P's choice of 0.3 as the intrasectoral ABS correlation parameter for CDO Evaluator (the first of the rating-agency Gaussian copula systems, released, as noted, in November 2001). The ABS CDOs of that period were far more diversified across sectors than later deals, and subprime residential mortgage-backed securities typically made up only 30 percent to 40 percent of their asset pools (Whetten and Adelson 2005, p. 20). In that context, the choice of correlation between sectors is at least as important to rating outcomes as correlations within them, because the correlation matrix will contain more intersectoral than intrasectoral correlations. S&P's choice of 0.1 for the former (Bergman, 2001) was more stringent than the figure of zero it employed for interindustry correlations and higher than the values of 0.04 to 0.06 Moody's was later to derive from analysis of ABS ratings transitions (Toutain et al., 2005, p. 13).

Among that backdrop, S&P's choice of 0.3 as the intrasectoral ABS asset correlation could actually be interpreted as cautious, more cautious, at least in the case of mortgages, than a purely econometric estimate: Parisi (2004) reports an average correlation of 0.06 of the losses on pairs of pools of US residential mortgages in the period 1995–2002. If the interviewee quoted above is correct in reporting that a major influence on the choice was the use of 0.3 as the intraindustry correlation assumption, then it was the transfer to the rating of ABS CDOs of an assumption that was at least sometimes seen in its original context as "overly conservative" (Chen et al., 2005, p. 3n). There was sharp controversy about one of the correlation assumptions in S&P's Evaluator, but it concerned the zero interindustry correlation (the remaining trace of the older evaluation practices incorporating stressed scenarios and conditional independence),[42] not the 0.3 intrasectoral ABS correlation. As far as I can tell, no one at the time foresaw, at least at all clearly,[43] that the effects of the choice of 0.3 would in fact be far from conservative.

If the choice of 0.3 or thereabouts as the intrasectoral ABS asset correlation was the chief proximate precondition of the arbitrage that fueled mezzanine ABS CDOs,[44] the background precondition was the separate evaluation first of the ABSs in the CDO's asset pool and then of the CDO itself. As suggested above, that was the "natural" way to map the evaluation task onto the organizational structure of the rating agencies, but it is also clear, with hindsight, that this two-step organizational division of labor fed the arbitrage. The justification of awarding high ratings to securities based on a pool of assets of only moderate credit quality is ultimately the diversification of that pool. In that sense, diversification can be a "free lunch": at little additional cost, it dilutes away almost all the idiosyncratic risk posed by an equivalently sized holding of a particular asset, leaving only the systematic risk posed by the exposure of all the assets to the same underlying economic factor or factors.[45]

In the two-step process, however, the lunch was frequently being eaten twice, so to speak. The rating of each ABS reflected the way in which the diversification of its pool of mortgages (including its geographical diversification) minimized idiosyncratic risk, and then diversification (in the form of the modest correlation assumption) was also taken to justify higher ratings of most of the CDO than of the component ABSs. Here is where the organizational analogy between the evaluation of a CDO made up of corporate bonds and a CDO made up of ABSs was treacherous. A corporate bond or loan will typically be high in idiosyncratic risk, hence the justification of giving higher ratings to tranches formed from a diversified pool of such bonds or loans than to its components. ABSs, however, often no longer contained much idiosyncratic risk that could be diversified away, but only systematic risk (exposure to common factors such as the risk of nationwide house price decline) that was not greatly reduced by packaging ABSs into a pool. There is some evidence that relations between the ABS specialists and the CDO specialists in the rating agencies were not always good (an interviewee reports that in his agency "communication between the ABS and CDO groups was very poor"),[46] but even if they had been harmonious this effect – the benefits of diversification being consumed twice – would have been created if each group had continued to follow its habitual practices.

This issue – that in the two-step evaluation process the free lunch of diversification was often being eaten twice – also bears upon an argument frequently invoked by market participants prior to the crisis as implying the safety of ABS CDOs: that the United States had never experienced a substantial nationwide house-price decline since the Great Depression, with sharp falls restricted to specific regions. If that could be extrapolated into the future (and of course we now know it could not be), it did mean that the safety of ABSs was increased by geographical diversification. However, it also was taken as indicating the even greater safety of ABS CDOs, which often added little further geographical diversification because the constructors of the underlying ABSs had already diversified them as much as possible to avoid ratings penalties.

From this viewpoint, it is worth considering what would have happened if, instead of splitting the evaluation of ABS CDOs into two steps, conducted by two separate groups (the ABS group and the CDO group), the rating agencies had allocated the entire task to just one of the groups and instructed it to use just its own techniques, developing those techniques as necessary, despite the very large amount of extra work that would have been created. To ask what would have happened if an ABS CDO had been evaluated using solely the logistic regression or hazard-rate models and historically based stress scenarios sketched in the second section of this chapter is an exercise in the counterfactual. It would have required merging the loan-level data from multiple ABSs, applying those models to the entire merged pool, then modeling the cash flow consequences for each ABS of the predicted defaults and recoveries, and finally modeling the knock-on consequences for the CDO. I have not found an instance of this being done, and interviewees seem to regard it as still not fully practicable, primarily for computational reasons.[47]

What does seem clear, though, is that had it been technically feasible to rate a mezzanine ABS CDO using only ABS practices, doing so would have been unlikely to permit the CDO to have large AAA tranches. When the mortgage default rates that characterized a AAA stress were applied to the giant merged pool, the cash flow to most of the BBB ABS tranches would most likely cease. Cash flow into the ABS CDO would then be greatly reduced, and in consequence even its higher tranches would default and would thus have had to be deemed not eligible for a AAA rating. (Indeed, that is in essence what has actually happened. The US mortgage market has suffered default rates that approach those of a AAA stress. The AAA tranches of subprime ABSs have so far generally survived that stress – while many have suffered ratings downgrades, only a few have defaulted, as shown in Table 1.1 – but their BBB tranches often haven't survived, and mezzanine ABS CDOs, which are composed mainly of those tranches, have therefore failed en masse.)

There are, however, not counterfactual but actual instances of the obverse: evaluating an ABS CDO using only CDO practices.[48] In around 2006, some CDO specialists at one of the rating agencies tried as "a case of intellectual curiosity," as one of them put it to me, to do just that. They applied the oldest and simplest of all the Gaussian copulas – Vasicek's model – to pools of mortgages, calibrating its correlation parameter to the typical ratings of ABS tranches (they found a value of between 0.3 to 0.4 to fit). They then "allocate[d] losses randomly to each ABS deal ... so that the frequency (and severity) with which each BBB ABS tranche defaulted could be recorded. This allowed the correlation between each pair of ABS tranches to be calculated." The result was far from the modest level of 0.3 that generated the ABS CDO arbitrage: "This correlation turned out to be very high indeed, in the region of 0.8." Unfortunately, however, these specialists did not at that point have organizational responsibility for ABS CDO evaluation ("it wasn't 'under our watch' at the time"), and they knew their "method was simplistic," so they "never wrote it up" and took the issue no further.

Table 1.1 CDO evaluator's three-year default probability assumptions versus realized default rate of US subprime mortgage-backed securities issued from 2005 to 2007

	CDO evaluator three-year default probability assumptions, as of June 2006 (%)	Realized incidence of default, as of July 2009 (%)
AAA	.008	.10
AA+	.014	1.68
AA	.042	8.16
AA–	.053	12.03
A+	.061	20.96
A	.088	29.21
A–	.118	36.65
BBB+	.340	48.73
BBB	.488	56.10
BBB–	.881	66.67

Sources: Adelson (2006a); Ertürk and Gillis (2009).

The analysis they had performed is what participants call a "drilldown," an evaluation of a structured financial instrument that does not simply reuse previous evaluations of its components but "drills down" to the assets underlying those components (in this case mortgages). Additional evidence that the organizational division of labor, and not simply the pursuit of fees, mattered to the ratings evaluation of ABS CDOs comes from the contrast in this respect between the evaluations of them and of the instruments whose structure most closely resembled theirs: CDO^{2}s ("CDO-squareds"). These are CDOs whose asset pools consist of tranches of corporate CDOs. CDO s did not cross organizational divides in the way ABS CDO^{2}s did: they were firmly within the remit of the agencies' CDO groups, which had responsibility for the evaluation both of the structure itself and of its components. In this case, drilldown analyses were performed. The CDO groups rated CDO^{2}s by merging the asset pools of the underlying CDOs and applying their Gaussian copula systems to the merged pool. This evaluation practice meant that the "free lunch" of diversification was eaten only once in the evaluation of CDO^{2}s, not twice as in the case of ABS CDOs. It also took into account another potential source of correlation: the frequent presence of the debts of the same corporation in several of the CDOs whose tranches made up the asset pool of a CDO^2. Drilldown evaluation muted the attractiveness of CDO^{2}s as arbitrage opportunities, and the sector never grew to approach anything like the scale of ABS CDOs.

ABS CDOs and the causes of the credit crisis

The overall performance of ABS CDOs is most easily tracked via the incidence of "events of default," which are triggered by very poor performance of the underlying assets.[49] While the ABS CDOs issued from 2001 to 2003 have not performed catastrophically by that metric, from 2004 on each successive vintage was worse than its predecessor. Events of default have been declared in around 30 percent of ABS CDOs issued in 2005; in over 40 percent of those issued in the first half of 2006; in over 70 percent of deals from the second half of 2006; and in over 80 percent of deals from 2007 (Sakoui, 2009). By March 2010, events of default had been declared in 418 CDOs totaling $371.6 billion, the vast majority of them ABS CDOs.[50] The exact losses are still unknown (only 27 percent of those deals had actually been liquidated at that point) but the IMF's October 2008 estimate, quoted in the introduction, of $290 billion still looks reasonable.

While losses on ABS CDOs have not been central to all the failures or near failures of major institutions (they played, e.g. only a small part in the bankruptcy of Lehman Brothers; see Valukas, 2010), their overall role has been large. They triggered the bankruptcy in the early summer of 2007 of two hedge funds run by Bear Stearns, which was the single most clearly identifiable trigger of the crisis. When the funds' main creditor, Merrill Lynch, seized $850 million of their ABS CDOs on June 15, it found it could sell them only at around 20 percent of their face value, "triggering the repricing of CDOs around the world" (Onaran, 2008). The world's largest insurer, AIG, was pushed to the brink of bankruptcy by write-downs of $33.2 billion (49.6 percent of its total losses) on credit default swaps via which it had sold protection on ABS CDOs. The world's largest bank, Citigroup, nearly suffered the same fate following $34.1 billion ABS CDO write-downs (61.6 percent of its total losses). Merrill Lynch incurred calamitous $26.1 billion ABS CDO write-downs, UBS a near-calamitous $21.9 billion, Ambac (a leading monoline insurer) $11.1 billion, Bank of America $9.1 billion, and Morgan Stanley $7.8 billion. Among the major institutions whose losses are analyzed by Benmelech and Dlugosz (2009), ABS CDO write-downs totaled around two and a half times the write-downs on residential mortgage-backed securities themselves.

Of course, ABS CDO losses came from ABS losses, and those in turn stemmed from mortgage defaults. By the end of 2009, 4.58 percent of all the residential mortgages in the United States were in foreclosure (a rate without precedent since the Great Depression) and a further 10.44 percent were delinquent (one or more payments overdue), with rates for subprime or Alt-A (mortgages assessed as being of higher quality than subprime but lower than prime) even higher: for example, 15.58 percent of subprime mortgages were in foreclosure, and a further 25.26 percent delinquent.[51] The result has been losses on ABSs hugely in excess of those assumed in the rating of ABS CDOs (see Table 1.1), and those losses are the ultimate cause of events of default in the majority of recent ABS CDOs.

These mortgage default rates have multiple, interacting causes, including the substantial falls in US house prices since 2006, the sharp rise in unemployment since 2007, and the well-documented decline in the standards of US mortgage underwriting in the years prior to the crisis. The burgeoning literature on the credit crisis has yet to reach a definitive judgment on the relative importance of these causes, and that is a task well beyond the scope of this chapter. Most directly pertinent here are mortgage underwriting standards. It is well established – three existing papers, using different methodologies, have all found evidence of it[52] – that the securitization of mortgages weakened the screening of applicants by the originators of these mortgages. The likely reason is similarly well understood and not unique to the current crisis: securitized lending creates an agency problem by transferring many of the costs of default from loan originators to investors, a problem that is exacerbated if – as was often the case – the originators of loans are remunerated, directly or indirectly, according to the volume of loans they originate. Problems of this kind undermined all the various pre-1930 waves of mortgage securitization in the United States (Snowden, 1995). For example, in the 1880s and early 1890s large numbers of mortgage companies issued bonds backed by Western farm mortgages. The 1890s depression saw most such companies fail, in part because "their local agents ... generally working on a commission basis ... were overgenerous in approving loans" (Bogue, 1955, p. 267).

For a quarter of a century from the 1977 rebirth of private-label mortgage securitization in the United States, this ever-present agency problem was largely held at bay. Clearly, one important set of gatekeepers in this respect was the rating agencies, and much attention has focused on the question of whether they loosened their standards of evaluation of mortgage-backed securities in the years prior to the crisis (see, e.g. Smith, 2008a, 2008b; Fligstein and Goldstein, 2010).

Unfortunately, the snowballing process led me predominantly to rating-agency interviewees who were CDO specialists, not ABS specialists, so my interview data do not answer this question. However, Ashcraft, Goldsmith-Pinkham, and Vickery (2009) examine trends through time in the fraction of subprime and Alt-A mortgage-backed securities that were rated lower than AAA, taking into account both the extent of other forms of credit support (insurance and excess spread) and the characteristics of the underlying mortgage pools (the FICO score of the borrower, loan-to-value ratio, local-area house price changes, etc.). They find that, controlling for all the other variables, the fraction rated below AAA went down by around 20 percent between mid-2005 and mid-2007 (see also Fligstein and Goldstein, 2010). This is consistent with a decline in rating standards, and while Ashcraft *et al.* (2009, p. 22) "remain agnostic" whether the cause is "innocent errors" or "agency problems due to the 'issuer pays' credit rating model," an extensive body of rating-agency email messages released in April 2010 by the Senate Permanent Subcommittee on Investigations does suggest both market-share pressures and a degree of internal doubt about the appropriateness of some ratings.[53]

It is worth noting, however, that this 20 percent decline in the fraction rated below AAA represents only a modest change in the structure of a typical subprime ABS: from lower tranches totaling around 24 percent of the structure to the 19 percent shown in Figure 1.3. The change is small relative to the huge differences – of between 12-fold and over 300-fold – between the previous historical experience of ABS defaults (which I have shown in Table 1.1 as it was captured in the default probability assumptions of CDO Evaluator)[54] and the actual incidence of those defaults during the crisis. Certainly, small causes can have big effects, but any analysis of the crisis that attributes it primarily to declining standards at the rating agencies would have to show a plausible mechanism by which that might have happened here.

It is, therefore, worth also considering the other gatekeepers, discussed in the second section: the traditional buyers of mezzanine ABS tranches, normally rated BBB (Adelson and Jacob, 2008b). By 2005–06, those investors, and the specialists who earlier had insured the mezzanine tranches, had been almost entirely displaced: "About 90% of the recently issued triple-B-rated tranches [of subprime ABSs] have been purchased by CDOs" (Adelson, 2006d, p. 5). The mezzanine ABS CDO managers who replaced them did sometimes try to be discriminating in their ABS purchases. One, for example, told me how he and his colleagues tried to avoid ABSs constructed by the subprime lender Ameriquest, because they felt its lending standards were lower than those of its peers. Another told me how, despite the fact that by 2005–06 the week that traditional mezzanine-tranche buyers had been given to analyse ABSs had often shrunk to less than a day, his firm had nonetheless set up the expensive tools needed for that analysis in such a way that much of it could be performed "in an hour or two."

However, what the constructor of a mezzanine ABS CDO could not do was avoid those tranches altogether. As another interviewee put it: "So, you know, you talk to people [CDO constructors], and they're complaining about the quality [of ABSs].... But they got a mandate to do the CDO, they got to get it done. They got to buy something. So, 'cause they want their fees." In particular, the constructors of ABS CDOs would still buy ABSs even when their spreads no longer seemed, to ABS specialists, to justify their risks: ABS CDOs "will not hesitate to bid spreads tighter than can be fundamentally justified so long as their "arb" [arbitrage] can still be made to 'work'" (Adelson, 2006d, p. 1). Indeed, the aggregate demand from ABS CDOs for mezzanine tranches of ABSs exceeded total supply (as an interviewee put it, CDOs "were so into it, that the amount of paper being created wasn't enough for them"), so even poorly regarded ABS constructors were still able to sell their mezzanine tranches, traditionally the hardest to place. The gatekeeper role of the traditional buyers of those tranches thus vanished entirely.

To the extent that the removal of this second set of gatekeepers facilitated the loosening of standards of mortgage lending, ABS CDOs contributed to their own downfall. They were also at the pinnacle of a broader change. From 1970 to around 2000, mortgage securitization in the United States could be described as predominantly being "securitization in order to lend" (a way of funding lending), and those who saw it like that had an incentive, over and above the presence of rating-agency and mezzanine-buyer gatekeepers, to avoid poor-quality lending: even if defaults on securitized loans no longer directly affected them to any great degree, they would indirectly damage their organization's reputation and thus endanger future funding. In the following decade, however, these priorities were often reversed. "Lending in order to securitize" became a dominant motivation, in other words, making loans in order to capture the arbitrage profits to be reaped by packaging them into ABSs, and then packaging those ABSs into CDOs. The "assembly lines" – as market participants often called them – that did this packaging needed an ample supply of raw material, in other words, of mortgages. Demand for the latter was so strong that mortgage brokers found themselves the objects of eager attention from "wholesalers," representatives of banks or other finance companies who would pay commissions to brokers for their clients' mortgage applications. Some wholesalers reportedly even offered sexual favors in addition to fees (der Hovanesian, 2008).

As already suggested, however, the resultant decline in mortgage-underwriting standards needs to be weighed up against other causes of high default rates such as falling house prices, and while the ample, relatively low-cost funding provided by securitization contributed to the house-price bubble that ended in these sharp house-price falls (see, especially, Mian and Sufi, 2008), it was not the only cause of the bubble. Furthermore, while mezzanine ABS CDOs were the crucial purchasers of the lower tranches of ABSs, high-grade ABS CDOs were only one source among others of the demand for higher tranches.[55] So the argument that ABS CDOs contributed importantly to the US mortgage crisis by removing a crucial set of gatekeepers and encouraging the "lend to securitize" imperative remains a hypothesis, albeit a plausible one.

More definitively identifiable are the roles played by two further imports from credit derivatives to the world of ABSs: credit default swaps and tradable credit indices. Credit default swaps on ABSs made it possible, effectively for the first time, for traders in hedge funds and banks directly to bet against subprime mortgages. Via a default swap, such traders could buy protection on an ABS tranche (normally a mezzanine tranche, with its high exposure to default) without needing to own the securities involved. If the tranche defaulted, they would receive from the protection seller any shortfall in the money due to an owner of the securities, which would be a handsome return for modest protection premiums.

Such purchases of protection grew rapidly, especially after the terms of credit default swaps were standardized in 2005. Even though they were underpinned by skepticism about the prospects for ABSs, they paradoxically had the temporary effect of further fueling the growth of ABS CDOs, because – in a situation in which, as noted, the demand from the constructors of ABS CDOs for mezzanine ABSs had outstripped supply – they made possible synthetic ABS CDOs. Instead of buying ABSs, the latter sold protection on them, via credit default swaps, to traders betting against subprime mortgages, and used the swap premiums to pay investors. The ABS CDO "system," if one can call it that, thus quite literally absorbed the dissent that underlay the purchases of protection. Indeed, as was highlighted by the April 2010 civil fraud action launched by the SEC against Goldman Sachs, in some cases the selection of ABSs for an ABS CDO reflected input from those (such as hedge fund manager John Paulson) who wished to use the CDO as a way of hedging their exposure to subprime or betting against it.

ABS credit default swaps and synthetic subprime ABS CDOs magnified the risks of mortgage lending. If losses on the underlying mortgages reached a level that caused an ABS tranche to default, then more was at stake than the consequent losses to direct investors in that tranche, such as cash CDOs. All the credit default swaps on the tranche would also be triggered, causing additional losses, for example, to synthetic CDOs that had sold protection on the tranche. As ABS defaults mounted, the eventual result was massive transfers of wealth from ABS CDOs and other sellers of protection to the buyers of protection: hedge funds such as Paulson's, and those banks – notably Goldman Sachs and Deutsche – that had also started to buy protection on a large scale, either as a way of hedging their positions or as a way of profiting from the coming disaster. The total amount of such transfers is not known, but something of their scale is indicated by the fact that John Paulson made $15 billion for his fund in 2007, mainly in this way (Zuckerman, 2009). To some extent, of course, these transfers were simply from one bank to another, but they were of sufficient size dangerously to erode the capital base of those banks that had been large net sellers of protection.

The second set of imports from the world of credit derivatives, tradable credit indices, rendered visible the extent to which banks' assets had lost value. Two new broadly canonical-mechanism tradable indices – the ABX, launched in January 2006, and its tranched version, TABX, launched in February 2007 – allowed traders to buy and sell protection on standard packages of subprime ABSs.[56] As the cost of buying protection on an ABX index rises, the level of that index falls, and because that level (unlike the price of individual ABS credit default swaps) was public, it rendered visible a decline in perceived creditworthiness. The result of a greatly increased demand from hedge funds and banks such as Deutsche and Goldman to buy protection was that the ABX indices fell sharply early in 2007, and then again from the late spring onward. By early 2008, ABX levels implied the expectation of almost total capital losses on the BBB and BBB tranches of the subprime ABSs they covered, and very large losses even on higher tranches (Fender and Scheicher, 2008).

The banks that owned ABS CDOs and ABSs (many of the latter in "warehouses" awaiting packaging into ABS CDOs) generally held them in what are called their "trading books," which meant – under current "fair value" accountancy regimes – that they had to be marked-to-market: that is, revalued as market prices changed. The ABX provided a market that could be used to do just that. There was fierce dispute as to its adequacy – "ABX and TABX don't really count as grown-up markets. The market participants needed to create proper two-way flows in ABX remain elusive" (Hagger, 2007) – and there were accusations that even though tradable credit indices apparently were proper canonical-mechanism markets, they could actually be manipulated (interview data; Hughes, 2008). However, there was strong pressure from auditors (some fearful after the scandals and criminal convictions earlier in the decade, notably concerning Enron and WorldCom, of "any impression that they are going soft on clients") to use the levels of the ABX to value banks' holdings. "It's cover-your-ass stuff," said one critic of the practice, but it meant that "banks that mark assets far from where the indices trade incur the ire of their auditors" (*Economist*, 2008, pp. 95–6).

Using the ABX, and such other market prices as were available, to value ABS and ABS CDO portfolios meant that such valuations were forward looking: those prices incorporated predictions of defaults to come, not simply those defaults that had already happened. In the eyes of the proponents of "fair value" accounting of this kind, these valuation practices appropriately rendered mortgage-related losses quickly visible. In the eyes of its opponents, they worsened the crisis by making these predictions self-fulfilling, because they produced accounting write-downs of such a magnitude that they spilled over into "the real economy," causing first an effective shutdown of subprime mortgage lending (leaving borrowers without opportunities to refinance, for example, when "teaser" rates ended) and then a general collapse of other credit that led, inter alia, to a sharp rise in unemployment. In so doing, those evaluation practices may have helped bring about the huge default rates on which they were predicated.

The final process that needs to be examined is how ABS CDO losses came to be highly concentrated in banking and insurance, given that instruments of that kind were expected to minimize the effects of losses of this sort by allowing the shedding of dangerous accumulations of credit risk. (Of the IMF's estimate of $290 billion ABS CDO losses, at least half was incurred by banks and a further 20 percent to 25 percent by insurers; see IMF, 2008, p. 9, table 1.1.) The chief cause of the concentration of losses was that the safest tranches of ABS CDOs – the AAA super-senior tranches that typically made up more than half of even mezzanine ABS CDOs (see Figure 1.4) – were hard to sell to outside investors, because the finite cash flow into an ABS CDO meant its super-senior tranche could offer only very modest spreads, usually around only 25 basis points (a quarter of a percentage point) over Libor, without overly reducing the spreads on the lower tranches.

Banks such as Merrill Lynch and Citigroup, with giant ABS CDO "assembly lines," thus had little option but to retain most of their super-senior tranches, leaving them with huge exposures when defaults threatened even those tranches. The credit default swaps via which banks bought protection on super-senior tranches from AIG and the monolines were the largest single causes of insurers' losses. Analytically most interesting, however (because they are most directly indicative of beliefs about super-senior ABS CDO tranches), are those cases in which traders at banks without large-scale involvement of their own in ABS CDOs nevertheless chose to buy super-senior tranches originated by other banks or to sell those banks protection on them via credit default swaps.

Most fascinating of all these cases is a trade put on by a proprietary trading group at Morgan Stanley from September 2006 to January 2007.[57] I first learned about this trade in a February 2010 interview, and a fuller, but almost entirely consistent, account was then given by Lewis (2010, pp. 200–19), on which I also draw here. The total loss on it was $9 billion, just over half of the total credit-crisis losses that temporarily threatened the survival of the world's second most prominent investment bank (Benmelech and Dlugosz, 2009, p. 163, table 1; Lewis, 2010, p. 215).[58] What makes the trade interesting is that the Morgan Stanley group responsible for it was among those skeptical of the prospects for the US mortgage market, and like others they had accumulated a large ($2 billion) "short" position in credit default swaps on BBB mezzanine tranches of ABSs, in other words, a position that would pay out, via the swaps, if those tranches defaulted. They were – rightly – convinced that the position would thus be extremely profitable, but until that happened it was what traders call a "negative carry" position: keeping it in place required expenditure (the premiums that had to be paid to the protection sellers). A common way of eliminating the negative carry of a "short" BBB position (and of hedging against the possibility that one's pessimistic view of creditworthiness is wrong) is to match it with a "long" AAA position in the sector in question, the rationale being that a decline in creditworthiness will have a far greater impact on BBB than on AAA assets, while the income from being long the latter (i.e. from holding them or selling protection on them) will eliminate the negative carry. So the Morgan Stanley group did just that in late 2006 and early 2007. Unfortunately, though, they did this not by going long AAA ABS tranches but going long AAA ABS CDO tranches. They matched their $2 billion of purchases of protection on BBB ABS tranches with $16 billion or more of sales of protection on AAA super-senior ABS CDO tranches. (The difference in size – again perfectly understandable – reflected the fact that BBB tranches are far more sensitive to declines in credit quality and have much higher credit default swap premiums than AAA.)[59]

The difference between an AAA position in ABSs and in ABS CDOs may seem minor, but it changed the nature of the trade utterly. The asset pools of the ABS CDOs in which the Morgan Stanley traders had a long position consisted largely of mezzanine ABS tranches of the kind they were short. In the terminology of the world of corporate CDOs, that made it a correlation trade, and had the position been shown to a correlation trader he or she would immediately have seen that the trade utterly depended on the correlation of those BBB tranches remaining at the modest levels reflected in the AAA rating. If correlation was high, and if some BBB tranches defaulted (as the Morgan Stanley traders expected them to), then it was probable that many other such tranches would also default. If that happened, even the AAA super-senior tranche of an ABS CDO composed of these tranches would be likely to default in its turn. Indeed, a corporate correlation trader, in a different section of the bank, would simply not have been allowed to take on such a gigantic exposure to correlation, as this position would have been understood, in that section, to involve.

The fact that the position was taken on indicates either belief that correlation was indeed low or simply belief that a tranche rated AAA must be much more creditworthy than a BBB tranche. (It is more likely that it was the latter, but my data do not allow me to be certain.) Crucially, the detailed history of the trade reveals that such convictions were not restricted to the Morgan Stanley group. Merrill Lynch turned down the latter's offer to buy $2 billion of its super-senior ABS CDO tranches because the 28 basis point spread Morgan Stanley demanded was greater than the 24 basis points Merrill was prepared to pay (Lewis, 2010, p. 208). The difference, as Lewis points out, was a mere $800,000 a year, a sum Merrill's traders would surely gladly have paid had they thought that there was any real risk of the tranches in question defaulting. Similarly, even as the crisis began to unfold in July 2007, two other banks, UBS and Mizuho Financial Group, purchased large chunks of Morgan Stanley's super-senior ABS CDO positions from it at what appears to be reasonably close to face value.

Within a matter of days, such sales could no longer be made. When Morgan Stanley finally extricated itself from some of the remainder of its super-senior position by selling it back to Deutsche, it received only 7 percent of its face value (Lewis, 2010, p. 214). In a single year, a $16 billion ABS CDO position that had been evaluated as AAA had apparently lost up to 93 percent of its value.[60] Repeated across the portfolios of many of the world's leading banks, falls of this kind helped push many of them close to, or beyond, the boundary of insolvency.

Conclusion

This chapter has shown how the clusters of evaluation practices surrounding ABS and CDOs differed and how (via the "convention" formed by the ratings-spreads nexus and the organizational division of labor in ratings agencies) those practices fueled an arbitrage that had the disastrous consequences outlined in the previous section. A number of questions nevertheless remain.

One question is substantive: since corporate CDOs themselves embodied an arbitrage similar in its nature to the ABS CDO arbitrage, why did they not have similar disastrous effects? The answer appears to be contingent. The capacity to sell on "leveraged loans" (loans that were used mainly for "leveraged buyouts," in other words debt-fueled takeovers) by packaging them into CDOs helped increase levels of leverage, and it did loosen lending standards in that sector, too. In particular, CDO funding was associated with less tight loan covenants (these covenants give rights to creditors and impose restrictions on borrowers). However, the other correlates of the packaging of leveraged loans into CDOs – cheaper and more readily available credit – had the countervailing effect of making it possible to finance leveraged buyouts of much larger firms. The fact that other things being equal such firms are safer – they "generated more free cash flows … and were less risky" (Shivdasani and Wang, 2009, p. 5) – seems to have counterbalanced the effects of the tendency to looser covenants.[61] As in other aspects of the account given here, specific contingencies (in this case, the presence in corporate lending of a countervailing effect absent in mortgage lending) matter greatly.

A more general issue, an analytical one, raised by my focus on evaluation practices concerns belief. Should we understand the conduct of those practices and the use of their results as having been driven by belief in them, or should it be seen as cynical, as driven simply by the pursuit of gain (e.g. by earning fees from ratings)? More broadly, were those involved self-interested rational actors freely choosing their actions, or did those actions, at least sometimes, "incorporate institutional rules by taking them for granted without much decision or reflection" (Meyer, 2009, p. 41)? Did "habit" (Camic, 1986) or even "habitus" (e.g. Bourdieu, 1984) play a role?

Of course, habits and social interests are interwoven: what is in our interest often becomes habitual (as, indeed, Bourdieu's work reminds us). Nevertheless, because of the understandable desire to assign blame it is easy in the aftermath of a calamity such as the credit crisis to adopt too simplistically what Vaughan (1996, p. 36) calls the "amoral calculator hypothesis." Certainly, reflexive, calculative action has played a major role in my narrative: what is arbitrage, after all, if it is not action of this kind, action that exploits discrepancies in others' evaluations (see Beunza and Stark, 2004)?[62] Yet the episodes discussed here include at least one set of cases (the super-senior ABS CDO trades outlined at the end of the previous section) that are hard to interpret without invoking belief either in evaluation practices or in the ratings that were their products. Nor, I think, would amoral calculation be a correct interpretation of the way the rating agencies evaluated ABS CDOs: I have found no clear evidence that they saw the danger of ABS CDOs and ignored it for the sake of fees. On the contrary, the evaluation of ABS CDOs using existing corporate CDO models and similar correlation values is plausibly interpretable as organizational routine: the extension to a new domain of evaluation practices that were familiar and convenient, and that did not involve the considerable development effort that analysing ABS CDOs in the alternative ways I sketched in that section would have needed.

The analogy with Vaughan's work also raises a second analytical issue: organizational structure. There is a sense in which the situation examined here contrasts quite sharply with that analysed in Beunza and Stark's (2004) discussion of arbitrage. In the trading room they studied, "the friction among competing principles of arbitrage" was productive: it "generates new ways of recognizing opportunities" (Stark, 2009, p. 16). While that is the case here too, it is so only temporarily: opportunities that are recognized are soon eclipsed by dangers that are not identified. Instead of Stark's "heterarchy" (flexible governance that makes friction productive by facilitating organizationally distributed "reflexive cognition," with, for example, elements of "self-management" and "lateral accountability" rather than simply "vertical authority"),[63] what I have found is more often reminiscent of the rigidities and barriers to information flow in the background of the Challenger disaster (Vaughan, 1996). As noted in the introduction, the ABS CDO seems less the productively polysemic "boundary object" of the social studies of science (Star and Griesemer, 1989) than a kind of epistemic orphan, cognitively peripheral to its parent worlds, and not the object of a new creole or even much of a pidgin (for which see Galison, 1997).[64]

What is in retrospect striking is how little sense there was before the crisis of the dangers that were accumulating in ABS CDOs. As noted in the introduction, the first interviews for the research reported here were conducted in 2006 and early 2007, before the crisis, and they concerned the evaluation practices surrounding corporate CDOs. The practitioners of these had their concerns – one rating-agency employee reported: "Some investors have said … to us … 'does a AAA mean the same thing as it meant five years ago?'" – but to the extent that those concerns had a specific focus it was a sophisticated form of CDO called a CPDO (constant proportion debt obligation), not the vastly bigger volume of the "boring" ABS CDOs. Similarly, the pre-crisis conference "trip reports" by Mark Adelson of Nomura (see, e.g. Adelson, 2006c, 2006d, 2007) reveal widespread awareness among ABS specialists of growing problems and high levels of fraud within the US mortgage market, but not the perception that the apparently safe

ABS CDOs were exquisitely exposed to those problems. To recognize the dangers of ABS CDOs, one had to have an awareness both of the risks accumulating in ABSs and of the pivotal role of the assumption of only modest correlation among those ABSs in the evaluation of ABS CDOs, and it seems as if few did. Certainly, those who were prepared on the very eve of the crisis to buy the super-senior tranches of those CDOs seem not to have had.

Again, the amoral calculator hypothesis is conceivable: that some of the almost complete pre-crisis silence on the dangers of ABS CDOs was a version of Bourdieu's "complicitous silence," the silence of those who could have spoken but did not do so.[65] Stark's work, however, suggests an alternative conjecture: that it would have taken heterarchical organization to fuse together the two institutionally separate insights needed fully to grasp those dangers. The conjecture is plausible: in particular, Goldman Sachs, reported by several of my interviewees to be more heterarchical in its organization than most other major banks (it was a partnership, not a public company, until 1999), escaped financially almost unscathed. Unlike almost all other banks, Goldman hedged or liquidated its ABS and ABS CDO positions several months before the crisis. However, the systematic, comparative organizational research needed to test the conjecture is, for reasons of access, currently impossible.

This is only one of the ways in which the account given here does not claim to be comprehensive. I have emphasized that my aim is to complement other explanations of the crisis, not to replace them, and the account I have given clearly needs to be integrated with broader analyses, for example of the causes of the generalized increase in risk taking in banking in the run-up to the crisis. (Although I've emphasized the crucial role of ABS CDOs in the crisis, some banks – such as Lehman and the United Kingdom's HBOS – rendered themselves insolvent or close to it mainly by old-fashioned reckless lending, particularly in commercial property.) Nor has my account exhausted the sociological interest of credit derivatives, which are, for example, a rich topic for Muniesa's (2007) "pragmatics of prices."[66] There are also at least two further ways in which other forms of the economic sociology of evaluation could be applied in this area. First, it has been crucial to the development of the credit default swap market that these swaps are not classed as insurance, because if they were the buyer of protection would have to own the asset in question or have some other "insurable interest" in it, and the seller would be governed by the regulatory framework surrounding insurance. The contested legitimacy of contracts that resemble insurance but do not have these features largely remains to be studied (though it is touched on by Huault and Rainelli-Le Montagner, 2009, pp. 559–60).

Second, in my interviews there is an intriguing hint of the presence of an "order of worth" (Boltanski and Thévenot, 2006; Stark, 2009) quite different from monetary calculation. One interviewee told me how, as mortgage defaults mounted, traders in his bank started to exclaim, "No respect for the obligation!" I confess that I was so unused to hearing moralism of this sort from City of London or Wall Street traders that I asked him whether they were being ironic and was told they were not: they were genuinely affronted by what they took to be violations of moral obligation. In other contexts it would be regarded as positively irrational if the owner of an asset who enjoys limited liability (as, de facto, American residential-mortgage borrowers generally do) does not default when the asset's market value falls far below the sum of debt that funds it.[67] This may be an indication that – even among Wall Street traders – personal debts, especially home mortgages, with all their entanglement in the world of domesticity,[68] implicitly enjoyed a special status, perhaps even that this special status in some way underpinned the pervasive sense that mortgage-backed securities were uniquely safe. That, though, is speculation, and certainly cannot be tested with the data I have.

I hope that in its focus on evaluation practices at the heart of the credit crisis, this chapter has thrown some light on that crisis and has also shown that attention to these practices is of interest to economic sociology more generally. If nothing else, the crisis has shown how dangerous it can be (e.g. to public policy) to assess market processes in abstraction from the cognitive and organizational reality of evaluation practices. In April 2006, the IMF noted: "There is growing recognition that the dispersion of credit risk by banks to a broader and more diverse group of investors, rather than warehousing such risks on their balance sheets, has helped to make the banking and overall financial system more resilient" (IMF, 2006, p. 51).[69] As we now know, quite the opposite was in fact happening. Driven in part by the evaluation practices and organizational processes discussed here, risk was being accumulated, not dispersed, and the financial system was growing more fragile, not more resilient. There can surely be no more vivid demonstration of the need for a broadening of the disciplinary basis of research on financial markets, and in that broadening economic sociology has a vital role to play.

Notes

1. I am extremely grateful to my interviewees, without whose generosity with their time and insights this chapter could not have been written. Several also provided helpful comments on early drafts, as did Patrick Aspers, David Bloor, Michel Callon, Neil Fligstein, Iain Hardie, Gavin Kretschmar, Horacio Ortiz, Martha Poon, Arthur Stinchcombe, and five anonymous AJS referees. As always, however, responsibility for errors remains mine alone. The research reported here was supported primarily by a grant (RES-062-23-1958) from the UK Economic and Social Research Council (ESRC) though funding for earlier relevant fieldwork also came from another ESRC grant (RES-051-27-0062), from the UK Engineering and Physical Sciences Research Council (EP/E001297/1), and from the Strategic Research Support Fund of the University of Edinburgh's School of Social and Political Science. Direct correspondence to Donald MacKenzie, School of Social and Political Science, University of Edinburgh, George d.mackenzie@ed.ac.uk.
2. ABSs and CDOs will be explained in more detail in the second and third sections of this chapter. For now, it is adequate to think of them as sets of claims on the cash flow from a pool of underlying assets such as mortgages (in the case of ABSs) or corporate debt (in "corporate" CDOs).
3. I write "evaluation," not "valuation," because I want to encompass practices such as credit rating that contribute to knowledge of economic value but do not themselves generate a monetary valuation.
4. On market making, see Abolafia (1996); on the way auctions can produce legitimacy and shared knowledge of value, see Smith (1989); on the varying "quality" of prices, see Muniesa (2007). The "efficient market hypothesis" of financial economics (Fama, 1970) is, in effect, the hypothesis that the price of a financial instrument in a canonical-mechanism market is the best guide to its value.
5. This last situation, famously formulated by Keynes (1936, p. 156), is among those emphasized by the "economics of convention": see Eymard-Duvernay et al. (2005) and, more generally, Eymard-Duvernay (1989) and Favereau and Lazega (2002). Clearly the process is an important contributor to bubbles in both the stock market and housing market. It is, however, not at the center of my analysis because the instruments discussed were usually held for the "spread" they offered (see below) rather than purchased primarily because it was anticipated that they could be resold at a higher price.
6. For an analysis of differences among evaluation practices in a different sphere, see Fourcade (2009).
7. Although the chapter focuses on evaluation practices relevant to the credit crisis, other sociological work on financial markets also suggests the existence of distinct clusters of practice. See, especially, the characterization of different approaches to assessing the value of stocks in Smith (1999).
8. The literature on science also employs a broader understanding of the "symbolic" than is sometimes found when "culture" is invoked in the wider social sciences. As Knorr Cetina (1999, p. 11) puts it, "symbolic structurings ... come into view through the definition of entities, through systems of classification, through the ways in which epistemic strategy, empirical procedure, and social collaboration are understood in the ... fields investigated." It should be noted, however, that symbolism in the ordinary sense is not entirely absent from the evaluation practices discussed here. In particular, AAA was a rating that had a real symbolic cachet, frequently being understood to mean effectively free of any risk of default.
9. Conceiving of clusters of evaluation practices as "communities of practice" (Lave and Wenger, 1991) would involve a similar risk: the term might be taken to imply higher levels of interaction among

practitioners than often was the case, especially in what appear to have been the rather fragmented practices surrounding ABSs.

10 While these postulates are presented here simply as summarizing the findings of this research, some (notably 1 and 6) are also hypotheses that could be explored elsewhere. For reasons of space, I concentrate in this chapter on the evidence for the first, second, third, and sixth postulates.

11 On path dependency more generally, see, e.g. Arthur (1984), David (1992), and Nunn (2009).

12 See also Beunza and Stark (2004), who demonstrate the spatial distribution of different evaluation practices across the different "desks" (subgroups) of the trading room they study.

13 For all their importance, the credit rating agencies have been the object of surprisingly little social science attention. The single best study of them is Sinclair (2005).

14 These spreads were never fully public knowledge, but knowledge of them circulated reasonably widely among both constructors of ABSs and CDOs and regular buyers of them.

15 For sociological discussion of arbitrage, see, e.g. Beunza and Stark (2004).

16 These factors include global economic imbalances – notably the "savings glut" in countries such as China with big trade surpluses – and an extended period of low interest rates, which prompted a "search for yield": widespread hunger for even fractionally higher interest rates (see, e.g. Turner, 2009).

17 Also relevant, though they do not discuss the crisis, are the sociological discussion of the development of credit derivatives in Huault and Rainelli-Le Montagner (2009) and the excellent ethnography of ABS purchases and ABS CDO construction at a French fund management company in Ortiz (2008).

18 Empirically determining the relative weight of amoral calculation versus other cognitive/organizational factors is very difficult. I return to this issue in the conclusion.

19 Six interviews were with two market participants and two involved three interviewees. Three participants were interviewed three times, and 14 were interviewed twice.

20 The remaining interviewees were two who provide hardware on which computationally intensive models are run, four who work for firms specializing in provision of price data, and an accountant with specialist knowledge of accounting for financial instruments.

21 For earlier developments, in the United States and elsewhere, see Bogue (1955), Snowden (1995), and Goetzmann and Newman (2010).

22 Usage of the term "ABS" is not consistent through time. Only once subprime mortgage securitizations became popular did it start to include mortgage-backed securities, and even then securitizations of prime mortgages were not generally referred to as ABSs. In this chapter, however, the term "ABS" always includes mortgage securitizations.

23 I draw these dates from the data tables in Roy and McDermott (2007), though see also Cantor and Packer (1994, p. 20).

24 See, especially, Bhattacharya and Cannon (1989), in particular their worked example (pp. 482–3).

25 The rating agencies were not unique in this. Thus Fabozzi et al.'s (2007) textbook of mortgage-backed-securities makes effectively no mention of correlation.

26 S&P's stress scenarios also differed in the assumptions made about the severity of losses following default, with higher severities assumed in the stress scenarios for higher ratings, the rationale being that the house price declines in high-stress scenarios would imply lower proceeds following foreclosure. See Securities and Exchange Commission (2008, pp. 32–4) for the practices at Moody's and Fitch.

27 "Excess spread" is the difference between the aggregate interest payments received from borrowers (net of fees and other expenses) and the interest payments to investors; it creates what is in essence a reserve. Overcollateralization means that the total principal sum of the loans in the pool is greater than that of the securities held by investors, either because the deal was structured that way initially or because of "turboing," the use of excess spread to repay some investors and thus reduce the amount of securities still outstanding (Fabozzi et al., 2007, pp. 102, 188).

28 They were what would later be called "market-value CDOs": the pool of junk bonds was revalued fortnightly, and if its value fell below a set threshold for more than two weeks investors could require that the pool be sold and their capital returned to them (Hourican, 1990, p. 333).

29 Thus, e.g. if both company A and company B have a default probability of 0.1, and their defaults are independent events, then the probability of their both defaulting is simply 0.1 # 0.1 p 0.01.

30 Moody's explicitly calculated a "diversity score" for each CDO's pool. Fitch appears not to have had an explicit concentration penalty in this period.

31 Options are contracts or securities that grant a right but not an obligation. For example a "call" option gives the right to buy a block of shares at a set price – the "exercise price" – on, or up to, a given future date. An interest-rate swap involves one party paying the other a fixed rate of interest on an agreed

notional principal sum, while the second party pays a floating rate (usually Libor) on the same sum. Introduced in 1981 (Beckstrom, 1988, p. 43), interest-rate swaps quickly became widely used by banks and other market participants to manage the risks of interest-rate fluctuations.

32 Because of their limited liability, the owners of a corporation's shares possess what is in effect a call option on its assets. If the market value of those assets is below the total amount of the corporation's debt when the latter falls due, shareholders rationally should simply allow the corporation to default (leaving their shares worth nothing). If the corporation's assets are at that point worth more than its debt, their shares are in aggregate worth the difference. Those outcomes are precisely the pay-off of a call option with an exercise price equal to the total amount of the corporation's debt, and this allows option theory to be used in what has become known as the "Merton model" of default (see Merton, 1974).

33 A copula function (a formulation introduced to mathematical statistics by Sklar, 1959) "joins together" the distribution functions of uniformly distributed variables in such a way as to yield a specific multivariate joint distribution function. (A "Gaussian copula" yields a multivariate normal distribution function.) Copula functions were brought to the study of credit risk by Li (1999, 2000), who used them to specify the dependence among the survival or hazard-rate functions that model the time at which a corporation defaults. When referring to "Gaussian copulas," I also include models such as CreditMetrics and the original 2001 version of CDO Evaluator (discussed below), which are single-period (all that is modeled is whether a corporation defaults during the period in question, not when), but in which what is in Li's terms the copula function is Gaussian.

34 See, e.g. Chen et al. (2005, p. 7, exhibit 3). Moody's had developed a distinctive approach in which a CDO's "diversity score" (see note 30) was used to map its asset pool onto a hypothetical pool of homogeneous assets whose defaults were independent events and to which, therefore, the binomial formula from elementary probability theory could be applied (Cifuentes and O'Connor, 1996). Its commitment to this "bi-nomial expansion technique," which is much simpler than Gaussian copula formulations, meant it embraced Gaussian copula models more slowly and more partially than S&P and Fitch.

35 Moody's also used correlations produced from analysis of market prices by KMV, a firm cofounded by Vasicek, which it bought in 2002. KMV employed an elaborated version of the option-theoretic model outlined in n. 32 to estimate corporations' asset values and default probabilities. In their choice of correlation assumptions, however, the CDO specialists at Moody's "tilt towards the ratings-based results" (Fu et al., 2004, p. 10).

36 To be more precise, what can be inferred is the "risk-neutral" probability of default (see Baxter and Rennie, 1996).

37 As far as I can tell, deals prior to 1999, such as what seems to be the first ABS CDO, the Alliance Capital/Paine Webber "Pegasus One Ltd," issued in June 1995, were mostly market-value CDOs (see note 28 above).

38 Data from the Securities Industry and Financial Markets Association, www.sifma.org.

39 See Smith (2008a, 2008b).

40 For example, the baseline correlation between US subprime residential mortgage securities assumed by Moody's was 0.22. That would be increased to take into account factors such as the closeness of the vintage (year of issuance) of the ABSs: e.g. by 0.1 for the commonly encountered case of pairs of mortgage ABSs of the same vintage (Toutain et al., 2005).

41 S&P's Evaluator was, at least originally, a single-period model that (in the case, say, of a pool of assets all with a five-year maturity) would encompass the entire five years in a single simulation run. Fitch's Vector was a multiperiod model that was run in annual steps: "At every annual step [in a simulation] an asset portfolio is updated by removing defaulted assets and recording amounts and recoveries upon default" (Gill et al., 2004, p. 9). As far as I am aware, the annual steps were serially independent, so as an interviewee put it, an asset "that survives the first period will start the second period with a 'clean slate'." Since the probability of default of any asset in a single year will normally be assumed to be much lower than default of the same asset over five years, this tends to have the effect of generating fewer cases with large numbers of defaults in a multistep model than in a single-step model with the same correlation parameters. In consequence, "we need to increase correlation [in a multistep model] to "match" the cumulative distribution of the single-step model" in this respect.

42 In an interviewee's words, "Everyone said, 'how can you have no correlation between industries?'" For examples of the criticism, see Chen et al. (2005) and Adelson (2006b).

43 Perhaps the closest was Adelson (2003), who argued that evaluation practices surrounding both ABSs and CDOs understated correlation and ignored the way in which it can rise in a downturn. Even

here, though, there was no specific focus on the intrasectoral ABS correlation, and though Adelson's hypothetical examples include a pool with a correlation of 0.6, the range of values (0.25 to 0.4) mentioned in his text (p. 59) as examples of when "correlation is higher" includes the value of 0.3 chosen by S&P.

44 The use for mortgage-backed securities of lower default probabilities and higher recovery rates than for equivalently rated corporate bonds was also a facilitator. Again, I can find no criticism of this at the time, and indeed default data seemed unequivocally to point in that direction.

45 There is a deeper issue here that cannot be explored fully for reasons of space. This logic applies only if instruments are being evaluated according to their default probabilities or expected losses (as they were by the rating agencies and implicitly by those investors whose decisions were shaped by ratings), but modern asset-pricing theory suggests that they should not be evaluated in this way: their price should reflect not this "total risk," but only its systematic component, precisely because its idiosyncratic component can be diversified away. Coval, Jurek, and Stafford (2009) argue that because of this the prices of corporate CDO tranches were too high by the standards of asset-pricing theory, and the ratings-spreads convention discussed in the introduction seems to be the cause: it led market participants unwittingly to compare instruments with high systematic risk (senior CDO tranches) to instruments with similar default probabilities but lower systematic risk (corporate bonds). Their article is thus a beautiful demonstration of a convention shaping patterns of prices and creating what is (if modern asset-pricing theory is correct) a very large and very persistent inefficiency.

46 See also Adelson and Jacob (2008a, p. 8): "A key problem at many firms has been reluctance on the part of professionals in the areas of CDOs and structured credit to seek and accept input from ABS/MBS experts [MBS are mortgage-backed securities] … Significantly, the problem was not confined to just one type of firm. It was endemic among CDO and structured credit professionals at all kinds of firms: banks, securities dealers, rating agencies, bond insurers, money managers, and others."

47 For example, the cash-flow modeling would involve use of the huge commercially available "deal library" maintained by Intex Solutions (a firm based in Needham, Massachusetts), and those who have experimented with an approach of this kind tell me that practical complications (notably the fact that many ABS CDOs included tranches of other ABS CDOs in their pools) can cause the layered Intex models to run very slowly. Considerations such as this remind us that (though I have not focused on this issue) evaluation practices are material practices, and their materiality is consequential. It is also worth noting that a different reason why it would not have been attractive to rate ABS CDOs in the way described in the text is that the managers of a CDO generally enjoy the right to sell assets from its pool and replace them with others with the same or higher ratings. While it is quick and easy to use the conventional two-step approach to reevaluate an ABS CDO whose pool has been changed in this way, the approach described here would have to be restarted from scratch, by forming and then reanalyzing a new merged pool.

48 Although analytically less relevant here because it concerned a bank, not a rating agency, it is worth noting that in around 2006 Goldman Sachs started modeling ABS CDOs in a way broadly similar to that described in the text (although the Goldman model of the underlying ABSs was calibrated to the spreads they offered, not their ratings). The results also seem to have been significantly more pessimistic than those of the conventional two-step approach. Unfortunately, my interview data do not throw light on whether these results played a role in Goldman's crucial late-2006 decision to liquidate or hedge its mortgage-related positions.

49 Though there are a number of event-of-default tests laid down in the documentation of most CDOs, the critical issue is whether ratings downgrades or other reductions of the value of the CDO's asset pool have been big enough to cause the pool's total value to fall below the aggregate face value of the securities making up the CDO's topmost tranches (those initially rated AAA). That typically constitutes an event of default, following which control of the CDO passes from its managers to the "controlling class" of investors (normally the holders of the super-senior tranche), who have the right to declare an "acceleration" (which usually means diverting all cash flow to themselves) or to wind up the CDO by selling the assets in the pool (Goodman et al., 2007). Either course of action will leave the holders of lower tranches facing losses that may be close to total, and even the holders of the super-senior tranche will in current circumstances incur substantial losses.

50 See www.totalsecuritization.com.
51 See www.mbaa.org.
52 Keys et al. (2008); Mian and Sufi (2008); Rajan, Seru, and Vig (2008).
53 See http://levin.senate.gov/newsroom/2010.

54 The ABS default probabilities in Evaluator were obtained by "scaling" corporate default probabilities (which because of the larger numbers of corporate defaults were easier to estimate statistically) by factors that reflected overall differences between ABSs and corporate debt. An interviewee told me that the "scaling factors were chosen to provide the best overall agreement with the (limited) historical data, such as the average transition behavior of ABS and corporate ratings."
55 These other purchasers of the higher tranches of ABSs included "conduits" and "structured investment vehicles" (SIVs), which also sought a form of arbitrage profit. They were created by banks to invest in long-term, relatively high-yielding assets such as ABS tranches, while funding themselves more cheaply by the issuance of "commercial paper" (short-term debt). It was, however, a genuine arbitrage only if commercial-paper funding remained available to the conduits and SIVs, which ceased to be the case once the crisis broke. The rating agencies had insisted that the parent banks provide their conduits with pre-agreed credit facilities should this happen, and banks often, for fear of damage to their reputations, felt obliged to support their SIVs as well. Those conduits and SIVs are thus another route, in addition to ABS CDOs, by which ABS losses were concentrated within the banking system.
56 The ABX consists of five indices, each made up of one tranche from each of 20 large recently issued subprime ABSs. (The 20 tranches making up the AAA ABX index all had initial ratings of AAA, and there are similarly constructed AA, A, BBB, and BBB indices.) Buying and selling protection on the ABX index means entering into a credit default swap on the aggregate of the tranches making up the index in question. Originally, a new set of benchmark ABSs was selected each six months, so creating a new "series" of the ABX. This ABX "index roll" was suspended in December 2007 because too few new ABSs were being issued (Creditflux, 2007), and it has not subsequently resumed.
57 Other cases of banks buying super-senior ABS CDO tranches seem mainly to be so-called negative basis trades, in which a trader would buy a super-senior tranche (yielding annually around 25 basis points over Libor), buy protection on it from AIG or a monoline (for a premium around 15 basis points per annum), pay a charge around 5 basis points per annum to his or her bank's treasury for tying up the bank's capital, and thus be left with a profit of 5 basis points per annum. (I draw these "round number" figures from an interviewee familiar with the trade. In the credit derivatives market, the "basis" is the difference between the cost of buying protection on an asset such as a CDO tranche and the spread that the asset offers; here the basis is negative, hence the trade's name.) Because the swap seemed to eliminate whatever modest credit risk was involved in the super-senior tranche of an ABS CDO, it enabled that tranche to be classed in banks' risk management and accounting systems as fully hedged, which in turn allowed the full present value of the 5 basis point per annum profit to be "booked" immediately as "Day 1 P&L" (immediate profit: "P&L" is profit and loss). UBS's traders, for example, bought super-senior tranches totaling $20.8 billion, $15 billion of them for negative basis positions, and the latter were all judged "Day 1 P&L eligible" by the bank's relevant division, Business Unit Control (UBS AG, 2008, pp. 14–15, 23). Some traders may privately have doubted whether, in the cataclysmic scenario in which widespread losses were incurred even on super-senior tranches, the monolines or even AIG would have the financial strength to pay out, but in order to secure Day 1 P&L, "people bought protection they knew was worthless but that they know they will never need," as a risk manager at another bank told me in an email message on April 8, 2008 (at which time the full extent to which they actually did need that protection was only gradually becoming clear). That quotation suggests belief that the position was safe (and so suggests that these cases are like the Morgan Stanley trade discussed in the text), and the interviewee who explained the economics of the trade also indicated to me that it involved genuine belief in the AAA ratings of super-senior ABS CDO tranches. It is worth emphasizing, in this context, that though the trade was conducted on such a giant scale that it could threaten the survival of UBS, its profitability was modest. At 5 basis points per year on $15 billion, the trade's profit was $7.5 million per annum, which for a major bank is almost immaterial.
58 Morgan Stanley's purchases of protection on other ABS CDO tranches generated a profit, hence the lower ($7.8 billion) total ABS CDO loss quoted earlier.
59 There is a discrepancy between my interview data and Lewis's account concerning the exact ratio of the two positions and the rationale for it, but fortunately that is not crucial to the analytical import of the episode.
60 I write "apparently" because, as indicated in the discussion of the ABX above, it remained the case that there was no fully definitive way of valuing positions of this kind.
61 See also Hu, Solomon, and May (2008), who show that loans packaged into CLOs (as CDOs whose pools are leveraged loans are called) suffered fewer downgrades on average than a control group of nonpackaged loans.

62 It would also, e.g. be quite mistaken to imagine that all ratings were believed in. Thus one of my rating-agencies interviewees reported a discussion with investors, prior to the crisis, about a type of market-value CDO (see note 28) called a CPDO (constant proportion debt obligation), which a different agency had rated AAA. He told them that in his view a more appropriate rating would be BBB. They agreed, but they still welcomed the AAA rating because of the lower regulatory capital-reserve requirement the higher rating brought with it.

63 Stark (2009, pp. 5, 113). The notion of "heterarchy" is of course the inheritor of a long-standing strand of work in organizational sociology, stretching back at least to the "organic management" identified by Burns and Stalker (1961) as suitable for fast-changing environments.

64 For example, while there were around a dozen textbooks of corporate CDO correlation modeling, and hundreds of publicly available technical reports and research papers stretching back at least to 1996, there was no textbook of the equivalent practices in regard to ABS CDOs, and I have been able to find only three publicly available research papers, all from the end of the period discussed here (2007–08) and by the same two researchers from the Franco-Belgian Bank, Dexia (e.g. Garcia and Goosens, 2008).

65 "The most successful ideological effects are the ones that have no need of words, but only of laissez-faire and complicitous silence" (Bourdieu, 1990, p. 133; see Tett, 2009a).

66 Restrictions on the dissemination of the prices of credit derivatives – even those traded in what are in other respects canonical-mechanism markets – mean that there is often no unique set of market prices. Dealers can, and do, quote different prices – narrower or broader spreads between the prices at which they will buy and sell protection – to different categories of market participant. Again, materiality matters, in this case via the technical possibility of capturing the email messages containing dealers' price quotations and extracting and then circulating the prices they contain, a possibility that some dealers have attempted to block by making their emails non-forwardable. CMA, a firm specializing in extracting prices in this way, has circumvented this by developing a system that in effect electronically "scans" these non-forwardable emails.

67 The postulate that a firm's shareholders will allow it to default when this happens is the foundation of the "Merton model" (see note 32) that informed the development of the Gaussian copula. Only in certain states, such as California, are home mortgages legally no-recourse loans, but in practice US mortgage lenders seem not to pursue defaulters' other assets, even when legally they can, because the costs of doing so tend to be larger than the sums recovered.

68 See Boltanski and Thévenot (2006, pp. 164–78) though what they mean is broader than the ordinary meaning of the domestic.

69 In fairness to the IMF, I should acknowledge that it did point out that while "pricing data are relatively easy to obtain … measuring the degree and effectiveness of risk transfer continues to present statistical and methodological challenges" (IMF, 2006, p. 78).

References

Abolafia, Mitchel Y. 1996. *Making Markets: Opportunism and Restraint on Wall Street*. Cambridge, MA: Harvard University Press.

Adelson, Mark. 2003. 'CDO and ABS Underperformance: A Correlation Story.' *Journal of Fixed Income* 13 (December): 53–63.

Adelson, Mark. 2006a. 'Bond Rating Confusion.' Nomura Securities, New York, June 14, www.securitization.net/pdf/Nomura/BondRating_14Jun06.pdf. Accessed February 11, 2010.

Adelson, Mark. 2006b. 'Rating Shopping – Now the Consequences.' Nomura Securities, New York, www.securitization.net/pdf/Nomura/RatingShop_16Feb06.pdf. Accessed March 16, 2010.

Adelson, Mark. 2006c. 'Report from Las Vegas: Coverage of Selected Sessions of ASF 2006,' www.securitization.net/pdf/Nomura/ASF2006_3Feb06.pdf. Accessed February 11, 2010.

Adelson, Mark. 2006d. 'Report from Orlando 2006: Coverage of Selected Sessions of ABS East 2006.' Nomura Securities, New York, November 13.

Adelson, Mark. 2007. 'Report from Las Vegas 2007: Coverage of Selected Sessions of ASF, www.securitization.net/pdf/Nomura/ASF07Notes_5Feb07.pdf. Accessed February 11, 2010.

Adelson, Mark, and David Jacob. 2008a. 'Risk Management Lessons from the Sub-Prime Problem.' Adelson & Jacob Consulting, LLC, March 4, www.securitization.net/pdf/Publications/Adelson_RiskMngmnt_Mar08.pdf. Accessed February 11, 2010.

Adelson, Mark, and David Jacob. 2008b. 'The Sub-Prime Problem: Causes and Lessons.' *Journal of Structured Finance* 14 (1): 12–17.

Arthur, W. Brian. 1984. 'Competing Technologies and Economic Prediction.' *Options* (April): 10–13.
Ashcraft, Adam, Paul, Goldsmith-Pinkham and James Vickery. 2009. 'MBS Ratings and the Mortgage Credit Boom.' Working Paper. Federal Reserve Bank of New York, April 12, http://economics.rutgers.edu/dmdocuments/AdamAshcraft.pdf. Accessed September 30, 2009.
Aspers, Patrik. 2005. *Markets in Fashion: A Phenomenological Approach*. London: Routledge.
Aspers, Patrik. 2009. 'Knowledge and Valuation in Markets.' *Theory and Society* 38: 111–31.
Barnes, Barry, David Bloor, and John Henry. 1996. *Scientific Knowledge: A Sociological Analysis*. Chicago: University of Chicago Press.
Barnett-Hart, Anna Katherine. 2009. 'The Story of the CDO Market Meltdown: An Empirical Analysis.' BA dissertation. Harvard College.
Baxter, Martin, and Andrew Rennie. 1996. *Financial Calculus: An Introduction to Derivative Pricing*. Cambridge: Cambridge University Press.
Beckert, Jens. 2009. 'The Social Order of Markets.' *Theory and Society* 38:245–69.
Beckstrom, Rod. 1988. 'The Development of the Swap Market,' pp. 33–59 in *Swap Finance*, vol. 1, edited by Boris Antl. London: Euromoney.
Benmelech, Efraim, and Jennifer Dlugosz. 2009. 'The Credit Rating Crisis.' *NBER Macroeconomics Annual* 24: 161–207.
Bergman, Sten. 2001. 'CDO Evaluator Applies Correlation and Monte Carlo Simulation to Determine Portfolio Quality.' Standard & Poor's, New York, November, www.standardandpoors.com.
Beunza, Daniel, and David Stark. 2004. 'Tools of the Trade: The Socio-Technology of Arbitrage in a Wall Street Trading Room.' *Industrial and Corporate Change* 13: 369–400.
Bhardwaj, Geetesh, and Rajdeep Sengupta. 2008. 'Did Prepayments Sustain the Sub-prime Market?' Discussion Paper no. 2009-09S. Tilburg University European Banking Center.
Bhattacharya, Anand K., and Peter J. Cannon. 1989. 'Senior-Subordinated Mortgage Pass-Throughs,' pp. 473–83 in *Advances and Innovations in the Bond and Mortgage Markets*, edited by Frank J. Fabozzi. Chicago: Probus.
Black, Fischer, and Myron Scholes. 1973. 'The Pricing of Options and Corporate Liabilities.' *Journal of Political Economy* 81: 637–54.
Bogue, Allan G. 1955. *Money at Interest: The Farm Mortgage on the Middle Border*. Lincoln: University of Nebraska Press.
Boltanski, Luc, and Laurent Thévenot. 2006. *On Justification: Economies of Worth*. Princeton, NJ: Princeton University Press.
Bourdieu, Pierre. 1984. *Distinction: A Social Critique of the Judgement of Taste*. London: Routledge and Kegan Paul.
Bourdieu, Pierre. 1990. *The Logic of Practice*. Cambridge: Polity.
Burns, Tom, and George Stalker. 1961. *The Management of Innovation*. London: Tavistock.
Calomiris, Charles W. 2009. 'The Subprime Turmoil: What's Old, What's New and What's Next.' *Journal of Structured Finance* 15 (Spring): 6–52.
Camic, Charles. 1986. 'The Matter of Habit.' *American Journal of Sociology* 91: 1039–87.
Cantor, Richard, and Frank Packer. 1994. 'The Credit Rating Industry.' *Federal Reserve Bank of New York Quarterly Review* (Summer–Fall): 1–26.
Cantor, Richard, Owain ap Gwilym, and Stephen Thomas. 2007. 'The Use of Credit Ratings in Investment Management in the US and Europe.' *Journal of Fixed Income* 17 (Fall): 13–26.
Carron, Andrew S. 1990. 'Structured Finance Turns 20.' *Standard & Poor's Credit Review* 10 (10): 1,45.
Carruthers, Bruce. 2010. 'Knowledge and Liquidity: Institutional and Cognitive Foundations of the Sub-prime Crisis,' pp. 157–82 in Lounsbury and Hirsch 2010.
Carruthers, Bruce G., and Arthur L. Stinchcombe. 1999. 'The Social Structure of Liquidity: Flexibility, Markets, and States.' *Theory and Society* 28: 353–82.
Chaplin, Geoff. 2005. *Credit Derivatives: Risk Management, Trading and Investing*. Chichester: Wiley.
Chen, Natasha, Arturo Cifuentes, Manish Desai, and Anik Ray. 2005. 'The Young and the Restless: Correlation Drama at the Big Three Rating Agencies.' Wachovia Securities, New York, February 22. Copy kindly provided by interviewee.
Cifuentes, Arturo, and Gerard O'Connor. 1996. 'The Binomial Expansion Method Applied to CBO/CLO Analysis.' Moody's Investor Services, December 13.
Collins, Harry. 2004. *Gravity's Shadow: The Search for Gravitational Waves*. Chicago: University of Chicago Press.
Coval, Joshua D., Jakub W. Jurek, and Erik Stafford. 2009. 'Economic Catastrophe Bonds.' *American Economic Review* 99: 628–66.

Creditflux. 2007. 'Dealers Line Up Paulson's Next Short, an Alt-A Index.' *Creditflux Newsletter* www.creditflux.com.
Damouni, Nadia. 2005. 'Synthetic ABS Is Hot Property.' Credit, April 1. www.creditmag.com.
Daston, Lorraine J. 2000. 'Introduction: The Coming into Being of Scientific Objects,' pp. 1–14 in *Biographies of Scientific Objects*, edited by Lorraine Daston. Chicago: University of Chicago Press.
David, Paul A. 1992. 'Heroes, Herds and Hysteresis in Technological History: Thomas Edison and "The Battle of the Systems" Reconsidered.' *Industrial and Corporate Change* 1: 129–80.
der Hovanesian, Mara. 2008. 'Sex, Lies, and Mortgage Deals.' *Business Week*, November 24, 71–4.
Economist. 2008. 'Don't Mark to Markit.' *Economist* 386, no. 8570 (March 8): 95–6.
Ertürk, Erkan, and Thomas Gillis. 2005. 'Principal Repayment and Loss Behavior of Defaulted US Structured Finance Securities.' Standard & Poor's, New York, January 10. Copy kindly provided by interviewee.
Ertürk, Erkan, and Thomas Gillis. 2009. 'Structured Finance Rating Transition and Default Update as of July 24, 2009.' Standard & Poor's, New York, July 31. www.standardandpoors.com. Accessed August 4, 2009.
Espeland, Wendy Nelson, and Michael Sauder. 2007. 'Rankings and Reactivity: How Public Measures Recreate Social Worlds.' *American Journal of Sociology* 113: 1–40.
Eymard-Duvernay, Francois. 1989. 'Conventions de qualite et forms de coordination.' *Revue économique* 40 (2): 329–59.
Eymard-Duvernay, Francois, Olivier Faverau, Andre Orléan, Robert Salais and Laurent Thévenot. 2005. 'Pluralist Integration in the Economic and Social Sciences: The Economy of Conventions.' *Post-Autistic Economics Review* 34 (October 30). www.paecon.net.
Fabozzi, Frank J., Anand K. Bhattacharya, and William S. Berliner. 2007. *Mortgage-Backed Securities: Products, Structuring, and Analytical Techniques*. Hoboken, NJ: Wiley.
Fabozzi, Frank J., and Franco Modigliani. 1992. *Mortgage and Mortgage-Backed Securities Markets*. Boston: Harvard Business School Press.
Fahmy, Dalia. 2005. 'Profile: Merrill Lynch.' http://db.riskwaters.com/public/showPage.html?pagep217371. Accessed February 20, 2009.
Fama, Eugene F. 1970. 'Efficient Capital Markets: A Review of Theory and Empirical Work.' *Journal of Finance* 25: 383–417.
Favereau, Olivier, and Emmanuel Lazega (eds) 2002. *Conventions and Structures in Economic Organization: Markets, Networks and Hierarchies*. Cheltenham: Edward Elgar.
Fender, Ingo, and Martin Scheicher. 2008. 'The ABX: How Do the Markets Price Subprime Risk?' *BIS Quarterly Review* (September): 67–81.
First Union Securities, Inc. 2000. 'CDO Quarterly Review, August 23, 2000.' www.securitization.net/pdf/CDO%20Quarterly%20Review%20August%202000.pdf. Accessed December 31, 2008.
Fligstein, Neil, and Adam Goldstein. 2010. 'The Anatomy of the Mortgage Securitization Crisis,' pp. 29–70 in Lounsbury and Hirsch 2010.
Fourcade, Marion. 2009. 'Cents and Sensibility: Economic Valuation and the Nature of "Nature" in France and America.' Paper presented to the Third Conference on Economic Sociology and Political Economy, Loveno di Menaggio, Italy, June 14–17.
Fu, Yvonne, Jeremy Gluck, Paul Mazataud, David Rosa, Rupert Schoder, and Olivier Toutain. 2004. 'Moody's Revisits Its Assumptions Regarding Corporate Default (and Asset) Correlations for CDOs.' Moodys, New York, November 30. www.moodys.com.
Galison, Peter. 1997. *Image and Logic: A Material Culture of Microphysics*. Chicago: University of Chicago Press.
Galison, Peter, and David J. Stump (eds) 1996. *The Disunity of Science: Boundaries, Contexts, and Power*. Stanford, CA: Stanford University Press.
Garcia, Joao, and Serge Goosens. 2008. 'One Factor Models for the ABS Correlation' http://ssrn.com/abstractp1274808. Accessed August 14, 2009.
Gill, Kenneth, Richard Gambel, Richard V. Hrvatin, Heidi Katz, Gilbert Ong, and David Carroll. 2004. 'Global Rating Criteria for Collateralized Debt Obligations.' www.fitchratings.com.
Goetzmann, William N., and Frank Newman. 2010. 'Securitization in the 1920's.' Working Paper 15650. National Bureau of Economic Research, Cambridge, MA. www.nber.org/papers/w15650.
Goodman, Laurie S., Daniel Newman, Douglas J. Lucas, and Frank Fabozzi. 2007. 'Event of Default Provisions and the Valuation of ABS CDO Tranches.' *Journal of Fixed Income* 17 (3): 85–9.
Green, Richard K., and Susan M. Wachter. 2005. 'The American Mortgage in Historical and International Context.' *Journal of Economic Perspectives* 19 (4): 93–114.

Guillén, Mauro F., and Sandra L. Suarez. 2010. 'The Global Crisis of 2007–2009: Markets, Politics, and Organizations,' pp. 257–80 in Lounsbury and Hirsch 2010.

Gupton, Greg M., Christopher C. Finger, and Mickey Bhatia. 1997. 'CreditMetrics: Technical Document.' J.P. Morgan, New York.

Hagger, Euan. 2007. 'Tranched ABX Is a World Away from CDOs of ABS.' *Creditflux Newsletter* www.creditflux.com.

Harris, Gus. 2001. 'Commonly Asked CDO Questions.' Moody's, New York, February www.moodyskmv.com/research.

Hourican, Thomas P. 1990. 'Junk Bond Securitization,' pp. 333–41 in *The Handbook of Asset-Backed Securities*, edited by Jess Lederman. New York: Simon & Schuster.

Hu, Jian. 2007. 'Assessing the Credit Risk of CDOs Backed by Structured Finance,' http://ssrn.com/abstractp1011184. Accessed November 11, 2008.

Hu, Jian, Russell Solomon, and William May. 2008. 'CLOs: History, Structure, and Perspectives.' Moody's, New York, August 1. Copy kindly provided by Moody's.

Huault, Isabelle, and Heine Rainelli-Le Montagner. 2009. 'Market Shaping as an Answer to Ambiguities: The Case of Credit Derivatives.' *Organization Studies* 30: 549–75.

Hughes, Jennifer. 2008. 'Fair Value Concept Prompts Cries of Foul.' *Financial Times*, www.ft.com. Accessed September 14, 2009.

IMF (International Monetary Fund). 2006. 'Global Financial Stability Report: Market Developments and Issues.' International Monetary Fund, Washington, DC, April.

IMF (International Monetary Fund). 2008. 'Global Financial Stability Report: Financial Stress and Deleveraging: Macrofinancial Implications and Policy.' International Monetary Fund, Washington, DC, October.

Karpik, Lucien. 2010. *Valuing the Unique: The Economics of Singularities*. Princeton, NJ: Princeton University Press.

Keller, Evelyn Fox. 2002. *Making Sense of Life: Explaining Biological Development with Models, Metaphors, and Machines*. Cambridge, MA: Harvard University Press.

Keynes, John Maynard. 1936. *The General Theory of Employment, Interest and Money*. London: Macmillan.

Keys, Benjamin J., Tanmoy K. Mukherjee, Amit Seru, and Vikrant Vig. 2008. 'Did Securitization Lead to Lax Screening? Evidence from Subprime Loans,' http://papers.ssrn.com/sol3/papers.cfm?abstract_idp1093137. Accessed March 26, 2009.

Khadem, Varqa, and Francis Parisi. 2007. 'Residential Mortgage-Backed Securities,' pp. 543–92 in *The Handbook of Structured Finance*, edited by Arnaud de Servigny and Norbert Jobst. New York: McGraw-Hill.

Knorr Cetina, Karin. 1999. *Epistemic Cultures: How the Sciences Make Knowledge*. Cambridge, MA: Harvard University Press.

Lave, Jean, and Etienne Wenger. 1991. *Situated Learning: Legitimate Peripheral Participation*. Cambridge: Cambridge University Press.

Lewis, Michael. 1990. *Liar's Poker: Rising through the Wreckage on Wall Street*. New York: Penguin.

Lewis, Michael. 2010. *The Big Short: Inside the Doomsday Machine*. London: Allen Lane.

Li, David X. 1999. 'The Valuation of Basket Credit Derivatives.' *CreditMetrics Monitor*, April, pp. 34–50.

Li, David X. 2000. 'On Default Correlation: A Copula Function Approach.' *Journal of Fixed Income* 9 (4): 43–54.

Lounsbury, Michael, and Paul M. Hirsch (eds) 2010. *Markets on Trial: The Economic Sociology of the US Financial Crisis*. Bingley: Emerald.

Lucas, Douglas J. 2007. 'CDO Fundamentals.' UBS PowerPoint presentation, March. Copy kindly provided by author.

Lucas, Douglas J., Kimberly O. Rhodes, Alan Backman, and Daniel J. Curry. 1991. 'Rating Cash Flow Transactions Backed by Corporate Debt.' Moody's, New York, March. Copy kindly provided by interviewee.

McDonald, Lawrence G., with Patrick Robinson. 2009. *A Colossal Failure of Common Sense: The Inside Story of the Collapse of Lehman Brothers*. New York: Crown.

McElravey, John. 2006. 'Residential Asset-Backed Securities,' pp. 363–88 in *The Handbook of Mortgage-Backed Securities*, edited by Frank J. Fabozzi. New York: McGraw Hill.

Merton, Robert C. 1973. 'Theory of Rational Option Pricing.' *Bell Journal of Economics and Management Science* 4: 141–83.

Merton, Robert C. 1974. 'On the Pricing of Corporate Debt: The Risk Structure of Interest Rates.' *Journal of Finance* 29: 449–70.

Meyer, John W. 2009. 'Reflections: Institutional Theory and World Society,' pp. 36–63 in *World Society: The Writings of John W. Meyer*, edited by Georg Krucken and Gili S. Drori. Oxford: Oxford University Press.

Mian, Atif, and Amir Sufi. 2008. 'The Consequences of Mortgage Credit Expansion: Evidence from the 2007 Mortgage Default Crisis.' Working Paper 13936. www.nber.org/papers/w13936. Accessed August 19, 2009.

Morgan, Glenn. 2010. 'Legitimacy in Financial Markets: Credit Default Swaps in the Current Crisis.' *Socio-Economic Review* 8: 17–45.

Muniesa, Fabian. 2007. 'Market Technologies and the Pragmatics of Prices.' *Economy and Society* 36: 377–95.

Newman, Daniel, Frank J. Fabozzi, Douglas J. Lucas, and Laurie S. Goodman. 2008. 'Empirical Evidence on CDO Performance.' *Journal of Fixed Income* 18 (2): 32–40.

Nunn, Nathan. 2009. 'The Importance of History for Economic Development.' *Annual Review of Economics* 1: 65–92.

Onaran, Yalman. 2008. 'Fateful Embrace.' *Bloomberg Markets*, February, p. 42.

Ortiz, Horacio. 2008. 'Anthropologie politique de la finance contemporaine: Evaluer, investir, innover.' PhD thesis. Ecole des Hautes Etudes en Sciences Sociales.

Parisi, Francis. 2004. 'Loss Correlations among US Consumer Assets.' Standard & Poor's, New York, February. Available for purchase from Standard & Poor's.

Perraudin, William, and Astrid van Landschoot. 2004. 'How Risky Are Structured Exposures Compared with Corporate Bonds,' pp. 283–303 in *Structured Credit Products: Pricing, Rating, Risk Management and Basel II*, edited by William Perraudin. London: Risk.

Podolny, Joel M. 1993. 'A Status-Based Model of Market Competition.' *American Journal of Sociology* 98: 829–72.

Poldolny, Joel M. 2005. *Status Signals: A Sociological Study of Market Competition*. Princeton, NJ: Princeton University Press.

Poon, Martha. 2007. 'Scorecards as Devices for Consumer Credit: The Case of Fair, Isaac & Company Incorporated,' pp. 284–306 in *Market Devices*, edited by Michel Callon, Yuval Millo, and Fabian Muniesa. Oxford: Blackwell.

Poon, Martha. 2009. 'From New Deal Institutions to Capital Markets: Commercial Consumer Risk Scores and the Making of Subprime Mortgage Finance.' *Accounting, Organizations and Society* 34: 654–74.

Pozner, Jo-Ellen, Mary Katherine Stimmler, and Paul Hirsch. 2010. 'Terminal Isomorphism and the Self-Destructive Potential of Success: Lessons from Subprime Mortgage Origination and Securitization,' pp. 183–218 in Lounsbury and Hirsch 2010.

Quinn, Sarah. 2009. 'Things of Shreds and Patches: Credit Aid, the Budget, and Securitization in America.' Working Paper. University of California, Berkeley, Department of Sociology.

Rajan, Uday, Amit Seru, and Vikrant Vig. 2008. 'The Failure of Models That Predict Failure: Distance, Incentives and Defaults,' http://papers.ssrn.com/sol3/papers.cfm?abstract_idp1296982. Accessed August 1, 2009.

Ranieri, Lewis S. 1996. 'The Origins of Securitization, Sources of Its Growth, and Its Future Potential,' pp. 31–43 in *A Primer on Securitization*, edited by Leon T. Kendall and Michael J. Fishman. Cambridge, MA: MIT Press.

Reoch, Robert. 2003. 'Credit Derivatives: The Past, the Present and the Future,' pp. 7–12 in *Credit Derivatives: The Definitive Guide*, edited by Jon Gregory. London: Risk Books.

Rheinberger, Hans-Jo. 1997. *Proteins in the Test Tube*. Stanford, CA: Stanford University Press.

Rona-Tas, Akos, and Stefanie Hiss. 2010. 'The Role of Ratings in the Subprime Mortgage Crisis: The Art of Corporate and the Science of Consumer Credit Rating,' pp. 115–55 in Lounsbury and Hirsch 2010.

Rosenthal, James A., and Juan M. Ocampo. 1988. *Securitization of Credit: Inside the New Technology of Finance*. New York: Wiley.

Roy, Ratul, and Glen McDermott. 2007. 'ABS CDOs,' pp. 335–70 in *The Structured Credit Handbook*, edited by Arvind Rajan, Glen McDermott, and Ratul Roy. Hoboken, NJ: Wiley.

Rule, David. 2001. 'The Credit Derivatives Market: Its Development and Possible Implications for Financial Stability.' *Financial Stability Review*, 10 (June): 117–40.

Sakoui, Anousha. 2009. 'Moody's Warns of Ratings Downgrade for CLO Debt.' *Financial Times*, July 21, p. 32.

Sanders, Anthony. 2008. 'The Subprime Crisis and Its Role in the Financial Crisis.' *Journal of Housing Economics* 17: 254–61.

Sanford, Charles S., Jr. 1993. 'Financial Markets in 2020,' pp. 227–43 in *Changing Capital Markets: Implications for Monetary Policy*. Kansas City, MO: Federal Reserve Bank of Kansas City.

Scheinberg, Marc, and Tim Bartley. 2010. 'Regulating or Redesigning Finance? Market Architectures, Normal Accidents, and Dilemmas of Regulatory Reform,' pp. 281–308 in Lounsbury and Hirsch 2010.

Securities and Exchange Commission. 2008. 'Summary Report of Issues Identified in the Commission's Examinations of Select Credit Rating Agencies.' SEC, Washington, DC. www.sec.gov.

Securities Industry and Financial Markets Association. 2008. 'Restoring Confidence in the Securitization Markets,' www.sifma.org.

Shivdasani, Anil, and Yihui Wang. 2009. 'Did Structured Credit Fuel the LBO Boom?' http://ssrn.com/abstractp1394421.

Sinclair, Timothy J. 2005. *The New Masters of Capital: American Bond Rating Agencies and the Politics of Creditworthiness.* Ithaca, NY: Cornell University Press.

Sklar, Abe. 1959. 'Fonctions de ren dimensions et leurs marges.' Publications de l'Institut de Statistique de l'Universite.

Smith, Charles W. 1989. *Auctions: The Social Construction of Value.* New York: Free Press.

Smith, Charles W. 1999. *Success and Survival on Wall Street: Understanding the Mind of the Market.* Lanham, MD: Rowman & Littlefield.

Smith, Elliot Blair. 2008a. 'Bringing Down Wall Street as Ratings Let Loose Subprime Scourge,' Bloomberg, www.bloomberg.com

Smith, Elliot Blair. 2008b. '"Race to Bottom" at Moody's, S&P Secured Subprime's Boom, Bust.' www.bloomberg.com. Accessed December 31, 2008.

Snowden, Kenneth. 1995. 'Mortgage Securitization in the United States: Twentieth Century Developments in Historical Perspective,' pp. 261–98 in *Anglo-American Financial Systems: Institutions and Markets in the Twentieth Century*, edited by Michael D. Bordo and Richard E. Sylla. New York: Irwin.

Standard & Poor's. n.d. 'Global CBO/CLO Criteria.' Standard & Poor's, New York, ca. June 1, 1999.

Star, Susan Leigh, and James R. Griesemer. 1989. 'Institutional Ecology, "Translations" and Boundary Objects: Amateurs and Professionals in Berkeley's Museum of Vertebrate Zoology, 1907–39.' *Social Studies of Science* 19: 387–420.

Stark, David. 2009. *The Sense of Dissonance: Accounts of Worth in Economic Life.* Princeton, NJ: Princeton University Press.

Stuart, Guy. 2003. *Discriminating Risk: The US Mortgage Lending Industry in the Twentieth Century.* Ithaca, NY: Cornell University Press.

Tett, Gillian. 2009a. 'The Financial Doublethink That Needs to Be Eliminated.' *Financial Times*, August 21, p. 26.

Tett, Gillian, 2009b. *Fool's Gold: How Unrestrained Greed Corrupted a Dream, Shattered Global Markets and Unleashed a Catastrophe.* London: Little, Brown.

Toutain, Olivier, David Rosa, Yvonne Fu, Paul Mazataud, Guillaume Jolivet, Laurent Lassalvy, Julien Sieler, Gareth Levington, Gary Witt, and Yuri Yoshizawa. 2005. 'Moody's Revisits Its Assumptions Regarding Structured Finance Default (and Asset) Correlations for CDOs,' Moodys, New York, June 27, www.moodys.com. Accessed September 14, 2009.

Tower, Jonathan. 1999. 'Ginnie Mae Pool No 1: A Revolution Is Paid Off.' *Seattle Times* http://seattletimes.nwsource.com.

Tung, Julia, Jian Hu, and Richard Cantor. 2006. 'Measuring Loss-Given-Default for Structured Finance Securities, Moodys, New York, www.moodys.com. Accessed July 21, 2009.

Turner, Adair. 2009. 'The Financial Crisis and the Future of Financial Regulation.' www.fsa.gov.uk.

UBS AG. 2008. 'Shareholder Report on UBS's Write-Downs.' UBS AG, Zurich, April. www.ubs.com.

Valukas, Anton R. 2010. 'United States Bankruptcy Court, Southern District of New York: In Lehman Brothers Holdings Inc., et al., Debtors.' Jenner & Block LLP, www.scribd.com/document_collections/2373484. Accessed March 14, 2010.

Vasicek, Oldrich. 1991. 'Limiting Loan Loss Probability Distribution.' KMV Corporation, San Francisco, privately circulated, www.moodyskmv.com/research/whitepaper/Limiting_Loan_Loss_Probability_Distribution.pdf. Accessed May 5, 2008.

Vaughan, Diane. 1996. *The Challenger Launch Decision: Risky Technology, Culture, and Deviance at NASA.* Chicago: University of Chicago Press.

Velthuis, Olav. 2005. *Talking Prices: Symbolic Meanings of Prices on the Market for Contemporary Art.* Princeton, NJ: Princeton University Press.

Whetten, Michiko, and Mark Adelson. 2005. 'CDO/CDS Update 04/25/05.' Nomura www.securitization.net/pdf/Nomura/CDOCDS_25Apr05.pdf. Accessed August 21, 2009.

White, Harrison C. 1981. 'Where Do Markets Come From?' *American Journal of Sociology* 87: 517–47.

White, Harrison C. 2002. *Markets from Networks*. Princeton, NJ: Princeton University Press.
Zelizer, Viviana A. 1994. *Pricing the Priceless Child: The Changing Social Value of Children*. Princeton, NJ: Princeton University Press.
Zelizer, Viviana A. 1979. *Morals and Markets: The Development of Life Insurance in the United States*. New York: Columbia University Press.
Zelter, Jill M. 2003. 'Highlights of Fitch's New Global Rating Methodology for CDOs.' www.mayerbrown.com. Accessed July 19, 2009.
Zuckerman, Gregory. 2009. *The Greatest Trade Ever: The Behind-the-Scenes Story of How John Paulson Defied Wall Street and Made Financial History*. New York: Broadway.

2

What's in a name? Provident, The People's Bank and the regulation of brand identity

Liz McFall

The front cover of the 15 October 1965 issue of *The Investors Chronicle* featured an illustration of a family standing on a document rendered, with the help of fringed edges and some graphic licence, as a magic carpet. The family – husband, wife, two children, one girl, one boy – look comfortable in that conspicuously modern 1960s style adopted by so much commercial imagery of the period. The magic carpet they are standing on is a Provident Check, a form of documentary credit that the issuing company, Provident Clothing and Supply, had then been trading in for just under 90 years. The cover referred to a featured article, 'Provident's New Image', that was prompted by the investment potential offered by the company since it listed on the stock exchange in 1962. In its short history as a public company Provident had performed well and, as the article counselled, had made certain adjustments that were poised to help it perform even better.

These adjustments had a sudden incongruity measured against the precedent of the company's history. For its first 80 years the Provident Clothing and Supply Company had been a profitable family business operating a remarkably stable business model. This model revolved around the doorstep distribution of documentary credit in the form of checks that could be redeemed at specific retailers. As the 'clothing and supply' descriptor implies, this was credit designed to supply everyday needs and it was targeted directly at poorer households. The company negotiated discounts with retailers and charged fees to customers in a system that worked to both spread and control the costs of credit. During that time the Provident cultivated a quiet, conservative image using trademarks, logos and standard information on internally printed corporate paperwork that seldom varied over decades. The 1960s, in contrast, saw a sudden burst into colour and the first representations of Provident customers enjoying the modern standards of living that credit could furnish began to appear.

For a company that had built its business in supplying the means to buy 'clothes, boots and coal' to those with very limited resources, this was quite a shake-up. It signalled the start of an era in which the business model, the products offered, the means of delivery and the corporate image would change frequently and substantially alongside the identity the company was striving to name. If Stuart Hall's lesson that identity is always 'a process of becoming rather than being' (Hall, 1996, p. 4) is attended to and extended from questions of cultural to those of corporate identity, Provident, by the early 1960s, had started trying to become something both like, and unlike, what it had been. Identity however is neither a fixed essence nor a free for all and the resources of history, language and regulation bear down upon it. It was ultimately the latter that thwarted the company's attempt to name itself what it meant to become: the People's Bank. In the firm's long history, regulation had rarely acted so decisively but it was nevertheless always at work, in negotiation with practice and language to shape, motivate, enable and constrain. Regulation, as Bill Maurer (2012) has argued, offers a selective ethnography of past practice in the way that it highlights the problems it's attempting to solve. Some of these problems arise when companies attempt to have, that is to acquire, things, properties, shares, names and identities that mark out contested forms, descriptions or rights of practice. At the same time as addressing these problems, regulation creates spaces and opportunities for forms of practice that fall outside its retrospective gaze to emerge and to thrive. Provident's identity as a company and market leader and the fate of its later attempts to establish a new 'brand' identity as the People's Bank were, in some substantial part, outcomes of regulation.

Provident and the identification of the clothing and supply sector, 1880–1950

> Actually identities are about questions of using the resources of history, language and culture in the process of becoming rather than being: not 'who we are' or 'where we came from', so much as what we might become, how we have been represented and how that bears on how we might represent ourselves.
>
> *(Hall, 1996, p. 4)*

Joshua Waddilove founded the Provident Clothing Club in 1880. Waddilove was an active Methodist who had witnessed the financial difficulties experienced by the poor first hand while working as an industrial assurance[1] agent and collecting premiums from door to door. In choosing the name Provident he followed the lead of insurance companies which had an established practice of adopting names, like the Prudential, the Rock, the Refuge and even in several cases the Provident, that were meant to signal thrift, judgement, foresight and security. Names like these were an overt attempt to identify companies with positive moral values and sentiments that was all the more important given the turbulent history of the financial sector in the nineteenth century.[2] The Provident was named in brazen, calculated – although not necessarily cynical – defiance of the dubious moral associations of credit. Waddilove set out to develop a form of credit with the capacity to correct the poor's moral shortcomings and instil self-discipline, thrift and sobriety that would hence be worthy of its frugal and farsighted name.

These moral undertones are marked within the form of credit, documentary check trading, the Provident offered. Check trading was based on the issue of checks that were redeemable by arrangement at local shops supplying necessary things like clothes, boots and coal. According to company lore (PFG, 1980b; PCS, 1930, 1970b) Provident checks originated as a philanthropic service Waddilove performed for the poorest housewives he encountered in his work as an insurance agent. This involved giving them promissory notes that could be redeemed at local shops with Waddilove later settling the bill. After being approached by prospective customers willing to pay for the notes Waddilove made a business out of issuing the checks for a fee. Within a decade, the Provident was trading in ten towns in Yorkshire and Lancashire, and in 1899 it was incorporated as Provident Clothing and Supply Company Limited. By then there were many locally or regionally based check trading companies offering what had become a significant form of credit provision for the poor.

Provident was the biggest player by far in check trading throughout the sector's history and it was the place where the core business model, methods and equipment were developed. As the system was originally set up, checks were bought and paid for in instalments over 20 weeks and initially goods were to be had only after six payments had been made or after one payment if a charge for 'poundage' was paid. By 1908, 95 per cent of customers preferred to pay the poundage fee rather than wait for their goods and the advance payment option was later dropped. Retailers were persuaded to accept the checks and grant the company a discount averaging around 12.5 up to 15 per cent (BPP, 1981; Leslie, 1971). In return turnover would increase while the risks of bad debt would diminish. As Waddilove put it 'where bad debts are incurred we ourselves pay them. We increase the purchasing power of the people. A tradesman has to look on the all-round effects of our system on his business' (PFG, 1980b).

The claim to encourage thrift was based partly on restrictions on the use of checks to necessary forms of consumption (they couldn't for example be spent on gambling or alcohol) but more importantly on the way the instalment system was operated through doorstep collection. Agents were recruited to sell checks and then collect payment in weekly home visits. The system relied upon careful selection followed by close and frequent personal contact. At first very small amounts of credit would be offered to new customers, with gradual increases allowed as payment histories began to be built up, in a system that was designed to 'train' borrowers and limit exposure to bad debt (PCS, 1963). Provident agents in the 1920s were instructed to keep credit low for those with young children, to raise it when older children started working but to be ready to lower it again when they left home (O'Connell, 2009). This was a method of credit control that combined past payment history with agents' 'screening' (Poon, 2009) of would-be borrowers' character judged through proxies like the condition of their houses, gardens and clothing, together with word-of-mouth recommendations from relatives, friends and neighbours.

Agents kept collection books, listing the details of all customers, their orders and payment histories. They also issued and filled in payment receipt cards that were held by customers. In addition to recording details of orders and payments received, the receipt cards briefed customers on the rules of the system. All orders must be paid up by weekly instalments in 20 weeks, all customers were 'urgently requested' not to take more orders than they could 'pay regular weekly payments upon' and customers 'must only obtain orders for their own use and the use of their families'. Agents also issued customers with another key artifact, the Shopping Guide. Shopping guides contained long lists, and sometimes illustrated advertisements for shops, explanations of the system and advertisements for agents. They pointed out to customers how and where their checks could be spent and were therefore critical in defining the utility and appeal of checks.

Within a decade of establishment, the Provident employed 325 agents, by 1910 there were 3000, rising to 4000 in 1920 and 11,000 in 1960. In 1900 these agents were spread across just under 30 branch offices mainly in Yorkshire and Lancashire. A decade later there were 84 branch offices and a push into southern counties resulted in 110 offices opening by 1920, rising to 160 in operation in 1930 and 288 by 1951.[3] This rapid growth was accompanied by an equally rapid extension in 'necessary' goods and the shopping guides record the possibility of using checks in the 1930s to pay for drapery, furnishing, hardware, stationery, tobacco, paints, wallpaper, wirelesses, baby goods, barometers and all sorts of 'fancy goods' at hundreds of different shops in each branch district (PCS, 1934). There were agreements in force with 14,000 different retailers by the 1930s rising to over 20,000 in 1961 (PCS, 1962).

This extending range of possibilities was the nub of Provident's system. Credit options for the poor have historically been linked to specific traders: credit drapers, local shops offering 'tick', clothing clubs and catalogues all provided borrowing facilities but only – as the Provident always reminded customers in its shopping guides – against their own products. The Co-operative, which had initially opposed credit mechanisms in its stores, also developed a credit club system in the interwar years in response to dwindling sales and a context in which hire purchase multiplied twentyfold between 1918 and 1938 (Tebbutt, 1983). But although the Co-operative offered far better terms than most forms of credit it still could not, as the Provident's Shopping Guides pointed out, compete with the portability of checks. This was 'the glory of them … you could take them to 20, 30, 40 or even more shops' using them 'just like as if you had money in your purse' (in Taylor, 2002, p. 128). Shopping guides listed every shop accepting Provident checks in the area and emphatically reminded customers of this vital affordance – 'Provident checks (or Orders) are TAKEN AS CASH by all the tradesmen on this list and 'have EXACTLY THE SAME PURCHASING POWER AS READY MONEY' (PCS, 1961b, 1957, 1954, 1934).

Beyond steady expansion, the details of the Provident system – the role of agents, the nature of arrangements with retailers, the 20 week collected instalments, even the nature and style of key artefacts like shopping guides and payment receipt cards – varied little over the years. The only real innovation that happened in the first 80 years of trading was the introduction of the 'travelling check', which enabled a single check to be spent gradually at several different suppliers (BPP, 1981). In Figure 2.1 the guide on the left was issued in 1954 and the other in 1934. The similarities in design continue inside in nearly identical text outlining the five features of 'The Provident System' and the seven 'Provident Points' that were designed to drive home the benefits. The wording used to convey the 'system' and 'points' was very similar in 1934 to that featured in Figure 2.2's extract from a 1957 guide. The only significant change was that the 1934

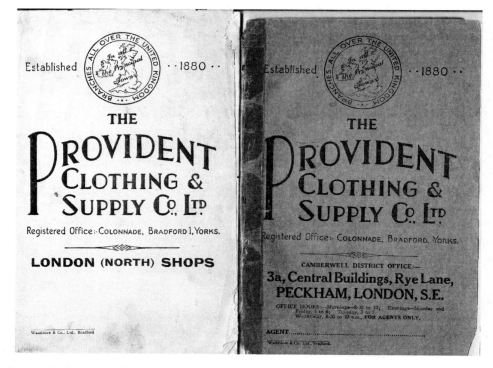

Figure 2.1 Provident shopping guides, 1954; 1934
Source: Photograph of author's own copies.

THE PROVIDENT SYSTEM

1.—Members get their Checks when ONE Weekly Instalment has been paid, together with a small charge for poundage.

2.—You can become a Member on payment of Sixpence per week or upwards, according to the value of the Order you take out.

3.—The Provident Checks (or Orders) are TAKEN AS CASH by all the tradesmen on this list and have EXACTLY THE SAME PURCHASING POWER AS READY MONEY. You simply go to any of the shops named herein, ask for what you want—very likely it will have its price marked—and present our Check in payment, which the shopkeeper will be pleased to take. Hand our Check to the tradesman AFTER your purchases have been completed.

4.—You have no need to spend the full amount of our Check at one particular shop. You can divide the amount amongst several tradesmen, until the face value of it is fully spent up, and in such cases the shopkeeper endorses the amount you have spent at his shop on the back of the Check, and returns it to you for future use. For instance, with a £2 Check, you can spend 20/- at any of the Clothiers on this list, 10/6 at any of the Booters, and 9/6 at any of the Milliners, and so on. If, before the Check is fully spent, there is no room for further endorsements, hand the Check to your Agent and ask him to obtain another Check for the unspent balance.

5.—You repay us the value of our Checks by instalments of 1/- in the £ per week, i.e., a 10/- Check must be paid up in regular weekly instalments of 6d. per week; a 20/- Check at 1/- per week; a 30/- Check at 1/6 per week; a £2 Check at 2/- per week, and so on, and all Orders must be fully paid up in 20 weeks.

PROVIDENT POINTS

1.—You can obtain AT ORDINARY CASH PRICES from the very best shops in your own district, every requisite for yourself, your family, or your home. You pay us by Easy Weekly Instalments. We pay the shopkeeper from whom you purchase.

2.—Our Agents call upon you for the payments weekly. All our Agents are local persons, known to you.

3.—We are giving, and will continue to give, the best and easiest weekly payment terms to the general public. Just give us a trial and see for yourself. No Entrance Fees. No Charge for Cards. No Fines.

4.—WE WANT YOU TO KNOW:—

(a) That Shopkeepers' Clubs give you no choice of shops. You are bound to go to one shop only, which is very often stocked specially for Credit trade

(b) That OUR PROVIDENT CHECK IS treated as Cash at ALL the Shops on this List, and you can divide the amount of the PROVIDENT CHECK amongst any of them until it is fully spent up. If you do not want to spend the balance of our Check now, keep it until you do want to spend it, and then pick your shop from this list. All the Shops on this List are CASH SHOPS and mark their goods at KEEN COMPETITIVE PRICES.

This fact alone is of great value to you.

(c) That the huge General Warehouses who issue tremendous catalogues of everything under the sun on the weekly payment plan, and who send you the goods you pick unseen from their Headquarters, give you no chance whatever of inspecting the goods yourself before you put your money down and bind yourself by signing their forms. In all these cases The Provident system fills a long-felt want, and in scores of other instances we can show you that the system of The Provident Clothing & Supply Co. Ltd. is the best and most popular Credit system ever devised, and a real boon to the respectable working-class. It is used by people who prefer to make their purchases in the time-honoured way, i.e., at the shops of their choice where they can buy in private.

5.—Keep your money in your own town. Join "The Provident" and buy from your own local tradesmen. You have greater choice; you can inspect all the goods yourself and see what you are buying, and you get the best possible value by buying your Drapery, Clothing, Boots, etc., from your own tradesmen, through the medium of a Provident Check.

6.—We have attained unparalleled success and popularity, and as a natural consequence there are hundreds of feeble imitators and mere copyists of the Provident system throughout the country. They have copied our system, tried to copy our methods and have even copied word for word our printed matter. But we ask you, for the sake of your own personal welfare, to be very careful and join only The Provident Clothing & Supply Co. Ltd., and not be misled into joining any other Company.

7.—The Provident has stood the test of over 75 years' experience. We give you the benefit of that experience; and hundreds of thousands of thoroughly respectable people throughout the largest towns in England, Ireland, Scotland and Wales, can testify that there is no Club or Weekly-Payment System like the "Good Old Provident," the original Company.

Figure 2.2 The Provident system, 1957 shopping guide
Source: photograph of author's own copy.

guide named its competitors as 'the Travelling Draper, Scotch Packman, Credit Draper, Tickman, Boot Clubman' while by the 1950s reference was made only to the disadvantages of 'shopkeepers clubs' and 'general warehouses'. The wording remained otherwise intact, and was placed somewhere in the inside covers until after 1962.

By the 1920s, Provident was still the only company trading nationally and until the 1960s almost all of its many competitors were small, local concerns. The 'clothing and supply' system it had established had spread across an estimated 600 firms by the 1960s.[4] Competitors included Bradford Clothing and Supply, People's Provident Supply, District Clothing and Supply, Practical Clothing and Supply, Crescent Premier Supply, National Clothing and Supply and Equitable Clothing and General Supply. Almost all of these companies were later bought out in the consolidation period that began after 1962 by Provident or by one of its two largest competitors, John Paget and Son established in Sheffield in 1900 and Hull Clothing and Supply founded in

1927 and trading as Cattle's (Holdings) Ltd in the early 1960s (BPP, 1981). As the near ubiquity of 'clothing and supply' in the company names of check traders implies, Provident had identified a system that was widely copied. There were:

> hundreds of feeble imitators and mere copyists of the Provident system throughout the country. They have copied our system, tried to copy our methods and have even copied word for word our printed matter. But we ask you for the sake of your own welfare, to be very careful ... hundreds of thousands of thoroughly respectable people throughout the largest towns in England, Ireland, Scotland and Wales, can testify that there is no club or weekly payment system like the 'Good Old Provident', the original company.
>
> (PCS, 1934)

This complaint was still being parroted in the 1961 edition of the guide and it bears some merit. Competitors clearly did identify the key features of check trading from the Provident's system and adopted very similar practices, regulations and artifacts. National Clothing and Supply (NCS, 1968), for instance, listed rules including 20 week instalments, customer responsibility for orders, renewal restrictions as well as advice to avoid shopping on busy Saturdays, all of which were features of the Provident. The stability of a system that barely changed in 80 years and its identification with just one company is remarkable. This however is not just down to Provident's perfection of the check trading system; it is also a function of how it developed outside the gaze of regulators.

Credit was largely unregulated until 1900, when the first Moneylenders Act required moneylenders to register with a magistrate and granted courts the power to dissolve agreements judged unfair. This attempt at credit regulation only tackled moneylending as the most controversial, and therefore most visible, form of credit. As O'Connell's authoritative history notes it was not a success and exposed 'the lack of knowledge about slum lending' and the difficulties of creating a workable model that could address 'the very different types of lending taking place in such diverse environments as the West End of London and the back streets of Liverpool' (O'Connell, 2009, p. 131). The revised law enacted in 1927 increased the costs of registration and introduced a nominal annual interest rate ceiling of 48 per cent that O'Connell documents led many moneylenders to return to illegal lending. By changing the moneylending environment it also inadvertently helped produce the conditions in which 'hire-purchase' systems could thrive. These were then left largely unregulated in England even after the toothless Hire Purchase Act 1938, until terms control orders were introduced in 1952 followed by the tougher Hire Purchase Act 1954 (Thornely and Ziegel, 1965). Check trading benefited from falling largely outside the scope of any regulatory efforts until the 1940s when conditions started to change. The major reshaping of the sector that began in the 1960s was a response to the constraints and opportunities that the regulatory framework presented in the context of post-war affluence.

Becoming Provident C&S

After decades of steady expansion the Provident and other check traders had a difficult war. Retailers had responded to the purchase tax and price controls that government had imposed on utility goods by reducing the discounts they allowed check traders and the latter had attempted to pass the cost back to customers with an increased poundage charge. This attempt coincided with the damning account of check trading published in 'Our Towns' by the Women's Group on Public Welfare, which informed the Board of Trade's decision in 1941 to prohibit the poundage charge entirely (O'Connell, 2009). Despite being queried in parliament[5] the prohibition remained in place until 1949 and by then the Provident had seen its customer base fall from 1,100,000 in 1939 to 535,000 in 1944. Customer numbers recovered somewhat when the prohibition was removed but by that time another problem was starting to emerge.

> Although Provident's customer numbers returned to their pre-war levels of just over one million in 1951, growth was more sluggish thereafter and it stalled in the late 1950s. Data from the company's archives also reveals that demand for checks became more seasonal in the late 1950s, with customer numbers rising by between 80,000 and 100,000 from the third to fourth quarter. The average value of checks taken out grew at a substantially slower rate than average earnings during the 1950s, rising barely at all between 1955 and 1959. This suggests that for increasing numbers of customers, checks were becoming less a part of their weekly routine and more of an additional option, at Christmas.
> *(O'Connell, 2009, p. 71)*

The challenge was to figure out how to counter the current of increasing affluence that would leave their product reserved for emergency use. The solution, of course, was to re-position their offering not against the current but within it. There were though, a few obstacles in the way. The things that Provident checks might supply had steadily increased in variety since the 1880s but the emphasis remained mainly on smaller, softer things like clothing and drapery while the hard, sought after durables of post-war Britain, the washing machines, vacuum cleaners and refrigerators were outside the scope of checks. These goods were primarily supplied to poorer customers through hire-purchase schemes that became subject to terms control orders after 1952. The 1952 Hire-Purchase and Credit Sale Agreements (Control) Order introduced a requirement that goods could only be purchased on hire purchase over an 18 month term and after a minimum 33 per cent cash deposit was paid. The sudden stringency of these terms led the Order to be described in parliament as 'a vicious piece of class legislation ... unnecessary and unfair discrimination against the poorer sections of the community'.[6] Terms control also opened up a potential space for check traders, whose low value products fell outside the scope of the various orders that were brought into effect at intervals until they were finally dispensed with in 1982 (cf. O'Connell, 2009).

To get into the market for the things hire-purchase schemes supplied, the 'dish washers, drying cabinets, ironing machines and irons, wringers and mangles, floor polishers, vacuum cleaners, water softeners and so forth, apart from all kinds of office furniture, bicycles, tricycles and practically every kind of mechanically-propelled vehicle',[7] required a new kind of product that could be used to borrow larger amounts over longer periods. The introduction of vouchers sounds like a relatively trivial matter but it was probably the biggest change in the company's operations since it was founded. Vouchers were the centrepiece of a strategy designed to respond to both the increasing seasonality of demand for checks and the 'interesting and even exciting possibilities' (PCS, 1962, p. 10) the new affluence afforded. One of the first changes the firm made was to quietly dispense with the limitations implied in the name 'Provident Clothing and Supply' by subtly altering it to Provident (C&S) Ltd in March 1961. The name change was part of a restructuring which saw a 'new' company acquire the whole of the share capital of the 'old' company and its subsidiary, the printing works Waddilove and Co. Ltd that had produced all their stationery since the 1890s, both of which were placed in voluntary liquidation at the end of the year (PCS, 1961). This technical restructuring was a precursor to the company's listing on the stock exchange in March 1962 and a change to the Articles of Association to permit the directors to borrow, without the prior consent of shareholders, up to five times the amounts paid up in share capital (PCS, 1962).

These changes were designed to give the company the liquidity to defer revenue and finance the increased supply of credit they anticipated providing after the introduction of vouchers in July 1961.

> In the past our check business was mainly restricted to clothing, shoes, drapery, linen and other soft household and family goods which could come within the 20 week payment period. Our customers had to look elsewhere for their other requirements. Now, however, vouchers provide our customers with a much more comprehensive service and can be used to acquire the whole wide range of domestic durable goods such as washing machines, cookers, refrigerators and the like with payment periods of up to 100 weeks. We have found this additional facility to be most welcome to customers and to shopkeepers.
>
> *(PCS, 1963, p. 10)*

Vouchers were heralded as a means of closing the gap between the company's traditional business, and emerging customer requirements. If this were to work it would take more than recognition of the opportunities afforded by the new, and already exhaustively debated, affluent desires of their customers. It also required technical planning and organisation to ensure that a fit could be engineered between new patterns of living and corporate experience. 'We', the annual report in the year of their introduction noted:

> have taken a searching new look at our organisation and methods – forging new links, examining incentives, setting up new sales promotion and generally initiating a policy of planned expansion. This policy must be soundly based and prudently executed if it is to produce lasting and reliable results.
>
> *(PCS, 1962, p. 10)*

All the firm's costing and debt experience was based on lending small sums up to a maximum of £20 over twenty week loan periods; offering sums of up to £100, for between 40 and a maximum of 100 weeks, was a different proposition and it was embarked on cautiously. One symptom of that caution was the decision initially to cap vouchers at £100 and to restrict them only to existing Provident customers. An increase in deferred revenue in 1962 was attributed to the introduction of vouchers and the longer periods of credit involved, and a further increase in 1963 combined with record turnover marked their secure establishment (PCS, 1962, 1963). Press headlines confirmed Provident's strong financial performance in 1963 and plans were announced later the same year for further expansion of the voucher business alongside the removal of their restriction to existing customers.[8] Another symptom of the organisational care taken was a delicate rebalancing of the role of agents in screening risk while promoting consumption.

By the late 1950s, the check trading labour market had shifted from being male dominated and part-time to almost three quarters female with many working full-time (O'Connell, 2009). This shift was part of a broader feminisation in sectors like mail order, which had cottoned on to the advantages of a labour supply with the 'natural' characteristics, interests and activities of women. Women agents were:

> after all, particularly sympathetic and alive to the nicely balanced details of the family budget. They sense in some cases better than men what their customers can or cannot afford ... operating as they do in their own communities they have a native ability to appraise the creditworthiness of the men and women around them.
>
> *(PCS, 1963b)*

All agents were 'inculcated' from the start 'with the basic idea that Provident checks are not meant to be frittered away on frivolous things' (PCS, 1963b). Agents' income was based on commission on both the total value of the collection *and* new business. The balance between these two sources of income had to be carefully managed given the regulatory sensitivities surrounding credit. Provident's assertion in the 1963 Annual Report that 'by far the greater part of the agent's remuneration is based on their total weekly collections and not from the value of new business introduced' was in part a sincere reflection of the firm's still relatively conservative lending policy. It was also designed to reassure brand new shareholders that, in a period in which there was a push for consumer credit controls with more teeth, Provident's lending was safe and unlikely to face tighter regulation.

This was not exactly the case. There was broad awareness that check traders escaped terms control and while this might have been tolerable when they were dealing only in short-term lending for smallish amounts, the introduction of vouchers brought them into effectively the same market as hire-purchase providers. As the market for vouchers grew, there were calls for the loophole to be closed. 'If we are leaving one wing of credit-sale distribution uncontrolled then there are dangers that malpractices in the uncontrolled wing will start to dominate the other', the Labour MP, Richard Winterbottom, argued before pointing to the difficulties of regulating the varieties of short-term credit (*HC Deb*, 24 June 1964, 697, c468). If the diversity of the sector and the scale, terms, relative affordability and 'necessaryness' of check credit had escaped much regulatory surveillance, a sense that credit providers in the affluent 1960s were 'running amok', led to increasing attention and ongoing deliberations about how best to respond. In the interim Provident did very well out of the regulatory gap as reported in *The Economist*:

> So far the Bank of England has not sent Provident Clothing a letter telling it to restrain its lending; but Provident is unlikely to be affronted by this lack of official recognition while its business continues to grow rapidly. The credit extended to its customers at December 31st was £26 million, £5 million (or 24%) higher than a year earlier. Provident has escaped the official net, it seems, because it cannot be treated as either a hire purchase company or a bank.
>
> (The Economist, 1966, p. 1047)

Provident, the article went on, had never had a 'traumatic bad debt period', which it attributed to the regular weekly visits by collecting agents who learn their customers' credit ratings quickly.[9] This was the same argument that Provident itself made – agents were incentivised to work for 'sound, dependable turnover' not to persuade families to enter into commitments they could not meet (PCS, 1963b).

This was true but it was also not quite that simple, particularly as the sector grew into the 1960s. The Provident's credit 'rating' system was qualitative and approximate. This didn't make it inefficient as the low bad debt ratio testified, but the introduction of vouchers also changed the qualitative calculations – what Franck Cochoy (2008) has characterised as 'qualculations' – that agents had to perform to control credit. The shift to a predominantly female, full-time agency workforce was part of this. Women were not only expected to be more sensitive to the family budget they were considered better attuned to building customers' appetites for the sort of things that would help shift the image of the company away from 'clothing and supply'. Women had a keen eye for all the necessities that would help 'keep the image of our service modern and bright without losing its traditional simplicity and integrity and to ensure that it reaches and is understood by the vast market of present and potential Provident users' (PCS, 1964, p. 10).

Maintaining a balance between 'bright modern-ness' and traditional simplicity was left to rest partly on the proclaimed superiority of women agents' social sensibilities. The majority of Provident customers were women and it was presumably a little easier for women agents to enter the homes of acquaintances and strangers and develop the kind of relationships that would allow them to 'see' the spaces in the home that credit could be summoned to fill. Women, as sovereign domestic consumers, were expected to have a better eye for any missing or worn-out domestic appliances that were essential for the modern home.

By 1964 Provident was representing itself to its shareholders as improving 'the wellbeing of people everywhere'. Its Annual Report that year boasted of helping 'equip better brighter labour saving homes'; enabling 'the family to be better clothed and equipped for all occasions'; providing the 'tools, books and equipment for acquiring skills' and 'encouraging sports and hobbies and holidays and leisure activities generally' (PCS, 1964, p. 10). The report continued the trend, established when the company first went public, of taking shareholders 'backstage' this time with a 'pictorial demonstration of the scope and social impact of the company's activities'. This demonstration eschewed the monochrome photographs of the previous two years in favour of comic book style colour drawings of a modern working class home. These sunny illustrations were designed to showcase the Provident's role in supplying the means for the expensive equipment, tools and appliances that every modern home now required. The company was upbeat that the strategy was working since it was also reporting its third successive year of record trading profit and a 55 per cent increase over the three year period at a time when overall economic conditions were difficult, with disappointing overseas trade figures and retail trade statistics that 'lacked sparkle'.

The imagery and mood of the 1964 Annual Report is a world away even from that published three years earlier just before the company went public. The change went across the board. Marketing materials began to appear that shed the subsistence credit image entirely. Even the resolutely functional and unchanging shopping guides were finally redesigned, and the guides to the Provident system rewritten in a way that emphasised customer focused values (see Figure 2.3). This was an atmosphere in which the *Investors Chronicle's* depiction of the voucher as a magical route to 'wellbeing' and 'clean modern living' was in accord with the Company's rebranding and the illustration was reproduced in the 1965 Annual Report. In reality, the average Provident customers lived in homes that were nothing like those beginning to be featured in company reports and marketing. Their customers remained throughout the decade resolutely 'in the CDE sectors, that is working class households where husband and wife are weekly paid' (Leslie, 1971, p. 24). The distance between the reality of customers' lives and their aspirations, as Provident's newly appointed marketing and consumer credit executives recognised, however was an opportunity, not a problem. By 1962, the firm's 'more youthful outlook, new ideas, new men and a new approach' (PCS, 1963, p. 10) led to the shopping guide system being supplemented with *Arcade*, a catalogue style magazine for customers, the launch of *Colonnade* an internal newspaper designed to improve communication with agents and an increased use of advertising, including for the first time, television advertising.

Mail order companies excelled at showcasing the goods on offer, rather than the credit means of their provision but as with store credit, customers could only buy what was in the catalogue or store – they couldn't shop around. What the changing regulatory environment helped Provident work out in the 1960s, was that they had to re-identify their product from subsistence clothing and supply credit to the means to a whole range of different ends from domestic hardware to foreign holidays, insurance services or even an 'Ashley Russell fur' (PCS, 1966b). Revamped marketing (see Figure 2.4) that hammered home the connections between all the different things that Provident credit would allow customers to have *right now* was part

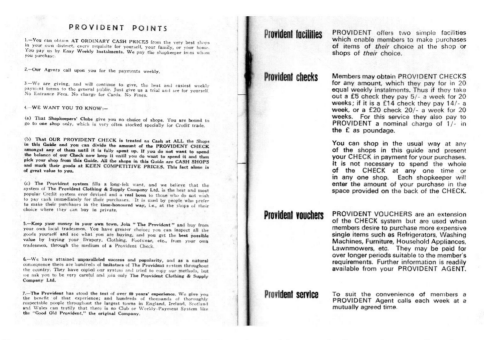

Figure 2.3 Provident points in the 1961 shopping guide reworked as customer values in 1966 shopping guide

Source: Photographs of author's own copies.

of that. Another part was the concentrated effort that led to agreements with retailers more than doubling from 20,000 in 1962 to 50,000 in 1965, including numerous multiples. Particular effort went into getting multiple retailers signed up. This included stores like Foster Brothers, Hepworths and Singer Sewing Machines and department stores like Frasers, Littlewoods and British Home Stores, which were enticed into the system through much lower discounts than were available to small independent stores.[10] This expanding range of destinations and ends helped Provident achieve a striking growth trajectory in the 1960s and sowed the seeds for it to pursue a strategy that would free it entirely from its associations with catalogues of things.

A bank for the people?

Provident described itself in its 1963 Annual Report as a 'fireside bank' and as 'the smaller man's friendly bank manager'. The idea of the Provident as 'the people's banker' had been around for years and reflected the fact that the services it provided stood in lieu of banking for customers who were primarily unbanked. Yet check traders, including the Provident, were not organised anything like banks at the start of the decade: most of the others were fairly small, local concerns, all were specialised in the provision of a limited, standard service and subject to strong constraints in how much they could lend and in how much they could borrow. As the 1960s progressed the technical organisation and structure of the Provident changed dramatically and in ways that would make the idea of it becoming a fully fledged bank much less unlikely. These changes reshaped Provident's identity from 'check trader' towards a much broader ranging

Figure 2.4 1965 Marketing sample
Source: Photograph of author's own copy.

provider of financial services. The changes in the customer-facing side of the business described above were part of that but they were entirely contingent upon a complete restructuring of the capital market side of the business. What the company became was a matter of what it acquired and ultimately what it failed to acquire.

In the years immediately following its 1962 restructuring and public listing the Provident began to get a fair amount of attention in the financial press. A series of articles like the *Financial Times*' 'Provident Clothing pays 2% More than Forecast' (21 February 1963) appeared referring to the company's 'good start', 'growth', 'interim up', 'good progress', 'payment raised' and 'moving ahead' over the next three years.[11] During this period the company was bullish and constantly on the lookout 'for acquisitions or amalgamations which might be capable of being arranged with other check companies' (PCS, 1963, p. 11). It embarked on a joint venture with United Dominions Trust, an industrial banker with large hire-purchase interests, to establish Paybonds Ltd, a company formed to launch a new form of consumer credit in 1964.[12] 'Paybonds' could be used to borrow up to £250 and were meant to bridge the gap between bank overdrafts and the Provident's other products. Unlike vouchers, paybonds were designed to be portable and could be spent at more than one retailer. They were intended to retain the business of retailers, particularly of electrical goods, who operated on narrow margins, and they involved a different spread of the costs of credit with a greater percentage borne by the consumer to cover the lower discount offered by the retailer. Their introduction was another indication of the diversification in the financial services the firm sought to offer. By 1965 the company was in talks with a US insurance company that would involve its agents selling policies and by 1967 talks with Barclays around their newly launched credit card were being reported.[13] In 1968 Provident acquired Practical Credit Service Limited and Bristol Clothing and Supply Company Limited (PCS, 1968). Profits almost doubled between 1961 and 1966, the record £8.53 million profit posted in 1973 was nearly five times that of a decade earlier, generating almost unvaryingly buoyant press coverage right through till 1973.[14]

In this atmosphere the idea that Provident could become a more mainstream provider of a full range of financial services was quite credible when the company took the most decisive, symbolic step in that direction.

> In December 1970, we made what could be our most important acquisition – The People's Bank Limited. At present this is a very small operation but the significance of the name to Provident and its relevance to the extension of a wider range of facilities to Provident customers and others are beyond doubt. This year we shall be preparing the Bank and making the necessary arrangements to enable it to take an increasingly important part in Group activities.
>
> *(PCS, 1970b, p. 7)*

Purchasing the People's Bank, according to Richard Davenport, who had succeeded Gordon Waddilove that year as the first chairman from outside the family, would reinforce a major branded consolidation and expansion of their activities to offer a 'totally comprehensive range of family and domestic financial services for the whole field of present and potential Provident customers' (PCS, 1971, 1972, p. 4). This change was enabled by the regulatory loophole that gave Provident relatively free reign in what was effectively the hire-purchase market. This circumstance had not gone unnoticed. The parliamentary debates on hire purchase and the regulatory environment surrounding consumer credit of the early 1960s culminated in the formation of the Crowther Committee in 1965. As evident in its reports to shareholders throughout the 1960s, the company was keenly aware that the committee's recommendation could entirely reshape the scope of their activities. Its diversification strategy was clearly expansionist but it was also anticipatory and defensive. The *Financial Times* reported that having come across the People's Bank by chance, Davenport was 'enchanted by the name (and vaguely uneasy that a competitor might get hold of it' (*Financial Times* 1965, p. 20). The article went on;

> Davenport says the purchase has nothing to do with the publication, probably next month of the Crowther Report on Consumer Credit. Even so, a banking status and exemption from the Moneylenders' Act is a pleasant hedge against any future changes in the credit law. More important, Provident's customers are getting more affluent over the years and the People's Bank will be able to provide the more sophisticated financial services they need.

The extent to which fear of Crowther was influencing Provident's strategy is moot, but the connections between it and the regulatory environment were widely reported.[15] If the Crowther recommendations were enacted, together with the Bank of England's credit control proposals, the effect, Morison (1971) concluded, would likely be to further blur the long established lines of demarcation in financial services as the clearing banks began to challenge finance houses for business and Provident's new banking subsidiary would 'square the circle'. Provident's customers were not clearing bank customers but they were widely expected to soon need banking services from somewhere and Provident would be well positioned to offer such services to the newly banked. There was considerable early confidence that this strategy was working. The People's

Bank received Section 123 banking status in April 1972 and a rights issue enabled the company to increase its borrowing ratio from 5 to 7 times capital and reserves in anticipation of the 'expected large volume of additional business' as the bank became fully operational (PCS, 1973, p. 4). The strength of the results in 1972 from Provident, and another firm Cedar Holdings, led the financial editor of *The Times* to remark.

> Both firms have already done much to refute earlier suggestions that their profitability depended on a restrictive credit environment in which the larger and more closely controlled lending institutions were at a competitive disadvantage. . . . This new potential is particularly important now that the People's Bank is fully operational. Its exemption from the workings of the Moneylenders Act came through only in April and it took another two months to start lending so it's early days yet for forecasting its impact on the lower end of the credit market. However the goodwill of Provident's existing customers, on whom the initial promotional effort has been concentrated should work in the company's favour.
>
> *(Financial Times, 7 September 1972, p. 18)*

The city's view through till 1974, was that the entry into broader financial services could not have been much better timed with the best profit outcomes having become an 'almost perpetual feature' at Provident.[16] Provident took a 26.7 per cent stake in its main, though still considerably smaller competitor, Cattles (Holdings) Ltd in 1973. In the same year it announced that it had become necessary to change its name to something that while 'retaining the word Provident of course' would more suitably indicate the range of the group's activities (PCS, 1973, p. 5). The 1973 report makes reference to the unstable interest rates and increases in money costs that were starting to unfold as the secondary banking crisis of 1973–74 took hold.[17] This was the biggest banking crisis of the twentieth century in the UK. It emerged after heavy lending to the property sector led to the failure of a number of secondary banks and threatened the liquidity of the entire banking system (Scott, 1996). By the middle of 1974 it was clear that Provident had not been entirely unscathed. The group reported that although it had not drawn upon the Support Group set up by the Bank of England it had been affected. Added to this it declared a £2.7 million loss caused by unauthorised trading in June of that year. In the following two years ebullient announcements were replaced with quieter claims that the group was weathering the downturn and awaiting improving conditions in which it could return to the 'bolder, more expansionist attitude which is more natural to us' (PCS, 1974; *Financial Times* 28 February 1975, p. 30). By the end of 1975 taxable profits rose again as the group returned to its core business of lending small amounts over short periods (*Financial Times*, 14 March 1977, p. 20).

This concentration on core markets was also at play in the bid to takeover Cattles in 1977. Had it been successful, this would have given the Group a better geographical spread since Cattles mainly had branches where the Provident had not, but the initial bid was rejected, subsequently increased and then lapsed following its referral to the Monopolies Commission.[18] Market research commissioned in 1975, after the worst of the crisis, confirmed a high degree of customer loyalty with two-thirds of customers using the firm for more than five years and a core market still concentrated amongst council house dwelling weekly wage earners aged between 25–44 (PCS, 1975). The Annual Report's coverage of the research emphasised the positive, but the survey also revealed a sharp falling off in custom from younger, better-off fractions of the working class. By 1979 customer numbers fell back again to 721,000 (BPP, 1981) and the Group reported that its newer acquisitions and activities 'supplement rather than challenge the preeminence of the traditional home service credit business' (PFG, 1979).

These were not quite the outcomes that were hoped for after the purchase of the People's Bank. In the wake of the secondary banking crisis the group did eventually introduce a greater range of financial services but it never succeeded in attracting a new, wider customer base. The 1974 Annual Report was entitled *Provident: the Peoples Bank* but changed to the more general *Provident Financial* in 1975. The proposal, reported in the *Daily Mail* in 1970, that all of Provident's larger branches would be rebranded as the People's Bank, was never realised. By 1980, the People's Bank operated only eight branches although there were plans for a further six. It was by then operating a full banking service that the *Financial Times* noted was 'open six days a week on a nine to five o'clock basis. There are no bank charges, current accounts earn 2 per cent interest and deposit accounts repay 15 per cent which is a point or so above that offered by the clearing banks' (*Financial Times* 16 January 1980, p. 6). These features might well have proved attractive enough for the more general expansion that had been planned but there was a further obstacle in the way.

One of the side effects of the secondary banking crisis was the enactment of a new Banking Act in 1979 that extended the supervisory responsibilities of the Bank of England over lenders. One of the Act's key provisions was that no new deposit taking business could be established without the Bank's permission and those already in operation had to be granted permission to continue (*Financial Times*, 21 September 1981, p. III). The Act distinguished been two types of business, banks and Licensed Deposit Takers (LDTs). In 1980 Provident applied for a licence to operate as a bank and thereby continue using the 'People's Bank' name as an integral element in restarting their long-held expansion plans. The Bank of England was not persuaded and classified the Provident an LDT. Provident did not, the Bank ruled, satisfy all the criteria of a recognised bank they had set out. A bank, according to the 1979 Act, should provide a wide range of banking services and enjoy 'high reputation and standing in the financial community' (*Financial Times*, 17 January 1981). Gordon Richardson, then Governor of the Bank of England asserted that 'classification as a licensed deposit taker is not to be seen of itself as impugning the status of an institution – and certainly not the integrity and competence of its management or the good name of the institution' (*Financial Times*, 21 September 1981, p. III).

This was scant compensation. Names in financial services, as Provident well understood, do a lot more signalling work than marking a 'good' or safe institution. They say something about the history, type and character of the business. There was no avoiding that LDT was a lower 'goat-like' status than bank (*Financial Times*, 16 January 1981, p. 6). Opening Provident's appeal against the decision in 1981, Anthony Graham-Dixon, QC, remarked that the name 'bank', meant people could expect 'probity, prudence, honesty, security and sufficient services in width and depth' to justify its use. LDT status not only did not convey such confidence but would prevent the company from continuing to trade under the People's Bank name. The 1979 Banking Act, Graham-Dixon argued, was essentially a piece of consumer protection legislation that was being loftily interpreted 'from the Ivory Tower of Threadneedle Street' and not from the user's point of view (*Financial Times*, 16 January 1981, p. 6). Provident's aim to bring full banking services to 17 million unbanked British adults primarily from the C2/D social categories, would be permanently halted if it was not allowed to call itself a bank. These arguments did not change the ruling, Provident published a bullish Annual Report in 1981 confirming their plans to roll out more People's Bank branches but in July their appeal was refused.

> The tribunal accepted that People's Bank provided four of the required services: current or deposit account facilities for members of the public or companies; overdraft or loan facilities; foreign exchange services; and financial advice. But it decided that the size of the business in relation to the last two services was not of sufficient nature or scope to provide

the wide range of banking services of a positive nature so as to entitle the appellants to recognition as a bank.

(Financial Times, *22 July 1981*)

Epilogue

Posterity offers no certain clues as to what might have happened if the decision had gone in Provident's favour. Perhaps a People's Bank offering a broad banking service on relatively favourable terms would have contributed to the development of a more inclusive financial services sector? The loss of the name to a new regulatory environment however confirmed Provident in an alternate strategy that was as much part of the kind of organisation they had been 'becoming' over their long history, and particularly over the previous two decades, as the 'poor man's banker'. The company had always been a provider of credit to customers with scarce means but by the end of the 1970s it was steadily moving away from its longstanding techniques of risk management by screening and stringent controls on the amount borrowed.

The introduction of vouchers offered a way of increasing the amount and the purposes Provident's credit facilities could be used for, but vouchers were still tied to particular retailers. Towards the end of the 1960s, following the introduction of the more portable 'paybonds', Provident had begun to explore other means of diversifying beyond documentary credit. A number of smaller check traders started offering cash loans in the 1960s, and although Provident did not join them until 1972, its loan service grew very quickly. By the end of the decade, all three of the largest documentary credit companies offered loans through their agents (BPP, 1981). Provident's loan book provided the group with £8.2 million of its £9.2 million pre-tax profit in 1979. Loans were a significantly more expensive form of credit than checks or vouchers where customers shared the lending costs with retailers, but this did not deter customers. Provident, and its main competitors, saw customer numbers increase steadily through the 1980s, even as the importance of voucher and check trading diminished, towards an estimated 3 million by the early 1990s (Rowlingson, 1994). Rather than expanding by moving into more mainstream banking services, Provident consolidated its position by specialising in an ever more tightly defined 'down' market of 'excluded', 'non-standard' or 'subprime' borrowers. This continued into the 1990s as mainstream credit providers responded to the negative equity housing crisis with a 'flight to quality' (O'Connell, 2009; cf. Burton *et al.* 2004; Langley, 2008). By the early 2000s, documentary credit trading had almost disappeared and Provident informed the Office of Fair Trading in 2011 that it no longer issued trading checks or bonds of any kind.

In 2016, the *Financial Times* described Provident Financial as a rarity among UK lenders in having 'had a good financial crisis' (20 January 2016). The company now has four main arms; a credit card business called Vanquis Bank, Satsuma an online instalment loan product, a motor finance unit and its home credit, or doorstep lending, arm that still employs 5,000 agents. Vanquis, a credit card with an APR around 40 per cent, now accounts for almost two-thirds of the group's products and the group is trying to scale back its doorstep loan business, which operates with APRs around 1000 per cent. Satsuma, which was launched in 2014 as a direct competitor to high profile payday loan companies like Wonga, has had little impact. The company's recent history shows how much it continues to be shaped by the regulatory environment. Satsuma was intended to take advantage of the expected clampdown on payday lenders, while Vanquis has done well out of the tighter prime lending environment after the crisis. As a name, Provident Financial is accommodating enough for the group to navigate its specialism through the non-standard and near prime credit markets moving up, down and around the stream as conditions permit. The name lacks the specificity of both 'clothing and supply' and 'People's

Bank' but this has ultimately allowed the group to operate fairly flexibly within the constraints set by its own history, language and regulation. With the benefit of hindsight, as an increasingly opportunistic lender that is not shy about pricing its specialist risks 'correctly', it may eventually have preferred the regulatory outcome it got. It is not so clear that its customers would agree.

Notes

1. Industrial assurance was a form of life assurance targeted at the poor and based on weekly doorstep collection that thrived in the UK, US, Australia, many parts of Asia and elsewhere until the late twentieth century. See McFall (2014).
2. Just how roguish Victorian financial capitalism was is a matter of debate cf. Klaus (2015) and Kynaston (1995) but the volatility of nineteenth-century insurance, credit and savings organisations is well recorded.
3. All data from PCS (1930); PCS (1951); PCS (1961–75); O'Connell (2009).
4. *HC Deb*, 20 May 1963 678 107.
5. *HC Deb*, 4 August 1942 382 825–6; *HC Deb* 11 September 1942 383 c506.
6. See 1952 *HC Deb* 13 March 1952 vol. 497 cc1695–719.
7. According to Eric Fletcher, MP Islington East HCD 13 March 1952 497 c1696; see also *The Economist* (1963).
8. *Financial Times, The Times* covered higher payments to shareholders than forecast on 21 February 1963.
9. A point *The Economist* also made in a 1963 article.
10. It probably also helped that Hugh Fraser was a shareholder; *The Times*, 9 November 1962.
11. See 'Provident Clothing expansion', *The Times*, Wednesday 4 March 1964, p. 17; 'Provident Clothing's good start', *Financial Times*, 26 March 1964, p. 18; 'Provident Clothing good progress', *Financial Times*, 18 February 1965, p. 16; 'Provident Clothing moving ahead', *The Times*, 31 March 1966, p. 19.
12. 'U.D.T. and Provident launch new personal credit scheme', *Financial Times*, 27 August 1964, p. 9; 'Paybonds', *The Economist*, 29 August 1964, p. 849; PCS (1964–66); BPP (1981).
13. 'Provident plan US insurance deal', *Sunday Times*, 14 February 1965, p. 30; 'Close link with Provident not likely, says Barclays', *Financial Times*, 5 June 1967, p. 5.
14. See PCS (1966, 1973) and 'Provident Clothing record £8.53m', *Financial Times*, 22 February 1974, p. 22. The *Financial Times* and *The Times* between them used words like 'confident', 'happy', 'peak' 'boom', 'boost', 'acceleration', 'strength' in article headlines at least 13 times between 1968 and 1974 not to mention numerous references to increases, more, up, lifts etc. The FT used 'Provident Clothing confident' alone four times between 1970 and 1974 (5 March 1970; 9 September 1970; 7 September 1972; 3 April 1974).
15. See especially Van Musschenbroek, K. (1970) featured article in the *Financial Times; Daily Mail*, 19 December 1970; *Financial Times*, 19 February 1969; 1 June 1970, *The Times*, 15 September 1971, 17 December 1973.
16. *The Times*, 22 February 1973, p. 24.
17. See Scott (1996) It was the biggest banking crisis of the twentieth century in the UK and occurred when heavy lending to the property sector led to the failure of a number of secondary banks and threatened the liquidity of the entire banking system.
18. *Financial Times*, 18 January 1977, *The Times*, 10 January 1977, p. 17, 22 February 1977, p. 24.

Bibliography

Burton, D., Knights, D., Leyshon, A., Alferoff, C. and Signoretta, P (2004) Making a market: The UK retail financial services industry and the rise of the complex sub-prime credit market. *Competition and Change*, **8**, 1: 3–25.

Cochoy, F. (2008) Calculation, qualculation, calqulation: shopping cart arithmetic, equipped cognition and the clustered consumer. *Marketing Theory*, **8**, 1: 15–44.

Hall, S. (1996) 'Who needs identity?' in S. Hall and P. du Gay (eds), *Questions of Cultural Identity*, Sage, London, pp. 1–17.

Klaus, I. (2015) *Forging Capitalism: Rogues, Swindlers, Frauds and the Rise of Modern Finance*, New Haven and London: Yale University Press.

Kynaston, D. (1995) *The City of London Volume 1: A World of Its Own 1815–90*, Bournemouth: Pimlico Publishing.

Langley, P. (2008) *The Everyday Life of Global Finance: Saving and Borrowing in Anglo-America*, Oxford: Oxford University Press.
Leslie, N. (1971) 'Check trading grows', *Financial Times*, 13 July, p. 24.
McFall, L. (2014) *Devising Consumption: Cultural Economies of Insurance, Credit and Spending*, London: Routledge.
Maurer, B. (2012) Regulation as retrospective ethnography: Mobile money and the arts of cash. *Banking and Finance Law Review*, **27**, 2: 299–312.
O'Connell, S. (2009) *Credit and Community: Working-Class Debt in the UK since 1880*, Oxford: Oxford University Press.
Poon, M. (2009) From new deal institutions to capital markets: Commercial consumer risk scores and the making of subprime mortgage finance, *Accounting, Organizations and Society*, **34**, 5, July: 654–74.
Rowlingson, J. (1994) *Moneylenders and their Customers*, London: Policy Studies Institute.
Scott, P. (1996) The new alchemy: Veblen's theory of crisis and the 1974 British property and secondary banking crisis, *Journal of Economic Issues*, **31**, 1: 1–11.
Taylor, A. (2002) *Working Class Credit and Community since 1918*, Basingstoke: Palgrave Macmillan.
Tebbutt, M. (1983) *Making Ends Meet: Pawnbroking and Working-class Credit*, London: Methuen.
Thornely, J.W.A. and Ziegel, J.S. (1965) Hire-purchase reformed. *The Cambridge Law Journal*, **23**, 01: 59–92.

BPP   British Parliamentary Papers
HCD   House of Commons Debate
NCS   National Clothing and Supply Company Ltd
PCS   Provident Clothing and Supply Company Ltd
PFG   Provident Financial Group

BPP (1981) Monopolies and Mergers Commission *Trading Check Franchise and financial services: a report into the supply of trading checks in the United Kingdom*.
Daily Mail. (1970) 'Forward with the People's Bank', 19 December, p. 8.
The Economist. (1963) 'The Check System', 16 March, p. 1046.
The Economist. (1964) 'Paybonds', 29 August 1964, p. 849.
The Economist. (1966) 'Provident Clothing: credit unsqueezed', 12 March, p. 1047.
Financial Times. (1963) 'Provident Clothing pays 2% more than forecast', 21 February, p. 14.
Financial Times. (1963) 'Provident Clothing forecast exceeded', 21 February, p. 14.
Financial Times. (1964) 'Provident Clothing's good start', 26 March, p. 18.
Financial Times. (1964) 'U.D.T. and Provident launch new personal credit scheme', 27 August, p. 9.
Financial Times. (1965) 'Provident Clothing good progress', 18 February, p. 16.
Financial Times. (1967) 'Close link with Provident not likely, says Barclays', 5 June, p. 5.
Financial Times. (1969) 'Provident's balance of probabilities', 19 February, p. 16.
Financial Times. (1970) 'What's in a name', 15 December, p. 20.
Financial Times. (1970) 'Provident Clothing confident', 5 March, p. 22.
Financial Times. (1970) 'Provident Clothing and other lenders', 1 June, p. 32.
Financial Times. (1970) 'Provident Clothing confident, 9 September, p. 28.
Financial Times. (1972) 'Provident Clothing confident, 7 September, p. 22.
Financial Times. (1973) 'Fine mesh needed for credit control', 12 December, p. 24.
Financial Times. (1974) 'Provident Clothing record £8.53m', 22 February, p. 22.
Financial Times. (1974) 'Provident Clothing confident', 3 April, p. 24.
Financial Times. (1975) 'Provident Financial down to £6.84m', 28 February.
Financial Times. (1977) 'Provident on target so far', 14 March, p. 20.
Financial Times. (1980) 'Credit outside the main lines', 16 January, p. 6.
Financial Times. (1981) 'Status appeal by People's Bank opens before Banking Act Board, 16 January, p. 6.
Financial Times. (1981) 'Decision on People's Bank recognition defended', 17 January, p. 3.
Financial Times. (1981) 'Bank of England's ruling on status upheld', 22 July.
Financial Times. (1981) 'Testing time over checks on liquidity', 21 September.
Financial Times. (2016) 'Provident Financial chases rewards where big banks fear to tread', 20 January, retrieved on 29 April 2016 from www.ft.com/cms/s/0/4df278f4-bab0-11e5-b151-8e15c9a029fb.html#axzz3z1pToWZL.
HCD (1964) 24 June 1964, **697**, c468.
Morison (1971) 'When the grass looks greener at the bank', *The Times*, 15 September, p. 12.

NCS (1968) Payment receipt card.
PCS (1930) *Fifty Years Progress 1880–1930*, Commemorative booklet.
PCS (1934) *Shopping Guide*, Camberwell district.
PCS (1951) Festival of Britain Banquet to Inspectors and Managers.
PCS (1954) *Shopping Guide*, North London.
PCS (1957) *Shopping Guide*, Bexley Heath.
PCS (1961b) *Shopping Guide*, Edgware district.
PCS (1961–75) *Annual Reports*, BOD.
PCS (1963b) *The Work of the Provident Agent*, Annual Report insert, BOD.
PCS (1966b) Shop with a Provident Check, *Shopping Guide*, Coventry.
PCS (1970b) *1880–1970 90 years of Provident Service*, Annual Report insert, BOD.
PFG (1974–5; 1979–80) Annual Reports, BOD.
PFG (1980b) *The Origins of Check Trading*, Annual Report insert.
Sunday Times (1965) 'Provident plan US insurance deal', Sunday Times, 14 February, p. 30.
The Times (1962) 'Provident link with Fraser shops', 9 November, p. 21.
The Times (1963) 'Provident Clothing exceed forecast by 2 points', 21 February, p. 18.
The Times (1964) 'Provident Clothing expansion', 4 March, p. 17.
The Times (1966) 'Provident Clothing moving ahead', 31 March, p. 19.
The Times (1972) 'Secondary lenders in the boom', 7 September, p. 18.
The Times (1973) 'Provident Clothing's defensive element', 22 February, p. 24.
Van Musschenbroek, K. (1970) 'Crowther and the credit iceberg', *Financial Times*, 21 September, p. 10.

3
Reflexivity of shadow banking

Benjamin Wilhelm

Introduction

Reflexive relations of finance and regulation point to the importance of shadow banking and its role for global financial hierarchies. Pierre Bourdieu discussing the production of the economic field accentuated the power struggle involved when it comes to processes of (economic) integration. This chapter, thus, highlights the role of shadow banking and its regulation for integrating the global financial field. Following Bourdieu, it argues that the homogenisation of the standard setting discourse, i.e. international financial regulation, after the recent financial crisis further concentrates the resources for domination on a global scale via the reflexive process of finance and its regulation along the problem of shadow banking.

Shadow banking is understood as a focal point for the performance of finance and its regulation. The chapter shows how these two fields interact and, indeed, how they constitute each other. The co-constitutive forces shape and make (shadow) banking, its bubbles, crises and they perpetuate dominance in the present, increasingly integrated 'global economic field' (Bourdieu, 2005). Globally shared standards and therefore an integrated financial and economic system provide for a synchronic experience of financial practices and crises (Nesvetailova, 2014; Kalemli-Ozcan, Papaioannou and Peydro, 2013; Frankel and Rose, 1998). Standards for such integration, however, put further emphasis on regulators as co-drivers for the perpetuation of dominance throughout the financial field.

The so-called run on the shadow banking system in 2008 had been followed by a reform agenda which is now at the point to integrate shadow banking practices into international regulatory frameworks, in particular via 'simple, transparent and standardised (STS) securitisation' (EC, 2015; BCBS and IOSCO, 2015). Whereas the Financial Stability Board (FSB) and others support 'non-bank credit intermediation' as it 'provides a valuable alternative to bank funding which supports real economic activity' (FSB, 2014b), it is still open for discussion what this actually means for the financial field and for relations of political dominance therein and beyond.

The chapter proceeds in two steps. First, it positions reflexivity on a field level and points to the central position of shadow banking for further homogenisation in finance. Second, the chapter provides a more granular reconstruction of the present regulatory discussion regarding the reflexivity of shadow banking which marks a central node for the further integration of the global financial field. The chapter concludes then with the central political and social implications of recent financial governance, i.e. an increasing dominance of an 'economistic' against a political-democratic rationale.

Politics of reflexivity

The use of reflexivity in social science broadly understood relates to the subject/object distinction and to their co-constitutive performance often applied to the researcher and her reflexive relation with the (social) world she studies (Hamati-Ataya, 2013; Leander, 2002; Lynch, 2000; Woolgar, 1988). Here, Pierre Bourdieu fosters the self awareness of the sociologist in analysing the sociality around her. Reflexivity in this way seems to be bound to individual (human) capacities to see the world and their part in the making of the (social) world. In economic sociology such an anthropological style of research contributed to a better understanding of practices and conditions of social exchange within the financial field (e.g. Zaloom, 2006; Riles, 2011; Abolafia, 1996).

Complementary, this section highlights a further style of reasoning when it comes to reflexive relations, i.e. to observe how homogenisation of the financial field has spread after the post-crisis reform agenda through the relation between financial practices and financial regulation. Not just in times of crisis, researchers may question their own stand to describe a reality not yet in place. However, an experience of crisis usually interferes with a taken for granted logic of how 'things' happen and such an experience therefore calls for more foundational adjustments. These may happen through a basic reconfiguration of categories within a theory in order to adapt to a new series of events and hence to change the normal behaviour of doing research.

Reflexivity and its subject

A reflexive understanding problematises standard positivist assumptions like objectification, generalisation or causation. Events of crises indeed may question the very definition of what such categories may refer to. Such events might question theoretical and methodological underpinnings (as well as delineation) of disciplines. Reflexivity in this sense is not only bound to the relation of a researcher and her object but also related to the performance of a social context which makes her a researcher, for instance a sociologist, and her object an object of study, for instance, perceived as being a (or in) crisis. Object and subject gain their specific role thereby not from an outer (empirical or scientific) world but through a specific compatibility of (or conflict within) social fields (Bourdieu, 1985). Events are thus not already present but are continuously constituted via compatible references regarding their presence.

The event of a financial crisis is thereby made obvious through how different observations relate to each other. For the present crisis two forms of observation seem indicative to understand its roots, consequences and how it is to be overcome: innovations in financial practices and their regulation. Both aspects share a considerable focus on the 'problem' of shadow banking. Indeed the notion of shadow banking itself is a by-product of a crisis experience represented in a recent and widely shared regulatory discourse. Such reflexive perspectives on the discursive conditions of crisis and finance had rather not been centre stage (for an indicative exception see Dorn, 2011).

Understandably, a probably larger social fraction demanded ways to compensate their losses or increase their profits within and after the financial turmoil. An investor's opinion on reflexivity might have been more useful than the one of a passed away sociologist. What Bourdieu, and indeed already quite a while ago, argued however was that an increasing homogenisation of economic fields in the context of fast information technology goes along with the perpetuation and strengthening of relations of dominance already present: 'We know that, as a general rule, formal equality in a situation of real inequality favours the dominant' (Bourdieu, 2005, p. 225).

Frequently, the notion of reflexivity seems to be reserved for the interaction of the researcher with her field. In contrast to this perception, more systemic approaches à la Parson or Luhmann account for the interactions of different fields (to stay with the Bourdieusian parlance) that contain and produce research subjectivities and their objects. The observation of such a reflexive interplay brings to light how second order observations (now to stick with a Luhmannian grammar) constitute and indeed are able to perform each other.

The regulatory discussion concerning shadow banking serves as an exemplar to show how the reflexive relation of the regulatory discourse interacts with the practice of banking and how this interaction performs systemic (in)stability. Whereas broader (economic) discussions understand this as a kind of feedback loop of regulation and innovation (sometimes referred to as 'reflexive governance', Voß, Bauknecht and Kemp, 2006), the point being made here is that the present state of the international financial architecture hardly allows for the distinction between the 'fields' of practice and prescription and thus for the assumption of pre-set entities (be it institutions or events) triggering each other.

Positivist approaches try to overcome this problematique of resemblance through an extension of 'surveillance' capacities, thereby gaining a higher degree of granularity regarding the field and thus being able to frame hypotheses accordingly (Fligstein and McAdam, 2012, p. 188). Consequently, a problem of explanation points to a problem of data availability and thereby forgetting about methodologically and theoretically rooted limitations of perspective. The constitutive practice of information computing, however, already and reflexively pre-sets the range of possible understandings in accordance with methodological/theoretical needs for explanation and surveillance techniques set in place. Thus, data generation is closely related to the structure of dominant modes of research that, in turn, points to the reflexive politics of an object/subject distinction.

In the case of financial regulation and financial practices respectively, the empirical fixation of the problem of shadow banking associated with data generation, the need for transparency, standardisation and complexity reduction, as useful as such enterprises may be, rather points to the already present structure of dominance which may hardly be separated from the form of knowledge production. The reflexivity of the financial field can thereby be traced along the making of the financial architecture concerning the 'problem' of shadow banking briefly outlined below.

Reflexive financial architecture

The new financial architecture after the crisis – and thus the practice of shadow banking – points to the plea for an economic sociology of law in recent years (Ashiagbor, Kotiswaran and Perry-Kessaris, 2013; Swedberg, 2003), as the transnational legal structure of finance highlights the convergence of different disciplinary perspectives. Indeed, what has already and often been shown is how the distinction of an economic, political, legal or social sphere rather resembles a modernist/positivist ideology of clear-cut categories to be found 'out there'. This is further accentuated via the performativity literature, which provides one entrance point to counter such macro causation short cuts via a focus on how (financial) things unfold (Callon, 2010; Aspers, 2007; MacKenzie, 2003). In this way, the 'problem' of shadow banking indicates the construction of certain perspectival categories and hence how such categories and their relations very much depend on reflexive relations.

International exchanges are not immediately visible on the banks' balance sheets though they are backed by shared legal understandings be it for appropriate collateral, haircuts or price-formations more generally. In this way, shadow banking provides a contemporary representation of how the global economic field is sustained and enlarged through rapid financial flows seemingly disconnected from national jurisdictions or other social formations. In contrast to a sovereign prerogative to contain markets, financial engineering not only synchronises financial categories like capital, profitability or the scope for transactions but this practice also functions as a constitutive driver for transnational harmonisation of financial standards.

Even though practices of shadow banking enable the circumvention of balance sheet restrictions, these practices are adaptive to international capital flows increasingly defined via international financial rules. Capital requirements in this respect are a central node to understand this evolution as they define the profitability of the bright as well as the gravity of the shady side of finance. This shared horizon for (shadow) banking activities defines and differentiates the notion of capital on a global scale and increasingly harmonises the strategies also for shadow banking activities. Indeed, the present regulatory agenda along the Basel III reforms put further emphasis on responsive capital standards based on respective financial or economic conditions. Legal, financial or economic rationales are thereby intertwined and create the space for shadow banking practices.

The problem of shadow banking for financial stability triggers a more responsive regulatory framework, especially regarding the structure of banks' balance sheets. This concerns, on the one hand, more transparent 'look through' capacities for regulators in order to see how banks relate to the shadow banking system via special purpose vehicles or the like (as a micro perspective); and, on the other hand, the new regulatory environment points to an automatic adaptation to more general economic conditions, for instance related to investment regions (bringing in a macro-prudential regulatory perspective). Both aspects further increase the reciprocity of different legal, financial and economic fields and provide for a deeper integration of global financial exchange.

Leading indicators such as GDP growth, main calculatory practices regarding risk or an inbuilt feedback loop to increase the sensitivity of regulatory practices point to the mechanistic understanding of closely interconnected financial machinery. Thereby, the political role of regulatory institutions or, more broadly, the reflexivity of social relations and financial exchanges are hidden behind a functional logic that excludes a more contested perspective besides efficiency, transparency or data mining. In the following section, two aspects (risk calculation and intermediation chains) of present financial practice are exemplary to show how harmonisation is enhanced via the reference to the shadow banking system and by leaving peripheral alternatives aside.

Reflexivity of shadow banking

Confronted with the global implications of shadow banking contraction, the G20 put up a regulatory agenda focusing on stabilising the financial system and thereby also the shadow banking sector. Even though the notion of shadow banking created a new epistemic basin for the present financial system as it brought together legal, economic and also political discussions regarding modern finance – its indicated fallacies had already been discussed some time before. The implications of complex securitisation (Plantin, 2011), the use of special purpose vehicles (Gorton and Souleles, 2005), problems of off-balance-sheet activities (BCBS, 1986) or the problem of systemic risk (Hellwig, 1995) and the need of macro-prudential regulation (Borio, 2005) had been on the table already before the notion of shadow banking came up though it further aligned these debates (FSB, 2013).

Considering that the shadow banking system generates 'benefits for the financial system and real economy, for example by providing alternative financing to the economy and by creating competition in financial markets that may lead to innovation, efficient credit allocation and cost reduction' (FSB, 2014b), *ex post* regulatory proposals can also be read as a blue print to normalise such intermediation chains and risk mitigation strategies. The different Basel frameworks for banking regulation connected the international banking system more closely by providing common standards especially for capital and capital transactions. Thereby, securitisation could be pursued within an internationalised market and via a common understanding of risk leading to financial exchanges decreasingly hindered through jurisdictional diversity.

Most recently, the problem of shadow banking provided for a focus on responsive instruments of international financial regulation. Regulatory standards for capital should be related to contextual conditions and they should account for new information about present and future developments of markets. These changes in turn affect the solidity of the capital basis of banking institutions. Such a new paradigm for regulatory standards sets the stage for a marketisation of regulatory adjustments. Shadow banking thus provides a central link for financial and 'regulatory markets'. Two discursive nodes are discussed below as they exemplarily show how, first, off-balance-sheet activities produce and sustain (shadow) banking and, second, how balance sheets are managed via calculatory practices of risk.

Off-balance credit intermediation

The sensitivity of financial regulation increased compared to the Basel I framework. Financial innovations structure asset portfolios in order to benefit from the more complex risk hierarchies implemented via Basel II. However, what appears in the first place as a success of the regulatory process turns out to trigger demand in tailored investment products off the banks' balance sheets. Shadow banking could produce such products and gained importance for (global) financial intermediation (Plantin, 2014). Or as the Joint Forum states: '[b]ecause the Basel II framework is more risk sensitive, it is likely to have a material effect on bank investors in terms of their interest in various types of securities' (Joint Forum, 2009, p. 18).

Such reflexive dynamisms display how the problem of shadow banking sustains the regulatory discourse with regard to the notion of risk. First, it positions the term as a central node for regulatory organisation and second it inscribes its implication into daily regulatory and bank governance. A further perspective points to how the transmission of credit through chains for intermediation further shifts the power from regulatory to bank governance, whereby the problem of shadow banking provides a catalyser for the enlarged authority of financial rationales in contrast to societal functions such as credit provision, financial stability or social security.

Most comprehensively, shadow banking is defined as non-bank intermediation (FSB, 2011). This points to the critical moment after the Lehman failure in 2008 triggering a run on the shadow banking system. What seemingly made traditional bank runs old fashioned did not apply to modern shadow banking as for this sector there was no deposit insurance scheme in place or an intervention routine by central banks. Hence, the collapse of the shadow banking sector and its opaque interconnectedness to the traditional banking sector is still a main target of the regulatory agenda (IMF, 2014; FSB, 2014a).

What was and sill is needed to manufacture money-like securities is a high degree of standardisation, i.e. a high degree of information insensitivity paired with broadly accepted standards for transparency. Both had been delivered through the standardisation of asset classes (like securities backed by prime mortgages) and external ratings provided by credit rating agencies.

Together these aspects define the regulatory capital needed in order to back up investments into such products. This combination created an 'opaque' and at the same time clear investment incentive in favour of asset-backed securities and securities thereof (Gorton, 2015).

The expansion of the shadow banking system reflected a shared feeling of having enough information about abstract categories, like a senior tranche of a mortgage portfolio. Further, risk calculations regarding the construction of the structured investment products made them appear to be immune to detailed disclosures of the performance of individual mortgages. Thereby the roll-over risk produced via the transformation of single mortgages with long-term maturity into short-term securities could be put aside not only to spaces off the balance sheets but also to a gullibility towards financial engineering. The construction of risk neutral special investment vehicles or entities had been central to facilitate the packaging and repackaging of such debt in the shadow banking system.

The calculation of risk relates to how banks interact (interconnectedness), their lending along economic circles (procyclicality), their indebtedness (leverage ratio) and the size of banking institutions (too-big-too-fail problematique). Each source of risk has now been counterbalanced via increased capital buffers or lending and borrowing limits to be fully implemented by 2019. Even though shadow banking has often been presented as the other side of banking, the largest (investment) banks made broad usage of the arbitrage opportunities via the cash flow structure of the shadow banking system (Joint Forum, 2015, 2009).

Within the new regulatory environment and via dynamic capital requirements for banks, shadow banking practices are increasingly connected to the traditional banking sector. Via more comprehensive transparency standards for banking, their trading books and an overall leverage limit, banks' balance sheets are now more reactive to developments in financial markets. This heightened reflexivity between regulation and the day-to-day practice of banking had been brought forward via the centrality of shadow banking for modern finance. The purpose of the new regulatory environment was hence rather directed to integrate the environment of complex securitisation into common international standards than to abandon these practices all together.

The shadow banking system enables banks to manage their balance sheet in a more attractive way for their shareholders when profitability increases (FSF, 2008). It creates financial products to still high and low risk appetite through its ability to differentiate risk exposures. It combines risk mitigation strategies through liquidity facilities, credit default swaps and cash flow waterfalls to produce what turned out as 'pseudo-risk-less' (Stein, 2010) securities being safe in good times and highly risky in bad ones.

Indeed, securities (i.e. collateral-backed financial instruments) can function as a form of money within and beyond the shadow banking system through which interconnections of the traditional and shadow banking sector are sustained. Similar to government bonds, highly rated collateral-backed securities serve as collateral for repurchase transactions - a highly liquid means for exchange of value. Thus, shadow banking opens up a way to create debt in a seemingly very profitable and at the same time low risk way as long as most parts of the financial system remain intact.

Despite the recent crisis, the failure of the shadow banking system showed the contemporary transformation of the credit system that is sustained via the post crisis approaches to make the financial architecture more resilient. The reflexivity of the shadow banking sector, in this sense, inscribes the exception of off-balance-sheet activities into the normality represented by the regulatory body. The implication of the present transformation of the financial system is thereby hardly one of reform with regard to social and political challenges but rather one of the mechanistic necessity to keep finance functional in and of itself.

Calculating risk

A further force for the increasing integration of the financial field goes along with the evolution of the concept of risk. Via the modern understanding of risk as an almost reified parameter, its calculability merged different aspects of the financial field and enabled connectivities to other social realms (Beckert and Berghoff, 2013; Kessler, 2007; de Goede, 2004). The following analysis turns to the role of risk within the context of shadow banking and its regulation. The discourse on the problem of the shadow banking sector highlights the limits of risk calculations during times of systemic changes.

Such events seemingly could not be translated into appropriate risk categories by rating agencies and associated losses could not be adequately dispersed via financial innovation. The 'black swan' became a sudden symbol for the limits of inductive reasoning in finance and thus of the modelling toolbox on which the shadow banking system relied. Contrary to the traditional banking sector, where central bank liquidity and regulatory capital provide certain resilience in times of unforeseen stress, shadow banking could operate in a (non)legal space of the balance sheets and hence outside of regulatory constraints on leverage (Ferrante, 2015; Plantin, 2014; Ordonez, 2013).

A central driver for this evolution was the inclusion of a portfolio invariant risk conception into regulatory standards. This established a singular understanding of risk, meaning that risk can be calculated and compared independently of its locality, temporality or associated agency (Kessler and Wilhelm, 2013). Thus, 'diversification effects would depend on how well a new loan fits into an existing portfolio' (BCBS, 2005, p. 4). The respective portfolio is made up of risk-weighted assets that undergo a mark-to-market valuation. In this way, banks are asked to manage their balance sheets according to market variations in a shared governance system to keep up with the regulatory demands concerning their respective capital requirements (and profitability).

The inscription of credit ratings for financial institutions and products produced a widespread standard along which the risk structure of a bank's balance sheet could be calculated. When market developments stay within the projected range of risk analyses, credit ratings provided the 'facts', which 'suffice to determine the capital charges of credit instruments' (BCBS, 2005, p. 4). However, the underlying formulas to calculate the needed capital contain intuitions about how markets should function. Though, looking at them after an event of crisis, these intuitions seem to apply only if they had not widely been built into the financial instruments aligning the banks' balance sheets to each other via regulatory 'incentives'.

One intuition in-built into capital requirements calculation is that capital charges for long-term obligations should be higher than for short-term exposure. Lower capital charges for short-term investments and similar investment strategies used, for instance, by money market funds created demand and thereby an investment incentive for an 'efficient' maturity transformation, i.e. to roll-over long-term investment via the issuance of short-term debt by off-balance-sheet entities. To do so, the shadow banking system made use of collateralised debt securities, which were increasingly assumed to be money-like liabilities that could be produced more efficiently than by the traditional and regulated banking sector (Plantin, 2014).

The notion of risk, also brought forward by joint regulatory standards, could thereby, on the one hand, align the demand for financial products and, on the other, sustain the institutional structure able to provide tailored investment products fitting the requirements of investors and thus of internationally shared understandings of financial regulation. Shadow banking in this sense is closely related to the specific understanding of risk sustained via regulatory demands. The notion of 'enhanced risk sensitivity' provides a further perspective into the dynamism of how a shared understanding of risk enables and limits possible practices in the shadow banking sector via increasing sensitivity to the calculatory standards of risk.

The European Banking Authority points 'to "qualifying" securitisations across the hierarchy of approaches, aimed at further increasing the risk-sensitivity of the bank capital treatment of securitisations' (EBA, 2015, p. 8). Thus, the practices of securitisation shall be further included into the regulatory body assuming that thereby banks follow the product structure to be set by the regulatory authorities. This indeed affects the business model of banking and therefore also the capital flows accordingly. The statement gives further insight into the understanding of risk. It is being seen as distinct from financial products. Risk could affect them but they are themselves not understood as part of risk creation. In this sense, the sensitivity approach becomes circular if risk is itself a very product of financial markets and not an external effect.

The Bank for International Settlements complements the view on the perception of risk as an external effect by arguing that some financial products are insufficiently sensitive to risk, especially sovereign exposures. Their preferential treatment indeed 'weakens the risk sensitivity of regulatory requirements' (BIS, 2015, p. 113). The implication of this statement seems to be rather close to the Bourdieusian argument that an increasing homogeneity of the financial field strengthens the structure of dominance already in place. The consequence of the argument above could be read as a differentiation of sovereign risk according to the compliance to the rationale of the financial architecture and hence financial dominance already in place.

The European Systemic Risk Board provides a further example of how the structure of dominance is not only sustained but how it could also be more effectively inscribed into regulatory demands. In a context of differentiated sovereign risk, banks are incentivised to widen their capital basis in order to provide a more resilient balance sheet (ESRB, 2015, p. 20). Thereby the hierarchy of sovereign risk indicated before gets institutionalised via the capital structure of banks. It increases demand for 'jurisdictional safe havens' again supporting the mechanisms of dominance in place and weakening or rather excluding alternatives for financial governance.

Conclusion

This snapshot of the regulatory context regarding the practice of shadow banking provides an indicative example of the reflexive drivers in favour of increasing homogenisation. Following Bourdieu, the standard setting discourse of international financial regulation after the recent financial crisis further concentrates the resources for domination on a global scale, especially as indicated via the perpetuation of shadow banking into international capital flows. It thereby fixates the prerogative of financial rationales and excludes political contestation, which might possibly be able to question the structure of dominance in place. Indeed, the post-crisis discourse on shadow banking vividly shows how financial practice and regulation further install the pre-crisis disciplinary and political hierarchy.

The notion of risk and the institutional structure in place provide for compatibility for financial exchanges, their profitability and their regulation. The focus on new rules for securitisation sets the stage for the shadow banking system to be come impregnated by the present distribution of dominance in financial markets. Policy prescriptions promoting heterogeneity to standards for financial activities are rather exceptional, whereas the intentional insertion of inefficiencies as provisions for higher resilience of financial entities (i.e. higher capital ratios) seems to be exactly what is omitted by the further evolution of market-based credit intermediation.

A new contextual phenomenon in contrast to prior histories of financial turmoil is that innovation now concentrates on time rather than on space. For instance, space related offshore settings to avoid taxes seem rather echoes from the past international order even though the recent 'discovery' of the so called Panama papers provides an excellent view into past and present possibilities for 'efficiency gains'.

Regarding time, we can observe at least two new forces, which expand (high frequency trading, Lenglet, 2011) and compress (risk calculation, de Goede, 2004) temporal horizons. The former tendency triggered a fragmentation of markets to the advantage of market operators and high frequency trading firms, whereas supervisory entities are hardly able to actually understand let alone prevent failure. The latter tendency uses accelerated computing capacity in order to run more complex risk modelling and thereby compressing more data about possible futures and opening up ever more possibilities for financial innovation.

These two dynamics complement each other in a way, which makes it more and more difficult to grasp not only the economic but also the political consequences of present financial markets. Subsequently the new shadow banking relies on a fragile and hidden framework for financial exchange generating profits in the present and deferring possible systemic failure, and hence widespread losses into a precarious future. The further evolution of shadow banking thus provides a wide opening for research into the reflexive interaction of financial innovation and regulation, not as separate forces but as an intersection which indicates how financial markets express contemporary hierarchies of domination seemingly very much apart from democratic decision-making about the societal location for international (shadow) banking.

References

Abolafia, M. (1996) *Making Markets: Opportunism And Restraint On Wall Street*, Cambridge, MA: Harvard University Press.
Ashiagbor, D., Kotiswaran, P. and Perry-Kessaris, A. (eds) (2013) Special issue: Towards an economic sociology of law. *Journal of Law and Society*, 40 (1).
Aspers, P. (2007) Theory, reality, and performativity in markets. *The American Journal of Economics and Sociology*, 66 (2), 379–98.
BCBS (1986) *The Management of Banks Off-balance-sheet Exposures*, Basel Committee for Banking Supervision, March 1986.
BCBS (2005) *An Explanatory Note on the Basel II IRB Risk Weight Functions*, Basel Committee for Banking Supervision, July 2005.
BCBS and IOSCO (2015) *Criteria for Identifying Simple, Transparent and Comparable Securitisations*, Basel Committee for Banking Supervision and International Organization of Securities Commissions, July 2015.
Beckert, J. and Berghoff, H. (eds) (2013) Risk and uncertainty in financial markets: A symposium. *Socio-Economic Review*, 11 (3), 497–576.
BIS (2015) *85th Annual Report. 1 April 2014–31 March 2015*, Bank for International Settlements, June 2015.
Borio, C. (2005) Monetary and financial stability: So close and yet so far?. *National Institute Economic Review*, 192 (1), 84–101.
Bourdieu, P. (1985) The social space and the genesis of groups. *Theory and Society*, 14 (6), 723–44.
Bourdieu, P. (2005) *The Social Structures of the Economy*, Cambridge: Polity Press.
Callon, M. (2010) Performativity, misfires and politics. *Journal of Cultural Economy*, 3 (2), 163–69.
de Goede, M. (2004) Repoliticizing financial risk. *Economy and Society*, 33 (2), 197–217.
Dorn, N. (2011) Policy stances in financial market regulation: Market rapture, club rules or democracy? In K. Alexander and N. Moloney (eds), *Law Reform and Financial Markets*, Cheltenham: Edward Elgar, pp. 35–68.
EBA (2015) *Report on qualifying securitisation*, European Banking Authority, 8 July 2015.
EC (2015) *Proposal for a regulation of the European parliament and of the Council laying down common rules on securitisation and creating a European framework for simple, transparent and standardised securitisation and amending Directives 2009/65/EC, 2009/138/EC, 2011/61/EU and Regulations (EC) no 1060/2009 and (EU) no 648/2012*, European Commission, 30 September 2015.
ESRB (2015) *ESRB Annual Report 2014*, European Systemic Risk Board, July 2015.

Ferrante, F. (2015) *A model of endogenous loan quality and the collapse of the shadow banking system*, Finance and Economics Discussion Series, 2015–021, Washington: Board of Governors of the Federal Reserve System, http://dx.doi.org/10.17016/FEDS.2015.021.

Fligstein, N. and McAdam, D. (2012) *A Theory of Fields*, Oxford: Oxford University Press.

Frankel, J.A. and Rose, A.K. (1998) The endogeneity of the optimum currency area criteria. *The Economic Journal*, 108 (449), 1009–25.

FSB (2011) *Shadow banking: Strengthening oversight and regulation. Recommendations of the Financial Stability Board*, Financial Stability Board, 27 October 2011.

FSB (2013) *Strengthening oversight and regulation of shadow banking. Policy framework for strengthening oversight and regulation of shadow banking entities*. Financial Stability Board, 29 August 2013.

FSB (2014a) *Transforming shadow banking into resilient market-based financing: An overview of progress and a roadmap for 2015*, Financial Stability Board, 14 November 2014.

FSB (2014b) *Strengthening oversight and regulation of shadow banking. Regulatory framework for haircuts on non-centrally cleared securities financing transactions*, Financial Stability Board, 14 October 2014.

FSF (2008) *Report of the financial stability forum on enhancing market and institutional resilience*, Financial Stability Forum, 7 April 2008.

Gorton, G.B. (2015) *The Maze of Banking: History, Theory, Crisis*. Oxford: Oxford University Press.

Gorton, G.B. and Souleles, N. (2005) *Special purpose vehicles and securitization*, NBER Working Paper, 11190.

Hamati-Ataya, I. (2013) Transcending objectivism, subjectivism, and the knowledge in-between: The subject in/of 'strong reflexivity'. *Review of International Studies*, 40 (1), 153–75.

Hellwig, M. (1995) Systemic aspects of risk management in banking and finance. *Swiss Journal of Economics and Statistics*, 131 (4/2), 723–37.

IMF (2014) *Risk taking, liquidity, and shadow banking: Curbing excess while promoting growth*, Global Financial Stability Report, 8 October 2014.

Joint Forum (2009) *Report on special purpose entities*, September 2009.

Joint Forum (2015) *Consultative document: Developments in credit risk management across sectors: Current practices and recommendations*, February 2015.

Kalemli-Ozcan, S., Papaioannou, E. and Peydro, J.-L. (2013) Financial regulation, financial globalization, and the synchronization of economic activity. *The Journal of Finance*, 68 (3), 1179–228.

Kessler, O. (2007) Performativity of risk and the boundaries of economic sociology. *Current Sociology*, 55 (1), 110–25.

Kessler, O. and Wilhelm, B. (2013) Financialization and the three utopias of shadow banking. *Competition and Change*, 17 (3), 248–64.

Leander, A. (2002) Do we really need reflexivity in IPE? Bourdieu's two reasons for answering affirmatively. *Review of International Political Economy*, 9 (4), 601–9.

Lenglet, M. (2011) Conflicting codes and codings: How algorithmic trading is reshaping financial regulation. *Theory, Culture and Society*, 28 (6), 44–66.

Lynch, M. (2000) Against reflexivity as an academic virtue and source of privileged knowledge. *Theory, Culture & Society*, 17 (3), 26–54.

MacKenzie, D. (2003) An equation and its worlds: Bricolage, exemplars, disunity and performativity in financial economics. *Philosophy and Social Criticism*, 33 (6), 831–68.

Nesvetailova, A. (2014) Innovations, fragility and complexity: Understanding the power of finance. *Government and Opposition*, 49 (3), 542–68.

Ordonez, G. (2013) *Sustainable shadow banking*, NBER Working Paper, 19022.

Plantin, G. (2011) *Good securitization, bad securitization*, IMES Discussion Paper Series, 2011-E-4.

Plantin, G. (2014) Shadow banking and bank capital regulation. *Review of Financial Studies*, 28 (1), 146–75.

Riles, A. (2011) *Collateral Knowledge: Legal Reasoning in the Global Financial Markets*. Chicago, IL: University of Chicago Press.

Stein, J. (2010) Securitization, shadow banking, and financial fragility. *Daedalus*, 139 (4), 41–51.

Swedberg, R. (2003) The case for an economic sociology of law. *Theory and Society*, 32 (1), 1–37.

Voß, J.-P., Bauknecht, D. and Kemp, R. (eds) (2006) *Reflexive Governance for Sustainable Development*. Cheltenham: Edward Elgar.

Woolgar, S. (1988) *Knowledge and Reflexivity*. London: Sage Publications.

Zaloom, C. (2006) *Out of the Pits: Traders and Technology from Chicago to London*. Chicago, IL: University of Chicago Press.

4
Interrogating the crisis
Financial instruments, public policy and corporate governance

Hugh Willmott

Introduction

> There is growing recognition that the dispersion of credit risk by banks to a broader and more diverse group of investors, rather than warehousing such risks on their balance sheets, has helped to make the banking and overall financial system more resilient.
>
> *(IMF, 2006, p. 51 cited in MacKenzie, 2009a, p. 73)*

What precipitated the global financial crisis of 2008 and why were structures of corporate governance unable to avoid or prevent it? The intention of this chapter is to offer some partial illumination of these questions by making corporate governance its focus. Its premise is that the way financial organizations, such as banks and insurance companies, do business, including their use of financial instruments, is contingent upon the conception and associated structures of corporate governance that are ostensibly designed to regulate – enable but also constrain – their activities.

When reflecting on the role and significance of governance in 'the corporate failures of the first decade of the 2000s', Deakin (2011) observes that a distinctive form of corporate governance – what he calls '*shareholder-value oriented corporate governance*' – 'provid(ed) an important part of the external context of financial instability, and exacerbate[ed] the misalignment of incentives within firms' (ibid, pp. 34–5). Shareholder-value-oriented corporate governance currently defines the parameters of 'best practice' by giving emphasis to a number of elements: the separation of chair and CEO roles, external monitoring, the presence of non-executive directors, and so on (see Veldman and Willmott, 2016). These elements, it will be argued, affirm rather than restrain, and effectively obscure rather than challenge, a conception of the corporation as a nexus of contracts in which, as Deakin (2011, p. 40) puts it, the corporate form 'is seen as an object of financial arbitrage', rather than, say, a legal fiction that is potentially amenable to serving a plurality of stakeholders (Stout, 2012).

The chapter seeks to shed light on why the calculations relating to financial products – notably, the rapid growth in securities taking the form of collateralized debt obligations (CDOs) that preceded the financial crisis – proved to be so recklessly optimistic, abjectly cynical or stunningly naïve. To this end, its focus is upon the normalization of the sale of subprime mortgages and their securitization during the years running up to the crisis. On the 'demand' side, the chapter attends to deregulation and, more specifically, to the relaxation of restrictions – specifically, those associated in the US with the reform of the Community Re-investment Act (CRA) – that fuelled the sale of huge volumes of subprime mortgages. Without the participation of previously 'redlined' communities in this market, far fewer subprime mortgages would have been packaged into CDOs. Turning to the 'supply' side of the normalization of the subprime mortgage market, I emphasize the limitations of the corporate governance of the financial institutions engaged in the securitization business. Other studies have highlighted failures of corporate governance in general terms (e.g. Loughrey, 2013; Vasudev and Watson, 2012; Sun, Stewart and Pollard, 2011). Here I take the example of American International Group (AIG), a company that had, in many respects, model governance structures, yet was found to be wholly incapable of monitoring and restraining its engagement in the writing of credit default swaps (CDSs) as hedges against the risks of defaulting CDOs, with catastrophic consequences.

The present analysis shares MacKenzie's (2009) assessment of the central role of CDSs and CDOs, including synthetic CDOs (see Roberts and Jones, 2009), in precipitating a financial crisis of such depth and duration. But it also qualifies and situates the explosive 'success' of these financial instruments in relation to other elements that comprised the 'perfect storm'. I focus upon securitization and corporate governance not least because, within organization studies, the paucity of analysis of financial institutions, products and markets is disproportionate to their influence. Moreover, scholarly consideration of corporate governance has been marginalized by regarding it as a specialist domain reserved for, or monopolized by, other academics (e.g. accountants, lawyers and behaviourists) rather than as a field of study integral to the analysis of organization(s).

The chapter begins with an overview of the context of the global financial crisis (GFC). Its anatomy is then examined, focusing upon the centrality of securitization in the meltdown before addressing directly the conditions which permitted the huge expansion of the subprime mortgage market. Having sketched some distinguishing features and backdrop of the GFC, attention is directed to the corporate governance of AIG, the firm that received the largest bailout. It concludes by reflecting upon the centrality of the shareholder value model in the run-up to the financial crisis as banks sought out new sources of such value in the subprime mortgage market and suggests that avoidance of a future crisis will require a radical change in the principles of corporate governance.

The context

During the decades running up to the financial crisis, a belief in the efficiency of markets combined with a shareholder-value oriented conception of corporate governance facilitated financially driven growth fuelled by access to sources of cheap credit. The 'new growth model', which Crouch (2008) has characterized as 'privatized Keynesianism', provided income streams by generating credit from available assets. In the UK context, the model promoted a permissive, re-regulation of financial markets which was announced in the UK by Big Bang (1986). At the heart of the 'new growth model' is a faith in markets as efficient allocators of resources and an antipathy to interventions by the state, including a philosophy of regulation of markets that must be light-touch and supportive. Concerns about 'society' and 'social justice' are marginalized as they are considered to be misconceived, given that the removal of restrictions and the operation of less fettered markets will 'lift all boats' as wealth 'trickles down' to benefit everyone. From the 1980s, successive administrations in the UK and the US seemed to assume that there was problem – such as meeting the challenge of making home ownership more widely available – for which the forces of the market, however convoluted and re-regulated, was not the solution. This philosophy is also evident in a conception of corporate governance that treats firms as bundles of assets to be analysed, restructured and traded using financial techniques; likewise, executives are incentivized with stock options and performance-related bonuses to pursue shareholder value maximization (Davis, 2009).

The chief threat to the 'new growth model' was identified as inflation: economists, regulators and politicians deemed the rate of inflation to be the primary benchmark of economic stability.[1] Preoccupied with its control, much less attention was paid to other risks, such as those associated with the neo-liberalization of financial markets and the possibility, however apparently remote, of their meltdown. The seemingly limitless expansion of the financial sector was celebrated as key to the miraculous rejuvenation of an economy that only twenty years earlier had been dubbed the 'sick man of Europe'.

Inflation, rather than any thought of a meltdown, exercised the minds of macroeconomic policy experts in the months preceding the GFC. The preoccupation with inflation is apparent in a speech given by the Governor of the Bank of England in January 2007, just a few months before the collapse of Northern Rock which precipitated the first run on a UK bank in 150 years. Flattering his audience of Birmingham businessmen, the Governor proclaimed that 'It is indeed much harder to run a business than to run a central bank' – an ostensibly self-effacing claim that was soon to be severely tested. The Governor then stressed that:

> it is our duty is to ensure that you do not experience the macroeconomic instabilities of the past *and that we keep inflation on track to meet our 2% target*. Stability is in your interest just as much as mine.
>
> *(King, 2007, emphasis added)*

The policy of maintaining a low rate of inflation, combined with a comparatively low cost of credit, resonated with an expectation of continuing growth undisturbed by 'macroeconomic instabilities'. There could be few clearer indications of how, amongst the guardians of financial institutions and markets, embodied in the figurehead of the Governor, the possibility of systemic risk and meltdown had seemingly been erased from their collective memory. It was, apparently, taken for granted that neo-liberal, market-centric policies and their associated, self-regulating practices would smoothly deliver a combination of low inflation and steady growth that, in the words of UK Chancellor Gordon Brown, would ensure 'no return to boom and bust'.

Confidence that stability and growth was assured so long as inflation was controlled encouraged ever-higher levels of gearing (debt-to-equity ratio) – not only by corporations, especially the investment banks, but also by consumers of financial products (e.g. households that take on mortgages and other forms of credit, such as loans for car purchase). Ballooning debt fuelled a rapidly expanding financial sector in which institutions competed to survive and grow by making highly leveraged acquisitions, the most spectacular of which was that of *ABN Ambro* by *RBS* and its minor partners *Fortis* and *Banco Santander*. The example of RBS, but also AIG which is considered in some detail in a later section, is illustrative of how, in the UK and the US, an unshakeable belief in continuing growth and financial stability followed from a subscription to the logic of neo-liberal economic policy.

Prior to 2008, there was, as the opening quotation from the International Monetary Fund (IMF) indicates a massive expansion in the development and use of financial instruments (notably, derivatives) facilitated by what the IMF terms 'the dispersion of credit risk'. Notably, there was an explosion of mortgage-backed securities (a form of CDO) as home loans were made more accessible to 'subprime' applicants, and applications were accepted which previously had been declined or redlined. Penetrating the home loans market more deeply, by making mortgages easier to obtain and cheaper to service through the alchemy of securitization, massively swelled the revenues of the financial institutions as well as the bonuses of traders dealing in those securities. Securitization was at the epicentre of a 'loads of money'[2] *Zeitgeist* in which 'maxing out' credit/accumulating debt became an imperative for consumers and corporations alike. For corporations, the substitution of debt for equity capital, tacitly underwritten by an apparently remorseless rise in asset values (e.g. property), offered an irresistible means of increasing dividends and capital growth. For consumers, equity release and/or juggling credit cards presented an effortless way of compensating for a squeeze on wages and related benefits. As an article published in *Harpers Magazine* in May 2006, two years before the financial meltdown, presciently observed in relation to the aspirational as well as the avaricious appeal of mortgage borrowing:

> the biggest incentive to home ownership has not been owning a home *per se* but rather the eternal hope of getting ahead. If the price of a $200,000 house shoots up 15 percent in a given year, the owner will realize a $30,000 capital gain.
>
> *(Hudson, 2006, p. 41)*

As the article goes on to note, referring directly to the guru of modern macroeconomic policy, Alan Greenspan, the home equity loan bubble made a substantial contribution to the US economy:

> In a study last year [2005], Alan Greenspan and James Kennedy found that new home-equity loans added $200 billion to the U.S. economy in 2004 alone ...
>
> *(ibid., p. 41)*

During the years preceding the global financial crisis (GFC), private indebtedness supplemented, and progressively replaced, public borrowing as a significant generator of economic activity. Consumers but also executives who failed, or declined, to avail themselves of cheap credit by leveraging their equity in order to invest in property (or go on acquisition sprees) were evidently financial dunces: they were 'missing a trick' and risked 'being left behind'. Those in possession of a modicum of *nous* eagerly plunged their snouts deeper into the credit trough as, obviously enough, asset prices were ever-rising. For homeowners, equity could be released or debts increased on the basis of paper capital gains. With regard to US-based investment banks, their leverage had, until 2003, been limited by the Securities and Exchange Commission (SEC) to 12 times capital. In 2004, it was raised to 40 times capital and compliance was made voluntary. In effect, the determination of the appropriate (prudent) ratio became a matter of internal corporate governance. Bonuses would be correspondingly boosted by raising these ratios to their upper limits. Unsurprisingly, in the absence of external regulation, asset-to-equity ratios in investment banks reached the upper 30s prior to the crisis. It was these ratios that resulted in the force and acceleration of the deleveraging dynamic that, in 2008, was precipitated by the crash in asset prices.

It transpired that the apparently relentless rise in asset prices depended upon a strong faith in the governance of the lenders about how the loans were financed, and how the pricing of risks attached to them were calculated (and hedged) using seemingly sophisticated models and opaque financial instruments, such as CDOs and CDSs. This faith turned out to be ill-founded – and possibly wilfully so – at least in the case of traders employed by the biggest of the financial institutions. They had not failed to notice that the rewards (e.g. performance related bonuses) were immediate and tangible, while sanctions were non-existent or distant and hypothetical. For others, as the *Harpers Magazine* article cited above anticipated, the 'real estate boom that began with the promise of "economic freedom" will, almost certainly, end with a large and growing number of workers locked in to a lifetime of debt service that absorbs every spare penny' (Hudson, 2006, p. 41).

When it appeared, two years before the meltdown, this assessment directly challenged the views of experts who advised that by raising interest rates to slow down activity in the housing market, the very worst that could happen would be a familiar and temporary bear market followed by a shallow and short recession. Seven years after the meltdown, the horrific scenario of workers locked into a lifetime of debt service sketched in the *Harpers* article seems almost benign. Today (June 2015), there is a scarier scenario of extended 'debt serfdom' in many economies. In this scenario, it is not anticipated that there will be a slow recovery involving a comparatively familiar experience of living standards rising less rapidly for a brief period following a normal, temporary slump. Instead, its dystopian vision foresees endless indebtedness with a substantial share of income being consumed by repayments of loans that are not eroded by inflation. In the UK context, the debt burden placed upon young people seeking a university education is illustrative of how such 'serfdom' is experienced. But the bigger picture is of wealth redistribution and the corrosion of savings through depressed interest rates and the use of quantitative easing. Sluggish growth, stagnant wages, deterioration in the terms and conditions of employment and deep cuts in public services are forecast as the price to be paid by the next generation. The foreseeable future is one of striving to deal simultaneously with huge, post-GFC social dislocations while seeking to reduce the massive debts piled up as a consequence of the taxpayer bailout of a financial sector modelled upon a shareholder-value conception of corporate governance. Because the US and especially the UK economies are so dependent upon the financial sector, it remains largely unreconstructed (e.g. with regard to scale, ownership and ethos). Moreover, the financial sector has become entombed in an increasingly baroque regulatory structure. While some areas of the financial sector are vibrant, others are unstable and probably unviable. Not only are they vulnerable to future meltdown but insofar as they reproduce and increase inequalities of wealth, power and opportunity, they further undermine an already precarious social cohesion.

Anatomy of the Global Financial Crisis

Securitization

It is instructive to situate the global financial crisis in the context of the preceding, exceptionally long, debt-fuelled economic boom marked by rising asset values, especially in property, that lasted, with a few minor interruptions and corrections, from the early 1990s.[3] The boom in house purchase and the refinancing of mortgages provided a steady flow of payments that could be securitized in the financial markets of New York and London as CDOs (see Box 4.1). The attraction of securitization was that it:

> *enabled much higher volumes of lending than would have been possible* if banks had been able to lend only the sums their customers had deposited: by the time of the credit crisis, *securitization funded more than half of all home mortgage lending in the US and a quarter of other consumer credit* (Securities Industry and Financial Markets Association 2008, exhibit 17, p. 37).
>
> *(MacKenzie, 2009a, p. 25, emphasis added)*

Box 4.1 Securitization: CDOs and CDSs in the run-up to the Global Financial Crisis

In principle, securitization, which includes the creation of CDOs, creates a secondary market for loans, such as home mortgages: it attracts capital in order to provide additional loans for conversion into securities and, by improving market efficiency, decreases their cost. CDOs graded by the rating agencies as investment grade (lowest risk), offered significantly better returns than gilts or corporate and government bonds. This competitive advantage resulted in their rapid and sustained growth and escalating complexity. Securitization has enabled financial institutions around the world to invest in, and thereby 'democratize credit'. It is these features and functions that the advocates of securitization, notably Alan Greenspan (Chairman of the US Federal Reserve, 1987–2006), prior to his epiphany, stridently celebrate.

For lenders, securitization provides the means of instantly realizing the value of any cash-producing asset. The payment stream is, in effect, received as a lump sum which can then be used to provide further loans, ad infinitum. The chief attraction of mortgage-based CDOs to insurance companies as well as pension funds and banks is their ability to offer a substantially better (up to 2–3 per cent) return than corporate bonds with an equivalent credit rating. Even when the rate of return was comparatively low, as in the case of the least risky, senior and super-senior tranches, banks bought the CDOs in volume as they could make a slender spread by borrowing at the marginally cheaper Libor rate (the rate at which banks borrow unsecured funds from other banks). The originators of CDOs often retain the very safest tranches because, although they offer the least attractive returns, they can be insured comparatively cheaply.

There is, however, another, often conveniently overlooked or downplayed, feature of securitization. The securitization and re-securitization of the loans is undertaken by investment banks in conjunction, or in cahoots,[4] with the credit rating agencies. Like the auditors of the financial institutions, the rating agencies have every reason not to ask challenging questions, even if they are supposed to possess the expertise required to ask them. Using historical data, the agencies did not contemplate or incorporate into their modelling the risk of a more systemic crisis, as contrasted with a temporary correction (Feirstein, 2009). The chance that defaults would cluster – referred to as the 'correlation rate' – was calculated by the rating agencies as 0.3.[5] All parties had every incentive to trust in the expertise of the agencies or suspend any doubts that they may have had in the credibility of their ratings. In any event, the traders who earned very tidy bonuses from selling the CDOs had no responsibility for the risks passed on to their purchasers.

Credit Default Swaps (CDSs) are privately negotiated contracts which offer an insurance against defaulting CDOs. They provide a low-cost hedge but they may also be bought speculatively in anticipation that a CDO will default. In 2003, they had a global value of around US$3 trillion which grew to US$45 trillion by 2007. Insurance companies, such as the giant AIG, provided the CDSs for clients wishing to hedge against defaults, or exceptionally to those who anticipated that certain CDOs would default.

Responsibility for assessing the risks of CDOs is the bread-and-butter business of the rating agencies. Paid by packagers of CDOs – the investment banks – the rating agencies compete for this lucrative business for which they are richly rewarded. During the years preceding the financial crisis, the models used by the agencies did not factor in the chance that the mezzanine and even senior tranches of the CDOs (see Appendix A) to which they assigned an investment grade rating might sink to speculative (or 'junk') status. The logic of the exclusion of this risk from their calculations was that it had never happened before. That undeniable fact was not, however, counterbalanced by the inconvenient fact that packaging subprime mortgages on an industrial scale was also wholly unprecedented. Nor was any consideration given to how sight could be quickly lost of where the risk was held. Supporters of extensive securitization emphasize the virtue of its de-concentration of risk, which contributes to reducing and thereby democratizes credit (see Appendix B). Its often wise-after-the-event critics, in contrast, have pointed to its obfuscation of risk and vulnerability to systemic contamination.[6]

Home loans, CDOs and CDSs

The massive expansion of credit associated with low interest rates was eventually curtailed by a series of US rate increases (2004) (see Appendix C) that progressively flattened property values and resulted in a rising number of loan defaults. Initially, these were interpreted as an indicator of a normal and expected cooling down of a slightly overheated market. However, by the summer of 2006, domestic property prices in the US started to *fall*; and by the end of November, the index of subprime mortgage bonds (ABX) indicated that borrowers were failing to make payments sufficient to pay off the very riskiest tranches of mortgage-backed securities. Despite this, where securities had received an AAA (investment grade) rating, the prices of the CDOs remained stable. It was six months later, in early 2007, that some misgivings were aired about the possible implications of falling US housing values for mortgage-backed CDOs. Yet, demand for the CDOs remained strong as a consequence of their delivery of comparatively high returns, and their ostensibly investment grade quality. Even as housing prices fell and foreclosures increased, few market players and commentators had sufficient cause to ask searching questions about the correspondence between the rating of CDOs and their contents. The profitability and associated bonuses delivered by the CDOs appeared to inhibit doubts about the solidity of AAA-rated CDOs and the prospect of them melting into air. Even when commentators presented explicit and detailed challenges to this assessment (e.g. Tomlinson and Evans, 2007), their siren voices were unheeded, or were dismissed as alarmist.

Wherever securities became widely traded, there was a demand for hedges – that is, protection against the risks attaching to possible, even if highly unlikely, falls in their value. Some holders of CDOs, and also for a few traders and institutions (e.g. hedge funds) spotted and seized an opportunity to make speculative bets against CDOs, in anticipation of their possible default. Those bets took the form of the purchase of CDSs (see Box 4.1). On the other side of these trades, the sellers of CDSs – notably, American International Group (AIG) – were eager to do business as their models predicted negligible risk of default.

Regardless of whether staff in investment banks (e.g. Lehman Brothers) and insurance companies (such as AIG) were engaged in packaging together and selling CDOs, or offering protection against CDO default, they had little reason to concern themselves with the reliability of the grading, or the dispersal and traceability, of the CDOs. For them, the more compelling, bonus-rewarded challenge was to obtain sufficient volumes of loans (e.g. mortgages) to package into CDOs. In turn, this mass production of CDOs fuelled demand for CDSs from which their providers derived seemingly riskless revenues and guaranteed bonuses. Maintaining the supply of CDOs was addressed by devising and stimulating innovative ways, legal and illegal, of expanding an untapped segment of the housing market: subprime. In the US, this segment had been opened up by an earlier change in US legislation, to be considered below, that was intended to correct a rather different problem of structural social disadvantage: the indiscriminate redlining of mortgage applications originating from certain disadvantaged neighbourhoods.

Risk, meltdown and bailout

The unexpected fall in property values in the US, following the rise in interest rates, triggered a higher level of defaults than had been predicted by the risk models. Supposedly impregnable tranches of CDOs were under water. Those who had not purchased CDSs to hedge their positions struggled to sell their holdings. Falls in the value of CDOs were further accelerated by the use of mark-to-market accounting, which tracked the highs and lows of market prices, irrespective of any reference to their book value or (presumed) underlying worth. Those who had hedged their positions called upon the issuers of CDSs, including AIG, to restore their collateral. Those calls induced panic selling. The markets froze as the solvency of all financial institutions was placed in doubt by the limited traceability of the toxic CDOs.

In the months preceding the GFC, analysts and traders had been content to trust the ratings provided by the agencies. Only in exceptional cases did they undertake the painstaking detailed forensic task of establishing how subprime mortgages had been packaged and graded. The few traders who closely investigated the provenance of many CDOs were able to purchase CDSs cheaply because the ratings agencies had assigned the CDOs an investment grade status. Their nerdish diligence paid off handsomely when the markets went into free fall (Zuckerman, 2009). Aside from the taxpayers who were assigned by political elites to pick up the very sizeable tab, the biggest losers were the employees, clients and shareholders of the counterparties, such as AIG, especially in cases where no hedge had been made against default, despite the low cost of doing so (ibid., p. 156).

As the markets crashed, it was no longer home owners who found themselves, or were suspected to be, in negative equity territory, and could obtain credit only at unattractively high rates. When it was impossible to determine which parties were left holding the toxic CDOs and/or remained solvent, interbank lending locked up as every financial institution hoarded whatever liquidity it had, or could acquire. The market for securities became increasingly unstable before completely drying up as collateral was demanded by counterparties, resulting in the balance sheets of heavily geared financial institutions being further weakened. Investment banks teetered at the edge of the void of insolvency, with Lehman Brothers, the most leveraged and least liquid of them, at the head of the line.

That no other investment bank stepped in to acquire Lehman Brothers, even at a knockdown price, indicated the magnitude of its exposures, notably in the mortgage-backed CDO market. As other institutions – banks and IAG – lined up behind Lehmans to go to the wall, greater respect could, at this point, have been shown for the 'laws' of neoclassical economics. That is to say, their fate could have been left to the Market: those that had lived and prospered by its sword would be cut down by it. Failing, lame-duck institutions would have been allowed to collapse, thereby, in principle, celebrating and restoring Market discipline and efficiency. Instead, and in unacknowledged defiance of the Market mantra, intervention by the US government averted the prospect of a repetition of Lehman's fate across the financial sector. Variants of this bailout scenario were repeated in the UK and elsewhere. Deemed to be 'too big to fail' (Sorkin, 2009), numerous investment banks and also AIG were saved through a huge injection of public funds that minimally restored their balance sheets. Either their toxic assets were bought up (the US approach) or the failing banks were placed in 'temporary' public ownership by holding preference shares and offering loan guarantees (the UK approach).

Lehman's collapse and its immediate aftermath pointed unmistakably to the existence of a toxic barrel of mutually contaminated rotten apples whose immanent insolvency threatened a cataclysmic global meltdown. As will be shown shortly, AIG was one of the largest and rottenest of these apples, and it received the largest bailout. It had sold huge volumes of CDSs without either investigating or hedging against the risk of CDOs being inadequately graded or becoming toxic. Only a massive injection of liquidity forestalled the demise of the zombie financial firms, thereby saving the financial sector from the forces of destruction that it had unleashed upon itself.

Home ownership and normalizing subprime: a political economy of mortgages

The economies of the UK and US are, as noted earlier, exceptional in the importance placed upon home ownership. It is reflected in the scale of the loans serviced by purchasers of domestic property that dwarfs other forms of personal borrowing (e.g. credit cards, overdrafts and finance for other assets, such as cars and white goods). Any fall, or even flat-lining, of property values is significant politically as well as economically as voters are generally more supportive of the party in power when the value of their assets, including their homes, is rising. It is this political sensitivity that leads governments to make interventions in the housing market that are intended to affirm, secure and/or enhance those values – for example, by opening up the market to new providers or by enabling access to capital markets for existing providers through demutualization (see Klimecki and Willmott, 2009). Such responsiveness extends to making legislative changes whose purpose is to improve the availability and affordability of loans to those previously denied access to them.

Such interventions are consistent with neo-liberal policy where the role of the state is to champion markets by enabling their more effective, unimpeded operation. The state may, for example, intervene to create conditions in which financial institutions are incentivized to demonstrate greater 'commitment to serving borrowers who may not meet traditional underwriting standards' (Schwartz, 2012, p. 332, citing Federal Reserve Bank of Boston, 1993). In the UK, 'Big Bang' incentivized building societies to demutualize; and it enabled banks to penetrate, and thereby shake up, a mortgage market previously dominated by mutuals (Klimecki and Willmott, 2009). The outcome was intensified competition in which the big proprietary banks, many of which were later to be bailed out by taxpayers, were the winners. They gained market share from the mutual. And comparatively small and undiversified demutualized societies struggled to deliver the capital growth demanded by shareholders. Northern Rock, for example, pursued a strategy of heavy reliance upon the wholesale markets. When these markets dried up, the resulting evaporation of liquidity contributed to its collapse. Its demise was followed by other demutualized building societies none of which survived the financial crisis.

Turning to the US, whose economy makes it much more important globally, the most significant state intervention in the housing market can be traced to a well-intentioned but ill-fated move by the Carter administration. In 1977, the Community Reinvestment Act (CRA) was introduced to tackle the issue of discriminatory 'redlining' of entire (disadvantaged) neighbourhoods. Redlining made it either impossible to obtain a mortgage by lower income groups, or made obtaining such loans conditional upon making substantively higher down payments and/or accepting shorter repayment periods.[7] With the objective of making home loans more widely available, the CRA gave the banks some comparatively gentle 'encouragement' to lend to (potentially riskier) borrowers from neighbourhoods that had previously been indiscriminately redlined. This 'encouragement' involved sanctioning lenders who showed a reluctance to issue such loans – for example, lenders' expansionist ambitions were blocked by providing unfavourable evaluations of their applications for new branches and mergers.

A subsequent and seemingly innocuous tweak to the 1977 CRA made in 1995 by the Clinton administration had the (unintended) consequence of normalizing as well as expanding, but never entirely legitimizing, the riskiest segment of the mortgage market. The tweak involved a substantial tightening of the supervision of banks, which became subject to more exacting compliance measures. An unanticipated outcome was the expansion of subprime lending by 'predatory lenders'. Crucially, the Clinton tweak also incorporated an invitation to community groups to complain when lenders were making loans below the amount calculated for each neighbourhood based on federal home-loan data. Community groups collected a fee from the lenders for marketing loans to target groups (Husock, 2000). In 2000, the Senate Banking Committee estimated that, in just three years, community groups had received $9.5 billion in services and salaries – which is an instructive indicator of the rate of expansion into the subprime segment of the mortgage market. So, a perverse effect of the Clinton tweak was greatly to increase, rather than to remove, the number and levels of activity of the shadowy businesses ('predatory lenders') that have traditionally serviced the subprime market[8]; and thereby to create a boom in this market segment. This boom was further fuelled by the Gramm–Leach–Bliley Act (1999) that repealed parts of the Glass–Steagall Act. It allowed local banks to offer a full range of investment services – a change explicitly welcomed by the Clinton administration as a way of expanding the reach of the CRA. As a consequence of these changes in legislation, growth in the subprime sector was rapid, propelled as it was by the simultaneous development of 'innovative' products – that is, 'interest only' but, more importantly, 'adjustable rate' mortgages – and payment methods tailored to lower income borrowers, including applicants with a patchy employment history.

The Clinton tweak to the CRA enabled many more loans to be made available to, and affordable by, lower and irregular income borrowers. It also legitimized and normalized the practice of lending to customers who previously had no prospect whatsoever of obtaining a home loan. By the early 2000s, the subprime segment was the most rapidly growing segment of the mortgage market; and this market was increasingly being serviced by shadowy, *non-*CRA lenders (e.g. independent mortgage companies such as *Ameriquest* and *New Century Financial*) as well as affiliates of banks or thrifts that were not subject to routine supervision or examination (Gordon, 2008). The numbers are dizzying. Between 1994 and 2003, subprime mortgage loans increased by *25 per cent every year* – that is, a ten-fold increase in nine years. Between 1997 and 2006, the price of the typical American house increased by 124 per cent. Brokers sold, or pushed, loans to almost anyone who could be persuaded to borrow, regardless of their immediate or projected ability to meet the monthly payments, if interest rates were to rise. By the third quarter of 2007, subprime *adjustable rate* mortgages in the US comprised about 7 per cent of those in arrears; and these accounted for nearly 50 per cent of the foreclosures which began during that quarter. This was roughly triple the rate of arrears and foreclosures in 2005. By January 2008, the equivalent rate of arrears had risen to 21 per cent, and by May 2008 it was 25 per cent. By August 2008, over 9 per cent of *all* US mortgages outstanding were either in arrears or in foreclosure.

The home loans had been arranged easily not just because interest rates prior to 2004 had been held low but also because investment banks were ready and eager to securitize the loans. It was the contents and rating of the CDOs that made those mortgages readily available. The ahistorical modelling of risk by the agencies, combined with the self-serving reliance of financial firms upon their ratings, meant that it was not just the high risk, 'junior' tranches that were adversely affected by defaults; it was also some of the other, ostensibly investment grade tranches. The securitization of subprime mortgages acted to accelerate the speed and depth of the financial meltdown as the value of CDOs plunged. As will be shown in a later section, the collapse is also attributable to the recklessness of counterparties, notably AIG, who were eager to provide a hedge, in the form of CDSs, against the risk of CDOs defaulting, without themselves hedging the risk of issuing the swaps. The question of why a company like AIG was able to take this business without itself adopting measures to hedge against the risk is considered in the following section.

Corporate governance: The case of AIG

'Corporate governance', Blair (1995) argues, extends to 'the whole set of legal, cultural and institutional arrangements that determine what publicly traded corporations can do, who controls them, how that control is exercised and how the risks and returns from the activities they undertake are allocated' (ibid., p. 3). In the analysis of AIG, the focus is principally upon the 'control exercised', and the allocation of risks and returns. Whether the 'set' of legal, cultural and institutional 'arrangements' actually '*determine(s)*' what corporations 'can do' (emphasis added), rather than condition(s) actions that are taken by corporate actors, is debatable. Nonetheless, Blair's inclusive conception of corporate governance is broadly endorsed here, and it should be born in mind when considering the case of AIG. The following analysis addresses the exercise of control and risk/reward allocations but it does so in relation what Blair plausibly characterizes as a comparatively narrow sense of corporate governance: one limited to *operations within companies* that include, for example, 'questions about the structure and functioning of boards of directors and the rights and prerogatives of shareholders in boardroom decision making' (ibid.). That said, Blair's broader vision of corporate governance explicitly includes 'aspects of corporate finance, securities law [and] laws governing the behaviour of financial institutions' as well as 'internal information and control systems' (ibid., pp. 3–4) – all of which are pertinent to the present analysis of the AIG case.

Strategic risk management

Led by the highly capable but autocratic Hank Greenberg, AIG expanded rapidly from the early 1970s when it comprised a modest collection of insurance businesses that had been created and carefully nurtured during the previous fifty years. The dramatic and unexpected collapse of AIG in 2008, which had been a highly regarded global player, begs questions about the responsibilities of its directors in monitoring and interrogating the source and exposures of its major revenue streams, notably the activities of AIGFP. In 1994, AIGFP generated a modest income of around $100m. By 2005, this had ballooned to $2.7bn, amounting to 25 per cent of AIG's net income. It was the operation of AIGFP within AIG that bankrupted the company. AIG's dramatic collapse casts doubt upon a model and structure of corporate governance that, at AIG, was in very many respects an exemplar of 'best practice', yet it failed spectacularly to challenge and forestall engagement in excessive, unhedged risk-taking.

Through a strategy of diversification as well as expansion of its established insurance business,[9] AIG under Greenberg's leadership had achieved consistently stellar returns of around 15 per cent compared to an industry norm of around half that. All AIG executives were 'asked to attain three targets: 15% annual revenue growth, 15% profit increases per year, and 15% return of equity increases annually' (Shelp and Ehrbar, 2009; Pathak *et al.*, 2013, p. 358). Based on its outstanding financial performance, the company and its tireless CEO enjoyed an unparalleled reputation in the industry. Notably, AIG benefited from a seemingly rock solid AAA credit rating that reduced the cost of the company's borrowing, thereby making it possible to undercut much of the competition and attract customers from whom concessions in price and risk could be 'negotiated'.

Of particular relevance for the present analysis, its AAA rating enabled AIGFP to compete effectively against investment banks in the long-term swaps market.

In late 1993, the AIG stock price reached $88 as investors regarded AIG as a safe-as-houses insurance company that, unlike the banks, was not operating in comparatively risky markets.[10] In 1996, AIG hired Charles M. Lucas from the Federal Reserve Bank of New York where he had directed its risk assessment and control systems. Lucas served as AIG's director of market risk management who oversaw the creation of a 'state-of-the-art risk enterprise system that addressed both credit risk and market risk' (Greenberg and Cunningham, 2013, p. 147; see also pp. 148, 229). Supported by this system, 'FP [Financial Product] managers, other independent AIG units, the company's outside auditors as well as the board of directors consistently monitored FP's risk portfolio' (ibid.), at least up until the time of the forced departure of its CEO from AIG in 2005.

In 1998, AIG had cautiously entered the CDS business when it accepted $194m from J.P. Morgan to insure the credit risk on $9.7bn AAA rated CDOs (see Boyd, 2011, p. 87 *et seq*; Tett, 2010, pp. 71–3). For AIG, this revenue seemed to be virtually risk-free as, following painstaking analysis, the chances of the AAA defaulting was shown to be infinitesimal (see Boyd, 2011, pp. 88–9). For J.P. Morgan, the deal released cash to make further investments (e.g. in CDOs) that would otherwise have been held in reserve in case of default.

'Money for nothing', reputational damage and the AIG indulgency pattern

In postmortems on AIG, considerable attention has been paid to the activities of AIGFP. Much less attention has been directed to how governance at AIG was entwined with its strategy for delivering its targets of 15 per cent annual revenue growth, 15 per cent profit increases per year, and 15 per cent return on equity. A sea change occurred at AIGFP when, in 2001, two years after the repeal of the Glass–Steagall Act, its head, Tom Savage, was replaced by his deputy, Joe Cassano. It has been widely reported that Cassano greatly appreciated the bonuses that flowed from the CDS business: he earned more than US$280m in cash during his final eight years (2000–08). While eager to maximize his compensation,[11] Cassano was less inclined to insist upon undertaking the highly detailed, stress-testing, analysis demanded by his predecessor. Of more importance, the bonus system at AIG incentivized engagement in trades, but did not encourage paying close attention to the analysis of risks.

For AIG, the repeal of the Glass–Steagall Act in 1999 was significant because it drew commercial banks, with their huge customer deposits, into the world of investment banking, to which the investment banks responded by borrowing huge amounts – between 30 and 40 times their equity capital by 2005–08. Much of this debt, borrowed cheaply when interest rates were held low, was used to purchase longer term, higher yield assets – notably, mortgages to be packaged as CDOs. When firms acted prudently, the CDOs were hedged by purchasing CDSs from companies such as AIG. For AIG, these trades appeared to deliver 'money for nothing': Rajan (2010) reports that 'Privately, AIGFP executives said the swaps contracts (CDSs) were like selling insurance for catastrophes that would never happen; they brought in money for nothing' (ibid., p. 135).

Until the late 1990s, Greenberg's 15/15/15 metric had been achieved through an expansion strategy of acquiring companies with profit potential. As the potential acquisition targets reduced in number and appeal, the established strategy yielded diminishing returns. It was also difficult to expand the existing CDS business that was based upon providing capital relief (see above). So, the pressure was on to identify other revenue streams. The pressures coincided with the company's involvement in a number of dubious deals, the most damaging of which was made with *Gen Re* in 2000, and which came to light five years later as a consequence of an SEC investigation of another insurer (Boyd, 2011). There are conflicting accounts of how this reputationally damaging deal occurred, with Greenberg insisting that his instruction had been misunderstood or miscommunicated (Greenberg and Cunningham, 2013).[12] Following the *Gen Re* scandal and some other damaging events (see note 9 for details), AIG's safe-as-houses reputation was placed in some doubt. Questions began to be asked about whether even the legendary Greenberg could 'control the far-flung businesses ... the way that he once had ... Where he was demonstrably losing his grasp was in the quest to bolster earnings via the use of ethically marginal financing techniques' (Boyd 2011, p. 117–18).

In the wake of the revelations about *Gen Re* and other lesser dents to AIG's reputation, it is remarkable that no AIG employee was 'reassigned' within the company, let alone fired. It is highly probable that this forgiving, or indulgent, attitude sent a signal to all AIG staff, including Joe Cassano, the head of AIGFP. It conveyed, or invited, the understanding that questionable, and perhaps even illegal, dealings were viewed by senior executives, notably Greenberg, as minor infringements that were almost unavoidable in a company as dynamic, dispersed and complex as AIG. If that were so, then it said as much about the acceptability, and perhaps unavoidability, of sailing dangerously close to the wind in order to deliver the 15/15/15 targets as it did about senior executives' commitment to AIG staff.

AIG's dubious deals attracted the attentions of a politically ambitious New York Attorney General, Eliot Spitzer. In the aftermath of Enron (Willmott, 2011), Spitzer sought to make his reputation by 'cleaning up' AIG. That, for him, meant claiming the scalp of Greenberg, a headline grabbing result that could only boost his populist appeal. Faced with this vocal and aggressive Attorney General, the AIG board, supported by the company's auditor, PwC, was disinclined to invite or provoke the closer attentions of Spitzer. They fired Greenberg (in 2005) in order to avoid Spitzer's threatened indictment of AIG over deals that, as Greenberg was keen to point out, amounted altogether to less than 1 per cent of its book value. As a consequence of the bad publicity associated with those deals, and compounded by Greenberg's outraged and noisy departure, AIG's treasured AAA rating was marked down to AA+. This triggered a series of collateral calls on the company amounting to $1.2bn, and turned out to be the beginning of the end of AIG.

Bounty hunt and nemesis

The rapid and dramatic change in the reputation and fortunes of AIG, reflected in pressures on its stock price, prompted Greenberg's successor, Martin Sullivan, to urge his staff to renew their search for other sources of good earnings. Sullivan's call was answered by a massive expansion of the CDS business, most of which, it later became apparent, was not hedged against the potential risks of it being called in. As Sjostrum (2009) comments, AIG was content to pocket the premiums, seemingly certain that the CDSs would expire untriggered. In the years running up to the GFC, sellers of CDSs, most notably AIG, were eager to take on vast liabilities as they seemed to be purely theoretical. In the event of loans defaulting, it was assumed that the investment grade CDOs covered by the CDSs would remain well above water: they would be the very last to default as the lower rated tranches would comfortably absorb any losses. Despite the reduction of the AAA rating to AA+, AIG continued to enjoy a very high credit rating: AIG was judged by the ratings agencies to be comfortably capable of covering any lossess. And its counterparties remained willing to pay a premium for protection against the remote possibility of investment grade CDOs defaulting.

The amounts involved were huge. According to Lewis (2010, p. 71), during 2005, '[i]n a matter of months, AIGFP, in effect, bought $50bn in triple-B-rated subprime mortgage bonds by insuring them against default' (see also Greenberg and Cunningham, 2013, pp. 231–2). And yet, as Lewis goes on to observe:

> no one said anything about issuing these CDSs – not AIG CEO Martin Sullivan, not the head of AIGFP Joe Cassano, not the guy in AIGFPs Connecticut office in charge of selling his firm's credit default swaps to the big Wall Street firms…The deals by all accounts, were simply rubber-stamped – stamped inside AIG, and then again by AIG brass.
>
> *(Lewis, 2010, p. 71)*

Moreover, many of the CDSs written by AIG incorporated credit support annexes (CSAs). These mandated that the CDS be marked to the market price of the CDO on a nightly basis. In what was, according to the risk models, the highly unlikely event of the market price of a CDO dropping by four percentage points or more, AIG would become liable to the counterparty for the equivalent sum.

In just six months, from December 2004 to mid-2005, AIGFP's CDS portfolio of $17.9bn had increased three-fold to $54.3bn. It was eventually shut down in the autumn of 2005 when there was about $73bn exposure to CDOs, many of them containing mortgages issued to economically marginal borrowers. This amounted to 75 per cent of AIG's equity base. *Yet, apart from Joe Cassano and his immediate colleagues, seemingly no one at AIG, not even the chief risk officer, knew about the CSAs. And no one thought to investigate the provenance of the CDOs despite, or maybe because of, their massive contribution to AIG's income.* AIG executives were, apparently, emulating 'the three monkeys' as they were incentivized to engage in wilful thinking and/or wilful blindness. Subsequent investigations of AIG did not identify 'a single instance of a senior manager sending so much as an inquisitive email about the swaps portfolio, despite it accounting for 75 per cent of AIG's equity base' (Boyd, 2011, p. 207). Nor is there any evidence of board members raising questions about what was a crucially important, rapidly growing source of AIG's revenues, its declared profits and its executives' ballooning bonuses. It seemed that the company's outstanding results in 2006 – it generated $113bn in revenues with profit margins of 19.1 per cent pre-tax – effectively silenced, or at least impeded, any potentially unsettling curiosity about the nature of the goose that was laying AIG's golden eggs, and so strongly disincentivized any potential inclination to raise challenging questions or engage in difficult conversations. In other words, corporate governance considerations were eclipsed so long as AIG was delivering bottom line results, and as long as members of the board, or the risk management committees, declined to raise any questions or voice any concerns about how these outstanding results were produced or what risks were attached to them.

In the summer of 2007, almost a year after borrower delinquencies were widely known to be growing, the ratings agencies finally began to downgrade residential mortgage-backed securities. The securities then traded well below par, resulting in collateral calls upon AIG where the CDSs carried a credit support annexe (CSA, see above) – notably, by Goldman Sachs who had been hedging their exposure to CDOs. As AIG responded to these calls, the company became progressively drained of liquidity. Even so, when the AIG compensation committee met in March 2008 to review the bonus allocation, CEO Martin Sullivan successfully lobbied the committee to exclude the losses when calculating the bonus pool. Again, it is relevant to ask: where was the corporate governance? Removing the losses from their calculations produced an overstated bonus of US$5.6m for the CEO and corresponding overstatements for other executives.

Robert Willumstad, who had become chairman of the AIG board in November 2006, succeeded Martin Sullivan as CEO in June 2008. He is reported to have remarked that if no one on the AIG board had been told that so much CDS business had been written, its scale and exposure should at least have prompted some consideration in risk management (Boyd, 2011, p. 245), thereby passing the buck from the board to an internal function. Here it may be asked: why were board members not actively asking questions about this major source of revenue rather than expecting to be informed about it? Greater vigilance from internal functions might have been reasonably expected but only if it is actively encouraged, or even demanded, by senior executives who, it appeared, were content to leave the activities of AIGFP unexamined, or were grossly incompetent with regard to their fiduciary duties. Why didn't members of the AIG board, which Willumstad chaired from late 2006 to June 2008, actively demand more information about where AIG's performance and profits were being generated, especially when the answer to this question pointed directly to the very rapidly expanding and known-to-be-risky area of AIG's activity: AIGFP? It was only after the event – when AIG was clearly in trouble in November 2007 – that its auditor eventually raised concerns about the source of AIGs revenues. In a report delivered to the board in early December, PwC emerged from a deep, seemingly self-induced, sleep to declare that the amount of collateral being called in on its CDSs might constitute a 'control deficiency' which was a violation of the Sarbanes-Oxley Act. Further investigation led PwC to file an 8-K statement that referred to a 'material weakness' with regard to the 'fair valuation of the AIGFP super-senior credit-default swap portfolio' (see Greenberg and Cunningham, 2013, p. 235 *et seq*). PwC's late intervention begs the question of how, and why, the auditor had failed to identify and/or register the risks associated with the ballooning of the CDS business much earlier. Only when there was a clear threat to the reputation of PwC, it seems, did the auditor sound the alarm.

Multiple failures of corporate governance occurred. Members of the board contrived to ignore 'The Elephant in the Room' because, as one supervisor put it, 'No one said anything at the board level because AIG worked where it mattered: the earnings release... "We knew it was crazy, but our job wasn't to worry about that; it was to ensure that good numbers came out"' (Boyd, 2011, p. 177). When the 8-K statement demanded by PwC was released, it resulted in an $11.47bn write-down that reduced AIG's earnings to $6bn from $14bn. AIG stock then dropped a further 11 per cent in addition to the previous month's fall of 14 per cent. In May 2008, AIG suffered yet another $9.1bn charge on its swaps book and announced a $7.81bn loss. The company simply could not keep up with demands for collateral because it could not sell its assets quickly enough to restore its liquidity. It then faced bankruptcy or bail out.

Reflection

Before AIG collapsed, the Federal Reserve stepped in with an initial huge taxpayer loan of $85bn that allowed the company to meet its immediate obligations to clients. The loan lubricated AIG's global insurance business as it provided $500bn of credit protection to its corporate clients. It also averted the threat of chaos and dislocation in equity and bond markets, with potential knock-on effects in product markets as well as annuities on a scale that that would have dwarfed the fall-out from the failure of Lehman Brothers. As AIG was one of the ten most widely held stocks in 401(k) retirement plans, its collapse also risked a run on mutual funds. This national and global dependence upon AIG would have been well understood by its directors, including its non-executive directors, who were content to 'serve' on the board of such a prestigious, global company. They received the material and symbolic rewards of their 'service' but were found to be contentedly asleep at the wheel. When roused from their slumbers, none of them accepted responsibility by tendering their resignation.

The initial loan to AIG was later supplemented by a further $100bn in exchange for 80 per cent equity ownership. The bailouts, which threw a lifeline to AIG and other zombie financial firms, were provided without any *quid pro quo* in the form of a rejection of, or even any substantial change in, the 'new growth model' spawned by neo-liberal thinking. The global financial system has been resuscitated by the bailouts and quantitative easing. Yet, the global economy remains, in 2015, plagued by counterproductive efforts to address structural instabilities that have spread from problems of corporate solvency to sovereign indebtedness. At the time of the bailout and since, attention to the structural basis of instability – notably, the 'too big' concentration in the sector compounded by competitive, short-term pressures to deliver shareholder value and the retention of associated incentives to do so – has tended to become dimmed and displaced. The focus has shifted to compensatory elaborations of the regulatory apparatus accompanied by some undemanding restructuring, and some rather vacuous calls to change the culture of the financial sector. With regard to AIG, it is notable that the Warren Report's detailed examination of the company's operation prior to the government rescue makes almost no reference to the role of AIG's corporate governance (Congressional Oversight Panel, 2010, pp. 18–57), preferring to focus instead upon the shortcomings of the regulatory regime, especially the role of the Federal Reserve Bank of New York, and the credit rating agencies.

The limited attention directed at AIG's corporate governance is lamentable precisely because, in formal terms, many of its features were exemplary. For example, its board membership comprised an overwhelming majority of outside, ostensibly independent directors – the ratio ranged from not less than 10:6 (2003) to as many as 14:2 (2007). Direct reference is made by AIG to the 'value of diversity of experience and views amongst Board members' and the company proclaimed that its size 'facilitate[s] substantive discussion by the whole board in which each director can participate meaningfully' (cited by Vasudev, 2009, p. 27). So, where were these independent experts during 2000–07, and what 'substantive' was their well rewarded expertise initiating or illuminating? A detailed examination of AIG disclosures and statements on its credit derivatives (CDS) business from 2002 to 2007 highlights a number of issues that could, and arguably, should have been picked up and examined by AIG's ostensibly high-powered board members (Vasudev, 2009). These include: the lack of explanation in the 2002 filings of why the default swaps business was handled by AIGFP rather than the insurance arm of AIG, and also a Derivatives Review Committee that was not a committee of AIG directors, and which did not examine the credit derivatives business at AIGFP as this was treated as an independent operation.

Members of the AIG board failed to question the basis for the claimed independence of AIGFP. And they were absent from the committee that reviewed its derivatives business. As early as 2002, AIG's filing acknowledged that the company was exposed to the credit risk associated with CDSs sold by the AIGFP: 'AIG guarantees AIGFP's debt and, as a result, is responsible for all AIGFP's obligations' (Vasudev, 2009, citing AIG Form 10-K, p. 50) This statement noted an 'upside', namely that AIG would be liable for payment only after default in the first 11 per cent of the portfolio. But absent from the statement was any equivalent recognition of the possibility of simultaneous defaults in different tranches, and there is no reference to any obligation to provide collateral in the event of a fall in the market value of the underlying securities. The latter obligation was disclosed only in the 2007 filing after such obligations were called in. In its filings for 2002–06, AIG quantified the 'fair value' of its *non-credit* derivatives portfolio and identified them as 'the maximum potential loss' that could be suffered by the company. But no equivalent figures were provided for its credit derivatives. No reference is made to procedures such as the monitoring of risk by the Derivatives Review Committee or seeking approval from the Credit Risk Committee. In the 2007 filing, AIGFP, which had been described the previous year as 'a specialized business, distinguishing itself as a provider of super senior investment grade credit protection' (Vasudev, 2009, citing AIG Annual Report for 2006, p. 34), declared a staggering loss of $11.5bn but with no further comment. A more sombre note is struck in the statutory filing for 2007 where there is an acknowledgment that 'AIG's risk management processes and controls may not be fully effective in mitigating AIG's risk exposures' (Vasudev, 2009, p. 18). This admission rather casts doubt on whether those formal controls had been even minimally effective in the preceding years when no reference was made to them in AIG's filings. These doubts are further fuelled by the apparent boilerplate of the 2007 filings' reference to 'review and oversight committees to monitor risks [and] set limits' (ibid.) as the expression of this commitment is 'not materially different from the perfunctory discussion of the management structure of the Financial Services division in the filing for 2002' (ibid.).

Conclusion

With hindsight and the benefit of many postmortems, it is becoming apparent that the financial meltdown of 2008 was the product of a 'perfect storm' of mutually reinforcing elements that, somehow and perhaps conveniently, went long undetected by those – economists (see Lawson, 2015, Chapter 6) but also investors and regulators – who profess expertise in the field of finance. In addition to sanctioning imprudently low interest rates, there was injudicious de-regulation, the transformation of investment banks from partnerships into proprietary companies,[13] the creation of highly complex financial instruments (e.g. CDOs) based upon ahistorical models, a reduction of the regulatory minimum capital required under Basel Accords, complicit rating agencies and auditors, flat real wages for many low and middle earners who sought to boost their income by borrowing against rising paper asset values, excessive leveraging by financial institutions, the use of mark to market accounting, avaricious executives and supine directors and, last but not least, accommodating models and practices of corporate governance.

When reflecting upon the preconditions and ongoing unfoldings of the global financial crisis, attention has been focused here on a rather obscure, if consequential, policy intervention, in the form of the Community Reinvestment Act (CRA). When tweaked by the Clinton administration, it unintentionally fuelled a rapid expansion and normalization of the subprime mortgage market as lenders were strongly incentivized to become responsive to previously 'redlined' applications. Combined with the partial repeal of Glass–Steagall, the Clinton tweak proved to be a thin end of a very large and unsteady wedge that contributed to the unprecedented growth and destabilization of the US housing market. It inadvertently prized open the flood-gates through which flowed a liquid wall of money produced by the sale of subprime mortgages and propelled by the use of securitization.

It was not just the Clinton tweak that inflated the subprime mortgage bubble but, rather, the mutually amplifying interconnectedness of a boom in this market and the securitization of subprime mortgages. The exponential growth of CDOs was a condition as well as a consequence of a seemingly limitless supply of credit. Operating within a neo-liberal regime fuelled by interest rates held artificially low, AIG embraced a conception of corporate governance geared to the maximization of shareholder value. The company complied formally with many vaunted features of corporate governance while it undertook 'a multi-billion dollar CDS business free from regulatory filings, mandated capital requirements, and government intervention' (Sjostrum, 2009, p. 989).

The 'new growth model' created business opportunities that offered quick wins, big bonuses and minimal personal risk. These were seized upon by the investment banks and AIG to expand the scale, complexity and reach of their operations. The beneficiaries were the smarter investors, and most of the bankers and traders, who collected their capital gains and dividends, salaries and bonuses prior to the meltdown. Traders and executives, like Joe Cassano and Martin Sullivan, made hundreds of millions of dollars in bonuses and pay-offs by piling up debts that taxpayers bailed out. Who were the major losers? Some of them were employees of financial institutions and their shareholders. But the majority were, and continue to be, 'ordinary' citizens and taxpayers – present and future. For years to come, the '99 per cent' will, in a variety of ways, be paying off the loans used to recapitalize financial institutions – institutions that had, in response to market-based incentives promoted by 'the new growth model' and its favoured, agency-theoretic conception of corporate governance, become too complex to manage, and too powerful to regulate or break up, as well as 'too big to fail'.

Given the further debts incurred to counter the worst effects of the economic slump in 2008, the prospect for most of the losers is a continuing deterioration in the provision of public services, increases in regressive taxes (VAT), cuts in social benefits and further degradation in the terms and conditions of employment (zero-hours contracts, erosion of employment security, reduced pensions, and so on), especially for those employed in the public sector. To justify such austerity, which is of greatest benefit to elites who are in a position to capitalize on others' distress (e.g. by acquiring public assets at knock-down prices), the debt is ascribed to excesses in public spending prior to the GFC when, arguably, it is a consequence of the unsustainability of the debt-fuelled 'new growth model' that elites now seek to rekindle (see Knights and McCabe, 2015). In the absence of concerted and determined efforts to discredit the model and replace it with a less socially divisive alternative, efforts to restructure and reform the governance of the financial sector are unlikely to result in more than cosmetic, weak and piecemeal reform.

As the impact of the meltdown becomes more widely felt, the losers may be prompted by their plight to reflect upon the role and credibility of the key financial institutions that remain in place, and now assume responsibility for the restoration of the financial system. Amongst them is the International Monetary Fund which in 2006, a year before the credit crunch occurred, confidently trumpeted the benefits of securitization (see opening quotation). Now, in 2015, the mandarins in the IMF are at least calling for a shake-up in banks' bonus-heavy pay structures and incentives that 'encourage excessive short-term risk-taking' (Donnan and Fleming, 2015; see also Johnson, 2015). The IMF is also warning that the financial sector in the US and other advanced economies is still too big, and continues to allow banking systems and financial systems to grow faster than its regulation can monitor (see Donnan and Fleming, 2015). But the IMF lacks the capacity and the mandate to do more than make calls that political and financial elites are at liberty to note but ignore, or simply disregard.

At the heart of a broken system is a shareholder-value model of corporate governance (Deakin, 2011) that since the crises, as Bainbridge (2012) shows, has been shored up, rather than challenged or substantially reformed. Reforms have generally 'empowered shareholders', rather than strengthened the governance role of other stakeholders, which 'make(s) the next crisis more likely and potentially more severe' (ibid, p. 13). It is improbable that shareholder-centricism will be remedied without radical and sweeping regulatory interventions by national and global governments. It is a view shared by Greenberg, the deposed CEO of AIG, who attributes much responsibility for the company's collapse to a shareholder-centric model of corporate governance that was unchecked *after* his departure. As he puts it, and with specific reference to the post-Enron era, the collapse of AIG followed a disastrous reconstitution of the AIG board which occurred in response to a 'national campaign for "shareholder democracy"' (Greenberg and Cunningham, 2013, p. 158). The avowed intent of the campaign was to curb the abusive exercise of power by executives. But, in Greenberg's eyes, the empowerment of shareholders was incapable of holding his successor properly to account (ibid., p. 158; see also p. 159). Indeed, Greenberg's successor, Martin Sullivan, and his fellow board members eagerly pursued the short-term shareholder value by recklessly permitting the expansion of revenues from AIGFP, thereby enabling the company to reach, and even exceed, its 15/15/15 targets. This hugely enriched AIG executives who were subsequently 'let go' with impunity. That said, it was Greenberg who had set up the 15/15/15 metric that AIG shareholders assumed could be indefinitely delivered.

Meaningful reform of the system requires, as Howson (2009, p. 50) notes, radical change that encompasses 'prudential regulation by public authorities'. But this is feasible only if the banks and insurance companies are broken up so that they are small enough to fail, as well as simple enough to audit and regulate. As Willumstad, who chaired the board before becoming its CEO, acknowledges but apparently lacked the time, capacity or will to address – the size of AIG and its labyrinthine complexity made it very difficult to monitor and control (see Boyd, 2011, pp. 174–6). Identifying much more wide-ranging reforms of corporate governance is one way to rebalance the distribution of benefits and costs arising from the financial sector. In the absence of such reform, established political and financial elites can be expected to 'push back' at even a minor tightening of control (e.g. over mortgage lending), as is evident in the US where the efforts by a coalition of banks and Republicans have repeatedly been directed at loosening the criteria for qualified mortgages through the proposed introduction of an alternative, market-based standard (see Jopson and McLannahan, 2015). The GFC has highlighted the 'limits of private law' (Howson, 2009, p. 50) that is at the centre of neo-liberalism, yet it remains in place because powerful vested interests are currently well served by it. Paradoxically, resistance to closer, more effective and publicly accountable global, as well as national, regulation of corporations and markets, makes it more likely that profit-seeking activities will result in systemic collapse.

Notes

1 This was reflected in the dramatic removal, within days of the election of a New Labour administration in 1997, of control of the base rate from the direct influence of politicians. A monetary policy committee, comprising five senior Bank of England executives and four experts selected by the Chancellor of the Exchequer, took responsibility with the objective of keeping inflation under 2.5%, principally by adjusting the base rate. This focus upon inflation is perhaps understandable in the UK context where it is so strongly associated with the traumas of stagflation and industrial conflict attributed to the diluted Keynesian policies of the 1970s.

2 The reference here is to a character created by Harry Enfield, a comedian, in 1986, the year of Big Bang. See http://knowyourmeme.com/memes/loadsamoney (retrieved 3 May 2016).

3 The boom was punctuated by occasional 'blips' and `bumps', such as the financial crisis in South East Asia in 1997 and the slowdown when the dot.com bubble burst in 2000. But it was the collapse of Long-Term Capital Management (LTCM) and the scandal of Enron that most clearly foreshadowed, and signalled warnings of the risks of securitization, including the use of financial models, at the heart of the global financial crisis.

4 It has been alleged that rating agencies routinely awarded investment grade status to tranches of CDOs constructed out of mezzanine or junior tranches from other CDOs. That is to say, the investment banks (e.g. Goldman Sachs but they were quickly imitated) are said to have gathered together the junior and mezzanine tranches of CDOs, and then 'persuaded the rating agencies that these weren't, as they might appear, all exactly the same things. They were another diversified portfolio of assets!...The rating agencies, who were paid fat fees by the firms for each deal they rated, pronounced 80% of the new tower of debt (i.e. new CDO) triple-A [top investment grade' (see Lewis, 2010, p. 73). To illustrate the point, it has been reported that Moody's, one of the rating agencies, downgraded a top, super-senior tranche of a mortgage-backed CDO given an AAA rating in April 2008 to a rating of B2 in November of the same year (MacKenzie, 2009).

5 An increase to 0.5 would have made CDOs significantly less attractive in comparison to gilts and corporate or government bonds receiving an equivalent investment grade rating.

6 An Alt-A grade, for example, means the claimed income or other key information of the borrower might not have been verified.

7 As an aside, Republicans rattled by the meltdown have identified the CRA as *the* (Democratic) source of the 'subprime crisis'.

8 Less shadowy lenders were willing to comply with CRA criteria because, following the introduction of the Riegle-Neal Interstate Branching and Efficiency Act (1994), passing a CRA review process was, as noted above, important when lenders wished to expand (e.g. through merger and acquisition).
9 AIG's labyrinthine complexities and opacity – paralleled by Enron (Willmott, 2011) – resulted, in part, from an acquisitions spree that included International Lease Finance Corporation, the market leader in aircraft leasing, and also SunAmerica leading provider of life assurance, savings products, annuities and mutual funds, in addition to its biggest US insurance competitor (American General Insurance).
10 This point was not lost on David Schiff in his 1993 article 'Swaps and Derivatives: AIG Hits Hyperspace'. Schiff subsequently highlighted a number of other dubious AIG dealings, including a reinsurance deal called Coral Re involving the giant Canadian Brewer Molson Companies whose CEO coincidentally joined the AIG board shortly afterwards, as well as Brightpoint that paid AIG about $15m in monthly premiums to retroactively cover an imaginary loss. AIG then made a payment of $11.9m that enabled Brightpoint to overstate its earnings by 61 per cent and so conceal the scale of its unanticipated losses. As Boyd (2011, p. 109) notes, this deal was remarkable since AIG allowed a longstanding subsidiary to risk the reputation of the company for a few million dollars in premium. It turned out to be even more remarkable when Schiff discovered that the 'Loss Mitigation Unit' of the subsidiary was openly advertising its services on AIG's website. For this, AIG was penalized $10m by the Securities and Exchange Commission. According to Boyd (2011, p. 110), Greenberg, the CEO of AIG, 'seethed at what he saw was the lack of proportion shown by the SEC and to an extent his board, who expressed displeasure to him in no uncertain terms'. This was to become a recurrent theme of Greenberg's attitude to regulators (see Braithwaite, 2015) and 'disloyal' members of the AIG board.

   A similar scam was undertaken in 2001 to provide banks with balance sheet relief. This was available though a product termed Contributed Guaranteed Alternative Investment Trusts (C-GAITS). Although Ernst & Young were initially content to suggest that these instruments were congruent with accounting standards, they withdrew this advice but AIG continued to market this product without drawing clients' attention to the potential accounting risk. By offloading $762m in three separate C-GAITS deals, PNC Financial Services Group was able to report a 52 per cent higher net income, for which AIG received $39.21m in fees (see www.sec.gov/litigation/complaints/comp18985.pdf retrieved 26 March 2015). The SEC settled for payment by AIG of $126m, and this was a 'deferred prosecution' to indicate that no one would be indicted so long at AIG complied until January 2006. This had a depressing effect upon the share price and further spooked the board. Even a pro-Greenberg board members is reported to have said of this period: 'No one thought that Brightpoint and PNC were the only deals that were [problematic]. The company was making money but we weren't sure where the next headache might come from' (Boyd, 2011, p. 117).
11 When Cassano's contract was terminated in 2008, no attempt was made by AIG to recover any of his compensation. Indeed, he was allowed to retain up to US$34m in uninvested bonuses and negotiated a US$1m per month retainer (see www.propublica.org/article/former-aig-exec-at-center-of-meltdown-got-paid-millions-for-little-work-101. Retrieved 24 July 2015).
12 The deal involved obtaining a loan of $500m from *Gen Re*, which looked as if it was a payment to reinsure an equal amount of risk but was deployed to improve a decline of $59m in AIG's general reserves that had sliced off $6 from its $99 share price.
13 The transformation of investment banks from partnerships into proprietary companies is important as it transfers risk, as well as reward, to shareholders. With this change, executives (no longer partners) have less direct personal interest in understanding and supervising risk; and they also find themselves under greater external pressures to maximize profitability.

Bibliography

Bainbridge, S.M. (2012) *Corporate Governance after the Financial Crisis*, Oxford: Oxford University Press.
Blair, M. (1995) *Ownership and Control: Rethinking Corporate Governance for the Twenty-First Century*, Washington, DC: Brookings Institute.
Boyd, R. (2011) *Fatal Risk: A Cautionary Tale of AIG's Corporate Suicide*, New Jersey: John Wiley.
Braithwaite, T. (2015) 'Hank Greenberg scores pyrrhic victory in AIG lawsuit', *Financial Times*, 15 June.
Congressional Oversight Panel (2010) *The AIG Rescue, Its Impact on Markets, and the Government's Exit Strategy*. Retrieved on 24 July 2015 from www.gpo.gov/fdsys/pkg/CPRT-111JPRT56698/pdf/CPRT-111JPRT56698.pdf.

Crouch, C. (2008) 'After privatized Keynesianism', Compass Think Pieces, Number 41. Retrieved on 14 June 2010 from http://clients.squareeye.com/uploads/compass/documents/CTP41Keynesianisam-Crouch.pdf.

Davis, G.F. (2009) *Managed by the Markets: How Finance Re-Shaped America*, Oxford: Oxford University Press.

Deakin, S. (2011) 'Corporate governance and the financial crisis in the long run' in Williams, C. and Zumbansen, P. (eds) *The Embedded Firm: Corporate Governance, Labor and Finance Capitalism*, Cambridge: Cambridge University Press, pp. 15–41.

Donnan, S. and Fleming, S. (2015) 'Christine Lagarde calls for shake-up of bankers' pay', *Financial Times*, 6 May.

Feirstein, B. (2009) *100 to Blame: The Community Reinvestment Act*, Corporate Skyboxes, and More, Vanity Fair, 10 September 2009. Retrieved on 12 May 2010 from www.vanityfair.com/online/daily/2009/09/100-to-blame-the-community-reinvestment-act-corporate-skyboxes-and-more.html.

Financial Services Authority (2009) *Mortgage Market Review*. Retrieved on 14 June 2010 from www.fsa.gov.uk/pubs/discussion/dp09_03.pdf.

Gordon, R. (2008) *Did Liberals Cause the Sub-prime Crisis?*, The American Prospect, 7 April. Retrieved on 12 May 2010 from www.prospect.org/cs/articles?article=did_liberals_cause_the_subprime_crisis.

Greenberg, M.R. and Cunningham, L.A. (2013) *The AIG Story*, New Jersey: John Wiley.

Howson, N.C. (2009) 'When "good" corporate governance makes "bad" (financial) firms: The global crisis and the limits of private law', *Michigan Law Review*, 108: 44–50.

Hudson, M. (2006) 'The new road to serfdom: An illustrated guide to the coming real estate collapse', *Harpers Magazine*, May: 39–46.

Husock, B. (2000), 'The trillion dollar bank showdown that bodes ill for cities' *City Journal*, Winter. Retrieved on 12 May 2010 from www.city-journal.org/html/10_1_the_trillion_dollar.html. Accessed 12 May 2010.

IMF (International Monetary Fund) (2006) *Global Financial Stability Report: Market Development and Issues*, Washington, DC: International Monetary Fund.

Johnson, M. (2015) 'Hedge fund pay down as top 25 managers bank total of $11.6bn', *Financial Times*, 5 May.

Jopson, B. and McLannahan, B. (2015) 'Democrats raise roof over mortgages', *Financial Times*, 14 May.

King, M. (2007) Speech made at the Birmingham Chamber of Commerce annual banquet. Retrieved on 18 June 2010 from www.bankofengland.co.uk/publications/speeches/2007/speech300.pdf.

Klimecki, R. and Willmott, H.C. (2009) 'From demutualization to meltdown: A tale of two wannabe banks', *Critical Perspectives on International Business*, 5, 1–2: 12–140.

Klimecki, R., Glynos, J. and Willmott, H.C. (2012) 'Cooling out the marks: The ideology and politics of the financial crisis', *Journal of Cultural Economy*, 5, 3: 297–320.

Knights, D. and McCabe, D. (2015) 'Masters of the universe: Demystifying leadership in the context of the 2008 global financial crisis', *British Journal of Management*, 26: 197–210.

Langley, P. (2009) *The Everyday Life of Global Finance: Saving and Borrowing in Anglo-America*, Oxford: Oxford University Press.

Lawson, T. (2015) 'Contemporary economics and the crisis' in T. Lawson, *The Nature and State of Modern Economics*, London: Routledge, pp. 130–41.

Lewis, M. (2010) *The Big Short: Inside the Doomsday Machine*, London: Allen Lane.

Loughrey, J. (2013) (ed.) *Directors' Duties and Shareholder Litigation in the Wake of the Financial Crisis*, Cheltenham: Edward Elgar.

MacKenzie, D. (2008) 'End-of-the-world trade', *London Review of Books*, 30, 9: 24–26. Retrieved on 14 May 2010 from www.lrb.co.uk/v30/n09/donald-mackenzie/end-of-the-world-trade.

MacKenzie, D. (2009) 'All those arrows', Review of G. Tett, *Fool's Gold: How Unrestrained Greed Corrupted a Dream, Shattered Global Markets and Unleashed a Catastrophe*, London Review of Books, 31, 12: 20–2. Retrieved on 14 May 2010 from www.lrb.co.uk/v31/n12/donald-mackenzie/all-those-arrows.

MacKenzie, D. (2009a) 'The credit crisis and a problem in the sociology of knowledge', Working Paper, School of Social and Political Science, University of Edinburgh.

Martin, R. (2002) *The Financialization of Daily Life*, Philadelphia: Temple University Press.

Morgan, G. (2010) 'Legitimacy in financial markets: Credit default swaps in the current crisis', *Socio-Economic Review*, 8, 1: 17–45.

Parker, M., Fournier, V. and Reedy, P. (2007) *The Dictionary of Alternatives*, London: Zed Books.

Pathak, J., Karim, K.E., Carter, C. and Xie, Y. (2013) 'Why do enterprise risk management systems fail? Evidence from a case of AIG', *International Journal of Applied Decision Sciences*, 6, 4: 345–71.

Rajan, R.G. (2010), *Fault Lines: How Hidden Fractures Still Threaten the World Economy*, Princeton, NJ: Princeton University Press.
Reed, M. (2011) 'The politics of crisis and the dynamics of organizational rule' Extended Review of A. Gamble, *The Spectre at the Feast: Capitalist Crisis and the Politics of Recession, Organization*, 18: 261–9.
Roberts, J. and Jones, M. (2009) 'Accounting for self interest in the credit crisis', *Accounting, Organizations and Society*, 34: 856–67.
Schiller, R.J. (2008) *The Subprime Solution: How Today's Global Financial Crisis Happened, and What to Do about It*, Princeton, NJ: Princeton University Press.
Schwartz, H.S. (2012) 'Anti-oedipal dynamics in the sub-prime loan debacle: The case of a study by the Boston Federal Reserve Bank' in Long, S. and Sievers, B. (eds) *Towards a Socioanalysis of Money, Finance and Capitalism: Beneath the Surface of the Financial Industry*, London: Routledge, pp. 321–34.
Securities Industry and Financial Markets Association (2008) 'Restoring Confidence in the Securitization Markets'. Retrieved on 29 August 2009 from http://sifma.org.
Shelp, R.K. and Ehrbar, A. (2009) *Fallen Giant: The Amazing Story of Hank Greenberg and the History of AIG*, New Jersey: John Wiley.
Sjostrum, W.K. (2009) 'The AIG bailout', *Washington and Lee Law Review*, 66, 3: 943–91.
Sorkin, A.R. (2009) *Too Big to Fail: Inside the Battle to Save Wall Street*, Harmondsworth: Penguin.
Stout, L. (2012) *The Shareholder Value Myth: How Putting Shareholders First Harms Investors, Corporations and the Public*, San Francisco: Berrett-Koehler.
Sun, W., Stewart, J. and Pollard, D. (2011), (eds.) *Corporate Governance and the Global Financial Crisis: International Perspectives*, Cambridge: Cambridge University Press.
Tett, G. (2010), *Fool's Gold*, London: Abacus.
Tomlinson, R. and Evans, D. (2007), 'CDO boom masks subprime losses, abetted by S&P, Moody's, Fitch', 31 May, Bloomberg.com. Retrieved on 10 June 2010 from www.bloomberg.com/apps/news?pid=newsarchive&sid=ajs7BqG4_X8I.
Vasudev, P.M. (2009) 'Default swaps and director oversight: Lessons from AIG', paper presented at the Risk Management and Corporate Governance Conference, Loyola University, Chicago, 1–2 October 2009. Subsequently published in *Journal of Corporation Law*, 35: 758–97.
Vasudev, P.M. and Watson, S. (eds) (2012) *Corporate Governance After the Financial Crisis*, Cheltenham: Edward Elgar.
Veldman, J. and Willmott, H.C. (2016) 'The cultural grammar of governance: The UK code of corporate governance, reflexivity, and the limits of "soft" regulation', *Human Relations*, 69, 3: 581–603.
Willmott, H.C. (2011) 'Enron narrative' in M. Painter-Morland and T. Ten Bos (eds) *Continental Philosophy and Business Ethics*, Cambridge: Cambridge University Press, pp. 96–116.
Zuckerman, G. (2009) *The Greatest Trade Ever: How John Paulson Bet Against the Markets and Made $20 Billion*, London: Penguin/Viking.

Appendix A: Collateralized Debt Obligations (CDOs)

CDOs are a form of bond whose complex structure was developed in the world of corporate debt. The first CDO was issued in 1987 but it was the late 1990s before they became established. By 2004, the global issuance of CDOs had reached $154bn and this increased rapidly to $520bn in 2006. In 2009, the global issuance of CDOs fell to $4bn. Mortgage-based CDOs have different risk classes comprising a number of tranches (junior, mezzanine, senior and super-senior) that offer different rates of return that, in the case of the most junior, high-risk tranches can be at least 12 per cent and as high as 15–20 per cent (see figure below).

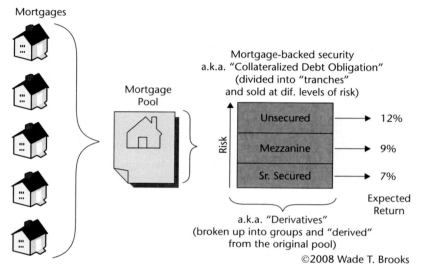

Source: http://en.wikipedia.org/wiki/File:Mortgage_backed_security.jpgSS (retrieved on 3 May 2016).

> If you took a million subprime mortgages, sliced 'em up, and shuffled the pieces around into smaller, seemingly random groups, you'd get CDOs – collateralized debt obligations. The idea was that they lowered the risk involved, which allowed for AAA ratings. It was all modeled on a mathematical formula called the Gaussian copula function, which looked something like this: Pr [TA< 1, TB< 1] = F2(F−1 (FA(1)), F−1 (FB(1),) (g). By 2006 some $4.7 *trillion* in CDOs had been sold. But there was just one small, tiny, little problem with the formula: it was based on "correlation," meaning you could predict the future by looking at the past. And in this case, the gamma function – g – was deduced from projections that house prices would continue to rise indefinitely, at the same rate as they had in the recent past. Obviously, they didn't. Which is why, when the first subprime mortgages began to default, the whole crazy apparatus that held up our financial high-wire act came tumbling down.
>
> (Feirstein, 2009)

Appendix B: The wonders of securitization

In November 2003, when speaking on behalf of the American Securitization Forum to the 'Hearing on Protecting Homeowners: Preventing Abusive Lending While Preserving Access to Credit' at the House of Representatives, Cameron L. Cowan, a Partner of Orrick, Herrington, and Sutcliffe, LLP, declared that:

> The success of the securitization industry has helped many individuals with subprime credit histories obtain credit. Securitization allows more subprime loans to be made because it provides lenders an efficient way to manage credit risk...Regulation that seeks to place disproportionate responsibilities on the secondary market will only succeed in driving away the capital loan purchasers provide in the subprime market.

He continued:

> I urge Congress to move with great care as it addresses the problem of predatory lending. The secondary markets are a tremendous success story that has helped democratize credit in this country. Well intended, but overly restrictive, regulation in this area could easily do more harm than good.

Source: http://financialservices.house.gov/media/pdf/110503cc.pdf
(retrieved 3 May 2016)

Appendix C

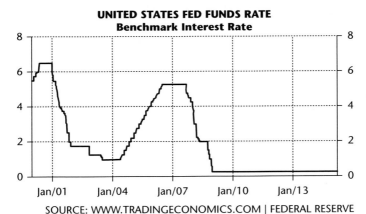

Part II
Critical perspectives on financial innovation

5

Reconceptualizing financial innovation

Frame, conjuncture and bricolage

*Ewald Engelen, Ismail Ertürk, Julie Froud,
Adam Leaver and Karel Williams*

This chapter argues for a reconceptualization of financial innovation which, as culprit and victim of the current crisis, is now damned by those who once praised it. But what is financial innovation? The dominant answers from mainstream finance and social studies of finance share variations on a rationalistic view whereby financial innovation is about improving markets or at least extending the sphere of rational calculability. Because improvisation is more important than the dominant perspectives can admit, this chapter proposes a new concept of financial innovation whose three main elements – frame, conjuncture and bricolage – are indicated by the title of this chapter. The importance of this problem shift is that it highlights the inherent fragility of this type of intermediary-led financial innovation where things will often miscarry and highlights the need for a more radical rethinking about policy responses to the financial crisis that began in 2007.

'Too much of a good thing': a crisis for financial innovation?

> In addressing the challenges and risks that financial innovation may create, we should also always keep in view the enormous economic benefits that flow from a healthy and innovative financial sector. The increasing sophistication and depth of financial markets promote economic growth by allocating capital where it is most productive. And the dispersion of risk more broadly across the financial system has, thus far, increased the resilience of the system and the economy to shocks.
>
> *(Ben Bernanke, Chair US Federal Reserve,
> New York, 15 May 2007)*

Not all innovation is equally useful. If by some terrible accident the world lost the knowledge required to manufacture one of our major drugs or vaccines, human welfare would be seriously harmed. If the instructions for creating a CDO squared have now been mislaid, we will I think get along quite well without. And in the years running up to 2007, too much of the developed world's intellectual talent was devoted to ever more complex financial innovations, whose maximum possible benefits in terms of allocative efficiency was at best marginal, and which in their complexity and opacity created large financial stability risks.

(Adair Turner, Chairman of the UK Financial Services Authority, The Economist's Inaugural City Lecture, 21 January 2009)

The media's 'credit crunch' of summer 2007 turned into a financial crisis of bank failure and bailout in autumn 2008 which then provoked a recession in 2009 and after. The results so far include not only huge write-offs of financial capital but also perhaps the largest, fastest destruction of intellectual capital in the past 100 years. Crunch, crisis and recession directly challenge the pre-2007 received wisdom about how, in the words of one elite investment banker, 'an innovations-based explosion of new financial instruments was a huge plus for market efficiency' (*Financial Times*, 27 October 2008). The first of the opening quotations, from Ben Bernanke (2007), illustrates how establishment figures uncritically praised the economic benefits of financial innovation right up to the credit crunch. They have, of course, since discovered that financial innovation can be less benign, and the second quote from a keynote speech setting out new principles of financial regulation from British establishment figure Adair Turner (2009) is an acerbic rejoinder to any contention that financial innovation has brought significant social and economic benefits. The consensus has thus now shifted so that by January 2009 Ben Bernanke had discovered that innovation can undermine the financial system and bring down a capitalist economy. This is, most obviously, a *crisis of financial innovation* because securitization represents innovation whose outcomes include frozen markets, failed and bailed banks and blocked credit. Significantly, it is also a *crisis for financial innovation* because these events have forced media commentators, politicians, officials and regulatory organizations to revalue this notion of innovation or at least to question the ability of banks and other institutions to manage innovation in the general interest.

The pre-crisis consensus on the benefits of financial innovation was such that regulators and officials were concerned to encourage more innovation and rehearse its many benefits. Consider, for example, the following views and positions all taken in the first half of 2007, weeks before the crisis started. The Financial Services Authority (FSA) in the UK was concerned that regulatory reforms should ensure that 'the UK continues to be Europe's recognized centre of financial innovation' (FSA, 2007). When praising financial innovation in his May 2007 speech, Ben Bernanke argued that 'in some respects financial innovation makes risk management easier' because it can be 'sliced and diced, moved off the balance sheet and hedged by derivative instruments' (Bernanke, 2007). His line about the 'great benefits of financial innovation' was echoed in a paper by Bank of England authors which argued that 'in recent years, there has been much greater scope to pool and transfer risks, potentially offering substantial welfare benefits for borrowers and lenders' (Hamilton, Jenkinson and Penalver, 2007, p. 226), including increasing 'the availability of credit to households and corporations' through a wider 'menu of financial products' (ibid., p. 230). While for Adrian Blundell-Wignall of the OECD, 'sub-prime lending is a new innovation ... the big benefit is that people who previously could not dream of owning a home share in the benefits of financial innovation' (Blundell-Wignall, 2007, p. 2).

With the credit crunch and problems about subprime after August 2007, this triumphalism about financial innovation was grudgingly revised and, in the first year of the crisis, the 'too much of a good thing' alibi was developed: an emerging crisis of financial innovation was reconciled with established views about the benefits of financial innovation by arguing that the problems were the result of *too much* (or the wrong kind of) innovation. Thus the Bank for International Settlements (BIS) in its 2008 Annual report accepted that securitization and the 'originate-to-distribute' model had not spread risk bearing because 'the way in which they were introduced materially reduced the quality of credit assessments in many markets and also led to a marked increase in opacity' (BIS, 2008, p. 8; see also Jenkinson, Penalver and Vause, 2008). This alibi initially softened criticism of financial innovation. As a *Financial Times* editorial argued, financial innovation was not 'mistaken in principle' because the problem was not turning mortgages into bonds but 'using securitization as way to dodge bank capital requirements, multiply fees and dump bad loans onto others' (30 December 2008). Second, if the problem was too much of the wrong kind of financial innovation, it was noted that regulators should guard against over-eager responses that might lead to too little innovation. The IMF's *Global financial stability report* of October 2007 argued that 'while recognizing that financial regulation needs to catch up with innovation, some Directors emphasized that actions to strengthen regulation should not stifle the creativity and dynamism of financial markets' (IMF, 2007, p. 126).

After the collapse of Lehman in September 2008, governments had to guarantee deposits and recapitalize banks in Europe and America. Understandably the balance of mainstream opinion then shifted, became much more hostile to financial innovation and more personalized with populist attacks on greedy bankers. Journalists in the financial press still used the alibi about the wrong kind of innovation and the language about costs and benefits: thus John Plender in a *Financial Times* feature (5 January 2009) described the 'double-edged nature of financial innovation ... throughout the ages'. But the politicians and intellectuals debating re-regulation and 'new financial architecture' are now much less kind. Most notably, several eminent mainstream economists have attacked financial innovation and flatly recommended less innovation. For example, Jagdish Bhagwati of Columbia University argued that financial innovation was unlike non-financial innovation because it generated more upheaval: 'with financial innovation, the downside can be lethal – it is "destructive creation"' (*Financial Times*, 16 October 2008). As implied in the opening quote from Adair Turner, we are now in a world where we can apparently distinguish good innovation from bad, while in December 2008 the Nobel Prize winner Robert Solow recommended 'a regulatory system aimed at insulating the real economy from financial innovation insofar as that is possible' and accepted 'that may require limits on the freedom of action of commercial banks' (*Financial Times*, 16 December 2008).

The (changing) consensus view is only a matter of making interpretative concessions after the agreed facts have changed. And there is something comic about how after 2007 journalists, officials, regulators and academics have salvaged as much as possible of their earlier positions on financial innovation when most of them acted like bishops blessing battleships. But the changes do raise some serious questions: how can there be too much of a good thing and how can such apparently good things suddenly (and quite unexpectedly) turn bad? There are also some interesting intellectual issues here. If everyone can agree that securitization and derivatives are examples of innovation, just what is (and is not) innovation? Where did ideas about financial innovation come from and why did the phenomenon enjoy such a positive reception for so long? When we answer these questions in the rest of this chapter, we find that media reports and the publications of official regulatory bodies reflect or at least are coherent with academic definitions. The arguments in these documents are tendentious because they represent financial innovation as a kind of heroic rationalism. Hence our main objective in this chapter is to propose a new concept of financial innovation whose three main elements of frame, conjuncture and bricolage combine to explain the fragile and variable results of financial innovation.

The chapter which develops these arguments is organized in a relatively straightforward way. The second section deals with academic representations of financial innovation in mainstream finance, as well as on the critical periphery in social studies of finance and financialization. Behind the concepts of 'financial engineering' and 'performativity' is a set of rationalistic assumptions which financialization rejects without finding an alternative concept of innovation. Section three argues that all these perspectives fail to engage with the improvisatory character of financial innovation. Sections four, five and six then propose our alternative account of financial innovation: section four outlines our ideas about a macro-frame of structural conditions, while section five outlines the changing field of conjunctural opportunities within which section six presents innovation as a work of bricolage. The concluding section explains how the re-conceptualization of financial innovation proposed in this chapter has implications for our understanding of the current financial crisis.

Current concepts of financial innovation: mainstream finance and social studies of finance

> What is recurrently ... described and celebrated as (financial innovation) ... is, without exception a small variation on an established design ... The world of finance hails the invention of the wheel over and over again, often in a slightly more unstable version. All financial innovation involves, in one form or another, the creation of debt secured in greater or lesser adequacy by real assets.
>
> *(Galbraith, 1990, p. 19)*

J.K. Galbraith would no doubt have dismissed derivatives and private equity in the mid-2000s as trivial variants on the junk bonds and leveraged buy-outs (LBOs) which he disparaged in 1990. His scepticism was theoretically grounded in heterodox political economics because Keynesian ideas about speculation or Minskian ideas about credit cycles both emphasize recurrence which devalues the differences and novelties of each new cycle in finance. This is important because it shows that financial innovation in the late 1980s was not an idea whose time had come but a metaphor making its way in a sceptical world. And this section tells the story of the two groups of academics who then promoted the concept: the financial economists put finance theory and theorists at the centre of a heroic process of extending and completing financial markets, while the social studies of finance produced an ethnography and history which did not break conclusively with the assumptions of the financial economists.

The first paradox here is that, with some exceptions (e.g. Molyneux and Shamroukh, 1999), the literature on financial innovation does not draw on the huge literature about (productive) innovation by mainstream and heterodox economists. Put another way, the main contributors to this (productive) innovation literature have not maintained Schumpeter's broad interest in finance. His 1934 text, *The Theory of Economic Development*, contains extensive discussion of credit and capital in the economic system and the growth of firms, as well as some discussion about money markets and their potential as a source of income. But, as O'Sullivan (2002) has noted, the links between finance and innovation have been 'largely neglected' in recent times, or dealt with very narrowly as institutional economists of different kinds are mainly interested in the role of financial institutions and markets in sustaining innovative productive processes and systems. Hence there is discussion of the role of venture capital (for example, in Lazonick, 2002) and of nationally specific firm finance relations that give rise to 'national systems of innovation' (see, for example, Nelson, 1993; OECD, 1997). If finance is seen as an input with consequences for production, the issue of innovation within finance is marginalized or denied. And this is manifest in the varieties of capitalism literature, including Hall and Soskice (2001) and Amable (2003) whose idea of national varieties resting on institutional complementarity effectively denies the possibilities of finance-led change (see also Engelen and Konings, forthcoming).

Hence, it was financial economists like Merton Miller (1986) who explicitly coupled the terms 'finance' and 'innovation' in the 1980s to create a leading metaphor. Their linguistic coupling was foundational because it associated developments in financial products and markets with standard economic ideas about innovation as a process with positive outcomes. Innovation can create losers as well as winners, but the standard economic definition of innovation is as something that results in a higher level of economic welfare, through enhancing either static efficiency or dynamic efficiency. In effect, the metaphor was positively charged and imparted a bias in favour of financial innovation when, as Merton claimed, there was a lot of it about. Writing in the mid-1980s, Miller asked the question, 'can any twenty-year period in recorded history have witnessed even a tenth as much new development?' (Miller, 1986, p. 460). Later writers remind readers of Miller's assertion that innovation cannot continue at the same pace and argue that it has indeed done so (Tufano, 2002).

But what exactly was innovation and how did it generate beneficial outcomes? The connection between innovation and more economic growth is explicitly made in some of the financial economics literature: for example, Miller (1986) defines financial innovation as something that produces economic growth in excess of what would otherwise occur. However, the financial economists were theorists of efficient markets (not modellers of contributions to economic growth). The financial economists thus added a link in the argument and, as theorists of financial markets, defaulted onto the idea that financial innovation is everything that makes financial markets more efficient and extends the sphere of financial markets; which, prima facie, should deliver higher growth and welfare gains. By the 2000s, with the hockey-stick growth of derivatives and other instruments, this definition had crystallized into the idea that the project of financial innovation in our time was the marketization of risk. And this definition was taken up by many, including behavioural financial economists like Robert Shiller, who did not believe in efficient markets and rational actors. Shiller defines 'radical financial innovation' as 'the development of new institutions and methods that permit risk management to be extended far beyond its former realm, covering important new *classes* of risk' (Shiller, 2004, p. 2).

This problem shift onto financial innovation as marketization creates at least three major problems: first, it makes the definition of financial innovation circular and tautological; second, it narrows the field of possible drivers of innovation; and, third, it encourages claims about benefits which have low empirical content.

1. The tautological problem is obvious if we consider Miller's claim that 'any surviving, successful innovation must have reduced deadweight transaction costs and expanded the reach of the market' (Miller, 1986, p. 463). In effect, any financial innovation that survives must have done so because it is truly *innovative* and has improved market efficiency. This is qualified in a modest way by Van Horne, who recognizes that 'enthusiasm' may 'allow certain deals to be masqueraded as financial innovation' where aggressive 'promoters' earning 'handsome' fees can temporarily confuse markets (Van Horne, 1985, p. 626), but that on an *ex post* basis such products would not be what Viñals and Berges (1988) denote as 'pseudo-innovation'. However, this is only a qualification to the tautological assertion that what survives must be innovative.

2. Logically, the narrow definition implies narrow causes as financial innovation responds to market signals, market failure and exogenous variables like technical change. Miller's early work applies a financial economics framework which highlights regulations and taxes as the 'impulse' to innovate (see also the idea of 'regulatory dialectic' discussed in Artus and de Boissieu, 1988, pp. 108 9), while Merton (1995) adds computer and technological advances as well as finance theory to the list of causes. Silber's economics-based approach includes

discussion of specific factors that can explain particular innovations (Silber, 1983, p. 91). As noted by Tufano (2002) and Ross (1989), much analysis is dominated by the idea that innovations are optimal responses to either market problems or arbitrage opportunities and that, significantly, they are often 'institution-free' (Tufano, 2002, p. 9).

3 It is easy to list but hard to measure the benefits of innovation. According to Tufano (2002), it is possible to measure the (considerable) benefits of retail process innovations that reduce transaction costs like ATMs or smart cards but, more generally, it is more challenging to measure the social welfare effects of new instruments in the wholesale markets. Where measurement attempts have been made, as with those collected in Allen and Gale's (1994) volume, the evidence suggests effects are mixed and complex: thus, with tools like short selling, there may be welfare gains from very limited use, but such gains are lost when the tactic is used without limit.

But, if we leave these problems to one side, financial economists do have a strong, simple and positive story about financial innovation, which serves as authority and source for all those pre-2007 lists of benefits by establishment figures. It is a rationalistic (indeed functionalist) account of financial innovations. New products and services allow funds to be moved across time and place, or to be pooled, risk to be managed, or asymmetric information or moral hazard problems to be addressed. And all this ultimately serves the teleological aim of constructing in the real world a perfect set of financial markets, making true the almost religious promise of instantaneous market clearing (see, for example, Merton, 1992). Within this frame, the work of financial innovation is a prosaic but heroic activity whose quality is captured in the notion of *financial engineering* used by some financial economists to suggest an apolitical, mechanical view of innovation focused on solving what are essentially technical problems of markets around information, pricing and so on.

The idea of financial engineering encourages lists of innovations and a cult of the engineer with Robert C. Merton playing the part of Isambard Kingdom Brunel. Hence we have classifications of types of financial innovation according to what they are designed to do (BIS, 1986; White, 1996), as well as shortlists of the most important innovations of recent times, with different academics arguing for their favourites (Miller, 1986). And, at this point, the financial economists themselves enter their own story because, if innovation is the completion of the market, those with technical hypotheses and algebra about markets and valuation surely have a privileged role in the remaking of the world. This is supported by chronology and popular history. Chronology is important because the huge expansion of derivatives trading after the 1980s postdates Merton's (1973) formulation of the Black–Scholes model and predates widespread use of the formula in valuing options and derivatives. All this was turned into popular history with Bernstein's *Capital ideas* about the migration of finance theory from academe to Wall Street as leading financial economists promoted a kind of modernization of finance theory which made Wall Street 'vital and productive' (Bernstein, 1992, p. 2). Bernstein's account is an explicit celebration of what is characterized here and elsewhere as a 'revolution' (see, for example, White, 1996, p. 6) whose heroes are the talented finance academics with ideas and new formulae.

Meanwhile, other parts of social science have taken up new ways of understanding finance. Social studies of finance have attracted a new generation of social constructionist sociologists with ethnographic and historical interests in describing and understanding what financial economists, traders and markets are about (see, for example, Knorr Cetina and Preda, 2004). At the same time, shareholder value and financialization have been taken up as interdisciplinary objects by an assortment of radicals from political economy and cultural economy (see, for example, the readings in Ertürk *et al.*, 2008). We would expect these academics to present a quite different account of financial innovation because their work gives due weight to the sociocultural, and does not construct the economy in terms of obstacles to market clearing. Furthermore, research from the social studies of innovation field has challenged notions that innovation is 'technology'-led and suggested caution about claiming the significance of new technologies in advance of the historical analysis that so often paints a more complex picture of effect (Edgerton, 2008). However, while the critical accounts of social studies of finance and of financialization are different, they do not succeed in breaking with the underlying heroic rationalism of the financial economist's account; or, more exactly, only the analysts of financialization dissent and they often do so by turning heroes into villains.

The social studies of finance have been both liberated and constrained by its founding problem shift towards social constructionism. An earlier generation of liberal sociologists protested that the categories of mainstream economics crudely misrepresented the complex world. Under French influence from Latour and others, social studies of finance in the 2000s have analysed how the categories of financial economics format the practical world. Thus, in MacKenzie's (2006) metaphor, theory is an engine not a camera so that financial theorems are characterized as 'producers' of market behaviour and prices, instead of 'cameras' which merely depict what is ontologically given. From this perspective, Black–Scholes and derivatives trading provide the perfect example, and Mackenzie (2006) has produced a nuanced and impeccably sourced history of all this which effectively provides scholarly support for a heroic view of theory-led financial innovation that is adumbrated by the finance literature and developed in the earlier popular histories. The a priori of this kind of approach is epitomized by the concept of performativity which is now widely used in social studies of finance. In general, the concept encourages studies which elaborate how economic theories and finance formulae are at the root of financial techniques and infrastructure, which have become the great facilitators of the recent development and spread of financial markets.

Performativity brings a new insight and there are several different variants on the concept which in English usage from Austin onwards recognizes misfires and mis-executions. But we doubt whether any of the concepts provides a sufficiently broad base for explaining financial innovation. Certainly, the preoccupation to date with the performativity of economic theory provides a very narrow lens. Unless one assumes that economic theory has some kind of ontological privilege which guarantees its primacy, the practical world is presumably one where multiple half-realized projects with contradictory discursive bases contend and coexist. In that case, we would expect problems arising from incremental change and interacting projects as well as a much larger role for 'unintended consequences' than most heroic rationalists would admit.

From this point of view, the financialization literature is interesting because it broadens the focus to consider many things other than the role of economic theory in financial innovation and generally takes a much more negative view of the consequences of financial innovation. The political and cultural economists in this group (see Ertürk *et al.*, 2008) hold to a view of capitalism where power is an important driver. Innovation since the 1980s is generally set in the context of sharply increasing inequalities of income and the rise of the 'working rich' and financial intermediaries in Europe and the United States (Duménil and Lévy, 2004). Beyond this, there are sharp differences between cultural and political economists about the nature of power and the capitalist process. From the cultural side, capitalism can be draped in the post-structuralist cloak of Foucauldian capillary power (de Goede, 2001, 2005; Langley, 2008), whereas in political economy from regulationists and neo-Keynesians capitalism is driven by the imperatives of capital accumulation (Aglietta, 2008; Stockhammer, 2008). Thus, the financialization literature has no founding orthodoxy but is instead a space of quarrelsome debate (Engelen, 2008).

The implications for views of innovation are quite interesting because the financialization literature both recapitulates all the tendentious positions we have previously criticized in financial economics and social studies of finance and succeeds in producing novelty by inversion as function becomes dysfunction and the prime movers become villainous intermediaries, not heroic academics. Financial economists explain innovation functionally as answers to real-world deviations from neoclassical market models (which ultimately make markets more similar to those models and hence more efficient); by way of contrast, Marxisant authors like Duménil and Lévy (2004) come up with a dysfunctional explanation as the interests of capital and the working rich are served by new kinds of class alliance with intentions and motives read off postulated class position. Other authors sidestep this position by emphasizing the incoherence and contradictions of financialized capitalism so that Froud *et al.* (2006) represent shareholder value as an unrealizable project with practical consequences. The same team has led the way in highlighting the role of financial intermediaries like investment bankers in financialized capitalism (Folkman *et al.*, 2007). They have dissociated themselves from ideas about intermediary capitalism partly through ideas about 'distributive alliance' where the bankers may not know what they do. But, in a curious way, they do invert the mainstream view of financial innovation as purposeful and heroic because the villain of financialization is the self-serving and greedy financier.

Empirical dissatisfactions: the need for reconceptualization

> I hit on the idea of a chocolate bar dispenser, but replacing the chocolate bar with cash.
> (*John Shepherd Barron, inventor of the first ATM*,
> Financial Times, *26/27 July 2008*)

This quote from the inventor of the first cash dispenser raises questions about what innovation is and how innovation takes place; it highlights the role of analogy and improvisation in the thinking which led to this important retail development. And this in turn raises the question of what the innovation is: is the major innovation the ATM, or its precursor the vending machine, or indeed the lateral thinking on vending that connects a new kind of machine for taking money out with existing machines for putting money in? The quote also suggests that these questions are empirical ones which could be answered only after talking to those involved at a practical level and by considering specific cases. A better concept of innovation cannot be obtained simply by avoiding the errors of rationalism and such like which were listed in the previous section.

If we begin by considering practitioners, the first point to make is that there is a large literature on financial markets and trading practices produced by practitioners or ex-practitioners. They are not cited by financial economists even though practitioner concepts like Soros' (2003) reflexivity or Taleb's (2007) 'black swan events' are widely used. Maybe this is because most of the insider accounts of business organization and market practice contradict the picture that arises from the self-knowledge of financial economists. The insider accounts suggest that the academic accounts overplay the rationality of agents as well as the role of finance theory and or new 'technologies of finance' in the actual practices of finance (Augar, 2001, 2005; Ellis, 2008; Knee, 2006; Lowenstein, 2001; Taleb, 2007). Haug and Taleb (2008) produce an alternative history of derivatives trading which emphasizes the importance of practitioner knowledge in valuing derivatives. They explicitly claim that the expansion of derivative trading did not require Black–Scholes algebra but could have been based on the heuristics used by traders. Equally challenging, other authors discuss the quotidian way in which bankers identify profit-making opportunities and continuously adapt themselves and the organization for which they work to changing conditions. These practitioners suggest a picture of improvised financial innovation which hardly fits with heroic rationality assumptions. At the same time, these accounts do imply that agents possess differentiated and continuously changing freedoms to exercise their limited powers (see, for example, Bookstaber, 2007; Dunbar, 1999).

If we then seek empirical cases, the problem is to find cases produced by authors who do not subscribe to the heroic rationalist assumptions that colour the more intellectualized accounts of the wholesale markets. In the period since the crisis began, we can turn to forensic journalism and newspaper accounts of where things have gone wrong and large losses have been chalked up. Here we will consider the case of Deutsche Bank which in the fourth quarter of 2008 issued a profits warning about a $4.8 billion loss after its proprietary traders had lost altogether some $2 billion in 2008. One star trader (Boaz Weinstein) apparently lost more than $1 billion, mainly in the final quarter before leaving to pursue opportunities elsewhere (*Wall Street Journal*, 15 January 2009). It is more difficult to find descriptions of things going right before 2007. But business school strategy cases and 'how to do it' teaching materials do present what might be called innocent descriptions of innovation in action, Here we will consider an IMD case (2008) which focuses on how J.P. Morgan successfully securitized some £850 million of Royal Bank of Scotland (RBS) subprime mortgage loans and took them off the RBS balance sheet. The two illustrative cases confirm the insights of practitioners but also suggest that financial innovation is not a discrete technical item but an improvised connection which takes the form of a chain of transactions within a configuration of asset prices and flows of funds.

The Deutsche Bank profits warning was a shock for stock market analysts and journalists. Deutsche had sustained relatively little damage in the first year after summer 2007 and this was widely attributed to the controlling intelligence of its senior investment bankers, under the leadership of Anshu Jain. Deutsche Bank may well have internal controls which prevent unauthorized trading of the kind practised by Jerome Kerviel at Société Générale, but the profits warning showed that Deutsche could not anticipate how shifts in flows of funds and asset prices would undermine a short, simple chain of offset transactions, where the profits had been reliably made by applying funds to earn more than it cost to source them from a previous trade. The best-known example of this in the 2000s was the yen carry trade but Deutsche and other banks had a variant, as described in the *Wall Street Journal Europe*, 15 January 2009. They borrowed to buy corporate bonds and then hedged the investments with derivatives because credit default swaps (CDS) allowed them to buy insurance against defaults on the bonds; the trade was profitable as long as the default insurance cost less than the corresponding income from the bonds. This all went wrong after the de facto nationalization of AIG and then the failure of Lehman Brothers in September 2007. With frozen credit markets the traders could no longer borrow to buy bonds and the price of CDS insurance rocketed. The secondary consequence was that bond prices then fell sharply, inflicting capital losses on all the players in the offset trade in bonds and CDS.

Our second illustrative case concerns a J.P. Morgan securitization of subprime loans for RBS in 2006 which depends on a much more complex long chain of transactions which is described in Figure 5.1 (IMD, 2008). Technically the chain is a synthetic CDO (collateralized debt obligation) using two special purpose vehicles with SPV1[1] (termed 'sequils') providing the funds and SPV2 (termed 'mincs') providing first-lost credit enhancement to SPV1. These transactions comprised a package ('sequils/mincs') that J.P. Morgan had introduced in 1999 and which had been successfully repeated for many other clients.

Any consideration of this chain brings out how it is both contingent and historically determined, lucrative yet fragile. The initiator is RBS, which is under pressure to improve capital adequacy under the Basel II regulatory framework by shifting subprime loans off the balance sheet. The result is a kind of alchemy as subprime loans go into the process and investment grade

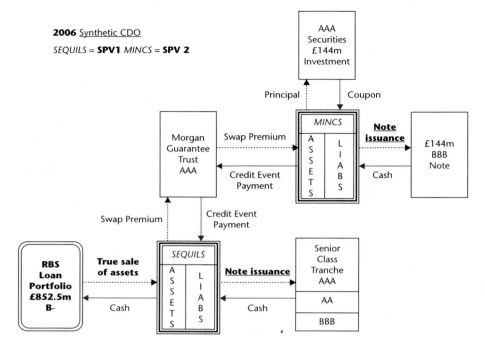

Figure 5.1 J.P. Morgan's securitization for RBS

paper comes out. This is very different from the original 1980s securitizations by Freddie Mac and Fannie Mae of mortgages or by Ford and GM of car loans, where it is the best-quality debt (in terms of default risk) that is passed on to allow credit expansion. The alchemical result for RBS depends on three techniques. The first of these is tranching to create different classes of coupon with some classes of coupon more remote from default. Second, a swap guarantee, which is a kind of insurance against default on the principal, is given by Morgan Guarantee Trust whose triple A rating then provides an uplift. Third, a further guarantee, which acts as a re-insurance scheme for Morgan Guarantee Trust, is a shell vehicle which attracts investors by offering them triple B returns on their principal which in turn has been invested in triple A securities.

This tiering of two SPVs and swap guarantees is the historically determined result of a decade's improvisation. J.P. Morgan has been doing this kind of securitization for seven years (IMD, 2008) and the separation of the funding and credit risks reduces the liabilities of Morgan Guarantee which would otherwise overwhelm its triple A rating. But it is also (just like Deutsche Bank's offset trade) contingent because its rationale and outcome depend on the prices paid and the flows of funds from investors into the coupons issued by SPV1 and SPV2. This, in turn, depends on market conditions, as well as on custom and regulation that prevents insurance companies from buying triple B coupons from SPV2, whose purchasers will include hedge funds (borrowing from banks like RBS). The practical limit is that the gain from the alchemy must be larger than the intermediary fees paid at each step and within this limit it is possible to conceive of securitization packages involving three or four SPVs to deal with loan guarantees and risks of different kinds.

In both Deutsche Bank's short chain and J.P. Morgan's long chain, some agents have to do the maths on what the derivatives are worth, probably (but not necessarily) using Black–Scholes.

The results of such calculations may have determined prices or served as a reference point, with Black–Scholes or another heuristic providing the same service as the trade price guide for the bidder at car auction. But the existence and saleability of the derivatives and their utility to the fee-earning coalition of intermediaries depends on all the conditions whose complexity emerges in the long-chain case. The chain exists in a 'field' strewn with techniques, cognitions, regulations and other social artefacts that may serve as the 'ready mades' feeding into the assemblages resulting from attempts by well-situated, but 'cognitively handicapped', agents to solve discrete problems. There are two important implications: first, innovation is not a substantial technical item but a series of chains or sets of relations; second, the intellectual task is to understand the conditions around the innovation chain which determine the form and complexity of innovation and, just as importantly, generated a multiplicity of fragile long chains in the years before 2007. On this basis, our alternative account of financial innovation seeks to develop some understanding of the conditions of existence of financial innovation.

Macro-frame: general conditions

> I have directed Secretary Connally to suspend temporarily the convertibility of the dollar into gold or other reserve assets, except in amounts and conditions determined to be in the interest of monetary stability and in the best interests of the United States.
>
> *(Richard Nixon announcing the floating of the dollar,*
> *Address to the Nation, 15 August 1971)*

Almost everybody who writes about financial innovation includes a descriptive list of general conditions which have enabled financial innovation since the 1970s. The quote above from Richard Nixon, announcing the 1971 floating of the dollar, is apposite because the end of the Bretton Woods fixed exchange rate system figures prominently on all such lists. Like Konings (2008), we would disagree with those who credit the breakdown of Bretton Woods with epochal significance (see, for example, Helleiner, 1994; Stockhammer, 2008). But we agree with those from right across the policy and discursive spectrum who argue or assume that general structural conditions of the kind discussed in this section collectively help to explain the rise of 'finance' in economic and political terms. In our view the changing structural conditions are relevant because they provide a kind of macro-frame around innovation and hence we describe them below before we go on to argue that such lists of facilitative conditions can only be part of an explanation of innovation.

The first condition has to do with the long-term process of state restructuring in response to the crisis of Keynesianism in the late 1960s/early 1970s. Forced by the spontaneous growth of the stateless Eurodollar market, states increasingly lifted earlier restrictions on cross-border financial transactions, resulting in the gradual development of a truly international market in foreign exchange contracts, which has transformed itself as an international interbank market, providing banks and other financial agents with sufficient liquidity and serving as the main supplier of the raw commodity out of which financial innovations were moulded (Grahl and Lysandrou, 2003; Helleiner, 1994). During the next two decades, the subsequent transnationalization of bond, equity and derivatives markets duly followed.

The unevenness of deregulation, as well as the continuing relevance of the state and national regulatory traditions, opened up numerous opportunities for 'regulatory arbitrage', which by the 1990s were being exploited by nimble players like hedge funds, private equity funds and other private capital-containing vessels domiciled in offshore financial centres. Periodic attempts to re-regulate financial markets, mostly in response to high-profile crises, were quickly undermined by the use of new techniques and instruments or by playing off different jurisdictions against one another. The knowledge, expertise and foresight of public regulators was increasingly not up to the task and Basel II capital adequacy requirements encouraged banks to develop the 'originate-and-distribute' practices that failed after 2007 (see Singer, 2007).

Second, financial pressures and ideological attractions have from the 1970s onward forced governments to retrench the post-1945 welfare arrangements they had set up to make amends for the great European wars and mass unemployment (see Judt, 2005). As a result, households across the Western world have seen state-backed guarantees eroded and have increasingly been obliged to turn to financial markets to gain access to goods such as housing, higher education and protection against unemployment or ill health (Hacker, 2006; Manning, 2000). This 'Big Risk Shift' has not only provided banks and other financial agents with an increased demand for financial debt instruments (credit cards, mortgages, loans) but also ensured a steady supply of new and stable income streams, a precondition for large-scale financial innovation (Leyshon and Thrift, 2007).

Third, as a result of pension reforms (the global replacement of pay-as-you-go systems by pre-funded pension systems), international trade imbalances and rising commodity prices (especially oil), there is a growing 'wall of money' facing global financial markets that is looking for investment opportunities. Prior to the September 2008 meltdown the volumes were truly staggering. The IFSL (2008) estimated total pension savings under management by pension funds in 2007 to be around $28.5 trillion. Mutual funds and insurers managed a further $27.3 trillion and $19.1 trillion respectively. Private equity and hedge funds had assets under management totalling $0.8 trillion and $1.9 trillion respectively. The fastest growth in assets under management, however, was booked by so-called sovereign wealth funds. At the high tide in late 2007 they managed assets in the order of $6.1 trillion, most of it deriving from rising commodity prices and the rest from foreign exchange reserves that are caused by global current account imbalances. In a recent report, the McKinsey Global Institute (2007) estimated that the size of these assets may reach over $15 trillion in 2012. It is, of course, the upscaling in the use of particular financial instruments as well as in the size of funds that has meant that the effects of financial innovation are felt widely as chains unravel.

Fourth, technological developments have been key for the growth and dispersion of modern financial products and markets. In wholesale as well as retail markets the introduction of new information and communication technologies (ICTs) has spawned new products and services, new modes of distribution and new techniques of pricing and risk management. No matter whether it is ATMs, ALM-models, remote access to the mainframes of exchange platforms, option price theory, the use of optic fibres to enhance transaction speed, automated or logarithmic trading, credit scoring, real-time information services (Bloomberg and Reuters) or the new HP Blade Workstation designed for hedge fund use, in all instances ICTs have allowed the rapid and radical transformation of the world's financial markets. In a general sense, it has been the virtualization of trade and the digitization of financial data that made up the precondition for the broadening and deepening of the financial markets. Only when the trade in claims on (future) income streams was decoupled from its physical carrier (the 'coupon' of Hilferding's time) could upscaling take place.

Finally, the development of new theoretical paradigms within economics has added substantially to the construction of a standardized set of techniques that allow anonymous traders, seated behind batteries of desktop screens, to legitimate their activities to an easily impressionable outside public and to recognize each other's expertise in the blink of an eye. The rise of finance as an economic subdiscipline, as described by MacKenzie (2006), has not only spawned a number of Nobel Prize winners but also a large number of mathematical formulae, models and theorems (Black–Scholes theorem; capital asset pricing model; option pricing model; value at risk), which can quickly be adopted and deployed in the new digital environment described above. While the heroic rationalist account almost overemphasizes the importance of these symbolic equations, they have increasingly become embodied in the financial technologies and discourse that surround present-day traders, bankers and analysts.

Taken together, these developments, which mix some intended policies with many unintended consequences, have resulted in a financial world in which funds are plentiful, capital is mobile, trading can easily be extended and there is a perpetual search for the next 'new, new thing'. These conditions are framework-setting and, as of early 2009, appear nearly irreversible in that finance continues to feed off mass savings in a deregulated, virtualized and border-crossing world even after the crisis. But these frame conditions are too general to explain the varying forms and direction of financial innovation in successive periods since the early 1980s. Or, put another way, within this general frame of facilitative conditions, the questions are about what happens, where and how. Our answer to these questions in the next two sections invokes Braudelesque ideas about conjuncture (between events and the *longue durée*) as the relevant span of time and to Lévi-Straussian ideas about bricolage as the unscientific process of improvisation. Together these concepts add two more conditions of innovation which help us to understand how financial intermediaries respond to opportunities created by specific sets of asset market conditions and retail identities and recently did so by creating long, fragile chains of innovation.

Meso-field: the conjuncture

We live in an era of very low predictability.

(Tony Blair, 8 January 2009, Paris, 'New World, New Capitalism' conference)

Tony Blair's post-crisis complaint conflates two separate developments. First, capitalism has been malfunctioning for all of us after the financial crisis and not responding to policy intervention. But also capitalism is not behaving as Blair expected it would to deliver growth and maintain employment. Blair and other members of the Western political class are surprised because they had an epochal concept of capitalism and no concept of conjuncture and therefore wrongly supposed that the conjunctural results of the 1990s or 2000s had epochal durability. If the distinction between (quasi-epochal) frame and conjuncture is important for social democratic analysis, it is crucial for understanding innovation which of course requires a (temporal and geographic) field where predictability and repeatability can be organized for a while. If facilitative conditions like deregulation, digital technology and changes in welfare provision constitute a sort of semi-permanent background frame, financial innovation also operates within a (more rapidly changing) conjunctural foreground whose field provides a distinct set of conditions around, for example, asset prices or retail products. Our argument is that the conjuncture is an important condition of innovation because it structures the immediate possibilities for and limitations of innovation.

Conjuncture can be understood as a distinctive but unstable combination of circumstances within which events and episodes happen to produce more quasi-resolution than permanent crisis. Our usage draws on Braudel (1982) in that it invokes the idea of multiple overlaid times and emphasizes the significance of something between events and the *longue durée* something astrological insofar as continuously changing arrangements of heavenly bodies have putative but unclear effects on earthly agents who may be influenced more by reading their horoscopes.

As a meso-economic field, a conjuncture is typically a four- to seven-year period partly defined by a capital market configuration of asset prices, flows of funds and interacting (competing, colluding) intermediaries. It is, in turn, supported by grand narrative, enacted by performance of key actors and then charged by mass subjectivities in societies like the US and UK where half have stock market savings and 70 per cent own houses. The narrative and performative elements ensure each conjuncture typically runs through a cycle of exuberance and asset price bubbles which fits with Keynes' and Minsky's perceptions about how market sentiment and lending behaviour determine changes in liquidity and asset prices so that the decision outcome connection is very variable. The agents include the masses and their representatives (states, mutual funds, pension funds and asset managers) as well as the elites.

Typically each new conjuncture crystallizes itself around different coupon instruments. The early 1980s saw the rise of the so-called secondary debt market, a newly constructed market for financial products where debt papers from sovereign debt holders were being recycled, generating great profit opportunities for many of the worlds' largest banks. In the second half of the 1980s that was overtaken by the junk bond craze and the leveraged buy-out madness that ended with the battle for RJR Nabisco between KKR and a number of other investment teams (see Burrough and Helyar, 1990). The early 1990s saw the rise of telecommunications and media as a new node for financial speculation which increasingly focused on equity, especially tech stock new issues which gradually became the Internet bubble in the late 1990s (Knee, 2006). The early twenty-first century gave rise to a new conjuncture, dependent on leverage and characterized by the use of derivatives with the securitization boom and the simultaneous rise of new actors – hedge funds, private equity funds and, in their wake, sovereign wealth funds.

In understanding these dynamic processes, we would argue against any general view that innovation drives the conjuncture. This is implicit in the conventional view of non-financial technical change in the broader economy, which supposedly slowly realizes the benefits of major innovations like electrical power. These arguments are central to ideas about economic growth implicit in work on business cycles and larger Kondratieff waves, also taken up by Schumpeter in the 1930s. The 'too much of a good thing' view of financial innovation represents a variant on that because innovation supposedly first helps to price risk and complete markets, then overshoots and ultimately helps to undermine certainty and paralyse credit markets, before they are turned into the stocks in trade of a new generation of market players embarking on the construction of a new set of financial innovations.

Rather, in our view, conjunctural opportunity structures the possibilities and limits of innovation and, in emphasizing this point, we endorse Schumpeter and others who emphasize the role of environment and context in innovation. The conjuncture after 2000 was not driven by the rediscovery of leverage (or borrowing to increase gains over an asset price cycle) which had previously figured in the late 1980s period of junk bonds. It was initiated by the US Federal Reserve's interest rate cut after the tech stock crash in the 2000s which made funds cheap and leverage more worthwhile. Improvisation then extended the field of application in the 2000s as debt was sold to banks using originate and distribute models, just as various techniques were carried forward into the 2000s from the 1980s, when US private equity general partners had first used limited liability partnerships to create two classes of equity holders, general and limited partners.

However, it is also the case that the conjuncture can be brought to an abrupt halt by the unintended consequences of financial innovation. A period when the specific forms of innovation and the conjuncture are mutually reinforcing regularly comes to an end with crisis, as was the case in 2008, and as has been demonstrated time and again by economic historians writing on the history of financial crises over the past 600 years (Galbraith, 1988; Kindleberger, 2000; Reinhardt and Rogoff, 2008). If innovation helps to shape the end of each conjuncture, so the form of the next conjuncture will in turn help define the opportunities and constraints for new kinds of financial innovation. It is also the case that in the next phase, as in previous ones, the conjuncture is shaped by narrative and politics as much as by technical finance and economics. Thus a conjuncture where the growth of financial markets is seen as conferring social as well as economic benefits is replaced by one where new financial architecture and re-regulation reining in unfettered finance are central to the narrative.

It should be clear that we are not arguing there is a functional, mechanical and automatic link between the conjunctural context and outcomes but think that, in a preliminary way, innovation could be defined as the attempt by financial intermediaries (within a given frame) to find profit by exploiting a conjunctural opportunity and to stop loss by recognizing conjunctural change in real time. The necessary qualification is that this is done under specific meso-technical and political conditions which give innovation its distinctive character and together define two kinds of collective imperative for senior intermediaries whose starting positions are typically themselves the transient legacy of previous periods of change. First, they must mobilize resources and upscale quickly to capture high margins before commodification sets in later in a short product cycle, generally four to seven years. Second, they must organize a political division of labour or ownership which diverts cash to well-positioned elite intermediaries (Godechot, 2008).

In the absence of a general system of property rights in financial innovation, novelty and rapid upscaling are critical because doing the same thing year after year brings in imitators and encourages commodification which reduces first-mover high profits for the institution and high bonuses for the individual. While newness in itself is no guarantee of success, novelty matters within each conjuncture. This incidentally also limits collective memory and respect for older, established members among intermediary groups. More exactly, what matters is scalable differentiation because the high margins on financial innovation are generally taken early in the product cycle. In a world where profit arithmetically equals margins times volume, the intermediaries of the financial sector (just like big pharmaceutical firms) need not have striking originality but can instead pursue differentiation and mass sales through a succession of blockbusters. The last conjuncture's blockbuster was securitization in the wholesale markets which spawned umpteen differentiations that could be scaled up, generating large volume and fees, above all because they connected with retail feedstock from mass saving and borrowing. As in pharma, the new blockbuster is often only trivially different from its precursors and competitors. Thus, the technique of securitization was not new because it dated from the 1930s and was first used on any scale in the US housing market in the 1970s. In the 1980s the BIS (1986) identified securitization as a key financial innovation yet it took another decade or more for its use to become widespread (Gotham, forthcoming). As Ertürk and Solari (2007) emphasize, upscaling was associated with institutional change as the banks reinvented themselves, with retail banks less dependent on intermediation as they shifted into the selling of mass financial products which generated retail feedstock. Meanwhile investment banks increased proprietary trading activities in wholesale markets including (new) instruments like derivatives.

But the conditions here are as much political as technical because elite intermediaries operate partly by targeting high returns in new upscalable activities and partly by constructing political divisions of labour and ownership which redistribute rewards to those like the head of the dealing room or the private equity general partner who position themselves to capture a substantial share of the returns. If we then distinguish between the position and the person occupying that position, we can guard against any tendency heroically to overestimate the efficacy of the individual agent. The rise and fall of various bonus-reaping positions in different conjunctures falls outside the agentic powers of any one individual. However, given a particular conjuncture and the hierarchy of positions that conjuncture entails, a strategic game takes place that is usually won by those with the properties required by these specific positions. Of course, the nature of those positions, the kind of individual properties (and hence people) required is very much determined by the conjuncture.

The political division of labour is emphasized by Godechot (2008) in his seminal article which represents the head of the dealing room as someone, like the putter-out in the industrial revolution, who creates a division of labour from which he benefits because the head makes himself indispensable as the only person who understands the whole business. In a related kind of argument, Froud, Johal, Leaver and Williams (2008) suggest that the general partner in private equity organizes a hierarchy of claims. Returns to debt are capped so as to benefit equity holders and subordinate outside equity investors disadvantaged under the '2 and 20' fee structure which generates handsome cash returns for the general partner regardless of success. In a second attempt at definition, financial innovation could be described as a political game of positioning played by initially well-situated and then well-adapted elite intermediaries. However, success in any one round of the game is no guarantee of success in the next as redundant heads of dealing rooms and embarrassed private equity partners now know; and success in any one round depends on some work of improvisation.

Bricolage (not rationality)

> [A]s long as the music is playing, you've got to get up and dance. We're still dancing.
> *(Chuck Prince, CEO of Citigroup,* Financial Times, *9 July 2007)*

Chuck Prince's now infamous remarks, a few weeks before the start of the credit crunch in the summer of 2007, gives us financial innovation in one image as a dance to the music of the time. Our qualification would be that the music is not in strict tempo and the dance movements are improvised. Our analysis of the frame and conjuncture conditions in the previous two sections brings out the complexities of time(s) but we must now consider the agent's work of flexibility, creativity and opportunism along the innovation chain. We understand this as bricolage but not in the common usage where bricolage associates with do-it-yourself bodging and making things from junk. Instead, we would use bricolage in a more precise Lévi-Straussian sense where, in terms of thought process, bricolage is opposed to the scientific mode of thinking, encompassing in this case both *techné* and *episteme*, and seems to be, in its practical orientation and its implicit criticism of the end means model of human action, more related to *metis* as described by the anthropologist James Scott (1998).

The term 'bricolage' has been previously and occasionally used in financial journalism or social studies of finance. Thus, Nicholas Hildyard (2008), writing for the Cornerhouse NGO, uses 'financial bricolage' as a descriptor of what finance was doing before the crash. More analytically, a concept of bricolage figures in the work of social studies of finance authors like MacKenzie or Beunza and Stark. MacKenzie (2003) uses the notion of bricolage and assimilates it into a rationalist frame as theoretically guided (not 'random') bricolage. Beunza and Stark (2003) too have employed 'bricolage' to describe the micro-level responses of financial agents to changing circumstances. In their narrative, bricolage is synonymous with 'improvisation', a mode of human action that functions as a fall-back when rational designs fall apart and as such is seen as a 'derived' or second-best type of human activity. Our concept of bricolage is rather different because we see it as a stand-alone activity which is in no way a poor substitute for (more) rational ways of knowing.

This is the point that Lévi-Strauss makes when he distinguishes rationalistic science from bricolage as a 'parallel mode of acquiring knowledge' (1966 [1962], p. 13). Bricolage involves 'build[ing] up structures by fitting together events, or rather the remains of events, while science, "in operation" simply by virtue of coming into being, creates its means and results in the form of events, thanks to the structures which it is constantly elaborating and which are its hypotheses and theories (Lévi-Strauss, 1966, p. 22). Lévi-Strauss distinguishes between the scientist and the bricoleur 'by the inverse functions which they assign to events and structures as ends and means, the scientist creating events (changing the world) by means of structures and the "bricoleur" creating structures by means of events' (ibid., p. 22). Lévi-Strauss's characterization of 'science' is inadequate or even sometimes misleading, that is not immediately a problem because the important point is his insistence that there is no implied negative value judgement of or inferred inferiority in bricolage compared with 'science'.

Of course, the notion of bricolage has been incisively used in areas of innovation outside finance. For example, Ciborra (2002) challenges heroic notions of the development of ICTs in helping firms establish a competitive advantage, emphasizing imitation rather than originality as the main force explaining development and uptake of new technologies. Using examples including the precursors to the internet, Ciborra argues that strategic information systems emerged where 'early adopters are able to recognize, in use, some idiosyncratic features that were ignored, devalued or simply unplanned' (Ciborra, 2002, p. 44). With bricolage, 'the practices and the situations disclose new uses and applications of the technology and the things' (Ciborra, 2002, p. 49); according to Ciborra, such practices are 'highly situated', exploiting local context and resources (ibid., p. 50).

We argue that bricolage has a particular double relevance to the process of *financial* innovation because it both describes the result of innovation, which in recent conjunctures has become a series of fragile long chains and it also characterizes the activity of innovation by the bricoleur at one nodal point in a chain. In emphasizing bricolage in this way we are challenging the dominant perspective on financial innovation in mainstream finance, social studies of finance and Marxist political economy which, all in different ways, argue or imply that science (represented by finance theory) or some other form of rationality (like class interest calculation) either is financial innovation or drives financial innovation. Against this, our argument is that financial innovation is contingent, resourceful and context-dependent, because bricolage in each new conjuncture reconstructs a world that escapes all rationalistic schemas. This point is practically important because it implies the problem lies with the current form of innovation (not too much innovation of the wrong kind): bricolage in a rapidly changing conjuncture produces inherently fragile long-chain innovation.

If we look back at the past conjuncture, the process of innovation could be defined holistically as a kind of supply-side bricolage to escape demand constraints through devising products which are either expandable or universal at the retail level and which connect the most mundane transaction to wholesale markets in the 'capitalization of everything' (Leyshon and Thrift, 2007). The universal financial product for the firm is the hedge because, as long as exchange rates, interest rates, fuel and commodity prices fluctuate, most firms will want to do some hedging. Meanwhile, at the retail level, consumers (hope to) escape the tyranny of earned income through taking out universal products such as pensions, revolving loans, mortgages and other financial products. A third piece of financial technique feeding into the bricolage of the twenty-first century was the security. Transforming illiquid and opaque income streams like mortgage payments, credit card payments, car loan payments and so on into tradable assets through the technique of securitization opened up huge fee-earning possibilities for financial intermediaries that stretched many different financial markets. The technical nature of the innovations after the mid-1980s was that, on the basis of this demand, in the last conjuncture it was possible to tier wholesale financial transactions one upon the other. Hedging transactions led to an almost infinite number of further derivative contracts of different kinds, just as retail loans to households provide the feedstock for CDOs and so on.

In this way, finance feeds finance in numerous (connected) long chains on a basis of precariously self-acting retail subjectivities, and consequently wholesale inventiveness and finance are not constrained by lack of demand until the conjuncture ends as the long chains collapse. On the upswing in the last conjuncture, the boosters celebrated the capacity of long chains to disperse risk without understanding the fragility of such chains because they had many points of disruption. If it had not been retail subprime mortgages and wholesale mortgage-backed securities, it would have been something else. If financial innovation did not produce a system, what went wrong was not a 'system accident' in the sense discussed by Charles Perrow (1999) and others in their analysis of Challenger, Three Mile Island and other catastrophes where the 'unanticipated interaction of multiple failures' leads to a failure of organizational intelligence. As our two examples illustrated, there never was a system or systems, only a ramshackle series of chain connections between heterogeneous objects found, constructed and imagined by a multiplicity of individuals and groups whose conduct was only temporarily aligned. Thus securitization of home loans and private equity, for example, were part of different long chains of financial innovation but they interconnect in several ways. Both are dependent on credit as the emblem of the conjuncture and the continuing willingness of overlapping buyers in these markets to take up unbundled debt products. Moreover, any crisis of confidence associated with financial products in one chain has contagious effects in others, though this point has not been understood by those who talk as though the banks have a quantum of bad assets as they originally had a small parcel of subprime lending.

Agents use justifications about marketizing risk, diversifying portfolios, maximizing returns or optimizing rewards, but these rationalizations are (just like shareholder value in the giant corporation) not realizable programmes, only rhetorics with effects. The practical issue for intermediaries is that a long chain of activity has a multiplicity of points or nodes where well-placed intermediaries are confronted with ever-changing conditions in each new conjuncture. The bricoleur is then the individual or group which turns the nodal possibility into a profitable position by using whatever instruments are to hand to create a business model from product or process. The 'bricoleur' is adept at performing a large number of diverse tasks; but, unlike the engineer, he does not subordinate each of them to the availability of raw materials and tools conceived and procured for the purpose of the project. His universe of instruments is closed and the rules of his game are always to make do with 'whatever is at hand', that is to say with a set of tools and materials which is always finite and is also heterogeneous because what it contains bears no relation to the current project, or indeed to any particular project, but is the contingent result of all the occasions there have been to renew or enrich the stock or to maintain it with the remains of previous constructions or destructions (Lévi-Strauss, 1966, p. 17).

This conceptualization is radical because it implies that the work of financial innovation does not have a one-on-one correspondence with or any necessary basis in a specific knowledge or technology; new instruments are less central than they seem to be in much obsessive recent discussion of the credit crunch because instruments are only part of the process and often conjuncture-specific. Not all acts of bricolage have the same outcomes: only some bricolage involves and implies a conceptual shift in the nature of products or a redefinition in the relation between products, parties and markets, while similar forms of bricolage in different conjunctures can give rise to divergent outcomes. Finally, it is worthwhile remembering that bricolage is a way of reconceptualizing what agents do, whereas innovation in financial economics is a term of praise used by third parties to denote the assumed qualities of a new product and which, in retrospect, is attached to the heroic innovator or heroic technique as a title of praise. Innovation in this last sense is an illusion to be dissipated or, at least, understood in social constructionist terms as something 'in the eye of the beholder'.

(Interim) conclusion

The re-conceptualization of financial innovation set out above is an argument rather than a report on the results of primary research. In the next stage, empirical work will play an essential role in exploring and developing this conceptualization further, but our intention in this chapter has been to focus on the concept because many academic understandings of financial innovation have been characterized more by assertion than by interrogation. The imperative to understand financial innovation is not purely academic; as politicians and regulators seek to outline new regulatory regimes and political frameworks for the finance sector, these are partly framed by the implicit assumptions about what exactly happened. While interesting texts written by journalists and former insiders are emerging which provide first-hand accounts of specific decisions, actions and personalities (see, for example, Tett's *Fool's Gold*, 2009, which focuses on Morgan Stanley), these do not provide any broader conceptualization that puts such micro-level detail into a meso- and macro-context.

By way of a conclusion to this conceptualization stage of our work, we have argued that financial innovation is not what it seems or, more precisely, not as it has been represented in a rationalistic frame. It is not the functionalist answer to real world deviances of financial markets from the neoclassical market model nor is it the product of heroic academic theorists or intermediaries. Instead, it is the outcome (or the emergent property) of the accidental coming together of structural preconditions, conjunctural situations and a repository of techniques, heuristic devices and skills that together form the resources of the cadre of (successful and unsuccessful) bricoleurs whose innovation is constructing chains.

As such, this view of innovation looks strikingly similar to the famous 'new combinations' definition of innovation given by Schumpeter in his 1934 classic. According to Schumpeter, there was nothing heroic about innovation nor could it be predicted or facilitated because entrepreneurs are lucky as much as smart. Innovation allows us to do things we could not do, combines different elements of the everyday and stumbles into novelty which, under happy conditions, is valued by others in hindsight as a true innovation. Our chapter shows how we can come to similar conclusions without buying into the premises of Austrian economics about the cognitive handicaps of human agents and the unintended information-processing capacities of collective arrangements such as markets. And Schumpeter's work raises many issues which remain relevant to future research on financial intermediaries which needs, for example, to consider the role of those who are outsiders by cultural identity, work history or generation. What is quite striking is that there is much that scholars of financial innovation can learn from those who have looked at other kinds of technology, including Edgerton's (2008) argument that it is the uses not the apparent inventions that should be the focus or Barry's (2001) concept of anti-invention which emphasizes private interests in the process of technological change of many kinds.

The redefinition of innovation points up the futility of castigating bankers and financiers for their 'greed' and turning the credit crisis into a morality play that calls into question the values of our so-called 'narcissistic societies'. No doubt, many investment bankers and hedge fund managers behaved egregiously and some were greedy. But that does not mean intermediaries are *solely* to blame for the banking crisis. At the level of individual agency, the main distinguishing characteristic of financial intermediaries is that they are well positioned to extract value from the chains of innovation, though they are all dancing to an irregular tune and must fear what happens when the music stops. Of course, when long chains of innovation fall apart there are many real losers, but the challenge is to avoid simple narratives of blame and causality which may be politically convenient but which in practice imply rather narrow prescriptions focused on the structure of compensation packages for bankers and traders, the regulation of particular financial instruments and so on. That is not to say that such proposals lack merit but equally they do not, even collectively, imply any radical response to the nature of the crisis. The questions asked by politicians, regulators and academics should be not simplistic ones about who is to blame, but they should be about the inherent fragility of bricolage in a changing conjuncture.

If, in quasi-moral terms, it is this whole form of innovation which is to blame, then it will be difficult to find regulatory 'solutions' to financial innovation. Many argue for a re-regulation of financial markets without recognizing the frame and conjuncture nature of innovation. The problem is that, in each new conjuncture, the regulators find themselves in the position of generals fighting the last war against irregulars who improvise new tactics and strategies. Most proposed solutions do not address the underlying, structural conditions, in particular the global 'savings glut'.

As long as there are huge amounts of savings and loans to process, there will be new opportunities for well-situated agents to practise bricolage. Many of the (discredited) household names of the financial markets of today will reinvent themselves to suit the new conjuncture of tomorrow, just as new groups of financial intermediaries will emerge with the opportunities a new conjuncture brings. It is less certain whether their critics have the same capacity for reinvention. A more effective response requires a narrative that goes beyond moral indignation about the consequences of bricolage and engages with the frame and conjuncture that facilitate its particular form.

Note

1 An SPV (special purpose vehicle) is a legal entity specially created to fulfil some legal and/or financial function. It may be wholly or partly owned by another legal entity, such as a public company. SPVs are commonly used in securitization to separate the parent legally from the obligations that arise from the securitization.

References

Aglietta, M. (2008). New trends in corporate governance: The prominent role of the long run investor. *Competition and Change*, 12(2), 203–22.
Allen, F. and Gale, D. (1994). *Financial innovation and risk sharing*. Cambridge, MA: MIT Press.
Amable, B. (2003). *The diversity of modern capitalism*. Oxford: Oxford University Press.
Artus, P. and de Boissieu, C. (1988). The process of financial innovation: Causes, forms and consequences. In A. Heertje (Ed.), *Innovation, technology and finance*. Oxford: Blackwell.
Augar, P. (2001). *The death of gentlemanly capitalism: The rise and fall of London's investment banks*. London: Penguin.
Augar, P. (2005). *The greed merchants: How the investment banks played the free market game*. London: Penguin.
Barry, A. (2001). *Political machines: Governing a technological society*. London: Athlone.
Bernanke, B. (2007). Regulation and innovation. Speech to the Federal Reserve Bank of Atlanta's 2007 Financial Markets Conference, 15 May, available at: http://www.federalreserve.gov/newsevents/speech/bernanke20070515a.htm.
Bernanke, B. (2009). The crisis and the policy response. Speech given at the LSE, London 13 January. Available at: http://www.federalreserve.gov/newsevents/speech/bernanke20090113a.htm.
Bernstein, P. L. (1992). *Capital ideas: The improbable origins of modern Wall Street*. New York: The Free Press.
Beunza, D. and Stark, D. (2003). The organization of responsiveness: Innovation and recovery in the trading rooms of Lower Manhattan. *Socio-Economic Review*, 1(2), 135–64.

BIS (1986). *Recent innovations in international banking.* Basel: Bank for International Settlements.
BIS (2008). *78th annual report.* Basel: Bank for International Settlements.
Blundell-Wignall, A. (2007). *Structured products: Implications for financial markets.* Paris: OECD.
Bookstaber, R. (2007). *A demon of our own design: Markets, hedge funds and the perils of financial innovation.* Hoboken, NJ: Wiley.
Braudel, F. (1982). History and time spans. In *Essays by Braudel* (trans. Sarah Matthews). Chicago, IL: University of Chicago Press.
Burrough, B. and Helyar, J. (1990). *Barbarians at the gate: The fall of RJR Nabisco.* New York: Harper & Row.
Ciborra, C. (2002). *The labyrinths of information: Challenging the wisdom of systems.* Oxford: Oxford University Press.
de Goede, M. (2001). Discourses of scientific finance and the failure of Long-Term Capital Management. *New Political Economy, 6*(2), 149–70.
de Goede, M. (2005). *Virtue, fortune and faith: A genealogy of finance.* Minneapolis, MN: University of Minnesota Press.
Duménil, G. and Lévy, D. (2004). Neo-liberal income trends: Wealth, class and ownership in the USA. *New Left Review, 30* (November-December), 105–33.
Dunbar, N. (1999). *Inventing money: The story of Long-Term Capital Management and the legends behind it.* Chichester: Wiley.
Edgerton, D. (2008). *The shock of the old: Technology and global history since 1900.* London: Profile Books.
Ellis, C. (2008). *The partnership: The making of Goldman Sachs.* Harmondsworth: Penguin.
Engelen, E. (2008). The case for financialization. *Competition and Change, 12*(2), 111–9.
Engelen, E. and Konings, M. (forthcoming). Financial capitalism resurgent: Comparative institutionalism and the challenges of financialization. In G. Morgan J. Campbell, C. Crouch, O. K. Pedersen and R. Whitley (Eds.), *The Oxford handbook of comparative institutional analysis.* Oxford: Oxford University Press.
Ertürk, I. and Solari, S. (2007). The reinvention of banks. *New Political Economy, 12*(3), 369–88.
Ertürk, I., Froud, J., Johal, S., Leaver, A. and Williams, K. (2008). *Financialization at work. Key texts and commentary.* London: Routledge.
Folkman, P., Froud, J., Johal, S. and Williams, K. (2007). Working for themselves. Capital market intermediaries and present day capitalism. *Business History, 49*(4), 552–72.
Froud, J., Johal, S., Leaver, A. and Williams, K. (2006). *Financialization and strategy: Narrative and numbers.* London: Routledge.
Froud, J., Johal, S., Leaver, A. and Williams, K. (2008). Ownership matters: Private equity and the political division of ownership. *CRESC Working Paper no. 61*, University of Manchester: CRESC.
FSA (2007). FSA publishes feedback and further consultation on Listing Reviews for Investment Entities. Press release, 29 June. London: Financial Services Authority.
Galbraith, J. K. (1988). *The great crash of 1929.* New York: Houghton Mifflin.
Galbraith, J. K. (1990). *A short history of financial euphoria.* New York: Penguin.
Godechot, O. (2008). What do heads of dealing rooms do? The social capital of internal entrepreneurs. In M. Savage and K. Williams (Eds.), *Remembering elites.* Oxford: Blackwell.
Gotham, K. F. (forthcoming). Creating liquidity out of spatial fixity: The secondary circuit of capital and the evolving subprime mortgage crisis. *International Journal of Urban and Regional Research.*
Grahl, J. and Lysandrou, P. (2003). Sand in the wheels or spanner in the works? The Tobin tax and global finance. *Cambridge Journal of Economics, 27,* 597–621.
Hacker, J. (2006). *The great risk shift: The assault on American jobs, families, health care, and retirement – and how you can fight back.* Oxford: Oxford University Press.
Hall, P. A. and Soskice, D. (Eds.) (2001). *Varieties of capitalism: The institutional foundations of comparative advantage.* Oxford: Oxford University Press.
Hamilton, R., Jenkinson, N. and Penalver, A. (2007). Innovation and integration in financial markets and the implications for financial stability. In C. Kent and J. Lawson (Eds.), *The structure and resilience of the financial system.* Canberra: Reserve Bank of Australia.
Haug, E. G. and Taleb, N. N. (2008). Why we have never used the Black-Scholes-Merton option pricing formula. Fourth version. January 2008. Available at SSRN: http://ssrn.com/abstract=1012075.
Helleiner, E. (1994). *States and the re-emergence of global finance: From Bretton Woods to the 1990s.* Ithaca, NY: Cornell University Press.
Hildyard, N. (2008). *A (crumbling) wall of money: Financial bricolage, derivatives and power.* Sturminster Newton: The Cornerhouse. Available at: http://www.thecornerhouse.org.uk/summary.shtml?x= 562658.
IFSL (2008). *Sovereign wealth funds.* London: IFSL.

IMD (2008). *CDO creative balance sheet risk management*. IMD -1-0261. Lausanne: IMD.
IMF (2007). *Global financial stability report, November 2007*. Washington, DC: International Monetary Fund.
Jenkinson, N., Penalver, A. and Vause, N. (2008). Financial innovation: What have we learnt? In P. Bloxham and C. Kent (Eds.), *Lessons from the financial turmoil of 2007 and 2008*. Canberra: Reserve Bank of Australia.
Judt, T. (2005). *Postwar: A history of Europe since 1945*. London: Penguin.
Kindleberger, C. P. (2000). *Mania, panics, and crashes: A history of financial crises*. New York: Wiley.
Konings, M. (2008). The institutional foundations of US structural power in international finance: From the re-emergence of global finance to the monetarist turn. *Review of International Political Economy*, 15(1), 35–61.
Knee, J. (2006). *The accidental investment banker: Inside the decade that transformed Wall Street*. New York: Oxford University Press.
Knorr Cetina, K. and Preda, A. (Eds.) (2004). *The sociology of financial markets*. Oxford: Oxford University Press.
Langley, P. (2008). *The everyday life of global finance: Saving and borrowing in Anglo-America*. Oxford: Oxford University Press.
Lazonick, W. (2002). The innovative firm. In J. Fagerberg, D. C. Mowery and R. R. Nelson (Eds.), *The Oxford handbook of innovation*. Oxford: Oxford University Press.
Levi-Strauss, C. (1966). *The savage mind* (Trans. from *La Pensée sauvage*, Paris, 1962). Chicago: University of Chicago Press.
Leyshon, A. and Thrift, N. (2007). The capitalisation of almost everything: The future of finance and capitalism. Paper presented at the IWGF workshop on Financialization, London, 12-13 February.
Lowenstein, R. (2001). *When genius failed: The rise and fall of Long-Term Capital Management*. New York: Random House.
MacKenzie, D. (2003). An equation and its worlds: Bricolage, exemplars, disunity and performativity in financial economics. *Social Studies of Science*, 33(6), 831–68.
MacKenzie, D. (2006). *An engine, not a camera: How financial models shape markets*. Cambridge, MA: MIT Press.
McKinsey Global Institute (2007). *Mapping the global capital market. Third annual report*. New York: McKinsey. Available at: http://www.mckinsey.com/mgi/publications/third_annual_report/ index.asp.
Manning, R. D. (2000). *Credit card nation*. New York: Basic Books.
Merton, R. C. (1973). Theory of rational option pricing. *Bell Journal of Economics and Management Science*, 4(1), 141–83.
Merton, R. C. (1992). Financial innovation and economic performance. *Journal of Applied Corporate Finance*, 4(4), 12–22.
Merton, R. C. (1995). Financial innovation and the management and regulation of financial institutions. *Journal of Banking and Finance*, 19, 461–81.
Miller, M. H. (1986). Financial innovation: the last twenty years and the next. *The Journal of Financial and Quantitative Analysis*, 21(4), 459–71.
Molyneux, P. and Shamroukh, N. (1999). *Financial innovation*. Chichester: Wiley.
Nelson, R. R. (Ed.) (1993) *National innovation systems: A comparative analysis*. New York: Oxford University Press.
OECD (1997). *National innovation systems*. Paris: OECD.
O'Sullivan, M. (2002). Finance and innovation. In J. Fagerberg, D. C. Mowery and R. R. Nelson (Eds.), *The Oxford handbook of innovation*. Oxford: Oxford University Press.
Perrow, C. (1999). *Normal accidents: Living with high risk technologies*. Princeton, NJ: Princeton University Press.
Reinhart, C. M. and Rogoff, K. S. (2008). This time is different: A panoramic view of eight centuries of financial crises. *NBER paper No. 13882*, March. Available at: http://www.nber.org/papers/w13882.
Ross, S. A. (1989). Institutional markets, financial marketing and financial innovation. *Journal of Finance*, 44(3), 541–56.
Schumpeter, J. A. (1961 [1934]). *The theory of economic development: An enquiry into profits, capital, credit, interest and the business cycle*. New York: Oxford University Press.
Scott, J. (1998). *Seeing like a state: How certain schemes to improve the human condition have failed*. New Haven, CT, and London: Yale University Press.
Shiller, R. J. (2004). Radical financial innovation. *Cowles Foundation Discussion Paper no. 1461*. Yale University.
Silber, W. L. (1983). The process of financial innovation. *American Economic Review*, 73(2), 89–95.
Singer, D. A. (2007). *Regulating capital: Setting standards for the international financial system*. Ithaca, NY: Cornell University Press.

Soros, G. (2003). *The alchemy of finance*. New York: Simon & Schuster.
Stockhammer, E. (2008). Some stylized facts on the finance-dominated accumulation regime. *Competition and Change, 12*(2), 184–202.
Taleb, N. N. (2007). *The black swan: The impact of the highly improbable*. New York: Random House.
Tett, G. (2009). *Fool's gold*. London: Little, Brown.
Tufano, P. (2002). Financial innovation. In G. M. Constantinides, M. Harris and R. M. Stulz (Eds.), *Handbook of the economics of finance*. (Vol. 1, part 1, pp. 307–35). Amsterdam: Elsevier.
Turner, A. (2009). The financial crisis and the future of financial regulation. Speech to *The Economists* Inaugural City Lecture, 21 January. Available at: http://www.fsa.gov.uk/pages/Library/Communication/Speeches/2009/ 0121_at.shtml.
Van Horne, J. C. (1985). Of financial innovations and excesses. *The Journal of Finance, 40*(3), 621–31.
Vinals, J. and Berges, A. (1988). Financial innovation and capital formation. In Heertje (Ed.), *Innovation, technology and finance*. Oxford: Blackwell.
White, L. J. (1996). Technological change, financial innovation and financial regulation in the US: The challenges for public policy. *Center for Financial Institutions Working Papers 97–33*. University of Pennsylvania, Wharton School Center for Financial Institutions.

6

Europe's toxic twins
Government debt in financialized times

Daniela Gabor and Cornel Ban

This chapter explores the links between the systemic shift to market-based finance and states' fiscal policy constraints. We draw on the literature on 'financialization' to introduce the concept of the 'collateral motive' – investors' demand for government bonds to mobilize as collateral in secured funding markets – and connect it to the shift to transnational, market-based, collateral-intensive banking. The resulting interdependence between banks and states has played a pivotal role in fiscal policy convergence around austerity. This policy outcome cannot be fully understood without analysing the processes through which impatient collateral management ignited a run on sovereign bond markets. Sudden stops left Eurozone governments as the only actors who could attempt to stabilize sovereign debt markets via austerity, at least until Mario Draghi promised to do whatever it takes.

Introduction

> it is often forgotten that collateral does not move by itself ... essentially, in the world of collateral, the bank funding desk is the pump.
>
> *(ICMA European Repo Council, 2014)*

Since the European sovereign debt crisis, it is common to deplore, pontificate about and seek to separate the toxic twins of Europe: governments and their banks, tied together in a deadly embrace through government bond markets. In the European periphery, the argument goes, worsening sovereign creditworthiness translated into poorly performing government bond markets that in turn showed up on the balance sheet of their (weak) banks, harming lending and exacerbating the crisis. Poor bank performance raised the prospect of bank rescues and so on, in a 'diabolical bailout loop' (Brunnermeier *et al.*, 2015).

For all their virtues, such accounts sideline the structural changes in finance that have bonded governments to their banks. Contrary to the common wisdom of a 'toxic' pact 'we guarantee your liabilities, you buy our debt', we stress the importance of the shift to market-based banking and financial innovations that transformed government bonds into high-quality collateral for raising short-term market funding. This has left the bond markets of European sovereigns increasingly vulnerable to sudden stops in capital flows. Without explicit central bank support, sudden stops pressure governments to adopt fiscal consolidations.

In this chapter we develop this argument by extending Ian Hardie's (2011) framework for analysing the financialization of government bonds markets in emerging countries. We introduce an additional dimension of investor loyalty in sovereign bond markets, which we term the collateral motive – investor demand for government bonds to meet funding or regulatory needs – and we link it to the increasing dominance of collateral-intensive banking models (Gabor and Ban, 2015; Cetorelli and Goldberg, 2012; Engelen et al., 2011; Hardie and Howarth, 2009; Pozsar et al., 2010). In sum, demand for sovereign bonds to use as collateral for the funding of the financial sector deepens government bond markets while eroding investors' loyalty. Sovereign risk affects banks' funding conditions such that banks' loyalty towards foreign or own governments is closely tied to the collateral (and safe asset) qualities of that debt. Changing perceptions of collateral quality forces governments to adopt fiscal austerity unless central banks commit to reverse the sudden stop. Absent a central bank willing to do so, as countries in the Eurozone have found out, and austerity appears as the only policy solution.

Austerity and financialization in government bond markets

The idea that sovereign bond markets constrain governments is not new. In a well-known scholarly account, Mosley (2000) persuasively showed that international financial markets can 'react dramatically' to government policies, but only do so in response to volatility in inflation or budget deficits. Confronted with such dramatic reactions, governments may have to please markets even if these are suspected of speculative intentions (Corsetti et al., 2012). Yet this is a self-defeating strategy when markets anticipate fiscal tightening to have negative growth consequences, further affecting government revenue and public debt sustainability. As a result, markets become 'schizophrenic', increasingly unable to distinguish between fundamentals and uncertainty in the pricing of sovereign risk (de Grauwe and Ji, 2012), a view accepted as far as the IMF (Ban, 2015). Doubts about the government's ability to service its debts become self-fulfilling (Gros, 2012), a development which in the Eurozone crisis helped bolster the 'expansionary austerity' thesis within influential niches of the EU crisis management elites (Helgadóttir, 2015; Blyth, 2013).

In these accounts, the 'market' is conceived of as a black box to which governments feed austerity plans and out come conflicting signals. But this black box that cannot explain why Spanish banks continued to buy Spanish government bonds or why French banks stopped doing so in early 2012, nor can it incorporate analytically the pervasive concerns with the interdependence between sovereigns and their banking systems, so often voiced in the European crisis (Buiter and Rahbari, 2012; Acharya and Viswanathan, 2011). Ian Hardie's (2011) research on the financialization of sovereign bond markets in emerging countries can unpack this black box because it explicitly considers the links between distinctive types of market participants, structural market features and governments' ability to undertake discretionary fiscal policies.

The core of Hardie's argument is that bond markets that attract short-term investors make it hard for governments to adopt countercyclical policies in recessions. Hardie defines financialization as 'the ability to trade risk', a process that affects both the market structure and market actors. The financialization of market structure is functionally equivalent to its liquidity: liquid markets increase the ability to trade risk because they allow frequent selling and buying with minimum price changes. It is such markets that attract impatient investors guided by short-term strategies. The increasing presence of financialized investors increases market liquidity, further financializing the market structure. In contrast, loyal investors that buy government bonds to hold to maturity have little incentive to trade and thus reduce market liquidity. As Hardie put it 'more (less) financialised investors are likely to increase (decrease) the financialization of market structure and more financialised markets attract more financialised investors'.

Critically, financialization puts new constraints on the state. Impatient investors undermine government debt sustainability because they tend to exit sovereign bonds markets rapidly when confronted with uncertain conditions. Conversely, loyal investors act as a stabilizing factor in times of crisis, preserving governments' ability to borrow. Although Hardie (2011) does not use the term explicitly, the distinction between loyal and 'impatient' investors sheds light onto the anatomy of sudden stops in sovereign bond markets, contributing to a growing literature that attributes sudden stops to resident capital flight (Rothenberg and Warnock, 2011) or to non-resident withdrawal from high-yielding markets (Gabor, 2012; Broner et al., 2011). If patient finance is what states need in hard times, the important question then becomes what makes investors loyal during a crisis.

Hardie's comparison of domestic banks in Brazil, Lebanon and Turkey suggests that loyalty has several regulatory and structural dimensions. The first is *relative exposure*. If banks hold significant portfolios of government debt relative to their overall balance sheet or the market size, they will face difficulties in exiting during a crisis. Regulatory caps on daily sale volumes or abrupt price changes, if banks try to sell large volumes, will cement banks' patience even when a sudden stop is anticipated. Some banks may not even have the option of exiting because their sovereign holdings are too high to liquidate. In contrast to the 'home bias'[1] literature that questions the benefits of banks' preference for home sovereign debt (see Fidora et al., 2007), the financialization lens suggests that the higher the relative exposure, the more loyal the bank and the lower the possibility that a sudden stop materializes.

Second, investors will be more loyal if they do not have *placement alternatives* readily available. In many less developed financial markets, banks have access to a narrow range of financial products, often with lower returns that government bonds. Therefore, even if banks can meet exit costs, they will remain loyal to preserve long-term profitability. Finally, a further important element is the ability to avoid *mark-to-market valuation*. Banks will buy during periods of market distress if they can hold sovereign bonds in the banking book rather than the trading book,[2] because the latter values bonds at market price (as opposed to the original buy value), exposing banks to market volatility. Conversely, holding bonds in the banking book discourages banks from selling since the sale would be accounted at market price, usually lower in a crisis (bar exceptional circumstances when a possible default is expected). Thus, banks that hold assets to maturity in the banking book are unlikely to lend these to impatient traders for shorting because the banking book valuation reduces the appeal of market volatility. In short, governments face significant challenges for funding deficits in financialized markets where investors have low relative exposure, readily available alternative investments and are subject to mark-to-market accounting practices.

Hardie warns that his insights did not directly apply to high-income countries because of their 'safe-haven status'. Even impatient investors prefer the liquidity of such government bonds during crisis, a widespread view in the literature (Dow, 2012), at least until the European sovereign debt crisis. Safety becomes the overriding motive for holding bonds, and trumps the determinants of loyalty discussed above. Without the constraint of bond markets, governments decide the fiscal path *a la* varieties of capitalism, as described above.

However, we argue, Hardie's theoretical framework can enrich the 'flight to safety' account if it includes an additional dimension of investor loyalty arising from the shift to collateral-intensive (shadow) banking. We term this the collateral motive: investors mobilize government bonds as collateral to access secured funding markets.

The collateral motive and the financialization of government bond markets

The framework we propose ties the collateral motive to fiscal policy choices in Europe in three steps. First, we explain how the changing nature of banking in high-income European countries during the decade prior to the crisis transformed sovereign bond markets into collateral markets and governments into providers of the most desired type of collateral – safe assets. Then, we show how in these conditions collateral management cultivated investor disloyalty, generating a coordination problem involving governments and their banking systems. We conclude by arguing that in the particular conditions of the European monetary union, this coordination problem could only be resolved by frontloading fiscal consolidation.

It is now widely agreed that banking models in high-income countries have changed. The outdated view of banks simply gathering domestic savings to lend out to domestic companies has been replaced with banking as an increasingly transnational, market-based and collateral-intensive activity (Gabor and Ban, 2015; Hardie et al., 2013; Gourinchas and Jeanne, 2012; Engelen et al., 2011). The IMF now treats global banks as key nodes in complex cross-border networks of international finance, super-spreaders of systemic risk though complex business models that involve yield search, tax and regulatory arbitrage (see Gabor, 2015). Transnational banks move liquidity through internal capital markets (Cetorelli and Goldberg, 2012) and rely on diverse strategies of funding (Bruno and Shin, 2012; BIS, 2011). Their leverage decisions have a significant impact on monetary conditions in developing countries (Bruno and Shin, 2012), reducing policy autonomy to a dilemma of either free capital flows or independent monetary policy (Rey, 2015).

These trends can be confirmed empirically by comparing the sources of funding for large banking systems (see Figure 6.1). Indeed, most European banking systems, whether from 'bank-based' or 'market-based' capitalisms, met less than half of their funding requirements from their traditional source, customer deposits, with France and Italy least reliant on deposit activity. Instead banks have turned to market funding, from the issue of debt securities[3] or direct borrowing on wholesale money markets, either domestic or cross-border (Hardie et al., 2013; Praet and Herzberg, 2008). Transnational banking also affects smaller banks without access to international markets. Transnational banks can easily channel foreign liquidity into domestic money markets and ease funding conditions for smaller banks even when the central bank attempts to tighten the monetary policy stance (Gabor, 2015; Bruno and Shin, 2012).

Private repo markets have quickly become the largest global source of wholesale funding (FSB, 2012; Gorton and Metrick, 2010). These are over-the-counter markets where the repo lender exchanges cash for assets (collateral), and commits to re-sell that collateral to the borrower at a later date (a day, a month or more). Global repo markets grew, on average, at almost 20 per cent between 2001 and 2007, driven by similarly rapid expansions in the US and Europe, a manifestation of the rapid growth in shadow banking with its collateral-intensive nature (Gourinchas and Jeanne, 2012).[4] Regulators applauded this growth because of the improved risk management provided by repo transactions. Since the lender becomes the legal owner of the underlying collateral, in the event of the cash borrower's default, the lender can recover her loan by selling the collateral. For example, the European Directive 2002/47/EC[5] removed obstacles to the cross-border use of collateral in European jurisdictions, citing improved distribution of liquidity and risk management (see also The Giovannini Group, 1999).

The most common collateral in secured transactions is a 'safe asset' that typically satisfies two conditions. First, it trades in highly liquidity markets. Higher liquidity implies less price volatility, which maintains the value of collateral close to that of the cash loan. Second, it is of high quality. Lower-quality assets require a higher haircut, which is the difference between the value

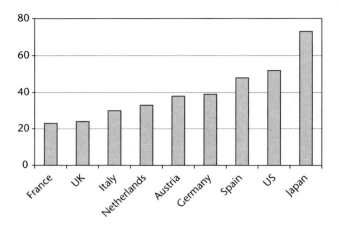

Figure 6.1 Share of customer deposit in total bank funding, June 2010
Source: BIS statistics.

of the cash loan and the value of collateral posted, to protect the lender against the risk that a rapid fall in the value of the collateral would result in loses if the cash borrower defaults. Prior to the crisis, the sovereign bonds of highly developed political economies best satisfied these conditions (Gorton and Metrick, 2010).

The pre-crisis growth in repo markets generated an increasing demand for safe assets as eligible collateral. When issuers of high quality sovereign debt did not satisfy the demand, responses varied depending on specific institutional and regulatory contexts. One avenue involved collateral mining[6] (Pozsar and Singh, 2011) that 'unearthed' sovereign debt instruments from 'buy to hold' portfolios of patient investors (such as pension funds) and introduced them in collateral portfolios. Similarly, collateral managers used the same sovereign debt instrument in various repo transactions if legal provisions allowed reuse (Singh and Stella 2012). Furthermore, according to the 'safe assets' literature, a collateral motive underpinned the production of structured securities at the core of the US financial crisis.[7] Shadow banks produced structured securities to address the shortage of the typical safe assets, US sovereign debt, prior to 2008 (Pozsar, 2011). Put differently, shadow banks increased leverage by generating structured securities that could be used as collateral in repo markets (Gorton and Metrick, 2010).

In the European markets, collateral demand triggered distinctive solutions to a similar problem. The rapid growth in European repo markets accompanying transnational banking could not be supported by the conservative fiscal stance of the primary 'safe sovereign', Germany (Bolton and Jeanne, 2011). Basically, Germany could not generate enough debt relative to the demand for it. To solve this problem, the European Commission proposed to address the shortage by regulatory reforms (The Giovannini Group, 1999). The Financial Collateral Arrangements directive 2002/47/EC provided a unified legal framework for the cross-border use of collateral and the essential techniques in collateral management (including reuse, substitution and collateral netting) that meant equal treatment of Eurozone sovereign debt in repo transactions[8] (Hördhal and King, 2008). The intention was to transform the bond markets of 'non-core' sovereigns into collateral – or safe asset – markets, and thus harness the forces of financial innovation to the European project of financial integration.[9]

At first, financial markets confirmed the Commission's expectations. Sovereign bond markets across Europe quickly became important sources of collateral. According to BIS (2011), up to 90 per cent of outstanding sovereign debt issued by Ireland, Italy, Greece, Portugal and Spain circulated as collateral in private European repo transactions before Lehman's collapse. The sovereign bond markets of these countries together provided around 25 per cent of sovereign European collateral, a share comparable to that of the 'safe' sovereign, Germany (ICMA, 2011). That European banks could raise repo funding on *identical* terms with German, Greek or Italian sovereign collateral testified to the success of the financial integration project (Hördahl and King, 2008). What later the European elites dubbed as the toxic twins of European finance, the ECB celebrated as evidence of the success of the repo-driven financial integration project.

In other words, banks (and other investors) did not enter European sovereign bond markets because of an 'accidental' yet collective mispricing of credit risk, as is the standard account of pre-crisis sovereign yield convergence (De Santis and Gerard, 2006). Instead, the collateral motive became an important driver of demand for European government bonds because European banks could access wholesale market funding by using collateral other than that issued by their own governments.

Indeed banks increasingly relied on other European government bonds as collateral to raise funding from other European financial institutions. According to ECB data, the share of own government collateral posted in private funding arrangements declined from 63 per cent in 2001 to 31 per cent in 2008, as other euro area institutions became the main counterparties. The collateral motive improved the liquidity of sovereign bond markets and helped 'periphery' sovereign debt migrate into the safe asset category, exactly as the European Commission and the ECB intended.

However, by 2008, policymakers in Europe started to voice concerns about the fragilities arising from the increasing importance of the collateral motive. Praet and Herzberg (2008) described the problem in the following steps:

1   'Interbank funding is itself becoming increasingly dependent on market liquidity as a growing proportion of interbank transactions is carried out through repurchase agreements'.
2   'This increasing reliance on secured operations means that (European) banks are mobilising a growing fraction of their securities portfolio as collateral'.
3   'Banks are increasingly mobilizing their traditional government and corporate bond portfolios to finance less liquid, but higher yielding forms of assets that again can be reused as collateral'.
4   'In periods of stress, margin and collateral requirements may increase if counterparties have retained the right to increase haircuts or if margins have fallen below certain thresholds'.
5   'Asset liquidity may no longer depend on the characteristics of the asset itself, but rather on whether vulnerable counterparts have substantial positions that need liquidating'.

While Praet and Herzberg (2008) did not use government bonds to illustrate the nexus asset liquidity/repo funding problems, their analysis does not exclude that possibility. When European banks mobilized their portfolios of government bonds as collateral (2 and 3), the potential runs in collateral markets could also include government bond markets in the European periphery (4), run that reflected more the funding pressures of large European banks involved in US shadow banking than the fiscal probity of sovereign (5).

Using Hardie's framework, collateral demand contributed to the financialization of the market structure for structured securities in the US, and 'periphery' sovereigns in Europe. It did so however at the price of building up the 'toxic twins' problem that would only become apparent in the crisis.

The collateral motive and investor loyalty

Demand for collateral changes the fundamental determinants of investors' loyalty vis-à-vis their sovereigns. Consider the example of commercial banks, traditionally the largest holder of government debt. As Table 6.1 confirms, banks demanded euro area collateral to diversify collateral portfolios, sharpening the internationalization of sovereign debt markets (Bolton and Jeanne, 2011). But diversified collateral portfolios conversely reduce banks' *relative exposure* – to use Hardie's phrase – to both home and foreign sovereign in terms of market size.

In the Eurozone, foreign banks held higher shares of government debt than domestic banks in all but three countries (Germany, Greece and Spain) by 2010 (see Table 6.1). Even in those three countries, non-bank investors (hedge funds, pension funds and other institutional investors) held close to or more than half of outstanding government debt. Where regulatory provisions allowed, buy-to-hold institutional investors (such as pension funds or insurance companies) chose to lend their securities to collateral 'miners', increasing the availability of alternative instruments.

Taken together, this diverse investor base and the availability of alternative sources of collateral reduced the costs of exit for investors faced with sovereign risk: loyalty became both expensive and counterproductive. Indeed, Angeloni and Wolff (2012) show that European banks reduced exposure to the five 'southern' Eurozone countries in the first nine months of 2011 as the European sovereign debt crisis intensified. French banks reduced their holdings by almost 22 per cent, and German banks by 15 per cent, mostly by withdrawing from the Italian sovereign bond market, the second largest source of collateral in Eurozone[10] according to ICMA (2011) statistics. The French banks' withdrawal is worth noting because the French banking system was highly market-dependent, funding around 23 per cent from interbank market sources for which it required high quality collateral (BIS, 2011 and Figure 6.1). As sovereign bond markets become collateral markets, the costs of exit in terms of relative exposure and alternative instruments become smaller, reducing the loyalty of market participants.

The collateral motive decreased loyalty in still more fundamental ways through valuation practices, Hardie's third dimension of investor (im)patience. At first sight, accounting practices in Europe should support investor loyalty. European banks hold only a small percentage of sovereign debt instruments on trading books that mark to market (Liikanen Report, 2012). In practice however, banks are exposed to collateral market volatility even when they hold

Table 6.1 Participants in sovereign bond markets (holdings as % of overall volume, 2010)

	Domestic banks	*Foreign banks*	*Non-bank holders*
Austria	6%	18%	76%
Belgium	9%	16%	75%
France	8%	8%	84%
Germany	34%	13%	53%
Netherlands	10%	16%	74%
Greece	19%	16%	65%
Ireland	7%	32%	61%
Italy	9%	12%	79%
Spain	41%	12%	47%
UK	6%	3%	91%

Source: EBA Stress Tests (2010).

bonds in the banking book because of the nature of collateral management. In traditional banking, deposit insurance protects the cash lender (the saver) from risks that the counterparty, the bank, may default. Collateral similarly enables the cash lender in repo transactions to mitigate counterparty risk (Gorton and Metrick 2010). But collateral does not eliminate *all* risk for the lender, in the way that deposit insurance does. Instead, it changes the lender's exposure from the counterparty to the market where that collateral trades. To paraphrase Hördahl and King (2008, p. 40) the main risk in a repo transaction is collateral market risk. If the counterparty defaults, the lender will fully recover her cash if she can sell that collateral at its posted value, that is if the market remains liquid and if the collateral has not fallen in value. For this reason, collateral managers typically worry about the liquidity of collateral markets, be it those of structured securities or sovereign debt markets, and mitigate these worries by mark-to-market valuations.

By definition then, collateral management is necessarily short-term and impatient regardless of whether it is either overnight, or at longer maturities. In the latter case, even if the repo has a three-month maturity, collateral managers still use mark-to-market practices to calculate the value of collateral portfolios on a daily basis, and trigger margin calls if prices are changing.[11] Indeed, a key requirement of collateral management is to ensure that the value of the collateral portfolio remains equal (close) to the cash loan in order to avoid credit risk. If, for instance, the collateral falls in price, the cash lender will trigger a margin call, asking the borrower to post additional collateral in order to match the original value of the loan.

For this reason, perceptions of collateral quality become crucial for collateral managers: margin calls makes 'volatile' collateral expensive because it requires borrowers to either hold (expensive) reserve collateral or have ready access to similar collateral. Collateral managers may chose 'cheapest to deliver' collateral (that they can buy cheaply) but only if they expect prices to increase in the future. In turn, perceptions of future price volatility associated with a sudden stop (decreases, equivalent to an interest rate increase) will reduce demand for that collateral because of the future margin calls on that asset. Thus, mark-to-market practices in collateral management erode investor loyalty, just as Hardie (2011) described in the case of international investors in emerging countries' bond markets.

Collateral managers must respond immediately to changes in either perceptions of collateral liquidity or overall confidence in valuations. The case of collateral markets supplied by governments (rather than shadow banks) stands apart because of the particular impact that crisis, financial or economic, has on government deficits. A crisis increases the fiscal burden either directly through the costs of bank rescue programmes (and these were high across Europe, see Engelen *et al.*, 2011) or if it triggers automatic stabilizers (higher welfare payments and lower tax revenue). Thus government deficits can increase even in the absence of discretionary stimulus measures. The higher supply of government bonds will push prices down (and yields up) unless private actors or the central bank increase demand. In a crisis, collateral managers have every incentive to abandon collateral markets that they perceive to be risky because a fall in the price of that asset may result in margin calls. Reduced demand reduces market liquidity, increases price volatility and margin calls further affecting demand – a vicious cycle that can precipitate a run on a collateral market. In other words, shifting perceptions of sovereign risk or confidence in valuations may trigger sudden stops in collateral markets.

Collateral damage in the euro crisis

The valuation of complex debt instruments often involves creative practices that retain credibility while investors remain confident. But financial crises typically erode confidence in valuations of risk and return (Dow, 2012). For instance, Lehman's collapse saw rising uncertainty about the value of structured securities. What ensued, Gorton and Metrick (2010) showed, was a sudden stop in the repo segment using structured products as collateral. In conditions of market uncertainty that reduces the value of collateral, collateral managers abandon higher-risk collateral markets or, if under serious funding pressures, may even resort to fire sales that further add to price volatility. By the end of October 2008, the only institution that still accepted structured securities as collateral was the US Federal Reserve, in its extraordinary liquidity injections.

This was a lesson that European policymakers appeared to have learnt from the US debacle in the early stages of the crisis. Similar to the US, private repo actors began questioning the 'safe-asset' tag attached, in this case, to sovereigns with well-documented domestic vulnerabilities (housing boom, high reliance on external funding). Concerns about sovereign risk saw an increasing shift in collateral demand for German safe assets and away from 'higher-risk' sovereigns such as Ireland or Greece. Repo transactions collateralized by Irish and Greek bonds fell in volume, as spreads to German debt widened (BIS, 2011). For all purposes, new concerns with sovereign risks and its impact on collateral liquidity appeared to ignite a run on the collateral markets supplied by 'periphery' sovereigns (Gabor and Ban, 2015).

However, country-specific factors and contagion from other sovereigns (Caceres et al., 2010) became important once the ECB refused to ease tensions in the Greek government bond market and instead insisted on withdrawing its extraordinary liquidity support for European banks (Gabor, 2014). In May 2010, the ECB signalled that it would not stabilize collateral markets if collateral was supplied by sovereigns, fearing a backlash from Northern countries. This started successive waves of runs on European collateral markets (Gabor and Ban, 2015). Indeed, the BIS (2011) reported that the share of repo transactions collateralized by Greek and Irish sovereign bonds halved between December 2009 and June 2010. Later that year, the Irish case offered the clearest example of a run on a sovereign collateral market that eventually forced the Irish government to ask for a bailout.

The Irish run featured a key repo market player named LCH Clearnet. This clearing house, Europe's biggest, acts an intermediary in repo transactions, and thus assumes the collateral risk that a cash lender would face in a bilateral transaction. For this reason, although repo transactions in Europe are mostly bilateral, strains in a particular collateral market (Irish sovereign bonds) will see lenders increasingly preferring to move repo activity through the clearing house.[12] The LCH Clearnet uses a rigid rule: if the yield on a sovereign bond increases by more than 450 basis points above a basket of AAA rated assets, it will trigger margin calls. When the Irish yield went above that threshold in November 2010, LCH raised margin requirements for banks that wanted to use Irish collateral to 15 per cent. Because Irish banks were not members of LCH, this mainly affected non-Irish banks holding Irish collateral (that incidentally held far higher holdings than the Irish banks). The changes in haircuts reduced demand for Irish government bonds, pushing yields further up, triggering a new margin call (FT Alphaville).[13] By 21 November, LCH had tripled the haircuts on Irish debt to 45 per cent. The run on the collateral market (worsened by short-selling) stopped only once the Irish government asked for an international bailout. Similar developments underpinned the Portuguese bailout, and the withdrawal of German and French banks from the Italian government bond market discussed earlier.

The limits of loyalty

The behaviour of domestic banks confronted with a run in the collateral market of their own sovereign offers a powerful example of why the collateral motive matters. It is worth remembering that in Hardie's framework, loyal domestic banks are crucial to preserving fiscal policy autonomy during crisis. From this perspective, except for Ireland, the periphery sovereign bond

Europe's toxic twins

markets should have benefited from the high 'home bias' of their domestic banks compared to Nordic countries. For example, both Spanish and Italian banking sectors held over 75 per cent of sovereign debt in home sovereign instruments in March 2010, before the sovereign debt crisis exploded (see Figure 6.2). At first, the benefits of loyal banks became apparent throughout 2009. The 'home bias' strengthened as banks used the long-term ECB liquidity to buy higher-yielding debt of their own governments, and post it as collateral for accessing ECB loans, just as Hardie's framework would have predicted.

But once funding conditions tighten, loyalty can became costly in collateral terms. The repo lenders may attempt to pre-empt a 'double exposure' by refusing to lend to a periphery bank seeking to borrow against periphery collateral. The ECB (2011) termed this the 'coordinated risks' on the repo market between counterparty (bank) and collateral (sovereign debt), or in the words of a bank collateral manager:

> an Irish bank pledging Italian debt as collateral is less desirable from a credit perspective than an Irish bank pledging AAA-rated security with no correlation to the European debt crisis. Where firms are declining PIIGS debt, collateral pledgers are sometimes faced with having to offer higher quality collateral.
>
> *(SLT 2011, p. 12)*

The 'coordinated risks' that affected Spanish (and Italian) banks throughout 2011 prompted these to curtail credit to the domestic economy (thus worsening the recession) to offset the loss of access to market funding.[14] It also triggered changes in their collateral strategy: to avoid such coordinated risks, both Italian and Spanish banks reduced exposure to their sovereigns from December 2010 to September 2011, the first by around 7 per cent and the second by almost 30 per cent (Angeloni and Wolff, 2012). Banks that manage significant portfolios of sovereign collateral as part of their market-funding strategies inevitably lose loyalty, in Hardie's sense, towards their home sovereign.

When sovereign bond markets become collateral markets, the sovereign-bank loop gets sharper (BIS, 2011, Acharya *et al.*, 2010). Governments have to absorb the costs of bank

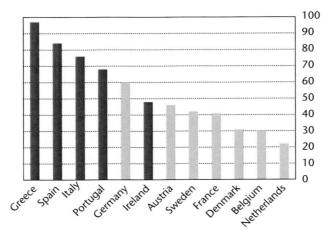

Figure 6.2 Share of domestic government debt in total government debt portfolios, selected European banking sectors, June 2010

143

restructuring or bank failure because bank runs would destroy the banking system. But if higher (countercyclical) spending increases sovereign risk, it can disrupt the collateral function of sovereign debt, with adverse effects on banks' funding conditions, particularly where those banks are 'loyal' banks.

The ingredients for a sudden stop in sovereign collateral markets are therefore always present because this interdependence between banks and sovereign creates a problem of coordination: who will assume responsibility for preventing a run on the sovereign collateral market? Private domestic banks cannot resolve this problem because of the impatient nature of collateral management discussed above. Central banks may be better candidates because theoretically there are no constraints to their ability to stabilize bond markets. As shown by the case of the Fed or the Bank of England, central banks can always create more base money to purchase government bonds (de Grauwe and Ji, 2012). The ECB's Outright Monetary Transactions provide an even more puzzling insight: collateral quality may be a question of a well-specified (verbal) commitment from central banks, commitment that private finance will be reluctant to test.

Absent the political and ideological conditions for such interventions, governments remain the only institution to stabilize their debt market. Expansionary fiscal policies that generate growth could be one option, yet the familiar time lags involved in fiscal expansions imply that in the first place, higher expenditures will increase funding needs in a financialized market guided by short-term considerations. Higher expenditures stand to worsen the crisis because the possible growth-inducing effects take time to materialize, whereas financialized sovereign bond markets are incompatible with medium-term strategies. In the Eurozone institutional context that prevents devaluations or inflation as alternative pathways, the remaining option is to reduce the supply of government debt until the ECB steps in, with OMT or quantitative easing.

Beyond the immediate stabilization measures that seek to contain the fragilities of the collateral motive, it is important to consider how, if at all, have states responded with regulatory shifts. In Europe, we have seen two conflicting trends. The first is for governments to successfully resist plans that put 'sand in the wheels' of the collateral motive. Indeed, immediately after the crisis, transnational regulatory bodies began asking critical questions about collateral-based financial systems. Recognizing that institution-based regulation can be easily avoided by moving in the shadows, the Financial Stability Board shifted attention to the direct regulation of repo markets, recast as securities financing transactions (SFT) markets. Yet direct regulation is proceeding at a slower pace than institution-based rules (EMIR, CRR, Basel III liquidity/leverage rules) that affect SFT markets indirectly, and, according to US regulators, at best marginally.[15]

At international level, the FSB watered down its plans for universal mandatory haircuts, excluding government bonds from its collateral regulation. Given the specific nature of European SFT markets – dominated by banks and intensive in government collateral – the FSB rules would only apply to less than 20 per cent of SFT transactions, failing to restructure the complex collateral chains between regulated and shadow banks that pose financial stability risks. In turn, European regulators have prioritized reporting and transparency of SFTs. While SFT transparency may shed much-needed light on systemic markets, the structural impact is limited. Excessive leverage occurs via SFT markets not (solely) because these are opaque, but because leverage is cheapest in SFTs with government bond collateral. European states dropped the more effective way of targeting the collateral motive, through the Financial Transactions Tax on repos with sovereign collateral, citing concerns with market liquidity (Gabor, 2016).

The second trend has been for central bankers, some Member States (Germany) and the European Commission to seek to create political momentum for the project of separating the toxic twins in an effort to conclude the Banking Union. This would involve caps on bank holdings of their own government's debt, and in the more radical version, removing the zero-risk weight attached to government bonds in capital requirements. That Germany would throw its support behind this project is not surprising. The economics of the collateral motive in a currency union suggest that a flight to safety episode triggered by concerns with collateral quality will always benefit Germany, because Germany issues safe asset of last resort. It remains to be seen whether this is yet another singular development of the complex political economy of the Eurozone, or the harbinger of a future where governments will have lost all their negotiating chips in their market funding arrangements.

Conclusions

The pre-crisis shift to transnational market-based, collateral intensive models of European banks' locked banks and sovereigns together in an embrace that led governments towards austerity rather than any other instrument of rebalancing.

Investors' disloyalty to their sovereign bond placements is an important determinant of austerity as policy. We show that it was the pre-crisis shift to transnational market-based, collateral intensive models of European banks' locked banks and sovereigns together in an embrace that led governments towards austerity rather than any other instrument of rebalancing.

What makes investors disloyal are their low exposure, the availability of alternative investment opportunities, the build-up of diversified collateral portfolios and a market dominated by mark-to-market valuation techniques. Although these insights were developed with emerging markets in mind, we found that investors in the sovereign bonds of the Eurozone's 'peripheries' behaved with the same impatience as investors in highly financialized bond markets for emerging economies. Before the crisis, the demand for sovereign bonds boomed, spurred on by the European institutions' policy of making all the sovereign debt for periphery countries equally eligible as collateral in ECB and private repo transactions. This provided more collateral at the cost of eroding banks' loyalty to their government's bonds, as the diverse investor base and the availability of alternative sources of collateral reduced the costs of exit for banks faced with sovereign risk. In sum, the Euro plus the repo turned ostensibly European lending into international lending in a common currency with disastrous results when the sudden stop occurred. Sovereign bond downgrades trigger margin calls, prompting managers to 'disloyally' head for the exits. This is precisely what happened in 2010, when downgrades of 'periphery' bonds rendered them ineligible or expensive to post as collateral due to higher haircuts. As a result, collateral managers in banks had no choice but reduce exposure to lower-value bonds, even if they were their own government's. Thus, banks' loyalty towards governments became closely tied to the collateral qualities of debt.

The situation in the Eurozone was further complicated by the fact that in early 2010 European Central Bank did not steadfastly commit to repair the damaged collateral function of 'peripheral' sovereign bonds, as it did in 2009 (Gabor and Ban, 2015; also Gabor, 2014). Just as downgrades chipped away at the collateral value of these bonds, making investors increasingly disloyal, the ECB withdrew extraordinary liquidity interventions. In these conditions, governments had to address the disruption of collateral markets for fear that bank runs would wreck their countries' banking systems and take the national economies down with them. Since the attempt to absorb these costs through expansionary fiscal policy could only make the problem worse given these constraints, leading to further downgrades, the onus fell upon European governments and the societies they governed to pay the price of stabilizing collateral markets. The collateral damage of collateralization is austerity.

Notes

1 The term illustrates the contradiction between the theoretical proposition that in efficient markets, as the markets of high income countries were routinely assumed to be, investors should have no preference for a particular issuer and the instances where bank sovereign portfolios were dominated by their own sovereign.
2 The trading book and banking book are accounting terms that refer to the practices through which banks account for their assets. Banks hold assets that are regularly traded in the trading book, and are required, under Basel II and III, to mark these assets to market daily. The trading book portfolio thus fully reflects market fluctuations. In contrast, banks account for assets held to maturity in the banking book, at their historical, rather than market, cost.
3 Including residential-backed mortgage securities, commercial mortgage-based securities, covered bonds and collateralized debt obligations.
4 The US repo market reached an estimated US$10 trillion or 70% of US GDP and the European repo market to EUR 6 trillion before Lehman (Hördahl and King, 2008).
5 Retrieved on 3 May 2016 from http://eurlex.europa.eu/smartapi/cgi/sga_doc?smartapi!celexapi!prod!CELEXnumdoc&lg=EN&numdoc=32002L0047&model=guichett.
6 Collateral mining 'involves both exploration (looking for deposits of collateral) and extraction (the 'unearthing' of passive securities so they can be re-used as collateral for various purposes in the shadow banking system)'.
7 This includes asset-backed securities, RMBS, CMBS, CDOs, CLOs.
8 In the US or UK, the sovereign collateral in funding-driven repos includes a homogeneous basket of sovereign debt instruments (so that the maturity of instruments does not matter). In contrast, the European sovereign rates are compiled on a basket of sovereign bonds issued by *any* of the euro area countries (Hördahl and King, 2008).
9 For the Commission, the new regulation was more than a pragmatic response to a policy problem. The Commission trusted the promises of financial innovation in repo markets: increased liquidity, improved risk management and better pricing tools (The Giovannini Group 1999; Engelen *et al.*, 2011). This expectation was grafted onto the European integration project itself. Financial innovation would achieve financial integration of both wholesale money markets and sovereign bond markets. It was the 'ever wider' union, financial market style.
10 For Italy, European Banking Authority data for 2010 show that the banks of the other European countries reduced their overall net exposure by €57 billion (of which €40 billion was by German banks alone). BIS data indicate that this exposure diminished further in the first half of 2011.
11 For example, a Spanish bank that posted Spanish sovereign collateral for a three-month repo initiated in March 2010 would have had to post additional collateral to compensate for the fall in the price of Spanish collateral triggered by contagion from the Greek crisis.
12 Indeed, the Spanish government welcomed the admission of Spanish banks to the LCH Clearnet platform in May 2010 because it would ease their access to repo funding collateralized with Spanish bonds.
13 Retrieved on 3 May 2016 from http://ftalphaville.ft.com/blog/2010/11/03/393051/when-irish-margins-are-biting/.
14 Retrieved on 3 May 2016 from www.ft.com/cms/s/0/1b6855b8-c404-11e0-b302-00144feabdc0.html#axzz24wgcv2mx.
15 Jeremy Stein on 'Fire Sales in SFT markets'. Retrieved on 3 May 2016 from www.federalreserve.gov/newsevents/speech/stein20131107a.htm.

Bibliography

Acharya, V.V, Schnabl, P. and Suarez, G. (2010) 'Securitization without risk transfer', National Bureau of Economic Research.
Acharya, Viral V. and Viswanathan, S. (2011) 'Leverage, moral hazard, and liquidity', *The Journal of Finance* 66, 1: 99–138.
Angeloni, C. and Wolff, G. (2012) 'Are banks affected by their holdings of government debt?', Bruegel Working Paper, March.
Ban, C. (2015) 'Austerity versus stimulus? Understanding fiscal policy change at the International Monetary Fund since the great recession', *Governance* 28, 2: 167–83.

Bank for International Settlements (BIS) (2011) 'The impact of sovereign credit risk on bank funding conditions', Committee on the Global Financial System Paper no 43.
Blyth, M. (2013) *Austerity: The History of a Dangerous Idea*, Oxford: Oxford University Press.
Bolton, P. and Jeanne, O. (2011) 'Sovereign default risk and bank fragility in financially integrated economies', NBER Working Paper No. 212.
Broner, F., Didier, T., Erce, A. and Schmukler, S.L. (2011) 'Gross capital flows: Dynamics and crises'. Retrieved on 16 May 2016 from http://papers.ssrn.com/sol3/papers.cfm?abstract_id=1825011.
Brunnermeier, M.K., Garicano, L., Lane, P.R., Pagano, M., Reis, R., Santos, T., Thesmar, D., Van Nieuwerburgh, S. and Vayanos, D. (2015) 'Breaking the sovereign-bank diabolic loop: A case for ESBies', *American Economic Review Papers and Proceedings*.
Bruno, V. and Shin, H.S. (2012) 'Capital flows, cross-border banking and global liquidity'. Retrieved on 3 May 2016 from http://ssrn.com/abstract=2020556 or http://dx.doi.org/10.2139/ssrn.2020556.
Buiter, W. and Rahbari, E. (2012) 'The European Central Bank as lender of last resort for sovereigns in the Eurozone', *JCMS: Journal of Common Market Studies* 50, 2: 6–35.
Caceres, Carlos, Guzzo, V. and Segoviano Basurto, M. (2010) 'Sovereign spreads: Global risk aversion, contagion or fundamentals?', *IMF working papers:* 1–29.
Cetorelli, N. and Goldberg, L. (2012) 'Follow the money: Quantifying domestic effects of foreign bank shocks in the great recession', *American Economic Review*, American Economic Association, 102, 3: 213–18.
Corsetti, G. (2012) 'Austerity: Too much of a good thing', A VoxEU.org eCollection of views by leading economists. London: Centre for Economic Policy Research (CEPR).
de Grauwe, P. and Ji, Y. (2012) 'Mispricing of sovereign risk and macroeconomic stability in the Eurozone', *JCMS: Journal of Common Market Studies* 50, 6: 866–80.
Dow, S. (2004) 'Uncertainty and monetary policy', *Oxford Economic Papers* 56, 3: 539–61.
Dow, S.C. (2012) 'What are banks and bank regulation for? A consideration of the foundations for reform', *European Journal of Economics and Economic Policies: Intervention* 1: 39–56.
Engelen, E., Ertürk, I., Froud, J., Johal, S., Leaver, A., Moran, M., Nilsson, A. and Williams, K. (2011) *After the Great Complacence: Financial Crisis and the Politics of Reform*, Oxford: Oxford University Press.
Fidora, M., Fratzscher, M. and Thimann, C. (2007) 'Home bias in global bond and equity markets: The role of real exchange rate volatility', *Journal of International Money and Finance* 26, 4: 631–55.
Financial Stability Board (FSB) (2012) 'Securities lending and repo: Market overview and financial stability issues'. Basel, April.
Gabor, D. (2012) 'Managing capital accounts in emerging markets: Lessons from the global financial crisis', *Journal of Development Studies* 48, 6: 714–31.
Gabor, D. (2014) 'Learning from Japan: The European Central Bank and the European sovereign debt crisis', *Review of Political Economy*, 26, 2: 190–209.
Gabor, D. (2015) The IMF's rethink of global banks: Critical in theory, orthodox in practice', *Governance*, 28, 2: 199–218.
Gabor, D. (2016) 'A step too far? The European FTT on shadow banking', *Journal of European Public Policy*, 23, 6: 925–45.
Gabor, D. and Ban, C. (2015) 'Banking on bonds: On the new links between states and markets', *Journal of Common Market Studies*, DOI: 10.1111/jcms.12309.
Glyn, A. (2007) *Capitalism Unleashed: Finance, Globalization, and Welfare: Finance, Globalization, and Welfare*, Oxford: Oxford University Press.
Gorton, G., and Metrick, A. (2010) 'Haircuts', *Economic Review* (November): 507–20.
Gourinchas, P-O. and Jeanne, O. (2012) 'Global safe assets', BIS Working Paper 151.
Gros, D. (2012) 'A simple model of multiple equilibria and default', CEPS Working Document 366.
Hardie, I. (2011) 'How much can governments borrow? Financialization and emerging markets government borrowing capacity', *Review of International Political Economy* 18, 2: 141–67.
Hardie, I. and Howarth, D. (2009) 'Die Krise but Not La Crise? The financial crisis and the transformation of German and French banking systems', *Journal of Common Market Studies*, 47, 5: 1017–39.
Hardie, I., Howarth, D., Maxfield, S. and Verdun, A. (2013) 'Banks and the false dichotomy in the comparative political economy of finance', *World Politics*, 65: 691–728.
Helgadóttir, Oddný (2015) 'The Bocconi Boys Go to Brussels: Italian economic ideas, professional networks and European austerity', *Journal of European Public Policy*: 1–18.
Hördahl, P. and King, M. (2008) 'Developments in repo markets during the financial turmoil', BIS Working Paper 34.

International Capital Markets Association (ICMA) (2011) 'European repo market survey', December.
ICMA European Repo Council (2014) 'Collateral is the new cash: The systemic risks of inhabiting collateral fluidity'. Retrieved on 16 May 2016 from file:///Users/d-gabor/Downloads/COLLATERAL%20IS%20THE%20NEW%20CASH%20THE%20SYSTEMIC%20RISKS%20OF%20INHIBITING%20-%204%20April%202014%20(1).pdf.
Liikanen Report (2012). 'High-level expert group on reforming the structure of the EU banking sector', Final Report, Brussels.
Merler S. and Pisani-Ferry, J. (2012) 'Hazardous tango: Sovereign-bank interdependence and financial stability in the euro area', Banque de France, Financial Stability Review, no. 16.
Mosley, L. (2000) 'Room to move: International financial markets and national welfare states', *International Organization* 54, 4: 737–73.
Pozsar A. (2011) 'Institutional Cash Pools and the Triffin Dilemma of the US Banking System', IMF Working Paper WP/11/190.
Pozsar, Z. and Singh, M. (2011) 'The nonbank–bank nexus and the shadow banking system', *IMF Working Papers*: 1–18.
Pozsar, Z., Adrian, T., Ashcraft, A. and Boesky, H. (2010) 'Shadow banking', *SSRN eLibrary* (15 July). Retrieved on 3 May 2016 from http://papers.ssrn.com/sol3/papers.cfm?abstract_id=1640545.
Praet, P. and Herzberg, V. (2008) 'Market liquidity and banking liquidity: Linkages, vulnerabilities and the role of disclosure', *Banque de France Financial stability Review*: 95–109.
Rajan, R. (2010) *Fault Lines*, Princeton, NJ: Princeton University Press.
Rey, H. (2015) 'Dilemma not trilemma: The global financial cycle and monetary policy independence', Working Paper No. w21162. National Bureau of Economic Research.
Rothenberg, A.D. and Warnock, F.E. (2011) 'Sudden flight and true sudden stops', *Review of International Economics*, 19, 3: 509–24.
Santis, R. De and Gerard, B. (2006) 'Financial integration, international portfolio choice and the European Monetary Union', *SSRN eLibrary* (May).
Securities Lending Time (SLT) (2011) 'Collateral management'. Retrieved on 12 March 2016 from www.securitieslendingtimes.com/sltimes/SLT-Colateral-Managment.pdf.
Singh, M. (2011) 'Velocity of pledged collateral: Analysis and implications', IMF Working Paper 11/256.
Singh, M. and Stella. P. (2012) 'Money and collateral', *SSRN eLibrary* (April). Retrieved on 3 May 2016 from http://papers.ssrn.com/sol3/papers.cfm?abstract_id=2050268.
The Giovannini Group. 1999. *EU Repo Markets: Opportunities for Change*. European Commission.

7
Variegated geographies of finance
International financial centres and the (re)production of financial working cultures

Sarah Hall

There is an established literature that examines how the international financial system is (re)produced through a small number of leading international financial centres (IFCs). Indeed, the importance of centres such as Wall Street in New York and the City of London is underscored by their position at the centre of the 2007–08 financial crisis. This chapter draws on economic geographical research and that from cognate social sciences to examine the variegated working cultures that exist in different financial centres. With a focus on investment banking in London, the chapter emphasizes the importance of knowledge and learning to shaping such working cultures. It is argued that this approach provides a valuable way of developing understandings of the (re)production of variegated working cultures between IFCs because education and training represents one set of practices that not only reflects variegation between IFCS but also acts to reproduce such difference, something that has been comparatively neglected in work on IFCs to date. Such an approach is important since it demonstrates how efforts to change working cultures in IFCs in the wake of the crisis needs to attend to both the formal regulatory environment and more informal social and cultural norms that are learnt through education and training.

The 2007–08 financial crisis is often labelled, in popular, academic and media outlets, as a *global* financial crisis. However, the label of global is in many ways erroneous. For example, whilst the crisis has undoubtedly had profound implications beyond its Anglo-American heartlands, for example through the ongoing Eurozone crisis, it remains the case that the initial source of the crisis lay in the specific banking practices of investment banks in Wall Street and subsequently in London and other European banking centres (Engelen *et al.*, 2012; Tett, 2010). Meanwhile, the term global also hides the heterogeneous ways in which the crisis has affected different people in geographically variable ways. For example, research has revealed the disproportionate impact of the crisis on minority ethnic and racial groups in the US in terms of the loss of their homes associated with the uncompetitive mortgage finance rates these groups were offered (Sidaway, 2008). In this chapter, I focus on international financial centres (IFCs) and work in economic geography in particular that has focused on documenting the distinctive working cultures associated with different IFCs. Such a focus is important since the distinctive working practices in New York and London throughout the 2000s that facilitated and legitimated the development of particular approaches to risk and new financial products, notably the development of securities, have been identified as being central to the origination and transmission of the crisis from

New York to other financial centres and the economy more generally (Wainwright, 2009). As such, research has called for attention to focus on how variegated institutional contexts shape the behaviour of highly skilled elites, including financial elites in the case of this chapter (Zald and Lounsbury, 2010).

In this respect, an established literature has developed in economic geography and cognate social sciences that has revealed the distinctive working cultures of IFCs and the relationship between them. For example, much has been made of the relationship of both competition and cooperation between London and New York that has typified their respective development as IFCs from the post-war period onwards (Beaverstock, 2005). However, whilst these differences have been well documented, the ways in which such variegation is produced and sustained has received comparatively less attention. In response, in this chapter I document recent work, predominately in economic geography, that has sought to address this oversight. In particular, I focus on financial knowledge practices and issues of learning and training within investment banking in London's international financial district to demonstrate how, alongside more formal regulatory environments, social and cultural practices inculcated through education and training contribute to the distinctive working cultures of IFCs. Intellectually, such an approach is important since it responds to recent calls that we need to move beyond simplistic accounts of the 'globalization of money' and instead 'reconceptualize' monetary space. We need to map its different layers and dimensions, its various constituent subspaces, and the myriad interconnections among them (Dodd, 2014, p. 221). Meanwhile, empirically, by better understanding how variegated working practices emerge in IFCs, it is possible to open up the space to act upon the levers that shape the international financial system more effectively in order to respond to the criticisms of the system in the wake of the financial crisis. The analysis in this chapter suggests that such efforts will be most successful if they focus on both the formal regulatory landscape but also more informal social and cultural norms and expectations concerning what are legitimate and normalized working cultures in particular IFCs.

I develop this argument over four further sections. First, I document how an interest in the types of knowledge used in wholesale finance has been used to specify the distinctive working cultures in different IFCs. Second, I introduce London's distinctive working culture in merchant and investment banking, paying particular attention to how this has changed over time. In the third section I consider how attending to processes of learning and education, rather than knowledge reveals how such variegation is sustained, alongside more formal regulatory environments that have been the main focus of research to date.

Specifying variegation within and between international financial centres

Clustering of financial services activity is not an entirely new phenomenon. For instance, financial services firms, notably banks, began to cluster in the City of London from the 1700s onwards, associated with supporting Britain's development as an imperial power (Cain and Hopkins, 1986, 1987). Nevertheless, financial services clustering has intensified in recent decades, leading academic research to identify a small number of international financial centres that continue to be vitally important to the system's reproduction (Choi et al., 2003). Research in this respect typically draws attention to New York, London and Hong Kong as well as noting the growing importance of centres in Southeast Asia including Shanghai, Beijing and Hong Kong (Lai, 2012). In many ways, this work builds on the significant contribution of Harvey (1982) in stimulating a research field around the geographies of money and finance. His approach stimulated work that examined the changing geopolitics of the international financial system and specifically how distinctive regulatory environments and associated working cultures gave rise to distinctive international onshore and offshore financial centres (Martin, 1999). In so doing, this work counters arguments that technological innovation and deregulation would signal the declining importance of location in shaping financial services activity as argued in O'Brien's (1991) 'end of geography' thesis for example. Indeed, such is the importance attached to IFCs that there is now a commonly understood hierarchy of centres (typically led by London and New York) and a consulting industry has emerged that seeks to document the relative strengths of different centres as well as offering advice on how centres could improve their standing (see for example Z/Yen, 2014).

In terms of theorizing the continued dominance of a relatively small number of IFCs within the international financial system, two complementary research approaches have developed. First, research has examined the intra cluster benefits of agglomeration within financial centres for financial firms and agents (Cook et al., 2007). This work takes as its starting point Clark and O'Connor's (1997) examination of the types of expert knowledge involved in the production, development and consumption of financial products. In this respect, they argue that financial products tend to be opaque in nature such that significant knowledge asymmetries can develop between financial services providers and their clients. As a result, firms co-locate in order to develop financial innovations and products at the boundary of financial firms and their corporate clients, increasingly involving other forms of expertise, notably that from corporate lawyers as well as informal knowledge spill-overs that take place within the cluster. In this way, financial centres are characterized by dense interpersonal and inter firm relations that give rise to what Bathelt et al. (2004) term 'buzz'. It is argued that it is this buzz that facilitates processes of innovation as financial service professionals use it to learn about the specific demands of their clients as well as the innovations being made by rival firms. Two further advantages arise from financial centre agglomeration. First, financial clusters facilitate market liquidity as customers and producers are co-located within the same financial centre. Second, the existing strengths of the cluster continue to attract further highly skilled labour which is required to sustain the financial services industry, due to its knowledge rich nature.

Beyond this work on intra cluster agglomeration economies, a second strand of research has examined inter-cluster relationships and the ways in which these sustain the dominance of a small number of financial centres. This research develops Castell's (1996) specification of a network society and emphasizes relations of complementarity, competition and commonality between IFCS, arguing that these relations are essential to the success of any given IFC. Wójcik (2013, p. 2) summarizes this approach when he argues that, 'from this perspective, international financial centres are viewed as a spatially distributed network of money and power, where the global and local processes intermesh and run into each other in a variety of ways'. In terms of IFCs themselves, much of this work has focused on the so-called NY-LON (New York London) connection (see Beaverstock, 2005; Wójcik, 2013) as well as relationships that have, temporarily at least, challenged the dominance of London and New York such as the perceived challenge posed to London's dominance as the leading European IFC by Frankfurt in the wake of the creation of the Eurozone (Faulconbridge, 2004). However, recent work has begun to examine the rise of other IFCs from this relational perspective. For example, work has been conducted into the changing relative power of different IFCs in Southeast Asia including Singapore, Hong Kong, Beijing and Shanghai (Lai, 2012). Meanwhile in terms of the substantive connections which are considered in this literature, particular attention has been focused on the global office networks of leading financial institutions and law firms, the geographies of stock markets that in many ways anchor IFCs and the flows of highly skilled individuals through migration and expatriation that support the development of specialist labour markets in IFCs (Beaverstock, 2004).

Taken together, this research has made considerable inroads into documenting the continued variegation between different IFCS. However, an understanding of how such variegation is reproduced and sustained has received less attention. In response, in this chapter I focus on the role of highly skilled individuals working in financial centres, particularly in merchant and investment banking in London's financial district to consider how a focus on their knowledge and learning practices may provide one important avenue through which such variegation is reproduced and sustained.

Specifying financial working cultures in London's financial district

An interest in London's financial working culture and its contribution to London's continued importance as an IFC is a longstanding research concern. Financial working cultures can be understood as comprising the ways in which financiers' daily working practices are co-constitutive of the regulatory, corporate and societal cultures of which they are a part. Perhaps most notably London's financial working culture, historically at least, has been characterized as being one of 'gentlemanly capitalism' (Augar, 2001). In part this reflects the highly gendered nature of merchant banking which was dominated by men who had been predominantly recruited based on their shared social and educational backgrounds at a small number of elite public (fee paying) schools and the Universities of Oxford and Cambridge. However, of critical importance for my interest in working cultures in this chapter, these social relations and the 'old boys networks' through which they were created (Cain and Hopkins, 1987; Michie, 1992) were used to form the basis of trust based relations between bankers derived from their shared backgrounds. As Thrift (1994, p. 342) notes, this 'narrative of the gentleman' was 'based on values of honour, integrity, courtesy and so on, and manifested in ideas of how to act, ways to talk [and] suitable clothing' (see also Tickell, 1996). Whilst McDowell (1997) has demonstrated how multiple masculinities existed in the City in the 1990s as the 'gentlemen' of merchant banks were accompanied by an increasingly aggressive macho masculinity associated with traders, it remains the case that the narrative of the gentleman was particularly important. Indeed, it has been argued that 'gentlemanly capitalism' underpinned London's historically light touch approach to regulation in which the Bank of England was based within close proximity of the banks it was regulating such that the Bank could use this location to fulfil its regulatory requirements based on a shared understanding between financiers and the Bank of England that a 'gentleman's word was his bond' (see Pryke, 1991).

This focus on the distinctive socio-economic context of working practices in London reflects the focus of economic geographical research into IFCs from the late 1990s which is characterized by a diversification in theoretical approaches beyond earlier work that focused on the geopolitics of money and finance. Rather, this more recent work has emphasized the social and cultural constitution of finance and argued that these dimensions are important when explaining and understanding the continued dominance of a small number of IFCs (Hall, 2011). Two strands of work have emerged within this wider approach. First, attention has been paid to understanding how developing interpersonal relations amongst financiers within and between IFCs is vital to the production and circulation of technical know-how which is central to the creation of financial products and the ability to tailor these to demands of corporate clients (Clark and O'Connor, 1997). Indeed, the importance of such relations has led a whole set of mobility practices within investment banking labour markets including short but frequent forms of business travel between financial centres as well as expatriation and longer forms of migration. Second, this research emphasizes that technical know-how is not the only form of knowledge that is important within financial services work. Rather this is accompanied by embodied forms of know-how that are typically more embodied in nature and give rise to the importance of bodily performances as signalled by Thrift's (1994) work on the narrative of the gentleman in London (Hall and Appleyard, 2009).

However, whilst research has suggested that gentlemanly capitalism was important, if not dominant, in terms of the working cultures of the City of London until at least Big Bang in 1986 and the considerable deregulatory changes that this brought about, significant changes to London's working cultures were seen following the internationalization of the City during the 1990s. In particular, the City went through a significant period of development in the 2000s in what can now be seen as a form of financialized development in which new banking products, notably securities grew significantly. Indeed, it was this period that laid the ground for the development of these products which were central to the causes of the 2007–08 financial crisis. The implications of this for the international financial system and the causes of the 2007–08 financial crisis have been widely debated (Augar, 2009; Tett, 2010). In this chapter, I examine the consequences of this in terms of the working cultures in London's investment banking sector. In what follows, I consider how examining the reproduction of these can be instructive in understanding how the distinctive working cultures of different IFCs is reproduced and the implications of this for the financial system more generally.

Financialized working cultures in London's financial district

Initially, the growing international make up of financial institutions in London from the 1990s onwards had relatively little effect on the working practices of wholesale bankers, and work tended to focus on established (US) investment banking activities through corporate finance activities, particularly offering advice to corporations on mergers and acquisitions. This work was supported by investment banks making loans to their clients in order to facilitate their M&A activities. Revenue for banks in this business model was generated by charging fees for M&A advice, usually at around 1.5 per cent of the value of the deal being considered (Folkman *et al.*, 2007). In so doing, despite the arrival of more overseas banks in London's financial district, this business model echoed in many ways that of merchant banks that had previously dominated in the City of London in which banking was typically based on long-term relationships between clients and their banks with clients usually using one bank for all their requirements rather than using different banks for different types of services (Hall, 2009). However, during the late 1990s and 2000s the profitability of this business model was challenged, primarily because more banks became involved in any one deal, thereby reducing the fee paid to any one bank (Hall, 2007). As a result, investment banks in London in the 2000s developed alternative business practices, particularly new, high margin activities including 'trading and principal investment where the investment bankers typically manages the investment bank's own account dealing in even more arcane coupons or undertakes asset management' (Folkman *et al.*, 2007, p. 563). Folkman *et al.* (2007) go on to argue that as a result, investment bankers are one component group of 'new capitalized markets' or what I've termed elsewhere 'financialized elites' 'who play a significant role in shaping processes of financialisation by not simply servicing the financial and banking requirements of large corporations but also increasingly by operating in financial markets in their own right' (Hall, 2009, p. 179).

This shift has led to a marked change in the working practices of London's financial district banking community. Previously, investment banking was a relationship based business as banks worked to develop long-term relationships with commercial clients. However, during the late 1990s, the nature of investment banking itself changed as, for example, undertaking an M&A

transaction increasingly involved not a bilateral relationship between a bank and a corporate client but centred on managing the relationships between a number of financial institutions including corporate finance boutiques, hedge funds and corporate law firms, all of whom have become increasingly important in delivering the increasingly complex financial advice demanded by corporate clients (Folkman et al., 2007; Hall, 2007). These working practices within investment banks changed even more markedly through the rise of structured finance, particularly securitization during the 2000s. This form of financial services work led to growing demand for individuals who were highly numerate, often holding postgraduate degrees in subjects such as maths, physics and computer science such that these individuals could perform 'socio-financial engineering' (Pryke and Allen, 2000) in which complex structured finance products were produced that offered 'the allure of high potential margins at a corporate level and personal remuneration through bonuses at the individual level' (Hall, 2009, p. 184).

This changed working culture, which is typified by a greater emphasis on technical and quantitative know how rather than relation based services, has been widely identified and debated, not least in terms of how it at least in part caused the international financial crisis (Tett, 2010). However, comparatively less attention has been paid to how this working culture was produced and sustained in London. In this respect, a number of factors are important including the changing makeup of London's financial district in terms of the types of firms operating there and the regulatory environment that favoured and permitted certain forms of financial services activity. However, in what follows, I return to the longstanding relationship between education and London's working culture to suggest that this represents an important but comparatively neglected set of activities and practices that shape the working cultures of the City.

Education and the (re)production of financialized working practices in the City of London

The internationalization of the City from the 1990s onwards, associated with the rise of new financial products, notably structured finance, meant that historic ways of recruiting bankers through 'old boys networks' associated with a small number of schools could no longer meet the demands of the City's labour markets (Leyshon and Thrift, 1997). This led to a widening of the educational backgrounds of those recruited into the City, albeit in only a limited way as recruitment became increasingly focused on the UK's elite group of Russell Group of universities (Jones, 1998). However, as the number of graduates seeking entry into these labour markets also increased, recruitment into financial services in the City is increasingly typified by positional competitions as individuals seek to obtain higher degrees and additional credentials in order to secure access, as well as undertaking internships (Hall and Appleyard, 2009). Indeed, in many ways the growing importance of an internship in securing employment in a leading investment bank is evidence of the ways in which vestiges of 'gentlemanly capitalism' remain since these openings are sometimes not widely advertised and are arranged by the personal and familial contacts of students wanting to undertake one. Moreover, they are often not paid, or if they are only nominally and as such undertaking an internship is limited to those with enough financial support to live in London.

This change in entry requirements into financial labour markets, and particularly those of investment banks, has been accompanied by a proliferation of postgraduate education and early career training which is increasingly seen as necessary in order to position oneself successfully to secure employment in the City (Hall and Appleyard, 2009). For example, recruits increasingly hold masters degrees, often in quantitative skills, or obtain an MBA later on in their career in order to maximize their positional advantage relative to other employees. This generic education is typically accompanied by firm specific training including graduate training schemes in which individuals work for a small period of time across a number of banking functions. Recent work in economic geography has begun to explore the importance of these educational activities not only in facilitating entry into elite labour markets but also in (re)producing the distinctive working cultures of particular IFCs (Faulconbridge and Hall, 2014). This approach draws on theories of practice to explore how economic practices are situated and normalized in particular geographical and institutional settings (see Gherardi, 2009; Shove, 2003). In particular, through a focus on London's early career financial and legal elite Faulconbridge and Hall (2014, p. 1683) examine 'how post-first-degree education represents an important means by which early-career elites are inculcated into the place-specific and organizationally specific meanings, competencies and technologies associated with financial business practices'.

This work builds on a longstanding interest in economic geography with the ways in which institutes sustain economic competitiveness and how these institutions develop over time (Saxenian, 1994; Storper, 2011). However, within economic geography, less attention has been paid to the creation and reproduction of institutional landscapes themselves. This is in contrast to work on the varieties of capitalism which places more emphasis on the ways in which institutions change, identifying education and training system as one element within this. Developing these insights, economic geographers have emphasized how education and training systems are both the product of, and shape, the institutional context in which they operate, thereby providing an important way of shaping both economic and financial practice but also the wider institutional context within which such practices take place. Research has shown how education, in the form of graduate training schemes for early career financiers plays, an important role in this process, as they are both tailored to the demands of investment banks operating in London whilst also serving to inculcate new recruits into what are deemed organizationally and geographically appropriate and desirable working practices. For example, in the case of investment banking, evidence suggests that banks are increasingly concerned about the limitations of the numerical skills held by UK graduates and are tailoring their training courses to reflect the different numerical ability of UK as opposed to EU and international recruits at a time when quantitative skills are increasingly desired by investment banks in the City (Faulconbridge and Hall, 2014).

Work such as this is important because it suggests that understanding how institutional landscapes are (re)produced is important since it opens up the space to consider how different forms of working cultures may be developed. Indeed, simply changing the content of educational programmes in and of themselves is rarely successful as the case of MBA curricula in the 2000s demonstrated. At this time, there was considerable debate about the nature of MBA curricula in light of the crisis in corporate America following the bursting of the dot com bubble. In particular there was a sense that MBA degrees needed to be less theoretical and better able to prepare managers for 'real world' issues (Mintzberg, 2004; Pfeffer and Fong, 2004). However, sceptics noted that rather than simply altering business school curricula, a more significant rethinking of the role of business schools in the corporate economy was needed in order to make effective change (Khurana, 2010; Starkey et al., 2004). This suggests that simply adjusting educational course content is unlikely to significantly change working practices in the City that have been the subject of considerable popular, political and media debate in the wake of the 2007–08 financial crisis. Rather, educational changes would need to be developed alongside changes to other dimensions of London's institutional landscape including its regulatory environment and the cultural and social norms that shape what counts as normalized and legitimate behaviour in the City.

Conclusions

Economic geographical research on finance, banking and IFCs has developed considerably over the last 30 years. Early work focused on the geopolitics of money and finance whilst more recent work has developed a stronger socially and culturally attuned reading of the nature of banking and finance. What unites these literatures is a concern with demonstrating how banking and finance have a distinctive geography that is important in understanding its operation, as evidenced by the uneven geography in terms of both its causes and consequences of the so-called 'global' financial crisis of 2007–08. Most notably, attention has focused on the continued clustering of financial and related services in a small number of IFCs. More recently, work has moved beyond simply demonstrating the differences between IFCS but has increasingly sought to document how differences in the institutional landscapes of different IFCs gives rise to geographically variegated working cultures.

In this respect, in this chapter, I have focused on the case of investment banking in London's financial district to examine how an interest in knowledge, learning and education has been developed within economic geography to reveal the ways in which education plays an important, but hitherto comparatively neglected role in reproducing London's cultures of work. This research is important in two main ways. First, it provides one way of examining how London's institutional landscape is reproduced – something that is particularly important given the ways in which these working cultures have been scrutinized in the wake of the financial crisis. Second, and following on, in so doing, it provides one way of developing a more politically and critically attuned reading of the cultural and social dimensions of money and finance, something that more recent work in economic geography has not developed as fully as earlier geopolitical approaches (Hall, 2011). In this respect, a focus on education and training within financial and banking labour markets in financial centres such as London is particularly instructive since it suggests that education is likely to have played an important role in reproducing and legitimizing the approaches to risks and their managements that characterized investment banking in the run up to the financial crisis. Revealing the role of education in this way is important because it points to the ways in which education might be used as a political and practical lever to shape behaviour in financial labour markets (see Faulconbridge and Hall, 2014) by, for example, demonstrating and drawing attention to the interconnected nature of global finance and the ways in which these networks were central to the transmission of the crisis itself.

More generally, economic geographical work on banking has made an important contribution to the burgeoning interdisciplinary approaches to banking and finance that have developed throughout the 2000s. For example, geographers have sought to develop the spatial vocabularies at work in research in financialization to move beyond a focus on the national scale but to instead reveal the complex geographies that are involved in reproducing financialized economies. Meanwhile, in terms of cultural economy approaches to money and finance, economic geographers have used their spatial interests to suggest that this might be one way in which this literature might develop a more critical tone. These inter-disciplinary avenues would seem to be the most appropriate for future research that continues to grapple with the changing geographies of banking and the ways in which these shape both the international financial system and the wider global economy.

Acknowledgements

The arguments presented in this chapter have been developed whilst working on project funded by the ESRC (RES-061-25-0071) and The British Academy (MD130065).

References

Augar, P. (2001) *The Death of Gentlemanly Capitalism: The Rise and Fall of London's Investment Banks*. London: Penguin.
Augar, P. (2009) *Chasing Alpha: How Reckless Growth and Unchecked Ambition Ruined the City's Golden Decade*. London: Bodley Head.
Bathelt, H., Malmberg, A. and Maskell P. (2004) 'Clusters and knowledge: Local buzz, global pipelines and the process of knowledge creation', *Progress in Human Geography* 28: 31–56.
Beaverstock, J.V. (2004) 'Managing across borders': Knowledge management and expatriation in professional service legal firms', *Journal of Economic Geography* 4 (2): 157–79.
Beaverstock, J.V. (2005) 'Transnational elites in the city: British highly-skilled inter-company transferees in New York City's financial district', *Journal of Ethnic and Migration Studies*, 31: 245–68.
Cain, P.J. and Hopkins, A.G. (1986) 'Gentlemanly capitalism and British expansion overseas. The colonial system 1688–1850', *Economic History Review* 39 (4): pp. 501–25.
Cain, P.J. and Hopkins, A.G. (1987) 'Gentlemanly capitalism and British expansion overseas II: New imperialism, 1850–1945' *Economic History Review* 40 (1): 1–26.
Castells, M. (1996) *The Rise of the Network Society*. Malden: Blackwells.
Choi, S.R., Park, D. and Tschoegel, A. (2003) 'Banks and the world's major banking centers, 2000', *Review of World Economics* 139 (3): 550–68.
Clark, G. and O'Connor, K. (1997) 'The informational content of financial products and the spatial structure of the global finance industry'. In Cox, K. (ed.), *Spaces of Globalization: Reasserting the Power of the Local*. New York: Guildford, 89–114.
Cook et al. (2007) 'The role of location in knowledge creation and diffusion: Evidence of centripetal and centrifugal forces in the City of London financial services agglomeration', *Environment and Planning A*, 39 (6): 1325–45.
Dodd, N. (2014) *The Social Life of Money*. Princeton, NJ: Princeton University Press.
Engelen, E. et al. (2012) 'Misrule of experts? The financial crisis as elite debacle', *Economy and Society*, 41: 360–82.
Faulconbridge, J.R. (2004) 'London and Frankfurt in Europe's evolving financial centre network', *Area*, 36 (3): 235–44.
Faulconbridge, J.R. and Hall, S. (2014) 'Reproducing the City of London's institutional landscape: The role of education and learning of situated practices by early career elites', *Environment and Planning A*, 46 (7): 1682–98.
Folkman, P. et al. (2007) 'Working for themselves? capital market intermediaries and present day capitalism', *Business History*, 49: 552–72.
Gherardi, S. (2009) 'Practice? It's a matter of taste!', *Management Learning*, 40: 535–50.
Hall, S. (2007) 'Relational marketplaces and the rise of boutiques in London's corporate finance industry', *Environment and Planning A*, 39 (8): 1838–54.
Hall, S. (2009) 'Financialized elites and the changing nature of finance capitalism: Investment bankers in London's financial district', *Competition and Change*, 13 (2): 175–91.
Hall, S. (2011) 'Geographies of money and finance I: Cultural economy, politics and place', *Progress in Human Geography*, 35 (2): 234–45.
Hall, S. and Appleyard, L. (2009) 'City of London, city of learning? Placing business education within the geographies of finance', *Journal of Economic Geography*, 9 (5): 597–617.
Harvey, D. (1982) *The Limits to Capital*. Oxford: Blackwell.
Jones, A.M. (1998) '(Re)producing gender cultures: Theorizing gender in investment banking recruitment', *Geoforum*, 29: 451–74.
Khurana, R. (2010) *From Higher Aims to Hired Hands: The Social Transformation of American Business Schools and the Unfulfilled Promise of Management as a Profession*. Princeton, NJ: Princeton University Press.
Lai, Karen P.Y. (2012) 'Differentiated markets: Shanghai, Beijing and Hong Kong in China's financial centre network', *Urban Studies*, 49 (6): 1275–96.
Leyshon, A. and Thrift, N. (1997) *Money Space: Geographies of Monetary Transformation*. London: Routledge.
McDowell, L. (1997) *Capital Culture*. Oxford: Blackwell.
Martin, R. (ed.) (1999) *Money and the Space Economy*. Oxford: Wiley.
Michie, R. (1992) *The City of London: Continuity and Change, 1850–1990*. London: MacMillan.
Mintzberg, H. (2004) *Developing Managers, not MBAs*. London: FT Prentice Hall.
O'Brien, R. (1991) *Global Financial Integration: The End of Geography*. London: Pinter.

Pfeffer, F. and Fong, C. (2004) 'The end of business schools? Less success than meets the eye', *Academy of Management, Learning and Education*, 1: 78–95.

Pryke, M. (1991) 'An international city going global: Spatial change in the City of London', *Environment and Planning D: Society and Space*, 9: 197–222.

Pryke, M. and Allen, J. (2000) 'Monetized time–space: Derivatives – money's new imaginary', *Economy and Society*, 2: 264–84.

Saxenian, A. (1994) *Regional Advantage. Culture and Competition in Silicon Valley and Route 128*. Cambridge, MA: Harvard University Press.

Shove, E. (2003) *Comfort, Cleanliness and Convenience: The Social Organization of Normality*. Oxford: Berg.

Sidaway, J. (2008) 'Subprime crisis: American crisis or human crisis?' *Environment and Planning D: Society and Space*, 26: 195–8.

Starkey, K., Hatchuel, A. and Tempest, S. (2004) 'Rethinking the business school', *Journal of Management Studies*, 41: 1521–31.

Storper, M. (2011), 'Why do regions develop and change? The challenge for geography and economics', *Journal of Economic Geography*, 11: 333–46.

Tett, G. (2010) *Fool's Gold: How Unrestrained Greed Corrupted a Dream, Shattered Global Markets and Unleashed a Catastrophe*. London: Abacus.

Thrift, N. (1994) 'On the social and cultural determinants of international financial centres: The case of the City of London'. In Thrift, N., Corbridge, S. and Martin, R. (eds), *Money, Power and Space*. Oxford: Blackwell, pp. 327–55.

Tickell, A. (1996) 'Making a melodrama out of a crisis: Reinventing the collapse of Barings Bank', *Environment and Planning D: Society and Space*, 14 (1): 5–33.

Wainwright, T. (2009) 'Laying the foundations for a crisis: Mapping the historico-geographical construction of residential mortgage backed securitization in the UK', *International Journal of Urban and Regional Research*, 33 (2): 372–88.

Wójcik, D. (2013) 'Where governance fails: advanced business services and the offshore world', *Progress in Human Geography*, 37 (3): 330–47.

Zald, M.N. and Lounsbury, M. (2010), 'The wizards of Oz: Towards an institutional approach to elites, expertise and command posts', *Organization Studies*, 31: 963–6.

Z/Yen (2014) *The Global Financial Centres Index 15*. London: Z/Yen.

8
The boundaries of finance as zones of conflicts

Sabine Montagne

Problematic: the boundaries of finance

Most studies in social science that have analysed finance (its institutions, its agents, its practices and norms) in the 1990s–2000s, have stressed, on the one hand, its peculiarity and, on the other hand, its ability/power to shape the other spheres along its own norms. On the one hand, the literature in ethnology confirms the distinctive features of the everyday financial work: distinctive habitus (Ho, 2009) and exceptional compensations (Godechot, 2007); seemingly high technical capabilities based on innovations that have been previously made in the academic sphere (Mackenzie, 2006). Finance is definitively a specific work area. The division of labour, inside the financial world, shows how some positions allow skimming value when other positions allow only to surf (Ertürk *et al.*, 2007). This diversity is also analysed as a proliferation of new actors who contribute to the investment decision-making process (Froud, Leaver and Williams, 2007). To a certain extent, finance seems to be a socio-economic 'laboratory' where new forms of labour, of knowledge and resource sharing are experimented.

On the other hand, literatures about 'financialization' state that financial deregulation has put pressure on firms and states, seeking not only to increase profits and dividends but also to force them to internalize new mental categories through its own performance metrics (Lazonick and O'Sullivan, 2000). The political economy that links the expansion of finance with the political neo-liberalism has described the effects of finance on everyday life as a 'deepening social connectedness', a network of binding processes that 'push ordinary people into financial mechanisms, confine their agency to the disciplinary mechanisms of borrowing and repayment' and, at the end, change their cultural dispositions (Konings, 2009, p. 115). This great ascendancy of finance over the other social spheres is largely viewed as a unilateral power that imposes through the contamination of mental categories and understandings. Financialization is colonization.

These perspectives come from very different sociological traditions and deal with different levels or scales. However they share three common points: they consider that finance is peculiar (finance is 'different'), autonomous (it creates its own norms), and has the power to export (finance imposes its own norms). So, finance is disentangled from the rest of the economy and the society and is able to deeply change them. Focusing on the peculiarity and the power of finance, these perspectives tend to give little attention to the processes through which finance is reciprocally determined by the other social spheres.

This reciprocal influence has been put into light by the financial crisis of 2007 and the direct governmental actions to support banks and save the financial system. The history of the intimate relationships between states and finance (Carruthers, 1996) has suddenly came back in the academic agenda. Sociologists and political historians have been increasingly re-interested in the economic-financial dimension of the state building (Lemoine, 2013; Polillo, 2013; Krippner, 2007). Beyond the partnership between state and finance, relationships between finance and other social spheres have been explored: for example, joint development of finance and French social work via microfinance (Moulévrier, 2013) or Brazilian trade unions (Chaves, 2013), that show how non financial agents (social workers and trade unions) have changed their world images and the meaning of their mission through performing joint tasks with financiers and, reciprocally, how their participation has influenced the form and scope of financial transactions.

All these works look at the expansion of finance *in connection to* the own dynamics of other leading social activities. The expansion of finance is viewed as part of a more structural or systemic (economic, political, and institutional) change. Several areas are changing at the same time and there is no need to assume *a priori* that finance is the first and leading engine of this change. Such a perspective allows focusing on non-financial agents and institutions and investigating processes and social forces that interfere with the social construction of financial institutions, practices and beliefs (Montagne and Ortiz, 2013). This perspective acknowledges the results of the sociology of finance that has focused on financial agents per se (traders, brokers, financial analysts, portfolio managers, bankers) and on their way to allocating money and that has focused on financial institutions per se (stock exchange, regulatory agencies, central banks) and their support to the expansion of finance. This systemic perspective supplements this corpus in emphasizing how non-financial agents and entities have supported (or resisted) this expansion.

This perspective is not exactly those of studies on financialization. Although there are at least three different approaches of financialization (Van der Zwan, 2014) we can consider 'financialization' a conceptual innovation that has rather consisted in describing finance as 'feeding upon itself' (Engelen, 2008, p. 112), as 'the growing share of finance-related income in non-financial firms' (Engelen, 2008, p. 114) and discussed 'general developments within capitalism, understood as a global system' (Engelen, 2008, p. 115). Of course socio-economic processes outside finance have been taken into account but have often been considered *conditions* of possibility for the expansion of financial activities or *effects* of the unilateral financial power. Conflicts of power and insider struggles, inside the other spheres, have hardly been examined as causal mechanisms or forces able to shape some institutional or organizational characteristics of finance. And yet we may wonder whether non-financial agents (corporates, labour, households, public officials) have used finance to serve their own interests, to deal with their own internal conflicts, and have become 'financialized' by their own strong acting much more than staying passive.

However, this first reformulation still gives too much credit to the very existence of a financial sphere isolated, detached and disentangled from the rest of the economy. Against this view, the British-style cultural political economy makes the point about the porosity of finance. According to these authors, 'financial institutions and actors are not coherent wholes with stable identities and shared interests', 'Financialization does not impose one new logic but makes and remakes the world in complex ways' (Froud, Leaver and Williams, 2007 p. 343). They reproach the studies on financialization that draw from functionalist economic views, for focusing too narrowly on the 'agency' between top managers inside giant firms and shareholders and for neglecting the other actors involved in shareholder value regime. Their alternative consists of taking into account the contribution of intermediaries outside firms (especially accountants and lawyers), who have yet greatly benefited from the permanent restructuring of these giant firms (Ertürk *et al.*, 2007). So, these authors invite us to investigate the wide range of intermediary positions that have been so much interested in the large variety of financial transactions and, consequently, have made what is called 'financialization' so strong. They invite us to surrender the vision of a separate social sphere defined by clear boundaries to the rest of economy.

We propose to push further and think out finance as processes of interaction with activities that are traditionally taken for non financial ones. Following Ertürk *et al.* (2007) who invite us to broaden the range of tasks, work and actors involved in finance, we suggest to extend this perimeter to labour relations. Moreover, we propose to assume that financial activities are a way to deal with conflicts that exist in the capital–labour nexus in exporting them to financial arenas and so, reshaping them through financial activities.

Such an attempt to 'dis-essentialize' finance is intellectually interesting since it contributes to a 'processual sociology'. Of course, financial work and rules establish professional jurisdictions but we have to give up a *substantialist* view of groups and cultures that are supposed to constitute Finance. The 'processual' sociology of Andrew Abbott (1995) thinks of cultural preferences, identities, and practices of groups not only as products of interaction with other groups but as a complex activity of *contingent building of boundaries* (Jeanpierre, 2010, p. 162). These preferences, identities and practices are not taken for causal determinants or for the origin of these groups. They are continuously redefined. As A. Abbott states 'social theories that presume given, fixed entities ... always fall apart over the problem of explaining change in those entities' (Abbott, 1995, p. 859). By contrast, he asserts that 'social entities come into existence when social actors tie social boundaries together in certain ways. Boundaries come first, then entities' (ibid., p. 860). If we follow him when he tells that 'Differences are things that emerge from local cultural negotiations' and 'that some events have stable lineages, thereby becoming what we call "actors", is something to be explained, not something to be assumed' (ibid., p. 863), we must consider how people and processes have created financial institutions and financial actors by linking old and new boundaries into units and so have finally constituted finance as a social entity.

This attempt to 'dis-essentialize' finance is also politically interesting since it helps to identify strategies that aim at escaping responsibility for social decisions. Here we follow Greta Krippner's analysis (2007). She shows how Federal Reserve officials discovered innovations in the policy process which 'enabled markets to do the FeD's work for it' (Krippner, 2007, p. 477) and allowed them to escape responsibility for economic outcomes in the context of continuing deteriorating economic conditions. In the same way, we propose to see the enrolment of workers and middle class households into finance by the corporate community and the federal government from the 1960s onwards, as a way to regulate labour and social conflicts in 'exporting' them to the financial sphere.

Such a relation between capital–labour nexus and finance has already been deeply analysed at the macroeconomic level. In the macroeconomic regime from the 1990s onwards, characterized by low wages, people have borrowed money to sustain their level of consumption. So credit has developed *because* (e.g. a macroeconomic causal mechanism) of the conjunction of a new capital–labour nexus and the upholding of consumer habitus. As for welfare policies, political scientists have explained how pension funds and mutual funds have been promoted in such a way that the government got rid of the task of expanding Social Security in the 1960–70s (Wooten, 2004; Hacker, 2002; Weir, Orloff and Skocpol, 1988). Then, employers got rid of taking the risk for funding sound pension funds for their employees from the 1980s: the financial portfolio risk has been re-allocated from employers to workers and households, so building up the so-called 'Defined Contribution Society' (Zelinsky, 2004). Nowadays, all aspects of the social life (retirement, children education, health, housing) must be planned through savings accounts and mortgage credit. If households cannot afford what they think they are entitled to, the system of the Defined Contribution Society lets them believe that it is their own individual fault.

The attribution of responsibilities for income and employment to real corporate employers and real macroeconomic policymakers has been reshaped into the anonymous and multidimensional exposure of workers to labour and financial markets. The struggle between well identified interest groups (unions versus corporates) and between relatively stable political coalitions (liberal-labour alliances vs. conservative coalitions) of the 1950–60s (Domhoff, 2013) has tended to dissolve into impersonal market forces. The Marxian subordination of labour – based on the absolute necessity for non-owners of selling their workforce – is redoubled by the necessity for non-owners to save from their wage and put their money into this specific social organization and hierarchy of positions called 'Finance'.

So, the problematic of the boundaries of finance seems to be a good entry to go beyond the skin-deep question of wealth inequality and to address the renewed deep-rooted question of the hierarchical subservience in employment that characterized capitalism (Lordon, 2015).

The case: Pension industry as an emergent entity

I will expand on this idea of finance as an emergent and porous entity, impregnated with outside conflicts, by analysing a well-known example, the case of US pension funds. It is a very good example to see how such an approach works. Pension industry has emerged in the 1950s. Before that, managing retirement promises was a task performed inside corporate firms, often as a 'pay as you go' device, not much connected with capital markets, sometimes delegated to insurance companies. From the 1950s onwards, specific professions, firms and transactions have developed and pension management has been disembedded from its corporate origin. The construction of a pension industry as a structured set of institutions and organizations has consisted of connecting the welfare paternalistic programmes of employers with wealth management activities to create a very novel space of practices and actors.

But pension funds have been still recognized as both creatures of capital/labour compromises – retirement benefits were a component of the long-term employment relationship – and powerful financial actors (Clark, 2000). So they seem to be located at the crossroads of two distinct social spaces (labour relations and financial work), two distinct institutional logics (social protection and financial speculation). One of the most striking features of this hybrid nature of pension industry is the fact that pension funds are ruled by the Department of Labor and not by the Securities Exchange Commission although they act definitively as financial investors.

Tensions between these logics interact in everyday transactions as well as in investment policies, governance and the constitutional status of pension funds. As for investment policies, for example, are pension funds just orthodox financial intermediaries that entirely comply with financial economics? Or are they influenced by other considerations because of the fact that they are managed on behalf of workers and under the control of employers? As for governance and power relations, do they manage the relation workers/financial markets as financial intermediaries do between shareholders and corporate managers? Or are they influenced by the fact that the beneficiaries (workers) of their services are subordinated to sponsors of pension funds (employers) through the job relation? We will show that investment policies and governance of pension funds are definitively influenced by the fact that pension funds are labour compromises. So, financial practices and beliefs of the pension industry are directly shaped by interest and conflicts between non-financial agents, workers and employers. In the words of Abbott (1995, p. 860), struggles between labour and employers come first; pension industry as a financial sphere emerges from their negotiations.

To examine this emergence, we will focus on the legal characteristics of these funds. The reason of this focus is that change in legal rules is one of the markers of the emergence and change of social entities. Law gives to nascent entities: materiality, regular and objective features, rules for their reproduction. Studying the history of the ruling of governance and investment policies, especially its actors, processes and mental categories, is a method to investigate the formation of the pension industry, its division of labour, its practices and system of classification.

The first characteristic that has influenced the governance of pension funds is the Trust: pension funds are Trusts. Trusts are a device of family law: they were traditional legal devices, intended to ensure the management of wealth of minors placed under supervision. They keep the control over property away from the proprietor and give it to a third party. Usually used by wealthy aristocratic dynasties, they were intended to keep safe patrimonial identities in avoiding young inheritors selling their estates and assets. Aware of the fact that families can have trouble and disagreement among their members, sponsors of trusts appointed a third party who was not a member of the family, for managing family wealth in compliance with their legal will (Harrington, 2009; Marcus and Hall, 1992). Trusts were also used by robber barons in the nineteenth century to despoil shareholders in minority within large holdings. Since that, Trusts have become the usual device for organizing the asset management of middle class savings. Therefore Trusts belong as well to the speculative capitalism of the last quarter of the nineteenth century as to the capitalism of pooled property of the last quarter of the twentieth century.

Several scholars have considered the peculiarity of this legal origin (Frankel, 2006) and affirmed it is directly responsible for the passivity of workers in pension funds (Alexander, 1993). The legal rules inherited from the ancient trust inhibit any active management that beneficiaries of pension funds could wish. The point of view of the Trust allows that the beneficiaries are *structurally* deprived of any power over asset management and that this deprivation is not an incident linked to a peculiar political conjuncture but has been intentionally institutionalized by employers and the state.

This perspective of the Trust opens the way for a structural or positional assumption: keeping beneficiaries at a distance away from asset management can be compared with the separation between salaried work and its wage compensation. In the same way as Marx defined the salaried work as the *absence of relation* between the product of the work and the price (salary) for this work, we can consider that the financialized labour (through pension funds expansion) is defined by the *absence of control* by workers over the management of assets saved on their behalf. From this perspective, we can consider pension industry a 'site of difference', an emergent entity (Abbott, 1995, p. 862) that is partly shaped by local interactions at the workplace and by nation-wide regulations dealing with the labour/capital conflict.

The second legal characteristic that has influenced investment policies is that these funds must invest according to fiduciary duties and especially according to the standard of prudence. Yet every asset manager is subject to this duty. However, the meaning given to it (by laws and courts) is not exactly the same for private banking, family office and pension funds. The difference is not only due to technical differences, temporal horizon, and risk adverse preferences. It is also due to the fact that capital/labour conflict is at stake in pension funds. By studying legislative, regulatory and judiciary processes together (Montagne, 2013), we have observed how transformations have affected the production and institutionalization of the standard over time. Its meaning has been negotiated both where the federal government's power to regulate meets the political sway of employers and financiers and at the junction between magistrates' procedural independence and the intellectual authority deriving from economic theories. The definition of prudence has grown out of a series of legal, regulatory and jurisprudential processes and is always a stake for employers, politicians, economists and jurists, who work at keeping the impact of the norm on investment behaviour – and more generally on relations between employees and the world of finance – under control.

So, the Trust and the standard of prudence are two legal institutions that show how the recent expansion of pension industry is politically anchored into conflicts of other social spheres and culturally anchored into the history of American economic institutions. Linking together the study of the Trust (as the 'structure' of pension funds) and the history of the prudent investor standard (as a 'multi process' definition of the investment norms) will illustrate our approach: anchoring emerged financial practices and agents into the changing socio-economic arrangements and into the history of economic institutions.

Theoretical and methodological considerations

Before giving more details about these legal characteristics and about how labour conflicts influence financial investing, we must come back to the theoretical background and the methodology. I claim that the influence of capital–labour conflict on finance is observable: (1) since investment norms (standard of prudence) which are financial tools, have not been crafted only by financiers and economists but also by employers and politicians; (2) since financial entities (pension funds) have used a legal device (Trust) inherited from the family sphere and yet used by financiers in the nineteenth century, because it fixed one of the major problems of employers, the control over their employees. In both cases, employers have tried to shape the structure of finance in order to fix problems they have *as employers*: control over the workforce.

The case of pension funds seems perfect for illustrating the view that finance is an emergent entity, anchored in outside conflicts, and is porous to them. Can such a type of investigation be generalized and become a research tool for testing emergence and porosity of finance in other contexts? We need a method that allow to articulate institutions, practices and beliefs of financial agents with institutions, practices and beliefs of non financial agents. One possibility is to look for what they share or what they borrow from each other. As for the example of pension funds, their legal rules have been borrowed from inheritance law (the law of Trusts) and their investment policies have been borrowed from the investment practices of corporate firms, as we will see in the following sections of this text.

Locating the analysis at this meta comparative level, those of shared system of classifications or practices or those of the circulation of meanings, leads us to consider a certain 'continuity of causation' (Hamilton, 1994, p. 185), not only across social space but also across time. Contrasting with the view that the recent expansion of finance is a break with the past, the perspective of shared rules puts into light historical continuities.

This circulation of meaning is particularly observable at the level of law. On the one hand, law diffuses principles across different domains of the social life. On the other hand, since case law largely refers to older cases and former meanings decided by courts decades ago, legal history shapes current economic activity too. These two effects of law (cross sectional and longitudinal) help us to bridge both past and present and 'here and there'. Because some legal principles have been used across time and in different social spaces, we are able to link these histories and spaces by comparing how they have used these legal principles.

We do not take legal rules as substantive and taken-for-granted meaning which would be alternatively used in different places and at different times. By contrast, legal rules must be considered 'contingent, culturally defined categories' (Fourcade, 2009, p. 13) - for example, produced by social processes. That means that our methodology does not consist in picking up these legal rules as if they were totally unambiguous and could be similarly used for an array of economic activities (and so, as 'variables', would affect these activities in similar ways). This mechanistic conception of the effect of law is replaced here with a more 'processual' one. That means that we must explore *why* they have been picked up and *how* they have been changed (or not) by these different activities and how they probably have addressed similar needs. We do not say that the same legal rules would be used in the same way for different activities and over time and that it would be the reason why these activities would be linked together or mutually influenced. By contrast, we assume that the meanings of legal rules are produced according to their specific use in different activities. But when employers organize their pension funds as Trusts, they take the same *pattern* of power nexus as those we find in the family area and in the robber barons' capture process. We will see in the next section that they deprive the beneficiary of control over asset management with the same legal device as the one used by the dynastic Trust or the financial Trust.

That also means that we must investigate *who* has picked them up and changed. This is a usual question for the sociology of law: the plurality of actors and logics emanating from distinct social spheres and impacting the meaning of legal categories. We will see how the example of the standard of prudence illustrates that in the last section.

Pension governance: a socially constructed and legally reinforced passivity of beneficiaries

The Trust is a mechanism of supervision. It began as a medieval arrangement which permitted the knight setting out on a crusade to place his fief in the hands of a peer, who was then bound to look after the family's upkeep. Whatever the kind of situation involved, the Trust always reveals the same need: transmitting wealth to legatees considered incapable of managing it themselves. When the Trust is created, there is a transfer of the ownership of the goods to the trustee, who then has a legal right over them. So Trusts are structures for depriving owners of control over their property. As Alexander analysed:

> Beneficiary passivity and the need for fiduciary protection were the primary purposes for creating the trust... Most trusts were created to benefit individuals (usually family members especially the settlor's wife and children and future generations of descendants) who were *socially constructed as dependent and passive*. Most settlors had a *paternalistic* motive for creating trusts: it was a surrogate for the settlor's personal protection of the beneficiaries... The trust itself took the place of the settlor as an actively *governing patriarch*. Modern pension law transplants the trust law assumption of beneficiary passivity to a quite different context.
>
> (Alexander, 1993, p. 132, emphasis added)

This passive model of ownership deviates from classical ownership which, historically promoted by the common law of property:

> consolidated in a single legal entity, usually an individual person, the relevant rights, privileges, and powers for possessing, using, and transferring assets... Under the passive model, beneficial owners of property rights lack the *authority* to decide how the assets in which they have a beneficial interest are used.
>
> (Alexander, 1993, p. 111)

Moreover pension law has greatly reinforced this characteristic. The federal statute passed in 1974, the Employee Retirement Income Security Act (ERISA) invites employers to delegate asset management to 'investment managers', by relieving them of liability for mismanagement of assets turned over to managers. Consequently, these professionals have got the responsibility for controlling the use of pension property even if employers formally control their selection, hiring and firing.

This mode of owning and managing pooled capital that had been set up for defined benefit schemes under ERISA has been extended to the new kind of pension funds, the defined contribution plans called 401k, from the 1980s on. These plans are Trusts and are regulated under ERISA. The same network of legal rules are implemented and enforced. However, rights, duties and responsibility are different since workers are formally entitled to decide how to invest their contribution. Does it mean that this autonomy breaks with the passive ownership structure and tends to mimic the classical liberal ownership?

ERISA formally authorized beneficiaries to make their own decision-making and the practical way for doing it is the now widespread 401k plans which mitigate trust law principles and liberal principles. This mix of two legal traditions does not seem to create a real mode of active property management (Ghilarducci et al., 2004; Stabile, 2002). The procedures, rules and habits that inhibit the autonomy of beneficiaries are rather powerful. First, the investment manager is unilaterally hired by the employer; beneficiaries have no word to say about this appointment. Second, the employer keeps his power to lock on the portfolios of beneficiaries and is able to prevent them from dealing on stocks. This possibility has been largely used to stop employees selling their company shares when stock prices are plummeting, especially in the case of the financial crash in 2000–3. In order to avoid massive selling, the employer can decide, for example, to replace the custodian: this administrative change has often been made because it allows for freezing portfolios for some days, weeks or even months. This duration is sometimes very long with respect to stock price movements. Of course, it is formally legal. But it prevents beneficiaries from enjoying the liquidity of capital markets. Third, the range of investment options that is available to beneficiaries is entirely chosen by the investment manager. Today, this range does not permit alternative investments that would be directed towards job creation, workplace democracy, and so on. 'Targeted investments' were prohibited – or at least made difficult to implement – by the Department of Labor in 1994, and unions' achievements in the 1950–60s have not have had lasting influence.

These examples show that the liberalization by the rules of 401k give beneficiaries a hybrid position: not yet the classical liberal owner but still not the protected beneficiary of the paternalistic welfare capitalism. The beneficiary is still a person who, as beneficiary of a Trust, must be protected: this inheritance justifies the fact that he is placed under supervision. But he has become an informed, advised and responsible person, as the autonomous investor protected by securities regulation. It seems that law has played with these two regimes, fiduciary and liberal, and radically changed the figure of the beneficiary. Admittedly he has the choice to decide which options to invest, but he cannot control the financial liquidity that would be necessary for this kind of decision-making, inside the classical liberal regime of property. He can neither get access to the whole universe of investments (available on markets) as his status of informed owner would allow him for.

The status of wage-earners, beneficiaries of pension funds, has shifted from the structural passivity, due to the traditional regulation by the Trust, to an 'autonomy under influence', characteristic of the 401k governance and pension management structure. This form of 'autonomy' has been inherited from the Trust. We can conclude that pension funds are not liberal financial devices. They are still embedded in the capital–labour nexus.

Investment policies: Who defined the rule of prudence?

The standard of prudence that rules investing decision-making in the USA has not been produced by the sole financial practitioners and academic economists. Investing prudently is as much a legal category applied by various legal professions as it is a scientific norm promoted by academic economists and defined in the corpus of academic articles and manuals of financial theory. It is also a professional standard, perceptible in the codes of conduct and regularities noted in the organization of the financial sector. With that in mind, one must pay attention to the interdependency of those representations and see how the processes that have led up to the legal standard participated in creating a concept with many meanings.

We will retrace the influences of those different social spheres by looking at the processes whereby legal and jurisprudential activities have injected new economic realities into the legal category of prudence and, in return, elicited new, 'best' financial practices. Three processes or procedures appear pivotal from the point of view of the transformation of the meaning of prudence: (1) the legislative elaboration of the standard of prudence during the 1960s, ending with the promulgation of the federal law ERISA; (2) the Administration's single-minded, regulatory form of interpretation during the 1970–80s; (3) and diversified decision-making applied by the bench as of the 1980s.

The pro-active interpretations of the Department of Labor

The Department embarked on the task of giving a precise definition of the new meaning of prudence in a series of Interpretative Bulletins. As of the early 1980s, it also brought to trial trustees or employers in order to effectively implement the new principles of prudence and build up jurisprudence. In a specific context – the outbreak of tender offers in the 1980s – the Department of Labor, helped by academics of the Law and Economics school, carried out the conceptual work that consisted in identifying the beneficiary's specific – financial – interest and clearly separating it from any other interests deriving from his/her position in the firm.

The Department made the sole financial interest of the workforce in their pension funds its main concern and *ignored their interest in* opposing the hostile takeover with the thought of *preserving their employment*. The argument also led to separating the average employee from the CEOs, by accusing the latter of wanting to salvage their own positions instead of acting in the stakeholders' economic interest. Employee-beneficiaries were portrayed as hostages to the directors and the trustees as subservient to management, puppets in a conflict of interests. The Department of Labor's court actions were thus an active contribution to disentangling the Keynesian alliance between capital and labour typical of the post-Second World War period (Helleiner, 1994) and to clear up the local compromises between industrialists, employees and politicians to oppose Wall Street's hostile attempts at takeover (Roe, 1994; Useem, 1993).

Reciprocally, firms were the active agents of the uses to which the pension funds were put: some companies used their fund's pension assets to direct the tenders and some large retirement plans by lending money participated in the hostile tenders directed by 'vulture' financiers; 'predators' such as the KKR firm (Kohlberg, Kravis & Roberts), became famous for having radically liquidated large American businesses.

Judges' detachment from financial theory

The position of the Labor Department on matters of investment norms rested on a scientific reference: the modern portfolio theory propounded by academic economists during the 1960s, mainly in the Chicago business school and at MIT. According to their 'pure' theory, diversification was one of the fundamental principles underlying the good investment norm and should theoretically have become the essential criterion for judging prudence. However, the equivalence between diversification and prudence was not introduced either by ERISA or by jurisprudence, encountering the hostility of employers as well as of certain financial sectors.

On one hand, employers obtained advantageous tax provisions from Congress and an official exemption allowing them to place the shares of their own companies in the different funds subjected to ERISA. Notwithstanding an obvious conflict of interests, the law did not prohibit those acquisitions. The commentators of Law and Economics expressed their disapproval in the face of an insufficiently orthodox interpretation of the financial theory (Langbein and Wolk, 1990; Fischel and Langbein, 1988). But employers' influence in Congress was still strong enough to uphold that policy. On the other hand, most financial managers remained reticent in the face of the modern portfolio theory (Clowes, 2000; Del Guercio, 1996; Bernstein, 1992; Longstreth, 1986), which was quite understandable since the theory rejected their claim of being able to choose the most profitable financial securities and reduced their so-called expertise to market charlatanism. In the course of those various departures from the theoretical conception, jurisprudence chose to lean on actual practices, thus tracing the contours of the definition of prudence. Rather than swallow the theory whole and its precepts as advanced by the Department, judges preferred to base themselves on conformity with acknowledged and generally widespread financial practices.

The selective use of the Efficient Market Hypothesis

Still, referring to the modern portfolio theory became more frequent as the new generations of financial practitioners, judges and lawyers became more familiar with it. The theory was in fact successfully taught in the business schools, from the 1970s on (Whitley, 1986) while the Chicago Law School initiated a programme to train judges in law and economics as of the mid-1970s (Duxbury, 1995). Finally, the appointments of judges by R. Reagan lastingly transformed the judiciary landscape.

Analysing the jurisprudence (Montagne, 2013) reveals that resorting to the efficient market hypothesis has however been far from systematic. Several examples testify to the fact that the same 'scientific' criterion – efficiency – can be applied in diametrically opposed ways. Several argumentative roads are in fact open to the judge: prudence as the strict application of the financial theory or as a balance of interests. The trials analysed in Montagne (2013) followed these two separate paths. These examples of judges' reasoning are nevertheless quite similar. The outcome of the trials is the same: the employees are thrown out. It is the result of the fact that, beyond the case at hand and the reference to the chosen interpretation, the judge has introduced a superior principle, of a political nature, which standardizes the decisions. That principle is the 'survival' of the industry, explicitly worded in the Congressional documents that participated in elaborating ERISA. For though the aim of the law is to protect employees' retirement, it means to do so by virtue of that concrete form of socio-economic organization represented by the 'pension industry'. Applying the law must not threaten the viability of pension funds as organized by the industry of finance.

The different facets of the production of the standard of prudence reviewed here allow us to see how the power of the state and employers has continued to obtain despite the growing empowerment of financiers. Of course, the deference of judges to the practices of finance, formulated in ERISA and reasserted by the Supreme Court, has made finance the legitimate institution when defining the investment norm. The fact that judges use organizational conformity as a criterion constitutes a devolution of the power to dictate the investment norm to the actors of finance, a devolution greatly encouraged by the federal government. But alternatively using another criterion – conformity with the financial theory – has allowed validating the financial uses applied by employers despite the intentions proclaimed by ERISA. The reference to the financial theory contained in decisions testifies to the fact that judges are capable of varying their interpretations of theoretical principles according to the situation and to the benefit of the employer class of litigants. So, defining prudence is not only defining the investment rules of the financial order (the money allocation); it is also defining a labour order where workers are subordinated to the logics of other groups.

Conclusion

The first aim of this chapter was to show how a financial sphere, the pension industry, has been built up *in connection with* what is perceived as the 'outside' of finance. We have seen how much the pension industry is a hybrid sphere, between capital–labour compromises and capital markets expansion. Its institutions and agents have invented the ruling of their own activities by borrowing ideas, understandings, categories and devices from other social areas. So doing, they have imported the main conflicts and the structure of power from inheritance law and from the capital–labour nexus to the financial sphere.

This importation has been developed *in connection with* some rules of the past. To some extent, pension industry's innovations have also borrowed from past economic traditions. The standard of prudence and the Trust are not minor details of the functioning of finance. They are its very institutional pillars. If we acknowledge their origin, history and transformations, we can frame pension industry into the history of economic institutions and into the patterns of major socio-economic conflicts.

To these two extents, the practices of this industry are not as much specific to a so-called 'financial world' as to the functioning of Anglo-American capitalist economies. The institutional change that has transformed the beneficiary, a legal minor, into an informed investor, that has replaced the prudent man rule with the diversification of risks promoted by financial economists, and pushed employers to delegate asset management to financial specialists, has not really deprived employers and the state of control over the circuits of money. So the US pension and mutual funds industries keep being shaped by the trustee–beneficiary relationship which belongs to the broader structure of domination that Hamilton (2010) calls the 'Western patriarchalism and patrimonialism'. Following Hamilton, we can consider the Trust a civilizational component of finance. But we cannot take it as a reified and per se institution that would be mechanically adopted and reproduced anywhere and anytime by economic agents. It is just a 'pattern of relationship that is held to have the ultimate validity' (Hamilton, 2010, p. 40). The question for sociological history is to show how this pattern is empirically used and transformed. We have seen that legal legacy, transplant, circulation and institutionalization of meaning are some of the main processes through which the Anglo-American form of subordination of the Trust has been renewed for managing labour savings.

The second conclusion to be drawn deals with the generalization of this approach. Can this kind of interactions between social spheres be generalized to other financial activities and especially to banking? Two kinds of works, institutional and ethnographic, open such a way. They introduce the effect of non financial institutions and non financial agents in the financial practices.

First, institutional analysis of the financial crisis of 2007 gives insights for such a perspective in comparing national political reactions to the crisis. In his comparison of the ruling of Special Purpose Vehicles in three European countries, M. Thiemann (2012) shows the importance of the national institutional matrix and of the intertwined links between economic and law spheres for the expansion/regulation of off-balance-sheet financing by banks. In Germany, the linkage of the credit law to the commercial law, the weak institutional position of the accounting standard setter to the ministry of justice and the specific importance of off-balance-sheet financing for the German economy in the 2000s, have prevented the modernization of accounting rules. By contrast, at the same time, France and Spain pushed for more stringent accounting rules that forced banks to account for the risks they took. This kind of comparative work allows us to measure the influence of state structure and public officials work on the banking rules.

Second, ethnographic studies of banking activities are another type of sociological approach that explores the construction of banking from the point of view of its (outside) clients. This approach follows Zelizer's tradition in focusing more on social links and social affiliations of the protagonists than on the social construction of credit markets (Lacan and Lazarus, 2015). Credit is essentially addressed as an object of relationships and as a practice. Based on the observation of interactions between clients and financial institutions, these studies show how commonly understood norms used by banks are built up 'from below'. They introduce the effect of non-professional agents (clients) in the making of banking activities.

As a third conclusion, we have to assess whether the notion of boundaries by Abbott is relevant to our approach of finance as an emergent and porous entity. We have seen that the emergence of the pension industry could be analysed as a historical process, starting with the dis-embedding from corporate employers and insurance companies, following with the anchoring in new wealth management activities, keeping on the legacy of Trust rules. Pension industry is now considered an 'industry' in the meaning of a set of distinct institutions and professions. In the same way, the asset management industry has grown out of a series of socio-economic events such as tax policies and the growing income of middle-upper classes. The credit sphere has also developed. From the 1980s onwards, financial firms and banks have begun to diversify and blur the boundaries made by the Glass–Steagall Act. Financial conglomerates have taken over a large variety of financial activities. Securitization has multiplied possibilities of financial commoditization and of new markets. In the 1990s, customers themselves have begun to play simultaneous roles: they borrowed money to buy stocks, acting simultaneously in the credit sphere and in the investment sphere. This is the 'financialization of daily life' which means an increasing exposure to a diversity of financial products and services for social groups that stood previously at a distance from capital markets. From the point of view of these financialized customers, is finance a 'social entity'? From the point of view of the academic observer, can finance be objectified as a 'social thing'?

Although all these financial activities deal with people's money, they were not a 'social entity' until this 'financialization': pension industry, asset management, hedge funds, credit sphere were distinct spheres, with their own culture, knowledge, techniques and professions. They addressed different needs and dealt with different types of customers. Finance was hardly an homogeneous field and, instead, consisted of several industries and different networks. What has changed from the 1980s onwards is on the one hand, the more connectedness between these financial activities and, on the other hand, the larger exposure of a larger number of customers to these activities.

So Finance has emerged as a social entity by aggregating financial activities that were previously considered separated. One example of this process is the connection between pension funds and hedge funds from the 2000 crisis onwards when pension funds reacted to serious financial troubles by starting to invest in hedge funds in order to increase their yield. But this aggregating process is not limited to reorganizing relationships between financial institutions. The history of the pension industry shows that its constitution as an entity is anchored on non financial institutions: inheritance law and capital–labour nexus. The case of pension industry illustrates how much this segment of finance has evolved alongside the mutations of American capitalism and has been concerned with several conflicts emanating from distinct social spheres.

With this example in mind, one must pay attention to the interdependency of the financial representations and practices and see how the processes that have led up to the connection of financial activities to each other participated also in reactivating the structure of domination and transmitting conflicts from other spheres to financial arenas.

This perspective is the kind for a cultural political economy that could help investigate the boundaries of finance as 'zones of action' because they are 'zones of conflicts' (Abbott, 1995, p. 857).

Bibliography

Abbott, A. (1995) 'Things of boundaries', *Social Research*, 62(4): 857–82.
Alexander, G. (1993) 'Pensions and passivity', *Law and Contemporary Problems*, 56 (1): 111–39.
Bernstein, P.L. (1992) *Capital Ideas, The Improbable Origins of Modern Wall Street*. New York: The Free Press, Macmillan.
Carruthers, B. (1996) *City of Capital: Politics and Markets in the English Financial Revolution*. Princeton, NJ: Princeton University Press.
Chaves Jardim, M. (2013) *Syndicats et fonds de pension durant le gouvernement Lula*. Paris: L'Harmattan.
Clark, G.L. (2000) *Pension Fund Capitalism*. Oxford: Oxford University Press.
Clowes, M.J. (2000) *The Money Flood, How Pension Funds Revolutionized Investing*. New York: John Wiley & Sons.
Del Guercio, D. (1996) 'The distorting effect of the prudent-man laws on institutional equity investments', *Journal of Financial Economics*, 40 (1): 31–62.
Domhoff, G.W. (2013) *The Myth of Liberal Ascendancy. Corporate Dominance from the Great Depression to the Great Recession*. London: Paradigm Publishers.
Duxbury, N. (1995) *Patterns of American Jurisprudence*. Oxford: Oxford University Press.
Engelen, E. (2008) 'The case for financialization', *Competition & Change*, 12(2), pp. 111–119.
Ertürk, I. *et al.* (2007) 'Against agency: A positional critique', *Economy and Society*, 36 (1): 51–77.
Ertürk, I., Froud, J., Johal, S. (2008) *Financialization at Work, Key Texts and Commentary*. London: Routledge.
Fischel, D. R., Langbein, J. H., 1988. ERISA's fundamental contradiction, the exclusive benefit rule. *The University of Chicago Law Review*, 55 (4): 1105–60.
Fourcade, M. (2009) *Economists and Societies, Discipline and Profession in the United States, Britain and France, 1890s to 1990s*. Princeton, NJ: Princeton University Press.
Frankel, T. (1998) 'Fiduciary duties' in Newman, P. (ed.), *The New Palgrave Dictionary of Law and Economics*, London: Macmillan, pp. 127–32.
Frankel, T. (2006) *Trust and Honesty, America's Business Culture at a Crossroad*. New York: Oxford University Press.
Froud, J., Leaver, A. and Williams, K. (2007) 'New actors in a financialised economy and the remaking of capitalism', *New Political Economy*, 12 (3): 339–47.
Ghilarducci, T. *et al.* (2004) *In Search of Retirement Security. The Changing Mix of Social Insurance, Employee Benefits, and Individual Responsibility*. New York: The Century Foundation Press.
Godechot, O. (2007) *Working Rich. Salaires, bonus et appropriation des profits dans l'industrie financière*. Paris: La Découverte.
Hacker, J. (2002) *The Divided Welfare State. The Battle over Public and Private Social Benefits in the United States*. Cambridge: Cambridge University Press.
Hamilton, G. (1994) 'Civilizations and the organization of economies', in Smelser, N. and Swedberg, R. (eds), *The Handbook of Economic Sociology*. Princeton, NJ: Princeton University Press, pp. 183–205.
Hamilton, G. (2010) 'World images, authority, and institutions. A comparison of China and the West', *European Journal of Social Theory*, 13(1): 31–48.
Harrington, B. (2009) *Trust and Estate Planning: The Emergence of a Profession and Its Contribution to Socio-Economic Inequality*. Cologne: MPIfG Discussion Paper 09/6.
Helleiner, E. (1994) *States and the Reemergence of Global Finance: From Bretton Woods to the 1990s*. New York: Cornell University Press, Ithaca.
Ho, K. (2009) *Liquidated. An Ethnography of Wall Street*. Durham, NC and London: Duke University Press.
Jeanpierre, L. (2010) 'Frontière' in Christin, O. (ed.), *Dictionnaire des concepts nomades en sciences humaines*. Paris: Métailié.

Konings, M. (2009) 'Rethinking neoliberalism and the subprime crisis: Beyond the re-regulation agenda', *Competition & Change*, 13(2): 108–27.

Krippner, G. (2007) 'The making of US monetary policy: Central bank transparency and the neoliberal dilemma', *Theory and Society*, 36(6): 477–513.

Lacan, L. and Lazarus, J. (2015) *A Relationship and a Practice. On the French Sociology of Credit*. Paris, Cologne: MaxPo discussion paper 15/1.

Langbein, J.H. and Wolk, B. (1990) *Pension and Employee Benefit Law*. New York: The Foundation Press, Westbury.

Lazonick, W. and O'Sullivan, M. (2000) 'Maximising shareholder value: A new ideology for corporate governance', *Economy and Society*, 29(1): 13–35.

Lemoine, B. (2013) 'Les dealers de la dette souveraine: politique des transactions entre banques et Etat dans la grande distribution des emprunts français' ('Dealers' of Sovereign Bonds. Transaction Policy between Banks and the Government regarding French Bond Distribution), *Sociétés Contemporaines*, 92: 59–88.

Longstreth, B. (1986) *Modern Investment Management and the Prudent Man Rule*. New York: Oxford University Press.

Lordon, F. (2015) 'Capitalism in the 21st century short on capital. Why Piketty isn't Marx', *Le Monde Diplomatique*, English edition, May. Retrieved on 26 October 2015 from http://mondediplo.com/2015/05/12piketty.

Mackenzie, D. (2006) *An Engine not a Camera. How Financial Models Shape Markets*. Cambridge, MA: The MIT Press.

Marcus, G., Hall, P. (1992) *Lives in Trust. The Fortunes of Dynastic Families in Late Twentieth-Century America*. San Francisco: Westview Press.

Montagne, S. (2013) 'Investing prudently: How financialization puts a legal standard to use', *Sociologie du Travail*, 55(1) English Supplement [online], c48–66. Retrieved on 26 October 2015 from www.sociologiedutravail.org/spip.php?article94.

Montagne, S. and Ortiz, H. (2013) 'Sociologie de l'agence financière: enjeux et perspectives' ('Sociology of Financial Agency: Questions and Perspectives'), *Sociétés Contemporaines*, 92: 7–34.

Moulévrier, P. (2013) 'Le crédit donné aux pauvres: droit à l'endettement et financiarisation de l'action sociale' ('Credit for the poor. Right to indebtedness and financialization of social action'), *Sociétés Contemporaines*, 92: 89–106.

Polillo, S. (2013) *Conservatives Versus Wildcats. A Sociology of Financial Conflict*. Stanford: Stanford University Press.

Roe, M. (1994) *Strong Managers, Weak Owners: The Political Roots of American Corporate Finance*. Princeton, NJ: Princeton University Press.

Stabile, S. (2002) 'Freedom to choose unwisely: Congress' misguided decision to leave 401(k) plan participants to their own devices', *Cornell Journal of Law and Public Policy*, 11(2): 361–402.

Thiemann, M. (2012) 'Out of the shadows?' Accounting for special purpose entities in European banking systems', *Competition and Change*, 16(1): 37–55.

Useem, M. (1993) *Executive Defense: Shareholder Power and Corporate Reorganization*. Boston, MA: Harvard University Press.

Van der Zwan, N. (2014) 'Making sense of financialization', *Socio-Economic Review*, 12 (1): 99–129.

Weir, M., Orloff, A. and Skocpol, T. (1988) *The Politics of Social Policy in the United States*. Princeton, NJ: Princeton University Press.

Whitley, R. (1986) 'The transformation of business finance into financial economics: The roles of academic expansion and changes in US capital markets', *Accounting, Organizations and Society*, 11(2): 171–92.

Wooten, J. (2004) *The Employment Retirement Income Security Act of 1974. A Political History*. Berkeley and Los Angeles: University of California Press.

Zelinsky, E.A. (2004) 'The defined contribution paradigm', *The Yale Law Journal*, 114 (3): 451–534.

Part III
New approaches to banking, risk and central bank role in the Eurozone

9

The new behemoth?

The ECB and the financial supervision reforms during the Eurozone crisis

Clément Fontan

When it was created in 1999, the ECB did not have supervisory powers over the Eurozone banking sector. Since the financial crisis, it gained macro and micro prudential supervisory authority over the whole Eurozone banking sector. As this concentration of power is not risk-free and other policy alternatives existed, why were these competences delegated to the ECB in particular?

In this chapter, I show that three main factors were at play during this delegation of competences. First, the ECB was very active in the legislative process and benefited from its original reputation based on the Bundesbank template. Second, Eurozone policymakers rallied on the ECB option for utilitarian reasons as they could import the ECB financial expertise in the new supervising bodies at no charge. Third, policymakers' misperceptions on the ECB's past positions of financial stability and unintended consequences from the ESRB creation explain why the ECB option prevailed on other policy alternatives. In conclusion, this transfer of competences cannot be described as 'controlled' by Eurozone policymakers and the ECB cannot present itself as 'neutral' agent in this process.

Introduction

Since 8 December 2009, when Fitch, the rating agency, rated down the Greek sovereign debt below A, the Eurozone crisis has been mainly framed as a fiscal and competitiveness crisis (Matthijs and McNamara, 2015). Hence, the main policy solution chosen by Eurozone policymakers to address the crisis was the imposition of austerity plans in the countries which needed financial help to refinance their debt and/or recapitalize their banking sector (Greece, Ireland, Portugal, Italy, Spain, Cyprus). This framing undermined the problematic role played by the banking sector in the aggravation of the public debt and in the build-up of the macroeconomic imbalances before and after the collapse of Lehman Brothers, in both debtor and creditor Eurozone countries (Dyson, 2014).

Indeed, since the creation of the euro, core European banks have been engaging in risky and massive lending to Eurozone periphery countries. The financial incentives driving these dynamics were very similar to the American subprime mortgage crisis, only with public debt instead of private debt. In the name of financial integration, the ECB created a basket of government securities in which the debt of any Eurozone country (Greece or Germany for example) has the same value when used as collateral in the ECB's refinancing operations[1] (Gabor and Ban, 2015, p.10). With the help of the European Commission, it encouraged financial operators to use government debts as collateral for the Eurozone's repo market[2] in an undifferentiated way. This policy revived the Eurozone's repo market: its size tripled between 2001 and 2008,[3] mostly because 75 per cent of the repo transactions used government debt as collateral for other risky financial operations (e.g. investing in the US mortgage subprime market). This recycling explains why Eurozone banks' balance sheets have more than doubled in size since Euro creation and how Eurozone financial imbalances built up.

It is thus no surprise that the first financial institutions hit by the subprime crisis were located in the Eurozone. After the collapse of Lehman Brothers, public authorities recapitalized their banking sector and thus aggravated their public debt. For example, when the Irish government decided to guarantee the liabilities of the Irish banks in September 2008, the Irish public debt rose from 40 per cent to 80 per cent of the GDP. When the Eurozone crisis erupted in early 2010, the core Eurozone banks were 'too big to bail'.[4] Consequently, the pain of the stabilization of their fragile balance sheets has been weighting on EU citizens through the imposition of austerity packages (Blyth, 2013, Chapter 3).

The Eurozone crisis has thus started with the banks and shall end with the resolution of this issue. Yet, the Eurozone authorities did not have the proper policy instruments to regulate neither the risky cross-border activities of the banks, nor to control the systemic consequences of a banking failure. Indeed, domestic regulatory authorities dominated the European financial supervision with a loose supranational coordination in the so-called 'Lamfalussy structure' (De Visscher, Maiscocq and Varone, 2008). In the words of M. King and C. Goodhart, the life of the banks was supranational while their death (e.g. the resolution of bank failures) remained national. Consequently, Eurozone policymakers decided to transfer more supervisory power to the supranational level in order to strengthen the supervision over the interconnected banking sector and 'restore the confidence' of financial market operators. This transfer has been done in two steps (Table 9.1).

First, the European System of Financial Supervision was established in 2010 to complement the Lamfalussy structure with a 'toothless' macro-prudential authority (the European Systemic Risk Board (ESRB)). Second, European authorities adopted a more integrated approach in

Table 9.1 Macro and micro prudential supervision in Europe

	History	Policy objectives	Policy instruments	Governance
The European Systemic Risk Board (ESRB)	Proposed in December 2008 Implemented in January 2010	Macro-prudential oversight of the Eurozone financial system	Non-binding recommendations (soft law)	General Council (35 people including 29 central bankers)
The Single Supervisory Mechanism (SSM)	Proposed in June 2012 Implemented in November 2014	Direct micro-supervision on the 130 largest banks Indirect supervision on less significant banks	On-site inspections Removal of banking licenses Adjust capital buffers (coercive instruments)	Supervisory board (27 people, 5 central bankers) submits drafts to ECB governing Council If disagreement, goes to mediation panel

2012 by layering a Banking Union over the existing system. This Banking Union is composed of a Single Supervisory Mechanism (SSM),[5] a Single Resolution Mechanism and a Common Resolution Fund. Macro-prudential supervision shed the light on the volatile and unstable nature of financial markets and the imbalances they cause, micro-prudential supervision is the classic control of single banks activities. Since it gained a prominent place in the governance of both the ESRB and the SSM, the major beneficiary of these reforms is the European Central Bank (ECB).

This chapter explains why and how the ECB, which was deprived from such competences at its creation, was delegated these new powers. In order to do so, I shall complement the existing literature, which focuses on utilitarian explanations, with constructivist approaches highlighting the role of policymakers' misperceptions, the ECB's organizational reputation and unexpected consequences stemming from past political choices. I explain first what were the Member States' and the ECB motivations for transferring supervisory power to the ECB. Then, I analyse the delegation process during the creation of the ESRB and the SSM. From a methodological point of view, I rely on an analysis of primary and secondary sources and on seven semi-structured interviews to examine the reform processes. These interviews were conducted between April 2010 and November 2011 with high-level officials from the DG Ecofin and Market of the European Commission, members of the European Parliament sitting at the Econ Committee and Member States representatives sitting at the Economic and Financial Committee (EFC), the key preparatory committee of the Ecofin meetings.

Financial supervision and central banking in the Eurozone

Since it was modelled on the Bundesbank template, the ECB was deprived from supervision competences when it was created in 1999. I explore first the theoretical motivations underpinning this institutional design in order to show that it is neither risk-free nor obvious for a central bank to be the supervisory authority for its banking system. Then, I examine the motivations of both Member States and the ECB to transfer these competences. Finally, I lay out two propositions to explain why the ECB gained these responsibilities.

The pitfalls of delegating financial supervision powers to central banks

When the ECB was created, it did not have any supervisory responsibilities: the only legal indications written down in the European treaties are at best very allusive or prospective. Article 127 (5) of the Treaty of their Functioning of the European Union only indicates an assistance mission to the existing regulatory bodies (advising clause) and Article 127 (6) stipulates that the European council, after consultation of the European Parliament and the ECB, can confer specific task to the ECB for the prudential supervision of credit institutions (enabling cause). This lack of competences is explained by the overarching influence of the *Bundesbank* template on the institutional design of the ECB (McNamara 1998).

Very schematically, central banking models can be placed on a continuum in which the two ends are the Anglo-Saxon and the continental templates. Either the central bank has a vast array of competences but its policies can be contested by political authorities (Anglo-Saxon model, the Federal Reserve and the Banque de France before 1993) or it is granted a high level of independence to focus solely on price stability (continental model, the *Bundesbank*). These institutional designs are anchored within different belief systems, which explain in turn the different trade-offs between the level of independence and the extent of the missions delegated to the central bank.

In the Anglo-Saxon model, central banks often exert financial supervision responsibilities in addition of their price stability objectives. The partisans of this model consider that inflation is more than a monetary phenomenon; hence, insider information on housing and financial assets' price evolution might help central bankers to keep prices stable. Besides, the de facto central bank's monopoly on liquidities is another argument for its supervision role. Through its daily refinancing operations, it has to make assessments about the financial assets held by commercial banks and has thus a better financial expertise than other agencies which are located further away from the markets (Goodhart, 2010). Besides, since central banks fulfil multiple policy objectives, their accountability is higher and their policies are likely to be regularly contested by elected bodies.

Supporters of the continental model consider that inflation is always a monetary phenomenon; central banks should neither follow indicators other than the evolution of money supply, nor pursue any missions other than price stability in order to avoid potential conflict of interests and moral hazard[6] (Issing *et al.*, 2001). For example, if ECB policymakers would learn *via* their supervisory role that a tightening of their monetary policy would endanger the financial position of a systematically important bank, they might refrain from doing so. As the supervised financial institutions would be aware of this potential conflict of interest, they might adopt risky (and lucrative) financial activities, which would undermine price and financial stability.

Moreover, the delegation of additional competences increases the risks of regulatory capture. According to Adolph (2013), chances of capture by private finance interests are correlated with a high-level of central bank independence. Since the ECB is one of the most independent central banks in the world, it is thus more likely to be captured by private interests. Moreover, when banking supervision responsibilities are concentrated in the hand of a single supervisor, the regulated industry has more incentives to capture the regulator (Boyer and Ponce, 2012).

In addition, granting new responsibilities to a central bank impacts the system of check and balances in democratic systems: the more competences an independent agency has, the more control should be exerted by elected bodies (Goodhart, 2010). In the eyes of the ECB, its accountability consists mainly in fulfilling its objective of price stability (Issing *et al.*, 2001). Consequently, the control exerted by the European Parliament on its activities is very weak in comparison with the auditions of the Fed chairman in front of the US Congress (Jabko, 2009). Since this low accountability is only justified by its narrow policy objectives, an extension of ECB's competences would need to be complemented by a stricter control over its activities from elected bodies.

Finally, the concentration of supervisory powers within the ECB was not the only available policy option. Indeed, Eurozone policymakers could have created a new supranational integrated supervisor following the template of the former UK Financial Services Authority. Alternatively, the European Banking Authority or even the European Commission could have been tasked with these supervisory powers (Bauer and Becker, 2014). Furthermore, the governance of new regulatory bodies (ESRB, SSM) could have been less overweighed by central bankers. For example, the US government created a new regulatory body in 2009 to achieve the same objectives as the ESRB.[7] Yet, its governing committee includes only one central banker out of ten committee members. To conclude, the delegation of supervisory competences to the ECB was neither the only available policy option, nor a risk-free solution.

The Member States' incentives for delegation

There are two ways of explaining policymakers' motivations in political science (Parsons, 2007, p. 13). The first way is a logic-of-position claim which focuses on the material and man-made incentives channelling someone into action. This claim also postulates policymakers' objective rationality. The second way is a logic-of-interpretation claim, which shows 'that someone arrives at an action only through one interpretation of what is possible and/or desirable'. Such interpretations are historically situated and they do not need to be irrational. The existing research on the reforms of financial supervision regimes in Europe mainly follows the logic-of-position claim. After reviewing it, I show the added value of the logic-of-interpretation claim.

First, neo-functionalist theories claim that spill-over effects motivate the delegation of competences. In the case of financial supervision, the concept of 'financial trilemma' informs that only two of three of the following objectives can be reached simultaneously in a given political system: financial integration, financial stability and national supervision (Schoenmaker, 2010). Since the two first objectives are already reached or have to be protected in the Eurozone, the author unsurprisingly recommends the transfer of supervision powers to the supranational level. Yet, this model of incompatibility does not explain why the ECB was the preferred supranational policy option.

According to liberal intergovernmentalists, Member States are inclined to transfer more power at the supranational level following an exogenous shock but they retain control over the extent of the transferred powers (Moravcsik, 1998). The choice of the specific supranational agency to endorse these powers is driven by Member States' utilitarian reasons such as feasibility and costs-effectiveness considerations. According to this theory, Member States want at the same time to benefit from the creation of a supranational supervisor and protect the interests of their national financial industry. Since the Eurozone hosts different banking models, Member States engaged in a power struggle to determine the form and extent of the transfer towards the ESRB and the SSM (Hennessy, 2014; Howarth and Quaglia, 2013).

Second, this focus on policymakers' rational calculations and material motivations should be complemented with a logic-of-interpretation claim. Indeed, Allison and Zelikow ([1971] 1999) underline that policymakers' rationality is limited in times of crisis while Jervis (1976) shows that policymakers' misperceptions have a significant impact on the final outcome of international negotiations. The concept of misperceptions encompasses policymakers' inaccurate inferences based on past events and miscalculations of consequences. I find it theoretically fruitful to link it with the concept of organizational reputation defined as 'a set of symbolic beliefs about the unique or separable capacities, roles, and obligations of an organization shared by a multiplicity of audiences' (Carpenter, 2010, p. 45). Organizational images are built through multiple and repeated interactions between the organizations' agents and their audiences In the case of the ECB, its main interactions with the Eurozone Member States take place in the Eurozone preparatory committees (Fontan 2013). The informality and the 'club feeling' of the working method adopted in these committees (Grosche and Puetter, 2008) leave room for the importance of the perceptions of its members of themselves on the decision-making process outcomes.

Since the ECB was modelled on the Bundesbank's template, the former inherited the 'conservative' orthodox reputation of the latter in the eyes of the Eurozone policymakers. As we shall see later, this reputation helped the ECB to gain financial competences, even though its past positions on 'light-touch' regulation encouraged problematic financial innovation. This paradox explains why I rely on the concept of misperceptions. Policymakers' misperceptions also explain why the delegation of competences to an independent agency can trigger unintended consequences on the next steps in the reform process (Pierson, 1996). Finally, economic beliefs also play a role in institutional reforms whether they are strategically used by political entrepreneurs or shaping their interests (Saurugger, 2013). In the case of financial supervision reforms, policymakers' normative conceptions about monetary policy shaped their interests in the delegation process whereas the ECB strategically adapted the belief system which modelled its original institutional architecture.

The ECB as a strategic player in search for new competencies

Once competences are delegated towards an independent agency, it often tries to extend its power beyond the agreed delegation contract (Elgie, 2002; De Rynck, 2016). Following this perspective, what can be the ECB's incentives to extend its original monetary competences towards the field of financial supervision?

Output legitimacy (Scharpf, 1997) is a first explanation. Since the ECB policymakers have the responsibility of promoting the smooth operation of payment systems,[8] they might believe that the gain of supervision powers could improve their control over the use of liquidities by the Eurozone banks, even more so in times of crisis. A former member of the board argues that in order to know whether its liquidity offers to the banking sector are adequate, the central bank needs to know the health of each bank (Bini-Smaghi, 2013, p. 89). This justification falls short since the banks' use of liquidity can be controlled through the settings of the ECB's monetary instruments, as exemplified by the Targeted Long Term Operations measures implemented in September 2014. Also, this control does not necessarily need to be done by the central bank that provided it.

A more compelling explanation is power-related: the governors of national central banks sitting at the ECB governing council want to regain the supervisory competences they lost at the national level in the last decade (on the role of national central banks in the financial supervision's reforms, McPhilemy, 2016).[9] Indeed, the rise of integrated regulators, notably in the UK and Germany, diminished the role of some central banks in the field of financial supervision from the end of the 1990s until the crisis. For example, the creation of the Austrian Financial Market Authority in 2002 was not well received by Austrian central bankers who have been trying to regain such competencies since then (Interview 1). Besides, the central banks that were deprived from banking supervision responsibilities, such as the Bundesbank, tried to gain such competencies to compensate their loss of power after the creation of the single currency (Schüler, 2004). The theoretical separation between central banks and financial supervision has thus less and less supporters in the ECB governing council.

Finally, the gain of financial supervision competences could endanger the ECB's orthodox reputation (cf. *supra*). Consequently, the ECB deployed multiple strategies to convince its Eurozone partners that the delegation risks were minimal while the potential gains could be important.

Two propositions

In summary, I lay out *two main propositions* to understand why and how the ECB managed to gain financial supervision competences during the crisis.

The first proposition focuses on the role of the states who have been the most crucial legislative players. The delegation process has been driven by Member States representatives' utilitarian motivations but they did not fully control the direction and the extent of this transfer. The ECB's central place in the supervision bodies should rather be understood as a result of policymakers' misperceptions and unintended consequences of their past policy choices.

The second proposition relates to the role played by the ECB in the legislative process. Even if it supposed to be independent and a neutral agent, this statute does not mean that it is detached from political considerations (Forder, 2002). On the contrary, ECB policymakers have incentives to gain new competences and they try to maintain and enhance their original reputation to maximize the extent of the transfer. The success of these tactics is thus the second element explaining the ECB's gain of competences.

The creation of the ESRB

I show first that, from the very beginning of the creation of the European Systemic Risk Board (ESRB) in 2008, the ECB was at the centre of the policymakers' proposals. Then, I examine how policymakers' motivations were driven by both logic-of-position and logic-of-interpretation in the legislative process. Finally, I analyse the ECB's strategies to protect and enhance its original reputation.

The framing of the reform by the central banks

When the Lamfalussy structure was created in 2000, the European Commission relied on a high-level expert group to frame the reform. It did similarly in the case of the ESRB with the creation of the De Larosière group in October 2008 whose mandate was to evaluate the existing system of supervision and submit proposals to reinforce it (De Larosière, 2009). High-level expert groups are used to bypass the domestic struggles triggered by the different national models of supervision and monetary policy:

> Everybody realized that sometimes we get stuck down in national dogma, and sometimes you need to bypass the national dogma, that's what we did with the group of wise men, and things got down in a way we would not have managed.
>
> *(Interview 1)*

The composition of the De Larosière group is crucial to understand why the ECB gained a prominent role in the ESRB. Indeed, most of the members of the De Larosière group use to be central bankers: the chairman of the group himself, Jacques De Larosière has been governor of the French central bank from 1987 to 1993; Otmar Issing was a member of the Bundesbank directorate from 1990 to 1998 and ECB chief economist from 1998 to 2006; Leszek Balcerowicz has been governor of the Polish central bank from 2001 to 2008; Rainer Masera has been chief of a directorate of the Spanish Central Bank from 1974 to 2006 and Lars Nyberg was deputy governor of the Swedish central bank from 1994 to 2005. Finally, only two out of the eight members of the group were not former central bankers (Onno Ruding and Callum McCarthy). Despite the presence of Otmar Issing, who has very mitigated views on integrating financial supervision tasks within central banks (Issing, 2012), the final report unsurprisingly recommended a strong role for the ECB in the future ESRB. As a concession to these internal critics, however, the report clearly states that it would not be desirable to grant micro-supervision powers to the ECB because of the increased risks of conflict of interests. Once the De Larosière group handled its report to the European Commission in February 2009, the EU legislative process started under the co-decision procedure.[10] The European Commission proposal was very similar to the report, then the Ecofin Council and the European Parliament needed more than a year to reach an agreement in November 2010.

The motivations of the Eurozone Member States

Eurozone Member States split into two groups because of disagreements over the ESRB's governance and the extent of its powers (Buckley and Howarth, 2010). On the one hand, a French-led coalition (including Spain, Italy and Belgium) wanted to maximize the transfer of competences at the supranational level. Officially, their main motivation was to reassure markets operators about the EU ability to break the vicious circle between the deterioration of periphery sovereign debt and Eurozone banks' balance sheets. Yet, French preferences were also tightly linked with their monetary policy beliefs as explained by a French negotiator preparing the Ecofin meetings:

> You have people thinking there is a plot behind the ESRB project. They claim that we are forcing the ECB to deviate from its objective of price stability by taking into account macro-prudential issues. Yet, we are thinking it is the best thing that can happen to the ECB. I remember when the ECB was explaining that it did not have to monitor financial assets developments, and thus the formation of speculative bubbles, since inflation is strictly a monetary phenomenon. Yet, the ECB should monitor financial assets, not to change directly its interest rates, it is not about that, but because it belongs to its field of responsibilities.
>
> *(Interview 2)*

In other words, economic beliefs shaped French negotiators' preferences who used the ESRB creation as a window of opportunity to counterbalance the original influence of the German template on the ECB. On the other hand, a coalition led by Germany and the UK governments (also including Finland and Netherlands) tried to minimize the transfer to the ECB for different reasons. The UK representatives did not want a concentration of power within the ECB since they are out of the Eurozone and they have no influence on it. Furthermore, they wanted to protect the City, the London financial centre, from supervisory oversight. Germany wanted to exclude its state-owned and regional banks from the supervision of a supranational body.

These resistances deprived the ESRB from coercive powers as it was only granted soft law instruments (Hennessy, 2014), but they did not question the ECB's central role within the ESRB because of two utilitarian reasons. First, the ECB is the only Eurozone's supranational player which is generating incomes and has control over its own budget.[11] The delegation of supervision competences to the ECB was thus costless for the Member States while the creation of an integrated regulator would have had a budgetary impact.[12] Second, macro-prudential oversight is highly dependent on an extended financial expertise to identify imbalances' risks. Besides, if the ESRB warnings are to be respected by domestic authorities, its expertise must be recognized by the latter. The ECB developed an extensive expertise on financial issues since it is assessing the quality of the bank's counterparts in its refinancing operations in a daily basis (compare with earlier discussion). It also has the biggest research centre on financial issues in the EU (on the processes of the ECB's hyper-scientization, Mudge and Vauchez, 2016) and it has developed a high level academic reputation thanks to a good bibliometric evaluation (Freedman et al., 2011). Importing the ECB's expertise within the ESRB was thus the second utilitarian motivation for the delegation of financial supervision competences to the ECB.

The Member States' misperceptions

Going beyond utilitarian explanations, policymakers' misperceptions on the ECB also played a central role in the ESRB creation. Domestic policymakers worried that the non-binding, but potentially reputation-damaging ESRB recommendations, could be used by some Member States against others. As they were looking to isolate the ESRB's governance from possible Member States pressures, they relied on the ECB since they perceived it as the most 'expert' institution among other supranational authorities. Misperceptions about expert neutrality (Radaelli 1999) show why policymakers had a favourable bias towards the ECB:

> The Commission is seen as a political body by many when the ECB is more an expert, people don't doubt their position, they don't see a political interest behind it, when they talk, it's closer to the truth.
>
> *(Interview 3)*

This bias was reinforced by policymakers' misperceptions on ECB's past policies:

> The ECB never believed in self-market regulation. If you look at Trichet[13] speeches on speculative bubbles, he talks about it since a long time. The criticism about the fact they lowered their interest rates too late, well people can talk, but everybody was in awe with Greenspan 10 years ago, now it is the opposite.
>
> *(Interview 4)*

Trichet has often been criticized in the EP by left-wing MPs because of the ECB high-interest rates. Now that we know that the crisis has been triggered by the relaxed US monetary policy decided by Greenspan, the ECB positions are more respected with the benefit of hindsight.

> *(Interview 5)*

In addition, the ECB's orthodox reputation was maintained and reinforced by the policy advices given by its representatives in the Eurozone committees:

> So, who's got the credibility? The ECB, because they got people who were so unpopular like Jürgen Stark,[14] in case you got budgetary deficit, Jürgen would stand in front of you and say 'this is a catastrophe' when we were not taking it seriously.
>
> *(Interview 1)*

Furthermore, when the Eurozone crisis erupted in 2010, the ECB became the lender of last resort for both Eurozone and Member States as it moved away from the *Bundesbank* template and implemented unconventional monetary policies (Buiter and Rahbari, 2012). The combination of its original reputation and its crisis policies caused the ECB to be perceived, in the eyes of Member States' representatives, as being an integral part of the solutions to the crisis and not being part of the problems that led to it (Interview 1). Following a classic logic of supranational alliances, the domestic policymakers' bias in favour of the ECB convinced agents from the Commission and the Parliament to put the ECB at the centre of the ESRB's governance:

> The ECB was the easy way. If we would have turned to the integrated regulator option, we would have needed to build its credibility. With the ECB, we had the credibility from the scratch towards the Member States.
>
> *(Interview 5)*

The moral authority is the reason we confirmed the ECB strong role. We are not ECB supporters for the sake of it, but if we had to create an ad-hoc body, there was no chance it could take the upper hand, and Barroso, it was even worse .... The debate was about: how can we create more European legislation? We wanted the ESRB recommendations to be effective, and when the ECB talks, it is listened to by the Member States.

> *(Interview 6)*

Consequently, the Eurozone policymakers' positive bias in favour of the ECB's past and present role explained partly the delegation process. These research results are consistent with the outcomes of other research on the role played by the ECB in the ESRB creation (McPhilemy, 2016, p. 533-534). I also underline that this bias was informed by policymakers' *misperceptions* on the ECB's past policies which, in fact, contributed to the Eurozone crisis. First, Eurozone economic imbalances were fuelled by the ECB's autonomous decision to calculate its interest rates with Eurozone average indicators. This decision led to real negative interest rates and speculative bubbles in many Eurozone countries, including Spain, Ireland and Greece (Ahrend *et al.*, 2008). Second, the financial innovation that caused the crisis follows past regulatory and political choices in which the ECB has been an active player rather than a powerless spectator. In addition of encouraging the recycling of periphery's debt on repo markets (cf. introduction), the ECB has been one of the promoters of the 'regulatory liberalism' paradigm in the EU (on the paradigm, see Mügge, 2011). Even though it did not have any kind of formal financial supervision competence before 2010, the ECB is part of the 'Basel Committee' forums and it delivers many legal opinions on supervisory issues. For example, Jean-Claude Trichet promoted markets' self-regulation as the best regulatory option at least until October 2007.[15] More precisely, he invited the hedge fund industry to 'review and enhance sound practices benchmarks' and to agree on a 'set of principles voluntarily prepared'.[16] Besides the actual ECB board members have been using legal but suspicious financial tools in their past activities. For example, Mario Draghi[17] was involved in the 'creative accounting' of Italian and Greek debt through the use of derivatives when he was head of the Italian Treasury in the beginning of the 1990s, and Goldman Sachs' vice-president between 2002 and 2005 (Landon and Ewing, 2011).

In conclusion, utilitarian motivations played a role in the transfer of financial supervision competences towards the ECB. Yet, this delegation cannot be understood without taking into account the role of misperceptions and inter-institutional struggles. Indeed, Member States' negotiators trusted the ECB because of its misperceived image of expert neutrality and economic orthodoxy. This trust explains in turn why supranational institutions were supporters of the ECB rather than another policy solution.

The ECB as a strategic player in the ESRB

Since its creation in 1999, the ECB has been advocating the delegation of financial supervision missions towards central banks at the national and European levels (Padoa-Schioppa 1999). In its monthly bulletin of April 2000, the ECB highlighted the stability risks caused by the lack of efficient supervision on cross-border banking activities within the Eurozone. It also underlined that relevant supervisory structures already existed within the ECB although they should be empowered. It is thus not surprising that the ECB played an active role in the legislative process of the ESRB creation:

> During the writing process of the legislation, we exchanged the drafts with the ECB many times and we gathered their comments. Exceptionally, they came with us many times at the Ecofin meetings. In the negotiating phase with the triangle Commission–Parliament–Council, they are not in the meetings anymore, but I still debrief them, when we readjust our position, we still gather their opinions.
>
> *(Interview 5)*

Besides this legislative involvement, the ECB has been promoting the concept of financial trilemma (cf. supra) to legitimize its gain of competences in press articles (Bini-Smaghi, 2009) and academic journals (Salines, Glöckler ant Truchlewski 2012). This strategy echoes with the use of other models of incompatibility, such as Mundell's 'impossible trinity' or Padoa-Schioppa's 'inconsistent quartet', by supranational players during the creation of the euro (Jabko 2006). In summary, the ECB developed a classic supranational strategy to gain supervision competences through its involvement in the legislative process and its promotion of incompatibility models.

Furthermore, the ECB has been minimizing the risks of this transfer in order to protect and adapt its original orthodox reputation. When the Commission consulted the ECB on the reform proposal, its legal staff proposed an amendment to underline that its new supervisory tasks should not be contradictory with its objective of price stability.[18] Since a new European regulation cannot contradict the terms of the treaties, the proposition was legally irrelevant and not adopted in the final ESRB legislation. Rather, the ECB repeated its commitment to price stability in order to protect its orthodox reputation.

This strategy has also been adopted during the ECB presidents' monthly press conferences and parliamentary hearings. Mr Trichet linked for the first time the objectives of price stability and financial stability in its October 2008 monthly press conference. In the very scripted ECB press conferences, he substituted the September 2008 sentence '[Price stability] will preserve purchasing power in the medium term and support sustainable growth and employment' by 'Price stability supports sustainable growth and employment and contributes to financial stability'. By doing so, Mr Trichet reminded the hierarchy between the objectives of price and financial stability in the orthodox economic theories and, at the same time, highlighted the potent ECB contribution to financial stability. Moreover, during its parliamentary hearings, Mr Trichet took advantage of a question on the compatibility between financial stability and price stability to repeat that 'the ECB is the ECB . . . it will not change its activities as the ECB', 'its primary mandate is price stability . . . it has the best result in terms of price stability for 50 years for the countries of the euro area'.[19] Then, he elaborated that 'the ESRB is a different institution. . . . It has been placed closed to the central banks because of their stake in the medium and long term, their independence and their stake in stability.'

Since 2010, this strategic discourse is completed with a symbolic staging where the ECB president does not answer to the questions related to the ESRB when he appears in front of the Parliament as the ECB president, and the other way round. Consequently, the ECB president claims that he has 'two hats' as he can strictly separates these two responsibilities. Since the presidents of the ECB and the ESRB are still the same person and their secretariats are located within the same building, this symbolic separation is only a mean to protect its reputation. The ECB's communication has thus been paradoxical and ambiguous: with the gain of supervision responsibilities it has been deviating from its original Bundesbank template, yet it has been constantly negating this move from orthodox principles.

The creation of the SSM

The creation of the SSM triggered a greater transfer of competences than in the ESRB case as the former has more coercive policy tools and intrusive capacities than the latter. Despite this discrepancy, the explaining factors for the SSM's creation were broadly similar to the ESRB case. Indeed, the ECB has been actively involved in the legislative process in order to maximize the extent of its supervisory realm. Besides, unintended consequences from the ESRB creation strengthened the recognition of the ECB's financial expertise. Finally, intergovernmental alliances were structured in the same manner as in the ESRB case.

The ECB as a strategic player

During the ESRB legislative process, the ECB asked for a maximization of the flow of information between the ESRB and the other micro-prudential supervision authorities[20] and an inclusion of the supervision of cross-border banks.[21] While the former point has been penned in the final legislation, the latter point was not even included in the De Larosière report (compare with earlier discussion). The ECB justified these recommendations with efficiency arguments: in order to better assess systemic risks, the macro-prudential supervisor should have better information on individual banks' activities and a direct watch on cross-border banks (micro-prudential responsibilities). The ECB also underlined that in case it could not fulfil properly its supervisory missions, the trust in the institution could be hindered. Yet, micro-prudential responsibilities increase the risk of policy failures and reputational damage to a bigger extent than macro-prudential responsibilities. It is quite obvious that the collapse of a supervised major financial institution or another recapitalization by the public authorities would be more dangerous for the ECB's reputation than an inaccurate ESRB non-binding report. Consequently, the ECB's willingness to extend its competences towards micro-supervision was driven by power concerns rather than efficiency concerns. More precisely, the ESRB was the ECB's 'Trojan horse' to regain the supervision over the whole banking system, as suggested by an EFC member in November 2010, two years before the Commission proposal on the SSM:

> I cannot show you the papers which are already circulating about the first meeting of the ESRB steering committee which will happen in December. But they are full of micro banking supervision items; the ESRB is the gateway to get all of the banking supervision under the central bank auspices. You will see in a few years' time, there will just be central banking supervision and insurances' supervision.
>
> *(Interview 1)*

Indeed, in the context of the 2012 Commission proposal on the Banking Union, the ECB President and Vice-President took first a proactive stand in favour of a centralized micro-supervisor at the European level[22] and then argue that central banks should gain this authority.[23] Besides, the ECB insisted that the SSM should have the final supervisory authority on the whole banking system, rather than on big banks only. The maximization of this transfer was justified once again with 'reputational risks' and efficiency reasons while the ECB repeated that these 'new tasks should not be mixed with its monetary responsibility tasks'[24] and reproduced the same symbolic separation than in the ESRB case.

Finally, the ECB pushed forward a last decisive argument for the gain of micro-supervision competences. From the beginning of 2012, an ECB legal team was tasked to determine what could be the maximum extent of the transfer in light of the 'enabling' cause of the European Treaties (Hennessy 2014, p. 11). In other words, the ECB was active to ensure that the gain of micro-prudential competences on the whole banking system would not need a Treaty change.

The unintended consequences of the ESRB

In this search for more competences, the ECB positions were strengthened by the unintended consequences of the ESRB creation on the balance of powers within the European statistical system. The economic statistics' production at the European level is shared between Eurostat and the ECB, the former is focused on general economic data while the latter collects financial statistics (European Central Bank and Eurostat, 2003). In order to strengthen the ESRB's oversight capacities, Eurozone policymakers made sure that the ECB could benefit from an important flow of micro-prudential information. The gain of macro-prudential supervision competences extended the ECB's range of data collection and on-site inspections, at the expense of Eurostat, on policy areas such as wages developments, pension funds, insurances and firms' activities. Policymakers' uncertainty in crisis times explains why they neglected the impact of their decision on the balance of power between Eurostat and the ECB:

> Before the crisis, you had to explain why you know something, all the time. Now, with the crisis, it is different. When you can explain uncertain developments or shed light on a specific policy item, nobody is asking you where the light is coming from.
>
> *(Interview 7)*

Crucially, the strengthening of ECB's powers, have not been and could not been anticipated by Eurozone policymakers as explained by a Eurostat agent:

> I have the feeling that the impact of the ESRB creation has not been understood and taken into account yet. It is not our role to say to the other European Commission DGs: are you aware that we lost the hand on financial supervision and maybe regulation? The European Commission lost power in the field, especially the Ecofin and Market DGs.
>
> *(Interview 7)*

Then, the increased recognition of the ECB's expertise helped its gain of micro-prudential supervision competences. Indeed, the initial September 2012 Commission proposal on the SSM creation and the December 2013 final regulation of the Council of the EU both stress out that 'as the Euro area's central bank with extensive expertise in macroeconomic and financial stability issues, the ECB is well placed to carry out clearly defined supervisory tasks with a focus on protecting the stability of Europe's financial system'. To conclude, the gain of supervision competences was self-enforcing since the unintended consequences of the ESRB creation partly explained the ECB's central role in the SSM.

Intergovernmental negotiations during SSM creation

During the creation of the banking union, Member States' alliances were broadly similar to the ESRB case (Howarth and Quaglia 2013). In 2010, Eurozone states were not ready to transfer micro-prudential supervisory powers for fiscal and sovereignty reasons, but the worsening of the Eurozone crisis shifted their positions. As the stakes were higher for the banking union than for the ESRB creation,[25] policymakers were also motivated by additional considerations.

First, in 2012, French public finances were too fragile for an eventual recapitalization of its banking sector that was heavily exposed to the peripheral sovereign debt.[26] When financial volatility spread to Spanish and Italian debt markets during the summer of 2011, French banks' balance sheets deteriorated alongside. In this context, banking union was envisioned by French policymakers as a mean to strengthen market operators' trust in the Eurozone institutions, and thus, to shelter the banks' balance-sheets from bond markets' volatility. Other Eurozone countries in a state of financial fragility, such as Spain and Italy, followed the French lead on that issue.

Second, the positions of German negotiators also shifted when the Eurozone integrity was threatened during the summers of 2011 and 2012. Furthermore, the German willingness to enforce stricter fiscal control mechanisms in the Eurozone's governance eased the compromise on banking union. Indeed, in the 'nested-games' logic prevailing in European integration processes (Tsebelis, 1990), the agreement on the banking union was used to loosen other states' resistances to the strengthening of fiscal control. Also, German negotiators managed to mitigate the extent of the transfer as they successfully sheltered the middle-sized domestic banking sector from direct supervision like in the ESRB case.

Finally, the ECB emerged again as the main winner of this transfer of competences despite the German reluctance to concentrate these powers within the ECB. In the context of high uncertainty triggered by the destabilization of Spain and Italy sovereign bond markets, the most straightforward policy solution was chosen and other policy alternatives were disregarded for the reasons exposed above. The Commission tried to change the SSM's host institution in favour of the European Banking Authority but such a transfer would have necessitated Treaty changes and the Commission did not have the necessary political authority to forge alliances in favour of this solution (compare with earlier discussion). Consequently, Germany lacked other political alternatives for the SSM and finally agreed on the ECB option.

Conclusion

This chapter explains why the ECB was granted macro-prudential and micro-prudential supervision powers after the 2007 financial crisis. I show first that this choice was neither automatic, nor risk free: other policy alternatives for solving the Eurozone's 'financial trilemma' were available and powers' concentration within a single institution rises conflict of interests' and regulatory capture's risks. Yet, three factors explain why the ECB has been the main winner of this transfer of competences. First, the ECB was very active in the legislative process and benefited from its original reputation based on the Bundesbank template. Second, Eurozone policymakers rallied on the ECB option for utilitarian reasons as they could import the ECB's financial expertise in the new supervising bodies at no charge. Third, policymakers' misperceptions on the ECB's past policies and the unintended consequences triggered by the ESRB's creation explain why the ECB's option prevailed on other policy alternatives. In conclusion, this transfer of competences cannot be described as 'controlled' by Eurozone policymakers and the ECB cannot present itself as 'neutral' agent in this process.

Additional unintended consequences could problematically unravel from such a concentration of powers within the ECB. Indeed, the first SSM's decisions do not show a clear break from previous ECB's positions in favour of 'light-touch' financial regulation. To date, the most important SSM policy was to assess whether the quality of capital held by the Eurozone's banks was sufficient in case of a crisis. Only minor peripheral banks fail the SSM's 'comprehensive assessment' which relied on a ratio comparing bank capital to risk-weighted assets. According to the Bank of England's chief economist,[27] this methodology is too complex and noisy, especially in times of crisis, and regulators should thus rely on the simpler and more efficient leverage ratio.[28] If the bank's robustness would have been tested with a leverage ratio, the core European countries' major financial institutions might have failed the test. Moreover, despite the fact that universal banks are strongly linked to the 'too-big-to-fail' problem in the Eurozone,[29] Danielle Nouy, the head of SSM, defends this banking model. Indeed, she stated that the Germany and French banking regulation reforms, which are considered to be the most protective of the universal banking models in the Eurozone (Couppey-Soubeyran, 2015), are 'sensible' and she 'would have serious reservations about going beyond that'.[30] This statement is in strong contrast with the global assessment that universal banking is a risk for growth and financial stability (Liikanen Report, 2012) and the US and UK regulatory efforts which adopted 'ring-fencing' measures. Finally, while the Bank of England advised to defer market operators' bonuses until their retirement, the ECB adopted a much lighter regulatory stance as it restricts the non-distribution of dividends only to the banks that failed the comprehensive assessment.[31]

List of interviews

Interview 1, EFC member, Brussels, November 2010
Interview 2, EFC member, Brussels, April 2010
Interview 3, EFC member, Brussels, November 2010
Interview 4, EC, DG Ecfin, Brussels, May 2010
Interview 5, EC, DG Ecfin, Brussels, May 2010
Interview 6, MP, Econ, Lyon, November 2011
Interview 7, Eurostat, Luxembourg, December 2010

Notes

1. Refinancing operations are the main policy tools of central banks. The central bank conducts an auction to loan a certain amount of liquidity to commercial banks at a certain rate against specified forms of collateral.
2. Repo markets are over-the-counter markets where banks exchange liquidity against collateral. They are part of the shadow banking system.
3. In 2008, the transactions made in the Eurozone repo market rose to €6tn (around 70% of the Eurozone GDP), In compression, the wholesale unsecured interbank market transactions reached €120bn.
4. As a consequence of the financial expansion permitted by the use of government debts on repo markets, the assets of the three biggest French banks were worth 250% of the French GDP in 2010.
5. In this chapter I focus solely on the financial supervision reform and not on the banking resolution item. Even though the linkage between these two items is crucial, my focus on the ECB gain of competences explains why banking resolution is out of the picture. This explanation applies for the lack of consideration about the issue of non-Eurozone countries.
6. In practice however, even the Bundesbank after 1975, the central bank most dogmatic about the overarching importance of money supply, took other factors into account to fixate its monetary policies.
7. The Financial Stability Oversight Council.
8. Art 105 (2) TFEU.
9. This goes against Hodson's (2011) argument that the ECB does not have any vested interest in the extension of its competences towards the field of supervision since the governors of the NCB sitting at the Council of governors want to protect their own national responsibilities.
10. Since the Lisbon Treaty, the European Parliament is a co-legislator in the field of financial supervision.
11. The ECB is generating incomes through its seigneurage activities, e.g. the financial revenue coming from the bank's refinancing operations' interest rates and the emission of banknotes.
12. Three EFC members indicated that the absence of cost has been the most important explanation for the ECB central place.
13. Former ECB chairman (2003–11).
14. Former ECB board member (2006–11), supporter of Bundesbanks' orthodoxy.
15. Speech of Jean-Claude Trichet, 3 November 2007. All the speeches are available on the ECB website www.ecb.europa.eu.
16. Speech of Jean-Claude Trichet, 5 June 2007.
17. ECB chairman since 2011.
18. ECB opinion (CON/2009/88), 26 October 2009.
19. Speech of Jean-Claude Trichet, 27 September 2010.
20. ECB legal opinion (CON/2010/5), 8 January 2010.
21. Speech of Jean-Claude Trichet, 7 December 2009.
22. Speech of Mr Draghi, 25 April 2012.
23. Speech of Vitor Constâncio, 7 September 2012.
24. Speech of Mr Draghi, 6 December 2012.
25. The ESRB secretariat triggered the hiring of 25 agents and an additional yet limited recruiting in the DG Research of the ECB. In comparison, the tasks linked with the operation of the SSM led to the hiring of more than 770 agents as in March 2014.
26. For example, the amount of the French bank's exposure to Italian debt reached 15% of the French GDP in 2011.

27 Speech of Andrew Haldane, 31 August 2012.
28 The assumption behind this proposition is that a financial crisis triggers the fall of all the asset prices.
29 All the European banks included in the Financial and Stability Board's 'too-big-to-fail' list are universal banks.
30 Interview of Danielle Nouy with Handelsblatt, 1 April 2015.
31 Recommendation ECB/2015/2 on dividend distribution policies.

Bibliography

Adolph, C. (2013) *Bankers, Bureaucrats, and Central Bank Politics: The Myth of Neutrality*. Cambridge: Cambridge University Press.
Ahrend, R., Cournède, B. and Price, R. (2008) 'Monetary policy, market excesses and financial turmoil', *OECD Economics Working Paper*, 5.
Allison, G.T. and Zelikow, P. ([1971] 1999) *Essence of Decision: Explaining the Cuban Missile Crisis*, 2nd edition. Harlow: Longman.
Bauer, M.W. and Becker, S. (2014) 'The unexpected winner of the crisis: The European Commission's strengthened role in economic governance', *Journal of European Integration*, 36: 213–29.
Bini-Smaghi, L. (2009) 'Europe cannot ignore its financial trilemma', *Financial Times*, 21 June.
Bini Smaghi, L. (2013) *Austerity: European Democracies Against the Wall*. London: CEPS Paperbacks.
Blyth, M. (2013) *Austerity: The History of a Dangerous Idea*. Oxford: Oxford University Press.
Boyer, P.C. and Ponce, J. (2012) 'Regulatory capture and banking supervision reform', *Journal of Financial Stability*, 8: 206–17.
Buckley, J. and Howarth, D. (2010) 'Internal market: Gesture politics? Explaining the EU's response to the financial crisis', *Journal of Common Market Studies*, 48: 119–41.
Buiter, W. and Rahbari, E. (2012) 'The European Central Bank as lender of last resort for sovereigns in the Eurozone', *Journal of Common Market Studies*, 50: 6–35.
Carpenter, D. (2010) *Reputation and Power: Organizational Image and Pharmaceutical Regulation at the FDA*, Princeton, NJ: Princeton University Press.
Couppey-Soubeyran, J. (2015) *Blablabanque. Le discours de l'inaction*, Paris: Michalon.
De Larosière, J. (2009) *The high-level group on financial supervision in the EU*, Brussels: Report for the European Commission.
De Rynck, S. (2016) 'Banking on a union: the politics of changing Eurozone banking supervision', *Journal of European Public Policy*, 23(1): 119–35.
De Visscher, C., Maiscocq, O. and Varone, F. (2008) 'The Lamfalussy reform in the EU securities markets: Fiduciary relationships, policy effectiveness and balance of power', *Journal of Public Policy*, 28: 19–47.
Dyson, K. (2014) *States, Debt, and Power: 'Saints' and 'Sinners' in European History and Integration*. Oxford: Oxford University Press.
Elgie, R. (2002) 'The politics of the European Central Bank: Principal–agent theory and the democratic deficit', *Journal of European Public Policy*, 9: 186–200.
European Central Bank and Eurostat. (2003) *Memorandum of understanding on economic and financial statistics between the Directorate General Statistics of the European Central Bank and Eurostat*. Brussels, 10 March.
Fontan, C. (2013) 'Frankenstein en Europe. L'impact de la Banque centrale européenne sur la gestion de la crise de la zone euro' *Politique européenne*, 42: 22–45.
Forder, J. (2002) 'Interests and "independence": The European Central Bank and the theory of bureaucracy', *International Review of Applied Economics*, 16: 51–69.
Freedman, C., Lane, P., Repullo, R. and Schmidt-Hebbel, K. (2011), *External evaluation of the directorate general research of the European Central Bank*. Frankfurt: European Central Bank, 25 January.
Gabor, D. and Ban, C. (2015). 'Banking on bonds: The new links between states and markets', *Journal of Common Market Studies*: 1–19.
Goodhart, C. (2010), 'The changing role of central banks', *Financial History Review*, 18(2):135–154
Grosche, G. and Puetter, U. (2008) 'Preparing the Economic and Financial Committee and the Economic Policy Committee for enlargement', *Journal of European Integration*, 30: 527–43.
Hennessy, A. (2014) 'Redesigning financial supervision in the European Union (2009–2013)', *Journal of European Public Policy*, 21: 151–68.
Hodson, D. (2011) *Governing the Euro Area in Good Times and Bad*. Oxford: Oxford University Press.

Howarth, D. and, Quaglia, L. (2013) 'Banking union as holy grail: Rebuilding the single market in financial services, stabilizing Europe's banks and "completing" economic and monetary union', *Journal of Common Market Studies*, 51:, pp. 103–123.

Issing, O. (2012) 'Central banks, paradise lost'. *Institute for Monetary and Economic Studies, Bank of Japan*, 30 May.

Issing, O. et al. (2001) *Monetary Policy in the Euro Area: Strategy and Decision-Making at the European Central Bank*. Cambridge: Cambridge University Press.

Jabko, N. (2006) *Playing the market: a political strategy for uniting Europe, 1985–2005*, Ithaca: Cornell University Press.

Jabko, N. (2009) 'Transparency and accountability', in Dyson, K. and Marcussen, M. (eds), *Central Banks in the Age of the Euro: Europeanization, Convergence and Power*. Oxford: Oxford University Press, pp. 391–406.

Jervis, R. (1976) *Perception and Misperception in International Politics*. Princeton, NJ: Princeton University Press.

Landon, T. and Ewing, J. (2011) 'Mario Draghi, into the eye of Europe's financial storm', *The New York Times*, 29 October.

Liikanen, E. (2012), 'Final report of the high-level expert group on reforming the structure of the EU banking sector', *European Commission*, 2 October.

McNamara, K. (1998) *The Currency of Ideas: Monetary Politics in the European Union*. Ithaca: Cornell University Press.

McPhilemy, S. (2016), 'Integrating macro-prudential policy: central banks as the 'third force' in EU financial reform', *West European Politics*, 39(3): 526–544.

Matthijs, M. and McNamara, K. (2015) 'The euro crisis' theory effect: northern saints, southern sinners, and the demise of the eurobond', *Journal of European Integration*, 37(2): 229–45.

Moravcsik, A (1998) *The Choice for Europe: Social Purpose and State Power from Messina to Maastricht*. Ithaca: Cornell University Press.

Mudge, S. L. and Vauchez, A. (2016), 'Fielding supranationalism: the European Central Bank as a field effect', *The Sociological Review Monographs*, 64(2): 146–69.

Mügge, D. (2011) 'From pragmatism to dogmatism: European Union governance, policy paradigms and financial meltdown', *New Political Economy*, 16: 185–206.

Padoa-Schioppa, T. (1999) 'EMU and banking supervision', *International Finance*, 2: 295–308.

Parsons, C. (2007) *How to Map Arguments in Political Science*. Oxford: Oxford University Press.

Pierson, P. (1996) 'The path to European integration', *Comparative Political Studies*, 29: 123–63.

Radaelli, C. (1999) *Technocracy in the European Union*. Harlow: Longman.

Salines, M., Glöckler, G. and Truchlewski, Z. (2012) 'Existential crisis, incremental response: The Eurozone's dual institutional evolution 2007–2011', *Journal of European Public Policy*, 19: 665–81.

Saurugger, S. (2013) 'Constructivism and public policy approaches in the EU: From ideas to power games', *Journal of European Public Policy*, 20: 888–906.

Scharpf, F.W. (1997) 'Economic integration, democracy and the welfare state', *Journal of European Public Policy*, 4: 18–36.

Schäuble, W. (2012) 'How to protect EU taxpayers against bank failures', *Financial Times*, 30 August.

Schoenmaker, D. (2010) 'The ECB, financial supervision and financial stability management', in De Haan, J. (ed.), *The European Central Bank at Ten*. New York: Springer, pp. 171–85.

Schüler, M. (2004) 'Integrated financial supervision in Germany', *ZEW Discussion Papers*, No. 04–35.

Tsebelis, G. (1990) *Nested Games: Rational Choice in Comparative Politics*. Berkeley, CA: University of California Press.

10
Varieties of capitalism and banking in the EU

Iain Hardie

Introduction

The title of this chapter might initially appear to suggest the covering of some relatively old academic ground. Banking, and in particular the 'dichotomous framing' of 'bank-based' and 'market-based' financial systems (Clift, 2007; Culpepper, 2005), have long been at the heart of the distinctions underpinning the varieties of capitalism literature. The patience of banks in bank-based systems, encouraged by the long-term relationships they form with non-financial companies (NFCs) shields NFCs from short-term market pressures. This allows, it is argued, long-term corporate investment decisions, worker involvement in company decision-making, effective training schemes (apprenticeship programmes), and stable long-term employment relations, including worker retraining and cooperative wage bargaining. Essentially, strategies can be followed that yield delayed returns, rather than short-term profit maximization. In contrast, in 'market-based' systems, banks are not providers of long-term capital and do not act as bulwarks against short-term financial market pressures on NFCs. Banks are predominantly short-term lenders and NFCs rely relatively more on equity and bond markets for finance.

The patient capital banks provide in the bank-based (archetypally German) financial system comes in two forms: equity and debt. Banks are long-term holders of the equity of the NFCs with which they have relationships and on whose boards bank employees often sit. In truth, these bank shareholdings were already in decline at the time of Hall and Soskice's seminal work (2001, p. 23; Jackson and Moerke, 2005). NFC cross-shareholdings and/or long-term pension fund holdings (Culpepper, 2005) of NFC equity arguably continued to have an influence, but banks now have little remaining influence as providers of long-term equity capital in Europe. In countries, such as Germany, where bank executive membership of NFC boards has been a source of influence, such membership has also declined, albeit replaced by NFC insiders (Hackethal, Schmidt and Tyrell, 2006).

The appropriate current focus for bank – NFC interaction is therefore bank lending. For Zysman (1983), there are two central distinctions between market-based and bank-based financial systems: first, between bank loans and securities; bank-based systems have persistently high aggregate bank lending in NFC finance (Beyer and Höpner, 2003; Vitols, 2004; Deeg, 2010). Zysman (1983, p. 63) makes the distinction between 'the impersonal arm's length dealings of capital markets' and 'the personal institutional ties of banks or lending institutions'. A second distinction, less commonly picked up by the subsequent literature, is between long and short-term bank lending. Patient banks in bank-based systems provide long-term loans. There are a number of assumptions implicit in Zysman's typology, some largely unaddressed in subsequent literature, some now questionable in the context of developments in banking in recent years. The focus of this chapter is on the latter, and on three assumptions in particular. The first is that banks and banking are synonymous. Zysman recognizes the existence of non-bank lenders, but rightly, given their small size when he was writing, largely ignores them. Subsequent literature on VoC has almost entirely ignored non-bank lenders; over time, and highlighted most dramatically by the financial crisis, this has become less defensible.

The second assumption is that loans are different from other types of financial instrument. 'What makes the financial systems different is the relative importance of two types of financial markets; capital markets and loan markets' (Zysman, 1983, p. 60). Borrowing through capital markets is to borrow in a way that exposes NFCs to the pressures of market prices, reducing their ability to make long-term decisions. The loan market, however, is in this typology different. Banks make loans, priced based on their own assessment of the creditworthiness of the borrower and of the long-term profitability of the relationship between bank and NFC. Not only are market pressures on NFCs mitigated by the 'financial power' of the banks, but banks are willing to engage in 'intertemporal transfers in loan pricing' (Boot, 2000, p. 13), lending at lower cost in the expectation of recompensing profit at a later date (Aoki, 1995; Aoki and Dinç, 2000; Rajan and Zingales, 2003; Aoki, Patrick and Sheard, 1995; Deeg, 1998). This widespread distinction underpins the categorization of financial systems by considering the provision of capital to NFCs (loan, bond, or equity)[1] or by the relative size of bank assets, equity stock market capitalization, and outstanding private bond market issuance (e.g. Allen and Gale, 2000). Crucial to the absence of market pressures on NFCs is the fact that loans remain on bank balance sheets and are valued 'at cost' – with a value the same as when the loan was made – unless there is severe credit impairment. Loans, unlike securities, are not traded instruments, with their price moving up and down with financial market prices.

This second assumption is concerned with the asset side of bank balance sheets and how market prices have an impact on those assets. The third assumption in Zysman's framework refers to the other, liabilities, side of the balance sheet. This assumption underlies all assumptions regarding banks as providers of patient capital: that banks are able, not just willing, to perform that role. Since banks are leveraged financial institutions, their capacity to lend is dependent on their ability to borrow.[2] In the early 1980s, when Zysman was writing, banks, even the investment banking operations of European universal banks, 'draw their funds from [individual and NFC customer] deposits', and depositors are loyal (Zysman, 1983, p. 61). These deposits could often be withdrawn on demand, but the overall volume was stable. Absent the rare event of a bank run, banks could be confident that they would have the deposits to fund long-term lending, despite the maturity mismatch. In the medium term, increased competition for deposits, and pressure from banks' own shareholders, could bring market pressures on to the banks themselves, but at this time banks in CMEs have the capacity to be patient in their lending.

This chapter explores these three core assumptions (the first briefly) in the context of developments in banking, particularly since the start of the century. The possibility of changes in banking has long been recognized in the VoC literature. Zysman encouraged future research into the impact of 'ever more elaborate financial markets' on national systems of capitalism (Zysman, 1983, p. 281), and Hall and Soskice (albeit focusing narrowly on regulation rather than also on innovation in banking practices) observed that '[f]inancial deregulation could be the string that unravels coordinated market economies' (Hall and Soskice, 2001, p. 64). These authors either recognized the static nature of their analysis (Zysman) or have been criticized for a lack of focus on processes of change (Hall and Soskice). Much of the VoC literature which followed them has indeed been centrally concerned with change, especially the extent of convergence between bank-based Continental European financial systems and their 'Anglo-Saxon' counterparts (see, for example, Berger and Dore, 1996; Crouch and Streeck, 1997; Kitschelt et al., 1999; Whitley, 1999; Schmidt, 2002). The question of change in Germany has figured particularly prominently. Yet throughout, this is a literature dominated by the issue of NFC financing: are NFCs increasingly reliant on securities markets for their financing, at the expense of bank loans? This literature suffers from two fundamental weaknesses (see Hardie et al., 2013; Hardie and Howarth, 2013a). First, and most important, it fails to question the fundamental dichotomy underpinning the VoC approach: the bank-based/market-based dichotomy. NFCs may (or may not – consensus has proved elusive) rely less on bank loans, but banks can still be patient and loans are different from securities. Related to this is a second weakness: a focus on the issue of convergence with an unchanging Anglo-Saxon capitalism. Change in the US and UK, the archetypal Anglo-Saxon economies, is rarely considered (although see Howell, 2007).

These weaknesses add up to a blind-spot regarding change in banks and banking. The view of banks has been very much within a narrative of disintermediation, of banks' role in the financial system reducing as securities markets become more important. There has been consideration on the response of banks, but it is focused on their contribution to this disintermediation. One of the few CPE scholars writing on banks, Deeg (2010), highlights the rise in 'deal-based banking', and the 'originate and distribute' business model. Outside CPE, the approach has been similar. Lall (2006; see also Allen and Gale, 2000) discusses traditional and 'new' financial intermediation by non-banks. Ertürk and Solari (2007) show change in the sources of bank profits, away from interest on loans towards fees.

Such approaches are problematic for one simple reason. If this is the dominant issue of change with banks in recent years, the expectation must be that banks would become smaller, perhaps absolutely, but certainly relative to the size of developed world economies. An alternative measure would be a reduced role for bank lending in NFC financing. This is not what has happened. Figure 10.1 shows bank assets/GDP for selected EU countries since 1980. Country experiences are not all the same, and there are some breaks in the data series. However, one thing is very clear. Banks have grown in size dramatically. The story of European banking since 1980, and especially since 2000, has not been about disintermediation. The importance of banks in the intermediation of financial flows in the European economy has dramatically increased, not declined. Prior to the financial crisis, the role of banks in NFC finance relative to securities markets similarly shows banks' increasing importance, not decline (Hardie and Howarth, 2013b).

One source of this increased size of bank balance sheets has been banks buying securities or 'trading assets' (see below). Aglietta and Breton (2001, p. 441) note that banks have added a 'new market portfolio' to their 'traditional credit portfolio' (see also Hardie and Howarth, 2009). Not only are banks making more loans to NFCs, but they are also becoming more important as the final purchasers of the securities whose development had been expected to result in banks' disintermediation. This would appear, on the surface, to suggest that EU economies (including the 'Anglo-Saxon' UK) were becoming more, not less, bank-based, as well as questioning the standard methodology of comparing the relative size of loan and securities markets.

This chapter does not, however, conclude that EU financial systems are becoming, more bank based. Rather, it questions these three assumptions underpinning the standard typology, as a way to consider present day financial systems and the role of banks within them. The next section examines the rise of banking activities performed by non-bank financial institutions: 'shadow banking'. The subsequent section focuses on the asset side of banks' balance sheets, and

Capitalism and banking in the EU

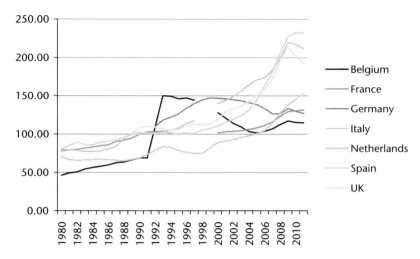

Figure 10.1 Bank assets to GDP, selected EU countries, 1980–2011
Source: World Bank global financial development database.

the extent to which they are subject to market forces, before a section focusing on the liability side of the balance sheet, and the changing nature of how banks finance not only their holdings of securities, but also their lending. This clear division of the two sides of the balance sheet is to some extent artificial (see discussion of the 'repo' market below), but serves a useful explanatory purpose. The aim of these two sections is to examine the 'financial power' of the banks (Zysman, 1983) through the concept of 'market-based banking'. Key to the conventional typology is banks having the power to act as bulwarks between financial markets and NFCs. This has spawned a considerable literature looking at the concentration of banks (though not banking) in individual countries, on the grounds that an oligopolistic market structure gives banks financial power (Byrne and Davis, 2003; Rajan and Zingales, 2003; Lall, 2006). I take a different view of financial power, arguing: (1) that changes in the loan markets have increasingly resulted in loans being the same as any other financial market instrument, actively traded and with the price determined in market trading; and (2) that lending is funded not only by patient depositors, but also be skittish financial market actors, whether other banks or NFCs making deposits or investors buying securities issued by the banks. The result is that the profitability of lending, and therefore its availability and pricing, is determined not by individual bank decision-making but by market prices. In traditional banking, banks make decisions on lending based on their own assessment of the correct terms for that loan and with little regard to pressures on their own borrowing; that borrowing being through stable customer deposits. Increasingly, both the terms of the loan and the cost of bank borrowing are directly determined by financial market prices. We have moved, to a varied extent across European national financial systems, to 'market-based banking' (Hardie and Howarth, 2013a; Hardie et al., 2013).

Shadow banking

The rise of shadow banking, in various guises, is one of the central explanations given for the financial crisis (e.g. Pozsar et al., 2010; Gorton, 2010; Gorton and Metrick, 2010). What these accounts highlight is the rise of credit provision by non-bank financial institutions, those entities rightly ignored by Zysman. In the crisis, the focus was on shadow banking in the US, but as regulators have increased the attention paid to this sector, the size of shadow banking in Europe has become apparent. As of end-2012, estimates from the Financial Stability Board ('FSB') put the assets of non-bank financial intermediaries in the euro area at 31 per cent of the total for the jurisdictions analysed, compared to 37 per cent for the US, with the UK a further 12 per cent (FSB, 2013, p. 10). Euro area assets were then US$22 trillion, and more than half the size of those of banks. The FSB regards non-bank financial intermediation as a 'conservative'[3] initial proxy for shadow banking.

There are nevertheless significant definitional uncertainties involved in any analysis of shadow banking. The term 'shadow banking' has been used to describe banking activity that is to a greater or lesser extent outside the commercial banking system (e.g. Pozsar et al., 2010; Tucker, 2010). Of importance here is the distinction between those activities that are off-balance-sheet of the banks and those that are not directly connected to the banks. Some have seen these as best defined separately, as 'shadow' and 'parallel' banking respectively (Adrian and Shin, 2010; Hardie and Howarth, 2013b; Hardie et al., 2013), with the term 'market-based banking' applied just to this shadow banking activity. Pozsar et al., (2010, p. 66) similarly differentiate between 'internal' and 'external' shadow banking and adopt a very specific definition of parallel banking related to the distinction between regulatory arbitrage and genuine competitive advantage. Gorton and Metrick (2010; also Gorton, 2010), in their focus on 'securitized banking', consider the funding of these securitized assets on the balance sheet, especially by the investment banks. However, shadow banking has been defined widely in recent debates, as policymakers seek to define banking and what should be regulated as a bank. The definition of shadow banking as 'the system of credit intermediation that involves entities and activities fully or partially outside the regular banking system' (FSB, 2013, p. 5) must now be regarded as broadly accepted. An accepted definition does not remove problems of analysis, however. Much of the activity of non-bank financial intermediation is not credit intermediation (for example, equity investment funds constitute 15 per cent of all non-bank financial intermediaries). A more granular analysis by the FSB of 20 jurisdictions suggests that less than two-thirds of non-bank financial intermediation can be considered shadow banking. This may change as data improves.

What is of interest to the VoC literature, and useful for cross-national comparison, may also remain somewhat at odds with the regulatory interest in the broadest data collection. A focus solely on even the narrowest areas of shadow banking, however, obscures as much as it reveals. It reveals one aspect of change while obscuring another, and for the EU in particular more important, development in financial systems: changes in the business activities of the banks themselves. Despite the very significant increase in the size of non-bank financial intermediation, it remains less than half the size of bank financial intermediation (end-2012; FSB, 2013, p. 8), with shadow banking even smaller. Confining the definition of market-based banking to shadow banking largely ignores the question of market-based banks. Changes in bank activities represent a potentially more important source of systemic change in financial systems. Those changes, and the rise of market-based banks as the central part of the rise of market-based banking, are therefore the main focus of this chapter, beginning with the next section's focus on bank assets.

The changing nature of bank assets

Albeit with considerable simplification, we can focus on two parts of the asset side of bank balance sheets: bank holdings of securities and bank loans. The argument for market-based banking depends on change in these three areas, evidenced by: (1) increased bank trading assets as a percentage of total assets; and (2) the changing nature of loan markets undermining their uniqueness amongst financial instruments. For example, 5 per cent of all non-bank financial intermediation in the FSB data, by volume, is by Dutch special financial institutions, and these entities represent around two-thirds of non-bank financial intermediation in the Netherlands. The FSB describes these entities as 'typically owned by foreign multinationals who use these entities to attract external funding and facilitate intra-group transactions' (FSB, 2013, p. 12). This is in the main multinationals issuing bonds through a Dutch subsidiary, guaranteed by the parent, and the motivation is generally avoiding withholding tax. While of interest to those focused on MNCs minimizing their tax bills, this does not represent any 'new' form of credit intermediation that would be of interest to analysis of financial system change. Such activity, however, results in the Netherlands having by far the highest volume of non-bank financial intermediation relative to GDP of the jurisdictions in the FSB data, in addition to representing over 15 per cent of all such intermediation in the euro area (intermediation which, as a result, is larger relative to GDP than in the US).

It is necessary, therefore, to be cautious in what we take from the recent work on shadow banking for considerations of VoC, and in particular regarding cross-national variation. We can say with confidence that non-bank credit provision increased rapidly in the years immediately preceding the financial crisis and that it has only reduced marginally since then. This is market-based financing of (amongst others) NFCs, and represents therefore secular change in the nature of NFC financing. It is change in EU financial systems as well as in the United States. We are as yet limited in the conclusions that can be drawn regarding intra-EU national variation, but the data available[4] is generally supportive of existing views of financial systems, with the possible exception (largely for the reasons noted above) of the Netherlands. Non-bank financial intermediation is far greater, relative to GDP, in the Netherlands and UK (all over twice GDP) than in France, Germany, Spain and Italy (all under half of GDP). This is entirely as we would expect, given the overlap between the volume of non-bank financial intermediation and the size of equity and bond markets in any individual country. Moreover, there appears little reason to expect – based on currently available data – any change in financial systems' relative positions (again, with the possible exception of the Netherlands) as a result of improvements in data allowing a focus on shadow banking that is more directly relevant to comparative political economy.[5]

The increase in financial assets

Increased financial assets – with their prices and therefore profitability determined by financial markets – represent a change in bank activities that has been acknowledged in the existing literature on financial system change, most notably in Aglietta and Breton's distinction between banks' 'new market portfolio' and 'traditional credit portfolio' (Aglietta and Breton, 2001, p. 441). The innovation in this development should not be exaggerated: European universal banks have long held securities on their balance sheets (including bank holdings of NFC equity which are central to CMEs). The change is rather the significant recent increases in this 'market portfolio' and the resultant fall in loans as a proportion of bank balance sheets. These increases show the extent to which banks, on the asset side, have moved away from the view that dominates the VoC literature. Simplicity, and some data limitations, suggests measuring both loans and advances, and holdings of financial assets that are sensitive to market movements,[6] as a percentage of total assets, as in Figures 10.2 and 10.3.

Hardie and Howarth (2009, 2013b) and Hardie et al. (2013) show that loans became a reduced part of commercial bank activities before the financial crisis, particularly from around 2000. An important question is whether the change represents a secular change in the nature of banks, or was rather the product of a particular period of market excess. It remains far too early to

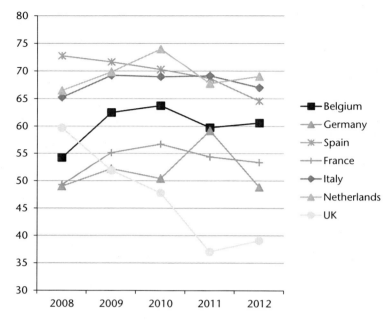

Figure 10.2   Loans and advances as a percentage of bank assets, selected EU countries, 2008–12
Source: ECB.[7]

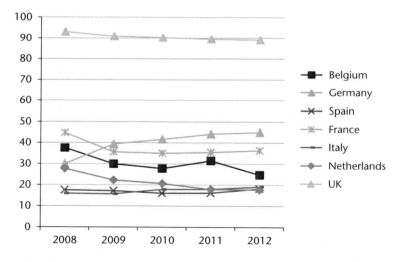

Figure 10.3   Holding of financial assets as a percentage of total bank assets, selected EU countries, 2008–12

Source: ECB.

answer that question definitively, given many unresolved problems in European banking, enforced government ownership and incomplete regulatory response. Figure 10.2, however, does not point to any dramatic reversal of the previous trend. Loans and advances are a marginally higher proportion of bank balance sheets in 2012 compared to 2008 in four of the countries shown, but the most marked changes have been in Spain and the UK, where the proportion of loans and advances to total assets has fallen, in the UK very significantly. There is also little sign of any convergence across the countries.

Figure 10.3 confirms this situation of little material change since the financial crisis, in the holding of financial assets. This includes financial assets held on banks' trading books, in addition to those deemed 'available for sale'. The differences between these accounting treatments are not a focus here (see Ryan, 2008; Hardie, 2012, pp. 48–50), but these are assets whose price movements will have a direct impact of bank profitability or equity. They can therefore be directly contrasted with the implied conception in the existing literature of bank assets as held 'at cost', with their profitability determined only by the quality of banks' initial decision-making regarding the creditworthiness of a borrower.

Any conclusions regarding secular change must also be regarded as premature with regards to this 'new market portfolio' (Aglietta and Breton, 2001), in particular because of the regulatory response to the financial crisis. This response has included various plans, at EU and national level, for 'ring-fencing' commercial from investment banking in the EU, with only the former likely to receive government support. Such regulation is clearly intended to reduce the holding of financial assets, but there is no sign in Figure 10.3 of this change taking place yet. Even focusing narrowly on assets held on trading books, in 2012 these were more than a quarter of total bank assets in the three largest European economies, France, Germany and the UK (including in the UK, loans valued at market prices). Indeed, as Howarth and Quaglia (2014) have argued, the nature of bank balance sheets may well, through their influence on national positions on bank regulation, have a significant influence on the limits EU regulation places on bank involvement in the buying and trading of financial assets (also Hardie and Macartney, 2016).

The changing nature of loan markets

Thus far, the discussion of the changing nature of bank assets has implicitly maintained Zysman's assumption that loans are a different kind of financial instrument. Hence, we can distinguish financial markets by the relative importance of loan and capital markets (Zysman, 1983, p. 60). Such a distinction no longer holds. NFC loans are increasingly traded financial instruments like any other, either directly or via securitizations such as Collateralized Loan Obligations and Commercial Mortgage Backed Securities. As these loan markets become market based, this alternative source of market pressures potentially challenges a view that change has occurred only at the level of large firms, through increased issuance of equity and bonds, but not at Small and Medium-Sized Enterprises (SMEs) (on Germany, see Vitols, 2004). Loan trading is most active in the United States; Gorton (2010, p. 42) sees the ratio of secondary market loan sales to outstanding commercial and industrial loans peaking in 2007 at over 25 per cent. Although 'relatively nascent' (Standard & Poor's 2010, p. 17), European markets had trading volumes in 2007 of US$225 billion (Axa Investment Managers, undated). The comparative importance of securitization between the US and Europe is similar. Although the US securitization market is far greater, European securitization reached US$453 billion equivalent by the crisis (European Securitisation Forum, 2008; see also ECB, 2009, p. 10), and both the Bank of England and the European Central Bank have joined the Federal Reserve in supporting securitization markets post-crisis, seeing such support as vital to improving the ability of NFCs to borrow (Cheun, von Köppen-Mertes, and Weller, 2009; on the link between securitization and credit growth, see Jiangli and Pisker, 2008; Sabry and Okongwu, 2009). Securitization is central to a decline in banks' financial power to limit the impact of the market on their clients (see Rajan and Zingales, 2003, p. 8). In securitization, not only is the pricing and availability of financing determined by the market, but the ability of banks to coordinate the rescue of companies in difficulty (Zysman, 1983, p. 64) is further undermined. The increasing use of Credit Default Swaps to trade and hedge corporate credit risk has contributed further to the extent to which the profitability of NFC lending, and therefore the decision on whether to lend and the interest rate to charge, has become determined not by bank decision-making but by market prices. When banks are 'originating to distribute' – making loans in anticipation of selling them via securitization, the pricing of the loan is determined by the anticipated price for which it can be subsequently sold. The availability of loans to NFCs therefore becomes set by the price at which they will be bought by financial market actors other than banks, or at which banks packaging them into securitization products will buy them. Market prices increase/decrease profitability, increasing/decreasing the ability to retain earnings to increase capital (Deutsche Bundesbank, 2009, p. 60), and, through the impact of profitability on bank share prices, increasing/decreasing the ability to raise new capital. Through 'value at risk' valuation of marked to market assets, increased volatility also increases the amount of capital banks require (Deutsche Bundesbank, 2009, p. 50; Commission Bancaire, 2009, p. 23). The issue, however, is not solely one of losses but is also a matter of procyclicality, as higher market prices can also increase profitability and lending capacity (Hellwig, 2009, p. 180; IMF, 2008).

The question of cyclical versus secular change is also important with respect to these developments. The picture is mixed. Securitization markets have seen major falls in volume, especially in Europe (excluding securitization to provide collateral for borrowing from the ECB) and some more esoteric financial products seem unlikely to return in anything like their previous form. The importance central banks attach to restarting certain forms of securitization, however, strongly suggests that this form of market-based lending will continue to be important. In the direct trading of loans, meanwhile, there have been a number of important developments. European secondary market trading volumes are down significantly, with quarterly volumes by the end of 2012 recovering to only a third of their 2007 peak, according to one market estimate (Markit, 2013). Such a significant fall – to volumes which represent a tiny fraction of NFC lending in Europe – obscures some significant developments which point also to significant secular change.

First, the trading of loans is no longer confined to 'leveraged' or non-investment grade loans. The initial development of this market, in both the US and Europe, was very much focused on this section of NFCs. However, as of the last quarter of 2012, the rapidly expanding trading of investment grade loans made up 21 per cent of European loan trading (Markit, 2013), suggesting a fuller range of NFC loans are being traded. Second, and more significant, institutional investors have been moving into the gap created by banks' difficulties, establishing loan funds to invest in loan markets. In 2012, banks only made up 52 per cent of the primary leveraged loan market in Europe (Forbes, 21 January 2014). With many of these loans not being traded (but still priced at market-driven yields), these developments will not show fully in data on secondary market trading.[8] Third, the regulatory attempts to move CDS trading onto exchanges will be likely to increase the visibility of these derivatives as the benchmark for pricing NFC credit in both bond and loan markets, thereby increasing the market element in loan pricing.

Changes in the securitization and trading of loans in Europe are not as yet at the levels of the United States, even in the United Kingdom, and there has been a significant reduction in this activity since the financial crisis. Nevertheless, even at the current levels, it is clear that these developments undermine the stark distinction between loans and securities markets. It is possible to distinguish financial systems by the extent to which these changes have occurred, but it is no longer possible to justify the (empirically simpler) typology using the comparative size of loan and securities markets.

The changing nature of bank liabilities

Changes in banks are not confined to just one side of their balance sheets. Market-based banking can be seen also in bank liabilities, and in particular in the way customer deposits have become a smaller component of bank borrowing. A 'traditional' bank borrows the money it lends from its customers through their deposits. Any holdings of securities are similarly financed by deposits (Zysman, 1983, p. 61). These depositors, even if their deposits can be withdrawn at any time, tend to be themselves patient. A bank run is possible, but, until Northern Rock in the UK in 2008, there had not been such a run in the UK since the nineteenth century. Furthermore, government guarantees to smaller depositors quickly returned depositors to their previous patience. As a result, banks funded by deposits do not face market pressures from this source to reduce lending or increase its cost (although note the role of increased competition discussed above). In contrast, banks financed through financial markets, including, importantly, from other banks,[9] face the possibility that these 'skittish' investors can withdraw almost instantly (see, for example, Basel Committee of Banking Supervision, 2008, p. 2). At the extreme, such as Northern Rock, this is the initial source of problems which lead to collapse.

The liability side of the balance sheet has moved far from the traditional conception of bank lending funded by customer deposits. First, as discussed by Gorton and Metrick (2010; also Gorton, 2010) in the case of 'securitized banking', holdings of financial assets are financed on a very short-term secured basis in the repurchase, or 'repo' market. The problems in this market have been well documented elsewhere in the case of the US, but were also significant in Europe. By August 2008, outstanding euro area repos totalled €6 trillion, 70 per cent of GDP (Gabor, 2012, p. 17). The market sensitivity and procyclicality of market-based assets are compounded when these assets are financed, as the vast majority are, by borrowing on a very short-term basis collateralized by the assets themselves. This is particularly the case in shadow banking by the investment banks. The importance of the repo market is highlighted by the analysis of the crisis in the US as a 'run on repo' (Gorton and Metrick, 2010; see also Acharya et al., 2010). The focus of these studies on the repo market serves to highlight that market-based assets are most commonly financed with market-based liabilities, and further shows the difficulties of seeking

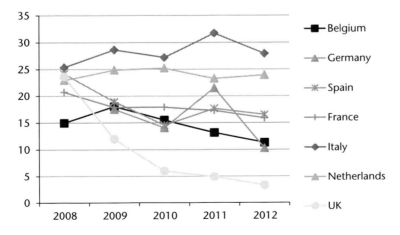

Figure 10.4 Customer funding gap,[10] selected EU countries, 2008–12
Source: ECB.

to disentangle the two sides of bank balance sheets. Although the securities financed in the European repo market include many unrelated to NFC lending (especially government securities), bonds issued by NFCs are also significant (Gabor, 2012, p. 19).

The second important area of market-based bank liabilities is in the financing of their customer lending activity. Very few banks have customer deposits equal to, or in excess of, their customer loans, creating a customer funding gap which can only be financed by borrowing from market sources (Bank of England, 2009, p. 37; ECB, 2009, p. 9; Raddatz, 2010). Financial market conditions have a direct impact on lending as a result. Kroszner, Laeven and Klingebiel (2007) show how credit-dependent sectors grow faster in normal times and are hit harder in tough times, while Ivashina and Scharfstein, 2010; see also Basel Committee on Banking Supervision, 2008, p. 11) show that banks with higher customer deposits (and therefore less market-based) reduced lending less during the financial crisis. Figure 10.4 sets out the size of that customer funding gap as a percentage of total bank assets, across the countries considered in this chapter.

These developments can also be placed in a longer term context: from 1980 to 2000, deposits represented a declining share of bank liabilities in G7 countries except Japan (unchanged) and France (Byrne and Davis, 2003, p. 159),[11] and this continued until the financial crisis (Hardie and Howarth, 2013b). In order to lend, banks have always needed to borrow;[12] at issue is the nature of that borrowing. To varying degrees across the countries considered here, by the financial crisis a large proportion of that borrowing was not from deposits, but through sources such as the interbank market (short-term borrowing from other banks), bonds issues or securitization. As a result, banks' ability to lend is heavily influenced by their own market access, limiting the 'financial power' that can shield NFCs from market pressures. This development is recognized in central bank surveys of lending conditions for NFCs: EU banks are now asked about 'the cost and availability of [their own] funding' as an influence on lending to NFCs. This is a question the traditional conception of banks could not envisage being asked.

The customer funding gap for banks in the countries considered here increased in the years before the financial crisis, with the exception of Germany (Hardie and Howarth, 2013b; Hardie et al., 2013). As a result, market forces became more influential on lending. Figure 10.4 shows that the situation post-crisis is slightly more mixed. The funding gap has fallen, 2008–12, in five of the seven countries, most dramatically in the UK. Overall, this is a clear reversal of the previous trend. However, it is only (with the exception of the UK) a partial reversal. Financial market financing of NFC lending remains substantial in Europe, including in countries generally seen as bank-based.

The caveat regarding premature conclusions regarding post-crisis banks applies in this area also. Some contraction of market financing of lending after 2008 was to be expected, but the situation when European banks finally overcome their problems remains highly uncertain. However, even if banks did shrink their lending sufficiently for customer loans to be anything like equal to customer deposits, the result could only be even greater increases in the size of shadow banking, and therefore continued growth of market-based banking. Anyway, the change in banking practices would be too great. When the funding gap on loans and the financing of securities is combined, the IMF (2010, p. 67) estimates UK banks total market financing at over $4 trillion (146 per cent of GDP) by end 2007. Separate country figures for the euro area are not given, but the Euro area total is US$12.4 billion (94 per cent of euro area GDP). Short-term (up to 1 year) bank market funding, the most immediate source of market pressure on bank lending, represented 65 per cent of UK GDP and 54 per cent of the euro area (IMF, 2010, p. 67; in comparison, the US figure is 'only' 32 per cent).

Any full analysis of the market pressures on banks as a result of financial market funding requires a more detailed consideration of the various sources of that funding. This is also necessary for any sensible comparison across countries. Empirically, this is challenging, as it involves an understanding of very similar markets in different countries. Both Italian and German banks, for example, rely relatively heavily on issuing unsecured bonds as a means of funding. In both cases, however, the nature of the purchasers of those bonds – the banks' own individual or savings bank customers – makes this a more stable source of borrowing than bonds sold to a broad range of institutional investors (e.g. Westdeutsche Landesbank, 2009, p. 97; Bayerische Landesbank, 2009, p. 33; Pagoulatos and Quaglia, 2013, p. 186). Similarly, banks in a number of countries issue covered bonds, a particular form of secured bond.[13] However, this market is longer-established and more stable in Germany (*Pfandbriefe*) than in other countries. A state guarantee on mortgages also makes Dutch securitizations more stable (Chang and Jones, 2013, p. 83). Any fuller attempt to outline these distinctions is beyond the scope of this chapter (for further discussion, see Hardie and Howarth, 2013a; Hardie et al., 2013). The bank funding markets can however, as an initial analysis, be distinguished in three ways. First, by the maturity of borrowing; shorter maturity liabilities, including borrowing from other banks, transmit market problems to banks' financing more quickly. The majority of unsecured interbank borrowing is short-term, often for less than a week (Bank of England, 2007, p. 34). Banks reliant on longer-term sources of funding (for example, Germany), such as various forms of bonds, face less immediate refinancing pressures. Second, wholesale markets must be distinguished by their fragility: the financial crisis has demonstrated that some wholesale markets are more fragile than others (Hardie et al., 2013; ECB, 2009, p. 11), making the impact on lending of market difficulties more immediate for those systems more dependent on those markets. Third (and empirically most difficult), market borrowing can be distinguished by who is being borrowed from – by the type of investor. Individual investors buying bonds may be largely indistinguishable in their behaviour from individual depositors. Borrowing from other banks has proved especially skittish, with borrowing from international banks and especially in foreign currencies particularly vulnerable in the event of market weakness. Institutional investors are also generally likely to exit. Overall, however, it must be recognized that exposure to financial market funding generally goes hand-in-hand with financing from less stable sources.

The implications of market-based banking for varieties of capitalism

This chapter has argued that the nature of banks and banking has undergone such profound change that the underpinning of the bank-based/market-based dichotomy has disappeared. Although there is no simple correspondence between typologies of financial systems and modes of capitalism (Deeg, 2010), this clearly has significant implications for the varieties of capitalism literature. As noted above, Hall and Soskice (2001) already saw the potential for change in banks to undermine CMEs, which depend on bank-based finance. If banks are just another group of financial market actors, as influenced by market prices as any others, it might appear sensible to consider an end to the long-running debates on convergence of CMEs with the LMEs. For VoC, if such a view is accepted, either a financial system underpinning of CMEs was always incorrect, or much of the VoC literature is in danger of finding itself in a cul de sac.

That is not the view taken in this chapter, for two reasons. First, considerable national variation in market-based banking remains, as the data presented above clearly show. In a number of the European countries discussed here, a significant amount of 'traditional' banking – loans to NFCs which remain on the banks' balance sheets, funded by customer deposits – remains. The extent of market-based banking is in itself a source of national variation. The post-crisis regulatory response could be as likely to heighten this variation as reduce it, though that must remain supposition at the time of writing (November 2015).

In terms of the direction of research, central bank desires to support securitization and the FSB's focus on a future for 'market-based finance' (Carney, FT.com, 16 June 2014) may point in another direction. While closer attention to the nature of banking in developed economies is overdue for comparative political economy, a research agenda considering the extent of national system moves from traditional to market-based banking should not be the main focus of future research on financial systems. A further, more promising, approach involves abandoning the existing dichotomy, and questioning the homogeneity not only of bank-based finance, but also of market-based. The underlying logic of patient capital protecting NFCs from short-term market pressures is maintained, but the assumption of banks as necessarily the only, or even the predominant, source of patient capital is abandoned. CPE has made small steps in that direction already: NFCs' long-term holding of each other's equity, for example, has long been central to financial systems in certain CMEs, and pension funds have been seen as a potential replacement for banks as patient owners of NFC equity (e.g. Culpepper, 2005). There is much further to go, with a research agenda targeted across the range of financial market providers of capital to NFCs. Such an agenda would require fundamental questioning of a number of the basic assumptions in the VoC literature. For example, does patient capital require a relationship between NFC and the provider of capital? What is the nature of market pressures on lenders? What is the role of voice versus exit? The list of potential questions is long, and the implications of the answers may well lead CPE to a very different conception of the varieties of financial systems.

Notes

1. This ignores both the maturity of bank lending and financing from companies' own retained earnings. See Murinde, Agung and Mullineux, 2004.
2. On the importance of long-term financing for the ability of German banks to make long-term loans to NFCs, see Vitols, 1998.
3. The FSB considers it currently covers around 90 per cent of global financial system assets. Data focuses on country of domicile, and does not cover many of the offshore financial centres where much shadow banking activity is domiciled. This results in underestimation of hedge funds in particular (FSB, 2013, p. 14).
4. For the UK, Netherlands, Germany, France, Italy, Spain and Switzerland.
5. Hardie et al. (2013) and Hardie and Howarth (2013b) focus also on banks' off-balance-sheet activities, especially asset-backed commercial paper. This market has collapsed, and much off-balance-sheet activity has moved back on bank balance sheets. Depending on regulatory developments, off-balance-sheet activities may once again become a key component of market-based banks.
6. Financial assets held for trading, financial assets designated at fair value through the profit and loss account, and available-for-sale financial assets. This excludes financial assets designated as held to maturity, and therefore valued at the purchase cost.
7. See www.ecb.europa.eu/stats/money/consolidated/html/index.en.html, accessed 13 July 2014.
8. Post-crisis, trading volumes in most financial instruments have fallen, as banks have been less willing to support secondary trading. Secondary loan trading volume needs to be viewed in this context.
9. Byrne and Davis, 2003, p. 156, show the increasing importance of interbank lending from 1970 to 2000.
10. Calculated as total loans and advances less total deposits other than those from credit institutions, all banks.
11. Increasing interbank deposits means customer deposits declined even more (Byrne and Davis, 2003, p. 155).
12. Including borrowing from the central bank, involving liquidity support in a crisis.
13. For further detail, see IMF, 2009, p. 90.

References

Acharya, V.V., Schnabl, P. and Suarez, G. (2010) 'Securitization without risk transfer'. February. Retrieved on 7 February 2012 from www.nber.org/papers/w15730.

Adrian, T. and Shin, H.S. (2010) 'The changing nature of financial intermediation and the financial crisis of 2007–09'. *Federal Reserve Bank of New York Staff Reports* no. 439 (April).

Aglietta, M. and Breton, R. (2001) 'Financial systems, corporate control and capital accumulation', *Economy and Society* 30 (4): 433–66.
Allen, F. and Gale, D. (2000) *Comparing Financial Systems*. Cambridge, MA: MIT Press.
Aoki, M. (1995) 'Monitoring characteristics of the main bank system: An analytical and developmental view'. In Aoki, M. and Patrick, M. (eds) *The Japanese Main Bank System: Its Relevance for Developing and Transforming Economies*. Oxford: Oxford University Press, pp. 109–40.
Aoki, M. and Dinç, S. (2000) 'Relational banking as an institution and its viability under competition'. In Saxonhouse, G. and Aoki, M. (eds) *Finance, Governance and Competitiveness in Japan*. Oxford: Oxford University Press, pp. 19–42.
Aoki, M., Patrick, H. and Sheard, P. (1995) 'The Japanese main bank system: An introductory overview'. In Aoki, M. and Patrick, H. (eds) *The Japanese Main Bank System: Its Relevance for Developing and Transforming Economies*. Oxford, UK: Oxford University Press, pp. 3–48.
Axa Investment Managers (undated), *Has the Dawn Risen on the European Loan Market?* Retrieved on 2 March 2011 from www.axa-im-structuredfinance.com/index.cfm?pagepath=investment_expertise&CFNoCache=TRUE&servedoc=266DA5E7-1708-7D7E-1B46D0085C4C613A.
Bank of England (2007) *Financial Stability Review* (October). London: Bank of England.
Bank of England (2009) *Financial Stability Review* (December). London: Bank of England.
Basel Committee on Banking Supervision (2008) *Liquidity Risk: Management and Supervisory Challenges*. Retrieved on 7 February 2012 from www.bis.org/press/p080221.htm.
Bayerische Landesbank (2009) *Annual Report 2008*. Retrieved on 7 February 2012 from www.ar08.bayernlb.com/bayernlb/annual/2008/gb/English/pdf/report.pdf.
Berger, S. and Dore, R. (1996) *National Diversity and Global Capitalism*. Ithaca, NY: Cornell University Press.
Beyer, J. and Höpner, M. (2003) 'The disintegration of organized capitalism: German corporate governance in the 1990s', *West European Politics* 26: 179–98.
Boot, A.W.A. (2000), 'Relationship banking: What do we know?', *Journal of Financial Intermediation* 9: 7–25.
Byrne, J.P. and Davis E.P. (2003) *Financial Structure*. Cambridge: Cambridge University Press.
Chang, M. and Jones, E., (2013) 'Belgium and the Netherlands: Impatient capital' in Hardie, I. and Howarth, D. (eds) *Market-Based Banking and the International Financial Crisis*. Oxford: Oxford University Press, pp. 79–102.
Cheun, S., von Köppen-Mertes, I. and Weller, B. (2009) 'The collateral frameworks of the Eurosystem, the Federal Reserve System and the Bank of England and the financial market turmoil', *European Central Bank Occasional Paper Series* 107, December.
Clift, B. (2007) 'French corporate governance in the new global economy: Mechanisms of change and hybridisation within models of capitalism', *Political Studies* 55 (3): 546–67.
Commission Bancaire (2009) *Annual Report 2008*. Retrieved on 21 February 2012 from http://bdfbs-ws01.heb3.fr.colt.net/gb/supervi/telechar/cbreport/annual-report-commission-bancaire-2008.pdf.
Crouch, C. and Streeck, W. (eds) (1997) *Political Economy of Modern Capitalism: Mapping Convergence and Diversity*. London: Sage.
Culpepper, P.D. (2005) 'Institutional change in contemporary capitalism: Coordinated financial systems since 1990', *World Politics* 57 (2): 173–99.
Deeg, R. (1998) 'What makes German banks different', *Small Business Economics* 10: 93–101.
Deeg, R. (2010) 'Institutional change in financial systems'. In Morgan, G., Campbell, J.L., Crouch, C., Pedersen, O.K. and Whitley, R. (eds) *The Oxford Handbook of Comparative Institutional Analysis*. Oxford: Oxford University Press, pp. 309–34.
Deutsche Bundesbank (2009) *Financial Stability Review 2009*. November. Retrieved on 22 February 2012 from www.bundesbank.de.
Ertürk, I. and Solari, S. (2007), 'Banks as continuous reinvention', *New Political Economy* 12 (3): 369–88.
European Central Bank (ECB) (2009) *EU Banks' Funding Structures and Policies*. May. Retrieved on 11 November 2010 from www.ecb.int/pub/pdf/other/eubanksfundingstructurespolicies0905en.pdf.
European Securitisation Forum (2008) *Securitisation Data Report Q1: 2008*. Retrieved on 8 November 2010 from www.afme.eu/document.aspx?id=2878.
Financial Stability Board (FSB) (2013) *Global Shadow Banking Monitoring Report 2013*. Retrieved on 15 July 2014 from www.financialstabilityboard.org/publications/r_131114.pdf.
Forbes (2014), 'Europe: Leveraged loan manager ranks grow for first time since 2007, 21 January'. Retrieved on 21 July 2014 from www.forbes.com/sites/spleverage/2014/01/21/europe-leveraged-loan-manager-ranks-grow-for-first-time-since-2007/.

Gabor, D. (2012) 'The power of collateral: The ECB and bank funding strategies in crisis'. Retrieved on 20 July 2014 from http://papers.ssrn.com/sol3/papers.cfm?abstract_id=2062315.

Gorton, G.B. (2010) *Slapped by The Invisible Hand*. Oxford and New York: Oxford University Press.

Gorton, G.B. and Metrick, A. (2010) 'Securitized banking and the run on repo'. Retrieved on 7 February 2012 from http://ssrn.com/abstract=1440752.

Hackethal, A., Schmidt, R.H. and Tyrell, M. (2006) 'The transformation of the German financial system', *Revue d'Economie Politique* 116: 431–56.

Hall, P.A. and Soskice, D. (2001) 'An Introduction to varieties of capitalism'. In Hall, P.A. and Soskice, D. (eds) *Varieties of Capitalism: The Institutional Foundations of Comparative Advantage*. Oxford: Oxford University Press, pp. 1–68.

Hardie, I. (2012) *Financialization and Government Borrowing Capacity in Emerging Markets*. Basingstoke: Palgrave Macmillan.

Hardie, I. and Howarth, D. (2009) *'Die Krise* but not *La Crise?* The financial crisis and the transformation of German and French banking systems', *Journal of Common Market Studies* 47 (5): 1017–39.

Hardie, I. and Howarth, D. (eds) (2013a), *Market-Based Banking and the International Financial Crisis*. Oxford: Oxford University Press.

Hardie, I. and Howarth, D. (2013b) 'Framing market-based banking and the financial crisis', in Hardie, I. and Howarth, D. (eds) *Market-Based Banking and the International Financial Crisis*. Oxford: Oxford University Press, pp. 22–55.

Hardie, I., Howarth, D., Maxfield, S. and Verdun, A. (2013) 'Banks and the false dichotomy in the comparative political economy of finance', *World Politics* 65 (4): 691–728.

Hardie, I. and Macartney, H. (2016) 'Too big to separate? EU ring-fencing and the defense of too big to fail banks', *West European Politics* 39 (3): 503–25.

Hellwig, M. (2009) 'Systemic risk in the financial sector: An analysis of the subprime-mortgage financial crisis', *De Economist*, 157 (2): 129–207.

Howarth, D., and Quaglia, L. (2014) 'The steep road to banking union: Constructing the single resolution mechanism', *Journal of Common Market Studies* 52 (1): 125–40.

Howell, C. (2007) 'The British variety of capitalism: Institutional change, industrial relations and British politics', *British Politics* 2: 239–64.

IMF (2008) *Global Financial Stability Report*. October. Retrieved on 2 February 2012 from www.imf.org.

IMF (2009) *Global Financial Stability Report*. October. Retrieved on 20 February 2012 from www.imf.org.

IMF (2010) *Global Financial Stability Report*. October. Retrieved on 7 February 2012 from www.imf.org.

Ivashina, V., and Scharfstein, D.S. (2010) 'Bank lending during the financial crisis of 2008'. *Journal of Financial Economics* 97 (3): 319–38.

Jackson, G., and Moerke, A. (2005) 'Continuity and change in corporate governance: Comparing Germany and Japan', *Corporate Governance* 13 (3): 351–61.

Jiangli, W. and Pisker, M. (2008) 'The impacts of securitization on US bank holding companies'. Retrieved on 8 February 2012 from http://ssrn.com/abstract=1102284.

Kitschelt, H. et al. (eds) (1999), *Continuity and Change in Contemporary Capitalism*. Cambridge: Cambridge University Press.

Kroszner, R.S., Laeven, L. and Klingebiel, D. (2007) 'Banking crises, financial dependence, and growth', *Journal of Financial Economics* 84: 187–228.

Lall, S. (2006) 'How to characterize financial systems'. IMF Global Issues Seminar Series, 25 October. Retrieved on 20 February 2012 from http://siteresources.worldbank.org/EXTABOUTUS/Resources/Lall-slides.ppt.

Markit (2013) *Markit European Loan Volume Survey*, 28 January. Retrieved on 21 July 2013 from www.markit.com/assets/en/docs/products/loans/Markit%20Euro%20Volume%20Survey%20Q4%202012.pdf.

Murinde, V., Agung, J. and Mullineux, A. (2004) 'Patterns of corporate financing and financial system convergence in Europe', *Review of International Economics* 12 (4): 693–705.

Pagoulatos, G. and Quaglia, L. (2013) 'Turning the crisis on its head: Sovereign debt crisis as banking crisis in Italy and Greece'. In Hardie, I. and Howarth, D. (eds) *Market-Based Banking and the International Financial Crisis*. Oxford: Oxford University Press, pp. 179–200.

Pozsar, Z., Adrian, T., Ashcraft, A. and Boesky, H. (2010), 'Shadow banking', *Federal Reserve Bank of New York Staff Reports* no. 458 (July).

Raddatz, C. (2010) 'When the rivers run dry: Liquidity and the use of wholesale funds in the transmission of the US subprime crisis', *World Bank* Policy Research Working Paper Series 5203.

Rajan, R.G. and Zingales, L. (2003) 'Banks and markets: the changing character of European finance', *CEPR Discussion Papers* 3865.

Ryan, S.G. (2008) 'Fair value accounting: Understanding the issues raised by the credit crunch'. Retrieved on 7 February 2012 from www.uic.edu/classes/actg/actg593/Readings/Fair-Value/Fair%20value%20accounting%20-%20Understanding%20the%20issues%20Ryan.pdf.

Sabry, F. and Okongwu, C. (2009) 'Study of the impact of securitization on consumers, investors, financial institutions and the capital markets'. 17 June. Retrieved on 21 February 2012 from www.americansecuritization.com/uploadedFiles/ASF_NERA_Report.pdf.

Schmidt, V.A. (2002) *The Futures of European Capitalism*. Oxford: Oxford University Press.

Standard & Poor's (2010) *A Guide to the European Loan Market*. January. Retrieved on 15 February 2011 from www.lcdcomps.com/d/pdf/European_Loan_Primer.pdf.

Tucker, P. (2010) 'Shadow banking, financing markets and financial stability'. Retrieved on 3 March 2011 from www.bankofengland.co.uk/publications/speeches/2010/speech420.pdf.

Vitols, S. (1998) 'Are German banks different?' *Small Business Economics* 10 pp. 79–91.

Vitols, S. (2004) 'Changes in Germany's bank-based financial system: A varieties of capitalism perspective' Discussion Paper SP II 2004-2003. Berlin: Wissenschaftszentrum Berlin.

Westdeutsche Landesbank (2009) *Financial Report 2008*. Retrieved on 9 February 2011 from www.westlb.de/.

Whitley, R. (1999) *Divergent Capitalisms: The Social Structuring and Change of Business Systems*. Oxford: Oxford University Press.

Zysman, J. (1983) *Government, Markets and Growth: Financial Systems and the Politics of Industrial Change*. Ithaca, NY: Cornell University Press.

11
The financialisation of local governments
Evidence from the Italian case

Andrea Lagna

Derivatives markets emblematically reflect the rise of finance in modern capitalism (Bryan and Rafferty, 2006; Wigan, 2009, a multifaceted process known as financialisation (Engelen, 2008). The notional value of global over-the-counter (OTC) derivatives was $553 trillion at the end of June 2015 (BIS, 2015). This huge sum raises questions concerning why individuals use derivatives and how these practices spread differentially across the world.

In this chapter, I examine how the expansion of derivatives markets, actors and technologies in Italy caused havoc amongst local governments, one the most important institutions of democratic life. By examining this case study, I argue that specific political struggles shape the global growth of derivatives – and financial innovation more broadly – into a complex and uneven process. Whether implicitly or explicitly, mainstream financial theory considers the development of derivatives markets in ahistorical terms. It refers to how derivatives and their speculative mechanisms provide investors with useful solutions to hedge risk in a calculated manner (Greenspan, 2003). Against this orthodox narrative, I demonstrate that actual politics and power relations underlie market-based financial innovation and its crisis-prone nature (Nölke, Heires and Bieling, 2013; Konings, 2010).

The analysis proceeds in three steps. In the first section, I rethink derivatives markets, instruments and actors as a universe of accounting deception. This facet of derivatives is very apt in the context of power struggles. In the second section, I examine the political-strategic reasons underpinning Italian municipalities and their overexposure to interest rate swaps. In the third section, I conclude by reviewing the current Italian scenario in a comparative European perspective.

Derivatives: weapons of hedging efficiency, speculative disarray and accounting dissimulation

What are derivatives? How do they work? Who are the actors using them and why?

According to a standard definition, a derivative contract is 'a financial instrument whose value depends on (or derives from) the values of other, more basic, underlying variables' (Hull, 2009, p. 1). In other words, the value of the derivative stems from the price volatility of its underlying asset. As mainstream textbooks (Hull, 2009; Kolb and Overdahl, 2007) commonly explain, there are four basic or 'plain vanilla' types of derivatives:

- *Forwards*, which are customised agreements between two parties to buy or sell an underlying asset at a specified price on a future date.
- *Futures*, which are similar to forwards but are standardised and traded on an organised exchange.
- *Options*, which are contracts that offers the buyer the right – but not the obligation – to buy (call options) or sell (put options) an underlying asset at an agreed-upon price during a certain period of time or on a specific date.
- Finally, *swaps* are agreements between two parties to exchange the cash flows of different assets at a future date.

Other exotic types of derivatives alter these primary instruments to create more complex and 'synthetic' products.

For a long time in history, contracts similar to forwards, futures and options were traded primarily on agricultural products and commodities (Swan, 1999). However, particularly after the emergence of swaps in the early 1980s (Geisst, 2002, pp. 248–52), derivatives contracts on financial assets became the most widely traded instruments. Listed in descending order according to market size (BIS, 2015), modern derivatives refer to five different categories of underlying assets:

- *Interest rate* such as interest rate swaps, interest rate futures and forward rate agreements.
- *Foreign exchange rate* such as currency swaps, currency futures, currency options and currency forwards.
- *Credit* such as credit default swaps, total return swaps and collateralised debt obligations.
- *Equity* such as stock options, warrants, index futures.
- *Commodity* such as commodity futures, commodity options and commodity swaps.

Other contracts are also traded on underlying variables such as property indexes, macroeconomic indicators, freight rates, weather forecast, CO_2 emissions and so on (Alizadeh and Nomikos, 2012; Sandor, 2012; Smith and Searle, 2010; Gurkaynak and Wolfers, 2006; Jewson and Brix, 2005). This indicates the possibility for derivatives-based techniques to be applied to many aspects of our economic, political, social and cultural reality (Bryan and Rafferty, 2011, 2006; Wigan, 2009; Shiller, 2003).

Derivatives contracts are bought and sold on two types of markets that differ in terms of trading arrangements, procedures and levels of risk. These two markets are: *organised exchanges* and *OTC markets*. An organised exchange is a centralised marketplace for buyers and sellers of derivatives contracts. Bids and offers can be based on an open out-cry system or on electronic trading. Today, most of the exchanges trade through computer-based platforms. Organised exchanges offer instruments that are standardised in terms of quantity, quality, expiration months, delivery terms and dates, minimum price fluctuations, daily price limits, trading days and hours. For this reason, contracts can be easily transferable to third parties through the market (Hull, 2009, pp. 1–2).

As Loader (2005) shows, the major benefit of organised exchanges is the use of the central counterparty system of clearing and settlements. Here, the clearing house sells the contract to the buyer and buys it from the seller, intermediating between the two parties by clearing and settling the contract. This method dramatically reduces the risk of default through the system of so-called margins according to which market participants are required to register an account with the exchange from which money is withdrawn or credited according to the daily profits and losses. These margins are usually very low compared to the control over large amounts of underlying assets an individual can exert. This means that with a relatively small amount of cash, investors can enter into derivatives worth much more than the required initial margin deposits – a characteristic known as leverage (Hull, 2009, p. 15).

Contrary to organised exchanges, OTC markets are decentralised networks where financial institutions tailor instruments to fit certain requirements of their clients. Due to the benefits of trading custom-made products, OTC markets expanded overwhelmingly compared to formal exchanges. However, these markets have no central clearing house and contracts are instead privately negotiated between the two parties – an aspect which implies a considerably higher exposure to credit risk (Hull, 2009, p. 2). For this reason, initiatives were developed to minimise risk on OTC markets. For instance, contract details are subject to market standard documentation such as the Master Agreement by the International Swaps and Derivatives Association (ISDA). In spite of this, it is evident that OTC markets simply function by linking various trading floors amongst the major financial institutions. There is 'no central mechanism to limit individual or aggregate risk taking, leverage, and credit extension, and risk management is completely decentralized' (Schinasi et al., 2000, p. 19). At the level of transparency, besides semi-annual surveys by central banks, 'information about market concentration and who owns which risks is generally unavailable; at best, a trading desk might know that some institutions are building up positions' (Schinasi et al., 2000, p. 19). After the 2008 global financial crisis, regulators pushed for a comprehensive reform of OTC derivatives markets with the objective of increasing transparency and reducing their systemic risk (FSB, 2010, 2014).

Why do derivatives exist? Who are the actors using them? The mainstream argument is that derivatives markets provide a fundamental function of risk management. To appreciate what derivatives-based risk management entails, let us refer to two examples of forward and futures contracts.

Imagine that instead of awaiting the crop to be ready and then trade wheat at the prevailing market price, a farmer and a miller agree in advance on a specific price, quantity and date of delivery of the wheat in the future.[1] Once the crop is harvested and ready to be sold, the market-prevailing price at harvesting time could be either above or below the price previously agreed on in the contract. The first case favours the miller. In fact, because of the contract, she pays less for the wheat than what she would pay if buying the commodity at the market-prevailing price. The second case favours instead the farmer who, due to the contract, is being paid more than what others pay on the market. In spite of this seemingly one-sided bet against the future price of wheat, both parties gain in business certainty and price stability.

In the second half of the nineteenth century, merchants in Chicago revolutionised the modalities of forwards-like contracts and established the first market for futures contracts at the Chicago Board of Trade (CBOT). Futures are contracts in which all details are specified, making it easy to be exchanged amongst traders. After the CBOT, other markets for futures soon flourished across the United States (US) (Markham, 2002, pp. 265–9). How does a futures market function?

An organised futures exchange is a centralised marketplace for buyers and sellers of futures contracts.[2] Let us imagine on 5 March the miller gives instruction to a broker to enter into a future to buy 5000 bushels of wheat in July. In the same period, the farmer instructs another broker to enter into a contract to deliver 5000 bushels of wheat in July. As the party who agrees to buy the commodity, the miller is in the long position (going long). The farmer is instead in the short position (going short) as she agrees to deliver the commodity. Each contract always involves both positions. Under an open outcry system, floor traders would meet up to agree on a price. On an electronic platform instead, brokers would match bids and offers via computer-trading networks. The price agreed – let us say $4 per bushel – is the current futures price for July wheat, which is subject to fluctuations in supply and demand.

Conceptually, futures are very similar to forwards since both contracts involve the future delivery of an asset at a price agreed today. However, there are three key differences. First, the two instruments are traded on different markets. Being standardised products, futures are bought and sold on organised exchanges. Second, the miller and the farmer do not meet up personally, but refer to their brokers who in turn relate to the exchange's clearing house as their counterpart. In other words, it is the clearing house which sells the wheat to the miller's broker and buys it from the farmer's broker, clearing and settling the contract. Third, and this is a fundamental innovation in derivatives trading, the two parties are not bound to exchange the actual commodity at the expiration of a contract. The majority of futures positions are closed out before being exercised at expiration, making the market for futures work practically through a process of cash settlement (Levy, 2006). Profits and losses are calculated on the basis of the daily price movements of futures, whilst the accounts of both long and short positions are adjusted for gains and losses at the end of each trading day.

Since futures can be easily closed out before expiration, exercising the contract for delivery is very unusual. Closing out a position means entering into a contract that is the opposite of the original one (Hull, 2009, p. 23). For example, the miller – who bought a July wheat futures contract on 5 March – can close out the position by instructing the broker to sell one July wheat futures contract on, say, 6 May. The farmer who is in a short position would do the opposite. In both cases, total gain or loss are determined by the difference in the futures prices between the day in which they entered the first contract (5 March for the miller) and the day when the contract is closed out.

To clarify the use of these mechanisms, let us refer to a historical case which is based on the insightful research conducted by Levy (2006, pp. 312–13). In February 1892, Andrew J. Sawyer – a grain trader and CBOT member – testified before the US House Committee on Agriculture during the Hatch bill hearings. This bill sought to curb speculation by restricting futures trading without the actual exchange of the underlying commodity (Markham, 2002, p. 320). Sawyer explained to the Committee how he used futures markets for hedging purposes: 'suppose we are handling 100,000 bushels a day and we can sell in Minneapolis, Buffalo, Montreal, or New York only 75,000 bushels a day, say that is all we can sell. We have then 25,000 bushels left on our hands which we can not sell, there being no market for it' (House Committee on Agriculture, 1892, p. 31). Sawyer could hold these 25,000 bushels, but what would have happened if after six months the price for wheat had declined even further? In this case, he needed to insure his business against such event. At this point Sawyer could sell wheat futures to traders in the CBOT pits. If two days after entering into the contract, the current market price was below the contract price, Sawyer would have profited. He would close out his position, obtaining the capital necessary to keep storing the 25,000 bushels. On the contrary, if the futures market price had turned against him, Sawyer would have incurred losses on his futures position. However, in this case, he would have at least delivered the 25,000 bushels of wheat on the cash market, where the actual commodity is bought on the spot.

Sawyer represented a typical example of *hedger*, a market participant who used futures as a form of insurance against the risk involved in his business operations. In other words, he speculated on futures markets, but only with the intention of either closing out his position before expiration – therefore making a profit to be reinvested in his business – or effectively delivering the actual commodity at the end of the contract. Besides hedgers, futures markets attracted many traders who were hardly interested in the actual exchange of wheat. In fact, contracts were only rarely exercised at expiration. How did advocates of futures trading justify the presence of *speculators* in the pits? Although compared to gamblers by the people outside the exchanges, speculators nonetheless appeared to other market participants as essential providers of liquidity. By buying and selling contracts in search for a profitable trend, they went long or short when they anticipated prices to respectively increase or decrease. In so doing, whilst satisfying their thirst for quick profits, speculators made sure that hedgers like Sawyer always found counterparts to their actual trading needs (Levy, 2006, p. 325).

Contemporary literature on derivatives widely acknowledges this distinction between hedgers and speculators. The two broad categories include myriad of market participants such as banks, institutional investors, central banks, governments, companies, wealthy individuals and retail investors. These actors, either directly or indirectly, enter into futures and other derivatives contracts to hedge risk or take risk.[3] Paradoxically, the two facets are intertwined and support each other.

In this study, I contend that such hedging-speculation dualism is of limited heuristic value because it fails to account for a pivotal dimension of derivatives markets: these instruments provide opportunities to avoid regulation and to window-dress accounting rules. To be sure, as long as we focus on trading in organised exchanges and futures or options as instruments, we can easily explain the use of derivatives-based techniques through the hedging–speculation dichotomy. Yet, things are quite different as soon as we examine OTC markets and particularly swaps instruments, a scenario that Partnoy (2009, p. 18) describes as the 'wild Wild West of trading'.

The swaps market expanded dramatically since the 1980s because investors found these tools useful to hedge their risk exposures towards volatility in interest rates and exchange rates (Markham, 2002, p. 192). According to the conventional argument – based on the theory of comparative advantage – the swap market makes possible for both parties to borrow and repay at the globally lowest costs in interest-rate structure and currency (Hull, 2009, pp. 147–76).[4] To be sure, these features are true to a certain extent. However, as Partnoy (2009, p. 46, my italic) explains in reference to the case of the investment bank Bankers Trust:

> companies would do swaps not necessarily because swaps allocated risk more efficiently, but rather because they were unregulated. *They could do swaps in the dark, without the powerful sunlight that securities regulation shined on other financial instruments.* And here was the crucial point: to the extent companies and their *financial officers could use custom-tailored swaps to avoid regulation or to hide risks*, Bankers Trust's profits from selling swaps to those companies might not disappear so quickly. Corporate treasurers hoping to benefit from such swaps would pay a premium – it wasn't their money, after all – if the swaps were structured in a way that created more opportunity for profit, but hid the risks from their bosses.

In the following sections, I attempt to uncover such dark side of derivatives by exploring the case of Italian municipalities and their use of swaps. I show how swaps can become tools of accounting dissimulation – or, as some financial journalists would put it, 'weapons of mass deception' (Dunbar, 2006; Norris, 2013). This aspect is crucial to explain the politically driven and differential expansion of derivatives practices. I base my analysis on previous research results which I published in Lagna (2015).

Italian municipalities and derivatives: a story of political resistance against fiscal austerity

The historical conditions for Italian local authorities to approach OTC derivatives markets emerged in the mid-1990s. During these years, a domestic alliance between centre-left politicians and neo-liberal-minded technocrats pushed for Italy to join the euro in 1999 by complying with the Stability and Growth Pact (SGP). European integration represented a leverage to their power position because it functioned as an 'external constraint' (Sbragia, 2001; Dyson and Featherstone, 1996) on the country's traditional political-cum-business establishment, which had until then relied on the dissipation of public finance (Pasquino, 2000, p. 79), full control over state-owned industrial and financial apparatus (Bianchi, 1987) and, finally, a corporate governance regime that worked to the advantage of private blockholders (Deeg, 2005; McCann, 2000).

At the same time, as Italy faced the imperative to reduce public debt and deficits under the dictates of the SGP (Cafruny and Ryner, 2008; Heipertz and Verdun, 2005, 2004), the neo-liberal coalition also advanced the benefits of a fiscal and administrative decentralisation (Alonso, 2012). The costs and benefits of decentralisation in Italy had been debated since the 1980s, but the process gained momentum only with the first 'Bassanini' law in 1997 (Italian Parliament, 1997). It was eventually finalised with the consolidated law on local authorities in 2000 (Italian Government, 2000) and, eventually, the reform of the constitutional law in 2001 (Italian Parliament, 2001a). The latter granted local authorities wider margins of autonomy in their revenue and expenditure decisions, a process which gradually continued until the present time (Italian Parliament, 2010b). These reforms opened up new scenarios for local authorities by dismantling the old system of sub-sovereign finance where the central government collected most part of the inland revenues and then transferred funds to local authorities. Moreover, when state transfers were insufficient, local administrators financed their investments through fixed-rate loans from public banks such as Cassa Depositi e Prestiti (Rosati, 2009, p. 4).

Thus, whilst the level of state transfers began to decrease in line with EU-imposed budgetary limits, local authorities gradually obtained more autonomy in the management of their revenue and expenditure flows. In this context, they faced the necessity – or the opportunity – of approaching financial markets, instruments and actors beyond the traditional public sphere (Saccomanni, 2007, p. 17). In a word, local authorities began to move within new institutions and discourses of a financialised kind. Derivatives and particularly interest rate swaps emerged as fundamental practices of this new environment. As a council member of a Southern Italian municipality explained in a bizarre comparison, 'swaps became very fashionable ... bank brokers contacted budget *assessori* relentlessly ... just like solar-panel companies are doing today' (Interview, 31 August 2012, my translation).[5]

The construction of a regulatory framework concerning the use of derivatives in local finance mirrored the course of events. Regulation acknowledged swaps for the first time in 1996. Local authorities were allowed to issue bonds since 1994 and, in this regard, they were obliged to enter into currency swaps contracts when bonds were denominated in foreign currencies (MEF, 1996; Italian Parliament, 1994). Besides this, there was no specific regulation concerning the adoption of other types of swaps up until the period 2001–04 (MEF, 2004, 2003; Italian Parliament, 2001b).[6] It is only at this point that a specific regulatory regime was put in place to discipline the growing use of derivatives in local finance. Although this regulation was updated in few occasions (Italian Parliament, 2006), its basic pillars remained substantially unchanged until the summer of 2008 when the government enacted a moratorium that prohibited local governments from entering into new contracts (Italian Parliament, 2008a, 2008b). This regulatory architecture can be summarised in the following six features (see Franco, 2009, pp. 18–22, 46; Rosati, 2009, pp. 9–11, 15–18):

- Local authorities were allowed to use derivatives only to hedge existing liabilities and not for speculative purposes.
- They were obliged to use currency swaps when issuing bonds in foreign currencies, as well as amortising swaps when issuing bonds (or taking out loans) with single repayments at maturity.

- They were allowed to use currency swaps, interest rate swaps, forward rate agreements, amortising swaps and interest rate options (caps, collars).
- They could have restructured their debt positions but could not have done so with the objective of postponing the maturity of the initial debt. Moreover, these operations could not have included an upfront sum above 1 per cent of the notional amount or an increasing flow of payments by the local authority to the counterparty over the duration of the contract.
- Local governments were obliged to enter into contracts with highly creditworthy dealers only and by using financial and monetary parameters belonging to G7-area. Moreover, for contracts of approximately €100 million (notional value), they should have limited exposure to a single intermediary at 25 per cent of the total notional amount.
- The Ministry of Economy and Finance (MEF) was responsible for monitoring derivatives activities every three months. Bank of Italy and the Italian securities market authority (CONSOB) were both responsible for controlling financial intermediaries and their derivatives operations with local authorities.

At this point, a key question arises: Why did local authorities adopt derivatives? Under growing financial constraints, they attempted to make a virtue of the new financialised practices. The mainstream economic understanding shows that these actors aimed at optimising the costs of the debt portfolio by restructuring the debt position. This was done in the attempt to free part of those financial resources that were previously used to serve the debt, therefore generating more liquidity in the budget at a time in which the latter was drying up.

For instance, a municipality in the Apulia region decided to restructure its debt by closing over 60 fixed-rate loans – of the total value of over €10 million – which were contracted with Cassa Depositi e Prestiti in the period 1997–2004.[7] At the same time, the municipality issued municipal bonds known in Italy as *buoni ordinari comunali* (BOC) at a fixed rate of 3.75 per cent for the same value and with a 20-year maturity. A specialised bank assisted the issuing process in all its phases and underwrote the entire lot of bonds. In other words, the municipality had the opportunity to extinguish its debt – in the form of loans – and issued bonds to 'catch the opportunity arising from favourable levels of market rates' (Interview, 4 September 2012, my translation). The interest rate swap entered the picture in 2006. How did it work in practice?

The very same bank proposed the municipality to enter into a fixed-to-floating interest rate swap. It is important to remember that this swap did not substitute the previous commitments that the municipality had on the 20-year-maturity bond. It was instead a separate contract that worked like a bet where the bank was the fixed-rate payer and the municipality was the floating-rate payer. In this type of swap, the nature of the bet was that the fixed-rate payer had a negative flow of funds towards the floating-rate payer when the interest rate went down and vice versa. Due to the interest-rate scenarios, the municipality had initially a positive flow of funds. In practical terms, the municipality still paid a fixed-rate of 3.75 per cent on its bonds, but this interest was discounted of certain basis points in line with the funds that derived from the swap bet in variable terms. However, as interest rates rose, the initial positive flows turned negative for the municipality.[8] Hence, the opportunity was not as attractive as it had been in the beginning.

Apart for the common economic rationale behind the use of derivatives by local authorities, there is another dimension of the story that relates to the Italian power relations. This story clearly highlights the politicised strategies of Italian local governments and how they attempted to challenge the neo-liberal institutions of fiscal austerity as constructed since the 1990s. In fact, by looking at several specific cases of municipalities, it becomes clear that the latter employed interest rate swaps because of a key accounting element, namely: the *upfront*.

This is a sum that the bank advanced to a given municipality to set the contract in a market-neutral position. It happened when the swap was of a 'non-par' type, meaning that, when the two parties entered into the contract, the swap presented a negative market value for one of the two parties – in this case, the municipality. As a result, the bank brought the contract to a par condition by advancing an upfront sum to the municipality which should be equivalent to the negative market value the local government was exposed to at the signing of the contract (Rosati, 2009, pp. 1–2). This aspect presented a crucial accounting artifice. Municipalities considered the upfront as a revenue rather than a debt. For this reason, they circumvented the budget constraint of 15 per cent of the debt-to-revenue ratio as imposed by the *patto di stabilità interno* – that is, the domestic equivalent of the SGP. In other words, local governments inflated the revenue side of the ratio whilst leaving the debt-side unchanged. Paradoxically, the upfront turned into a virtue to be potentially used for creating mass consensus at a local level (Carlini, 2010). Indeed, as Sanderson, Dinmore and Tett (2010) pointed out:

> In the revolving-door world of Italian local politics, each new administration wanted its own upfront, so asked their bankers to restructure the deal to release more cash in advance. The terms of the swap tended to become more restrictive each time. Some banks covered the cost of the upfront fee by pricing the interest rate swap more aggressively, so that only in unusual circumstances would the entity receive more each period than it paid out.... In other cases, upper and lower limits on the movement of interest rates ensured the upside for the local authorities was reduced and downside risks were magnified.

Current trajectories in Italy and other European countries

When the global financial crisis occurred in 2008, Italian local authorities had already spurred a heated controversy concerning their use of financial derivatives, particularly owing to the substantial losses they incurred. According to data from the Bank of Italy (Bankitalia, 2009, p. 22; 2014, p. 22), 349 local governments – including regions, provinces and municipalities – had a negative mark-to-market exposure to derivatives of €600 million in December 2005. This figure increased to 600 local authorities with a negative market value of €737 million by December 2006. In December 2008, the number of local governments declined to 474 but the negative market value went up to approximately €1 billion. Since then, although the number of local authorities with currently open derivatives positions declined, the amount of losses increased to above €1.2 billion in June 2014 (latest data available), with a peak of €1.5 billion in December 2012. It is important to note that these data only concern the activities of financial intermediaries that operate in Italy. Yet, larger local authorities typically contracted with foreign operators, which account for an approximately 60 per cent market share. In other words, the data represent an approximation that underestimates a much broader phenomenon (Franco, 2009, pp. 26–7). Losses could even reach €10 billion according to the *Financial Times* (Sanderson et al., 2010). In this context, the government imposed the above-mentioned moratorium that prevented local administrations from entering into derivatives contracts until a new regulation was agreed upon.

After this, the events concerning the use of derivatives in local finance evolved along two major paths. First, regions, provinces and municipalities either closed out their contracts – in the majority of cases, at a loss – or filed lawsuits against financial intermediaries in the attempt to invalidate their contracts. Media became very attentive to several trials involving major cities, most notably Milan (Sirletti and Martinuzzi, 2014; Martinuzzi, 2013). Second, regulators began to work on a new regulatory framework to discipline the matter whilst the parliament led a two-year investigation on the matter (Italian Parliament, 2010a). In September 2009, MEF (2009) released a provisional draft of this regulation that was also discussed by the parliament. The draft focused on three main aspects:

- The types of derivatives contracts available to local authorities.
- The derivatives components that local authorities could have included in their financing strategies.
- The transparency of information to be presented both in the contract profiles and the annual budget report.

Although the first two dimensions did not present substantial innovations, the last aspect concerning transparency implied instead important changes. To begin with, besides being obliged to communicate to the client the par value and the implicit costs of the contract at least every three months, intermediaries were supposed to include in the contract profile elements such as: a full description in Italian language of all the contract details; the par value at the start of the contract; an analytical description of all the factors that constitute not only the derivative instrument per se, but the entire portfolio in which the derivative contract is included; a numerical simulation about the implicit cost of the contract – this aspect led to a controversial debate between those who preferred probability analysis and the Italian Banking Association (ABI) which proposed instead sensitivity analysis (Italian Parliament, 2011). In addition to this, the new regulation increased also the controls over the specific procedures that local administrators would undertake when using derivatives. In this regard, municipal treasures had to indicate – both in the annual budget report for the next year (*bilancio di previsione*) and for the previous year (*rendiconto*) – the full picture of derivatives activities, including: the type of operation; the notional principal amount; the underlying liability; the past and expected negative and positive flow of payments. Furthermore, local authorities had to indicate the ratio between the debt that the derivative operation refers to and the total debt position. Finally, they were required to establish a so-called 'risk fund' to cover the negative payments which could incur in the derivatives positions.

Eventually, owing to its complexity, the debate reached a stalemate. Thus, in December 2013 – five years after the enactment of the moratorium – the short-lived government led by Enrico Letta opted to permanently prohibit local authorities from using derivatives, leaving only the possibility to use interest rate caps on their actual loans (Italian Parliament, 2013). This solution is similar to the British case where local authorities are prohibited from entering into derivatives transactions because they do not possess the necessary knowledge and skills. The House of Lords took this exemplary decision in 1989 after the London borough of Hammersmith and Fulham incurred losses of several hundred million pounds in one of the most infamous derivatives fiascos (Geisst, 2002, pp. 260–3).[9]

Whilst Italian regulators took this course of action, other European Member States did not follow it and still allow local governments to embrace financial innovation. This is the case despite the fact that large derivatives debacles involving municipalities occurred in countries such as Germany and France (Dodd, 2010) – see for instance the City of Saint Etienne (Katz, 2010) and Pforzheim (Hendrikse and Sidaway, 2013).

Concluding remarks

Alan Greenspan (2003) – Chairman of the US Federal Reserve System from 1987 until 2006 – commented on the global growth of derivatives markets with the following words:

> For at least the past twenty years, the process of financial globalisation has been rapidly advancing. The development of new financial products, notably a wide variety of OTC

derivatives, and the removal of many barriers to international capital mobility has tightened linkages among global financial markets. As a result, capital has flowed more freely across national borders in search of the highest risk-adjusted rates of return. At some point, globalisation undoubtedly will reach maturity. Financial innovation will slow as we approach a world in which financial markets are complete in the sense that all financial risks can be efficiently transferred to those most willing to bear them.

This perspective is common amongst mainstream financial theorists, who understand the striking expansion of derivatives in the light of how these instruments give investors the tools necessary to hedge risk in a calculated manner. Derivatives are fundamental to make financial markets 'complete' in the theoretical sense given by Arrow and Debreu (1954).

Against this view, I have contended that it is necessary to transcend the orthodox narrative on derivatives to explore the actual politics and power relations underlying the global spread of modern financial innovation. In fact, the striking growth of derivatives is a global process that unfolds differentially depending on context-specific political struggles. To substantiate this argument, I have attempted to explore the 'underbelly' of derivatives markets, a scenario that is made of regulatory arbitrage and accounting dissimulation. Wielding derivatives as 'weapons of mass deception' (Dunbar, 2006; Norris, 2013) is a very useful practice in the context of power conflicts. After this, I have focused on the case of local governments in Italy and how they employed derivatives to challenge the regime of fiscal austerity that – imposed by domestic neo-liberal forces since the 1990s – left local communities at the end of their tether.

Notes

1. The example of forward contracts is based on Bryan and Rafferty (2006, p. 41).
2. The example of futures contracts is based on Hull (2009, pp. 21–43).
3. Besides hedgers and speculators, there are also market participants – known as *arbitrageurs* – who attempt to identify valuation discrepancies and profit from them (Hull, 2009, pp. 14–15; MacKenzie, 2003).
4. The theory of comparative advantage applied to a fixed-to-floating interest rate swap would work in the following way – the example is based on Hull (2009, pp. 147–76) and Valdez and Molyneux (2013, pp. 434–41). Imagine that company A and company B need to borrow funds. A is able to borrow more cheaply than B at either a fixed or floating interest rate, but has a greater comparative advantage in a fixed interest rate. Yet, A would prefer borrowing at a floating interest rate. On the contrary, B prefers a fixed interest rate but – owing to its lower credit rating – such fixed rate is not as attractive as the floating one. To sum up the hypothetical scenario: (a) A can raise fixed-rate funds at 7% or floating at the Libor rate. A prefers floating interest rate, but has a comparative advantage on fixed-interest-rate borrowing; (b) B has to pay a fixed interest rate of 10%, whilst can borrow floating at the Libor rate +1%. Company B prefers fixed interest rate, but the floating rate is cheaper than the fixed one. Hence, A raises funds from its lender at 7% fixed interest rate, whilst B borrows from its lender at a floating rate equal to the Libor rate +1%. However, both companies decide to enter into an interest rate swap on a given notional principal amount – which will not be exchanged – and for a given period of time. The terms of such swap agreement are the following: (a) A agrees to pay B the floating rate, which equals to the Libor rate; (b) B agrees to pay, let us suppose, 8% fixed interest rate to A. In other words, the swap allows: (a) A to pay 7% fixed interest rate to its lender, but the company receives 8% fixed interest rate from B. This is a profit of 1% which in actual terms makes A pay B the Libor rate − 1% – even less that what A would pay if the company borrowed funds directly with at a floating interest rate; (b) B pays Libor rate +1% to its lender, but receives the Libor rate from A. This is a cost of 1%, which adds up to the 8% fixed interest rate B pays to A, for a total of 9% fixed interest rate. This last rate is still less than the 10% fixed interest rate B was required to pay if the company had borrowed funds directly at a fixed rate. Please note that the swap contract is distinct from the respective contracts in which the two companies previously enter into. In other words, A still pays its fixed interest rate of 7% and B pays Libor +1%. The example above is simplified to the extent that it does not take into account of differences in

5 The interviewee agreed that the information given to me was not be individually ascribed. Italian municipalities are governed by a mayor (*sindaco*), a municipal executive (*giunta comunale*) and a municipal council (*consiglio comunale*) as the legislative body. The interviewee refers to the *assessori comunali* who are the members of the executive. Each *assessore* has responsibility for a specific department such as budget, urban affairs, sport and so on. Council members are instead known as *consiglieri comunali*.
6 The use of derivatives by private actors was instead regulated by the 1998 consolidated law on finance (Italian Government, 1998).
7 The following case is based on two interviews (4–5 September 2012) with the head of the financial services of the municipality in question, as well as the official documents that were kindly provided by the interviewee after request to the mayor. The interviewee agreed that the information given to me was not be individually ascribed and the name of the municipality was not to be mentioned – although the official documents concerning the specific swap operation are publicly available via request to the mayor.
8 From 2009 onwards, interest-rate scenarios changed and started approaching 0%. However, the municipality kept losing money due to the interest-rate collar. The specific interest rate was the 6-month Euribor.
9 See Dunbar (2014) for an analysis of how several banks circumvented British regulation by embedding derivatives inside contracts known as lender option borrower option (LOBO).

References

Alizadeh, A.H. and Nomikos, N.K. (2012) 'Ship finance: Hedging ship price risk using freight derivatives'. In Talley, W. (ed.) *The Blackwell Companion to Maritime Economics*. Chichester: Wiley & Sons, pp. 433–51.

Alonso, S. (2012) *Challenging the State: Devolution and the Battle for Partisan Credibility: A Comparison of Belgium, Italy, Spain, and the United Kingdom*. Oxford: Oxford University Press.

Arrow, K. and Debreu, G. (1954) 'Existence of an equilibrium for a competitive economy', *Econometrica*, 22 (3): 265–90.

Bankitalia (2009) *Debito Delle Amministrazioni Locali*. Rome: Bank of Italy. Retrieved on 15 December 2015 from www.bancaditalia.it/pubblicazioni/debito-amministrazioni/.

Bankitalia (2014) *Debito Delle Amministrazioni Locali*. Rome: Bank of Italy. Retrieved on 15 December 2015 from www.bancaditalia.it/pubblicazioni/debito-amministrazioni/.

Bianchi, P. (1987) 'The IRI in Italy: Strategic role and political constraints', *West European Politics*, 10 (2): 269–90.

BIS. 2015. *OTC derivatives statistics at end-June 2015*. Basel: Bank for International Settlements. Retrieved on 15 December 2015 from www.bis.org/publ/otc_hy1511.pdf.

Bryan, D. and Rafferty, M. (2006) *Capitalism with Derivatives. A Political Economy of Financial Derivatives, Capital and Class*. Basingstoke: Palgrave Macmillan.

Bryan, D. and Rafferty, M. (2011) 'Deriving capital's (and labour's) future', *Socialist Register*, 47: 196–223.

Cafruny, A.W. and Ryner, M.J. (2008) 'Is the SGP crisis also the crisis of the EU? Assessing the EMU from a structural, transatlantic perspective'. In Talani, L. and Casey, B. (eds) *Between Growth and Stability. The Demise and Reform of the European Union's Stability and Growth Pact*. Cheltenham: Edward Elgar, pp. 60–84.

Carlini, V. (2010) 'Ecco Come La Finanza Creativa Ha Danneggiato Gli Enti Pubblici', *Il Sole 24 Ore*, 22 March. Retrieved on 15 December 2015 from www.ilsole24ore.com/art/SoleOnLine4/Finanza%20e%20Mercati/2010/03/derivati-comuni-truffa-raggiro-ente-pubblico-P_A.shtml.

Deeg, R. (2005) 'Remaking Italian capitalism? The politics of corporate governance reform', *West European Politics*, 28 (3): 521–48.

Dodd, R. (2010) 'Municipal bombs', *Finance & Development*, 47 (2): 33–5.

Dunbar, N. (2006) *Risky Finance: Weapons of Mass Deception*. Retrieved on 15 December 2015 from www.nickdunbar.net/articles-and-reviews/risky-finance-weapons-of-mass-deception/.

Dunbar, N. (2014) *Lost Lobos*. Retrieved on 15 December 2015 from http://nickdunbar.net/2014/10/24/lost-lobos/.

Dyson, K. and Featherstone, K. (1996) 'Italy and EMU as a "vincolo esterno": Empowering the technocrats, transforming the state', *South European Society and Politics*, 1 (2): 272–99.

Engelen, E. (2008) 'The case for financialization', *Competition & Change*, 12 (2): 111–19.

Franco, D. (2009) *Indagine Conoscitiva sull'Utilizzo e La Diffusione degli Strumenti di Finanza Derivata e delle Cartolarizzazioni nelle Pubbliche Amministrazioni*. Rome: Italian Senate. Retrieved on 15 December 2015 from www.bancaditalia.it/pubblicazioni/interventi-vari/int-var-2009/Audizione_Senato_080709.pdf.

FSB (2010) *Implementing OTC Derivatives Market Reforms*. Basel: Financial Stability Board. Retrieved on 15 December 2015 from www.financialstabilityboard.org/2010/10/fsb-report-on-implementing-otc-derivatives-market-reforms.

FSB (2014) *Overview of Progress in the Implementation of the G20 Recommendations for Strengthening Financial Stability*. Basel: Financial Stability Board. Retrieved on 15 December 2015 from www.financialstabilityboard.org/2014/11/overview-of-progress-in-the-implementation-of-the-g20-recommendations-for-strengthening-financial-stability-5.

Geisst, C.R. (2002) *Wheels of Fortune. The History of Speculation from Scandal to Respectability*. Hoboken: Wiley.

Greenspan, A. (2003) *Global Finance: Is It Slowing? Remarks by Chairman Alan Greenspan at the Banque de France International Symposium on Monetary Policy, Economic Cycle, and Financial Dynamics, Paris, France*. Retrieved on 15 December 2015 from www.federalreserve.gov/BOARDDOCS/SPEECHES/2003.

Gurkaynak, R. and Wolfers, J. (2006) 'Macroeconomic derivatives: An initial analysis of market-based macro forecasts, uncertainty, and risk', NBER Working Paper No. 11929.

Heipertz, M. and Verdun, A. (2004) 'The dog that would never bite? What we can learn from the origins of the stability and growth pact', *Journal of European Public Policy*, 11 (5): 765–80.

Heipertz, M. and Verdun, A. (2005) 'The stability and growth pact – theorizing a case in European integration', *Journal of Common Market Studies*, 43 (5): 985–1008.

Hendrikse, R.P. and Sidaway, J.D. (2013) 'Financial wizardry and the golden city: Tracking the financial crisis through Pforzheim, Germany', *Transactions of the Institute of British Geographers*, 39 (2): 195–208.

House Committee on Agriculture (1892) *Fictitious Dealing in Agricultural products. Testimony Taken before the Committee on Agriculture during a Consideration of Bills Nos. 392, 2699, and 3870, Restricting and Taxing Dealers in Futures and Options in Agricultural Products, and for Other Purposes*. Washington, DC: United States House Committee on Agriculture.

Hull, J.C. (2009) *Options, Futures and Other Derivatives*. Upper Saddle River, NJ: Pearson Prentice Hall.

Italian Government (1998) *Law Decree No. 58 (24 February)*. Retrieved on 15 December 2015 from www.normattiva.it.

Italian Government (2000) *Law Decree No. 267 (18 August)*. Retrieved on 15 December 2015 from www.normattiva.it.

Italian Parliament (1994) *Law No. 724 (23 December), Article 35*. Retrieved on 15 December 2015 from www.normattiva.it.

Italian Parliament (1997) *Law No. 59 (15 March)*. Retrieved on 15 December 2015 from www.normattiva.it.

Italian Parliament (2001a) *Constitutional Law No. 3 (8 October)*. Retrieved on 15 December 2015 from www.normattiva.it.

Italian Parliament (2001b) *Law No. 448 (28 December), Article 41*. Retrieved on 15 December 2015 from www.normattiva.it.

Italian Parliament (2006) *Law No. 296 (27 December), Article 1 (736–739)*. Retrieved on 15 December 2015 from www.normattiva.it.

Italian Parliament (2008a) *Law No. 133 (6 August)*. Retrieved on 15 December 2015 from www.normattiva.it.

Italian Parliament (2008b) *Law No. 203 (22 December), Article 3*. Retrieved on 15 December 2015 from www.normattiva.it.

Italian Parliament (2010a) *Indagine Conoscitiva sull'Utilizzo e La Diffusione degli Strumenti di Finanza Derivata e delle Cartolarizzazioni nelle Pubbliche Amministrazioni (Documento Conclusivo)* Rome: Italian Senate. Retrieved on 15 December 2015 from www.parlamento.it/service/PDF/PDFServer/BGT/470072.pdf.

Italian Parliament (2010b) *Indagine Conoscitiva Sulla Finanza Locale*. Rome: Italian Chamber of Deputies. Retrieved on 15 December 2015 from http://documenti.camera.it/_dati/leg16/lavori/documentiparlamentari/indiceetesti/017/009/intero.pdf.

Italian Parliament (2011) *Resoconto Stenografico No. 19*. Rome: Italian Senate. Retrieved on 15 December 2015 from www.senato.it/service/PDF/PDFServer/DF/253243.pdf.

Italian Parliament (2013) *Law No. 147 (27 December), Article 1 (572)*. Retrieved on 15 December 2015 from www.normattiva.it.

Jewson, S. and Brix, A. (2005) *Weather Derivative Valuation: The Meteorological, Statistical, Financial And Mathematical Foundations*. Cambridge: Cambridge University Press.

Katz, Alan. (2010) 'The city that got swapped', *Bloomberg*, 22 April. Retrieved on 15 December 2015 from www.businessweek.com/magazine/content/10_18/b4176100989666.htm.

Kolb, R.W. and Overdahl, J.A. (2007) *Futures, Options, and Swaps*. Oxford: Blackwell.

Konings, M. (2010), 'The pragmatic sources of modern power', *European Journal of Sociology*, 51(1): 55–91.

Lagna, A. (2015) 'Italian municipalities and the politics of financial derivatives: Rethinking the Foucauldian perspective', *Competition & Change*, 19 (4): 283–300.

Levy, J.I. (2006) 'Contemplating delivery: Futures trading and the problem of commodity exchange in the United States, 1875–1905', *The American Historical Review*, 111 (2): 307–35.

Loader, D. (2005) *Clearing and Settlement of Derivatives*. Burlington: Elsevier.

McCann, D. (2000) 'The 'Anglo-American' model, privatization and the transformation of private capitalism in Italy', *Modern Italy*, 5 (1): 47–61.

MacKenzie, D. (2003) 'Long-Term Capital Management and the sociology of arbitrage', *Economy and Society*, 32 (3): 349–80.

Markham, J.W. (2002) *A Financial History of the United States. From Christopher Columbus to the Robber Barons (1492–1900)*. Armonk: M.E. Sharpe.

Martinuzzi, E. (2013) 'JPMorgan, UBS tricked Milan in swaps case, Judge says', *Bloomberg*, 4 February. Retrieved on 15 December 2015 from www.bloomberg.com/news/2013-02-04/jpmorgan-deutsche-bank-tricked-milan-in-swaps-case-judge-says.html.

MEF (1996) *Ministerial Decree No. 420 (5 July)*. Retrieved on 15 December 2015 from www.dt.tesoro.it/it/debito_pubblico/enti_locali/nota_espl_normativa_enti_territoriali.html.

MEF (2003) *Ministerial Decree No. 389 (1 December)*. Retrieved on 15 December 2015 from www.dt.tesoro.it/it/debito_pubblico/enti_locali/nota_espl_normativa_enti_territoriali.html.

MEF (2004) *MEF Memorandum No. 128 (27 May)*. Retrieved on 15 December 2015 from www.dt.tesoro.it/it/debito_pubblico/enti_locali/nota_espl_normativa_enti_territoriali.html.

MEF (2009) *Schema di Regolamento Ministeriale di Attuazione dell'Articolo 62 del Decreto Legge 25 Giugno 2008, N. 112, Convertito con Modificazioni dalla Legge 6 Agosto 2008, N. 133, come Sostituito dall'Articolo 3 della Legge 22 Dicembre 2008, N. 203 (Documento di Consultazione)*. Retrieved on 15 December 2015 from www.dt.tesoro.it/export/sites/sitodt/modules/documenti_it/regolamentazione_bancaria_finanziaria/consultazioni_pubbliche/Derivati_enti_locali_-_regolamento_ex_articolo_62_d.l.pdf.

Nölke, A., Heires, M. and Bieling, H.J. (2013) 'Editorial: The politics of financialization', *Competition & Change*, 17 (3): 209–18.

Norris, F. (2013) 'Wielding derivatives as a tool for deceit', *The New York Times*, 27 June. Retrieved on 15 December 2015 from www.nytimes.com/2013/06/28/business/deception-by-derivative.html.

Partnoy, F. (2009) *Infectious Greed. How Deceit and Risk Corrupted Financial Markets*. New York: Public Affairs.

Pasquino, G. (2000) 'Political development'. In McCarthy, P. (ed.) *Italy since 1945*. Oxford: Oxford University Press, pp. 69–94.

Rosati, A. (2009) *Indagine Conoscitiva sulla Diffusione degli Strumenti di Finanza Derivata e delle Cartolarizzazioni nelle Pubbliche Amministrazioni*. Rome: Italian Senate. Retrieved on 15 December 2015 from www.consob.it/documenti/Pubblicazioni/Audizioni/audizione_rosati_20090318.pdf.

Saccomanni, F. (2007) *Le Problematiche Relative agli Strumenti Finanziari Derivati*. Rome: Italian Chamber of deputies. Retrieved on 15 December 2015 from www.bancaditalia.it/pubblicazioni/interventi-direttorio/int-dir-2007/saccomanni_061107.pdf.

Sanderson, R., Dinmore, G. and Tett, G. (2010) 'Finance: An exposed position', *Financial Times*, 8 March. Retrieved on 15 December 2015 from www.ft.com/cms/s/0/0d29fbdc-2aef-11df-886b-00144feabdc0.html#axzz2Ldv9pQZa.

Sandor, R. (2012) *Good Derivatives: A Story of Financial and Environmental Innovation*. Hoboken: Wiley.

Sbragia, A. (2001) 'Italy pays for Europe: Political leadership, political choice, and institutional adaptation'. In Green Cowles, M., Caporaso, J. and Risse, T. (eds) *Transforming Europe. Europeanization and Domestic Change*. Ithaca: Cornell University Press, pp. 79–96.

Schinasi, G.J. et al. (2000) *Modern Banking and OTC Derivatives Markets. The Transformation of Global Finance and Its Implications for Systemic Risk*. Washington, DC: International Monetary Fund.

Shiller, R.J. (2003) *The New Financial Order. Risk in the 21st Century*. Princeton, NJ: Princeton University Press.

Sirletti, S. and Martinuzzi, E. (2014) 'JPMorgan, UBS convictions overturned in Milan swaps case', *Bloomberg*, 7 March. Retrieved on 15 December 2015 from www.bloomberg.com/news/2014-03-07/jpmorgan-ubs-convictions-overturned-in-milan-swaps-case.html.

Smith, S.J. and Searle, B.A. (2010) *The Blackwell Companion to the Economics of Housing: The Housing Wealth of Nations*. Chichester: Wiley & Sons.
Swan, E.J. (1999) *Building the Global Market, a 4000 Year History of Derivatives*. London: Kluwer Law International.
Valdez, S. and Molyneux, P. (2013) *An Introduction to Global Financial Markets*. Basingstoke: Palgrave.
Wigan, D. (2009) 'Financialisation and derivatives: Constructing an artifice of indifference', *Competition & Change*, 13 (2): 157–72.

Part IV
Regulation of misconduct in banking

12

Libor and Euribor

From normal banking practice to manipulation to the potential for reform

Daniel Seabra Lopes

Introduction: a brief history of reference rates

Libor and Euribor are the reference interest rates that set the average cost of loans among a restricted group of banks. The major relevance of Libor and Euribor relies, however, on their being metonymically associated to international interbank money markets in which banks engage in a series of mutual over-the-counter lending operations. These markets are only half a century old. They started to develop in Europe in the late 1950s and throughout the 1960s, giving rise to a London-based transactional structure known as the Eurodollar market, whose activities went uncontrolled by either national central banks or the Bretton Woods fixed exchange rate system institutions (Arrighi, [1994] 2010, p. 310). The quick expansion of such an informal market – which soon became a fundamental source of funding for large banks and multinational corporations (BIS, 1983, pp. 11–12) – sometimes gets interpreted as a reopening of the international financial circuits that had otherwise stayed shut since 1929 (see Ridley and Jones, 2012; Engelen *et al.*, 2010, p. 47). The breakdown of the Bretton Woods Accord in 1971 symbolized a new era of fluctuating rates, with banks and corporations increasingly recurring to financial derivatives so as to actively manage risk: interest rate swaps, forward rate agreements as well as currency options and swaps became associated with Eurodollar lending operations as from the late 1970s onwards (Kirti, 2014). In 1981, the calculation of the Libor rate was for the first time based on a daily poll arranged by the Chicago Mercantile Exchange, officially launched as an index of the same Eurodollar market in 1985 under the supervision of the British Bankers Association. At the same time, similar rates appeared in Europe, such as Pibor, Fibor or Aibor, which would later merge into Euribor. This later rate was introduced in 1999 under the administration of the European Banking Federation and soon became the leading benchmark for interbank lending operations within the Eurozone.

This brief historical sketch serves to properly situate the emergence and centrality of reference rates such as Libor and Euribor. Though credit is usually presented as the lifeblood of the economy, enabling the regular circulation of money among producers, distributors and consumers, or among employers, employees and a host of different business counterparts (cf. Tett, 2009, p. 28), the systemic importance of international interbank loans is a relatively recent event stemming from coalescent economic, political, organizational, technological and even theoretical developments. One of such developments has to do with a long post-Second World War process of both liquidity and mass consumerism enhancement (Westbrook, 2010, pp. 30–1; Marron, 2009, pp. 79–98), first supported by the state during the heyday of Keynesianism and progressively assumed by private actors (namely banks via retail credit) under a neo-liberal deregulatory framework. This transition was paralleled and indeed further reinforced by the computerization and synchronization of financial markets (cf. Knorr Cetina and Bruegger, 2002), which deepened the internationalization of interbank borrowing supported by electronic transfer systems and enabled Eurodollar market access to smaller domestic banks. Finally, and though this may appear as a lateral process, conceptual developments in the area of finance – e.g. the famous Black–Scholes–Merton option pricing model (cf. MacKenzie, 2006) – liberated the expanding realm of derivatives from the negative connotations associated with gambling and speculation. Finance thus began to appear as a highly technical and measurable process, assisted by a host of theoretical constructs such as the efficient market hypothesis, random walk theory or the capital asset pricing model, giving a new breadth to the industry of indices and benchmarks.

This industry currently publishes over a million indices every day, whether exclusively concerning financial markets or markets with which finance closely interrelates, such as the energy, real estate and maritime transportation markets or even non-market realities such as global warming and longevity rates. Investment strategies, insurance and pension plans, savings accounts and retail loans are now commonly interlinked with the rise and fall in one or more of such indices. In this respect, the Libor story becomes quite illustrative. Throughout the 1970s, a reference interest rate with the same name began to get adopted by groups of banks to price Eurodollar adjustable rate lending operations known as syndicated loans: every three or six months, when the interest rates of these loans were about to be readjusted, the banks forming the syndicate communicated to each other their respective funding costs, whose averaged value would consist of the adjusted interest rate for the new period arising. The Libor rate in those days was, in many respects, a club instrument devised and employed by those most committed to using it (see Rauterberg and Verstein, 2013, p. 4), in a circular scheme that clearly suggests self-reference. This scheme was largely maintained when a centralized calculation of Libor based on a daily poll was put into practice by the Chicago Mercantile Exchange in 1981 (MacKenzie, 2009, p. 81) and, four years later, officially assumed by the British Bankers Association, with rate production continuing to derive from quotes provided by Libor's biggest users. By the mid-1980s, however, the relevance of Libor had already gone far beyond syndicated loans to encompass both the derivatives and the retail credit markets. The rate had become what Ashton and Christophers (2015, pp. 190–1) call a 'legal technology of arbitration', serving as an external referent enabling the creation of a multiplicity of new contractual relationships. In the words of Minos Zombanakis, an old Greek banker who took part in those pre-1981 Libor indexed syndicated loans (cited in Ridley and Jones, 2012): 'We started something which was practical and convenient. We never had in mind that this rate would spread to mortgages and things like that...'

Astonishment is, of course, a frequent after-the-fact reaction to financial turmoil and scandal, and one that may divert attention from processes of strategic recombination and exponential imitation that actually make up the contemporary financial world. This chapter intends to follow the road that leads from convenient practice to contagious expansion to manipulation and, finally, to a promise of reform. In this respect, three things deserve properly underlining. The first is how the Libor rate was nurtured by influential players strategically positioned at the convergence points of international finance and thus endowed with a capacity to set new rules and thereby extend a game they were already playing. The second stems from a tendency towards continuing to do things along previously stipulated lines, following what sociologist

Niklas Luhmann ([1997] 2012, p. 41) describes as operationally closed organizational practices – and we will see that manipulation attempts fit this picture more as a rule than as an exception. The third factor embodies a cluster of nexuses or associations that expands while – indeed also because – old habits remain. Thus, when Euribor came to being in 1999 and replaced former interbank rates in francs, marks and other currencies, it soon became clear that it would no longer indicate a single, circumscribed reality – the average interest rate practised in lending operations among a restricted group of banks. As with Libor at that time, Euribor was supposed to signal a wider interbank money market and even the whole economy (to the extent this gets perceived in accordance with the conditions imposed on the international interbank lending funded retail credit supply). In this sense, both Libor and Euribor may also be viewed as multi-referential and multifunctional rates with a notable aggregation capacity.

That, in a nutshell, constitutes the main argument of this chapter. The trail of both Libor and Euribor is here followed in relation to an organizational complex combining specific material infrastructures, legal arrangements, communication channels, representational devices and workplace routines (while impossible to describe in detail all the facets composing this complex and across various countries, some concrete examples are provided). The chapter proceeds as follows. The next section presents Libor and Euribor in their contemporary, multi-referential guise. The third section offers some ethnographic evidence of how these rates are employed in routine banking practices, highlighting their somewhat diverse usages and implications (i.e. their multi-functionality). The fourth section introduces the Libor/Euribor manipulation scandal, which became a public issue in the spring of 2012. The fifth section describes some of the efforts taken towards the reform of both rates. The sixth section puts forward the conclusions reached. The research underlying this chapter was mainly supported by two post-doctoral grants awarded by the Portuguese Foundation for Science and Technology (FCT): SFRH/BPD/37785/2007 and SFRH/BPD/78438/2011. Additional funding was provided by the FCT's strategic project for research units (PEst-OE/SADG/UID428/2013) and a FAPESP grant for visiting scientist (Process No. 2014/04977-1).

Libor and Euribor as multi-referential benchmarks

As stated, Libor (the London Interbank Offered Rate) and Euribor (the Euro Interbank Offered Rate) indicate the average interest rates practised in unsecured lending operations among a selected group of banks, termed 'panel banks'. Libor refers to transactions occurring in the London interbank money market through different real-time gross settlement systems (RTGS). At present, this rate contemplates five different currencies: pound sterling, euro, yen, Swiss franc and, most notably, the US dollar – whose rates usually correspond to the meaning of the word 'Libor' in the absence of any further specification. Euribor refers to transactions in the Eurozone money market made through the Trans-European Automated Real-Time Gross Settlement Express Transfer System (TARGET2) controlled by the Eurosystem. Contrary to Libor, Euribor is focused exclusively on the euro currency. The calculation processes of the two rates bear many similarities being based not on actual interest values but rather on individual estimates regularly submitted by panel banks to an external calculation agent – Thomson Reuters/Intercontinental Exchange (ICE) for Libor and Global Rate Set Systems Ltd for Euribor. These calculation agents collect the information received and perform the computation on behalf of the entities currently responsible for administering each rate. On 3 February 2014, the Libor administration was transferred from the British Bankers Association to ICE Benchmark Administration Ltd (a private network of exchanges and clearing houses), while Euribor is presently managed by the European Money Markets Institute, previously known as

Euribor-EBF, a nonprofit international association founded in 1999 and under the auspices of the European Banking Federation.

The information available on Libor and Euribor computation processes does not yet contemplate these recent replacements at the calculation and administration levels even while the overall delegation structure remains the same. Basically, the calculation takes about an hour and a half to complete and combines both automated and manual input procedures (cf. EEMI, 2014; EBA and ESMA, 2013, pp. 10–11; MacKenzie, 2009: 81–2). Every business day at around 10:00 (Greenwich Meridian Time in the case of Libor, Central European Time in the case of Euribor), Thomson Reuters and Global Rate Set Systems clean all information regarding previous data and open up their systems so that each panel bank can electronically submit the newest estimates via private pages accessible only to the calculation agents and the bank in question – the submissions including lending offers of no stipulated amount for a group of maturities ranging from overnight (Libor only) to 12 months – see Table 12.1. The system remains open for about an hour before there follows a smaller period during which panel banks can revise and correct the information provided or be notified by the calculation agent in case of communication failure or any other such anomaly. Then the window closes and the rate calculation begins: for each maturity, a percentage of the highest and lowest quotes (25 per cent in the case of Libor, 15 per cent in the case of Euribor) is automatically eliminated, with the remaining rates averaged and rounded off to five (Libor) or three (Euribor) decimal places. Around 11:30, the calculation agent will publish the newest rate values, which become accessible to subscribers and can subsequently be further disseminated (Figure 12.1).

The further dissemination of the Libor and Euribor rate reflects both their relevance and the current structural significance of these two benchmarks. As mentioned in the introductory section, both Libor and Euribor are now widely employed as reference rates in multiple over-the-counter and exchange-traded derivatives contracts such as interest rate futures, options and swaps or forward rate agreements, while at the retail level the two rates also integrate into a variety of products, from corporate loans to mortgages to student loans to credit cards (Ojo, 2014; Kiff, 2012). In this vein, the US dollar Libor acquired the reputation of being the most important series of numbers in the whole world (*Money Week*, 2008), with Euribor taking on an equally prominent status though in a less ample market context. Hence do we here refer to both Libor and Euribor as multi-referential and aggregative rates. Though originating in an elite circuit of interbank lending, the two rates have clearly escaped that primary context to become involved in the calculative and legal arrangements of other financial markets. Indeed, the usage

Table 12.1 Excel spreadsheet used for internally informing of the Euribor rate values in one Portuguese retail bank

	LAST	LAST 1	LAST 2	LAST 3
SW	4,405	4,405	4,386	4,388
1M	4,484	4,484	4,485	4,484
2M	4,757	4,756	4,757	4,757
3M	4,964	4,963	4,964	4,963
(...)	(...)	(...)	(...)	(...)
1Y	5,321	5,306	5,314	5,301
	22-08-2008	21-08-2008	20-08-2008	19-08-2008

Notes: English in the original: reading from left to right, the first column indicates the maturities, with 'SW' standing for Spot Week; the second column (titled 'LAST') displays the newest Euribor values, with the following columns presenting the values of the three previous days, for the purposes of comparison (the corresponding dates appear below).

	LIBOR					EURIBOR
Market context	London Interbank Money Market					Eurozone Interbank Money Market
Administration	ICE Benchmark Administration Ltd					European Money Markets Institute
Currencies	USD	GBP	EUR	JPY	CHF	EUR
Number of panel banks	18	16	15	13	11	24
Tenures	Overnight, 1 week, 1–3 months, 6 months, 12 months					1–2 weeks, 1–3 months, 6 months, 9 months, 12 months
Calculation agent	Thomson Reuters/Intercontinental Exchange (ICE)					Global Rate Set Systems Ltd
Dissemination of results	Real time for subscribers and with a 24 hour delay for the public in general					

Figure 12.1 Generic information about Libor and Euribor, December 2015

of such reference rates in retail credit contracts is now usually reinforced by national jurisdictions, sometimes with concrete specifications regarding employable tenures or averaging procedures as in Spain, Portugal or Italy (I return later to this point), while in countries such as Belgium, the use of Libor and Euribor as reference rates for retail credit is strictly forbidden – with all mortgages indexed to Belgian sovereign bonds instead (see Zachary, 2009).

Libor and Euribor in normal banking practice

The closest example to an ethnography of Libor calculation may be found in MacKenzie (2009, pp. 1–2). In this section, I propose to complement his impressions by putting forward a picture of how Euribor rate numbers are processed outside panel banks and at the level of normal banking practice. Until recently, public dissemination of both the Libor and Euribor values was made in real time and shortly after the calculation agent had published the newest rate values. In 2014, both administrators introduced a 24-hour delay. The following empirical description refers to a period before this alteration was implemented, though the cognitive, interactive and bureaucratic procedures remain valid today. The action takes place inside the financial department of one Portuguese retail bank. In the dealings room of this financial department, there was a person in charge of the interbank money market operations. This same person was also responsible for informing the bank's marketing and commercial branches of the newest Euribor values. Thus, every day, around 11:30 CET (10:30 in Portugal), she accessed the calculation agent's page on one of her computer screens from which she copied the latest Euribor values and pasted them into a previously prepared Excel spreadsheet as shown in Table 12.1.

The Excel file was then renamed and immediately sent to other banking departments. One can thus observe how, at a very immediate level, reference rates enter the realm of organizational practice also as expedients that maintain specific communication channels (both internal and external) open and active.

What gets communicated through these channels subsequently serves as the basis for further action. The fact that both Libor and Euribor are now incorporated into many retail credit products with adjustable interest rates means that the two indices have transcended the boundaries of what they supposedly indexed (the interbank money market) to begin performing new functions – in this case, employed as base rates in retail credit products – in other financial market segments. A link between wholesale and retail finance thus becomes established. For this purpose, the official rate values require some further adjustment. In terms of calculation, the Euribor rate used in Portuguese retail credits is subject to another new round of averaging. The values regularly provided by the calculation agent and internally released through documents such as in Table 12.2, thus undergo compilation at the end of each month and then divided by the corresponding number of days, the resulting simple mean consisting of the more mundane Euribor indexer – or base rate – used in retail credit and which would have to be incorporated into retail contracts coming into effect the month thereafter (note the lag effect that also accompanies the transition from wholesale to retail finance). The rules of this calculation have been declared mandatory by a specific Portuguese law (*Decreto-lei 240/2006*), which added that banks were only permitted to round up the rate's fourth decimal place. At this point, the Euribor rate ceases to be the trimmed average of projections regarding lending prices in the interbank money market to become an actual interest rate component, applied uniformly to retail credit contracts along with a spread depending on individual risk scores.

Because of this multifunctionality, both Euribor and Libor are now omnipresent in regular banking practice. Updated Libor/Euribor values must be regularly incorporated into online credit simulators, a procedure far from automatic – usually implying a series of trial and error operations and, in most cases, mobilizing human resources from different banking departments. Current Libor/Euribor values may also be present in calculations associated with product developments, especially regarding the choice of tenures in relation to specific credit modalities. Moreover, banks are frequently prompted by the media and consumer or industry associations to provide information regarding their supply with this usually involving similar comparisons between different rate maturities. In addition, Libor/Euribor play an important role in reports depicting business evolution or in budgetary activities (where future profits are anticipated according to a projection of future rate values). As such, documents and graphs describing the history of Libor or Euribor along with the tables displaying the newest values provided by their calculation agents emerge as relevant sources of information for marketers, risk analysts and other banking professionals working at the commercial branches (one fieldwork recollection regards a dossier titled 'Home Loans/Interest Rates 2008' where one marketer could readily pick up Euribor values relative to any previous month).

Most of these cases incorporate a pragmatic view of Libor/Euribor, that is, a perspective in which the information provided by the calculation agent and subsequently recalculated for retail

Table 12.2 List of the main public consultations on financial benchmarks, in chronological order

Consultation paper	Leading institution	Dates	Number of published responses	
			Institutional	Personal
Functioning and Oversight of Oil Price Reporting Agencies	IOSCO	2012-03-01/2012-03-30	15	3
The Wheatley Review of Libor: Initial Discussion Paper	Financial Services Authority (UK)	2012-08-10/2012-09-07	Over 60 (unpublished by the FSA)	
Consultation on Market Manipulation: Lessons and Reform post-Libor/Euribor	European Parliament/ Economic and Monetary Affairs Committee	2012-08-20/2012-09-17	43	2
Consultation on the Regulation of Indices	European Commission	2012-09-15/2012-11-29	75	—
The Regulation and Supervision of Benchmarks	Financial Services Authority (UK)	2012-12-05/2013-01-16 and 2013-02-13	24	—
Financial Benchmarks Consultation Report	IOSCO	2013-01-11/2013-02-11	55	2
Principles for Benchmarks-Setting Processes in the EU	EBA and ESMA	2013-01-11/2013-02-15	67	—
Principles for Financial Benchmarks Consultation Report	IOSCO	2013-04-16/2013-05-16	42	1

purposes is mostly taken for granted, with actors merely accounting for acute number reproduction from reliable sources – often a chart like Table 12.2, prepared for dissemination by entitled professionals within each bank – to new documents, files and calculation instruments. What counts as Libor or Euribor is the list of percentages reputedly stemming from such reliable sources, distributed along a network that starts in the calculation agent's online page and may end in several retail credit simulators available on bank web pages and local branches – with one stop for reproduction in the bank's financial department and another in the marketing department in the case of the two Portuguese banks where I did my fieldwork. Since there was only one desktop and screen per desk in the marketing areas of both banks, a common strategy was to print out the source of Euribor values so as to better verify that the same values had been correctly inserted into newer reports, tables and devices. During credit simulator rates updating, for example, marketers in charge of this task would make recourse to a printed table exhibiting the newest Euribor indexer values while testing the simulator prototype available on screen to ensure that no mistakes had been made. In such cases, Euribor percentages were compared to each other, either confirming that there was a perfect match or evaluating the rate's movements over a specific period, and with absolutely no concern for questions such as whether those percentages adequately reflected the current interbank lending conditions or whether there was any substantial difference between the Euribor rate published by Thomson Reuters and the nationally prescribed calculation of the Euribor indexer (I am here simply making an ethnographic statement, and not implying that retail banking actors *should* have this kind of concern around Euribor descriptions and representative capabilities).

It is thus possible to speak of a routine principle of reproduction in which bankers keep in line with past organizational practices. This principle both relates with operational imperatives and remains necessarily closed to marginal interrogations. Libor and Euribor, as taken-for-granted facts, are thus mandatorily copied from one station to another, from one document to another, with actors more concerned with accurate 'reproduction' than with the supposed 'accuracy' of that being reproduced.

There is, however, more to the story. Not only are both Libor and Euribor laterally involved in a multitude of financial instruments and investment strategies but they also act as trading targets. Betting on trends in Libor or Euribor now represents common practice even while the classification of such a move as an 'investment' has equally involved specific legal arrangements in the respective different jurisdictions (see MacKenzie, 2009, pp. 75–8). Such trading strategies are usually developed within global megabanks acting as brokers and subsequently handed down with a delay to smaller players under a contracted business relationship (see Box 12.1 for an example).

[Name of broker]

Euribor: cheap upside printing, possible protection against EBC aggressive rate policy shift – Paper bot 10K ER 95 25 / 95 50 1 x 2 with Libor remaining at current levels (7 bps above repo fin rate), trade targets almost 50bps of easing by yr end. . .

Box 12.1

Long call ladder option strategy sent from a then Euribor/Libor panel bank via a Bloomberg chat room to a Portuguese retail bank. The strategy bets on a Euribor rate cut of 50 basis points – note how the projection also takes the Libor values into consideration (English in the original).

Source: Author's fieldnotes.

Trader reactions to such 'broker tips' are far from mechanical not only due to the cryptic jargon but also because additional information is usually required: special, subscribed website pages run by important news providers such as Bloomberg or Reuters may thus be accessed to view graphs with Libor/Euribor predictions plus information regarding the instrument or strategy under analysis, such as its profit and loss curve or the latest transaction prices. The capacities of smaller banks to invest must also be taken into consideration as many strategies will only pay off when the bank enters the market with a number of contracts larger than those internally affordable to its own trading portfolio. In these cases, banking actors are no longer merely copying information from one platform to another but rather prospecting information and gathering knowledge in order to reach an investment decision. The knowledge itself is, however, equally based on standardized market indices and devices, with traders seldom questioning the adequacy of the information coming from the news providers. Libor and Euribor thus remain unquestioned presuppositions under which new questions may be asked, regarding not the interbank money market itself but, for example, the options and futures markets, whose fluctuations are comparably faster.

In sum, whereas marketers oscillate between the reproduction of Libor/Euribor daily and monthly rates, traders ignore both to concentrate mainly on the real time evolution of Libor/Euribor derivatives markets as displayed on trading terminals, waiting for the right moment to step in or step out. In all cases, Libor and Euribor are taken as established *facts* – i.e. something largely taken-for-granted and thus serving as an unproblematic basis for further activities (see MacKenzie, 2009, pp. 9–10) – with careful reproduction specifically intended to preserve their facticity.

Manipulation scenarios

The so-called Libor manipulation scandal erupted in June 2012 out of a sequence of investigations by the former UK Financial Services Authority. Controversy around Libor does, however, hold a longer history. MacKenzie (2009, p. 82) situates the emergence of this controversy in 2007–08, in close association with the bailouts of UK banks Northern Rock and Bear Sterns. MacKenzie's account, though, still highlights Libor's facticity. The rate is thus presented as 'an example of a measure that *has* usually been taken as an adequate representation of the underlying market' (ibid., p. 79, emphasis in the original), and whose 'fixing is designed to be *sociologically* robust, so to speak' (ibid., p. 82, again, emphasis in the original). Suspicions around possibly deflated Libor values in the midst of the 2008 financial turmoil were communicated by the panel banks themselves to the British Bankers Association and the Bank of England (Mollenkamp, 2008). In 2009, the UK Financial Services Authority undertook a systematic investigation of the institutions involved in the Libor submission process, with cooperation from regulators and public authorities in other jurisdictions whose currencies then integrated the list of Libor rates – namely the United States, Japan, Switzerland, the European Union and Canada (which would later withdraw its currency from the Libor list) (cf. *The Wheatley Review of Libor: Final Report*, 2012). This investigation found evidence of regular rate rigging inside certain panel banks from at least 2005 onwards thus confirming what previous accounts based on econometric screening models designed to detect signs of possible conspiracy and manipulation had hesitantly hinted at (cf. Abrantes-Metz *et al.*, 2008). However, some media sources have subsequently reported statements from traders dating obscure practices as of the late 1980s (*The Economist*, 2012) – thus encompassing almost all of Libor's official history.

Rate rigging means the submission of Libor values inflated or deflated according to the bank's investments in derivatives or loan portfolios. The extent of US bank and Euribor/Libor panel member Citigroup's swap operations in early 2009, for example, was susceptible to providing significant returns should the Libor value drop (Snider and Youle, 2010). Profits deriving from bank retail credit portfolios might also prove substantial in case of deliberate rate increase as this would correspondingly increase the monthly instalments of millions of borrowers with Libor indexed loans – hence the lawsuits filed by US homeowners against a number of panel banks accused of strategically inflating Libor submissions at the beginning of each month just when most adjustable rate mortgages got reset (see Touryalai, 2012). This type of manipulation is usually described as 'positional' (Rauterberg and Verstein, 2013, pp. 31–2) or 'portfolio driven' (Snider and Youle, 2012) and requires some form of coalition between the employees submitting rate information, traders and even senior administrative staff all of whom are working for the same bank (see *The Economist*, 2012; Snider and Youle, 2012, pp. 8–9). Barclays Bank – that took centre stage during the scandal and was fined for manipulation attempts – also admitted the existence of tacit agreements among certain panel members to foster portfolio driven rate rigging. Collusion has indeed been at the heart of the whole Libor scandal, as testified to by another lawsuit lodged by the US Federal Deposit Insurance Corp against panel members (Raymond and Viswanatha, 2014).

A second type of rate manipulation has already been alluded to: the submission of rate values lower than those actually obtained so as to safeguard the bank's creditworthiness in times of lower liquidity levels. Such a strategy was intentionally deployed during the 2008 financial freefall and with every likelihood of having required the acknowledgement and approval of senior staff. There is, thus, some variety in the procedures to that which constitutes rate manipulation and the coalitions that need establishing in order to bring this about. Enough evidence has been provided of manipulation attempts involving horizontal *internal* collaboration between traders and staff members in charge of submitting rate values. No one seems to doubt that vertical internal collaboration, forming a triangle with the upper edge occupied by senior directors, also occurred. Finally, allegations of collusion point clearly towards both horizontal and vertical *external* collaborations, i.e. taking place across different panel banks. Of course, from a sociological point of view, horizontal/vertical and internal/external emerge as situational coordinates revealing the highly composite and flexible character of contemporary global banks. In fact, such global banks seem closer to being clusters of independent operational networks rather than uniform organizations – and it is perhaps important to stress that these same panel banks were among the first to report possible attempts at manipulation with the settlement of the whole Libor affair having largely benefited from the cooperation of bank employees acting against some of their colleagues and directors.

All this brings us back to the issue of self-reference. Let us recall that the official Libor rate was calculated on the basis of information submitted by Libor's most important users and on behalf of a bankers association. In a way, Libor never ceased to be the 'club good' that the pre-1981 Eurodollar community tailored for its own practical purposes. Evidence gathered by authorities and journalists suggests that false reporting has all along featured as part of Libor's official history – to a greater or lesser extent similar to the investment activities described in the previous section – and not just as a consequence of market turbulence or liquidity problems at particular times. In this sense, we may approach Libor manipulation as an example of financial innovation performed by well positioned and well adapted elite intermediaries acting as *bricoleurs* (cf. Engelen *et al.*, 2010, pp. 53 and 56). Indeed, while Ashton and Christophers (2015, p. 197) view rate rigging as a variety of arbitrage, we take it here as an example of financial bricolage or innovation in its crudest sense, since – as the same authors acknowledge (ibid., p. 198) – rate rigging meant the creation, and not just the discovery, of new price differentials through specific arrangements only accessible to certain panel bank employees.

On this basis, two things deserve highlighting. The first is that such an innovation soon became routine: apparently some traders needed but a Mars bar to persuade their cash desk colleagues to indulge in such a scheme, as told by a former UBS and Citigroup trader (see Marston, 2015). The second is that the same principle of strategic invention remains valid even when moving from the globally to the nationally circumscribed circuits of financial convergence. We have already described how Euribor rates were subjected to a second round of averaging before their application to mortgages in countries such as Portugal. In this respect, Portuguese banks have already also faced allegations from citizens and consumer associations of discretionarily averaging the Euribor mortgage indexer through both the rounding up of the fourth decimal case and the use of a 365-day basis for annual credit interest calculation while annual deposit interest was estimated solely on a 360-day basis (the idea, in this latter case, obviously incorporates that of increasing the amount of interest receivable to the detriment of that payable). These practices, which were subsequently regulated by a series of bills (see Lopes, 2013, p. 22, note 6), clearly reveal how Portuguese banks were also creatively deploying their capacity to play with basis points and incorporating this into their routine practices.

Reaction and reform

Rigging suspicions soon extended from Libor to Euribor and other interbank rates (cf. European Commission, 2012, p. 2), leading both to the inclusion of financial indices manipulation in the 2012 revision of EU Market Abuse Directive and to extensive reviews of financial and market benchmarks led by international political organizations such as the European Commission and the European Parliament, and international supervisory authorities such as the International Organization of Securities Commissions (IOSCO, founded in 1983), the European Banking Authority (EBA, established in 2011) and the European Securities and Markets Authority (ESMA, also established in 2011) (see Table 12.2 for a list of the public consultations around this issue). The Board of Governors Economic Consultative Committee of the Bank for International Settlements contributed to the debate with a report entitled 'Towards Better Reference Rate Practices: A Central Bank Perspective' (March 2013). All these regulatory work streams were paralleled by efforts towards establishing new benchmark principles and codes of conduct, and as developed by industry associations such as the Global Financial Markets Association, the Index Industry Association, ASSIOM Forex (the Financial Markets Association of Italy), or by private index providers acting in cooperation such as Argus, Platts and ICIS.

The participants in these discussions were mostly institutional: alongside industry associations there were national and international regulators, banks, brokers and asset management firms, stock exchanges and other index providers, and, to a lesser extent, consumer associations. Furthermore, a considerable number of these institutions participated in more than one public consultation (often recycling their responses to previous consultations given the juxtaposition of content). Such is the case of the main index providers and industry associations whose collaboration with the authorities also included attending private meetings. Notwithstanding the global scope of the subject under consultation and the leading institutions' receptivity to contributions from anywhere, the geography of respondents inevitably reflected global asymmetries, with the United States and the main European Union countries (the UK, Germany and France) massively represented, along with other rarer contributions from South Africa, Australia (both only in the IOSCO consultations) and Japan, with the total absence of Russia, China, India, South America and other African countries.

Within these debates, issues around facticity and representational accuracy were paramount to regulators. According to the European Commission consultation paper (2012, p. 2), benchmarks are thought to rigorously reflect the economic realities that they intend to measure – hence the allusion to transaction based evidence as the ultimate constituent of market reality. Or, as ESMA executive director Verena Ross stated during one public hearing held in Paris (13 February 2013), with Libor and Euribor in mind, 'there must be some reality check between what the benchmarks say and what transactions say'. Libor and Euribor represent, in this respect, an interesting case, in that the interbank market they were supposed to reflect largely ceased to exist in the wake of 2007–08, at least for maturities of over one month as duly noted by many respondents to these consultations and acknowledged by the authorities themselves. This was attributed to a series of interrelated causes, ranging from the European sovereign debt crisis and rating downgrade to the growing influence of central bank lending facilities to Basel III new liquidity coverage ratio measures to – last but not least – the Libor scandal itself. In the words of former US Commodity Futures Trading Commission Chairman Gary Gensler, during an IOSCO public roundtable held in Washington also in February 2013 (YouTube, 2013), 'this is a world in which banks are being asked to quote something that might not even exist'. Indeed, with reference to the over thirty day Libor and Euribor rates, 'if the benchmark isn't benchmarking something, then what is it that we have here?'

We have a fiction, perhaps a 'convenient fiction', as one *New York Times* journalist once put it (Norris, 2012), echoing concerns first expressed by bankers (see Tett, 2007); but we clearly do not have a fact. Furthermore, as both regulators and actors, as well as sociologists of finance, maintain, trust in financial markets stems from facts and not from fictions. A reliable 'fact', in this case, means a number seen as adequately reflecting market reality, preferably anchored in actual, observable transactional data and susceptible to being incorporated into normal bureaucratic practices without any further concerns. One of the main conclusions of these rounds of public consultations regards the supremacy of prices as practised in authentic deals over price estimates as the basis for index production. Some participants – namely stock exchanges and related venues – even advanced rather Manichean distinctions between 'objective' and 'subjective' benchmarks or 'neutral' and 'panel based' index providers (EUREX, 2013; STOXX, 2012). From a sociological perspective, however, the production of facticity depends on a set of arbitrary conventions and discretionary judgements sustained by a community of fact users who also oversee fact production. The several original Libors applied to syndicated loans shared this characteristic. Commenting on a specific Scott Paper Company contract involving the production of a Libor rate by a small group of banks under the eye of a larger banking committee, Gary Gensler noted approvingly in the same IOSCO public roundtable that 'it's like living in a small town, or in a small village: it's less prone to misconduct because the community keeps you in line' (YouTube, 2013).

Even liquidity, so often regarded as the ultimate source of price objectivity, may be understood as a consequence rather than the cause of index creation, as indeed stressed by some respondents to these public consultations who explained that, by providing standardized, easily accessible information about a certain market sector or commodity, a new index may increase the visibility of such a sector or commodity, ending up stimulating further negotiation (see AFG, 2013, p. 3; ICE, 2013, p. 4). This means that benchmarks, in addition to being multi-referential and multifunctional, also prove performative, and this both in the positive sense – when a market develops in their image – and in the negative sense – when the represented market ceases to exist (see MacKenzie, 2006, pp. 16–20, for a discussion of the different performativity modalities). However, such a tension between facticity and what may be called fictionality emerges only episodically in these various discussions around index production, with regulators insisting upon the relevance of actual transactions (or, alternatively, of quotes committed to actual transactions) and internal governance mechanisms to ensure accurate reporting.

In the end, some minor changes were introduced into the production of Libor and Euribor – although the reform process is not yet complete. Apart from the already mentioned replacements at the administration and calculation levels, the number of tenures was considerably reduced (from 16 to 7 in the case of Libor and 15 to 8 in the case of Euribor) and a 24-hour delay of rate public release was introduced. A significant exodus of Euribor panel members (from 44 to 24) also deserves mention, especially because it forced regulators to intervene by declaring Libor and Euribor panel membership mandatory – a move that may indicate the club days are now over. Finally, efforts towards the development of parallel interbank rates drawing more substantially on actual transaction data are currently underway: private company STOXX has launched two rival benchmarks in 2013 while both the Federal Reserve and the European Money Markets

Institute are still working on viable substitutes to, respectively, Libor and Euribor. In this respect, the G20 has requested the launching of an alternative to Libor by 2016.

Conclusion

Notwithstanding the historical resilience of certain accounting standards and the irreversible character of computer technology, there is much about global finance and credit that appears precarious and fragile (cf. Carruthers and Ariovich, 2010, p. 3). The recent Libor/Euribor affair is but an episode of a turbulent saga of devaluations and miscalculations that intensified after the 2008 financial meltdown and brought forth the issue of financial reform as a more or less permanent necessity (see Lanchester, 2013 for a review of recent banking scandals). In such circumstances, it is obviously difficult to come up with straightforward answers and clear-cut solutions. In any case, the perspective outlined in this chapter suggests that other issues should be taken into consideration alongside facticity enhancement through recourse to transaction-based evidence and internal governance mechanisms. The history of Libor configures a movement from convenient practicality to contagious expansion that favoured innovative manipulation attempts and ended up in mandatory reproduction to avoid panel exodus and any immediate index discontinuation. Contrary to what some might think, such a movement is far from surprising, this chapter having proposed a few arguments that clearly help in illuminating why this is so.

First, the Libor rate was invented by elite international banks acting in a highly deregulated market (the London Eurodollar market) and committed to finding a solution for handling long-term interest rate risk. These actors were in very favourable position to setting the rules of the game: they gathered privileged data from among themselves and developed a new calculation. Thus, in a sense, they were innovators (or *bricoleurs*). However, what passes for innovation is quickly followed by imitation, and even more so in the case of finance. Most financial activity is indeed composed of repetitive goal-directed routines – to borrow an expression from sociologist Anselm Strauss (1993, p. 195). Even inside dealing rooms and other similar hot spots there are lots of things that still tend to be done according to previous lines of procedure – patterning and standardization enabling time economization and more efficient problem solving. As such, the same Libor rate began being used repeatedly for interbank borrowing, and later indexed to other products and starting to perform new functions. This aggregation capacity is mainly explained by the rate's multi-referential and multifunctional potential, which stems from a conjugation of factors: the extant connections between interbank lending and other financial markets, the absence of any patent registration restricting further Libor uses or the emergence of similar rates (such as the antecessors to the Euribor) and the fact that these rates consist of a list of numbers easily copiable from one station to another (as seen in section three a propos Euribor).

Libor's exponential success as a benchmark for the international interbank money market and beyond opened up new possibilities for the former club members then converted into panel banks. What is now recognized as manipulation is but a calculation prerogative of these players which shares many similarities with other forms of financial innovation. One may counter that Libor manipulation was not openly assumed by those practising it, and that these people surely knew that they were themselves cheating and could eventually be caught. The boundaries between right and wrong are, however, not as clear-cut as one might think. There are other financial innovations which appear wrapped up in a veneer of technical expertise before getting described as pure scam in many after-the-fact stories such as the Madoff case. Alternatively, to give a slightly different example, consider the subsequent rounds of calculation and averaging involved in Euribor adaptation to retail loans or deposits: in this case, the new calculations performed opened up the possibility of gaming with rounding off and year extension in a way that forced national regulators to intervene and legislate – though banks were merely capitalizing on a legal void rather than actively manipulating the results. Innovation, just like manipulation, is mainly the result of an advantageous position that subsequently becomes amplified by repetition.

References

Abrantes-Metz, R., Kraten, M., Metz, A. and Seow, G. (2008) 'Libor manipulation?' Retrieved on 13 December 2015 from http://ssrn.com/abstract=1201389 and http://dx.doi.org/10.2139/ssrn.1201389.

AFG (2013) AFG response to the ESMA & EBA consultation on 'Principles for benchmarks-setting processes in the EU'. Retrieved on 13 December 2015 from www.esma.europa.eu/system/files/div_4066_02_afg_response_to_esmaeba_financial_benchmarks_consultation.pdf.

Arrighi, G. [1994] (2010) *The Long Twentieth Century: Money, Power, and the Origins of Our Times*. New York: Verso.

Ashton, P. and Christophers, B. (2015) 'On arbitration, arbitrage and arbitrariness in financial markets and their governance: Unpacking Libor and the Libor scandal', *Economy and Society*, 44(2): 188–217.

BIS (1983) *The International Interbank Market: A Descriptive Study*. Retrieved on 13 December 2015 from www.bis.org/publ/econ8.pdf.

Carruthers, B. and Ariovich, L. (2010) *Money and Credit: A Sociological Approach*. Cambridge: Polity Press.

EMMI-European Money Market Institute (2014) *Euribor® Code of Conduct*. Retrieved on 13 December 2015 from www.emmibenchmarks.eu/assets/files/Euribor_code_conduct.pdf.

Engelen, E., Ertürk, I., Froud, J., Leaver, A. and Williams, K. (2010) 'Reconceptualizing financial innovation: Frame, conjuncture and bricolage', *Economy and Society*, 39(1): 33–63.

ESMA-EBA (2013) 'Principles for benchmark-setting processes in the EU'. Paris: ESMA.

EUREX (2013) 'Eurex response to IOSCO consultation report on financial benchmarks'. Retrieved on 13 December 2015 from www.iosco.org/library/pubdocs/399/pdf/Eurex,%20Frankfurt.pdf.

European Commission (2012) 'Consultation document on the regulation of indices'. Retrieved on 13 December 2015 from http://ec.europa.eu/internal_market/consultations/docs/2012/benchmarks/consultationdocument_en.pdf.

ICE (2013) 'Public comment on financial benchmarks (CR01/13 IOSCO consultation report on financial benchmarks)'. Retrieved on 13 December 2015 from www.iosco.org/library/pubdocs/399/pdf/ICE%20Futures%20Europe%20%20ICE%20Clear%20Europe%20Ltd.pdf.

Kiff, J. (2012) 'What is Libor? The London Interbank Rate is used widely as a benchmark but has come under fire', *Finance and Development*, 49(4): 32–3.

Kirti, D. (2014) 'What are reference rates for?' Retrieved on 13 December 2015 from http://scholar.harvard.edu/dkirti/publications/what-are-reference-rates.

Knorr Cetina, K. and Bruegger, U. (2002) 'Inhabiting technology: The global lifeform of financial markets', *Current Sociology*, 50(3): 389–405.

Lanchester, J. (2013) 'Are we having fun yet?', *London Review of Books*, 35(1): 3–8.

Lopes, D.S. (2013) 'Metamorphoses of credit: Pastiche production and the ordering of mass payment behavior', *Economy and Society*, 42(1): 26–50.

Luhmann, N. [1997] (2012) *Theory of Society, Vol. 1*. Stanford: Stanford University Press.

MacKenzie, D. (2006) *An Engine, not a Camera: How Financial Models Shape Markets*. Cambridge, MA: The MIT Press.

MacKenzie, D. (2009) *Material Markets: How Economic Agents Are Constructed*. Oxford: Oxford University Press.

Marron, D. (2009) *Consumer Credit in the United States: A Sociological Perspective from the 19th Century to the Present*. New York: Palgrave Macmillan.

Marston, R. (2015) 'Libor rates could be exchanged for a Mars bar, court hears'. Retrieved on 19 December 2015 from www.bbc.com/news/business-33448210.

Mollenkamp, C. (2008) 'Libor fog: bankers cast doubt on key rate amid crisis', *Wall Street Journal*, 16 April. Retrieved on 13 December 2015 from www.wsj.com/articles/SB120831164167818299.

Money Week (2008) 'Libor: the world's most important number'. Retrieved on 13 December 2015 from http://moneyweek.com/libor-the-worlds-most-important-number-13816/.

Norris, F. (2012) 'The myth of fixing the Libor', *New York Times*, 28 September, B1. Retrieved on 13 December 2015 from www.nytimes.com/2012/09/28/business/the-myth-of-fixing-the-libor-high-lowfinance.html?_r=2&ref=business&.

Ojo, M. (2014) 'Libor, Euribor, and the regulation of capital markets: a review of the Efficient Market Hypothesis', *Strategic Change: Briefings in Entrepreneurial Finance*, 23: 119–24.

Rauterberg, G. and Verstein, A. (2013) 'Index theory: The law, promise and failure of financial indices', *The Yale Journal on Regulation*, 30: 1–61.

Raymond, N. and Viswanatha, A. (2014) 'US regulator sues 16 banks for rigging Libor rate'. Retrieved on 13 December 2015 from www.reuters.com/article/2014/03/14/us-fdic-libor-idUSBREA2D1KR20140314.

Ridley, K. and Jones, H. (2012) 'A Greek banker spills on the early days of the Libor and his first deal with the Shah of Iran'. Retrieved on 13 December 2015 from www.businessinsider.com/history-of-the-libor-rate-2012-8.

Snider, C.A. and Youle, T. (2010) 'Does the Libor reflect bank's borrowing costs?' Retrieved on 13 December 2015 from http://papers.ssrn.com/sol3/papers.cfm?abstract_id=1569603.

Snider, C.A. and Youle, T. (2012) 'The fix is in: detecting portfolio driven manipulation of the Libor'. Retrieved on 13 December 2015 from www.dartmouth.edu/~tyoule/documents/main_paper_2%281%29.pdf.

STOXX (2012) 'STOXX Ltd. response to public consultation by the European Commission on the regulation of indices'. Retrieved on 13 December 2015 from http://ec.europa.eu/internal_market/consultations/2012/benchmarks/registeredorganisations/stoxx_en.df.

Strauss, A. (1993) *Continual Permutations of Action*. New York: Aldine de Gruyter.

Tett, G. (2007) 'Libor's value is called into question', *Financial Times*, 25 September. Retrieved on 13 December 2015 from www.ft.com/cms/s/0/8c7dd45e-6b9c-11dc-863b-0000779fd2ac.html#axzz3QECI8aIw.

Tett, G. (2009) *Fool's Gold: How Unrestrained Greed Corrupted a Dream, Shattered Global Markets and Unleashed a Catastrophe*. London: Little, Brown.

The Economist (2012) 'The Libor scandal: The rotten heart of finance' (7 July). Retrieved on 13 December 2015 from www.economist.com/node/21558281.

Touryalai, H. (2012) 'Banks rigged Libor to inflate adjustable-rate mortgages: Lawsuit'. Retrieved on 16 January 2015 from www.forbes.com/sites/halahtouryalai/2012/10/15/banks-rigged-libor-to-inflate-adjustablerate-mortgages-lawsuit/.

YouTube (2013) 'CFTC public roundtable to discuss IOSCO consultation report on financial benchmarks'. Retrieved on 19 December 2015 from www.youtube.com/watch?v=duUODyMdnsE.

Westbrook, D. (2010) *Out of Crisis: Rethinking Our Financial Markets*. Boulder, CO: Paradigm.

Zachary, M.D. (2009) 'The Belgian mortgage market in a European perspective', *Economic Review* (National Bank of Belgium), III, pp. 93–108. Retrieved on 13 December 2015 from www.nbb.be/doc/ts/publications/economicreview/2009/revecoiii2009e_h5.pdf.

13
Hedge funds
Past and present

Photis Lysandrou

Introduction

Hedge funds are a unique type of financial institution. Unlike banks that traditionally perform a 'transformation' function (liquidity, risk or maturity transformation) hedge funds merely perform a 'transfer' function in that assets placed under their management by clients are redeployed with the aim of generating better returns than is possible for those clients. Freed from the type of regulatory and fiduciary constraints that are binding on other institutional investors such as pension and mutual funds, hedge funds are not obliged to factor risk on anything like the same scale into their return generating strategies, a feature which explains why the latter are usually classified as 'absolute return' strategies. Finally, the multiplicity of their investment strategies are what distinguish hedge funds from the more specialised private equity firms that represent the other major type of 'alternative investment' vehicle. Before reviewing these strategies and their wider implications, we begin with a brief history of hedge fund development.

The development of hedge funds

The story of hedge funds is usually said to begin with Alfred Jones' partnership, 'A.W. Jones and Co', established in the US in 1949. The latter's basic strategy, based on what Jones called his 'hedge principle', was to combine long positions in stocks that were deemed undervalued with the short selling of stocks that were deemed overvalued. Jones' success in generating unusually high returns over the next two decades (one estimation puts the cumulative returns between 1949 and 1968 at around 5000 per cent) helped to spawn imitators, particularly following the publication of a profile of Jones in *Fortune* magazine in 1966 in which the term 'hedge fund' was first used. A 1968 survey by the Securities Exchange Commission found that about 140 hedge funds had been established in the US by that time. Since then, the hedge fund industry has grown to a size sufficient enough to make it a powerful force in the global financial landscape: an estimated 10,000 funds were operating in 2007 on the eve of the financial crisis (approximately 70 per cent of which were based in New York with a further 26 per cent based in London) with assets under their management totalling approximately $1.5 trillion. Although the hedge fund sector, in common with many other financial sectors, suffered a decline in 2009–10 following the devastations of the subprime crisis, this decline has since been more than reversed as evidenced by the fact that by mid-2015 assets under hedge fund management were in the region of $2.7 trillion (Barclay Hedge, 2015).

The expansion of the hedge fund industry over the past six and a half decades can be divided into three distinct phases: (1) 1950–80; (2) 1980–2000; (3) 2000–present. The factors demarcating the first and second of these growth phases broadly relate to differences in the general investment philosophy of the hedge funds on the one hand and to differences in the general economic environment in which they operated on the other. Where the hedge funds of both periods were quintessentially speculative vehicles, borrowing heavily to leverage up their bets, the early hedge funds would typically avoid market risk by combining their bets in a particular asset class with offsetting positions in the same asset class, while their later counterparts would on the contrary typically embrace market risk. This is why some commentators argue that 'wager' or 'speculative' funds are now a more accurate description of hedge funds than is this latter term. Similarly, while the conservative, market risk avoiding approach of the early hedge funds was broadly reflective of an era where a battery of government controls and regulations ensured that the financial sector remained relatively small in scale and largely passive in character, the aggressive, market risk embracing approach of the later hedge funds was entirely in keeping with the opportunities offered by the new realities of the post Bretton Woods era, chief amongst these realities being the huge growth in the scale and volatility of the now largely deregulated financial markets.

The third period of hedge fund growth beginning in the early 2000s sees further changes in hedge fund investment strategy, which will be documented below, but the more significant change that occurred at this time was the 'institutionalisation' of the hedge fund client base. From 1950 right through to 2000, rich individuals (the so-called 'high net worth individuals') were the only major source of money pouring into the hedge funds. From this time on, however, institutional investors including pension funds, endowments and funds of funds, also became an important source of investments in hedge funds as can be gauged by the fact that while individuals accounted for 95 per cent of hedge fund assets in 2000 their percentage share had fallen to approximately 50 per cent in 2007 (IFSL, 2008). The principal development triggering this very sudden change in the hedge fund client base was the fall in yields in all of the major US bond markets in the early to mid-2000s (initially caused by the low federal fund rate and then sustained by the huge influx of foreign public and private investments funds into the US).[1] In their search for yield, institutional investors turned to the hedge funds as part of the solution to the problem.

Hedge fund strategies

Hedge fund investment strategies divide into two broad categories: 'market-neutral' and 'directional'. The market neutral category aims to obtain returns that are uncorrelated with market movements and include 'arbitrage' strategies (these exploit price differences within and across financial markets) 'event-driven' strategies (these exploit opportunities created by specific transaction events such as mergers, spin-offs and share buy-backs or by specific situations such as corporate bankruptcies) and equity market-neutral strategies (these exploit price differences in equity markets through long/short combinations). The directional category aims to obtain returns by speculating on market movements and includes 'macro' strategies (taking bets on movements in stock market prices, interest rates, currency exchange rates and commodity prices) and 'emerging market' strategies (investing long in emerging markets' sovereign debts and corporate securities).

Up to the late 1990s, directional strategies were the most popular amongst hedge funds with the 'macro' subcategory alone accounting for approximately 55 per cent of all assets under management in 1997. Of the many examples of how hedge funds profited handsomely from macro strategies in this period, two of the most prominent involved speculative bets against currencies' fixed exchange rates. The first case concerns the British pound's rate in the European Exchange Rate Mechanism. Established in 1990 when Britain joined the ERM, sterling's rate against the Deutschmark came under massive attack from macro hedge funds led by George Soros' Quantum Fund that had built up a short position in sterling over the summer of that year to the tune of about $10 billion. Although the Bank of England raised interest rates on 16 September 1992, following weeks of spending huge amounts of its foreign exchange reserves (about $15 billion), it was forced later that day ('Black Wednesday') to admit defeat and take the pound out of the ERM. The pound's immediate depreciation against the Deutschmark brought immediate profits for the hedge funds and other speculators with Soros alone making an estimated profit of about $1 billion. The same speculative tactics were used five years later in the summer of 1997, when the Thai baht and subsequently a number of other Asian currencies were forced off their dollar pegs through the massive short selling of these currencies, the resulting devaluations again generating substantial windfall profits for Soros' Quantum Fund and for other macro hedge funds.

By the mid-2000s, hedge fund assets were not only more evenly divided between the directional and market neutral strategies but also more evenly spread across the different subcategories. Thus 'macro' strategies accounted for only about 12 per cent of assets in 2007, compared to 55 per cent a decade earlier, while arbitrage and event driven strategies increased their share to 26 per cent and 21 per cent respectively (Blundell-Wignall, 2007). This shift towards a greater diversity of hedge fund strategies was only one of the manifestations of the new competitive pressures in the hedge fund industry accompanying the increase in the number of firms operating within it (this number doubled between 2002 and 2007, from 5000 to the 10,000 figure noted above). Other important manifestations of the new competition were the increased use of derivatives and other sophisticated financial instruments in the execution of investment strategies (such instruments barely figured in the currency speculation episodes of the 1990s described above) and the exploitation of new advances in computerised trading technology.

Of particular importance in respect of this last point is the advent of High Frequency Trading, a subset of Automated Trading (the other subset comprising of Algorithmic Trading) conducted primarily, if not exclusively, by the hedge funds so as to extract profits from any price disturbances in the major equity markets. As such disturbances, typically associated with the equity portfolio balancing trades of mutual funds and other large institutional investors, are likely to be very small (due to an assortment of price-minimising trading techniques deployed by these investors that include the use of crossing networks and dark pools, the 'slicing and dicing' of large orders and their simultaneous routing through multiple trading platforms) hedge funds programme their computers to trade the same stocks many times over, as many as forty or fifty times a day, so as to extract any profits from these trades. This fact helps to explain why hedge funds currently account for a very large percentage of the daily trading in the major equity markets even while they hold a much smaller fraction of the total shares outstanding (Stowell, 2012).

Not all hedge funds can consistently deliver above average returns and thus justify their above average fees, and when those that do, it is not only because of the sophistication of their investment strategies or because of the superiority of their knowledge and technical expertise. It can also be because, unencumbered by the moral or ethical considerations that constrain other more socially responsible investors, hedge funds can pursue return maximising strategies that go beyond what is normally considered acceptable.

A good illustration of this point is the deal called ABACUS 2007-AC1 arranged between Goldman Sachs and the hedge fund manager John Paulson. Paulson approached Goldman Sachs in late 2006 saying that he wanted to bet against risky subprime mortgages using derivatives. Goldman Sachs knew that the German bank IKB was willing to buy the exposure that Paulson was looking to short but that IKB would only do so if the mortgage securities were selected by an outsider. Thus in January 2007, Goldman approached ACA Management LLC, a bond insurer, which agreed to work with Paulson in constructing a portfolio of subprime-backed securities (CDOs) that would then be marketed by Goldman Sachs. IKB took some $150 million of the portfolio's risk exposure while ABN Amro, a Dutch bank recently acquired by a consortium led by Royal Bank of Scotland, took $909 million of exposure. What Goldman Sachs (that had received a $15 million fee from Paulson) never told ACA or IKB and ABN Amro is that Paulson had shorted the toxic securities that he himself had picked, a clear example of conflict of interest (ACA was in fact led to believe that Paulson wanted to own some of the riskiest parts of the securities). In the summer of 2007 with the outbreak of the subprime crisis, IKB lost all of its $150 million investment while RBS in late 2007 unwound ABN's position in ABACUS by paying Goldman Sachs $840.1 million. Most of that money went to Paulson who made a total profit of about $1 billion. Interestingly, when Paulson appeared before a US congressional hearing on the financial crisis in December, 2008, along with other hedge fund leaders including George Soros, he claimed that he knew nothing of the highly toxic nature of the CDOs that were at the epicentre of the crisis (Kirchgaessner and Sender, 2008).

A more general form of unethical behaviour on the part of hedge funds is the notorious 'hold-up' strategy, one which has understandably led those hedge funds that use this strategy to be categorised as 'vulture funds'. This strategy refers to the practice whereby hedge funds buy the bonds of indebted countries cheaply, resist their debt restructuring proposals, and then sue for full repayment. One example is when Themis Capital and Des Moines Investments Ltd won a case concerning $18m of debt from the Democratic Republic of Congo, in which they had invested. A New York judge ordered the country to repay the investors the full amount borrowed plus interest, an amount that came to $70m, as the debt originated from the early 1980s under the Mobutu regime. Another example is that when Greece restructured almost €200bn of bonds in 2012, hedge funds holding €6bn worth held out against the deal, and were repaid by Greece in full. Yet another example concerns the Argentinian government's continuing resistance against the litigious attempts of certain hedge funds, such as the US based Elliot Associates controlled by Paul Singer, to be paid the full face value plus interests of Argentinian government bonds issued in 2001 even though these had been purchased by the hedge funds at a fraction of their face value. A powerful blow against the 'hold-up' strategy deployed by hedge funds was delivered in September, 2014, when the United Nations General Assembly voted overwhelmingly to adopt a new global framework for sovereign debt restructuring, one that would strengthen nations' right to seek protection from creditors.

Benefits and costs of hedge funds

Hedge funds are said to confer a number of benefits, the foremost of which concern market liquidity and financial innovation. In addition to High Frequency Trading, many of the other hedge fund strategies that were outlined above involve heavy trading with the result that the share of hedge funds in the daily trading volumes in many financial markets is out of all proportion to the size of their assets. Thus the hedge funds' share of trading represents a high ratio not only in the major stock exchanges, but also in the bond markets (Institutional Investor, 2012). The trading behaviour of hedge funds is said to be beneficial in that by improving the liquidity of the financial markets they thereby enhance price discovery and reduce the possibility of pricing inefficiencies all of which in turn helps to lower the costs of financing for corporations. Hedge funds are also said to have a beneficial impact on the financial markets insofar as they force the pace of development of new financial instruments and technologies that can in turn facilitate a more efficient allocation of risk across market participants and a better management of risk within portfolios.

On a wider note, hedge funds are said to help promote economic efficiency by virtue of acting as a vital intermediary medium through which market discipline is imposed on governments. Thus when George Soros' Quantum Fund and other hedge funds came under criticism for making substantial profits from speculating the British pound out of the ERM in 1992 and from speculating the Asian currencies off their dollar pegs in 1997, their standard line of defence was that the targeted governments had no business in setting exchange rates according to political priorities rather than according to market fundamentals and that all that their speculative actions had done was to allow these fundamentals to reassert themselves. Similarly, those 'hold-out' hedge funds that today face heavy criticism from their attempts to extract maximum pay-outs from indebted governments typically argue that, as this indebtedness was invariably the result of poor economic governance in the past, the up-side of their hold-out strategy is to force better economic governance in the future.

On the cost side of the equation, the chief dangers posed by hedge funds are that they can greatly increase market volatility and systemic risk. Take first market volatility. As already stated, hedge funds account for a substantial proportion of trades in many markets and while the spreading of trades across assets can help improve liquidity and price efficiency it is also possible that a particular event or disturbance can lead to 'herding' i.e. the concentration of trades on particular assets or the convergence in particular strategies, which can subsequently amplify the effects of the original disturbance. A good example of this type of problem was the US' stock exchanges 'flash crash' of 2010, when on 6 May of that year, shortly after 2.00pm, the Dow Jones Industrial Average fell by about 1000 points (9 per cent) before a near full recovery was made a few minutes later. Although the initial decline was triggered by a mutual fund selling an unusually large number of financial contracts tied to the S&P 500, that decline was subsequently amplified by the hedge funds' high frequency trades of the same contracts.

Take next systemic risk. Hedge funds are still comparatively small in size, but their heavy use of leverage means that should one fail at any time this could create contagion across asset classes as its positions are unwound. Furthermore, the failure of a highly levered hedge fund could have a general destabilising on the banking system as a consequence of interlocking financial ties. The difficulties of Long-Term Capital Management in 1998 illustrates the point. Founded in 1994 by John Meriwether, a former bond trader at Saloman Brothers, and having amongst its principal partners Myron Scholes and Robert Merton (future Nobel Prize winners for their work on the pricing of options derivatives), this hedge fund specialised in using complex derivatives to leverage up absolute-return trading strategies. The principle instrument traded were government bonds, and the principal bet was that government bond prices would tend to converge in the new era of the 'great moderation' and globally integrated financial markets. However, following first the Asian crisis of 1997 and the Russian rouble crisis of 1998 (when the Russian government defaulted on its bonds), the price differences between emerging market bonds and advanced market bonds widened significantly as investors sought the safety of the latter. As a consequence, far from making substantial profits, LTCM quickly ran up a debt of over $3 billion on its derivative exposures. Its collapse may or may not have brought down the US banking system, but the fact remains that Alan Greenspan, the then chairman of the US Federal Reserve, was not prepared to take the risk. Under his supervision, an agreement was reached on 23 September 1998 under which 16 leading US banks put up a $3.6 billion bailout fund. While LTCM survived thus eliminating its threat to the US banking, the firm was eventually closed down two years later. Another, more recent example of the potential systemic risk posed by hedge funds is provided by the events surrounding the subprime crisis and the immediate after effects over the period 2007–08. Although the collapse of the conduits and of other shadow banking vehicles were in this period the principle source of the pressures that threatened the very survival of the banking system and that required heavy government intervention to fend off this threat, another important source of that pressure was the collapse of some 3500 of the 10,000 hedge funds operating at that time (King, 2011).

In addition to the economic costs of hedge funds there are also the social costs, chief amongst which are those connected with wealth redistribution. If the unprecedented levels of wealth concentration amongst the world's high net worth individuals represents the single the most important source of hedge fund's finance, so do the latters' investment activities help to further accelerate this global wealth concentration. Thus when Paulson pocketed for himself and his wealthy clients about $1 billion profit from the ABACUS deal, the bulk of that money (over $800 million) had come from British taxpayers inasmuch as it was the British Labour government that had bailed out RBS when it faced bankruptcy owing to its exposure to that disastrous deal. Taxpayers were also similarly hit when hold-up hedge funds succeeded in extracting billions of dollars from Greece and other indebted countries in the more recent period. That this represents wealth redistribution on a large scale becomes even more clear when one takes into account that it is the low to mid income households who bear the majority of the tax burden given that they simply do not have the means of exploiting the same sophisticated tax avoidance or tax minimising schemes as do the very high income individuals.

Role of the hedge funds in the subprime crisis

The realisation that hedge funds have the potential to seriously disrupt the financial markets has prompted calls for these private investment vehicles to be made subject to the same disclosure standards and regulatory constraints as are currently binding on the public investment vehicles. While these calls began to be made before the outbreak of the subprime crisis in 2007, they became louder and more insistent after the crisis. Given that what began as a crisis in the market for subprime-backed securities rapidly mutated into the worst global economic crisis since the Great Depression, it stands to reason that the hedge funds would have been clamped down very quickly had it been generally recognised that these institutions bore the major responsibility for the growth of the toxic securities. However, this was not the case. Rather, the general consensus was that it was the banks and their associates who created the structured finance CDOs that were chiefly responsible for the subprime crisis. Even in continental Europe, where the drive towards closer regulation of the hedge funds is at its most powerful, it is still widely accepted that the hedge funds played a secondary, amplifying role in the crisis rather than a primary, causal one. To quote from a report published in February, 2009, by the High-Level Group on Financial Supervision in the EU: 'Concerning hedge funds, the Group considers they did not play a major role in the emergence of the crisis. Their role has largely been limited to a transmission function, notably through massive selling of shares and short-selling transactions'.[2]

This conclusion is wrong. The hedge funds may have played no part in the actual construction of the CDOs that were at the epicentre of the crisis but this is not the point. The point is that had it not been for the hedge funds' unique intermediary position between the investors seeking yield on the one side and the banks who created the high yielding securities on the other, the supply of these securities could never have reached the proportions that were critical to causing the collapse of the whole financial system. There should never have existed a mass market for CDOs given that their complex and opaque structure broke all the rules of commodity exchange and without the hedge funds such a market would not in fact have existed. Wealthy individuals did not have the requisite expertise to participate in this market while liquidity and other considerations prevented institutional asset managers from having more than a limited participation. In both cases, the preferred solution to the yield problem which was becoming increasingly acute after 2001 was to pour money into the hedge funds who in turn believed that one of the surest ways of satisfying the demand for yield was to redirect substantial proportions of this money into CDOs.[3]

By the end of 2006, there was approximately $3trillion worth of CDOs outstanding with about one-third of this sum comprising of 'cash' CDOs and the other two thirds comprising of 'synthetic' CDOs (Borio, 2008). It has been estimated that the hedge funds held about 60 per cent of the cash CDOs and about 30 per cent of the synthetic CDOS while the banks, insurance companies and pension and mutual funds held the rest.[4] After the subprime crisis, the hedge funds played the role of the innocent and gullible investor,[5] but far from being lured by the banks into buying the CDOs they on the contrary pressured the banks into accelerating the rate of supply of these products, particularly of the super senior and senior variety.[6] They did so because these triple-A rated products served a double purpose for the hedge funds in that on the one hand they generated a higher return than did US treasuries even while having the same rating and on the other hand they could be used as collateral in credit arrangements on account of their high rating. Given that hedge funds borrow heavily from their prime brokers to leverage up their various exposures it was only logical that they should use CDOs as collateral to reduce borrowing costs, while the prime brokers for their part were obliged to accept the CDOs as collateral in reverse repos given that it was they themselves who helped to create these structured credit products in the first place.

Regulation of the hedge funds

The privileges that are unique to hedge funds and certain other types of private investment vehicle have traditionally been divided into two categories: (a) they have not been subject to strict disclosure rules regarding their investment strategies and (b) they have not been subject to tight restrictions regarding the financial products and practices that they can use to implement these strategies. The fact that policymakers acknowledged the complicity of the hedge funds in the subprime crisis means that these vehicles will henceforth lose the first of their traditional privileges. Thus, following the enactment of the Dodd–Frank act in July 2010, hedge funds operating in the United States are required to register with state or federal financial authorities and to comply with their guidelines regarding transparency and disclosure.[7] Similarly in Europe, hedge funds will in the future only be allowed to operate across all of the Member States of the European Union if they register with the newly created European Securities and Markets authority and agree to comply with its reporting standards.[8]

However, the fact that policymakers continue to believe that the hedge funds did not play a major causal role in the subprime crisis means that these institutions will not lose the second of their traditional privileges. Although financial authorities will have the right to impose restrictions on hedge funds' use of certain products (e.g. swaps and other derivatives) and trading practices (e.g. short selling) whenever deemed necessary, the more substantive point is that the hedge funds will continue to be generally exempt from the constraints that are currently binding on the activities of other financial vehicles such as pension and mutual funds.

Hedge fund resurgence

Following a temporary stall in the immediate post-subprime crisis period, assets under hedge fund management have again started to grow at a rapid pace. This hedge fund resurgence is likely to continue for the foreseeable future for two sets of reasons, one to do with enablement and the other to do with motivation.

The key enabling factor is that hedge funds will, as has just been observed, continue to face far lighter regulation than do other types of institutional investor. Hedge funds may find the new transparency and reporting constraints to be an unwelcome nuisance, but these constraints will do little to hamper their use of unconventional, and often unethical, techniques and strategies to generate above average yields, which is what after all gives hedge funds their raison d'être. It should be further noted that hedge funds have escaped heavier and more effective regulation not only because they were largely absolved from complicity in causing the subprime crisis but also because of the political weight that they carry in the two major countries where they are based, the US and the UK. If the Republican Party in the US is opposed to any further tightening of hedge fund regulation, this is not a little to do with the fact that hedge funds are an important donor of funds to the Party as holds true in the case of the UK's Conservative Party where hedge funds, together with private equity firms, now account for about 27 per cent of all donations (Mathiason and Bessaoud, 2011).

Foremost among the motivating factors driving hedge fund resurgence is the parallel resurgence of global wealth concentration. While the combined wealth of the world's high net worth individuals fell from about $40 trillion in 2007 to an average of $36 trillion in 2008–09, that wealth has again grown, reaching $56.4 trillion in 2014 (Capgemini-RBC Wealth Management, 2015). Much of this wealth is stored in an assortment of relatively safe assets (ranging from blue chip corporate securities and government bonds to real estate and cash), but a significant proportion continues to be allocated to the higher yield-higher risk alternative investments class, including hedge funds. Another, equally important driver behind the new phase of hedge fund growth are the extremely low yields on major government securities, a fact that recalls similar developments in the run up to the financial crisis. The problem is that although the global demand for safe haven US treasuries and other advanced economy government bonds continues to rise in the current era of low economic growth and heighted uncertainty, the rate of supply of good quality investable government bonds has been constrained by fears that overstepping a specified government debt to GDP threshold (the Reinhart–Rogoff 90 per cent threshold figure being the most widely invoked) would spell disaster. As if these fears did not have a powerful enough dampening effect on government bond supplies, and thus on bond yields, what has served to make matters even worse is the reliance on monetary policy, in the form of Quantitative Easing, as a major way of lifting domestic economies out of recession. With bond yields at or close to zero by virtue of central bank bond purchases, it is little wonder that institutional investors such as pension and mutual funds who have to meet obligations to their clients are increasing their investments in hedge funds in a desperate attempt to find extra yield. There can be no better illustration of this desperation than the fact that, despite facing heavy criticism in bartering its moral principles for material gain, the Church of England has recently increased its exposure to hedge funds from about 4 per cent of its £600 million pension fund to over 10 per cent (Jones, 2012).

Conclusion

The fundamental question that arises out of the above discussion is whether hedge funds are necessary to the functioning of the contemporary financial markets and thus to the continued development of capitalism. Aside from the hedge funds themselves, there is a body of academic and official opinion that answers this question in the affirmative.[9] However, the peculiar circumstances surrounding the emergence and subsequent growth of the hedge funds point to a different answer. The idea of hedge funds may have originated in 1949 when Alfred Jones went long in some assets to hedge his short positions in other assets, but they only became properly established as private pools of capital in the 1980s with the shift towards neo-liberal macro policies and the consequent rise in the scale and concentration of private wealth. Since that time the hedge funds have grown in tandem with the growth in the number of high net worth individuals and in the volume of assets owned by them, but if this trend towards the increasing concentration of wealth ownership was ever to be reversed the flow of cash into the hedge funds originating from this particular source would dry up in an instant. So also would the flow of cash originating from institutional investors if bond and other securities markets were to become more developed in Asia, Latin America and in other parts of the world. These investors would not have become major clients of the hedge funds in the early- to mid-2000s had the rate of growth in the global supply of investable securities kept with up with the rate of growth in global demand, for in this event the yield problem would not have become as acute as it did and consequently the need to rely on the hedge funds for yield would not have become as intense. The same line of argument also holds true today in that were the global supply and demand for investable securities more evenly matched, there would not be a yield problem on the scale forcing institutional investors into the arms of the hedge funds. In the final analysis, hedge funds continue to exist and continue to grow because of continuing anomalies in the global capitalist system rather than because they constitute an essential part of that system.

Notes

1 For more detail on this point see Goda, Lysandrou and Stewart (2013).
2 The High Level Group on Financial Supervision in the EU (2009).
3 For a more detailed exposition of this argument see Lysandrou (2011).
4 Blundell-Wignall (2007); House of Commons (2008).
5 When the heads of some of the biggest US hedge funds were called before a US Senate hearing on the subprime crisis in November, 2008, they declared that they were in no way to blame for the financial carnage. The 'focal point of carnage', to quote Kenneth Griffin one of the hedge fund chiefs, was not us 'but the regulated institutions, the commercial banks who originated and securitised the subprime mortgages and the investment banks who then used these securities as backing for Collateralised Debt Obligations and other structured financial products'. By their 'fanciful' ratings of these products, to quote James Simmons another of the hedge fund chiefs, the credit rating agencies must take particular blame for the carnage in that they facilitated the sale of 'sows ears as silk purses' (Kirchgaessner and Sender, 2008).
6 To quote from testimony given by Gerald Corrigan of Goldman Sachs at the 2008 House of Commons hearing on the financial crisis: 'To a significant degree it has been the reach for yield on the part of institutional investors in particular that goes a considerable distance in explaining this very rapid growth of structured credit products' (House of Commons, 2008).
7 Under the terms of Article IV of the Dodd–Frank act, only hedge funds with less than $25 million assets under management (AUM) will retain private investor exemption. hedge funds with between $25 million and $100 million AUM will be required to register with the state in which they operate, while hedge funds that operate in over 15 states or have over $100 million AUM will be required to register with the Securities and Exchange Commission. A further point worth noting is that in order

to limit the potential risks to commercial banks from hedge fund activities, Article VI of the Dodd–Frank act sets the limit to bank shareholdings in hedge funds at 3 per cent.

8   The initial position of some EU states, including France, was to require foreign hedge funds operating in Europe to register with the financial authorities of each Member State; however, following opposition from the United States and the United Kingdom, which argued that this policy would not only be cumbersome but also highly discriminatory, a compromise solution was reached in October 2010 whereby, after an initial transition period, pan-European marketing rights (the so-called 'EU passports') will also be available to foreign hedge funds. See Tait (2010).

9   See, for example, McKinsey Global Institute (2007), or Danielsson et al. (2004), or Stulz (2007).

References

Barclay Hedge (2015) Alternative Income Database.

Blundell-Wignall, A. (2007) 'An overview of hedge funds and structured products: Issues of leverage and risk', OECD.

Borio, C. (2008) 'The financial turmoil of 2007?: A preliminary assessment and some policy considerations', BIS Working Papers No 251, March.

Capgemini-RBC Wealth Management (2015) World Wealth Report.

Danielsson, J., Taylor, A. and Zigrand, J.P. (2004) 'Highwaymen or heroes: Should hedge funds be regulated?', London School of Economics, November.

Goda, T., Lysandrou, P. and Stewart, C. (2013) 'The contribution of US bond demand to the US bond yield conundrum of 2004 to 2007: An empirical investigation', *Journal of International Financial Markets, Institutions and Money*, 27: 113–36.

House of Commons. (2008) Treasury Committee, *Report on Financial Stability and Transparency*, 26 February.

IFSL (2008) Hedge funds 2008, retrieved on 3 May 2015 from www.ifsl.org.uk.

Institutional Investor. (2012) 'Study confirms hedge funds are taking over bond trading from banks', 28 August.

Jones, S. (2012) 'Church of England doubles hedge fund investments'. *Financial Times*, 30 November.

King, M. (2011) 'We prevented a Great Depression', *Daily Telegraph interview*, 11 March.

Kirchgaessner, S. and Sender, H. (2008) 'hedge fund chiefs blame the system for financial crisis', *Financial Times*, 13 November, available at www.ft.com.

Lysandrou, P. (2011) 'The primacy of hedge funds in the subprime crisis', *Journal of Post-Keynesian Economics*, 34, 2.

Mathiason, N and Bessaoud, Y. (2011) 'Tory Party funding from City doubles under Cameron', *The Bureau of Investigative Journalism*, February.

McKinsey Global Institute. (2007) 'Hedge funds: From mavericks to mainstream', Chapter 4 of *The new power brokers: How oil, Asia, hedge funds and private equity are shaping global capital markets*, October.

Stowell, D. (2012) *Investment Banks, Hedge Funds, and Private Equity*. London: Academic Press.

Stulz, R. (2007) 'Hedge funds: past, present and future', *Journal of Economic Perspectives*, 21, 2.

Tait, N. (2010) 'Brussels agrees tougher rules for hedge fund', *Financial Times*, October 19, available at www.ft.com/intl.

14
Offshore financial centres and tax evasion in banking

Silke Ötsch and Michaela Schmidt

Offshore finance is a sector that has grown considerably since the 1970s. For the majority of banks and a large number of companies, the use of offshore jurisdictions tends to be the rule rather than the exception. Offshore economies are not only significant because of their dimensions; in our view, they embody a parallel set of economic rules used by financial and economic elites to circumvent democratic rules on financial regulation and the repartition of funds. In this chapter, we will explain the notion of the offshore economy and its related terms; introduce some academic approaches and theories on the offshore sector; describe the development of offshore finance and tax evasion; outline its actors, techniques, dimensions and effects; and we will finally address regulation. We underline that offshore and onshore economies are closely linked. Offshore finance evolved due to sociocultural, economic, political and technical factors. This is why we have chosen an interdisciplinary approach to outline this complex phenomenon.

The offshore world: tax havens, secrecy jurisdictions and shadow banks

The global financial system has become heavily reliant upon practices and jurisdictions that are known as tax or regulatory havens, offshore financial centres, secrecy jurisdictions and shadow banking entities. There is not a universally accepted, precise definition for what a tax haven or an offshore financial centre is, nor is there broad consensus regarding on what terms this phenomenon should be named. The term *tax haven* – in addition to the French term *paradis fiscal*, or financial paradise – should evoke positive associations and suggest that a tax haven is a desirable place remoted for regulators Yet, tax havens are currently associated with tax evasion and criminality; therefore, most tax havens prefer to call themselves 'offshore financial centers (OFCs)' (Hampton and Christensen, 2007; Palan, 2003, pp. 18–21; for a definition see Palan, Murphy and Chavagneux, 2010, pp. 23–8 and Zoromé, 2007). OFCs have become the denotation of choice by international organizations like the Organisation for Economic Cooperation and Development (OECD) and the International Monetary Fund (IMF) as well. The term offshore denotes all jurisdictions whose regulation and/or taxations vastly differ in comparison to onshore economies (Rixen, 2009, p. 11). The very term 'tax haven' suggests that tax avoidance and tax evasion are the only problems that can arise through these jurisdictions.

Yet, since the early 1960s, they also laid the foundation for a new phenomenon: the occurrence of the little regulated Euromarket (see paragraph *The Evolution of Offshore Finance*) and unregulated financial institutions, or so-called shadow banks. Offshore jurisdictions make it possible for financial institutions to circumvent domestic supervision and regulation (Palan and Nesvetailova, 2014). This is why the Tax Justice Network (TJN), a coalition of researchers, non-governmental organization (NGO) staff members, and activists prefer the term *secrecy jurisdiction* to articulate that the problems extend far beyond taxation, and that such jurisdictions 'provide facilities for people or entities to get around the rules, laws and regulation of other jurisdiction, using secrecy as their prime tool' (TJN, 2013a).

Other researchers use the terms *tax haven* and *regulatory haven* to distinguish between havens that are used for tax evasion and avoidance purposes from those that are used to circumvent financial supervision and regulation (Schmidt and Ötsch, 2014; Rixen, 2013, 2009; Troost and Liebert, 2009). *Tax havens* are then defined as jurisdictions that offer low or nil taxation in addition to secrecy provisions, such as banking secrecy laws, and they are used by non-residents to avoid and/or evade taxes (Palan, Murphy and Chavagneux, 2010, pp. 30–5). Moreover, there is no or restricted exchange of information about non-residents with other jurisdictions (Rixen, 2009, p. 10). *Regulatory havens* are characterized by lax financial regulation, e.g. the nondisclosure of beneficial ownership, a lack of interest of the national supervisory authority, and the possibility to circumvent regulatory capital requirements (Troost and Liebert, 2009, p. 79); the majority of financial institutions are controlled by non-residents and the scale of the financial sector exceeds the needs and the size of the home economy (Rixen, 2009, p. 10). Tax and regulation aspects often complement each other (Schuberth, 2013, p. 126) – the tax system favours the financing of investment via debt capital, especially since interest payments can be deducted as costs, whereas dividend payments cannot. Secrecy jurisdictions exacerbate the debt bias of investments in two ways: the circumvention of capital requirements enables higher debt levels (regulatory aspect), and the (higher) interest payments lower the onshore tax burden, maximizing the offshore profit (tax aspect).

Recently, the Asian crisis and the global financial crisis revealed another set of alternative conduit spaces and entities that emerged in the offshore world: so-called shadow banks. Although secrecy jurisdictions and shadow banks are two different phenomena, they are closely connected: financial actors use shadow banks to circumvent financial regulations, and a majority of shadow banks are located at secrecy jurisdictions (Rixen, 2013, p. 435). The term *shadow banking* is relatively new and is commonly credited to Paul McCulley, who observed in a 2007 speech to the Federal Reserve Conference a growth of 'unregulated shadow banks that (unlike regulated banks), fund themselves with uninsured short-term funding . . .' (McCulley, 2009, p. 257). In examining the financial crisis, some researchers conclude that the shadow banking system played a major role in the crisis, or it may even lie at the heart of it (Palan and Nesvetailova, 2014; Rixen, 2013, 2009; Stewart, 2013; Troost and Liebert, 2009; Murphy, 2008).

In this chapter we will use the terms *tax* and *regulation havens* as per their described definitions. From our understanding, tax and regulatory havens are subcategories of secrecy jurisdictions or offshore jurisdictions, respectively, as they are defined by the TJN.

Research on offshore finance

Despite the high losses in tax income and the enhanced financial market instability, until the crisis of 2008, there was only little research on offshore banking. Research was conducted by international institutions (e.g. Bank for International Settlements (BIS), Financial Stability Board (FSB)/Financial Stability Forum (FSF), IMF, OECD, United Nations, United Nations

Conference on Trade and Development) and civil society actors, especially by the TJN. The database is fragmentary due to political considerations and the lack of political will to collect data (Sullivan, 2007a); in addition, there are also methodical difficulties associated with collecting data on illegal businesses and markets (Beckert and Wehinger, 2013; Palan, Murphy and Chavagneux, 2010, p. 47). There are also legal grey areas and an ignorance of the issue of offshore markets that do not fit into standard economic models (Palan and Nesvetailova, 2014, p. 28). Some authors gave an overview regarding the phenomenon of offshore economies and societies (Urry, 2014; Chavagneux and Palan, 2012; Shaxson, 2011; Brittain-Caitlin, 2005; Palan, 2003; Hampton and Abbott, 1999; OECD, 1998; Hampton, 1996), as well as regarding offshore or shadow banking (FSB, 2011; Pozsar, Ashcraft and Boesky, 2010; Ricks, 2010; Errico and Musalem, 1999). Until the point of the financial crisis, international institutions conducted research with a regulatory purpose that – up until the financial crisis and the consequent rise of public critique – was characterized by political considerations due to the pressure of lobbies and certain countries. As a consequence, institutions, such as the OECD, had to moderate demands, revise definitions, and so on (Ötsch, 2012, pp. 32, 35) (we will mention the most important body of the literature on regulation below).

The international TJN, founded in 2003, has special merits in research and advocacy in international taxation and secrecy jurisdictions, with a focus on tax havens. When the network began, there was little systematically collected information on the offshore economy. The network compiled key data on the dimensions, techniques and strategies, and actors and regulations of these economies. Furthermore, the TJN developed a method through which to rank secrecy jurisdictions based on data pertaining to the score of secrecy jurisdictions, and on the scale of its financial activities. The resulting list is called the 'financial secrecy index' (for more, see explanations about offshore jurisdictions below; TJN, 2015, Christensen, 2012). It also contains country reports. Researchers associated with the TJN underlined the negative impact of secrecy jurisdictions on developing countries in the overall overview of global financial flows (Cobham, 2012; Shaxson, 2011, pp. 147–65; Palan, Murphy and Chavagneux, 2010, pp. 153–88; Missbach, 2009, pp. 104–5; Henry, 2003; Oxfam, 2000).

It is not easy to summarize academic debates about offshore banking given that for a long time, mainstream academia neglected the offshore economy. Research was performed by a diverse group of academics from different disciplines, such as international political economy (IPE), geography, international development and relations, law, accounting, economics, sociology and history.

Literature from the field of IPE especially deals with the role of the state and its transformation, the role of capitalism, law, professional groups and elites. Susan Strange inspired an important strand of research. She assumed that in a competitive situation in which states aspire to attain the largest possible share in global markets, economic actors increasingly escape the control of the state, whereby financial services dominate other parts of the economy (Strange, 1998, 1996, 1988, 1986). As a consequence of laissez-faire politics, and rather than active regulation, forms of non-state governance emerged – namely in the field of organized crime (illegal markets and banking, especially money laundering) and as tax and regulatory havens (Strange, 1998, pp. 123–38). This finally undermines democratic institutions (Strange, 1998, pp. 179–83).

Based on empirical historic studies on the evolution of offshore legislation, Sol Picciotto (1999a, 1999b, 1992) describes 'offshore statehood' as a catalyst for the restructuring of the international state system. According to Picciotto, the scope of effective exercise of states' powers, 'far from being circumscribed in precise and mutually exclusive terms' is 'flexible, overlapping and negotiable' due to the economic and social relations that transcend state boundaries (Picciotto, 1999a, p. 44). International investors, especially transnational companies

(TNCs), and their advisers exploited 'the elastic scope of state sovereignty' (Picciotto, 1999b, p. 1) and created, initially supported by state authorities, an 'offshore statehood' that provides the legal structures 'for routing global flows through the use of artificial persons [e.g. corporations] and transactions' (Picciotto, 1999a, p. 43). Picciotto further elaborated upon the propositions for global regulation, including global taxes and the unitary taxation for TNCs (Picciotto, 1999b).

Ronen Palan takes up this strand of research by explicitly focusing on the offshore economy. In his book, *The Offshore World*, he stresses the importance of tax havens for modern political economy and draws the attention to the powerful, who take 'advantage of opportunities' (Palan, 2003, p. XII). He provides an overview of the different forms of offshore economy (offshore finance and tax havens, export processing zones, flags of convenience, electronic commerce, online sex, casinos and so on) and 'its ability to expand into new realms' (Palan, 2003, p. 7), as well as its history and dimensions (Palan, 2003). In the book *Tax Havens*, Palan, Murphy and Chavagneux (2010) provide more technical details and an updated and systematized description of tax havens.

Like Picciotto, Palan dissociates himself from a simple dichotomy of the states versus the economy. In his view, the offshore economy did not emerge because of rising taxation and regulation; rather, it 'enabled onshore, or the modern nationally based state, to emerge in the first instance' (Palan, 2003, p. 11). Once the modern national state emerged, the ruling classes were keen to avoid conflict with financiers and introduced extra rules for international investors, which resulted in a 'bifurcation of law' (Palan, 2003, p. 10). One of Palan's (2003, 2002) core concepts is 'commercialized sovereignty'. This means that 'offshore jurisdictions are offering sovereign protection or a right of abode, whether real or fictional, and using this as a source of revenue' (Palan, 2003, p. 59, pp. 175–8). Recently, Palan and Nesvetailova proposed a Veblenian approach to the offshore economy based on the ideal type of businessman who, in Veblen's view, is a central actor in capitalism. The businessman's key competence is in buying, selling and avoiding the competition as much as possible. The 'most likely source of rent-seeking opportunities' would be the state and the law (Palan and Nesvetailova, 2014, p. 29). When applied to offshore business, providers and users of offshore services try to use the technique of sabotage – in this case, using the law 'to secure some special advantage or preference, usually of a business-like sort' (Palan and Nesvetailova, 2014, p. 27); thus, they use legal mechanisms, but not in the spirit of the law (Palan and Nesvetailova, 2014, p. 34).

Approaches from sociology draw attention to further conditions explaining the phenomenon of offshore economies. In contrast to a pointed idea regarding globalization-based market behaviour, Matthew Donaghy and Michael Clarke (2003) suggested to also consider factors that culturally constitute markets. They proposed five heuristic tools to conceptualize OFCs and to understand their diversity and dynamics – namely, (1) monetary ambience, which is a type of cultural form that is used to deal with money, especially at the micro-level in social interactions; (2) onshore patronage, which represents the relations between an onshore state and a specific offshore jurisdiction; (3) legal culture relating to 'collective philosophies, ideas and practices', including informal practices; (4) regulatory jingoism, a tactic of OFCs to circumvent international pressure; and (5) local embeddedness, which encompasses the ability of institutions to adapt to immediate local conditions (Donaghy and Clarke, 2003, pp. 385–91). John Urry interprets 'offshoring' as a strategy of class warfare from above, which encompasses hiding activities of organized crime, corruption, and 'white-collar financial crime' (Urry, 2014, p. 16). He relates these concepts to the role of secrecy in society, modelled after Georg Simmel's concept of money. Urry interprets 'offshoring' as an advanced form of secrecy that is challenged by new claims for visibility (Urry, 2014). Other authors point to the role of discourses and the effects of a deeply anchored figurative and metaphorical language and discourses used to gain social acceptance of the non-democratic offshore system (Ötsch, 2016, 2014; Ötsch and Di Pauli, 2009). Regarding elites, professional groups, and their influence and preserving power, Prem Sikka assumes that accountancy firms, which earn income from consultancy services in tax avoidance and privatization (which is necessary due to declining public revenues and the resultant need to raise private funds, or to replace public by private services), have a special impact on the offshore economy (Mitchell and Sikka, 2011; Sikka, 2008, 2003; Sikka and Hampton, 2005). Brooke Harrington draws the attention to the profession of trust and estate planning (including tax avoidance) and its impact on inequality (Harrington 2012).

Researchers in geography, anthropology and international relations have provided significant contributions towards better understanding the phenomenon of offshore economies from the 1990s onwards. Instead of dealing with abstract flows of money, researchers put an emphasis on 'place as socially constructed and dynamic'; hence, transactions depend upon 'trust among various actors out of processes of competitive deregulation' and 'places are remade and their borders redrawn by a wide variety of local and extra-local actors' (Hudson, 1998, p. 915). Researchers provided an overview of offshore economies by bringing together perspectives from economics, geography, international law and international politics (Hampton and Abbott, 1999); by assembling empirical data from case studies on secrecy jurisdictions; and by discussing regulation and its impact on different spaces, regions, or types of jurisdictions, and the different local actors involved (Sharman, 2012, 2011, 2010, 2006; Wainwright, 2011; Hampton and Christensen, 2007, 1999; Rawlings, 2004, 1999; Roberts, 1995). Secrecy jurisdictions as 'small island economies' and their relationship to onshore states are widely discussed (Hampton and Christensen, 2011, 2007, 2002; Sharman, 2010, 2009; Maurer, 2008; Van Fossen, 2008; Vlcek, 2008, 2007; Rawlings, 2005; Cobb, 1998). In many cases, regulatory pressure from the OECD is criticized because larger developed countries would be in a better situation than small jurisdictions (Vlcek, 2008, 2007), and as the strategy of 'naming and shaming' focuses on small jurisdictions with little political power, whereas offshore institutions located within OECD states are not listed, although their regulation might be less effective or might contain elements of typical offshore jurisdictions (Haberly and Wójcik, 2014; Sharman, 2011, 2010, 2009; Maurer, 2008). Thus, research should focus on the effects of power (Sharman, 2011). More recent contributions in geography propose to take a closer look at the interconnections between global financial and global production networks – and thereby on the co-evolution of globalization and financialization (Coe, Lai and Wójcik, 2014; Palan and Nesvetailova, 2014; Hall and Leyshon, 2013) – and connect the literature on financial geographies, advanced business services, world cities and offshore financial centres (Wójcik, 2013).

Discussions of offshore jurisdictions are usually missing from economic textbooks. According to Palan and Nesvetailova, the mainstream economy often uses a simple dichotomy of the state as a regulator and as a business that maximizes its profits; this dichotomy does not depict interconnections. Abstract economic theory usually does not address the difference between pre- or post-tax profits (Palan and Nesvetailova, 2014, p. 29). Nonetheless, heterodox economists provided useful insights in debates on tax competition that were related to offshore jurisdictions (Genschel and Schwarz, 2011; Genschel, Rixen and Uhl, 2007), and they also contributed to questions of regulation (Zucman, 2014; Johannesen and Zucman, 2014; Rixen, 2013, 2011, 2008; Kudrle, 2008). Jim Stewart provided insights into the offshore legislation in Ireland, namely in the field of tax evasion (Stewart, 1989), tax incentives, and financial flows in multinational companies (MNCs) (Stewart, 2005), as well as in terms of high profits and minor employment effects in treasury management firms (Stewart, 2008). These firms receive fees for administration functions (Stewart estimates that local expenses do not exceed 3 per cent of total administrative expenses), whereas the respective Financial Vehicle Corporations are performed outside the secrecy jurisdiction (Stewart, 2008, pp. 8–10). Stewart showed how offshore legislation destabilizes the financial system, which was at the forefront of the crisis (Stewart, 2008). The shadow banking sector is often located in secrecy jurisdictions, where regulatory requirements such as equity-to-assets ratios and transparency regarding the ownership of assets are low. Above, they offer quick procedures to register funds. Banks located onshore purchased Special Purpose Vehicles registered in secrecy jurisdictions (such as Ireland) and speculated using high gearing ratios and often short-term forms of refinancing. A subsidiary of the German Depfa Bank registered in Ireland acted as an insurance company without fulfilling the requirements for insurance companies (Stewart, 2008). Once the speculation went wrong, Financial Companies without banking license had no access to central bank money. As a consequence, their owners (often banks located in places with stricter supervisions and legislation) had to take over the losses in their balance sheets. So, offshore legislation and practices affected regulated financial centres. Economists and accountants also compiled, analysed, and presented data from a wide variety of sources and helped to better estimate the various dimensions of the offshore economy, the direction of monetary flows, and the effectiveness of regulation (Zucman, 2013; Rixen, 2013, 2011, 2008; Desai, Foley and Hines 2006; Desai, 2005).

The evolution of offshore finance

According to Palan, Murphy and Chavagneux., the fundamental instruments for systematically circumventing regulation and taxation have been created since the late nineteenth century (Palan, Murphy and Chavagneux, 2010, pp. 107–11). American corporate law, which emerged from the 1870s–90s, was a blueprint for several juridical forms of the offshore economy. To attract firms from New York and Massachusetts, New Jersey introduced the legal form of the corporation, removing restrictions concerning size, market share, time limits on corporate charters, mergers, acquisitions, and purchases, and permitted the corporation to own equity in other companies – a legislation that facilitates profit shifting within one corporation (Palan, Murphy and Chavagneux., 2010, p. 110). Similar legislature was copied and elaborated upon in Delaware.

With regard to taxation, Picciotto (1992) outlines that conflicts emerged with the rise of direct taxation and the appearance of TNCs after 1914. While in principle, countries like the United States apply the source principle – which means that taxable revenue is taxed at the source where it is generated – other countries, such as the United Kingdom, use the residence principle, which is based on taxing individuals who reside in the country. Once the impact of TNCs increased, the authorities were confronted with questions about how to tax these corporations while avoiding double and non-taxation (Picciotto, 1992, p. 14). In an important case in 1929, a British court decided that a company – even if registered in the UK – is not liable to pay taxes there if the company is controlled from abroad (Picciotto, 1992, p. 14). That specific decision on 'virtual residences' led to the appearance of a number of tax havens, due to the fact that the policy was applied to British colonies such as Bermuda, the Bahamas and, later, the Cayman Islands, as well as to Hong Kong (Palan, Murphy and Chavagneux, 2010, pp. 112–15). Moreover, countries negotiated bilateral taxation agreements that should prevent double taxation.

Some scholars refer to the important role of the trust. The legal construction of the trust is rooted in the important status of the professional secret in Anglo-Saxon law from the fourteenth century (Strange, 1998, p. 130). In a trust, ownership and control is separated, and lawyers control the trust and thus conceal the real owners (Zaki, 2010, pp. 75–7). Banking secrecy is another key instrument for a different kind of offshore jurisdiction. One important step was the introduction of the Swiss banking law in 1934, which forbids the transmission of any kind of relevant information about bank accounts and their clients. The law was introduced following a banking crisis and served as a concession for the banks' agreement on tightened banking supervision (Palan, Murphy and Chavagneux, 2010, pp. 120–2). Other jurisdictions such as Beirut, the Bahamas, Liechtenstein and Panama took over similar legislation, and Luxembourg and Austria introduced an even stronger kind of banking secrecy (Palan, Murphy and Chavagneux, 2010, p. 122).

The creation of the Eurodollar market in London in the 1950s was an important step towards establishing and extending offshore banking to bypass regulation and the Bretton Woods system (Burn, 2006, 1999). According to Gary Burn:

> the advent of a new international money market . . . marked the beginning of a fundamental shift in international financial relations, from one directed towards the furtherance of distinct 'national' regimes of accumulation, based on a system that was almost wholly regulated, to one that is today mostly responsive to the demands of global speculation and almost wholly unregulated.
>
> (Burn, 1999, p. 226)

In the 1950s, the Bank of England did not intervene once London bankers began to treat financial transactions between non-residents (in terms of foreign currency) as if they did not fall under the British banking regulation, even when the transactions took place in London (Burn, 1999, p. 230). As Burn writes, the 'prefix "Euro" is a misnomer, in that it defines what is an *offshore currency*, held and used *outside* the country where it acts as legal tender, and traded in a market which exists outside the system of state-prescribed banking jurisdiction' (Burn, 1999, p. 226). As a consequence, the inflow of money in British financial services rose, and because of the 'politically independent' decision-making power of the Bank of England in terms of monetary policy, the monetary policy corresponded to the interests of London's financial services, whose members were heading the Bank of England (Burn, 1999, p. 248). In the following decades, those that engaged in the British financial service tried to improve favourable legislation in the dependent territories (Palan, Murphy and Chavagneux, 2010, pp. 135–40).

From the beginning of the 1960s, the volume of offshore finance increased significantly (Palan, Murphy and Chavagneux, 2010, pp. 140–9). In the late 1960s, Singapore established an offshore market of the Asian Currency Unit, which operates similarly to the Euromarket to attract banks. From 1998 onwards, the government of Singapore introduced further legislation, such as tightened banking secrecy (which is in comparison to Switzerland), aiming to become the leading financial centre in Asia (Palan, Murphy and Chavagneux, 2010, p. 142). Beginning in the 1980s, Hong Kong started to abolish taxes on different kinds of financial transactions and interest, and its market subsequently grew to become the second largest financial centre in the Asian region (TJN, 2015; Palan, Murphy and Chavagneux, 2010, p. 143).

Further, the European offshore finance system became more established. The Netherlands identified MNCs as a target group, lowered their taxes, and created shell companies (Van Dijk, Weyzig and Murphy, 2006). Ireland established the Irish Financial Centre in Dublin in 1987, known for its lax or non-existing regulation (Stewart, 2013, 2008; Troost and Liebert, 2009).

Luxembourg tailored 'specific legislation in sector after sector through a "light touch", tax light, rather secretive "offshore" model' (TJN, 2013b; see also Zucman, 2014, pp. 39–41, 50–2, 96–102).

Although the United States (or its federal states such as Florida, Wyoming, Delaware and Nevada) rarely appears as an offshore centre in official records, they play an important role in offshore business (TJN, 2015; Zaki, 2010). States such as the Virgin Islands and the Marshall Island have close links to the US financial services sector (Shaxson, 2011, pp. 18–21, 166–92). Shaxson outlines that the American offshore sector played a role in the deregulation related to subprime crisis by circumventing maximum interest rates from the 1980s, and in introducing regressive tax advantages for big banks (Shaxson, 2011, p. 170), by allowing shadow banks to engage in the insurance sector and by facilitating the creation of trusts and lowering the protection of creditors (Shaxson, 2011, pp. 184–92).

Today's offshore jurisdictions

From time to time, institutions like the OECD, the IMF or the European Commission and national tax authorities publish lists for research reasons, to 'name and shame' offshore jurisdictions or to implement sanction within the national legislation. In many cases, the criteria used to classify jurisdictions are not made public. While in the 1990s, indicators such as low taxes were used (OECD, 1998), other approaches have compared numbers from national accounts, tax payments, and the declared profits of companies (Bach, 2013; Jarass and Obermaier, 2005), or their liabilities and assets (Lane and Milesi-Ferretti, 2010). Lane and Milesi-Ferretti (2010) counted that only 32 small international financial centres (IFC) with a population of not even 13 million people had – as per their gross international balance sheet (the sum of their external assets and liabilities) – over 18 trillion US dollars in 2007, as the net asset value of the Cayman Islands was over 2.2 trillion US dollars, and that of the British Virgin Islands was 1.6 trillion US dollars (Lane and Milesi-Ferretti, 2010, p. 23). These IFCs do not even include Switzerland, Luxembourg, Ireland, Cyprus, Hong Kong, or Singapore. Based on Lane and Milesi-Ferretti's method, as well as based upon datasets from the Swiss National Bank, Zucman argues that in regard to international investment statistics, there are two anomalies that probably originate in tax evasion: (a) the high amount of European securities without an identifiable owner; and (b) from the 1990s onwards funds flow from poor to richer countries (Zucman, 2013, p. 1322).

The TJN uses secrecy indicators (legal barriers to prevent information flow to the relevant authorities, which include tactics such as banking secrecy or anonymous forms of ownership) and the scale of financial flows to rank financial secrecy jurisdictions (TJN, 2015; Christensen, 2012). The world's ten largest secrecy jurisdictions in the index in 2015 are: (1) Switzerland; (2) Hong Kong; (3) the USA; (4) Singapore; (5) Cayman Islands; (6) Luxembourg; (7) Lebanon; (8) Germany; (9) Bahrain; and (10) the United Arab Emirates (TJN, 2015). However, national categories depict the phenomenon of offshore only to some degree. If secrecy jurisdictions were regarded in terms of their functional interaction, the network consisting of British banks and financial enterprises headquartered in London, and the financial enterprises and services registered in dependent territories and former colonies, would be at the top (TJN, 2015; Shaxson, 2011, p. 15). It is striking that unexpected offshore jurisdictions appear in the index; these jurisdictions have legal devices for financial secrecy that, up to now, have often been overlooked (for Germany see Meinzer, 2015).

Secrecy jurisdictions usually cooperate with one another. According to Zucman (2014, p. 43), 60 per cent of the foreign assets invested in Switzerland come from tax havens using letterbox companies such as Panama or the British Virgin Islands. Thus, unlike what the common assumptions and several tax haven lists suggest, offshore economies are not only a matter of small islands or countries; rather, they are legal instruments that were introduced or tolerated by offshore and, apparently, onshore jurisdictions. Onshore and offshore finance economies are closely interconnected, especially when considering shadow banking and onshore banking (Palan, 2003; Errico and Musalem, 1999), the use of correspondent accounts (see techniques of avoidance), the fact that most states have tax legislation offering advantages to specific sectors (TJN, 2015; Palan, Murphy and Chavagneux, 2010, pp. 40–5. For Gemany see Meinzer 2015), the financial flows of foreign direct investment between offshore and onshore jurisdictions (Haberly and Wójcik, 2014), 'real' and financial economies (Coe, Lai and Wójcik, 2014; Palan and Nesvetailova, 2014; Hall and Leyshon, 2013), or in the taxation of TNCs in grey areas of legality (Troost, 2013b; Picciotto, 2012). Given the interconnectedness of offshore and onshore finance, it is not enough to simply look at jurisdictions; instead, it is important to take a closer look at actors, especially MNCs and TNCs, owners of capital, and the professional groups involved in offshore services.

Actors

According to the FSF (2000, p. 10), offshore jurisdictions are used by (1) international companies to maximize profits, protect assets and issue securitized products through special purpose vehicles (SPV); (2) individuals to protect assets from potential claimants; (3) financial institutions to minimize income and withhold tax to avoid regulatory requirements, and to assist customers in minimizing income and withholding tax; (4) insurance companies, to accumulate reserves and avoid regulatory requirements; and (5) criminals and others to launder proceeds from crimes through the banking system.

Banks seem to use secrecy jurisdictions more extensively than non-financial companies. They have particularly large number of subsidiaries in secrecy jurisdictions (TJN, 2009) and they seem to primarily employ schemes for profit shifting for tax avoidance (Merz and Overesch, 2014). Based on the empirical analysis of subsidiary-level bank data from the international bank database, Bankscope, Julia Merz and Michael Overesch (2014) found that the 'magnitude of the tax sensitivity of reported profits [of multinational bank subsidiaries] is almost twice compared with effects found in previous studies for MNEs [multinational enterprises] outside the financial sector' (Merz and Overesch, 2014, p. 3). Offshore jurisdictions are further used by shadow banks (Rixen, 2013, p. 435). The shadow banking system is huge in size: the FSB estimates that in 2011, its assets made up about 67 trillion dollars, which accounted for 25 per cent of the global financial system (FSB, 2012, p. 3).

According to Sikka (2003, p. 365) professional intermediaries, such as accountants and lawyers, play a key role in secrecy jurisdictions as well. The Big Four accounting firms (KPMG, PricewaterhouseCoopers, Deloitte & Touche and Ernst & Young) are present in all of the world's significant tax havens (Palan, Murphy and Chavagneux, 2010, p. 13). According to Mitchell and Sikka (2011, p. 4), they are in fact the driving force behind the creation of global tax avoidance schemes.

Techniques of avoidance

There are many techniques that underlie the use of the offshore economy. Many avoidance models are complex and combine instruments from several jurisdictions. To circumvent new regulation, the techniques constantly change (for more specific information about avoidance techniques, see country reports of the financial shadow index TJN, 2015, 2013a; AABA, 2014;

Tax Research, UK, 2014; and websites of providers of offshore services). Two major tools for tax evasion are the banking secrecy and legal forms that enable anonymous ownership or, more precisely, 'entities and arrangements – whether trusts, corporations, foundations or others – whose ownership, functioning and/or purpose is kept secret, and sometimes where the very legal basis of ownership becomes muddied' (TJN, 2014).

In a jurisdiction that adopts banking secrecy, banks are not allowed to forward information about an account holder and/or account information to the responsible authorities (except in special cases, which vary in each jurisdiction – e.g. once criminal proceedings are already in progress). Until now, most secrecy jurisdictions do not respond to 'fishing expeditions' (that means the request for information about the data of a group of persons with special characteristics – e.g. from tax authorities) but only to a degree of 'reasonable suspicion'. These requests are a little promising; thus, authorities need to know (for example) what amount of money is in an account, so as to provide reasons why a holder is suspected of holding untaxed or illegal money.

In entities with an anonymous ownership structure, capital can be hidden because ownership and control are often formally separated (Zaki, 2010, pp. 75–8). In the case of a trust, ownership is transmitted to a nominee, who manages it for a third party (Palan, Murphy and Chavagneux, 2010, p. 92). Furthermore, there is no register for these transactions and the persons involved; as such, the legal constructs imply that the entities and persons involved are registered in different jurisdictions, and that avoidance models use shell companies (Zaki, 2010, pp. 156–8). According to TJN (2014), there is still a third avoidance strategy – namely, a kind of sabotage of information exchange. Even if there are agreements on information exchange, jurisdictions do not dispose of information because they do not collect locally-held information.

Correspondent banks are important facilities to transfer money from offshore to onshore legislations and vice versa. Correspondent accounts are based on agreements between banks from different countries. The original function is to provide banking services in foreign countries to the banks' clients without establishing a subsidiary in the country in question. Correspondent accounts are misused for money laundry and tax evasion which is possible because the authorities of one of the partner banks have low transparency standards (see Meinzer, 2015, pp. 80–1; US Senate Committee on Homeland Security & Governmental Affairs, 2001).

Tax avoidance by companies is an important issue, as value creation increasingly shifts to the field of intangible assets. Enterprises manipulate the local allocation of profits or the capital structure of the MNC/TNC in tax systems that are still tailored to the production of goods. A large amount of tax evasion is not conducted in the spirit of the law; rather, it is formally legal. Enterprises especially use double taxation agreements (Troost, 2013a). Originally, these bilateral agreements should prevent taxpayers from being taxed twice. Usually in practice, authorities do not systematically control whether companies misuse double taxation agreements. As a result, some enterprises do not pay taxes in any country. The European Commission (EC) now speaks of double non-taxation (EC, 2014). According to Merz and Overesch (2014, p. 5), due to their special business model, banks have additional strategies for profit shifting – namely, 'interest margins, allocation of services and hedging instruments' and the 'disclosure of loan loss provisions'.

Dimensions and effects

The existence and size of secrecy jurisdictions have various impacts. First, tax havens that are used for tax evasion and avoidance consequently lead to *tax loss* in the residential countries. There is little data about the amount of money channelled through secrecy jurisdictions. Since

2003 when, according to Palan, Murphy and Chavagneux (2010, p. 61), not even rough estimates on these values were available, researchers have undertaken various approaches to provide concrete figures (Zucman, 2014; Henry, 2012; Palan, Murphy and Chavagneux 2010; Sullivan, 2007b). The tax loss caused by tax avoidance and evasion of companies is estimated at 2 per cent to 2.5 per cent of the gross domestic product (GDP) (Palan, Murphy and Chavagneux., 2010, p. 66), corresponding to an annual tax loss of 270 to 335 billion dollars in the European Union. James Henry (2012, p. 4) calculated that up to 32 trillion dollars (about 26 trillion euros) of unreported private financial wealth was held offshore at the end of 2010 by high-net worth individuals. These figures only include financial wealth and therefore exclude real estate, yachts and other non-financial assets. Zucman (2013, p. 1323) estimated that 8 per cent of the private financial wealth (about 5.8 trillion dollars) of wealthy individuals is being stashed away in tax havens, leading to an annual tax loss of 130 billion euros under the assumption that 75 per cent of the wealth is untaxed. However, the figures only refer to private financial wealth, whereas tax losses through tax avoidance by MNCs are not included. According to Troost (2013a, p. 13) the tax losses that are encountered through the tax avoidance strategies of MNCs are twenty times higher than those associated with the tax evasion of wealthy individuals. More than 80 per cent of the 100 largest publicly-traded US corporations have subsidiaries in tax havens (GAO, 2008, p. 4).

Aside from the actual tax loss, the existence and size of offshore jurisdictions also have important and indirect implications. According to Genschel and Schwarz (2011) and Genschel, Rixen and Uhl (2007), tax havens contribute to an *international tax dumping*. An analysis by the IMF (2014) on 'spill-overs' in international corporate taxation (the impact that one country's tax practices has on another) arrives at the conclusion that these effects on corporate tax bases and rates through profit shifting are significant and sizeable (IMF 2014, pp. 19–20), especially for developing countries. In some cases, the IMF found that tax losses through weaknesses in the international tax regime reached up to 15 per cent, relative to all tax revenues. Palan, Murphy and Chavagneux (2010, p. 157) concluded that tax havens contribute to a distributional shift in taxation; wealthy individuals and MNCs reduce their tax bills, whereas the general public, including small- and medium-sized businesses that compete with MNCs, has to compensate for these tax losses (through higher income and consumer taxes).

Due to the financial crisis, there is another aspect of secrecy jurisdictions that demands attention: the consequences of secrecy jurisdictions on financial stability. International organizations, regulatory and supervisory authorities, as well as the European Commission have analysed the risks of the shadow banking systems on financial stability (see European Commission, 2012; FSB, 2011; Pozsar, Ashcraft and Boesky, 2010 and Ricks, 2010 for the Federal Reserve (Fed); IMF, 2010). However, according to some authors, the offshore aspects of the shadow banking system (and, therefore, of the financial crisis) were overlooked in recent studies (Palan and Nesvetailova, 2014, p. 4; Stewart, 2013, p. 2). The authors argue that secrecy jurisdictions are central to the daily operation of the global financial system, and that they keep threatening overall financial stability. There are numerous linkages between the shadow banking system and the offshore system, although studies on these linkages are still in their early stages (see e.g. Beyer and Braeutigam, 2014; Rixen, 2013; Stewart, 2013; Schmidt, 2012). First, the offshore world and the shadow banking system overlap significantly (Rixen, 2013, p. 437). Second, the risks for financial stability, which are referred to by researchers and international organizations as the shadow banking system, apply to secrecy jurisdictions as well; secrecy jurisdictions reinforce each of these individual risks (Schmidt, 2012, pp. 212–14). These risks include the significant growth of assets and liabilities in secrecy jurisdictions, as well as the numerous linkages to onshore banks that increase the risk of contagion effects. Furthermore, secrecy jurisdictions abet the suspected growth of the off-balance-sheet activities of financial institutions (FSF, 2000, p. 1). The lax oversight and lack of cooperation with onshore jurisdictions enables financial institutions to hide the risks involved in their offshore subsidiaries from regulators (Rixen, 2013, p. 438) and, therefore, restrains the global regulation and supervision of the financial system (FSF, 2000, p. 1).

Tax avoidance and regulation are often reduced to a problem of missing state revenue. In fact, the very nature of offshore economies means that there is a loss of democratic decision-making, namely in terms of financial regulation, in opportunities for public investment (this is relevant because of the allocation of resources for desired projects and due to macroeconomic effects) and the incentive effect of taxes (e.g. environmental taxes). A shift away from the public sector to private households and enterprises also means that political spending and decision-making power decreases. Missing revenues are only partly compensated for by charity, whereby benevolent persons exercise more power than others (Hartmann, 2013). Different authors speak of a tendency of 're-feudalization' due to a growing inequality enforced among others by offshore economy (Neckel 2010; Kissling, 2008). The rich withdraw their wealth from taxation using private trusts, whereas average citizens' tax money is used to bailout banks (Neckel, 2010, p. 14). The moral background of the bourgeoisie (embodied by Josef Schumpeter's ideal type of the entrepreneur) is replaced by the rentier. Owners bear no risk and belonging or success beat achievement (Neckel, 2010).

Regulation: reality and requirements

Until recently, the use of offshore economies was seen as a peccadillo. Thus, regulation was merely lax and politicians did not use pressure to exert power over this issue (Ötsch, 2013, pp. 80–93). However, since the financial crisis, the debate on how to tackle tax and regulatory havens has deepened because of two different reasons. First, some researchers argue that regulatory havens, together with the shadow banking system, keep on threatening the overall financial stability (Palan and Nesvetailova, 2014; Rixen, 2013, 2009; Stewart, 2013; Troost and Liebert, 2009; Murphy, 2008); therefore, tight regulation is necessary. Second, tight national budgets, as well as increased media attention on tax avoidance and tax evasion, have led to new initiatives to tackle the offshore economy (Ötsch, 2014, p. 57; for an overview on long-term regulation processes see Dietsch and Rixen, 2016, pp. 1–24). The G20 announced a bundle of requirements to regulate secrecy jurisdictions (G20, 2013, pp. 12–13; G20, 2008, p. 3) – namely, (1) promoting automatic information exchange (AIE); (2) dealing with beneficial ownership; (3) addressing base erosion and profit shifting by MNCs; and (4) addressing the risks posed by the shadow banking system, while protecting the financial market against illicit finance risks arising from non-cooperative jurisdictions.

Here, we mainly focus on the use of offshore jurisdictions for tax evasion and avoidance. Hence, we focus on (1) AIE; (2) beneficial ownership; and (3) addressing base erosion and profit shifting. Regarding the use of offshore tools for the avoidance of financial market regulation, we refer to the chapter on shadow banking in this book. However, we would like to mention that according to Rixen (2013), the regulatory response towards secrecy jurisdictions and shadow banks fall short of what would be needed. Rixen argues that the regulatory reform is only incremental rather than radical, serving more a symbolic purpose than having any actual effects.

We will focus on the regulation that was implemented starting in the late 1990s, especially since secrecy jurisdictions did not attract much attention by international politics, media or professional literature before then, although there were rare exceptions. Historically, the years from 1998 to 2000 saw the beginning of international efforts to tackle tax havens (see Palan, Murphy and Chavagneux, 2010, pp. 203–25 for a detailed overview), as national governments delegated the responsibility to tackle tax and regulation havens to international organizations (for an overview on the concerned institutions and their responsibilities, see Gonzales and Schipke, 2011, p. 44).

Automatic information exchange

According to Itai Grinberg (2012) there are three stages concerning the evolution of tools for international taxation. The basic instrument of choice is AIE, a major instrument that is used to prevent tax evasion. The first phase is exchange upon request (pp. 6–11), the second is the anonymous withholding of taxes (pp. 12–31), and the third phase includes AIE (pp. 33–62). In the case of exchange upon request, authorities need to give reasons as to why a specific holder of an account is suspected of holding illegal money. In international negotiations states agreed upon withholding taxes and fixed certain tax rates. Banks and authorities of the offshore jurisdiction then collect the money and transfer the aggregated sum to the home country of the holder of an account. As the holders are kept anonymous, authorities cannot verify whether the amount originally deposited into the account was taxed, or whether it was illegal money. On the contrary, AIE means that 'jurisdictions obtain financial information from their financial institutions and automatically exchange that information with other jurisdictions on an annual basis' (OECD, 2014, p. 3) Therefore it is a systemic and periodic transmission of taxpayer information by the source country to the resident country (OECD, 2012, p. 3). It concerns various categories of income (e.g. dividends, interest, royalties). In the past, the OECD and its Global Forum had promoted information exchange upon request, and they claimed that the AIE was technically not feasible (Meinzer, 2014, p. 97); however, they changed their position in a report published in 2012, arguing that 'automatic exchange of information proves to be a useful way to implement enhanced international tax-cooperation' (OECD, 2012, p. 2) and that they will develop a multilateral platform to facilitate that practice. The OECD (2012, p. 18) argues, that AIE has a number of benefits: (1) it can provide timely information on non-compliance; (2) it can help detect non-compliance where tax authorities have had no previous indication of non-compliance; (3) it has deterrent effects and therefore increases voluntary compliance; (4) it can educate tax payers in their reporting obligations and (5) leads to higher tax revenues and ensures that all tax payers pay their fair share of tax. However, the success of AIE depends on the quality of information that is exchanged and on low related costs through, for instance, common standards and processes (OECD, 2012, p. 2). In 2013, the G20 accepted the AIE as the new single global standard, expecting that their members would begin to implement it by the end of 2015 (G20, 2013, p. 13).

In the past, tackling tax evasions has been of secondary importance in the EU. Yet in 2003, a Saving Tax Directive fixed the AIE as standard (European Commission, 2003). However, the directive has loopholes and limitations: first, EU member states with a banking secrecy (Belgium, Austria and Luxembourg), as well as its dependent territories, are allowed to apply a withholding tax during a transitional period. Second, the directive only applies to interest payments, whereas other capital returns (e.g. dividends, royalties) are not included. Finally, it only applies to individual persons, whereas other legal entities (e.g. private companies and trusts) are excluded. In 2014, an amendment was approved (European Commission, 2014). The revisited directive should be adopted by member states by 2016, in an attempt to close several of those loopholes. It adopts the new global standard on Automatic Exchange of Information (AEOI) developed by the OECD. The Foreign Account Tax Compliance Act (FATCA), a US federal law that was issued in 2010, has increased the pressure towards the introduction of the AIE as well. It requires foreign financial institutions to report information-related assets that are held overseas by US persons to the revenue service of the US government (Grinberg, 2012); yet FATCA has been criticized because the information exchange is not fully reciprocal.

Beneficial ownership

The effectiveness and efficiency of AIE depends upon the disclosure of beneficial owner information, which is currently rarely collected and transmitted (OECD, 2014, p. 3). In particular, trusts and similar constructions are often not obliged to document the true beneficial owners that benefit from the ownership, even though its ownership is in the name of another entity, often a trustee. Although the use of a trustee does not change the position regarding tax liability, these constructions are used to evade taxes. To prevent this, countries must require the collection and disclosure of beneficial ownership and share this information with other countries by making it public (Troost, 2013b, p. 10). On behalf of the disclosure of the beneficial owner, a new proposal for a directive on the prevention of the use of the financial system for the purpose of money laundering and terrorist financing (European Parliament, 2014) represents a significant advantage. It states that Member States should ensure that beneficial ownership information is stored in a central register and that this information is made available to competent authorities, obliged entities and other persons with legitimate interest (e.g. investigative journalists). How a legitimate interest is defined will probably be at the heart of legal disputes (Meinzer, 2015, p. 103). The proposal commits legal entities and corporations to collect information of the true beneficial owners if they hold more than a 25 per cent share (Troost, 2013b, p. 10). Yet, the Member States can decide that a lower percentage may already be an indication of ownership or control. The proposal turned in the fourth Anti-Money (AML) Directive that will take effect from June 2015 (European Commission, 2015). EU countries will have two years from then to implement the rules. However, it should be noted that the directive will not impact non-European tax havens.

Base erosion and profit shifting

The still ongoing crisis of the public finances in Europe, as well as the spectacular cases of tax evasion and avoidance by corporations (e.g. Google, Starbucks, Amazon and Apple), turned the focus to base erosion and profit shifting via MNCs. In 2013, the G20 charged the OECD with analysing the problem. The OECD focused primarily on the analysis of the misuse of double-tax treaties, the taxing of the digital economy, as well as on the abuse of transfer prices (OECD, 2013, pp. 10–23). To tackle the tax avoidance through MNC, a variety of measures has been discussed (e.g. the Base Erosion and Profit Shifting Initiative of the OECD). Some of these measures, e.g. unitary taxation or country-by-country reporting would imply fundamental changes in the international tax system.

For instance, a fundamental change in the international tax system would be achieved by engaging in a shift towards assessing MNCs on a unitary basis, coupled with a principled basis for appointing tax liability. Current OECD international guidelines are based on the arm's-length principle, meaning that transfer prices between companies of MNCs are the same as if the two companies involved were indeed two independent companies, and not part of the same corporate structure. This ensures that transfer prices are established on a market value basis. However, MNCs have been able to misapply those rules to 'separate income from the economic activities that produce that income and to shift it into low-tax environment' (OECD, 2013, p. 19).

The OECD analysed that this is achieved, in part, by transferring intangible assets and other mobile assets for less than full value (p. 19). In contrast, a unitary approach is based on the assumption that the income of a firm is earned by that firm as a whole and that tax should be paid where the economic activities take place (Picciotto, 2012, p. 10). A unitary tax base is then taxed with the national tax rate. A coordination of these tax rates could be necessary to reduce the incentive for states to offer low tax rates in an attempt to attract investment (Picciotto, 2012, p. 13).

A so-called country-by-country reporting could be a first step to unitary taxation and would require that MNCs name each country in which it operates, disclose all subsidiaries and their performances, and disclose details on the costs, tax charges, assets, and employees (Palan, Murphy and Chavagneux, 2010, p. 246). Therefore, income could be taxed where its economic activity was produced, eventually even based on an international unitary taxable base.

Unitary taxations already exist in certain states of the US; in the EU, some discussions about this have taken place since the 1990s (Troost, 2013b, p. 6). The European Commission tabled a proposal for unitary taxation, the so-called Common Consolidated Corporate Tax Base (CCCTB) to apply to all companies within the EU (Picciotto, 2012, p. 15). The new Capital Requirement Directive of the EU, which started in 2015, contains an obligation for country-by-country reporting that pertains to credit institutions and investment firms that hold residence in one or more of the EU Member States; it also applies to companies with activities in the extractive industry and those that log primary forests (Troost, 2013b, p. 5), as these companies are often associated with a great source of wealth in resource-rich developing countries. An analysis of this first country-by-country reporting of 26 EU based banks suggests, that they overstated profits in identifiable low tax and offshore jurisdictions and under-reported them in those places they mainly operate (Murphy, 2015).

Conclusion

The field of research on offshore economies and societies is not yet systematically evolved. There are many valuable contributions from different disciplines, but these approaches do not form a coherent body of research on tax havens and offshore practices (except in regard to the TJN). Whereas literature and policy actions on tax evasion and avoidance through offshore jurisdictions have increased since the financial crisis in 2008, there is still a lack of research on (1) the consequences of secrecy jurisdictions for financial stability and (2) possible linkages between secrecy jurisdictions and the shadow banking system. International organizations, regulatory and supervisory authorities have analysed the risk of the shadow banks on financial stability, yet they might have overlooked the offshore aspect of the shadow banking system. The studies on linkages between the shadow banking system and secrecy jurisdictions are still in their early stages. It might be useful to combine research on tax evasion and avoidance as well as on financial stability from different fields such as regulation and technical issues, economics, sociology, public finance, politics and finance.

Concerning policy action and connected areas of future research, we conclude that the use of secrecy jurisdictions is increasingly discredited in public opinion, and that politicians and regulatory bodies announce measures to tackle the problem. Yet, an evaluation of the reform politics following the financial crisis has produced mixed results. Tax evasion for private persons has become more difficult in certain jurisdictions, especially due to enforced Automatic Information Exchange. Moreover, the regulation of corporate taxation on the international level is a crucial issue, because if corporate tax base erodes, the taxation of individuals will also be at question, as individuals likely would invest in companies. In regard to the political process, regulatory approaches such as country-by-country reporting, beneficial ownership and the mid-term implementation and configuration of unitary taxation will probably be on the agenda of civil society, researchers and regulators.

Nonetheless there seems to be a shift towards less regulated jurisdictions (Johannesen and Zucman, 2014; Zucman, 2014, p. 11; TJN, 2015). Furthermore, even if at the moment there seems to be a political will to tackle tax evasion and avoidance, it is not sure whether politics will maintain that pressure. Regarding complex issues of the taxation of international companies, it is possible that politicians take missing international coordination as pretext to pursue a politics of competition between jurisdictions by offering tax advantages. On the other hand, there is a danger, that announcements concerning tackling secrecy jurisdictions are, first and foremost, symbolic, and that the measures will get diluted once put into practice. This likely has to do with the public's low level of interest in finance; the pointed interest of professional groups, lobbyists, companies and other users; as well as the amount of collaboration of certain authorities and politicians with offshore jurisdictions and actors. Therefore, Zucman asks for far-reaching measures – namely, (a) progressive taxation of wealth on the global level; (b) a worldwide registry for finance; and (c) a radical reform of corporate taxation (Zucman, 2014, p. 15, pp. 85–116). Additionally, economic and financial sanctions should be used to address tax evasion (Zucman, 2014, pp. 85–116). Regulation of offshore practices is an area of continuous development. The regulation of offshore finance is not only a technical question, it is also a question of political will and of the overall economic structure; thus, onshore and offshore economies and society are closely linked. The increasing complexity of tax and financial systems poses a threat to the democratic control of these systems. How can these systems be steered according to democratic decisions if there is no international political coordination, if those who can afford paying for expertise have advantages in using regulatory gaps and influencing politics and if the affluent use know-how to push through special interests?

References

AABA (2014) *Association for Accountancy & Business Affairs*, Essex. Retrieved on 9 November 2015 from http://visar.csustan.edu/aaba/home.html.
Bach, S. (2013) 'Unternehmensbesteuerung', *DIW Wochenbericht*, 22/23.
Beckert, J. and Wehinger, F. (2013) 'In the shadow: Illegal markets and economic sociology', *Socio-Economic Review*, 11 (1): 5–30.
Beyer, K. and Braeutigam, L. (2014) 'Offshore aspects of shadow banking'. In Ötsch, W., Grözinger, G., Beyer, M. and Bräutigam, L. (eds) *The Political Economy of Offshore Jurisdictions*. Marburg: Metropolis, pp. 7–23.
Brittain-Caitlin, W. (2005) *Offshore: The Dark Side of the Global Economy*. New York: Farrar, Strauss and Giroux.
Burn, G. (1999) 'The state, the city and the euromarkets', *Review of International Political Economy*, 6 (2): 225–61.
Burn, G. (2006) *The Re-emergence of Global Finance*. Basingstoke, Hampshire: Palgrave Macmillan.
Chavagneux, C. and Palan, R. (2012) *Les paradis fiscaux*. Paris: la Découverte.
Christensen, J. (2012) 'The hidden trillions: Secrecy, corruption, and the offshore interface', *Crime, Law and Social Change*, 57 (3): 325–43.
Cobb, C. (1998) 'Global finance and the growth of offshore financial centers', *Geoforum*, 29 (1): 7–21.
Cobham, A. (2012) 'Tax havens and illicit flows'. In Reuter, P. (ed.): *Draining Development?* Washington, DC: World Bank, pp. 337–71.
Coe, N., Lai, K. and Wójcik, D. (2014) 'Integrating finance into global production networks', *Regional Studies*, 48 (5): 761–77.
Desai, M. (2005) 'The degradation of reported corporate profits', *The Journal of Economic Perspectives*, 19 (4): 171–92.
Desai, M., Foley, F. and Hines, J. (2006) 'The demand for tax haven operations', *Journal of Public Economics*, 90 (3): 513–31.

Dietsch, P. and Rixen, T. (2016): 'Global tax governance: What it is and why it matters'. In Dietsch, P. and Rixen, T. (eds) *Global tax governance. What is wrong with it and how to fix it*. Colchester, United Kingdom: ECPR Press, pp. 1–24.

Donaghy, M. and Clarke, M. (2003) 'Are offshore financial centres the product of global markets?', *Economy and Society*, 32 (3): 381–409.

Errico, L. and Musalem, A. (1999) *Offshore Banking: An Analysis of Micro- and Macro-Prudential Issues*. Washington, DC: IMF.

European Commission (2003) *European Union Savings Directive (EUSD)*, formally Council Directive 2003/48/EC of 3 June 2003 on taxation of savings income in the form of interest payments. Brussels: European Commission.

European Commission (2012) *Green Paper Shadow Banking*. Brussels: European Commission.

European Commission (2014) *The internal market: Factual examples of double non-taxation cases*. Brussels: European Commission.

European Commission (2015) *The fourth Anti-Money Laundering (AML) Directive* on the prevention of the use of the financial system for the purposes of money laundering or terrorist financing. Brussels: European Commission.

European Parliament (2014) *Proposal for a Directive of the European Parliament and of the Council on the Prevention of the use of the Financial System for the Purpose of Money Laundering and Terrorist Financing*. Brussels: European Parliament.

FSB (2011) *Shadow Banking: Strengthening Oversight and Regulation*. Basel: Financial Stability Board.

FSB (2012) *Global Shadow Banking Monitoring Report*. Basel: Financial Stability Board.

FSF (2000) *Report of the Working Group on Offshore Centers*. Basel: Financial Stability Forum.

GAO (2008) *International Taxation. Report to Congressional Requesters*. Washington, DC: United States Government Accountability Office.

Genschel, P. and Schwarz, P. (2011) 'Tax competition: A literature review', *Socio-Economic Review*, 9: 339–70.

Genschel, P., Rixen, T. and Uhl, S. (2007) 'Die Ursachen des europäischen Steuerwettbewerbs', *Politische Vierteljahresschrift*, 48 (2): 297–320.

Gonzales, M. and Schipke, A. (2011) 'Bankers on the beach', *Finance & Development*, June: 42–5.

Grinberg, I. (2012) *Beyond FATCA: An Evolutionary Moment for the International Tax System*. Retrieved on 9 November 2015 from http://scholarship.law.georgetown.edu/cgi/viewcontent.cgi?article=1162&context=fwps_papers.G20 (2008) *Declaration Summit on Financial Markets and the World Economy*. Washington, DC: G20. Retrieved on 9 November 2015 from http://georgewbush-whitehouse.archives.gov/news/releases/2008/11/20081115-1.html.

G20 (2008) *G20 Leaders' Declaration*.Washington, DC Summit: G20. Retrieved on 9 November 2015 from http://www.g20.utoronto.ca/2008/2008declaration1115.html.

G20 (2013) *G20 Leaders' Declaration*. Saint Petersburg Summit: G20. Retrieved on 9 November 2015 from http://en.g20russia.ru/news/20130906/782776427.html.

Haberly, D. and Wójcik, D. (2014) 'Tax havens and the production of offshore FDI', *Journal of Economic Geography*, 15 (1): 75–101.

Hall, S. and Leyshon, A. (2013) 'Editorial: Financialization, space and place', *Regional Studies*, 47 (6): 831–3.

Hampton, M. (1996) *The Offshore Interface: Tax Havens in the Global Economy*. London: Palgrave Macmillan.

Hampton, M. and Abbott, J. (eds) (1999) *Offshore Finance Centers and Tax Havens*. West Lafayette (Indiana): Purdue University Press.

Hampton, M. and Christensen, J. (1999) 'Treasure Island revisited', *Environmental Planning*, 31 (9): 1619–37.

Hampton, M. and Christensen, J. (2002) 'Offshore pariahs?', *World Development*, 30 (9): 1657–73.

Hampton, M. and Christensen, J. (2007) 'Competing industries in islands', *Annals of Tourism Research*, 34 (4): 998–1020.

Hampton, M. and Christensen, J. (2011) 'Looking for Plan B: What next for island hosts of offshore finance?', *The Round Table*, 100 (413): 169–81.

Harrington, B. (2012) 'Trust and estate planning: The emergence of a profession and its contribution to socioeconomic inequality', *Sociological Forum*, 27 (4): 825–46.

Hartmann, M. (2013) *Soziale Ungleichheit – kein Thema für die Eliten?* Frankfurt: Campus.

Henry, J. (2003) *The Blood Bankers*. New York: Four Walls Eight Windows.

Henry, J. (2012) *The Price of Offshore Revisited*. TJN (ed.). Retrieved on 9 November 2005 from www.taxjustice.net/2014/01/17/price-offshore-revisited/.

Hudson, A. (1998) 'Placing trust, trusting place: On the social construction of offshore financial centres', *Political Geography*, 17 (8): 915–37.
IMF (2010) 'Understanding financial interconnectedness', Washington, DC: IMF.
IMF (2014) 'Spillovers in international corporate taxation', Washington, DC: IMF.
Jarass, L. and Obermaier, G. (2005) *Geheimnisse der Unternehmenssteuern*. Marburg: Metropolis.
Johannesen, N. and Zucman, G. (2014) 'The end of bank secrecy?' *American Economic Journal*, 6 (1): 65–91.
Kissling, H. (2008) *Reichtum ohne Leistung. Die Feudalisierung der Schweiz*. Zürich: Rüegger.
Kudrle, R. (2008) 'The OECD's harmful tax competition initiative and the tax havens: From bombshell to damp squib', *Global Economy Journal*, 8 (1): 1–26.
Lane, P. and Milesi-Ferretti, G. (2010) *Cross-Border Investment in Small International Financial Centers*. Washington, DC: IMF.
McCulley, P. (2009) *The shadow banking system and Hyman Minsky's economic journey*. Retrieved on 9 November 2015 from www.cfainstitute.org/learning/products/publications/rf/Pages/rf.v2009.n5.15.aspx.
Maurer, B. (2008) 'Re-regulating offshore finance?', *Geography Compass*, 2 (1): 155–75.
Meinzer, M (2014) 'Current practice of automatic tax information exchange in selected countries'. In Ötsch, W., Grözinger, G., Beyer, M. and Bräutigam, L. (eds) *The Political Economy of Offshore Jurisdictions*. Marburg: Metropolis, pp. 97–133.
Meinzer, M. (2015) *Steueroase Deutschland*, Munich: C.H. Beck.
Merz, J. and Overesch, M. (2014) *Profit Shifting and Tax Response of Multinational Banks*. Retrieved on 9 November 2015 from http://papers.ssrn.com/sol3/papers.cfm?abstract_id=2479818.
Missbach, A. (2009) 'Die Schweiz als Steueroase', *Prokla*, 39 (1): 101–17.
Mitchell, A. and Sikka, P. (2011) *The Pin-Stripe Mafia: How Accountancy Firms Destroy Societies*. Essex: Association for Accountancy & Business Affairs. Retrieved on 9 November 2015 from http://visar.csustan.edu/aaba/PINSTRIPEMAFIA.pdf.
Murphy, R. (2008) *Tax havens creating turmoil*. London: Evidence submitted to the Treasury Committee of the House of Commons (ed. TJN).
Murphy, R. (2015) *European Banks' Country-by-Country Reporting. A review of CRD IV data*. Norfolk: Tax Research LLP. Retrieved on 10 November 2015 from www.parlamento.euskadi.net/pdfs_berriak/8158.pdf.
Neckel, S. (2010) 'Refeudalisierung der Ökonomie. Zum Strukturwandel kapitalistischer Wirtschaft', *MPIfG Working Paper* 10/6. Retrieved on 13 June 2012 from www.mpifg.de/pu/workpap/wp10-6.pdf.
OECD (1998) *Harmful Tax Competition. An Emerging Global Issue*. Paris: OECD Publishing. Retrieved on 9 November 2015 from www.oecd.org/tax/transparency/44430243.pdf.
OECD (2012) *Tackling Offshore Tax Evasion*. Paris: OECD Publishing.
OECD (2013) *Addressing Base Erosion and Profit Shifting*. Paris: OECD Publishing. Retrieved on 13 February 2013 from http://dx.doi.org/10.1787/9789264192744-en.
OECD (2014) *Standard for Automatic Exchange of Financial Account Information*. Paris: OECD Publishing. Retrieved on 25 September 2014 from www.oecd.org/tax/exchange-of-tax-information/Automatic-Exchange-Financial-Account-Information-Common-Reporting-Standard.pdf.
Ötsch, S. (2012) 'Die Normalität der Ausnahme: Finanzoasen als Parallelökonomie', *Momentum Quarterly*, 1 (1): 27–44.
Ötsch, S. (2013) 'Time for socio-economic peace-making'. In Preiss, B. and Brunner, C. (eds) *Democracy in Crisis*. Vienna and Berlin: LIT-Verlag, pp. 79–109.
Ötsch, S. (2014) 'Our banking secrecy is a strong castle', In Ötsch, W., Grözinger, G., Beyer, M. and Bräutigam, L. (eds) *The Political Economy of Offshore Jurisdictions*. Marburg: Metropolis, pp. 39–60.
Ötsch, S. (2016) 'The offshore coalition, its tactics and strategies', *American Behavioral Scientist*, 60 (30): 321–9.
Ötsch, S. and Di Pauli, C. (eds) (2009) *Räume der Offshore-Welt*. Frankfurt am Main: Attac Trägerverein.
Oxfam (2000) *Tax Havens: Releasing the hidden billions for poverty eradication*. Retrieved on 9 November 2015 from http://policy-practice.oxfam.org.uk/publications/tax-havens-releasing-the-hidden-billions-for-poverty-eradication-114611.
Palan, R. (2002) 'Tax havens and the commercialisation of state sovereignty', *International Organization*, 56 (1): 153–78.
Palan, R. (2003) *The Offshore World*. Ithaca and London: Cornell University Press.
Palan, R. and Nesvetailova, A. (2014) 'Elsewhere, ideally nowhere: Shadow banking and offshore finance', *Politik*, 16 (4): 26–34.

Palan, R., Murphy, R. and Chavagneux, C. (2010) *Tax Havens. How Globalization Really Works*. Ithaca and London: Cornell University Press.

Picciotto, S. (1992) *International Business Taxation*. London: Weidenfeld.

Picciotto, S. (1999a) 'Offshore: The state as legal fiction'. In Hampton, M. and Abbott, J. (eds) *Offshore Finance Centers and Tax Havens*. West Lafayette: Purdue University Press, pp. 43–79.

Picciotto, S. (1999b) *Redrawing the Line between the State and the Market*. Conference Paper. Robarts Centre, Toronto. Retrieved on 21 September 2011 from www.lancaster.ac.uk/staff/lwasp/endoff.pdf.

Picciotto, S. (2012) *Towards Unitary Taxation of Transnational Corporations*. Retrieved on 9 September 2013 from www.taxjustice.net/cms/upload/pdf/Towards_Unitary_Taxation_1-1.pdf.

Pozsar, Z., Adrian, T., Ashcraft, A. and Boesky, H. (2010) *Shadow banking*. Staff Report. New York: Federal Reserve Bank. Retrieved on 11 October 2015 from www.ny.frb.org/research/staff_reports/sr458.pdf.

Rawlings, G. (1999) 'Villages, islands and tax havens', *Canberra Anthropology*, 22 (2): 37–50.

Rawlings, G. (2004) 'Laws, liquidity and Eurobonds: The making of the Vanuatu tax haven', *The Journal of Pacific History*, 39 (3): 325–41.

Rawlings, G. (2005) 'Mobile people, mobile capital and tax neutrality', *Accounting Forum*, 3 (29): 289–310.

Ricks, M. (2010) *Shadow Banking and Financial Regulation*. Columbia Law and Economics Working Paper. Retrieved on 11 October 2015 from http://corpgov.law.harvard.edu/2010/09/18/shadow-banking-and-financial-regulation/.

Rixen, T. (2008) *The Political Economy of International Tax Governance*. Basingstoke: Palgrave.

Rixen, T. (2009) *Paradiese in der Krise: Transparenz und neue Regeln für Steuer-und Regulierungsoasen*. Berlin: Heinrich-Böll-Stiftung.

Rixen, T. (2011) 'From double tax avoidance to tax competition', *Review of International Political Economy*, 18 (2): 197–227.

Rixen, T. (2013) 'Why reregulation after the crisis is feeble: Shadow banking, offshore financial centers, and jurisdictional competition', *Regulation & Governance*, 7 (4): 435–59.

Roberts, S. (1995) 'Small place, big money: The Cayman Islands and the international financial system', *Economic Geography*, 7 (1): 237–56.

Schmidt, M. (2012) 'Steueroasen und Regulierungsoasen – Auswirkungen auf die Stabilität des Finanzmarkts und politische Implikationen', *Momentum Quarterly*, 1 (44): 203–62.

Schmidt, M. and Ötsch, W. (2014) 'The political economy of offshore jurisdictions. An introduction'. In Ötsch, W., Grözinger, G., Beyer, M. and Bräutigam, L. (eds) *The Political Economy of Offshore Jurisdictions*. Marburg: Metropolis, pp. 7–23.

Schuberth, H. (2013) 'Tax policies and financial stability – lessons from the crisis'. In Braude, J., Eckstein, Z., Fischer, S. and Flug, K. (eds) *The Great Recession: Lessons for Central Bankers*, Cambridge: MIT Press, pp. 123–63.

Sharman, J. (2006) *Havens in a Storm. The Struggle for Global Tax Regulation*. Ithaca: Cornell University Press.

Sharman, J. (2009) 'The bark is the bite: International organizations and blacklisting', *Review of International Political Economy*, 16 (4), pp. 573–596.

Sharman, J. (2010) 'Shopping for anonymous shell companies', *The Journal of Economic Perspectives*, 24 (4): 127–40.

Sharman, J. (2011) 'Testing the global financial transparency regime', *International Studies Quarterly*, 55 (4): 981–1001.

Sharman, J. (2012) 'Chinese capital flows and offshore financial centers', *The Pacific Review*, 25 (3): 317–37.

Shaxson, N. (2011) *Treasure Islands*. London: Bodley Head.

Sikka, P. (2003) 'The role of offshore financial centres in globalization', *Accounting Forum*, 27 (4): 365–99.

Sikka, P. (2008) 'Enterprise culture and accountancy firms', *Accounting, Auditing & Accountability Journal*, 21 (2): 268–95.

Sikka, P. and Hampton, M. (2005) 'The role of accountancy firms in tax avoidance', *Accounting Forum*, 29 (3): 325–43.

Stewart, J. (1989) 'Transfer pricing: Some empirical evidence from Ireland', *Journal of Economic Studies*, 16 (3): 40–56.

Stewart, J. (2005) 'Fiscal incentives, corporate structure and financial aspects of treasury management operations', *Accounting Forum*, 29 (3): 271–88.

Stewart, J. (2008) 'Financial flows and treasury management firms in Ireland', *Accounting Forum*, 32 (3): 199–212.

Stewart, J. (2013) *Low Tax Financial Centres and the Financial Crisis: The Case of the Irish Financial Services Centre*. Retrieved on 11 October 2015 from www.tcd.ie/iiis/documents/discussion/pdfs/iiisdp420.pdf.
Strange, S. (1986) *Casino Capitalism*. Oxford: Blackwell.
Strange, S. (1988) *States and Markets*. London: Pinter.
Strange, S. (1996) *The Retreat of the State*, Cambridge: Cambridge University Press.
Strange, S. (1998) *Mad Money*. Manchester: Manchester University Press.
Sullivan, M. (2007a) 'Lessons from the last war on tax havens', *Tax Notes*, 30 July.
Sullivan, M. (2007b) 'Tax analysts offshore project', *Tax Notes Today*, 10 October.
Tax Research UK (2014) *Richard Murphy's tax blog*. Retrieved on 11 October 2015 from www.taxresearch.org.uk/Blog/2006/09/19/tax-competition-dealing-with-the-myth/.
TJN (2009) *Where on Earth are You? Major Corporations and Tax Havens*. Revised Version. Retrieved on 11 October 2015 from www.taxjustice.net/cms/upload/pdf/45940CCBd01.pdf.
TJN (2013a) *Financial Secrecy Index – 2013 Results*. Retrieved on 1 March 2014 from www.financialsecrecyindex.com/introduction/fsi-2013-results.
TJN (2013b) 'Narrative report on Luxembourg', TJN (ed.) *Financial Secrecy Index*, p. 2. Retrieved on 11 October 2015 from www.financialsecrecyindex.com/PDF/Luxembourg.pdf.
TJN (2014) *The Mechanics of Secrecy*. Retrieved on 11 October 2015 from www.taxjustice.net/topics/secrecy/the-mechanics-of-secrecy/.
TJN (2015) *Financial Secrecy Index – 2015 Results*. Retrieved on 11 October 2015 from www.financialsecrecyindex.com/introduction/fsi-2015-results.
Troost, A. (2013a) 'EU: Steuerflucht als Geschäftsmodell', *Blätter für deutsche und internationale Politik*, 12: 13–16.
Troost, A. (2013b) *Die Europäische Union bläst zur Jagd auf Steuersünder*. Berlin: Rosa Luxemburg Stiftung.
Troost, A. and Liebert, N. (2009) 'Das Billionengrab Von Steueroasen und Schattenbanken', *Blätter für deutsche und internationale Politik*, 3: 75–84.
Urry, J. (2014) *Offshoring*. Cambridge: Polity.
US Senate Committee on Homeland Security & Governmental Affairs (2001) *Correspondent Banking: A Gateway for Money Laundering*. A Report by the Minority Staff of The Permanent Subcommittee On Investigations. Washington.
Van Dijk, M., Weyzig, F. and Murphy, R. (2006) *The Netherlands: A Tax Haven*. Amsterdam: Centre for Research on Multinational Corporations (SOMO).
Van Fossen, T. (2008) 'Why are tax havens in small states?' In Pillarisetti, R. (ed.) *Small Economies and Global Economics*. New York: Nova Science Publishers, pp. 221–31.
Vlcek, W. (2007) 'Why worry? The impact of the OECD harmful tax competition initiative on Caribbean offshore financial centres', *The Round Table*, 96 (390): 331–46.
Vlcek, W. (2008) 'Competitive or coercive?', *The Round Table*, 97 (396): 439–52.
Wainwright, T. (2011) 'Tax doesn't have to be taxing: London's 'onshore' finance industry and the fiscal spaces of a global crisis', *Environment and Planning*, 43 (6): 1287–304.
Wójcik, D. (2013) 'Where governance fails: Advanced business services and the offshore world', *Progress in Human Geography*, 37 (3): 330–47.
Zaki, M. (2010) *Le secret bancaire est mort, vive l'évasion fiscale*. Lausanne: Favre.
Zoromé, A. (2007) *Concept of offshore financial centers: In search of an operational definition*. IMF. Retrieved on 11 October 2015 from www.imf.org/external/pubs/ft/wp/2007/wp0787.pdf.
Zucman, G. (2013) 'The missing wealth of nations: Are Europe and the US net debtors or net creditors?', *The Quarterly Journal of Economics*, 128 (3): 1321–64.
Zucman, G. (2014) *Steueroasen. Wo der Wohlstand der Nationen versteckt wird*. Berlin: Suhrkamp.

Part V
Limits of post-crisis bank regulation

15
Post-crisis bank regulation and financialized bank business models

Ian Crowther and Ismail Ertürk

Post-crisis regulatory objectives: de-risking and re-capitalizing banks for a safer financial system

Major regulatory initiatives after the 2007 banking crisis aim to make banks safer for depositors and taxpayers by introducing measures to de-risk and re-capitalize banks. The Basel III framework amended the pre-crisis Basel II risk algorithm for capital adequacy and increased the required amount of loss absorbing capital for banks. Basel III also includes a de-risking element in the form of liquidity management for safer funding. National regulatory initiatives aim both to de-risk banks by measures that separate risky investment banking from the utility retail banking and to re-capitalize them by strengthening the Basel III capital requirements. To achieve the latter objective the Liikanen Review in the EU proposed higher risk weights for bank assets than Basel III, the Vickers Report in the UK proposed higher minimum capital required than Basel III and the Dodd–Frank Act in the US empowered the newly created Financial Stability Oversight Council to impose a tougher leverage ratio than Basel III on banks that are deemed to pose systemic risk. Although all these three structural reform initiatives have not been implemented in full for various specific reasons in these three jurisdictions, the driving principles of these reform initiatives – de-risking banks through de-leveraging/re-capitalizing and reducing reliance on wholesale funds – remain intact despite various types of resistance to these reforms.

The section 619 (the Volcker Rule) of the Dodd–Frank Wall Street Reform and Consumer Protection Act banned proprietary trading in investment banking units (Dodd–Frank Act, 2010b). In the UK, the Vickers Report (ICB, 2011) ring-fenced the utility retail banking from risky investment banking. This ring-fencing by the Vickers Report constituted the core of the UK coalition government's Financial Services (Banking Reform) Bill of 2013 (HM Treasury, 2013). In the EU, the Liikanen Review in principle followed a similar path to the Dodd–Frank Act and the Vickers Report and proposed protection of vulnerable retail clients of banks. The White House website announced the Dodd–Frank Act with the following statement:

> To make sure that a crisis like this never happens again, President Obama signed the Dodd–Frank Wall Street Reform and Consumer Protection Act into law. The most far reaching Wall Street reform in history, Dodd–Frank will prevent the excessive risk-taking that led to

the financial crisis. The law also provides common-sense protections for American families, creating a new consumer watchdog to prevent mortgage companies and payday lenders from exploiting consumers. These new rules will build a safer, more stable financial system – one that provides a robust foundation for lasting economic growth and job creation.

(White House, 2010)

The 2,319-page-long Dodd–Frank Act aimed to de-risk the banks through a combination of supervisory surveillance, curbing certain bank activities and creating a legal framework for an orderly winding down of complex banking giants (Dodd–Frank Act, 2010a). The Liikanen Review in the EU too primarily aimed at curbing 'excessive risk taking' and stated that: 'The risk-taking was not matched with adequate capital protection, and strong linkages between financial institutions created high levels of systemic risk.' (Liikanen, 2012).

Both the Dodd–Frank Act and the Liikanen Review are more comprehensive than the Vickers' report in the sense that the former two aim for a more comprehensive structural reform of banking. However, the Libor scandal forced the politicians in the UK to increase the scope of the Vickers Report and a Parliamentary Commission on bank standards was set up in the UK. The final legislation on banking reform, The Financial Services (Banking Reform) Act 2013, therefore kept the Vickers Report's ring-fencing as its core logic of banking reform in the UK. The Liikanen Review proposes a bank resolution programme in the EU, bail-in bonds to supplement risk absorbing capital, improving risk weights used in calculating minimum capital under Basel, and improvement to governance mechanism at banks (Liikanen, 2012). As such all these post-crisis regulatory interventions in banking imagine a safe banking system for the society. Regulators accessorize their regulatory frameworks with various forms of stress testing that emphasize the priority of the safety of the banks and the banking system.

The Basel capital adequacy accord adjusted its risk algorithm for loss absorbing capital after the crisis and proposed re-capitalization of banks by increasing the minimum capital required against risk and also by redefining what qualifies for capital. Re-capitalization of banks under Basel III addresses both micro-prudential bank level risks and macro-prudential systemic risks (BCBS, 2011). In addition to the re-capitalization of banks Basel III also aims at de-risking highly leveraged banks by proposing a liquidity coverage ratio that encourages less reliance on short-term volatile funds to finance bank assets (BCBS, 2013). Basel's epistemic approach to banking is neutral to size and unlike the national banking reform initiatives covered above Basel does not directly and explicitly deal with too-big-to-fail problems in banking. As long as banks keep sufficient risk weighted capital and the right kind of liquidity, the size does not seem to matter for the Basel framework.

The implementation of these post-crisis initiatives aiming to de-risk the banks and to create a safer banking system naturally has been subject to a set of nationally specific resistances, debates, interpretations and delays. Although the Dodd–Frank and the Vickers initiatives have finally become legislative rules to reform banking in the US and the UK, the Liikanen initiative in the EU has still not been converted into a legislative form. In the EU, the Credit Requirement Directive IV (CRD IV) and Credit Requirement Regulation address the capital adequacy, leverage and liquidity related de-risking issues. The Bank Recovery and Resolution Directive complements the de-risking measures by aiming to protect the taxpayers and national finances from future bank failures. The EU Commission sees these de-risking measures as pieces in the bigger puzzle of the Banking Union (European Commission, 2014). However, the Commission still acknowledges that the Liikanen Review's aim to structurally reform the Eurozone banking by separating risky investment banking from the utility retail banking has not been addressed by the Banking Union framework:

Nevertheless, some EU banks may still remain too-big-to-fail, too-big-to-save and too-complex-to-resolve. Further measures are therefore needed, notably a structural separation of the risks associated with banks' trading activities from its deposit-taking function. Today's proposals aim to strengthen the resilience of the EU banking sector while ensuring that banks continue to finance economic activity and growth.

(European Commission (a & b), 2014)

Although all major post-crisis structural reform initiatives in the US, the UK and the EU that aim to de-risk the banking system have not been fully implemented and have experienced and continue to experience dilutions, delays and resistances their key philosophical tenets regarding the location of systemically important risks in banking firms have not been questioned. Our objective in this chapter is to argue that systemically important risks in banking are product of bank business models and as such their locations within the banking firm tend to conjuncturally vary as bank business models change. Therefore the starting point of any structural reform framework should be the business models of banks rather than their ephemeral risk profiles and capital structures. In the next section we will explain financialized business models of banks and then we will give examples of potentially systemic risks that financialized bank business models are capable of producing and that escape the analytical insights of the major structural bank reform initiatives in the post-crisis period.

Financialized bank business models

The financialization literature covers a cross-disciplinary space in academic research that includes political economy, sociology, management studies, cultural studies and geography (Zwan, 2014; Engelen and Konings, 2010; Treeck, 2009, Ertürk *et al.*, 2008). In this chapter we are interested in exploring the behaviour of financialized banking firm and therefore will draw upon the work of CRESC researchers in Manchester on financialization where the political and cultural economy critique of the shareholder-value principle in present day capitalism is the major focus (Engelen *et al.*, 2011, Ertürk *et al.*, 2008, Froud *et al.*, 2006). Maximization of shareholder value in firms with dispersed ownership is both prescribed by mainstream corporate finance books and consultancy firms and practiced by the management. Froud *et al.* (2006) discuss the mainstream finance inspired work of consultancy firms that sold to and implemented shareholder-value practices in corporations in the neo-liberal era since the 1980s. Lazonick and O'Sullivan (2010) explore the historical rise of shareholder-value maximization principle as the dominant corporate governance practice in the US corporations where distributing profits to shareholders through high dividends and share buybacks is preferred to retaining profits for long-term investments. Share price is influenced immediately by current cash payments to shareholders. Retaining profits to invest, on the other hand, does not have the same immediate effect on share price.

Such behaviour was exhibited by Citigroup in 2006 when Citigroup's profitability alone could not drive the share price up. The relative financial performance of the Citigroup was disappointing in 2006 and therefore a $7 billion share buyback was carried out to increase the share price to compete in shareholder-value creation with other banks. Share buyback helped to deliver a 20 per cent appreciation in share price: 'Our total shareholder return was nearly 20 per cent for the year, a level that placed us in the middle of the pack of a group of financial services companies' (Citigroup, 2007). In the same year Deutsche Bank proudly announced to its shareholders that '(t)hese outstanding results enable us to deliver excellent value to our shareholders. Our share price rose 24% during the year, outperforming both the DAX and the Euro-STOXX banks indices,…' (Deutsche Bank, 2007). In the post-crisis environment Deutsche Bank, like almost all banks who suffered significant reduction in market value, could not deliver a meaningful share price increase. But this did not stop Deutsche Bank from announcing shareholder-value maximization as its top priority: 'While we're pleased with the year-on-year improvement, we're not satisfied with this level of profitability. We have the potential to deliver more for our shareholders, and Strategy 2015+ is designed to deliver that potential' (Deutsche Bank, 2013). The principle of shareholder-value maximization is adopted even by the UK government who bailed out Royal Bank of Scotland at a record cost to the taxpayer at £46 billion in 2008. The remuneration package of the CEO Stephen Hester for the 80 per cent state-owned bank included £6.4 million worth of long-term incentives that were linked to an increase in share price (BBC News, 2009). The UK government saw the taxpayers as shareholders in RBS and believed that an increase in the share price that generated an £8 billion return was a justifiable performance target.

In a financialized economy corporations compete in the stock market to deliver shareholder value and banks are no exception to this financialized form of competition even under state ownership as the case of RBS in the UK shows. In Anglo-Saxon economies and to a certain extent in coordinated market economies (CMS) like Germany and France the objective of the publicly listed company's management is to maximize shareholder value, which is measured by the performance of share price in the stock market. There is a sizeable literature on whether coordinated market economies like Germany and France, where banks are believed to be providers of patient capital to productive firms and not to prioritize return to shareholders, are becoming financialized or not like the firms in Anglo-Saxon economies, where stock markets demand quarterly reported financial performance. It is beyond this chapter's scope to cover these debates. But as the Deutsche Bank example above demonstrates, CME-based public firms also prioritize shareholder-value maximization, especially when they have institutional shareholders from Anglo-Saxon economies that demand shareholder-value-driven corporate governance.

In a financialized economy where the hegemonic corporate governance form requires firms seeking maximization of shareholder value and the remuneration of the managers is linked to the achievement of this objective then return on shareholders' funds becomes the key financial metric to measure firm performance. Consequently, return on equity has become a universal metric to measure financial performance in all publicly listed banks including the ones in CMEs. Both academics like Engelen *et al.* (2011) and regulators like the Bank of England's economist Haldane (Haldane, 2009) agree that high, unrealistic returns on equity targets in shareholder-value-driven banks that compete in stock markets encouraged excessive risk taking by management. Haldane, in one of his post-crisis writings on the causes of the crisis, comments that:

> First, the downward slope is consistent with global banks targeting a ROE, perhaps benchmarked by peers' performance. The Bank's market intelligence in the run-up to crisis suggested that such 'keeping up with the Jones's' was an important cultural influence on banks' decision-making. Second ... banks kept up in this competitive race by gearing-up. Banks unable to deliver sufficiently high returns on assets to meet their ROE targets resorted instead to leveraging their balance sheets.
>
> *(Haldane, 2009)*

Engelen *et al.*'s (2011) empirical research into returns on equity in pre-crisis banking finds that there is a consensus rate of 15 per cent that banks universally aim to achieve. Figure 15.1 demonstrates how between 2002 and 2007 the average return on equity of the Eurozone banks caught up with that of Anglo-Saxon banks in the kind of competition that Haldane describes above based on his insights as a regulator.

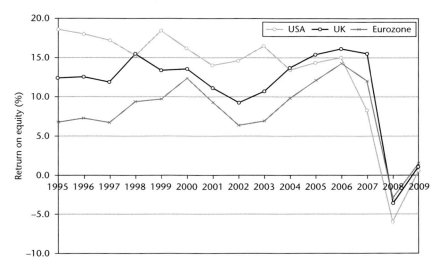

Figure 15.1 Convergence to 15% ROE in pre-crisis banking
Source: Engelen *et al.* (2011).

Since the crisis in 2007 banks have had difficulty in achieving the pre-crisis return on equity profitability of 15 per cent and above. But the industry still uses return on equity as a shareholder-value-creating performance metric and a new post-crisis consensus rate of about 11 or 12 per cent seems to be emerging:

> Deutsche's new co-chief executives are expected to make a decisive break with the decade-long era of Josef Ackermann, their predecessor, when they will drop a target of generating a 25 per cent pre-tax return on equity. Analysts estimate that the new goal could be in the region of 12 to 13 per cent ROE after tax – a benchmark more commonly looked at by investors than the pre-tax figure. Two weeks ago, the new chief executive of Deutsche's main European rival Barclays lowered the bank's target to at least its cost of equity, currently 11 to 11.5 per cent. 'A return on equity target of 12 per cent would be a very good number for a top tier investment bank in the current environment,' said Kian Abouhossein, analyst at JPMorgan.
>
> *(Wilson, 2012)*

There are also other key metrics that are used by bank equity analysts such as fee income and cost ratio to evaluate a bank's financial performance in a financialized economy. Before the 2007 crisis the growth of bank balance sheets and mergers and acquisitions to create banking conglomerates were also encouraged by the stock market in creating shareholder value. And the regulators were not discouraging such stock market-driven creation of large complex financial institutions. RBS, which was the largest corporate failure in the UK in terms of losses suffered, was congratulated by the markets when it bought ABN-Amro because it had finally joined the global league of super-sized banks.

Too-big-to-fail is an *ex post* risk that regulators today try to deal with through various de-risking and re-capitalization measures. However, before the crisis stock markets encouraged banks to increase size through acquisitions and leverage. Belgian, Austrian and Italian banks went on a spending spree to buy banks in Eastern Europe to achieve both higher return on equity in these higher margin banking markets and asset growth. When acquisitions were not possible for aggressive growth for a small regional bank like Northern Rock in the UK, Northern Rock instead used securitization to finance aggressive asset growth. Basel II risk algorithms did not regard Northern Rock's collateralized real estate lending as risky. Northern Rock, which had to be bailed out by the UK government after a run on the bank in 2008, exploited the internal rating-based methodology for risk calculation under Basel II and operated with lower capital when the bank was taking more credit risk in the mortgage market and liquidity risk in wholesale funding markets. Figure 15.2 shows how Northern Rock reported its lower capitalization under Basel II internal rating-based methodology.

Northern Rock had relied heavily on securitization of its mortgage assets to finance the phenomenal growth of its mortgage book that was praised by the bank analysts. Thus, according to ING in September 2006, 'Northern Rock has managed to transform itself into one of the UK's top residential secured lending powerhouses. . . We expect asset and profit growth to continue to outpace the market, and Northern Rock is the envy of its peers' (Sarangi, 2006). In announcing its 2006 preliminary results Northern Rock stated that 'Northern Rock has four distinct funding arms enabling it to attract funds from a wide range of customers and counterparties on a global basis. In recognition of our broad and innovative access to a cost effective and diverse capital markets investor base, Northern Rock was awarded the prestigious International Financing Review's 2006 Financial Institution Group Borrower of the Year award' (Northern Rock, 2007).

Not only did the securitization of its mortgage loans provide liquidity to fund its phenomenal growth, it also allowed Northern Rock to achieve favourable capital adequacy ratios under Basel II. Residential mortgages constituted 77 per cent of the total assets of Northern Rock in 2006 and securitization under Basel II meant, as Figure 15.2 demonstrates, their risk weights were significantly reduced. Since management compensation in financialized banks is determined by share price in the stock market where the equity analysts' and activist hedge fund shareholders' opinions on bank strategy, as the Northern Rock example above shows, are crucially important, actual risk taking behaviour is not likely to be influenced by the regulators' views on risk. Academics like Bebchuk and Spamann (2009) who study corporate governance and optimal

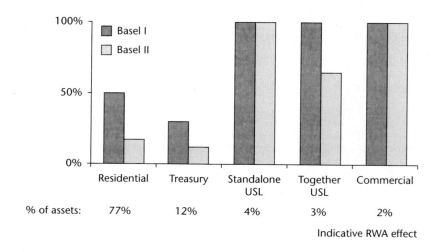

Figure 15.2 Northern Rock's lower capitalization under Basel II

Source: www.northernrock.co.uk, www.n-ram.co.uk/~/media/Files/N/N-RAM/content/results-presentations/stockex070124.pdf\ (accessed on 9 February 2010).

executive remuneration contracts draw regulators' attention to this fundamental gap in regulators' thinking about risk in banking: 'Moreover, as long as management's incentives are tied to those of shareholders, management might have an incentive to increase risks beyond what is intended or assumed by the regulators, who might often be one step behind banks' executives. Regulators should attempt to make management incentives work for, rather than against, the goals of banking regulation' (Bebchuk and Spamann, 2009).

Since the introduction of the Basel capital adequacy accords from the late 1980s onwards, the calculation of return on equity in banking has become more creative. The regulatory focus of Basel is optimum equity allocation against balance sheet and off-balance-sheet risks in banking. Basel capital adequacy accords have developed an algorithm where each bank activity, both on balance sheet and off balance sheet, has a precise risk weight that determines how much capital a bank keeps against this quantified credit or market risk. For example, under Basel I, banks had to keep $8 capital against $100 loan to a private company with no credit rating. However, lending to the national government through the purchase of sovereign bonds, according to Basel I risk algorithm required zero capital because sovereigns are assumed to have zero default risk. Similarly, lending to other banks is assigned a 20 per cent weight because shorter-term lending to other banks compared with corporate lending is considered to be one-fifth less risky. With Basel II, credit derivatives were allowed to be used as credit risk mitigation methodologies and banks started to buy large amounts of credit default swaps to shift the credit risk on their balance sheets to the insurance companies.

Therefore banks could enhance their return on equity ratio by reducing their denominator, as the OECD economists Blundell-Wignall and Atkinson (2010) have shown, by creatively applying the Basel risk algorithm that is influenced by modern finance theory. As Engelen *et al.* (2011) have argued, bank business models are driven by the objective of maximizing share price in the stock market in financialized capitalism. Stock markets universally demand 15 per cent return on equity from banks. Therefore financial innovation tends to create lower risk weighted assets for banks to achieve this metric. Credit derivatives and securitization were examples of such financial innovation before the crisis. Sovereign bonds, interbank lending and real estate lending too were lower risk weighted than corporate and SME lending. Since the crisis, central bank monetary policies aim to cheaply fund SMEs and corporations to spur economic growth by keeping cost of funds to the banking system very low. However, banks are unwilling to lend to SMEs and corporations because such banks, assets are subject to higher risk weight under Basel capital rules and hence tend to reduce return on equity. In the UK especially the government's funding for lending scheme that aimed to improve credit flow to SMEs has been spectacularly unsuccessful causing public criticism of new Basel capital rules by the coalition minister for business Vince Cable (Ridley, 2013). Not only do the re-capitalization efforts under Basel III discourage capital flow to SMEs and to the industry, according to the OECD economists Blundell-Wignall, Atkinson and Roulet, 'Basel risk weighting and the use of internal bank models for determining them leads to systematic regulatory arbitrage that undermines its effectiveness' (Blundell-Wignall *et al.*, 2013).

Bank business models increasingly attract the critical attention of economists who problematize the analytical soundness of bank risk modelling by the regulators. Ayadi and de Groen (2014) studied the relationship between bank business models and financial instability in the European Union to gain a better insight into systemic risk properties of different bank business models. Roengpitya *et al.* (2014) studied a larger sample of banks including non-European banks to see whether bank business models have changed after the crisis. They found that there is a tendency towards commercial banking business models that are associated with less earnings volatility. Although such studies emphasize the importance of studying business models in banking in order to develop more nuanced and effective regulatory frameworks, they do not include in their analysis how stock market valuation of these business models influences the risk taking activities. Bank managers shape bank business models and bank strategies to satisfy shareholder value in the stock market rather than serving regulators and other stakeholders. After a survey of banking executives in 2013 *The Banker* magazine concluded that 'banks can use the process of complying with new regulations to inform strategy and steer it in the direction of securing sustainable returns for shareholders' (Alexander, 2014).

In the following section we will present three post-crisis case studies where in pursuit of generating high return on equity, shareholder-value-driven banks have relocated risks to areas that were not covered by the post-crisis de-risking regulatory initiatives. In all three cases banks suffered losses that were not insignificant. The case of Barclays is chosen to argue that post-crisis regulation fails to address explicitly (a) re-located risks that arise from new forms of regulatory arbitrage and (b) moral hazard that arises from unregulated financial innovation. The J.P. Morgan Chase case is chosen to argue that the post-crisis regulation has failed to address the risks that arise from modelling and reporting of risks in non-investment banking activities in large financial conglomerates that aggressively pursue 15 per cent return on equity. The third case study involves UK retail banking where the mis-selling of financial products rather than risky investment banking activities caused incalculable losses that erode the capital base of systemically important financial institutions. In the UK the ring-fencing of retail banking under The Financial Services (Banking Reform) Act 2013 assumes that the source of fragility in the financial system lies in investment banking activities of banking conglomerates. Similarly, the Liikanen report in the EU ignores the potential systemic destabilizing risks against which there are no regulatory re-capitalization measures. The failures in risk management in banking in proprietary trading and investments in CDOs in the investment banking units of banks were the major concerns of all post-crisis regulatory frameworks. However, these three case studies involve two banks, Barclays and J.P. Morgan Chase, which came out of the crisis with their investment banking activities receiving praise in risk management. Bob Diamond who was the head of Barclays Capital, the investment banking unit of Barclays, was promoted to become the CEO of Barclays as his unit continued to deliver high return on equity within the bank and for the bank. J.P. Morgan Chase's CEO Jamie Dimon boasted about his banks' mastery of risk management in investment banking in the aftermath of the crisis.

Post-crisis examples of relocated risks in shareholder-value-driven banks

Case study 1: Barclays' Protium SPV

The de-risking measures that are introduced by the major regulatory initiatives since the crisis are likely to be one or two steps behind the banks' ability to manufacture returns, generating new risks that become possible in a field of conjunctural market and regulatory arbitrage opportunities. One example of such conjunctural regulatory arbitrage opportunities is the creation by Barclays of Cayman Islands-based fund called Protium Finance LP. In order to improve its capital adequacy ratio under Basel II and reduce the volatility of reported earnings under mark-to-market accounting rules soon after the banking crisis of 2007 Barclays moved $12.3 billion (£7.5 billion) of its toxic assets (residential and commercial mortgage-backed securities, collateralized loan obligations, and so on), which had to be otherwise mark-to-market with huge potential losses, from its balance sheet to a special purpose vehicle called Protium (Salz, 2013). And then a group of Barclays managers left the bank, as part of the deal, to set up a fund management company called C12 to manage the assets of Protium. Barclays lent a 10-year loan of $12.6 billion to Protium, slightly more than the value of credit assets transferred to Protium, for Protium to buy the toxic assets from Barclays (Barclays PLC, 2010a). Basically a $12.3 billion (£7.5 billion) of toxic mortgage-backed securities on Barclays' balance sheet were replaced by a loan of almost the same amount, which required less capital under Basel II, and improved Barclays' reported return on equity. Barclays justified the transaction at the time by explaining how it would 'enhance shareholder value in three ways' by (1) reducing volatility of earnings, (2) increasing risk adjusted returns on equity and (3) securing long-term access to a specialist management team (Lucas, 2009). According to the *Financial Times*, this accounting trick allowed Barclays to pay less tax and to report higher profits as well as avoiding capital deficit.

> Tax experts say that aside from dodging potential short-term impairment and capital charges, the benefit for Barclays' bottom line – bigger profits in 2009 – allowed the bank to crystallise a large volume of tax losses racked up amid the financial crisis. Hence the bank's tiny £113m corporation tax bill in a year when it made a record £11.6bn in pre-tax profits.
> *(Jenkins and Murphy, 2011)*

In the face of growing post-crisis public and political criticism of banks Barclays rather arrogantly stated in its 2009 Annual Report that 'Regulation needs to be strengthened but it must not result in a financial system that cannot serve the needs of the global economy'. It was dubious though how an accounting trick like Protium, as the *Financial Times* described it, could be of service to the global economy (Barclays Plc, 2010b). The new capital adequacy accord of Basel III removed the regulatory arbitrage advantages of Protium under Basel II and in 2010 Barclays bought back the toxic assets from Protium at £6 billion, incurring a loss of about £1.7 billion in the process (Jenkins, 2011 and Murphy; Barclays Plc, 2012). According to the *Wall Street Journal*, new Basel III rules would triple the capital that Barclays had to keep against the loan to Protium and would reduce Barclays' return on equity impacting negatively its share price (Nixon, 2011). But the Barclays managers who left Barclays to manage Protium continued to receive their guaranteed fees. Basel III could not stop the moral hazard that benefited the managers at the expense of shareholders and taxpayers. The legal structure of Protium was such that Barclays ended up paying a total amount of £735 million to wind down the special purpose vehicle.

Although the losses incurred by Barclays in the Protium saga were not high enough to cause insolvency, the example shows that the de-risking initiatives of national regulators fail to see the location and nature of new risks in complex financial institutions that harm taxpayers but are financially beneficial for bank managers and have potential systemic risk implications because markets can overreact to the loss consequences of complex and opaque financial transactions. This example also shows how bank managers can circumvent bonus caps by re-hiring themselves at favourable terms as fund managers to manage the toxic assets that they themselves in the first place created. Barclays have not fully disclosed the structure of Protium and the deals agreed with the ex-Barclays managers. The media coverage of the Protium deal suggests that senior managers at Barclays' Structured Capital Markets division who helped Barclays to arbitrage and mitigate tax in the past were involved in the creation of Protium, and that these senior managers financially benefited from the Protium structure (Sunderland, 2013). Post-crisis regulatory initiatives aim to have living wills from large complex banks but are very unlikely to prevent the creation of off-balance-sheet mechanisms like Protium that can threaten the well-being of a complex bank. Also, there are no provisions in the ring-fencing regulation in the UK against legitimate accounting tricks that banks employ to re-locate and represent risks in pursuit of high return on equity. In its 2011 Annual Report Barclays stated that:

Our primary objective is to maximise returns for shareholders and in doing so, we aim to deliver top quartile TSR (total shareholder return). ... Over the past five years there has been a clear relationship between TSR and return on equity (RoE) with the market value of the shares improving with higher reported RoE.

(Barclays Plc, 2012)

Case study 2: J.P. Morgan Chase's 'Big Whale' trading losses

In the example of Barclays' Protium the new risk was manufactured in a legitimate regulatory arbitrage space that was created by risk accounting rules and Basel II capital adequacy rules. In the case of J.P. Morgan Chase, on the other hand, the risk did not arise at the proprietary trading desks that the Dodd–Frank Act aims to remove from banks but in mundane investment of excess cash in the Chief Investment Office (United States Senate, 2013). Usually excess cash at J.P. Morgan Chase would be invested in safe assets like government bonds. But the quantitative easing policies of the Federal Reserve that aim for zero-interest rates for economic recovery reduced returns from such liquid safe assets. Financial media have reported that J.P. Morgan Chase had a different view on the riskiness of such safe assets and its CEO Jamie Dimon publicly stated, 'If you own Treasuries folks, you could be taking a lot of risk' (Makan, 2012). Therefore, in this context of subjective risk perceptions, in order to achieve higher returns the investment officers at J.P. Morgan Chase had invested in credit derivatives and then hedged the risk by shorting their long positions. It was such complex hedging activities outside investment banking that caused the loss, which was estimated to be around $6 billion. But the exact size of the loss could not be calculated accurately by J.P. Morgan Chase. J.P. Morgan Chase first announced that the loss was $2 billion and then gradually increased the size of the loss to $6 billion, creating uncertainty in investors and regulators regarding J.P. Morgan Chase's ability to control the risk of the portfolio. Although like Barclays' Protium the reported loss was not big enough to threaten insolvency for J.P. Morgan Chase, it nevertheless showed that a bank like J.P. Morgan Chase, which had come out of the banking crisis of 2007 with flying colours in risk management, might not after all be good at managing and reporting risk under the conjunctural market conditions created by quantitative easing policies of the Federal Reserve.

Jamie Dimon, the CEO of J.P. Morgan Chase explained, in the bank's 2012 Annual Report, that the failings in risk management were due to complacency created by high returns in CIO: 'Given the portfolio's success over time, we had become complacent, and we weren't as rigorous and sceptical as we should have been' (J.P. Morgan Chase & Co, 2013).

However, the portfolio's problems were known by the outsiders in the credit derivatives market before J.P. Morgan Chase publicly acknowledged it. The *Wall Street Journal* reported the market rumours on 6 April 2012 (Zuckerman and Burne, 2012). The CEO Jamie Dimon responded to the media reports of J.P. Morgan Chase's risky trading portfolio a week later by describing them infamously as 'a complete tempest in the teapot' (Benoit, 2012). It was only a month later, on 10 May 2012, that J.P. Morgan Chase admitted that they made a loss from the reported trades at the bank's Chief Office of Investments. J.P. Morgan Chase's first estimate of the loss in May 2012, was $2 billion, but this figure was later raised to $5.8 billion, in July 2012, creating uncertainty over the actual size of the loss.

Value at Risk (VaR) in Figure 15.3 is an estimation of losses from the investment portfolio in the Chief Investment Office of J.P. Morgan Chase. Big banks like J.P. Morgan Chase are trusted by the regulators to use their own risk measurement models. Similarly, under Basel capital adequacy rules regulators allow banks to use their own internal rating based risk weights in calculating required regulatory capital. The lines in Figure 15.3 show the probabilistic tail end

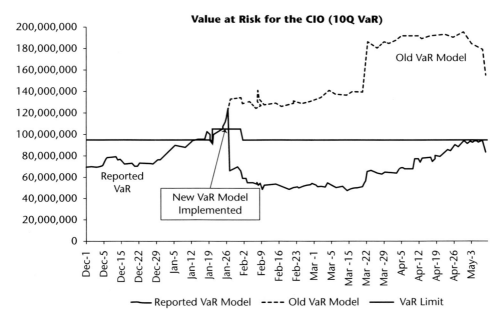

Figure 15.3 Manipulation of risk valuation models at J.P. Morgan Chase
Source: United States Senate (2013).

losses from the investment portfolio at CIO. One of them shows the losses under the old Value at Risk (VaR) model that was used until January 2011 and the other shows the losses under the new VaR that was implemented after January 2011. Starting from January 2011 the investment portfolio at the CIO was making losses that were higher than the allocated capital can support – the level shown by the VaR Limit line in Figure 15.3. J.P. Morgan Chase changed its model in January 2011 to hide the losses. The losses reported under the new VaR model were less than the limit. But even under the manipulated new model losses were exceeding the VaR limit and J.P. Morgan Chase had to disclose its losses and made them public after having denied earlier rumours reported in the media.

This case did not involve risk trading that is financed by wholesale funds or over-the-counter derivatives that the post-crisis Basel liquidity regulation and the Dodd–Frank Act aim to control. J.P. Morgan Chase was using its own liquidity, customers' deposits, to generate extra returns in its CIO, not in its investment banking division. It is not an accident that such high risk trading happened at a bank that aggressively pursues shareholder value and reports 15 per cent return on equity as its target profitability (J.P. Morgan Chase). At the time of the London Whale trade saga J.P. Morgan's competitor US banks like Bank of America Merrill Lynch and Citigroup were investing in safer US government guaranteed bonds of 85 per cent and 49 per cent of their available for sale assets against J.P. Morgan Chase's 30 per cent (Makan, 2012). J.P. Morgan Chase's annual reports regularly show the share price performance of J.P. Morgan Chase against its competitors. Of course, the higher share price performance of J.P. Morgan Chase could be due to variety of other factors. But since risk and return are positively correlated in financial markets higher profits at J.P. Morgan Chase must be associated with higher risks as the London Whale trade case has shown. But the risk management models that are not regulated by the Dodd–Frank Act can be manipulated by banks with aggressive shareholder-value-driven business models to hide the risk and return relationships in transactions. The US Senate Permanent Subcommittee on Investigations that investigated the J.P. Morgan Chase's Big Whale trades concluded that J.P. Morgan Chase had manipulated risk models to reduce capital requirements for higher risk derivatives trading:

> In contrast to JP Morgan Chase's reputation for best-in-class risk management, the whale trades exposed a bank culture in which risk limit breaches were routinely disregarded, risk metrics were frequently criticized or downplayed, and risk evaluation models were targeted by bank personnel seeking to produce artificially lower capital requirements.
>
> *(United States Senate, 2013)*

In shareholder-value-driven bank business models reporting high return on equity is the primary objective, as discussed earlier in this chapter. And, as Figure 15.3 shows, the unregulated risk modelling allows banks to report artificially low required capital, resulting in higher return on equity. Ertürk *et al.* (2013) analyse such bank behaviour to show that capital adequacy regulation unintentionally provides opportunities for banks to report high artificial return on equity rather than adequately capitalizing banks against risks. De-risking banks is not likely to be meaningfully achieved without regulators seriously evaluating bank business models that publicly promise the consensus unrealistic and unsustainable return on equity of 15 per cent that the stock market in a financialized economy demands from banks for shareholder value.

Case study 3: Mis-selling by the UK retail banks

After the banking crisis of 2007, between 2009–14 the UK retail banks collectively have paid £17 billion to their customers in redress because they mis-sold payment protection insurance (PPI). PPI is an insurance product that enables consumers to insure repayment of loans if the borrower dies, becomes ill or disabled, loses a job, or faces other circumstances that may prevent them from earning income to service the debt. The UK retail banks sold such products to customers who were not qualified and/or who were not properly informed about the product. Morgan Stanley estimates that the total cost to the UK banks could reach £27 billion by the end of 2016 (*The Economist*, 2015). This amount is larger than the £24 billion loss that RBS suffered in 2008, which was then the largest loss in UK corporate history.

Mis-selling costs weaken the capital base of the UK banks because both actual costs and provisions against probable future claims by customers reduce retained earnings and hence the equity. Therefore the post-crisis regulatory measures to re-capitalize the UK banking system to make it more resilient against economic shocks and possible deteriorating economic conditions in the future are hampered by high and incalculable costs of mis-selling. Lloyds Banking Group suffered most financially in mis-selling PPI by providing £9.8 billion between 2011 and 2015, and the bank is unable to estimate accurately the total cost of mis-selling:

> The total amount provided for PPI represents our best estimate of the likely future costs, albeit a number of risks and uncertainties remain, in particular complaint volumes, uphold rates, average redress costs, the scope and cost of proactive mailings and remediation, and the outcome of the FCA Enforcement Team investigation. The cost of these factors could differ materially from our estimates, with the risk that a further provision could be required.
>
> *(Lloyds Banking Group, 2014)*

Such a high cost of mis-selling weakens Lloyds Banking Group's capital base and the bank was one of the three banks in the UK out of a total of eight that could not pass the Bank of England's

2014 stress test (Bank of England, 2014). Mis-selling is a result of banks' goal to increase fee income that stock markets demand for higher share price performance. Fee income generating activities of banks usually are not risk weighted under Basel capital adequacy rules and therefore do not require risk capital to back them. Fee income increases return on equity as the numerator can increase without a corresponding increase in the denominator. Also, fee income tends to be non-cyclical unlike trading and interest income. The Financial Conduct Authority's investigations into mis-selling at Lloyds TSB and Bank of Scotland between 2010 and 2012 found that when the customer demand for investment products fell after the crisis these banks adjusted their business models to sell more insurance products. At Lloyds TSB, during that period, sales of cyclical investment products decreased by 54 per cent but sales of protection products increased by 65 per cent (Financial Conduct Authority, 2013). It is not unusual for shareholder-value-driven banks to act aggressively in search of fee income generation. Retail banks have an advantage over investment banks in generating fee income because they have a much larger retail banking customer base and a much bigger sales force. Bank staff in branches are incentivised to sell products to their financially illiterate retail customers. The UK Financial Conduct Authority reported that:

> We were concerned to find that incentive schemes with high-risk features and the potential for sales staff to earn significant bonuses were common across the firms we assessed. Most firms did not have effective systems and controls in place to adequately manage the increased risks of mis-selling arising from their incentive schemes.
>
> *(Financial Services Authority, 2013)*

Mis-selling happened both before and after the crisis. Between January 2010 and March 2012 Lloyds Banking Group (Lloyds TSB, Halifax and Bank of Scotland) mis-sold over one million products to nearly 700,000 customers (Financial Conduct Authority, 2013). The financial cost of mis-selling to the UK retail banks is significant and weakens the capital base of these banks when the regulatory initiatives aim to re-capitalize them for a safer banking system. As Ertürk and Solari (2007) have argued, the business models of shareholder-value-driven retail banks require aggressive selling of retail products to financially illiterate customers because in a financialized economy banks are likely to achieve high share prices in the stock market if they meet the required financial performance metrics in return on equity and fee income. An equity analyst report by Deutsche Bank in 2006, before the crisis, commented positively on the cross selling of retail banking products by 'retrained branch staff' at Lloyds TSB:

> The focus thus far has been improving the customer proposition through the branch network and increasing the sales performance of branch staff. Although we believe this will ultimately result in an increase in current account and other major product sales, one immediate uplift has been to the cross sell of life, pensions and long-term savings products. This has been achieved as the product range was simplified and the branch staff retrained. This is a positive development and is key to the strategy of taking an increasing share of each customer's wallet.
>
> *(Deutsche Bank, 2006)*

Lloyds TSB's stock market valuation is influenced by such analyst reports on bank business models, and the bank management responds to such reports to deliver shareholder value. After the crisis, however, what Lloyds TSB had taken away from each customer's wallet has to be returned to the customers' wallet with great cost to the stability of the banking system in the UK.

As reported above, mis-selling at Lloyds Banking Group continued after the crisis between 2010 and 2012. Shareholder-value-driven bank business models shape the incentive and remuneration systems in banking and the post-crisis regulatory initiatives do not have analytical frameworks to deal with such business model risks.

None of the post-crisis bank regulatory frameworks has explicitly addressed the risks in sales-driven retail banking. The US Consumer Financial Protection Bureau and the UK Financial Conduct Authority were established after the crisis to protect consumers through minimizing informational asymmetries, promoting transparency in pricing and aiming to punish misbehaving financial intermediaries. However, the risks to the financial systems that arise from sales driven business models in retail banking are not adequately addressed. Selling mortgages to subprime borrowers at teaser rates was a retail banking business model before the crisis that the stock market rewarded handsomely. In the post-crisis UK the government encourages competition in retail banking and retail banks compete for customers by marketing deposit products at introductory rates without disclosing the real long-term costs and benefits. The assumption in post-crisis regulatory initiatives that retail banking has to be ring-fenced and protected from risky investment banking needs to be revisited as retail banking rather needs to be ring-fenced from the unrealistic return on equity expectations of stock markets.

Conclusion

This chapter aimed to argue that the post-crisis regulatory initiatives that are meant to de-risk and re-capitalize banks to create financially sound individual banks and consequently a stable financial system do not take into account return on equity-driven bank behaviour in a financialized capitalism. In a financialized economy banks compete in the stock market to maximize shareholder value. Investors in the stock market identify key financial performance metrics that influence market capitalization of banks. In banking return on equity is the primary metric and a rate of 15 per cent was the pre-crisis norm. Remuneration of managers in a financialized economy is tied to the delivery of shareholder value. Therefore bank managers are incentivised to achieve a high return on equity ratios in banking and Basel capital adequacy rules allow managers to carry out regulatory arbitrage to achieve high return on equity targets. In retail banking high fee income is another important financial metric that influences market capitalization of banks. Mis-selling in the UK retail banks is a consequence of financialized bank behaviour that aims high fee income through cross-selling.

By using three post-crisis case studies, two from investment banking and one from retail banking, we argued that shareholder-value-driven banks re-locate risks to areas that remain in the blind spot of post-crisis de-risking and re-capitalizing regulatory initiatives. To achieve a safer financial system bank regulators need to specifically address the regulatory challenges of financialized bank business models. To this effect we would propose that investment banking and retail banking have to be completely separated for both risk and stock market purposes. Investment banking is a higher risk cyclical business and therefore would offer a different risk and return proposal than less risky and less cyclical retail banking to stock market investors. Less risky utility retail banking should not come under pressure from the stock market to deliver unrealistic and unsustainable 15 per cent return on equity. However, we need to exclude proprietary trading from investment banking as proprietary trading is a higher risk activity than customer driven investment banking activities like underwriting bond and equity issues. Proprietary trading and similar high risk investment strategies would be more appropriate for hedge fund like intermediaries. Modern finance theory argues that risk diversification can be and should be done by investors themselves not by the companies, and modern corporate and investment practices reflect this rationality. However, if large complex banks exist for national political purposes rather than for economic purposes, as the CEO of J.P. Morgan Chase Jamie Dimon said recently (Glazer, 2015), and as we have observed in creation of national giant banking firms through mergers and acquisitions since the early 1990s, then we need to think of a totally new kind of governance and ownership structures for them that need to be democratically discussed for the benefit of taxpayers. If risky banking conglomerates are a political choice for nation states then they should not be managed for shareholder value in a financialized economy, and it is not the re-capitalization but the re-design of capital structure and governance that we need (Blundell-Wignall and Atkinson, 2010).

References

Alexander, P. (2014) 'Banks try to stay ahead of regulatory tide'. The Banker Special Report – Transforming the Bank: Regulation and Strategy. January, p. 2.
Ayadi, R. and de Groen, W.P. (2014) *Banking Business Models Monitor 2014 Europe*. Brussels: Centre for European Policy Studies and International Observatory on Financial Services Cooperatives.
Bank of England. (2014) 'Stress testing the UK banking system: 2014 Results', p. 7.
Barclays Plc. (2010a) 'Annual Report 2009', p. 7.
Barclays Plc. (2010b) 'Annual Report 2009', p. 114.
Barclays Plc. (2012) 'Annual Report 2011', p. 41.
BBC News. (2009) 'RBS boss set for £9.6m pay deal'. Retrieved on 4 May 2016 from http://news.bbc.co.uk/go/pr/fr/-/1/hi/business/8112199.stm.
BCBS. (Basel Committee on Banking Supervision) (2011) 'Basel III: A global regulatory framework for more resilient banks and banking systems', June, Basel. Retrieved on 4 May 2016 from www.bis.org/publ/bcbs189.pdf.
BCBS. (Basel Committee on Banking Supervision) (2013) 'Basel III: The liquidity coverage ratio and liquidity risk monitoring tools', June, Basel. Retrieved on 4 May 2016 from www.bis.org/publ/bcbs238.pdf.
Bebchuk, L.A. and Spamann, H. (2009) 'Regulating bankers' pay'. Harvard John M. Olin Center for Law, Economics, and Business. Discussion Paper No. 641. Retrieved on 4 May 2016 from www.law.harvard.edu/programs/olin_center/.
Benoit, D. (2012) 'J.P. Morgan: A London whale? He is more of a shrubbery'. *Wall Street Journal*, 13, April.
Blundell-Wignall, A. and Atkinson, P. (2010) 'Thinking beyond Basel III: Necessary solutions for capital and liquidity'. OECD Journal: *Financial Market Trends*, (1): 1–23.
Blundell-Wignall, A., Atkinson, P. and Roulet, C. (2013) 'Bank business models and the Basel system: Complexity and interconnectedness'. OECD Journal: *Financial Market Trends*, (2): 1.
Citigroup. (2007) 'Annual Report 2006', p. 5.
Deutsche Bank. (2006) 'Lloyds TSB: Dial T, for turnaround', p. 4.
Deutsche Bank. (2007) 'Annual Review 2006', p.2.
Deutsche Bank. (2013) 'Annual Review 2012', p. 3.
Dodd–Frank Act. (2010a) Retrieved on 4 May 2016 from www.govtrack.us/congress/bills/111/hr4173/text.
Dodd–Frank Act. (2010b) 'Dodd–Frank Wall Street Reform and Consumer Protection Act'. Retrieved on 4 May 2016 from http://housedocs.house.gov/rules/finserv/111_hr4173_finsrvcr.pdf.
The Economist (2015) 'British banks: The $43 billion-dollar bill', 7 February.
Engelen, E. and Konings, M. (2010) 'Financial capitalism resurgent: comparative institutionalism and the challenges of financialization'. In Morgan, G. et al. (eds) *The Oxford Handbook of Comparative Institutional Analysis*. Oxford: Oxford University Press, pp. 601–24.
Engelen, E. et al. (2011) 'After the great complacence: Financial crisis and the politics of reform', Oxford: Oxford University Press.
Ertürk, I. and Solari, S. (2007) 'Banks as continuous reinvention', *New Political Economy*, (12): 369–88.
Ertürk, I. et al. (2008) *Financialization at Work: Key Texts and Commentary*. London: Routledge.
Ertürk, I. et al. (2013) '(How) do devices matter in finance?' *Journal of Cultural Economy*, 6 (3): 336–52.
European Commission. (2014) 'Banking Union: restoring financial stability in the Eurozone', 14 April. Brussels. Retrieved on 5 May 2016 from http://ec.europa.eu/finance/general-policy/docs/banking-union/banking-unionmemo_en.pdf.

European Commission. (a & b) (2014) (a) 'Structural reform of the EU banking sector – Press Release', 29 January. Brussels. Retrieved on 5 May 2016 from http://europa.eu/rapid/press-release_IP-14-85_en.htm?locale=en('PEU credit institutionshttp://eurlex.europa.eu/legal-content/EN/TXT/PDF/?uri=CELEX:52014PC0043 &from=EN.

Financial Conduct Authority. (2013) 'Final Notice to Lloyds TSB Bank plc and Bank of Scotland plc', p. 6.

Financial Services Authority (2013) 'Final guidance: Risks to customers from financial incentives', p. 6.

Froud, J. et al. (2006) *Financialization and Strategy: Narrative and Numbers*. London: Routledge.

Glazer, E. (2015) 'J.P. Morgan's Dimon says big is beautiful'. *Wall Street Journal*, 14 January.

Haldane, A. (2009) 'Small lessons from big crisis'. Retrieved on 5 May 2016 from www.bankofengland.co.uk/publications/speeches/2009/speech397.pdf.

HM Treasury. (2013) 'Department for Innovation and Skills: Banking reform: A new structure for stability and growth'. Retrieved on 5 May 2016 from www.gov.uk/government/uploads/system/uploads/attachment_data/file/228995/8545.pdf.

ICB. (Independent Commission on Banking) (2011) 'Final Report: Recommendations'. London. Retrieved on 5 May 2016 from http://webarchive.nationalarchives.gov.uk.

Jenkins, P. and Murphy, M. (2011) 'Protium assets return to haunt Barclays'. *Financial Times*, 27 April.

J.P. Morgan Chase & Co. (2013) 'The 2012 Annual Report'.

Lazonick, W. and O'Sullivan, M. (2010) 'Maximizing shareholder value: A new ideology for corporate governance', *Economy and Society*, 29 (1): 13–35.

Liikanen, E. (2012) 'High-level Expert Group on reforming the structure of the EU banking sector – Final Report'. Brussels. Retrieved on 5 May 2016 from http://ec.europa.eu/internal_market/bank/docs/highlevel_expert_group/report_en.pdf p. i.

Lloyds Banking Group (2014) 'Annual Report and Accounts 2013'.

Lucas, C. (2009) 'Barclays announces the restructuring of $12.3bn of credit market assets', Speech by Chris Lucas, Barclays Group Finance Director to investors'. Retrieved on 5 May 2016 from www.barclays.com/content/dam/barclayspublic/docs/InvestorRelations/IRNewsPresentations/2009Presentations/Speech by Chris Lucas, Barclays Group FinanceDirector – 16 September 2009.pdf.

Makan, A. (2012) 'JPMorgan takes more risk than rivals'. *Financial Times*, 23, May.

Nixon, S. (2011) 'Barclays pays a heavy price for protium ruse', *Wall Street Journal*, 15 February.

Northern Rock. (2007) 'Annual Report 2006'. Retrieved on 5 May 2016 from www.ram.co.uk/~/media/Files/N/NRAM/content/results-.

Ridley, A. (2013) 'Blame bank regulation for Britain's stagnation', *Financial Times*, 12 August.

Roengpitya, R., Tarashev, N., and Tsatsaronis, K. (2014) 'Bank business models', *BIS Quarterly Review*, December: 55–67.

Salz, A. (2013) 'The Salz Review: An independent review of Barclays' business practices'. Retrieved on 5 May 2016 from www.barclays.com/content/dam/barclayspublic/documents/news/875-269salz-review-04-2013.pdf.

Sarangi, A. (2006) 'Northern Rock: This train has left the station'. ING Equity Markets. p. 2.

Sunderland, R. (2013) 'Arrogant and obsessed with winning at all costs: Barclays' moral flaws laid bare in damning report'. This is Money.co.uk.

Treeck, T. Van. (2009) 'The political economy debate on 'financialization' – a macroeconomic perspective', *Review of International Political Economy*, 16 (5): 907–44.

United States Senate. (2013) 'JP Morgan Chase whale trades: A case history of derivatives risks and abuses'.

White House. (2010) 'Dodd–Frank Act'. Retrieved on 5 May 2016 from www.whitehouse.gov/economy/middle-class/dodd-frank-wall-street-reform.

Wilson, J. (2012) 'Deutsche to break with Ackermann target', *Financial Times*, 9 September.

Zuckerman, G. and Burne, K. (2012) 'London whale' rattles debt market', *Wall Street Journal*, April.

Zwan, N. van der. (2014) 'State of the art: Making sense of financialization', *Socio-Economic Review*, 12: 99–129.

16
Financial market regulation
Still a regime removed from politics?

Nicholas Dorn

Introduction

Financial market policies and regulation are inherently political issues, the implications of which run wider from markets themselves and their robustness or fragility, to encompass questions of political authority (technocrats or politicians?). Yet, in the long run-up to the financial crisis beginning in 2007, the governance of financial markets was accepted as being 'beyond' democratic direction. The first objective of this chapter is to explore aspects of de-democratisation, as it emerged historically in the UK and became a model for the EU. The second objective is to ask whether the crisis provided an opportunity to extend the perimeter of democracy to cover questions of the design of financial markets, or whether the converse occurred. A final objective is to think about the (potentially diverse) normative stances that might be taken within financial markets, and within international regulatory networks, vis-à-vis the prospect of democratic control. An important proviso is that it is not the purpose of the paper to argue for 'more regulation', or for 'less', indeed it is argued that the posing of regulatory questions in more or less terms obscures the more important underlying issue of 'regulation by whom'.

Classic commentaries on crisis, including those by Harold Minsky and Joseph Schumpeter, share the view that the tendency to crisis is inherent in the market system (Minsky, 2003; Schumpeter, 1939). Such ideas are now commonly shared by a wide range of commentators – market liberals, neo-Keynesians, neo-Marxists and central bankers – all of whom accept that fragility is the inherent condition of finance. Where commentators differ hugely is over what (if anything) should and could be done about the instability of financial markets: enjoy the thrills and spills, put some sand in the wheels, imagine a transformed system, or what?

Of course, different schools of thought deploy different assumptions, languages and forms of evidence. However, at the core of the debate is one fundamental question, which is about analytical breadth: narrow or wide – mono-disciplinary or interdisciplinary? This question is very much up for grabs. Although classical economics, with its notions of equilibrium, is no longer in vogue, regulators still seem broadly to assume that a reformed economics can provide a master framework. That continuing assumption, be it implicit, apologetic or explicitly declared, carries with it a considerable exclusionary effect, since most policymakers – let alone citizens – soon glaze over. Economics as a discipline reinforces and polices the perimeter against democratic intrusions.

Happily, against that mono-disciplinary tendency, there is much contemporary work that develops a much wider perspective. Some of this wider corpus tries to build bridges between economics and sociology (Pixley *et al.*, 2013), between market theory and law (Pistor, 2013) or between political economy and crisis management (Gamble, 2014). To take as an example Gamble's 2014 book, *Crisis without End? The Unravelling of Western Prosperity*, he attempted to take into account contemporary issues around governance and legitimacy (troubling), expectations of continuing growth (dashed) and states' fiscal conundrums (dire). All of which clearly loom large in the wake of the crisis from 2007 onwards, particularly in the Eurozone. On governance and legitimacy, Gamble remarked as follows in an interview:

> We've become so used to technocratic economic management. For a lot of the time democratic electorates were quite willing for responsibility to be ceded to technocratic elites. But that sense that so many voters have that there's nothing to choose between the mainstream parties any longer – which has always been there in the background but in the last years or so has become particularly strong in western states – is reinforced when it seems that the only solutions are technocratic ones which all point in the same direction. That is breeding a big problem about democratic consent and it's leading to some political manifestations, like the surge in populism, which to a technocratic, cosmopolitan elite look highly irrational and atavistic. But actually a lot of it is the product of bewilderment at the sort of world we seem to be entering, one in which no one is really in control. People have lost a lot of confidence in the ability of technocrats to guide us and to solve problems.
>
> *(Andrew Gamble interviewed by Derbyshire, 2014)*

Such remarks locate the starting point for the present chapter: the structural discontinuity between democratic processes and financial market regulation. Historically, three opportunities to address this separation were passed by (Dorn, 2014). First, at the time of the UK general franchise in 1918, private regulation of financial markets sidestepped the realm of public politics. Second, after the Second World War, private regulation adopted a public guise at home and a networked persona internationally. Third, within the European Union, recent signs have not been entirely encouraging, mechanisms being put in place to save the Eurozone and its banks, and to expand capital markets, whilst binding its citizens.

'A regime removed from politics'

Consider the following extract from the minutes of the Court (non-executive directors) of the Bank of England, meeting in 2008, in the context of a realisation of the seriousness of the then financial crisis:

> In relation to defining a special resolution regime, there was a discussion about the Treasury's current thinking and *how it fell short* of the Bank's view. HM Treasury were largely considering options centred on their own role and issues concerning the transfer of property rights from shareholders. The present draft legislation amounted to adapting the emergency powers that had been taken for Northern Rock. HM Treasury were considering the mechanical instructions that would be required to enact the powers that ministers would have, *which therefore politicised the process* of dealing with failing banks. In the Bank's view, what was required was *a regimen removed from politics* with well defined processes and responsibilities rather than one centred on ad hoc decisions by the Chancellor of the day.
>
> *(Bank of England, 2008, p. 194, italics added)*

These and other minutes of the Court of the Bank of England from 2007 to 2009 were released in early 2015, triggering widespread and sometime ironic commentaries on the competency (or lack thereof) of the Bank's non-executive directors in exerting any meaningful check or control over the executives of the Bank (see, for example, Giles, 2015). Andrew Tyrie, Member of Parliament and chairman of its Treasury Committee, lambasted both the executives and non-executives of the Bank for 'groupthink':

> There is very little sign from the minutes of any differences of view among the senior executives of the Bank who were informing the Court about what was happening. Nor did the non-executive directors attempt to examine the different policy positions that might have been considered. The Bank appears to have been a very hierarchical organisation, with clear signs of 'groupthink' among its leadership. The executive rarely acknowledged possible weaknesses in its views or, other than grudgingly, admitted that it might have been unprepared for the crisis. . . . The Court does not seem to have challenged the executive strongly. Even after the crisis, the Governor's view (in the draft strategy for his second term) that monetary policy should remain the main purpose of the Bank, and that financial stability work should be merely ancillary to monetary policy, was examined only mildly, with a suggestion that the Bank's financial stability role be given more emphasis. The non-executives acted on occasion more as cheerleaders for the executive's views, and accepted its policy priorities.
>
> *(Tyrie, 2014)*

Mr Tyrie's comments underline the extent to which policymakers' concerns, which initially focused on financial markets and their conduct, widened to encompass the regulators and *their* conduct. What specifically comes out of the chairman of the Treasury Committee's observations on the governance of the Bank of England – leaving aside the irony with which they are expressed – is the sense conveyed of the *cognitive interiority* of the regulator. Much mention was made in the years following the financial crisis of the possibility that regulatory capture of the regulator by the industry may have played a part – although this accusation is often softened by reference to cognitive capture rather than revolving doors and corruption. On reflection, however, the idea of openness conveyed by references to capture may, rather ironically, be wide of the mark. The regulator – or rather, the regulatory community, blending into national, regional and international networks and bodies – may be too self-contained, too self-referential. As the present author has put it elsewhere:

> [R]egulators 'crowd', 'herd' and sometimes merge, so mimicking and exacerbating financial market tendencies towards similarity and contagion, and drawing regulators and markets into the same vortex. . . . Crowding comes to the fore when regulators become reliant on similar mindsets, information sources and regulator rationales and objectives. Such was the case in the long period of complacency prior to the crises of 2007 onwards (Engelen *et al.*, 2012). It was not just that the regulatory mindset models were wrong but rather that they were so similar; hence allowing the same basic business model to proliferate so widely. More diversity would have been safer. There was a temporary disruption in the convergence in regulatory thinking, as the response to crisis precipitated some radical re-thinking. 'Post crisis' re-thinking then quite rapidly re-coalesced around the new notion of macroprudential regulation, which recognizes that problems arise not only with specific firms and trades but also systemically, in the interstices, connections and similarities. A similar recognition is needed in relation to regulation itself.
>
> *(Dorn, 2015, p. 162)*

Such a recognition may haunt the minds of the brightest regulators. However, the implications would be far from being easily digested by either regulators or policymakers (by which is meant here elected politicians). The conclusions that have been drawn from the crisis have been too limited, concerned too much with regulatees (firms, markets and their interconnectedness and herding) and insufficiently with regulators (and *their* interconnectedness and herding).

As far as conceptual interconnectedness within regulatory systems – and cut-outs between them and politicians and their constituencies – are concerned, the 'post-crisis' record is decidedly mixed. Initially, chastened by the depth and persistence of the crisis and subsequent depression (particularly in Europe), regulators themselves made their apologies, admitted that they had blind spots, pointed to lessons learned and to new tasks acknowledged, and promised to do better in future. In doing so, regulators made themselves yet more powerful. There has been a deluge of regulation and a stepping up of cooperation at national, regional and international levels (see Chapters 15, 17, 18 and 19 in this volume and for a useful EU compendium, Lannoo, 2015).

So, are we now safe in their hands: is the problem solved in principle? Not quite, because the problem is not one that can be adequately specified or answered in terms of the amount, detailed content or vigour of regulation; rather it concerns underlying assumptions concerning regulatory thinking and governance. Although having been cast into doubt by the crisis, the assumption that *expertise* can steer the ship is remarkably tenacious. 'Econocrats' (Froud *et al.*, 2012, p. 44) formulate policies in relation to financial markets, so supposedly safeguarding economies, states and citizens. Technocratic steering goes hand in hand with an upward drift of agenda making, from the national (or more specifically city) level, to international networks. What have been the results? There has been an international convergence of regulatory thinking and of rule making, levelling the playing field. This may have been to the advantage of large transnational financial market participants – but at the same time it provided the conditions for an exacerbation of market herding, too-similar business strategies, connectedness, contagion and the potential for crisis.

In short, regulatory autonomy (from social and political systems) and herding (with each other) sanctioned the same characteristics in financial markets.

Admittedly, there have been some counter-pressures, notably in resolution planning, where the need for states to ensure manageability of restoration and/or resolution of entities within their jurisdictions has led to what Ben Bernanke refers in an interview as 'national treatment':

> The Federal Reserve moved recently in the direction of enhancing its oversight of foreign subsidiaries and foreign banks that are located in the United States. So there is some movement towards socalled national treatment. Banks complain that that's going to Balkanise the capital markets. But, as Mervyn King [former governor of the Bank of England] said so beautifully, banks live globally and die locally. So, for that reason if no other, there's some case for having regulators look at the subsidiaries of foreign firms, as well as their own domestic firms.
>
> *(Bernanke, in interview with Wolf, 2015, p. 3)*

Such toleration of so-called Balkanisation is, however, still regarded as exceptional in the US and EU financial markets, being accepted only insofar as it seems necessary to achieve resolution, as Bernanke's acceptance of it makes clear. The more general tendency is to strive for close alignment of national and regional regulatory systems, if not harmonisation (the clearest example being in the Eurozone). Why this is so has something to do with the interests of large, would-be global financial firms but also has to do with the dynamics between regulatory systems and politics. Following the onset of the financial market crisis, when it became clear that expertise had been illusionary, the regulatory community hastened to declare that expertise must be re-built. This was welcomed by policymakers who – having been genuinely scared by regulatory failures and having been obliged to be seen as being in the driving seat in the years immediately following the crisis in the mid to late 2000s – thereafter became fatigued by having to devote some much time to these perplexing matters. So, by the mid-2010s, policymakers were keen to step back and to let regulators take up the reigns once more. The financial markets themselves, having been subjected to considerable re-regulation, hardly objected to de-politicisation of regulation and to the return of something approaching regulation-as-normal.

Thus, on all sides there have been pressures for resumption of the pre-crisis mode of regulation – and for some fine-tuning of its content, backing away from aspects politically agreed in the heat of crisis and its immediate aftermath, yet found burdensome by the industry. Some examples follow. In the US, UK and wider EU, policy intentions for bank separation and/or ring-fencing were softened at implementation stage (Binham and Dunkley, 2015; Hardie and Macartney, 2015). The UK Fair and Effective Markets Review (HM Treasury et al., 2015) effectively re-cast market conduct issues in terms of partnership. A UK policy proposal that would have laid the onus of proof on senior managers to show that they had taken reasonable steps to prevent regulatory breaches was dropped (Pinsent Masons LLP, 2015; HM Treasury 2015). These retreats from what had been seen as 'banker-bashing' were underlined by a change at the top of the Financial Conduct Authority (Fortado et al., 2015).

The EU Capital Market Union (CMU) underscores the intention to rehabilitate banks, shadow banks and securitisation processes between them. As part of the construction of CMU, the European Commission invited the industry to submit evidence of crisis-era regulation that might, perhaps through interactions between the admittedly by now extensive and complex rules, have 'unintended consequences' (European Commission, 2015). As presented by Commissioner Lord Hill, this is to be more of a regulatory tidying-up exercise than a bonfire (Hill, 2014a). As he put it when speaking as Commissioner-designate in hearings before the European Parliament: 'If, during this process [of review of regulation], evidence appears that we have not got it quite right, we should not be afraid to make quick and effective adjustments' to regulation (Hill, 2014b, 3). CMU generally – and the broad regulatory review process that it entails – clearly give some satisfaction to those in the industry who hanker after the lighter touch they enjoyed prior to the crisis (Van Steenis, 2014). Depending on political contingencies in the late 2010s and beyond, there is indeed considerable de-regulatory potential, especially when these matters are taken within the European Commission's broader 'better regulation' agenda (Pesendorfer, 2016).

Considering the mid-2010s signs at national and EU levels – and the controversies no doubt to be generated by the backing-away from some prior policy commitments – we can expect a continuation of arguments over 'more' or 'less' regulation. What we have referred to as the quantity perspective on regulation seems set to continue to frame the policy argument.

These are important issues; however, this chapter is not primarily concerned with 'more' or 'less', regulatory toughness or slackness, or signs of (re-emergence of) capture. The main concern here is the return of regulation to its pre-crisis conditions of cognitive interiority and political autonomy. Temporarily put in question by the crisis, since then these conditions have been almost totally restored.

This restoration is partly but not completely explicable in terms of relations between regulators, policymakers and the markets. What about political parties? Looking at the contexts within and levels at which financial market regulation occurs – the restricted disciplinary circles involved, regional and international networking and detachment from party politics concerns – one notices the low level of political parties' interest in and engagement with financial market regulation before the crisis. Even following the outbreak of the crisis, financial market issues were politicised very unevenly, despite the lives of so many in the US, the EU and in particular the Eurozone having been deeply touched by down-turns in investment and by austerity measures (the latter being deepened as a consequence of bailouts of holders of senior bonds of troubled banks). There has been public anger, yet this has taken the forms of 'banker bashing' and widespread cynicism over elites, rather than attempts to move banking and other financial services into the centre of political debate and democratic decision-making.

It has been left to new political parties and hitherto (but no longer) 'fringe' parties to engage with citizens on issues around financial markets, paying for failure, austerity and so on. With the exception of the more distressed Eurozone countries, where the issues were so stark as to be unavoidable, established mainstream political parties have sought to avoid party political debate around financial markets. They focus and defer 'upwards' to elite policy and regulatory circles, rather than 'downwards' in a debate with citizens. Thus the latter are presented with decisions already taken rather than with an agenda for debate (cf. Dyson, 2013 on austerity policies). The moving of financial market regulatory issues off the political agenda stems from mainstream political parties' acceptance of the technocratic proposition that, whilst financial markets may have political effects, these effects, the processes that lead to them and the choices to be made are matters to be understood by experts.

How has this handover of political responsibility come about? The origins of financial market regulation's political detachment and herding tendency can be located within a historical perspective.

From city clubs to offshore networks: a short history

In the UK in 2014, in the context of very serious debate on constitutional reforms, notably for Scotland, a more light-hearted debate was fabricated on the question of whether London should declare independence from the United Kingdom. According to an online poll, one in five of those Londoners answering said that it should (Moore-Bridger, 2015). Meanwhile, there is a feeling in other parts of the UK that London is already another country, with its own distinct economic, cultural and political arrangements, facing more out to the rest of the world than in to the rest of the UK (for one perspective on this, see O'Brien, 2012). Thus London, including the financial markets which make it a world city (Sassen, 2007), seems autonomous.

There is a historical truth in this, which can be traced through centuries, through trade guilds and the professions (condensing Dorn, 2014). Up until the twentieth century, rule making and enforcement in such groups were rooted in direct social contacts between traders, who were clustered in geographically and culturally specific communities. Each of these economic communities had its own cultural, moral and (self-) regulatory coherence. Max Weber referred to such communities as 'status groups' and as 'closed clubs' – language that led to the notion of 'club regulation' (Weber, 2000, pp. 326–7; see also Preda, 2005, p. 455). Such self-organisation served practical purposes within economic communities (resolution of disputes, and so on) and it also had political boundary-maintaining purposes, in two senses. The economic activities in question were reserved for those who had been accepted into the group (guild, club, cartel). Moreover, club regulation or private regulation (as we would call it today) kept at bay outside interference in the rules of the game.

According to noted economic historians Cain and Hopkins (1987), London's financial markets 'were regarded as being beyond the realm of party politics'. As Daunton (1989, p. 154) has put it 'The ancient right that the monarch could not enter the City without the permission of the lord mayor survived and this privilege had, in a sense, been inherited by the commercial and financial institutions of the City'. Replace the word 'monarch' in Daunton's statement with 'parliament' and one arrives at a definition of financial market regulation that proved resilient in the face of the emergence of democracy. The general franchise of 1918 did not touch financial market club regulation, whose autonomy was defended by sectoral cartels and by the Bank of England. Democracy had arrived, yet financial market self governance carried on as before, the two running in parallel universes. Other authors have made broadly similar observations-for example, George Gilligan (2014, p. 21) refers to the 'relative autonomy' of City of London, whilst Pixley *et al.* (2013, p. 33) refer to a dynamic between public control and 're-privatisation' of the Bank of England.

In the post-Second World War period, the governance arrangements arrived at for London financial markets made a journey into the state – to be clear, market governance entered the state, not the other way around – and from there on to the European Union and international networks and bodies. The Bank of England began a slow process of opening up banking to international competition, with attendant loosening of historical, locally determined and culturally embedded modes of self-regulation. This was the beginning of a transition in occupational culture and style of self-regulation, from the quite specific, localised, socially-grounded club form, to diverse and more free-wheeling forms (Schooner and Taylor, 1999; see also Kerr and Robinson, 2012). The Bank gave (initially cautious) assent to financial innovation and to the new players (especially foreign ones) who were willing to drive it. These new forces were allowed to be even more self regulating than the established banks had been.

The Bank also aligned its agenda with a pro-market vision of the European Community, going as far as 'technical' involvement in planning for monetary union (*Guardian*, 1989). And the Bank initiated, encouraged and shaped international networking between regulatory peers, such networks functioning as channels for diffusion of views and regulatory influence (Moran, 1994, p. 162). By widening its networking, from local to European and international channels and whence back down to national, the Bank played a key role in maintaining and elaborating financial regulation as a de-politicised space. Through these means, City firms and the Bank of England together re-invented London, within a global perspective, as a kind of 'offshore'.

This internationalisation was driven from the 1950s onwards by the City and the Bank more than by government. Only after the main outlines had been laid and found to work – from the point of view of providing London with a considerable international competitive advantage – did the state step in, from the 1970s onwards, to consolidate, generalise and formalise arrangements (resulting in the so-called Big Bang, a Securities Investment Board and eventually the Financial Services Authority, which inherited banking regulation from the Bank of England). These historical developments had a consistently democracy-excluding effect, which was deepened by international networking and convergence of thinking amongst regulators. The resulting introversion provided the breeding ground for transatlantic regulatory herding and hence for crisis.

Could international regulatory networks be reconciled with democracies?

Following the crisis from 2007 onwards, Western-led regulatory clubs were somewhat discredited. At the same time, the drop in competitive advantage of US and European banks vis-à-vis their global peers opened up regulatory spaces – such as the Basel Committee on Banking Supervision and the Financial Stability Board – to wider international membership (Helleiner and Pagliari, 2011). It has been suggested that the opening up of such regulatory nodes may not necessarily mean fragmentation; rather it could be understood, and to some extent managed, as 'cooperative decentralization' (ibid., p. 196). In such a scenario, tasks falling to the international levels would include 'looser forms of cooperation such as principles-based international standards, information-sharing, research collaboration, international early warning systems, and capacity building' (ibid., p. 196). Yet that possibility raises many issues. For example, 'information sharing': what information and for what purposes? Consider also 'international early warning systems'. There is already a big impetus to collect and share information about trading, through exchanges of data depositories between regulators, supported by legislation in the US and EU. Equally, 'capacity building' (Helleiner and Pagliari, 2011) might sound anodyne to some; however the political science literature on the role played by international organisations in country development suggests otherwise.

These apparently technical and information-orientated endeavours raise issues about interpretation (at what levels and against what objectives?) and about who makes the recommendations for action (and on what basis?). Encapsulating such issues in as neutralised terms as 'information exchange' hardly does justice to the questions raised. If information is power, then information-centralising proposals merit political scrutiny.

What should be the basic policy design for financial markets, in the service of which information should be collated? The Warwick Commission on International Financial Reform found that countries have 'different national political priorities, financial structures and institutional capacities', which should be safeguarded:

> It seems heretical to argue against 'level playing fields', but in certain areas of finance, an unlevel playing field has merit. . . . We need a financial system that is robust to shocks, and that requires diversity, not homogenous behaviour derived from the blanket application of the same rules and standards on valuation, risk and trading. An unlevel playing field between countries is also desirable so as to best take into account different national political priorities, financial structures and institutional capacities.
>
> *(Warwick Commission, 2009, p. 9)*

The question of capacity 'for what' requires particular careful scrutiny in the context of sensitivity to the risks posed by similarity. It is arguable what forms of *techne* could safely be adopted at the top, then routed down to regional and country levels and hard-wired in, so becoming universal templates for the forward development of regulatory institutions, skills and thinking. If an in-principle acceptance of democracy is accompanied by an in-practice programme of capacity building that assumes a common core, then the former may be enveloped and trumped as the latter expands. Apparently soft modes of international cooperation may have rather hard effects, especially on thinking.

To make these observations is not to argue that information, capacity building and cooperation cannot be public goods. Rather, it is to point to some difficulties of defining, in an operational manner, their relation to regulation, democracy and protection of the potential for diversity in financial markets. Debate is needed on whether international regulatory networking is best driven in a top-down manner, through elite networking and technical expertise; bottom up, through some system of representation of democratic choices (which international organisations and also it seems regional organisations have yet to find a way to facilitate); or via some mix of the two (which, although messy, might remain more transparent and open). There are some serious intellectual and institutional design challenges here.

Could market participants be reconciled with democracies: *cui bono*?

This chapter has offered a historical account of technocratic regulation of financial markets and has allied itself with those calling for democratic direction in the interests of stability. We now open up the question of how market participants might take sides on this: on what grounds might market participants think that democratic direction of market regulation is either worth facilitating or opposing? This is partly a question about interests in the narrow sense – hence the section heading used above, *cui bono* – but it also potentially opens up normative questions, concerning market participants' wider senses of societal structure and right and wrong.

The remarks offered here will be very tentative. There is no general answer about market participants' acceptance or rejection of the claim that financial market regulation should be embedded within and subordinated to democracy. Much remains contingent, so there is much to play for. On the one hand, one cannot say that financial markets are 'naturally' in opposition to democracy. On the contrary, witness, for example, the pro-democracy role of financial markets in developing countries, in ex-communist states and in countries acceding to the European Union, where George Soros' foundation is notably active (for a critical review of Soros' thinking, see Major, 2008). Yet in earlier years, this same Soros successfully bet against the British pound sterling, forcing the UK out of a precursor to the euro. In retrospect, Soros might be seen as having done the UK a favour; however he hardly did so in a spirit of helping or democratisation. The relations between financial market participants and democracy are not cast in stone.

It is not difficult to find signs of disinterest in, exasperation with and even contempt for the democratic process. For example, in the context of public discussions in Brussels, the present writer witnessed middle-level finance industry executives bemoaning the so-called Meroni doctrine – which to some extent has circumscribed the ability of officials of the European Commission and of the European Supervisory Agencies to make decisions without reference back to the European Parliament (for an update, see Pelkmans and Simoncini, 2014). The efforts expended in lobbying the European Parliament are considerable (Corporate Observatory Europe, 2014) and it might be more convenient for the industry to be able to focus on the European Commission and on regulatory authorities. Even so, at the present the European Parliament to some extent *contains* debate, thus acting as a substitute for wider polities. Those financial market executives whose political impatience is such that they would circumvent the parliament should perhaps be careful what they wish for.

Cutting across these somewhat polarised attitudes – pro and anti-democracy – there are no doubt many aspects of financial markets that we could characterise in terms of *indifference* to democratic process – unless the latter seem to get in the way, when hostility may arise. Consider, for example, venture capital and private equity. Venture capital generally operates at or near the point of business start-up, providing speculative funding to develop and bring to market new product or services. Venture capital shades off into wealthy individuals who act as business angels; and into crowd-sourcing, through which many individuals of modest means come together to back projects that appeal to them (and/or whose products they may want to adopt). Somewhat by contrast, private equity targets mature and allegedly flabby firms. It came to public attention from the 1980s onwards, deploying leverage to buy out underperforming industrial firms and restructure them, so changing the industrial landscape and also labour markets. As a UK parliamentary report put it, there has been 'a debate in the case of some large-scale private equity takeovers about how much of the profit can be attributed to financial engineering compared with value extraction and creation' (House of Commons Treasury Select Committee, 2007, p. 3).

On the one hand, there seems little reason to think that such firms, individuals or loose collectivities would be sympathetic to democratic claims over financial market regulation. On the other hand, there might be some contingencies when such market participants themselves champion democratic principles, albeit for purely tactical and self-serving reasons. Consider for example the following statement by the British Private Equity and Venture Capital Association (2014, p. 226):

> It is vital that ESAs [European Supervisory Authorities] do not have the ability to introduce through guidance and technical standards legislative provisions which were rejected during Level 1 negotiations. For example, the European Securities and Markets Authority ('ESMA') AIFMD Remuneration Guidelines apply the remuneration rules to delegates, a concept not provided for in the Level 1 Directive. If confidence in ESMA is not to be undermined it is vital that it is subject to proper constitutional arrangements and does not have the ability to legislate 'through the back door'. Its apparent ability to do so seriously undermines regulatory certainty and means that firms cannot be sure that the position set out in Level 1 or Level 2 materials will be the final position.

Here the Private Equity and Venture Capital Association waves the flag of constitutionality in order to block what it sees as back-room, intra-regulatory and unmerited rule-making. This is an interesting spectacle. Whilst there is quite a distance between sectional self-defence and an in-principle commitment to democratic steering of financial market regulation, there may be times when at least interesting conversations can be attempted, on a tactical basis.

Finally, it is important to acknowledge the possibility of ideational, cultural and political cleavages within sectors and within financial markets. Differences in terms of background, experience, ages and position within firms may also sometimes be important. These are under-researched areas. Focusing on private equity, Froud *et al.* (2012) reported on social relations between partners of firms, portraying these relations in terms of 'strong assertion of absolute trust [which is] accompanied by an equally strong assertion of uncompromising exclusion of anybody who infringed that trust' (Froud *et al.*, 2012, p. 4). The context is that private equity has time horizons that are relatively long – up to a decade, certainly much longer than in investment banking – over which time key relationships have to be maintained. By contrast, in the words of one of Froud *et al.*'s private equity interviewees, investment banking is regarded as having 'lost its moral bearings [and] short-term gain. . . . People are contemplating longer careers here [in private equity], so that means more of a relationship, less the transactional' (interviewee cited by Froud *et al.*, 2012, p. 17). Thus, 'while there is public distrust of private equity, this does not mean that there is no personal trust within the organization' (ibid., p. 7).

As for whether private equity, or other sectors of financial markets, have a sense of a public interest, it is difficult to say. Probably not much, once self-serving rationalisations and public communication strategies are set aside. Even so, differentiation between sectors might occasionally offer opportunities for tactical alliances with democratic forces.

Conclusion: persistence of expertise and of the quantity perspective

To summarise the argument, there are two broad perspectives from which regulatory failure can be approached. The first, which after 2008 became the conventional view, focuses on the quantity and intensity of regulation. Within a quantity perspective – or quantity delusion, as the current author would describe it – regulation is described in 'too little' or 'too much' terms. Many maintained before the crisis, and some still after it, that there is too much regulation (see Mayer, 2014). In the years following the outbreak of the crisis the consensus became that there had been too little regulation; that regulatory forbearance, de-regulation, under-regulation and insufficient regulatory cooperation and expertise open the door to crisis. The implication was taken that what is needed is more regulation, better and more extensive information, filling lacunae more robustly and more evenly implemented across all jurisdictions. Although that mode of thinking has been dominant since the emergence of the financial crisis, it has been impeded by some practical difficulties and conundrums – for example, in connection with bank resolution, where subsidiarisation may assist regulators in dealing with what would otherwise be tightly interlocked parts of complex international groups (see Bernanke quote above and, for a critique of subsidiarisation, see Myles, 2014). Within a quantity perspective on regulation, such difficulties are seen as specific sticking points, whilst the broader drive is towards continuing internationalisation of regulation.

A distinct view, advanced here, focuses not on quantity of regulation but on the historical de-politicisation of financial market regulation and on contemporary prospects for its politicisation (we cannot say re-politicisation, for the historical reasons set out above). In concrete terms, politicisation implies shifting systemic regulatory oversight responsibilities away from independent agencies, to government bodies and/or departments, which are not simply held accountable to their parliaments and electorates (Bianculli et al., 2015) but are strongly driven by the latter. This would offer citizens some voice and decision-making power in relation to 'their' financial markets and – highly relevantly in the context of austerity policies – in relation to any public subsidies (Haldane, 2010) that they might wish to make available to particular categories of market participants.

These two perspectives – on quantity or intensity of regulation and on its relationship to democratic political processes – are competitive. That is to say, a focus on quantity implies that there is an ideal level of regulation, which can be determined on technical grounds: if so, public scrutiny is properly restricted to post-hoc accountability of regulators to administrations and parliaments, by way of giving justifications for what has been decided. In that case, party politics and citizens do not make policy inputs. By contrast, politicisation of financial market regulation is based on the proposition that there need not be one unitary regulatory approach, applied across all justifications. To the contrary, a global patchwork of regulatory difference may be valued – both normatively, because it reflects the (still) national basis of democracy, and functionally, because diversity of regulation avoids the all-eggs-in-one-basket danger inherent in expertise-based regulatory convergence.

How one appraises recent developments in the structure and functioning of regulation depends on which of the above two perspective one takes. Since 2008, there have some significant changes, especially within the EU. From a quantitative perspective, these changes may drive broadly in the right direction, whilst from the politicisation perspective, they unfortunately go in the wrong direction. The EU, which before the onset of the crisis had an institutionally complex but functionally rather loose financial market regulatory structure, has moved further in the direction of centralisation, under three Authorities: national regulators keep their place at the table but are more tightly bound together than hitherto (Moloney, 2014). Unsurprisingly, the crisis functioned an opportunity to push forward on market integration. This has gone furthest in the Eurozone: Banking Union provides for more centralised governance than in the case of securities regulation or insurance regulation. However, in all these areas there is considerably more dense regulation than prior to the crisis.

Clearly, the quantity perspective on financial market regulation has carried the day. Yet, despite more regulation and more convergence, the crisis continues and indeed deepens in Europe, with zombie banks, negative economic growth, unemployment and associated dissent. The economic and political connotations of the Eurozone and of Banking Union have changed – from excitement and achievement, through ambiguity, to disillusionment and distress. Capital Markets Union provides a policy motif that is at least less *distressing* than is the Eurozone (Sandbu, 2015), yet it is if anything more politically distant. We might ask if CMU could be more inclusive in the sense of citizens' involvement in its design. The extent to which this comes across as a frankly silly question is a measure of something very fundamental not having been learnt by European technocratic elites. The reference points and detail of consultations on

CMU are well attuned to market stakeholders but, needless to say, would go well over the heads of citizens – were they to try to engage. Which they do not, not surprisingly, since neither do the political parties that seek to represent them, so fundamental design issues are never brought to citizens.

This is a multi-level failure: political parties fail to engage with questions of what financial markets are for and how they should be structured; this leaves governments free to deal with such issues off the political agenda, in the context of industry lobbying and regulatory claims; and except at turning points, regulators are generally left to sort these issues out between themselves. Citizens are conceptualised, if at all, as eventual beneficiaries: all decided, nothing to worry your head with. If we take a bird's eye view, such as one that might be adopted in the context of international country development, then flown-in international advisors and commentators would wag their fingers and draw attention to the need for elites to foster wider debate, in order to satisfy the requirements of democratic legitimacy and also to generate 'local ownership'. *Chez nous*, there is a long way to go. Regulatory ownership is indeed the issue, its current direction being normatively objectionable and functionally dangerous. Historically, London has a lot to answer for; however, that does not excuse continuation of the game according to the historic rules.

References

Bank of England 2008 *Committee of Non-Executive Directors (NEDCO) Meeting Wednesday 12 March 2008, minutes*, released by the Bank on 7 January 2015 as part of *Court Minutes 2008 Book I*, 136–273. London: BoE. Retrieved on 5 May 2016 from www.bankofengland.co.uk/archive/Documents/archivedocs/codm/20072009/codm2008b1.pdf.

Bianculli, A., Fernández-Marín, X. and Jordana, J. (eds) (2015) *Accountability and Regulatory Governance*. Basingstoke: Palgrave Macmillan.

Binham, C. and Dunkley, E. (2015) 'Banks score victory on ringfencing rules'. *Financial Times*, 15 October. Retrieved on 6 May 2016 from www.ft.com/intl/cms/s/0/53986f2e-7317-11e5-bdb1-e6e4767162cc.html.

British Private Equity and Venture Capital Association (2014) 'Written evidence (FRF0010)'. In House of Lords European Union Committee (ed.), *Review of the EU Financial Regulatory Framework. Written and Oral Evidence*, pp. 223–229. London: Stationary Office. Retrieved on 5 May 2016 from www.parliament.uk/documents/lords-committees/eu-sub-com-a/EU-FRF/review-of-the-eu-financial-regulatory-framework-evidence.pdf.

Cain, P. and Hopkins, A. (1987) 'Gentlemanly capitalism and British expansion overseas, 1950–1945', *Economic History Review*, XL (1): 1–26.

Corporate Observatory Europe (2014) *The Fire Power of the Financial Lobby*, A Survey of the Size of the Financial Lobby at the EU level. Brussels: Corporate Observatory Europe. Retrieved on 6 May 2016 from http://corporateeurope.org/sites/default/files/attachments/financial_lobby_report.pdf.

Daunton, M. (1989) "Gentlemanly capitalism' and British industry 1820–1914', *Past & Present*, 122: 119–58.

Derbyshire, J. (2014) 'Crisis without end? A conversation with Andrew Gamble', *Prosect Magazine*, 30 July. Retrieved on 6 May 2016 from www.prospectmagazine.co.uk/blogs/jonathan-derbyshire/crisis-without-end-a-conversation-with-andrew-gamble.

Dorn, N. (2014) *Democracy and Diversity in Financial Market Regulation*. Abingdon: Routledge.

Dorn, N. (2015) 'Regulatory herding versus democratic diversity: History and prospects', *Journal of Financial Perspectives*, 3 (2): 161–74.

Dyson, K. (2013) 'Sworn to grim necessity? Imperfections of European economic governance, normative political theory, and supreme emergency', *Journal of European Integration*, 35 (3): 207–22.

Engelen, E., Ertürk, I., Froud, J., Johal, S., Leaver, A., Moran, M. and Williams K. (2012) 'Misrule of experts? The financial crisis as elite debacle', *Economy & Society*, 41 (3): 360–82.

European Commission (2015) *Call for Evidence EU: Regulatory Framework for Financial Services*. Brussels: EC. Retrieved on 6 May 2016 from http://ec.europa.eu/finance/consultations/2015/financial-regulatory-framework-review/docs/consultation-document_en.pdf.

Fortado, L., Parker, G., Arnold, M. and Binham, C. (2015) 'Martin Wheatley resigns as chief of Financial Conduct Authority', *Financial Times*, 17 July. Retrieved on 5 May 2016 from www.ft.com/intl/cms/s/0/61f867fa-2c76-11e5-8613-e7aedbb7bdb7.html.

Froud, J., Nilsson, A., Moran, M. and Williams, K. (2012) 'Stories and interests in finance: Agendas of governance before and after the financial crisis', *Governance* 25 (1): 35–59.

Gamble, A. (2014) *Crisis Without End? The Unravelling of Western Prosperity*. Palgrave Macmillan.

Giles, C. (2015) 'BoE governing body kept in dark during crisis', 7 January, *Financial Times*. Retrieved on 6 May 2016 from www.ft.com/intl/cms/s/0/849be4dc-95c0-11e4-a390-00144feabdc0.html.

Gilligan, G. (2014) '"Bad" behaviour in international financial markets: National and multilateral perspectives'. In O'Brien, J. and Gilligan, G. (eds) *Integrity, Risk and Accountability in Capital Markets: Regulating Culture*. Oxford: Hart Publishing, pp. 21–39.

Guardian (UK newspaper), 1989, 'Delors: Now for Two-speed EC?', 19 April. Retrieved on 7 May 2016 from www.cvce.eu/content/publication/2002/12/19/9f43953e-aed7-4a92-977c-275bc86ce80f/publishable_en.pdf.

Haldane, A. (2010) *The 100 Billion Question*. London: Bank of England. Retrieved on 6 May 2016 from www.bankofengland.co.uk/archive/Documents/historicpubs/speeches/2010/speech433.pdf.

Hardie, I. and Macartney, H. (2015) 'Too big to separate? A French and German defence of their biggest banks', blog. Brussels: Finance Watch. Retrieved on 5 May 2016 from www.finance-watch.org/hot-topics/blog/1067.

Helleiner, E. and Pagliari, S. (2011) 'The end of an era in international financial regulation? A postcrisis research agenda', *International Organization*, 65, 169–200.

Hill, J. (2014a) *Capital Markets Union – finance serving the economy* (speech). Brussels: European Commission. Retrieved on 5 May 2016 from http://europa.eu/rapid/press-release_SPEECH-14-1460_en.htm.

Hill, J., 2014b, *Answers to the European Parliament Questionnaire to the Commissioner-Designate Jonathan Hill Financial Stability, Financial Services and Capital Markets Union*, 1 October, 6, Brussels: European Parliament. Retrieved on 5 May 2016 from http://ec.europa.eu/commission/sites/cwt/files/commissioner_ep_hearings/hill-reply_en.pdf.

HM Treasury (2015) *Senior managers and certification regime: Extension to all FSMA authorised persons*. London: HM Treasury. Retrieved on 5 May 2016 from www.gov.uk/government/publications/senior-managers-and-certification-regime-extension-to-all-fsma-authorised-persons.

HM Treasury, Bank of England and Financial Conduct Authority (2015) *Fair & Effective Markets Review. Final Report*. London: Bank of England. Retrieved on 5 May 2016 from www.bankofengland.co.uk/markets/Documents/femrjun15.pdf.

House of Commons Treasury Select Committee (2007) *Private Equity. Tenth Report, session 2006–2007*, volume I. London: Stationary Office. Retrieved on 5 May 2016 from www.publications.parliament.uk/pa/cm200607/cmselect/cmtreasy/567/567.pdf.

Kerr, R. and Robinson, S. (2012) 'From symbolic violence to economic violence: The globalizing of the Scottish banking elite', *Organization Studies*, 33 (2), 247–66.

Lannoo, K. (ed.) (2015) *From Northern Rock to Banking Union. A Guide to the EU and the Financial Crisis*. London: Rowman & Littlefield International and Brussels: CEPS.

Major, A. (2008) 'Markets and knowledge: A review of Robert Shiller's The Subprime Solution and George Soros's The New Paradigm for Financial Markets', *Socio-Economic Review*, 7 (2): 369–74.

Mayer, T. (2014) 'In search of a more stable monetary and financial order', *Journal of Financial Perspectives*, 2 (1): 1–7.

Minsky, H. (2003) 'The financial instability hypothesis'. In Stilwell, F. and Argyrous, G. (eds), *Economics as a Social Science: Readings in Political Economy*. North Melbourne: Pluto Press, pp. 201–3.

Moran, M. (1994) 'The state and the financial services revolution: A comparative analysis', *West European Politics*, 17 (3), 158–77.

Moloney, N. (2014) *EU Securities and Financial Markets Regulation*. Oxford: Oxford University Press.

Moore-Bridger, B. (2015) 'One in five Londoners want the capital to become independent', 10 September, *London Evening Standard*. Retrieved on 5 May 2016 from www.standard.co.uk/news/uk/one-in-five-londoners-want-capital-to-split-from-rest-of-uk-and-become-independent-9722652.html.

Myles, D (2014) 'Subsidiarisation: the next risk to financial stability', *International Financial Law Review*, 3 March. Retrieved on 5 May 2016 from www.iflr.com/Article/3315115/Subsidiarisation-the-next-risk-to-financial-stability.html.

O'Brien, N. (2012) 'London is a different country – it needs bigger thinking', 13 April, *The Evening Standard*. Retrieved on 5 May 2016 from www.standard.co.uk/comment/comment/london-is-a-different-country--it-needs-bigger-thinking-7643011.html.

Pinsent Masons LLP (2015) 'Bankers' 'presumption of responsibility' removed from senior managers' regime, Out-law blog, 19 October. London: Pinsent Masons LLP. Retrieved on 5 May 2016 from www.out-law.com/en/articles/2015/october/bankers-presumption-of-responsibility-removed-from-senior-managers-regime.

Pelkmans, J. and Simoncini, M. (2014) *Mellowing Meroni: How ESMA can help build the single market*, CEPS Commentaries, 18 February. Brussels: Centre for European Policy Studies. Retrieved on 5 May 2016 from www.ceps.eu/book/mellowing-meroni-how-esma-can-help-build-single-market.

Pesendorfer, D. (2016) 'EU capital markets union: Tensions, conflicts, flaws', in Dorn, N (ed), *Controlling Capital: Public and Private Regulation of Financial Markets*, Abington: Routledge, pp. 41–57.

Pistor, K. (2013) 'A legal theory of finance', *Journal of Comparative Economics*, 41 (2): 315–30.

Pixley, J., Whimster, S. and Wilson, S. (2013) 'Central bank independence: A social economic and democratic critique', *The Economic and Labour Relations Review*, 24 (1): 32–50.

Preda, A. (2005) 'Legitimacy and status groups in financial markets', *British Journal of Sociology*, 56 (3): 451–71.

Sandbu, M. (2015) *Europe's Orphan: The Future of the Euro and the Politics of Debt*, Princeton, NJ: Princeton University Press.

Sassen, S. (2007) *A Sociology of Globalization*. New York: W.W. Norton.

Schooner, H. and Taylor, M. (1999) 'Convergence and competition: The case of bank regulation in Britain and the United States', *Michigan Journal of International Law*, 20, 595–655.

Schumpeter, J. (1939) *Business Cycles: A Theoretical, Historical, and Statistical Analysis of the Capitalist Process*. New York and London: McGraw-Hill.

Tyrie, A. (2014) *Tyrie comments on Bank of England financial crisis minutes*, press release, 7 January. Dods Parliamentary Communications Ltd. Retrieved on 5 May 2016 from www.actuarialpost.co.uk/article/bank-of-england-release-financial-crisis-minutes-7088.htm.

Van Steenis, H. (2014) 'Europe needs a more flexible financial market', *Financial Times*, 1 October.

Warwick Commission on International Financial Reform (2009) *In Praise of Unlevel Playing Fields*, Warwick University. Retrieved on 5 May 2016 from www2.warwick.ac.uk/research/warwickcommission/financialreform/report.

Weber, M. (2000) 'Stock and commodity exchanges' [Die Börse], *Theory & Society*, 29 (3): 305–38.

Wolf, M. (2015) 'Lunch with the FT: Ben Bernanke', *Financial Times*, life & arts section, 24 October, p. 3. Retrieved on 5 May 2016 from www.ft.com/intl/cms/s/0/0c07ba88-7822-11e5-a95a-27d368e1ddf7.html.

17
Prudential regulation in the age of internal models

José Gabilondo

Some of the most significant changes in banking law since the global financial crisis involve attempts to make banks more financially stable through more rigorous requirements about how they finance their lending and investment activities. Central to this is the growing use of quantitative models by banks and their regulators to conduct financial war games that simulate how a bank would fare under adverse market conditions. These models – known as "internal models" because they are often proprietary and non-public – attempt to simulate how future states of the market would impact a bank's financial structure, in particular its ability to absorb losses without interrupting operations.

Regulators first approved these internal models in the 1990s to track some of the risks in bank investments held for trading. Since then, regulators have authorized model-based approaches for a wider range of financial risks – including credit and liquidity risks – and for some nonbank financial entities, like broker-dealers. Today, many banks use these models to comply with prudential regulation about safety and soundness.

During the past financial crisis, however, these models did not perform as expected. In particular, the models did not estimate how severe the market downturns would become and how much value assets would lose during these extremal conditions. To resolve illiquid and insolvent banks, governments had to spend large sums, leaving the public wondering why bank risk management and regulatory oversight had not worked as planned. The resulting legal reforms have emphasized regulatory capital, increased liquidity requirements, and added new constraints on the use of internal models. In particular, banks must now periodically "stress-test" these models by running them through adverse market scenarios to better appreciate how banks would weather large losses.

Though questions remain about their efficacy, model-based approaches to compliance and regulatory oversight are here to stay. Therefore, this chapter provides a framework for understanding model-based stress-tests. The first section introduces the regulatory capital framework in which these stress-tests take place. The second section reviews the current state of stress-testing practices and uses those of the Federal Reserve as an example. The final section concludes with some observations on a market stress that has once again become relevant for the banking sector – rising interest rates.

José Gabilondo

Internal models for prudential oversight

The backdrop to these developments is the growth during the past thirty years of a global regulatory bureaucracy that has engineered a uniform approach to prudential standards for banks, formerly the province of domestic legislation. This process gathered momentum in 1987, when central banks active in the Basel Committee on Banking Supervision proposed the Basel Capital Accord (Accord) (1996).[1] The Accord introduced a "risk-based" framework that tied a bank's minimum capital to a variety of risks assigned to their asset portfolios. Stress-testing of internal models grew out of the Accord and its major revisions in 1996, 2004, and 2010. First intended for globally active banks, these risk-based standards have become a default rule for most banks.

Risk-based approaches to regulatory capital

Conventionally, banks distinguish between two kinds of loss: expected and unexpected. Insofar as banks can anticipate the loss in underwriting loans and other investments, this expected loss is provisioned for by siphoning off current earnings to set up a reserve intended to absorb these losses. This way, when the expected loss materializes, it is recognized for accounting purposes along with an offsetting charge to the loss reserve, thereby minimizing any impact on current earnings. In contrast, unexpected loss refers to risks implicit in the same portfolio of investments but incapable of being meaningfully estimated during the underwriting process. When these unprovisioned-for losses materialize, they must be absorbed out of current or retained earnings or an impairment of capital.

Private firms deal with unexpected loss by having an equity capital cushion that partially insulates creditors from the risk of loss. Similar to market capital standards, regulatory capital also addresses unexpected losses, in particular those caused or amplified by the bank's role in intermediation. A bank's equity capital reassures regulators that the bank will be able to weather unexpected losses that could threaten its operations. More so even than in private firms, these losses loom prominently in banks because—to serve their role as credit intermediaries—they intentionally maintain a mismatched balance sheet in which short-term, effectively floating rate funds finance long-term assets like mortgages and investments in securities.

The deep structure of the Accord's approach to provisioning for unexpected loss as established by the Accord is a pro forma regulatory balance sheet intended to capture the financial risks faced by the bank. This pro forma balance sheet is derived from the financial balance sheet by making some regulatory adjustments to the bank's financial balance sheet.

Imagine a bank with the financial balance sheet in Figure 17.1.[2]

The goal of the regulatory capital balance sheet is to estimate the bank's ability to absorb unexpected losses. The first step in doing this is to deduct assets with no actual liquidity with which to absorb loss, in this case goodwill. To balance the deduction on the asset-side, the equity account must also be adjusted dollar-for-dollar, because equity bears the first loss arising from asset loss. Thus, the balance sheet "shrinks up," increasing the bank's leverage as measured by regulatory metrics.

The next step is to classify assets—or fractions of assets—based on their risk of unexpected loss. Admittedly, this is a somewhat contradictory proposition because what makes a loss unexpected also makes it difficult to measure in a meaningful way. Nevertheless, the Accord introduced factor weights that assigned different degrees of risk to assets: 0 percent, 25 percent, 50 percent, and 100 percent. The greater the perceived risk of unexpected loss in the asset, the higher would be the applicable risk factor. The gross value of the asset multiplied by the

BANK'S FINANCIAL BALANCE SHEET				
Assets		Liabilities		
Cash	2,450,000	Demand Deposits		5,000,000
US Treasuries	1,500,000	One year CDs		1,000,000
		Medium-term notes		1,000,000
Residential mortgages	2,000,000	Subordinated debt		2,400,000
Unsecured loans	2,000,000	Equity		
Corporate debentures	2,000,000	Noncumulative perpetual preferred stock		200,000
Goodwill	50,000	Common stock		400,000
Total	**10,000,000**	**Total**		**10,000,000**

Figure 17.1 Bank's financial balance sheet

respective risk factor produced the asset's "risk-weighted" value. These are the values to be booked, carried, and funded on the (pro forma) regulatory balance sheet.

In our example, the cash and the government securities are deemed so free of risk that a bank could fund them entirely with debt rather than with any equity. Hence, they get a 0 percent risk-weight. No portion of their value appears on the regulatory balance sheet. Like the deduction for intangibles, the deduction of risk-free assets also results in an offsetting deduction on the right-hand side of the balance sheet, this time taken from the liabilities at the top. These deductions for risk-weighted assets produce the opposite effect of the intangibles deduction by reducing the bank's leverage because the same amount of equity capital remains to support less debt.

Residential assets, however, entail more risk of loss than either cash or government securities, so the mortgages receive a risk-weight of 50 percent, which means that one-half of their value is booked on the regulatory balance sheet. Only risk-weighted assets (or the fraction of whole assets remaining after the factor discounts) appeared on the regulatory balance sheet and became subject to capital standards. In this example, half of the mortgage entry can be funded entirely by debt, but the remaining half must be funded by some qualifying blend of debt and equity. Getter (2012, pp. 3–10) suggests that although sorting assets into four different risk "buckets" made the capital standard more responsive to a bank's risk, this scheme still lets banks game the weighting by letting them pick riskier assets—with a better chance of return—within each risk bucket. The all-in regulatory capital cost for the mortgages would reflect this blend of blends, i.e. the weighted average of (1) the all-debt financing and (2) the equity-stopped debt financing. The loans and debentures receive a risk-weight of 100 percent, which means that the entire amount of the bank's investment in them must be funded—for regulatory purposes—by equity-stopped debt. For example, assuming that a firm had to set aside $8 of equity for every $100 of risk-weighted asset exposure, an asset in the 100 percent bucket (like the unsecured loan) would have to be financed by qualifying equity capital up to 8 percent of its value. The rest of its value (92 percent) could be financed by borrowing.

This system still left banks with discretion in terms of how assets would be classified. Insofar as a bank could convert high risk-weighted investments into assets with lower risk weights, i.e. a 0 percent factor rather than a 50 percent one, the bank could reduce its regulatory requirement to issue equity. Because equity costs the bank more than borrowing, doing so would reduce the bank's overall funding costs.

The Accord also classified capital by its ability to bear unexpected loss. Debt obligations that involve contractual obligations have no capacity to bear loss since any deviation from the contractual terms exposes the bank to breach. In contrast, balance sheet values assigned to common stock can absorb loss because the stockholder cannot force the corporation to make any distribution. Instruments in between debt and equity—like preferred stock—had some loss-bearing capacity based on the permanence of the capital contribution.

After calculating the risk-weighted assets and the amount of qualifying regulatory capital (net of intangibles deducted), the regulatory balance sheet (which will never balance because of the risk-weighting) is complete (Figure 17.2). It is this pro forma balance sheet that is tested against capital adequacy standards and—as discussed in the section below—"stressed" to see how it holds up in different states of the world.

By today's standards, the approach was relatively simple. It focused on credit risk rather than the various other kinds of risks to which banks are subject. The mathematics involved were straightforward: subtracting or discounting assets and dividing subsets of equity by the resulting asset values to determine the equity cushion. The framework also converted off-balance-sheet items to on-balance sheet equivalents, but—though the assumptions used to measure these contingencies could be disputed—the calculation was simple. In effect, this framework imposed across-the-board capital requirements for banks, which were left with relatively bounded discretion to manipulate the capital evaluation process.

For example, banks were expected to have at least 8 percent of Tier I capital, a category of equity deemed to absorb loss well. Dividing the qualifying capital by the risk-weighted asset base results in Tier I equity ratio of 11 percent (the sum of the preferred and common). The rest of the risk-weighted asset base (89 percent) is funded with borrowed money. Assuming that the minimum required of Tier I equity is 8 percent, the bank substantially exceeds the

REGULATORY BALANCE SHEET — NET OF INTANGIBLES, WRITE OFFS, AND DEBT-FUNDED ASSETS AND LIABILITIES			
Risk-Weighted Assets		**Regulatory Capital**	
Residential mortgages	1,000,000	Preferred stock	200,000
Unsecured loans	2,000,000	Common stock	350,000
Corporate debentures	2,000,000		
Total	**5,000,000**	**Total**	**550,000**

Figure 17.2 Regulatory balance sheet – net of intangibles, write offs, debt-funded assets, and liabilities

minimum. Its risk-weighted leverage ratio is about 1:8, i.e. the bank borrows $8 for every $1 of equity.

This tiered approach to classifying and measuring bank capital would become a permanent part of the Basel framework. The standard way of calculating capital would also become a permanent part of regulatory capital architecture. Soon, however, regulators would introduce a major change by letting banks use internal models that provided more discretion when determining whether the bank's capital was sufficient.

Model-based approaches to evaluating risk

The Accord framework was not inflexible because it gave regulators discretion to adjust the amount of regulatory capital—and the consequent compliance burden on banks—in four ways. Excluding intangibles from the requirement that they be deducted relaxed the regulatory burden. Adjusting the risk-weightings determined what share of a bank's assets needed to be considered for regulatory capital purposes. Accepting hybrid instruments as forms of regulatory capital gave banks more flexibility in financing themselves. Finally, calibrating the final ratios that established capital adequacy let regulators reduce or increase the brunt of regulatory capital requirements.

Despite this internal flexibility, business practices soon overtook the Accord and began to challenge its conceptual integrity. Banks resisted the leverage constraints that regulatory capital imposed. Regulators also wanted more freedom to respond to changing conditions. Before banks participated extensively in securitizing credit, a bank's assets could be divided into separate asset "books" with distinctive risk qualities. The bank's credit book held its real estate, commercial, and personal loans. It also included contingent credit commitments like letters of credit or credit lines which—once drawn upon, would mature into assets. This book was exposed to credit and interest-rate risk. Separately, the bank also had investments and securities, some held for active trading and some intended to be held to maturity. The "trading" or securities book was exposed to market risk, which included interest rate risk and other risks related to price movements in the secondary markets for these investments.

As banks participated more in securitization, however, this neat division between the credit book and the trading book broke down. Banks began to convert whole loans into a more heterogeneous blend of assets: long-term, short-term, and structured in different ways with different risks. Whole mortgages would remain exposed to interest rate risk during the relatively long term of the mortgages. A bank that made a loan with an eye to securitizing still assumed credit risk based on the borrower's creditworthiness. However, securitization would have reduced this risk by shortening the horizon for default while on the bank's books.

The certificates issued by the securitization vehicle in the secondary market, however, were viewed as separate products subject to market risk. So the bank was now dependent on the ongoing functioning of secondary markets for securitized products. In effect, the originate-to-distribute model changed the risk profile of banks by making market risk more important. Market risk—also known as "price risk"—referred to changes in interest rates, equity prices, commodity values, and foreign exchange rates. A better way of tracking market risk was needed.

To this end, in 1996, banking regulators modified the Accord to provision better for market risk in the bank's trading book (Basel Committee on Banking Supervision, 1996). This became an opportunity for proponents of more quantitative, though arguably subjective, approaches to bank capital to challenge the mathematically simple approach of the 1987 Accord. It was in this context that regulators first let banks use internal models to comply with prudential regulation.

Using quantitative models to estimate financial risks was nothing new. For example, the International Monetary Fund had been using model-based stress-testing since the 1990s as part of its Financial Sector Assessment Program, which evaluated a country's exposure to financial risks (Blaschke et al., 2001). The 1996 market risk amendment, however, would be the beginning of a process in which internal models came to dominate both private compliance by banks and prudential oversight by regulators. Securities regulators would later allow some large broker-dealers to use a similar model-based approach to comply with capital regulation.[3]

These internal models grew out of probability theory, in particular the branch that addresses "stochastic" processes, i.e. those that involve random outcomes. Probability assigns a likelihood that a distribution of future random outcomes will occur. In this case, the future random outcomes were price movements in interest rates, equity prices, foreign exchange rates, commodities prices, and options. Market risk included two elements: price movements affecting the market as a whole (general market risk) and movements that affected the particular instrument, issuer, or position (specific risk).

The 1996 market risk amendment provided a default system for measuring these market risks. Banks could also request permission from their regulator to use their own internal risk models to measure market risk. Value-at-risk (VAR) became the most common technique used in these internal models. VAR estimated the maximum loss that a bank would be likely to incur for a given confidence interval, i.e. 99 percent of the time. When financial simulation suggested that a bank's risk of unexpected loss increases, the bank could provision for this increased risk by increasing its equity capital. For example, the bank might decide not to issue dividends that could otherwise be retained by the bank to bear unexpected loss.

In order to secure regulatory approval to use these internal models, banks had to satisfy qualitative criteria to ensure that these models were sound and that they were integrated into a firm's risk management.[4] One of the requirements for regulatory approval was that the bank subject these models to further stress-tests to ensure that they estimated the impact to the bank of major market disturbances (Basel Committee on Banking Supervision, 1996, pp. 46–7). Stress-testing attempted to model what happens to banks during "extreme" situations that occur infrequently but that involve exceptionally serious consequences to the bank's financial stability. Typically, these involve market conditions in which asset prices fell, loan defaults increased, and macroeconomic conditions worsened, while the demands on the bank to provide liquidity and credit increased.

A stress-testing exercise involved three distinct steps essentially similar to those involved in VAR analysis. First, the exercise would identify states of the world deemed so extreme that they would pose material risks to a financial firm or a sector. These scenarios could be based on historical scenarios or hypothetical ones involving financial crises or economic crises that impacted the financial sector. For example, stylized scenarios posit certain price movements deemed extreme in themselves, for example interest rate movements greater than 100 basis points or stock index movements greater than 10 percent. Hypothetical scenarios consider the impact on prices of nonfinancial events, such as earthquakes, wars, or terrorist attacks.

After identifying the target scenarios, the stress-test predicts what would happen to asset prices or cash flow during each one of these alternative extreme states of the world. The predictions depended on assumptions about how price movements in the market were correlated. Once completed, this phase of the exercise would have generated a map of hypothetical market prices. The final step of the stress-test was to estimate how a particular portfolio or firm would behave in these alternative states of the world. This part of the analysis would require assumptions about whether losses could be hedged or shifted.

Stress-testing and VAR both involve attempts to estimate how the bank's financial structure would respond to changes in market conditions, but they operate at different probability ranges, with stress-testing emphasizing more remote outcomes. Berkowitz (1999) suggests that the notions of value-at-risk models and stress-testing have developed on separate tracks, but there is no necessary theoretical difference between the two. Stress-testing should enhance VAR analysis by considering four distinctive conditions that may be missed by VAR: (1) to model market shocks that have never occurred; (2) to model shocks that are more likely to occur than suggested by historical observation; (3) to model market conditions in which traditional price co-relations between asset classes break down; and (4) to model "structural breaks" that could occur (Berkowitz, 1999).

In 2004, Basel II modified the Accord to expand the use of these internal models, which could thereafter be used for credit risk as well as market risk. Banks that opted for models could rely on statistical assumptions provided by regulators or develop their own assumptions.[5] In effect, Basel II gave banks substantial discretion in picking how their regulatory capital would be calculated. Some banks welcomed this discretion because it allowed them to comply with regulatory capital rules more cheaply.

Post-crisis enhancements to stress-tests

In the years leading up to the financial crisis of 2007, the occurrence of several extreme events created more interest in stress-testing.[6] However, it would take the vicissitudes of the crisis—more than twenty years after the 1996 market risk amendment to the Accord—for regulators to require banks to take these qualitative and stress-testing requirements seriously. In part, this was because the financial crisis of 2007 highlighted the shortcomings of these internal models. A report of the Bank for International Settlements (2009) found that the scenarios in the stress-tests used before the crisis did not anticipate extreme conditions, that firms had not integrated stress-testing into governance, and that critical risks—including those from securitization—had been overlooked. It would seem, then, that these models failed to estimate the losses in precisely those extreme situations for which these models had supposedly been designed.

In particular, the models had failed to internalize the risk that certain markets would freeze up. One of the markets where this was most relevant was the interbank funding channel in which banks adjusted their short-term position. In particular, secured borrowing—for example, repurchase agreements—within this market displayed price and liquidity shortages that surprised observers. The same was true about secondary markets for securitized credit. When secondary market demand for credit dried up, whole loans became stranded on the balance sheets of originating banks, which found that—making matters worse—they also had to fund contingent credit commitments made to a variety of other financial intermediaries.

Having crossed the Rubicon in terms of approving these models, however, regulators opted to fine-tune them rather than return to the standardized approaches first put in place by the Accord. Regulators have also validated the model-based approach by using it to conduct system-wide regulatory assessments of the financial sector. The following discussion examines how the new round of stress-tests work and focuses on some of the initiatives of the Federal Reserve (Fed) in this area.

In general

In response to the global financial crisis, many financial regulators resynthesized their financial regulation paradigm to take better account of lessons learned from the crisis. This resulting regulatory consensus continued to include pre-existing ideas like the emphasis on tracking counterparty credit risk and on promoting sound capital structures. After the crisis, however, macro-prudential regulation provides the frame for these ideas, which are now subsumed under the goal of promoting financial stability and managing systemic risk.[7] The same is true about the renewed interest in stress-tests. Macro-prudential disturbances often form the basis of the scenarios used in these stress-tests. Also, stress-tests are intended to help regulators assess how the financial dynamics of individual firms and sectors can contribute to financial stability.

During the crisis, banking regulators conducted stress-tests to evaluate the status of the banking sector.[8] Building on these experiences, after the crisis regulators have made stress-testing a routine aspect of their programs. Compared with their policies before the crisis, however, regulators have now become more directive about these tests by mandating the content of the scenarios, when the tests should be conducted, and how the results are to be made public.

In effect, these changes are remedial efforts that tacitly recognize that the 1996 market risk amendment did not fully succeed in implementing effective supervisory oversight of internal models. After all, stress-testing techniques predated the global financial crisis. What the crisis helped to underwrite was the political resolve to put teeth into regulators' original supervisory guidance about using internal models.

Regulators in several jurisdictions, including Hong Kong, Ireland, Japan, Sweden, the European Union, and the United States, now perform some form of stress-testing at least annually, although they vary substantially across jurisdictions (Bank of England, 2013, p. 11). Internationally active banks may be subject to these requirements in more than one jurisdiction, for example in the United States and the European Union. In general, the stress-tests form part of a more comprehensive assessment by regulators of the financial health of the banking sector. For example, the European Central Bank (2014b) performed a comprehensive assessment of the banking sector, including results of stress-tests into its overall analysis of the sector. Some regulators publicly disclose the methodology used to conduct these tests while others have kept that information confidential. Some regulators require banks to publicly disclose the results of their stress-tests, but the majority of regulators publish only the results of system-wide aggregate stress-tests. For example, the press release of the European Central Bank (2014a) about its comprehensive assessment, revealed capital shortfalls at several banks and required substantial discounting of bank assets.

Most stress tests involve scenarios identified by the regulator as well as scenarios developed by the individual bank. When setting out the adverse scenarios that banks should use, regulators take pains to stress that the scenarios are not meant as forecasts. Regulators intentionally consider the results of several kinds of scenarios and models because they are trying to gain a more nuanced view of how firms might be affected by financial instability. Rather than functioning as a static evaluation of one point in time, the goal is for regulators to trace the path of how a firm or market may behave during an entire cycle (Bank of England, 2013, p. 10). Moreover, regulators recognize that differences between individual banks will influence how they are affected by adverse scenarios. Regardless of whether any particular stress-test accurately anticipates how adverse market conditions will affect a bank or a market, the process of being regularly engaged in these financial war games may leave regulators better prepared to deal with adverse scenarios when they do materialize.

The stress-tests used by regulators reflect different risk philosophies. For example, for its 2015 stress-tests, the Fed used an approach that combines stylized and hypothetical scenarios by building them around stylized scenarios based on recessions in the US that took place after the Second World War (Board of Governors of the Federal Reserve, 2015, p. 23). The Fed's approach includes both adverse and severely adverse scenarios. In the adverse scenario, at the global level there is a "weakening" in economic activity and the US experiences a mild recession. In the severely adverse scenario, globally there is a substantial reduction in economic activity and a drop in asset prices and in the US there is a severe recession with unemployment rising 4 percent to 10 percent. These scenarios are based on a problem with the real economy—a recession—that goes on to impact the financial sector. In contrast, the scenario put forward by the European Banking Authority scenario is built more directly on trends in financial markets (European Systemic Risk Board, 2014). In the exercise designed by the European Systemic Risk Board, a flight to quality from long-term debt leads investors to sell assets, which spills over into the real economy.

Federal Reserve stress-tests

To provide more granularity, the following discussion takes up how the Fed operates its stress-testing program. The Dodd–Frank Act of 2010 (the primary post-crisis law reform in the United States) imposed several stress-testing requirements. Each year the Fed releases the supervisory scenarios that will form the basis of the stress-tests.

The particular stress-tests vary with the size of the banking institution. All financial companies with $10 billion or more in assets regulated by a federal financial regulator must conduct annual internal stress-tests. The Fed must conduct annual stress-tests for all systemically important companies under at least three scenarios: baseline, adverse and severely adverse. These companies must also conduct semiannual internal stress-tests. Also, the Fed may also require stress-tests for non-systemically important companies. Community banks are effectively exempt from these stress-tests. Banks with total assets between $10 billion and $50 billion are subject to the basic stress-tests. Banking organizations with more than $50 billion in assets are subject to additional requirements.

The stress-tests form part of a more interventionist strategy about bank capital on the part of regulators, who now seem willing to impose more substantive limits on bank capital policy, risk management practices, and the business model. Much as legal capital rules limit when a corporation can issue dividends to its shareholders, the new regime puts in place a series of conditions that must be met before the bank reduces its equity capital base. In effect, the new rules attempt to standardize dividend policy for banks. For example, the Fed rule suggests a rule of thumb that a bank must reinvest at least 70 percent of its after-tax net profit rather than release it to shareholders through dividends. Banks subject to the Fed's jurisdiction must also now develop and codify capital policies that comprehensively address the sources and uses of capital (Board of Governors of the Federal Reserve, 2014, p. 17). The Fed would seem to be backtracking from the broad discretion previously given to banks to estimate their capital.

Ongoing changes in bank business practices that blur neat divisions between different kinds of risks continue to influence how these regulations are designed. The Fed's instructions to banks on how to prepare their capital plans reflect notions of financial risk that transcend the market risk-credit risk dichotomy. These instructions draw special attention to the financial risks from securitization, loan syndication, and bank exposures that are particularly vulnerable to market risks (Federal Reserve, 2014, p. 18). The notion of "pipeline risk," for example, combines market and credit risk into an expression typical of securitization. In particular, this warning addresses the risk that changes in market conditions (in particular investment demand for securitized credit in the secondary market) may cause the bank's balance sheet to expand as more credit products linger or become stranded in the pipeline.

Will these new requirements work? Only time will tell whether the Fed uses its stated authority over qualitative business process, but, taken at face value, the admonitions to banks about qualitative assessments appear to signal a willingness to look deeply at whether a bank has meaningful internal controls about capital. However, if the past is a precedent, the Fed may be somewhat reticent to use the full measure of its prudential authority.

José Gabilondo

Rising interest rates

One of the major potential stresses facing banks is rising interest rates, coming after a long period in which central banks kept money loose to help stabilize financial markets. Stress-testing addresses this scenario by simulating how the bank's financial position would change if rates change a certain amount over a one-year interval, e.g. a 200 basis point increase or decrease in a one-year period. How would rising interest rates affect the banking sector? In this case, the past may not be a precedent. Historically, banks tended to welcome rising interest rates because they increased their net interest margin, thereby boosting the bank's net profit. Due to changing in bank funding and investment patterns, today it is less certain how tighter money will impact any particular bank. In large measure, it depends on the bank's particular asset-liability mix. This key factor must be kept in mind when conducting or interpreting stress-tests.

The return of tight money

For many years, central banks have implemented highly accommodative stances in monetary policy. Many central banks have kept nominal interest rates at near zero interest rates, typically through open market operations involving short-term public debt. To supplement this loose money policy, central banks also provided additional liquidity to banks and other firms through large-scale asset purchases ("quantitative easing") in which central banks purchased long-term rather than short-term government debt. Especially during 2008, central banks also provided nonbank financial intermediaries with supplemental liquidity by making last resort lending available on the strength of nonconventional collateral.

For example, in the United States the Fed did not raise rates between 2008 and December 16, 2015, a period during which the target policy rate (the nominal Fed funds rate) did not rise above .25 (25 basis points). Moreover, United States banks also enjoyed extraordinary access to low cost funding from the Fed, which allowed them to stockpile reserves at the central bank, which, in addition to portending inflation risk, have kept banks liquid. The Fed's modest increase on December 16, 2015 of .25 to the target federal funds rates could signal the start of a new period of less accommodative monetary policy. The risk that interest rates will rise is not an extreme risk but, rather, a quite routine risk. The extreme risk involved is that rates will rise steeply or reach an unusual point or that financial markets will respond to these routine interest rate increases in an unexpected manner.

Forecasting the likely path of rising rates involves two major issues. First, how high might interest rates climb during the short term, often measured for this purpose as a one-year period? When imagining shocks to interest rates, many stress-tests use a 200 basis point increase within one year. Though it might seem high, such an increase is more common than one might imagine. Interest rates went up by at least 200 basis points in over 30 percent of the one-year periods between 1995 and 2008; during this same period, interest rates went up by at least 300 basis points nearly 16 percent of the time (Federal Deposit Insurance Corporation, 2010). Given the frequency of these substantial intra-year rate increases, using the 200 basis point standard in a stress-test may understate the real risk to the bank.

A second set of issues concerns how the yield curve responds to rising rates. Interest rates can rise in at least three major patterns, each of which impacts the bank's net interest margin in different ways. If both the short-term and the long-term rates rise in tandem, then the yield curve simply moves up to establish a parallel curve above the previous one. In this situation, the bank's borrowing costs have increased but so have the rates that the bank can charge its borrowers.

However, if short-term rates rise without a concomitant increase in long-term rates, the yield curve gets flatter, losing its normal upward-sloping shape. This means that the bank will have to pay more for its short-term borrowing but may not be able to increase its long-term lending rates. For banks that borrow at short terms and lend at long terms (the traditional maturity intermediation model), a flattening yield curve reduces profits, eats into capital, and, if it continues, may undermine the bank's financial stability.

In the converse situation, long-term rates rise more than short-term rates and the yield curve steepens. In this case, the bank's short-term borrowing costs rise, but these increased funding costs are more than offset by the additional profit made by charging more for long-term loans and investments. For many banks that borrow at short-term rates but lend at long-rates, this last outcome is the best because it will increase the bank's net interest margin.

Scenarios that test increase rate changes often assume a simple parallel shift upward. For better stress-testing results, however, interest rate scenarios should also consider how yield flattening and yield steepening will impact the bank's financial position. Moreover, the yield curve may reflect all three modes—parallel shifts, flattening, and steepening—as market interest rates adapt to the central bank's monetary policy decisions.

As central banks implement the shift from loose money to tight money, they may rely on relatively new policy tools to manage the exit from accommodative policies. For example, after the 2007 financial crisis, the Fed and the Bank of England began paying interest to banks on their excess reserves, i.e. amounts on deposit with the central bank in excess of the regulatory minimum. Several other central banks, including the European Central Bank and the Bank of Japan, also remunerate banks for their reserve deposits (Bowman, Gagnon, and Leahy, 2010). During the crisis, paying interest on bank reserves gave central banks a tool with which to establish a floor for interest rates. Similarly, raising the rate paid on excess reserves will help these central banks to influence market interest rates on their path upward.

The Fed and, perhaps, other central banks will also draw on open market operations to absorb monetary liquidity (that way making money more dear) through reverse repurchase agreements. In a reverse repo, the Fed "sells" a security to its banks and nonbank intermediaries, thereby absorbing monetary liquidity from these counterparties and leaving the bank less liquid because they have traded cash for government securities, still a highly liquid asset but less so than cash or central bank reserves. The Fed induces counterparties to enter into these deals not by fiat but by the price mechanism, i.e. the central bank must pay a market premium for the securities. In the aggregate, that market premium helps to increase interest rates. By determining the term of the reverse repo, i.e. deciding whether to roll-over the sale each day, the central bank can use these open market operations to adjust the overall liquidity supply.

Implications for banks

Historically, banks have not welcomed long periods of low interest rates. This was so because low interest rates depressed the bank's return on credit assets more than they lowered the bank's borrowing costs. So, low interest rates lead to persistent compression of the funding margin, cutting into bank profits. Consequently, the conventional wisdom is that banks welcome rising interest rates because it enhances their net interest margin. Rising interest rates may increase a bank's funding costs, but, to a larger extent, these rising rates mean that the bank can charge even more for making loans.

However, how banks fund themselves has changed in the years leading up to the 2007 financial crisis. Core deposits, which remained relatively stable even as rates rose, have been replaced with wholesale funds belonging to other financial intermediaries that will reallocate these funds to better earning investments as interest rates rise. Some banks have also issued more variable-rate debt whose servicing costs will increase as interest rates rise. At the same time, the asset composition of many banks has also changed. The decline of secondary market demand for structured credit products like asset-backed securities and collateralized debt obligations means that banks have had to hold on to assets—many of them issued at fixed-rates—longer than intended. These shifts in funding and asset composition will impact how rising interest rates impact any particular bank.

Moreover, going forward banks will have to contend with some important new funding constraints introduced in Basel III and implemented in national legislation: the liquidity coverage ratio and the net stable funding ratio. The former requires the bank to keep a minimum amount of its investments in lower-yielding liquid assets; the latter requires the bank to reduce its reliance on short-term debt by borrowing at longer-terms, an improvement in the bank's leverage structure that is certain to cost more than relying on short-term debt. The concurrent application of these ratios may render banks more liquid and more stable but, perhaps, less poised to exploit their traditional advantage in a rising rate environment to increase their net interest margin by funding high yield, long-term illiquid assets with low cost, short-term borrowing.

Given these changes in bank asset–liability structure, are rising interest rates still expected to increase the bank's interest margin? The answer is less clear, in part because interest rate increases impact a bank's financial structure in independent, somewhat offsetting ways. As a result, the net impact of any interest rate increase will depend on the particularities of a bank's balance sheet. Stress-tests should help to understand how the idiosyncratic financial structure of any particular bank will respond to such an increase in interest rates.

In order to understand the overall effect of an interest rate increase, consider how it will impact three key aspects of a bank's balance sheet: (1) its proportion of fixed-rate assets; (2) its reliance on rate-sensitive wholesale funds ("hot money"); and (3) its existing fixed-rate borrowing.

Insofar as the bank holds floating-rate assets, rising interest rates are less likely to result in loss because the coupon rate paid on these assets steps up to the new market rate of interest. As rates rise, however, the market value of the bank's fixed-rate assets (including loans and securities) will decline. Accounting rules may not require the bank to recognize unrealized loss on certain assets, but in real terms these unrealized losses reduce the bank's net worth. Moreover, prepayments on these fixed-rate assets will also decline as borrowers prefer to keep their lower-rate debt; as a result, the maturity of these fixed-rate assets will increase as they linger on the balance sheet longer than intended by the bank. The bank may be able to securitize these assets, but cashing out discounted assets means that the bank will have to recognize any built-in losses.

Rising interest rates also impact the other side of the bank's balance sheet, i.e. the bank's funding. To the extent that the bank has a strong deposit base, funding costs may not rise significantly because these depositors may not demand a corresponding increase in return as the market rate of interest climbs. Wholesale lenders, however, invest in the bank at arms-length (without the benefit of deposit insurance). Keenly aware of changes in market rates, wholesale lenders are likely to withdraw funds from the bank as soon as a better rate becomes available from another investment. To induce these lenders to roll-over any maturing investment in the bank, it may be forced to pay more interest, thereby increasing its funding costs.

In contrast, rising interest rates will not impact the bank insofar as it has previously borrowed at fixed-rates. Just like its own borrowers who refrain from prepaying mortgages and loans taken at previous interest rates that were lower, the bank will benefit from any long-term debt taken on when rates were low. Because rates have been low for some time, however, it may be that few banks have been able to lock-in sizeable amounts of fixed-rate, long-term debt.

To appreciate how these separate financial effects of rising interest rates converge in any particular bank, assume two different bank business models. The first one reflects the traditional maturity intermediation model: the bank's assets are long-term, fixed-rate, and illiquid; and its funding comes from core deposits and some wholesale lenders. As rates rise, this maturity mismatch, insofar as it has not been hedged away, will eat into the bank's profitability. In this case, its outstanding mortgage and securities inventory will be repriced downward insofar as it contains fixed-rate obligations. As its short-term borrowings mature, the bank will have to pay more to rollover its funding, especially that coming from wholesale lenders. Insofar as the bank makes new loans, however, it can exploit the rising rates by charging more, that way enhancing its net interest margin.

The second business model also has a maturity mismatch, but the asset-liability pattern is different from the traditional model: this bank invests in more short-term, liquid assets and it has issued more long-term, fixed-rate debt. Alternatively, its basic funding profile may be like the one above but the bank may have used swaps, credit transfer mechanisms, and other financial derivatives to replicate a balance sheet with liquid assets and long-term debt.

A bank in this position can profit from the increase in rates because of the favorable maturity mismatch. As short-term investments mature, the bank can lock in a higher return on new assets paying a market rate of interest. Because its assets mature faster than those of the traditional model, this bank will be able to favorably reprice its asset portfolio more easily. At the same time, the longer term of its borrowing means that the bank need not reenter the short-term funding market (in which rates are rising). Instead, it can wait until borrowing conditions are better. In many ways, this is the funding model that the new Basel funding rules point towards: the Liquidity Coverage Ratio will increase the bank's short-term liquid assets while the Net Stable Funding Ratio will increase the term of the bank's liabilities.

★ ★ ★

In effect, post-crisis legal reforms of financial markets amount to a substantial re-regulation of banking that, implicitly at least, recognizes that previous light-touch strategies for supervising banks did not work as expected. In particular, post-crisis reforms have changed the way that banks must track and provision for financial risks. The stress-testing techniques examined in this chapter are one important example of this re-regulation. Properly administered, stress-testing under prudent parameters should help banks and their regulators spot growing fragility in bank balance sheets before it ripens into a liquidity or solvency crisis. That said, since these stress-testing requirements are being implemented during a period in which banks must contend with several major regulatory and market shifts, these new requirements will probably require ongoing modification to make good on their promise.

Notes

1. The Committee's original members were Belgium, Canada, France, Germany, Italy, Japan, Luxembourg, the Netherlands, Spain, Sweden, Switzerland, the United Kingdom, and the United States.
2. In this chapter, the stylized balance sheets used to illustrate regulatory capital requirements make several simplifying assumptions such that they do not reflect actual capital requirements for these portfolios.
3. Firms regulated as broker-dealers had had to comply with net capital standards imposed by the Securities and Exchange Commission. In response to lobbying by financial conglomerates that included both banks and broker-dealers, in 2004, the Securities and Exchange Commission amended the net capital rule to allow some broker-dealers to meet their net capital requirements using these internal risk-management models. The requirements to use this method are found in Appendix E to 17 CFR 240.15c3-1. The change grew out of a pilot project conducted by the General Accounting Office (1998, p. 14) with six large securities firms that used proprietary risk models to estimate risks in their over-the-counter derivatives portfolios.

4 Because this technique attempts to measure how a bank's financial position would change based on changes in market conditions, the quality of the data used is key. An insurmountable shortcoming in the data is that it is not possible to accurately anticipate what the future states of the world will be. Concretely, this shows up in the limited ability to predict price behavior during the most important periods—extreme periods that show up as the negative tails in a normal distribution.
5 In the basic and more conservative approach, the bank would estimate the probability of a default on its assets and the regulators would provide the expected loss given default, the bank's exposure at default, and the maturity at exposure. Using the advanced approach, the bank would use its own values rather than those of the regulator.
6 These events include Black Monday (1987), the Asian financial crisis (1997), Russia's debt default (2001), and the terrorist attacks on the United States (2001). Each of these events impacted financial markets in important ways. There were also "extreme" events that turned out not to have much impact, for example the Century Date Change.
7 In addition to these stress-tests, Basel III imposes two other funding requirements that involve stress-testing liquidity and funding. Before the crisis, regulators imposed relatively "soft" expectations on banks with respect to how they managed liquidity. Though not called stress-tests, two other new regulatory requirements also involve simulations of bank financial conditions: the liquidity coverage ratio and the still inchoate stable asset funding ratio. By virtue of the Liquidity Coverage Ratio and the Net Stable Funding Ratio, global regulators have codified these liquidity norms as binding requirements, akin to the regulatory capital norms on which they are modeled.
8 For example, as part of the Capital Assistance Program conducted under the Emergency Economic Stabilization Act of 2008, the US Treasury and the Fed ran stress-tests of the 19 largest bank holding companies (Congressional Oversight Panel, 2009, pp. 8–27).

References

Bank for International Settlements (2009). *Principles for Sound Stress-testing Practices And Supervision*. Basel: Bank for International Settlements, p. 2.

Bank of England (2013). *A Framework for Stress-testing the UK Banking System*. London: Bank of England, pp. 10–11.

Basel Committee on Banking Supervision (1996). *Amendment to the Capital Accord to Incorporate Market Risks*. Basel: Bank for International Settlements, pp. 46–7.

Berkowitz, J. (1999). *A Coherent Framework for Stress-Testing*. Board of Governors of the Federal Reserve System Finance and Economics Discussion Series Paper 99–29.

Blaschke, W., Jones, M., Mainoni, G. and Martinez Peria, S. (2001). *Stress-testing of Financial Systems: An Overview of Issues, Methodologies, and FSAP Experiences*. International Monetary Fund Working Paper. Washington DC: International Monetary Fund.

Board of Governors of the Federal Reserve (2014). *Supervisory Expectations for a Capital Adequacy Process, Comprehensive Capital Analysis and Review 2015*. Washington DC: Federal Reserve, pp. 17–18.

Board of Governors of the Federal Reserve (2015). *Policy Statement on the Scenario Design Framework for Stress-testing*. Washington DC: Federal Reserve, p. 23.

Bowman, D., Gagnon, E. and Leahy, M. (2010). *Interest on Excess Reserves as a Monetary Policy Instrument*. Board of Governors of the Federal Reserve, International Finance Discussion Papers. Washington DC: Federal Reserve.

Congressional Oversight Panel (2009). *Stress-testing and Shoring Up Bank Capital*. Congressional Oversight Panel, pp. 8–27.

European Central Bank (2014a). *ECB's In-depth Review Shows Banks Need to Take Further Action*. Frankfurt: European Central Bank.

European Central Bank (2014b). *Note on the Comprehensive Assessment*. Frankfurt: European Central Bank.

European Systemic Risk Board (2014). *EBA/SSM Stress-test: The Macroeconomic Adverse Scenario*. London: European Banking Authority.

Federal Deposit Insurance Corporation (2010). *Nowhere to go but Up: Managing Interest Rate Risk in a Low-rate Environment*. Federal Deposit Insurance Corporation.

General Accounting Office (1998). *Risk Based Capital, Regulatory and Industry Approaches to Capital and Risk*. Washington, DC: General Accounting Office, pp. 7–14.

Getter, D. (2012). *US Implementation of the Basel Capital Regulatory Framework*. Washington, DC: Congressional Research Service, pp. 3–10.

18

Defences against systemic risk
A greater role and responsibility for bank lawyers? Judgement-based bank supervision*

Joanna Gray and Peter Metzing

Introduction to judgement-based supervision

The years since 2008 have seen much public blaming, naming and shaming of a wide range of individuals and institutions. These include senior management of financial institutions, individual traders in certain wholesale financial markets as well as those both within out side regulatory bodies who set the intellectual tone and strategic direction for financial regulation prior to the financial crisis of 2008. That latter category has encompassed the regulator's political masters, as well as the regulators themselves, insofar as a virtue was made by certain politicians of the competitive advantage of the 'light touch' and 'principles based' regime of financial regulation that pertained in the UK prior to 2008, and indeed of the initial political judgement of New Labour in the UK that led to the creation of the FSA as a unitary financial regulator in 1998 and the removal of direct powers of bank supervision from the Bank of England that accompanied it. Indeed, even the UK Queen was reported to have expressed interest and concern in the effectiveness of the powers of financial supervisors to achieve their objectives in an observation made during a recent visit to the Bank of England, that the Financial Services Authority did not have any 'teeth' (Rayner, 2012).

She was far from alone in reaching this conclusion and the UK has redesigned its regulatory architecture to confer direct powers of bank supervision on a new regulatory body that forms part of the Bank of England, the Prudential Regulatory Authority (PRA) that seeks to achieve a general objective to promote the safety and soundness of those whom it authorises.[1] A wholly separate regulatory body, the Financial Conduct Authority (FCA), has assumed responsibility for the licensing and supervision of institutions carrying out exclusively or primarily non-wholesale financial market business as well as integrity and conduct of business issues. Both FCA and PRA are subject to the powers of direction and recommendation by an important new Committee of the Bank of England, the Financial Policy Committee (FPC), which is tasked with guarding against risk to the financial system as a whole and will perform the difficult task of macro-prudential financial regulation remaining vigilant to the multifaceted yet persistent reality of systemic risk.

The UK pre-crisis operating framework of financial regulatory supervision was often characterised by both the FSA itself and by academic commentators as being risk driven and risk responsive (Black, 2004), but this descriptor has been displaced post-crisis by the need for supervisory action to be informed by and responsive to *judgements* formed by supervisors as to the risks posed by regulated institutions and key individuals working within or associated with them.

Giving primacy and practical effect to the judgements formed within the new UK financial regulatory bodies, the Financial Policy Committee (FPC), the Prudential Regulation Authority (PRA) and the Financial Conduct Authority (FCA), was identified by the UK government as being essential in order to achieve the core objective of a more stable and efficient financial system (HM Treasury, 2011, 1st para. foreword). 'Judgement' is seen to be synonymous with 'expertise' and it is the judgements of the aforementioned three new expert regulators, rather than risk scorecards, that are to form the driving force of the post-2008 financial regulatory system. Despite the centrality of judgements to the way in which regulators exercise their supervisory and intervention powers there has been little discussion of what distinguishes 'judgement' from its range of possible alternates (depending on context), such as 'opinion', 'view', 'decision' or 'step'. The OED defines 'judgement' as a quality, being an ability to 'make considered decisions or come to sensible conclusions'. But on what basis are such judgements made safely? And at what point in time? judgements can of course be formed about the past, present and future and can be based on all manner of things. The increasing use of the term 'judgement' by financial supervisors may be one of several examples where there is room for misunderstanding between those from different disciplines and culture with supervisors (especially those with a background primarily in financial economics) and lawyers using the term to mean different things, thereby attaching different degrees of importance to the various components of a 'judgement'.

Necessary links between micro and macro prudential supervision

The new legislation lays the foundations for closer and more intense scrutiny of those financial institutions to be authorised by the PRA. This is so not only from the perspective of their individual prudential health but also from the contextual perspective of their place in the firmament of the wider financial system. For the PRA is directed to seek to achieve its general objective with an eye to potential impacts or adverse effects upon the stability of the UK financial system.[2] It is thus clear that micro-prudential supervision of PRA-authorised institutions looks set to involve judgements being made that will necessarily require the application of macro-prudential or system wide factors to the case of a specific institution under PRA supervision. For if there is one central policy lesson that emerges from the global financial crisis it is the need for regulators to marry up and follow through with concrete practical actions and interventions the very many layers of abstraction in which financial risk can be manifest, from the level of broader global macroeconomic indicators right down to the level of the culture on the trading floor or failures in IT data systems within a specific business division of a regulated firm (Turner Review, 2009). Therefore it is important to bear in mind in any discussion of how the PRA should deliver judgement-based supervision that some of the underlying judgements to supervisory action will inevitably include judgements about sources of systemic risk that lie in the broader financial and economic environment beyond the influence, and sometimes even beyond the awareness, of specific authorised institutions. But the force and immediate effect of PRA supervisory action will be felt at the micro-level of the institution subject to supervision and it is at this juncture that we see one of the main obstacles to a judgement-led approach to supervision emerging in practice. The second part of this chapter considers this issue in greater detail along with other potential obstacles in response to some of the questions of practical policy of relevance to regulatory data gathering in particular, which were raised in the course of scoping out the BoE/CCBS workshop from which this paper developed. The first part of the paper summarises what the PRA has outlined as being the essential qualities and mechanisms of 'judgement-based supervision' but first examines its origins.

Origins of judgement-based supervision

When supervisors first began in this most recent round of wholesale regulatory reform to identify the need for a more judgement-led approach to their role it became clear that the term was being contrasted with a formulaic, mechanistic 'box-ticking' approach to supervision. Paul Tucker of the Bank of England, contrasted the two supervisory modes and emphasised the prospective, forward-looking nature of supervisory judgement when he began to publicly think through the implementation of macro prudential regulation. He emphasised:

> [T]he necessity of reviving supervision. By that, I do not mean checking compliance with rules after the fact, punishing breaches; punishing offenders does not bring back to life a bank or the customer businesses that have collapsed with it. I mean forward-looking judgements about the prudence of a firm's management and the resilience of its business.
> *(Tucker, 2009, p. 4)*

However, as the UK Turner Review pointed out, the approach to supervision employed by the FSA in the period leading up to the financial crisis was never stated to be a light touch checklist of compliance with rules (Turner Review, 2009, p. 86). Instead the FSA's whole approach to financial supervision had been carefully developed, crafted and refined to be expressed and implemented within a sophisticated risk-based operating framework within which both firm-specific and environmental risks were expressed and scored against broader risk categories that related to risks to the FSA's original four statutory objectives. This ARROW supervisory framework was employed by the FSA within a broader risk-based philosophy of regulation that worked alongside then prevalent intellectual assumptions now revealed to have been flawed. Turner saw these as being threefold: first, a belief in the ability of markets to accurately price and smoothly clear financial risk; second, the view that the appropriate primary responsibility for business risk be with the firm and not the regulator; and third, an assumption that a combination of lightly regulated and vigorous wholesale markets with conduct of business regulation applied mainly in retail financial markets would better protect financial customers than would product regulation or direct intervention in markets.

In many ways then it is unfair to characterise the pre-crisis supervisory approach of the FSA as being mechanistic and box-ticking in contrast to the more subtle and nuanced judgement-led approach now being developed. For the ARROW supervisory framework developed by FSA could hardly be described as being about checklist type compliance with rules. It was always intended to be much more than that and indeed its was presented as being far more multidimensional and broader in the reach and focus of its inquiry about the regulated subject than approaches to financial regulation that preceded it. Indeed, if we recall the origins of the FSA as a unitary financial regulator, it is worth noting that its disparate predecessor bodies charged with financial regulation from 1988 until 2001 were castigated by another Chancellor of the Exchequer in another political era as 'not delivering the standard of supervision and investor protection that the industry and the public have a right to expect'.[3] One of the most infamous examples of supervisory failure came to light in 1991 with the orchestrated and large-scale theft from the occupational pension fund of Mirror Group Newspapers by the founder of the Mirror Group. The supervisor then charged with the responsibility for the two investment management companies that ran the MGN pension funds was the Investment Management Regulatory Organisation. Its supervision of the companies concerned, Bishopsgate Investment Management Ltd. and London and Bishopsgate International Investment Management plc, was criticised as revealing an approach to supervisory monitoring that was too mechanistic, insufficiently critical and failed to spot emerging problems and sources of risk.[4] Delving even further back in time to the periods preceding the emergence of formal systems of statute-based financial regulation in the UK, in the Banking Act 1987 and Financial Services Act 1986, the rigour and effectiveness of largely self-regulatory and informal supervisory mechanisms in force in the 1970s and early 1980s attracted criticism too and led to the formal empowerment of the Securities and Investments Board (SIB) in 1988 (Gower, 1984). Much was then made of the enhancement to supervisory effectiveness that would flow from the SIB's statutory basis and its potential to use the power of formal law as opposed to suasion and regulation by membership contract.

And so every regulatory era grapples with the problem of how to supervise to bring about better outcomes. Each era has its dominant mood music being sounded by supervisors and it is clear that that of the coming decades is set to be 'judgement-led supervision' just as that of the past two decades has been 'risk-based supervision' within its attendant framework of 'principles-based regulation' as considered by Black (2010). This latter term has been conflated by politicians with 'light-touch' regulation in crisis demonology and does not feature at all in the reformed post-crisis legislative and regulatory framework.

Components of the new supervisory approach

It is possible to engage in extensive debates about the differences between 'regulation' and 'supervision' for the two terms are often used interchangeably but they do actually refer to different things. Regulation is an empty vessel and little more than dangerous window dressing without the myriad of day-to-day steps and processes that give it its legs and intelligence base. Those steps and processes constitute supervision. Regulators can know nothing and decide nothing unless they engage in continuous supervision of those to whom they have admitted to a regulated sector. The term 'monitoring' was used more often in the early days of UK financial regulation but this suggests a degree of passivity that no good regulator can afford. Supervision suggests a more dynamic and engaged regulator and not a mere bystander doing little more than watching and recording. Supervision can also be distinguished from enforcement, rule-making and many of the other functions that a regulator must undertake. The legislative framework requires the PRA (and indeed the FCA too) to maintain arrangements for the supervision of those whom it authorises[5] and these arrangements are contained in the more detailed handbook of rules and guidance that operates at the regulatory level to set the parameters of the legal framework in which the new supervisory approach will take place (FSA, 2011).[6]

Although the supervisory process is a continuous one, the key 'bite points' for PRA supervision, the points in time at which supervisory judgements will be made or reviewed and at which the legal powers of supervisory intervention may be exercised, are at authorisation in assessment of whether or not a firm meets the stipulated Threshold Conditions for PRA authorisation[7] and upon approval of individuals undertaking PRA-controlled functions[8] (certain critical roles within an authorised firm where the conduct and tone set by that individual could have an impact on the prudential culture within the firm – these are mostly characterised by the legislative framework as 'significant influence' functions). These are not simply one-off events but subject to regular review and continuing supervision, and the PRA's powers to modify the extent of a firm's authorisation or even cancel outright should the PRA judge it to have fallen below the expected conditions are seen as key backup mechanisms to following through on its judgements should less formal action and dialogue with the firm fail. Information gathering and investigation in the course of supervision are clearly vital processes, for good judgements depend on becoming and being kept well informed. The data challenges to effecting judgement-led supervision are considerable and are considered further below in the context of obstacles to judgement-led supervision. Suffice it to note at this point that legislative powers of information gathering and investigation have been amended in order to support a broader and more intensive data collection effort by supervisors.[9] The special reporting responsibilities of auditors of authorised firms (whereby auditors are placed under certain notification obligations intended to support supervisors in their role) have been extended to include auditors of recognised investment exchanges.[10]

The language of risk, however, has not disappeared from the framework being developed for PRA supervision, for judgements must be made *about* something and it is at this point that risk features again in the new supervisory framework. For in elaborating the elements of its new supervisory approach the PRA sees judgements about risk to its objective being made about firms both as regards current risks and also those that could 'plausibly arise in the future', and will focus its efforts on firms and issues according to the risk they pose to the stability of the UK financial system, thereby necessitating another set of judgements that entail risk assessments (Bank of England, Prudential Regulation Authority, 2012, p. 6).

This change in focus to the language of judgement and to a more prospective and forward-looking mode of viewing risk acknowledges the inherent and essential uncertainty about an unknown future world. Thus it seems a more realistic and appropriate descriptor for the task facing the supervisors than does the language of assessment.

The PRA will supervise institutions by making judgements about risks that might be posed to its objectives of safety and soundness and stability. In so doing it will consider three categories of risk – those that arise from the external economic context and the business model of the firm, but it is clear that the *key* judgement that matters most in determining the intensity of supervision is of the potential impact that a firm could have on financial stability.[11] The five categories by reference to which the significance of a firm to the stability of the UK financial system will be judged are differentiated by the extent to which its size, complexity, interconnectedness and business type have the capacity to cause disruption to the UK financial system by the firm's failure or its carrying on business in an unsafe manner.[12] These are the judgements that will be hardest for the PRA to make and may leave the greatest room for disagreement with those subject to them. Having made a judgement about the 'Gross Risk' surrounding a firm, the PRA supervisors will net off certain 'Mitigating factors' having also made judgements about these. Although the three categories of mitigating factors - Operational (management and governance, risk management and controls), Financial (Capital and liquidity) and Structural (Resolvability) - are all within a firm's control, any firm that is a Category 1 High Impact firm cannot escape intensive supervision by being squeaky clean with respect to all the mitigating factors. This is because the PRA has stated that it will still direct a wider range of its supervisory tools to High Impact firms regardless of the mitigating factors it identifies.[13] The FSA learned the hard way about the dangers of wrongly estimating the probability that a potentially High Impact firm could fail when the consequences of the categorisation of Northern Rock under the ARROW framework as a High Impact/Low Probability firm became clear (FSA, 2008). One lesson that emerged from the subsequent enquiry into its supervision of Northern Rock was that had the probing of Northern Rock's business model, financial strategy, liquidity coverage and so on been more extensive and a more critical and sceptical mindset been applied to the results of those probes (this is the 'judgement' part that was lacking) then a rather different risk categorisation might have been made. So it seems that despite a High Impact firm's record as regards the

Mitigating factors in the risk matrix that reduce its 'Gross Risk' to PRA objectives, it will still be subject to the same supervisory tools and checks as others in the same category without its talent for mitigation. In a financial system where even the best run, soundly capitalised and speedily resolvable firm may be brought down by external shock and the resulting contagion it makes sense for the supervisor to subject it to more intrusive supervision than a firm whose profile and position raises no systemic risk. Hence Low Impact firms are to be subject to only a minimal baseline level of supervision.

When the FSA first proposed the introduction of what are now very extensive rules and guidance on expected arrangements for senior management responsibilities, governance and risk management within an authorised firm was at pains to reassure firms and their advisers that they would not be seeking to impinge on the business judgement of firms or prefer any business culture over another (FSA, 1999). Indeed it made clear it did not expect to see any detailed plans relating to the firm's business strategy and it talked of the need to embed and support development of a compliance culture throughout the firm (FSA, 1999). Prudence and stability were never uppermost in its mind in what it had to say about culture and business strategy. The supervisory approach of and expectations the PRA will have in relation to the way in which a firm sees, lives and breathes its business could not be more different. For the PRA makes clear that its supervisors will be looking for and expect to see evidence that a firm has learned the lessons of 2008 and can withstand future siren calls of lucrative risky strategy and practices that may have external costs. Indeed this task of watching out for and countering any future backsliding on the priority attached to prudence and safety is seen by the PRA as being the key task of prudential regulator. Just as the FPC will seek to lean against the prevailing winds of the economic cycle in its directions and recommendations to the PRA and FCA as to how best to counter systemic risk, so too will the PRA provide the micro prudential counterweight to a firm's own internal cycle of growth. Clearly supervisors cannot and will not be at every Board meeting but they will be very much across the details of what is making a firm tick now and how it will meet the future, especially High Impact firms:

> [t]he PRA will aim to understand a business model's sustainability and vulnerabilities ... [f]or those firms posing greater risk to the stability of the system, the analysis will be more detailed. It will include a review of the drivers of profitability, risk appetite, performance targets and underlying assumptions, and a firm's own forecasts and their plausibility ... [and] if the PRA believes that mitigating measures alone cannot adequately reduce material risks to the safety and soundness of the firm, it will require the firm to change its business model.
> *(Bank of England, Prudential Regulation Authority, 2012, p. 17, paras 56–7)*

There are many other examples that could be highlighted of how and where judgement-led supervision looks set to be more intrusive than its predecessor. Another aspect of a more forward-looking supervisory perspective is that intervention action, in order to be effective in countering prospectively judged future risks, will often occur at an earlier stage and to a greater extent than it in the past. The planned 'Proactive Intervention Framework' (PIF) through which PRA supervisory intervention will be modelled and escalated necessarily involves assessment of risks to the viability of the firm. It will be placed in one of five categories of 'proximity to failure' and this category will determine the nature and pace of supervisory action. The potential impact of a firm on stability of the UK financial system and its resolvability will not be used in placing a firm on the PIF scale since these two factors tell us nothing about an individual firm's viability, unlike the external context, business risks, operational and prudential factors specific to a firm. It is at this point then that 'doing well' on its mitigating factors in reduction of its gross risk may reward a firm with a lower PIF categorisation. This is similar to the probability part of the Impact x Probability calculus used by the FSA in its categorisation of firms under the ARROW framework. For obvious reasons the PRA is not proposing to publish its PIF categorisation of a firm – not even to the firm itself in case this should trigger an obligation on the firm to disclose it to the market. We can thus expect to see much comparative activity, sharing of intelligence about life under the new supervisory regime and educated guesswork as firms try to form a view of how they are perceived by the PRA as opposed to how they see themselves.

The PRA makes it clear that its senior staff will be regularly involved in the risk assessments that feed into its judgements about supervisory action, and major supervisory judgements will be taken by experienced staff. In conveying its views and judgements to the firm as part of the ongoing supervisory process it is clear that, although it acknowledges that it expects to see the firm take the lead in ensuring good regulatory outcomes are delivered, if need be it will direct the firm how to act.[14] It will inform the firm what it judges the key risks and concerns relevant to that firm to be, will share its 'root cause analysis' of why this is so and how supervisory intervention can address the causes of PRA concerns about financial stability.[15] PRA intends to involve the Audit Committee of a firm and its non-executive directors in ensuring follow up action is taken by the firm in response to the issues raised by PRA.

Obstacles to a judgement-led approach to supervision?

People

While resourcing and staffing supervisory bodies for any high skill/high remuneration sector is acknowledged to be a perennial problem, it is a particular problem for a model of supervision that relies to such an extent on judgement. Getting hold of and retaining a sufficient number of the right mix of people with the right mix of skills and seniority to implement this more nuanced approach to supervision was identified as a potential problem by many witnesses before both the Joint Parliamentary Committee that scrutinised the (now enacted) Draft Financial Services Bill (hereafter referred to as the 'Draft FSB Committee') (Joint Committee on the draft Financial Services Bill, 2011).[16] It described the human resources challenge facing the PRA thus:

> Forward looking supervision is a key cultural change for the regulators and it will require a different approach and skillset. Effective judgement led regulation will require intellectual capability, an understanding of the complexities of financial markets and a willingness and confidence to challenge senior staff within firms. The lack of senior, experienced regulatory staff able to exercise judgement in an increasingly complex financial services market may constrain a shift in this direction.
> *(Joint Committee on the draft Financial Services Bill, 2011, para. 199)*

It recommended the human capacity of the supervisors be kept under regular review and that both bodies publish their plans to ensure both that they have the right calibre of staff and develop a public service ethos in which is embedded a career development trajectory around supervision, publishing progress updates in their annual reports.[17] The government's response to this recommendation, while fully alive to the importance of the 'people question' to a judgement-led approach to supervision, preferred instead to see this as an issue that fell within the operational autonomy of a supervisor, and respecting that autonomy was itself a pre-requisite of enabling the conditions for judgement-led supervision to flourish.[18] More recently the Parliamentary Commission on Banking Standards in its questioning of witnesses has voiced concerns about the new Supervisors' ability to attract and retain the right kind of staff, given the inevitable pay differentials between regulator and regulated and the fact that the need for industry to adjust to the new regulatory environment is adding to the problem of shortages of skilled risk and compliance staff who might be useful to supervisors (Cohrs et al., 2012, Q. 61–85). One interesting witness response to the perennial problem of incentives for a career in public service emphasised the intellectual demands and challenge of a 'career' in regulation as opposed to a 'job' in banking, and suggested that more be made of the differential in non-pecuniary rewards (Cohrs et al., 2012, Q. 40).

But there is more to this 'people question' than technical skills and experience for, as the Draft FSB Committee acknowledged, the changes in culture and philosophy needed for forward-looking supervision requires staff with the right approach and attitudes as well as experience. The new supervisory framework calls for vision and imagination. Supervisors will be needed with a capacity for broader and holistic vision as well as an ability to handle detail and technicality. So too will they need to be able to imagine different (perhaps highly unlikely and even far-fetched) futures and then think through their practical implications.

The need to see 'emergent risks' suggests an acuity of vision, which is the sum of more than just market experience and being quick on the uptake. It calls not just for one-dimensional lateral thinking but also an ability to see connections between apparently disparate institutions, markets, products and indeed across time. If judgements are to be formed that can be based on the kind of counterfactual insights that were missing in recent supervisory decision-making then there is a need to see not just plausible risks but also envision even implausible ones. For it is in the nature of decision-making under conditions of uncertainty that what may appear implausible, and even fanciful, viewed prospectively can turn out to be devastatingly real in hindsight. O'Malley, a leading commentator on the problems that risk and uncertainty present for governance, has talked of a need to 'beauraucratise imagination' and recommends a greater willingness to use other disciplines and mindsets than those that have traditionally prevailed in any particular supervisory domain in order to do this (O'Malley, 2012, p. 44 himself quoting from National Commission on Terrorist Attacks Upon the United States (2004), p. 344).

Yet the importance of imagination as a quality in efforts to develop the kind of counter-factual thinking that supervisory judgements may need to employ is missing in PRA's explanation of its approach to staffing (Bank of England, Prudential Regulation Authority, 2012, pp. 40–1). After all, lawyers, auditors, regulators and financiers who will still inevitably dominate the supervisory game, even under a judgement-led approach to supervision are essentially utterly practical people charged with solving problems, building structures and value chains and refereeing and managing expectations. They are used to real world games played in the here and now, the lived present, basing action and inaction on realised events and observable data rather than dreams, guesses and 'mere' fancy. Even economists, as they develop more imaginative stress and scenario testing techniques to use in the course of supervision, can be defeated by the sheer outlandishness of chance. For the predictive techniques of economics are bound by the endogeneity of the game we already know (Danielsson, 2000; Sollis, 2009). By way of example, O'Malley highlighted imagination as being the missing ingredient in the morass of intelligence data and possibilities that resulted in the failure to foretell 9/11 (O'Malley, 2012). The same could yet be true of efforts to make sense of the deluge of supervisory data and intelligence that will come the way of the PRA under its new approach to supervision. Yet what may seem to be an intractable information challenge to our predictive vision posed by the unknowable that surrounds systemic risk, may equally be a result of our own failure to treat the process of imagination as seriously as that of scientific theorising and reasoning.

Data challenges

Among the many questions that arise around supervisory data is how intrusive should a supervisor be in order to operationalise a more forward looking and judgement-led approach to supervision? Clearly, as Tucker remarked when, in 2009, he began to sketch out some of the practical challenges to placing judgements (as opposed to rules) at the heart of macro-prudential regulation, this new approach to supervision will be a 'data intensive endeavour' (Tucker, 2009). The Financial Services Acts of 2010 and 2012 have made changes the net effect of which is to strengthen the supervisor's formal data collection powers, but these formal powers are only one part of the toolkit used to compile the databases used to feed into supervisory judgements. The PRA will be receiving a vast amount of data under firms' reporting obligations, will make use of information about firms already in the public domain, and has signalled it intends to involve senior and operational staff of firms in helping it compile information. It will request from time to time firm-specific information such as management information and forecasts and will make use of risk, compliance and internal audit functions within the firm to help it identify risks pertinent to judgement formation (Bank of England, Prudential Regulation Authority, 2012, paras 173–6).

It is clear then that the PRA envisages many different channels of data flow which will yield both the routinely reported data that has been prepared for the specific purpose of inclusion in regulatory returns but also more raw and potentially sensitive information (such as management information or internal audit reports) that, under a less intensive supervisory regime may not have been accessed by a supervisor in original form if at all. The challenge for the PRA will be ensuring that in seeking to ensure 'firms … submit sufficient data of appropriate quality, to inform their judgements about key risks' (Bank of England, Prudential Regulation Authority, 2012, para. 173), it does not become overwhelmed and submerged with data flow from firms of a quantity and quality from which it is all but impossible to extract meaningful information. There was considerable discussion of this risk by witnesses before the Draft FSB Committee, which highlighted the poor quality of much risk data held within firms prior to 2007 and recommended the development of information standards for use within industry be a formal duty of the PRA.[19] Although this recommendation did not find its way into the legislation, the development and use of data standards within the financial sector is very much seen as key to getting better quality data to supervisors and this is discussed below in the context of the LEI initiative. The challenge for the PRA will be winning firms over to an understanding that, despite the fact that their own data collection and reporting obligations have increased significantly with the introduction of a common European framework for supervisory and financial reporting,[20] the PRA will still ask, from time to time, for additional information from different parts of the firm and will expect it to be applied within a very short time frame. Such requests will not always be welcome or even, seen from the perspective of the firm, may not seem relevant or appropriate. However, there are distinct advantages in having the ability to dig around different departments of a firm and make specific further data requests for raw internal information rather than receiving information in a state prepared for a reporting template. The collapse of Barings plc illustrates this, for had the Bank of England had access to the Internal Audit report prepared in July 1994 within the Barings group containing its assessment of the activities of its Singapore subsidiary it may have led it to closer scrutiny of Barings plc and perhaps averted or at least reduced the scale of Barings 1995 collapse.[21]

Obviously, supervisors would prefer that any specific request for information they make of an authorised person generates voluntary compliance. But the *in terrorem* value of the formal supervisory power contained in section 165 FSMA 2000 to require the disclosure by authorised persons of either specific or generic information and documents was recognised in the extension of the ambit of its reach in 2010 with the insertion of s165A, by which the power to seek information encompasses those beyond the regulatory perimeter where the information sought is considered relevant to financial stability.[22] The Draft FSB Committee recognised the value of such a power to the objective given to the Financial Policy Committee in surveying sources of systemic risk that might arise outside of the regulated sector and that there might be circumstances where the FPC would need to be able to use such a power directly itself to examine the murkier corners of shadow banking rather than relying on the PRA to gather the information sought.[23] The government response to the Draft FSB Committee's recommendation that the FPC be given a reserve power to use the s165A tool directly (rather than via the PRA) was to amend the legislation so as to preserve the hierarchy as to the use of the power but to reduce the potential for delay whenever the FPC makes a recommendation that the PRA be given power to look beyond the regulatory perimeter for information pertinent to financial stability.

It will be interesting to see how far outside the regulatory perimeter this power is used, for it affords the PRA and FPC a potentially very useful tool to gather data from a wider range of intermediaries, middlemen, advisors and some of the newer forms of financial intermediation which populate a changing financial system. Since the legal basis for its use will owe much to a supervisor's assessment of the relevance of specific information or classes of information to financial stability it may be difficult to gain acceptance for the use of this power and legal challenges to its use may be made. Firms will resist any requests they feel are mere fishing expeditions and may probe the reasoning that links information held or generated within their (unregulated) business to broader systemic stability. Although it did not involve the s165A power, the way in which the Court of Appeal was asked recently in Financial *Services Authority and others v Amro International and Goodman Jones LLP (interested party)*[24] to probe the exact extent of the FSA's powers to require information and disclosure from third parties in the course of an investigation carried on behalf of an overseas regulator, shows the kind of resistance that might yet emerge to the use of s165A. More intrusive and frequent data requests of those who lie beyond the immediate jurisdiction of the supervisors based on judgements about the possibility that they may help plot wider systemic risk will not be universally popular. And yet they may provide some of the most vital sources of data to fill in missing links in any useful map of systemic risk.

There has been a growing trend to harness the skills and perspective of third parties, be they obvious gatekeepers such as auditors of regulated firms, or expert skilled persons able to conduct forensic inquiries and review exercises within firms to assist supervisors. Singh (2003) has considered the genesis of third party involvement in bank supervision along with some of its advantages and disadvantages. The use of auditors' reports and skilled persons' reports has increased in recent years, with the statutory responsibilities conferred on auditors providing a potentially invaluable tool to supervisors insofar as auditors may disclose to regulators not just relevant information which arises in the course of his appointment but also opinions on that information.[25] Since interpretation of data is the key to forming supervisory judgement it behoves the supervisors to solicit and garner others' reading of data, especially where those others are closest to its source. Although such a suggestion would meet with howls of protest and defences of legal professional privilege the imposition of similar requirements, or at least the use of s165A(2)(d) in relation to law firms which act for systemically important financial institutions might afford the PRA, which can often understand and see potential risks posed by a firm's business model more clearly than can the firm itself, another channel into the network of advisory relationships.

The Draft FSB Committee regretted the weakening of the kind of close working relationships between bank auditors and supervisors than had existed prior to the transfer of banking supervisory responsibility from the Bank of England to FSA and highlighted the fact that:

> In 2006 there was not a single meeting between the FSA and the external auditors of either Northern Rock (PwC) or HBoS (KPMG), and only one meeting between the auditor of RBS (Deloitte) and the FSA. In 2007 there was only one FSA/auditors meeting with each bank auditor.
>
> *(Draft FSB Committee Report, 2011, para. 234)*

Their recommendation of a statutory duty for the PRA to meet regularly with bank auditors was not adopted, being seen instead as a matter of operational autonomy for the supervisor. However, the PRA has indeed signalled it expects firms' auditors' to fully engage and assist in its prudential supervision of firms and will be looking to them to disclose any 'emerging' concerns they may have about firms and will see such disclosures as being within their responsibilities under the Code of Practice governing the relationship between supervisor and external auditor, which provides guidance as to the extent of auditors' responsibilities under supervision rules (Bank of England, Prudential Regulation Authority, 2012, para. 177).[26]

The PRA plans greater use too of the Skilled Persons reporting mechanism to complement other channels through which it can obtain supervisory data (Bank of England, Prudential Regulation Authority, 2014, para. 178 PRA). Amendments have been made to the existing section 166 FSMA 2000 pursuant to which skilled persons can be appointed so that the regulator may now make a direct appointment of an appropriate third party to report to it on matters of interest relating to an authorised person rather than requiring the authorised person itself to commission the report. This shortened and more direct mandate for such experts will further enhance their use by regulators.[27] So too will the new s166A, which enables regulatory use of the skilled persons reporting mechanism as a useful follow-up regulatory tool for verification of firm data where a firm has failed to collect the data itself. Firms are obliged under the legislation to cooperate with and make full disclosure to skilled persons so appointed to investigate and report into their affairs or to collect and update data they hold. Nonetheless recent litigation, during the course of which pre-trial discovery has been sought of skilled persons supervisory reports into their affairs by investors and counterparties seeking to establish breach of common law or statutory duty on the firms' part, has not ruled out the possibility that such reports or information in them may be discoverable in certain circumstances.[28] This may mean that the conduct of skilled persons enquiries may in the future assume the tenor of a more formal investigation rather than the full and frank exchange of queries and information that a supervisor might prefer.

The discussion so far presumes that, in order to make full use of these enhanced powers and more various channels of data gathering, the regulator will know, or at least have a good idea as to what categories of data to request and of whom. While this may be true of categories of data pertinent to micro-prudential firm specific concerns, it is important to remember the macro-prudential objective inherent in the PRA's mission and its need for data to help it compile a systemic risk map. This adds a whole new dimension to the use of data collection and request powers. But in order to know what data firms may be in possession of that can meaningfully populate and illuminate that systemic risk map further the PRA must first have a view of the likely shape of the risk map itself – and forming those initial shapes involves a different kind of data exercise, which firms may at first have difficulty in seeing the need for. It is at this stage that the new Legal Entity Identifier initiative or 'LEI' comes into its own.

LEIs and the data challenge

Haldane (2012a) has vividly illustrated the need for policy to shift thinking about the behaviour of financial systems from accepting normality in terms of reversion to a mean to the way in which networks behave and build up in a financial system characterised by non-linear dynamics, self-organised criticality, preferential attachment in a way that incubates fat tail risk and contagion effects of catastrophe (Haldane, 2012a).

Clearly the data challenges to constructing the kind of multidimensional, jurisdictional and temporal systemic risk map needed (Haldane, 2012a), in order to effect macro-prudential supervision are very considerable indeed. The variety and kinds of indicators and data points needed to populate such a map of the financial system are infinite. Additionally, in order to be at all useful in gauging factors such as connectedness and contagion risk, lines will need to be drawn between apparently disparate data points separated by time, jurisdiction, product and legal entity for risk patterns to emerge to, in turn, be subjected to different interpretations and scenario tests. Only then can reasoned and grounded judgements be formed. Haldane recently employed the metaphor of the challenge facing Captain Kirk on the Star ship *Enterprise* making sense of the meanings behind the ever changing galaxies before him on the Observation Deck.[29] Supervisors have to do more than star gaze for patterns of connectivity or clustering of risk around nodes of activity but have the advantage of the ability to be able to work across jurisdictional borders through judicious use of their data collection powers across and beyond the perimeter of the regulated industry so as to begin to standardise and organise the morass of disparate transactions that appear systemically innocuous when viewed individually but, when aggregated, reveal patterns that cause supervisors concern.

In any attempt to understand and map systemic risk it seems crucial to disentangle and understand the legal interconnectedness of regulated financial institutions themselves. While this is certainly important, systemic risk has a further dimension which calls for minute and forensic plotting of the legal status of all entities which are, at any stage and in any point in time, privy to or otherwise exposed to a risk originated upon the creation of financial security. For it was the failure to appreciate the systemic risk created by the extensive use of off-balance-sheet special purpose entities in lengthy chains of securitisation which apparently insulated the parent entity from risk while, in reality, it created channels of contagion and risk concentration that represented perhaps *the* greatest intellectual failures of the crisis. Mason and Rosner (2007) show that what made perfect sense from an individual bank's perspective created the perfect conditions for systemic risk to spread by decoupling returns from responsibilities.

In order to better inform the regulators in the future a proposal for a Legal Entity Identifier (LEI) was developed by the Financial Stability Board (FSB) (2013). The aim of this initiative is to make transactions between legal entities more transparent and thus it represents the first step towards mapping the legal interconnectedness which in turn ought to help plot economic links. While the early stages of the LEI framework was facilitated by the FSB in conjunction with an advisory panel drawn from industry and the International Standards Organisation, the

G20 summit on 5 November 2012 agreed to empower a Global LEI System Regulatory Oversight Committee (ROC) to progress the LEI initiative. An LEI should comprise 'the official name of the legal entity, the address of the headquarters of the legal entity, the address of legal formation, the date of first LEI assignment, the date of last update of the LEI, [and] the date of expiry' (Financial Stability Board, 2012, p. 16), together with a unique 20-digit code to clearly identify any entity. So, every company, every subsidiary and every proprietary entity will carry a unique LEI to be quickly identified as such. During the collapse of Lehman Brothers regulators, competitors and even the Lehman's management could not identify their exact financial exposures to one another on a timely basis which contributed to the systemic effects of its demise (Office of Financial Research, 2012). One aspect of the LEIs is especially useful to gaining a broader picture of systemic risk since the use of special purpose entities ought to become more transparent as ROC charter also requires '[f]or entities with a date of expiry, the reason for the expiry should be recorded, and, if applicable, the LEI of the entity or entities that acquired the expired entity' (Financial Stability Board, 2012, p. 16).

The concept and definition of the LEI represents an attempt to begin to construct a standardised taxonomy for the financial sector along the lines of the barcode for financial transactions recently suggested by Haldane (Haldane, 2012b). Similar to a unique barcode attached to consumer goods, the supply chain would be made more transparent to all participants, including the final consumer at the end of the chain, the originator of the investment, intermediaries such as institutional investors scattered along the chain across jurisdictions and, of course, supervisors at national, regional and global level with an interest in using the LEIs to help more accurately map pockets of systemic risk.

However, LEIs will be worse than useless and could confuse an already confused picture should there not be clear agreement across all jurisdictions as to consistent use of the concepts underpinning the LEI. The fact that different national laws afford legal personality in different ways to entities that might seem on the face of it identical could yet limit the utility of the LEI unless there is a consensus that is then respected by national Courts as to the meaning of one type of legal entity as opposed to another. For if a legal entity faces challenges from creditors as to its validity and ability to be recognised in law then this is of potential significance to issues of ownership of assets, security taken and liabilities owed much further along the supply chain. A degree of independent legal expertise will be needed to verify any data submitted in compiling LEIs so that they do not become conduits for legal risk along the chain of financial intermediation.

As the LEI framework develops it may assist supervisors to formulate specific data requests to understand better how finance supply chains are constructed, but a considerable data collection and verification exercise is needed to compile, maintain and verify the data within the LEI framework itself first.

Product Identifiers would be a logical extension of the rationale behind LEIs but the granularity of the legal issues involved and hence the challenge of collecting component data to such product codes cannot be overstated. Proposals that have been made for common origination criteria for asset-backed finance shows just how detailed the legal issues that arise in tracking risk levels and patterns in just one lending sector are.[30] The more transaction-specific and proprietary any data sought by supervisors (or indeed any industry standards body that may take on the role of developing product standards) is the harder it will be to prise out of lenders and borrowers. Yet such product identifiers, if they could be superimposed onto chains and networks of LEIs could be an immensely powerful informational tool to provide context for the exercise of supervisory judgement.

Contestability of judgements

Legalism is the enemy of supervision and litigators can and will from time to time throw sand in the wheels of judgement-led supervision. The PRA acknowledges the risk that supervisory judgements will be open to contest:

> Firms will sometimes disagree with the PRA's decisions. This is inherent in a forward-looking system.
>
> *(Bank of England, Prudential Regulation Authority, 2012, p. 34, para 195)*

When such judgements have to be made by a supervisor *ex ante* on the basis of aggregations, disaggregations, combinations, re-combinations and finally interpretations of pieces drawn from a vast data cloud comprised of units and levels that come from many different sources and vary over time then the potential for real and genuine disagreement is compounded about what constitutes a 'plausible risk' and thus a proper use of supervisory power.

Tucker (2009) foresaw the increased litigation and reputational risks of this new mode of supervisory decision-making when he warned:

> If we are to tolerate supervisors where necessary substituting their judgement for that of managers and boards, then commentators, appeal tribunals and even parliamentarians will need to give supervisors the benefit of the doubt occasionally.
>
> *(Tucker, 2009, p. 5)*

When a firm feels the force of a supervisory intervention power following a judgement about the risk it might plausibly pose to a PRA objective of stability of the financial system it may well wish to probe the evidence bases and interpretive processes that led to that judgement. When the judgement results from a complex and finely balanced mapping of macro systemic risk analysis with micro analysis of factors specific to that firm then the firm itself may well argue that it sees the contours of the map very differently. It may argue that the map data could not possibly be said to reveal the risk pattern on which the supervisory judgement is based and hence could not possibly signal an emergent risk or a plausible risk to any PRA objectives. Under the previous UK legislative and regulatory framework such a challenge has already been made to supervisory intervention in 2008 in relation to the Icelandic banks. In a challenge to the UK government's Transfer Order made under the Banks (Special Provisions) Act 2008 in relation to deposits held by Kaupthing Singer & Friedlander (KSF) the UK subsidiary of Kaupthing hf, arguments were advanced about lack of proper evidence for any specific threat posed by KSF to the stability of the UK financial system.[31] The argument was made for the Icelandic bank that no attempt was made by HM Treasury to attribute any *specific* threat to UK financial stability arising from KSF's difficulties, and that it was therefore highly unlikely that KSF's difficulties were specifically responsible for any loss of consumer confidence in UK banking that may have been taking root in October 2008, especially given the enormity of emergency assistance measures for much larger UK deposit-takers announced at the very same time as the intervention in KSF. In other words, in the grand scheme of things that could be said to be responsible for rocking the systemic stability of the UK banking system in late 2008, the events at KSF were of relative insignificance. Looking forward to a judgement-led model of supervision it is likely that the constant need for supervisors to conjoin macro- and micro-prudential regulation could result in far more interventions based on judgements about the way in which macroeconomic and macro-prudential factors might plausibly affect safety and soundness of a specific firm or firms, and in turn how micro issues pertinent to a firm or firms may feedback into the financial system so as to raise broader systemic stability concerns. As Tucker put it '[w]hat all this amounts to is framing micro prudential regulation and supervision to deliver *macro* prudential objectives' (Tucker, 2011).

To some extent the recent legislative changes made to the jurisdiction of the Upper Tribunal[32] in relation to references of supervisory notices made by the PRA and FCA will go some way to limiting the ability of those aggrieved by a supervisory judgement to unpick its underlying reasoning. For, should it disagree with a supervisory decision, the Tribunal now may not make its own determination for that of the appropriate regulator but instead may simply refer the matter back for the regulator's determination with directions as to fact, law, matters to be taken into account in decision-making or procedural steps to be taken.[33] Crucially it may not substitute its own judgement on the supervisory issue in dispute for that of the regulator. In response to criticism made by those likely to be affected by this curtailment of the efficacy of a right to independent review[34] the Draft FSB Committee accepted the government's and regulators' arguments that 'allowing the Tribunal to substitute its own opinion for that of the regulator would undermine the principle of judgement-based regulation'.[35]

However, the marriage of macro and micro that judgement-led supervision demands could yet engage the legal process, much as it may seek to exclude it, since wherever competing interpretations or multiple accounts of reality are possible lawyers have a tendency to test the arguments by way of legal challenge and indeed this is seen as one of the many virtues of 'The Rule of Law'. It is easy to see more such challenges to supervisory intervention coming before the Courts once the legal profession adjusts to thinking and arguing probabilistically in terms of systemic risk and picking holes in systemic risk analysis underlying supervisory judgements.

The PRA is clearly cogniscent of this very real risk and at this stage can do little more than counter it with the assertion that its supervisory decisions 'will be rigorous and well documented, consistent with public law' with the 'most significant' of its supervisory judgements to be taken by its full Board headed by the Bank Governor with the discipline of a framework of accountabilities to parliament, the MPC and FPC (Bailey, 2012, p. 356).

The dawn of the regulatory state has been accompanied by a culture of vigorous pubic law litigation into which Human Rights jurisprudence has now taken root and employed at an increasing rate in the financial sector.[36] This makes it almost inevitable that the analysis and interpretation underlying PRA judgements on such highly contestable concepts as the reflexive relationship of systemic risk with a specific firm will mean that at some stage when the stakes are sufficiently high, supervisory interventions will come under the scrutiny of public law.

Conclusion

The reformulated legislative framework within which judgement-led supervision will operate has been crafted to allow for a prospective and highly discretionary form of decision-making to trigger intervention. But its success will hinge not just on the logistics of gathering, maintaining and verifying some very big data indeed across jurisdictions and across time but also on the vision and expertise of those charged with its interpretation. Some of that expertise will need to be granular and highly specialist legal expertise to unpick the transactions that constitute products and entities in a financial chain. There will be a need to spot how legal uncertainties within data being fed into the risk mapping exercises of the supervisor can affect the quality and value of those maps. There will be a need also to ensure that judgements are made and presented in a way that makes them robust enough to withstand challenges that delay their effectiveness.

Notes

* This chapter first appeared in *Journal of Banking Regulation*, 14 (3/4): 228–40 and the authors and editors of this work are most grateful to the publishers of the Journal of Banking Regulation, Macmillan Publishers Ltd, for permission to reprint it.
1 ss 2b (2) Financial Services and Markets Act 2000 (hereafter 'FSMA 2000').
2 ss 2B(3) FSMA 2000.
3 Chancellor of the Exchequer Gordon Brown, Statement to House of Commons, 20 May 1997.
4 SIB Report into IMRO's Supervision of BIM and LIM (FT Report 10 July 1992).
5 Section 2J FSMA 2000 (as amended).
6 The new PRA and FCA regimes relating to authorisation and supervision were the subject of detailed consultation in Financial Services Authority Consultation Paper 12/24 'Regulatory Reform: PRA and FCA regimes relating to aspects of authorisation and supervision' CP12/24, September 2012 (FSA 2012). Retrieved on 10 May 2016 from www.fsa.gov.uk/library/policy/cp/2012/12-24.shtml.
7 Section 55A FSMA 2000 (as amended).
8 Section 59 FSMA 2000.
9 Part XI Financial Services and Markets Act 2000.
10 Part XXII FSMA 2000 (as amended).
11 Bank of England, Prudential Regulation Authority. (2012) The PRA's approach to banking supervision at p. 11, para. 37.
12 Ibid., at pp. 16–17.
13 Ibid., at p. 31.
14 Ibid., at para. 190.
15 Ibid., at para. 191.
16 Joint Committee on the draft Financial Services Bill. (2011) *Draft Financial Services Bill*.
17 Ibid., *at* para. 201.
18 Joint Committee on the draft Financial Services Bill (2012) Government Response. 1 February, at para. A.60. Retrieved on 6 May 2016 from www.parliament.uk/documents/joint-committees/Draft-Financial-Services-Bill/Government-Response-FSB.pdf.
19 Para 243 Draft FSB Committee Report December 2011.
20 FINREP and COREP ushered in new common templates for supervisory reporting as of 1 January 2013.
21 *Re Barings plc and others (No 5), Secretary of State for Trade and Industry v Baker and others (No 5)* [2000] 1 BCLC 523.
22 FSMA 2000 s165A – s165C.
23 Para 148 Draft FSB Committee Report December 2011.
24 [2010] EWCA Civ 123.
25 S342(3) FSMA 2000.
26 The current Code of Practice introduced by the Bank of England and FSA forms part of regulatory guidance accompanying SUP 3.8.
27 According to Financial Services Authority (2007–12) Annual Reports, FSA consistently exercised power to commission s166 skilled persons reports from 18 in 2006/07 to 111 in 2011/12.
28 *Real Estate Opportunities Ltd v Aberdeen Asset Managers Jersey Ltd and others* [2007] EWCA Civ 197; *Zaki and others v Credit Suisse (UK) Ltd.* [2012] EWCA Civ 583.
29 Comments made in Keynote address at Centre for Central Banking Studies (2013) Workshop, the future of regulatory data analytics. Bank of England, 17 January 2013.
30 Clifford Chance LLP, Commercial Mortgage Lending – a need for Common Origination Criteria. November 2012.
31 *R v HM Treasury ex parte Kaupthing hf* (High Court 2009).
32 The Financial Services and Markets Tribunal was abolished and its functions transferred to the Upper Tribunal by the Transfer of Tribunals Functions Order 2010 (SI 2010/22) as part of a broader re-organisation of the Courts and Tribunals service.
33 S 133 (6) and (6A) FSMA 2000.
34 Written evidence of BBA to the Joint Parliamentary Committee on the Draft Bill – quoted by Committee in Joint Committee on the draft Financial Services Bill (2011), at para. 347.
35 Ibid., at para. 348.
36 Such as the challenge by Harbinger Capital Partners (to the Upper Tribunal's refusal in *Northern Rock Applicants v (1) Andrew Caldwell (2) HM Treasury* [2011] UKUT 408 (TCC) to set aside the valuation

assumptions used to determine compensation payable to Northern Rock shareholders, see Financial Times (2013) Northern Rock appeal in court. 20 January, www.ft.com/cms/s/0/fca32d10-6303-11e2-8497-00144feab49a.html#axzz2KVOjowpJ.

References

Bailey, A. (2012) 'The Prudential Regulatory Authority', *Bank of England Quarterly Bulletin*, 52(4): 354–62.

Bank of England, Prudential Regulation Authority. (2012) *The PRA's approach to banking supervision*, October, Bank of England. Retrieved on 10 May 2016 from www.bankofengland.co.uk/publications/Documents/praapproach/bankingappr1210.

Black, J. (2010) 'The rise, fall and fate of principles based regulation', *LSE Law, Society and Economy Working Papers* 17/2010.

Black. J. (2004) *The development of risk based regulation in financial services: Canada, the UK and Australia*. Retrieved on 16 October 2015 from www.lse.ac.uk/collections/law/staff%20publications%20full%20text/black/risk%20based%20regulation%20in%20financial%20services.pdf.

Cohrs, M., Foot, M. and Huertas, T. (2012) *Corrected transcript of oral evidence on Regulatory Approach*, HC 821-i. Parliamentary Commission on Banking Standards, 11 December 2012. Retrieved on 10 May 2016 from www.publications.parliament.uk/pa/jt201213/jtselect/jtpcbs/c821-i/c82101.htm.

Danielsson, J. (2000) 'VaR: A castle built on sand', *Financial Regulator*, 5(2): 46–50.

FSA. (1999) *Senior management arrangements, systems and controls*. Consultation Paper 35. Published December 1999, retrieved on 10 May 2016 from www.fsa.gov.uk/pubs/cp/cp35.pdf.

FSA. (2007–12) *Annual Reports*. London: FSA.

FSA. (2008) *The supervision of Northern Rock: A lessons learned review*. March 2008, FSA. Retrieved on 10 May 2016 from www.fca.org.uk/static/documents/fsa-nr-report.pdf.

FSA. (2011) *FSA handbook, high level standards block*. SYSC module of FSA Handbook in force in 2011. This and other previously in force versions of the Handbook can be viewed at www.handbook.fca.org.uk/handbook/SYSC/1/1A.html?date=2011-05-12 (accessed 10 May 2016).

FSA. (2012) *Regulatory reform: PRA and FCA regimes relating to aspects of authorisation and supervision*. Consultation Paper CP 12/24. September 2012. Retrieved on 10 May 2016 from www.fsa.gov.uk/static/pubs/cp/cp12-24.pdf.

Financial Stability Board. (2012) *Charter of the Regulatory Oversight Committee for the Global Legal Entity Identifier (LEI) System*. Retrieved on 10 May 2016 from www.leiroc.org/publications/gls/roc_20121105.pdf.

Financial Stability Board. (2013) *Fifth progress note on the Global LEI initiative*, 11 January. Retrieved on 14 February 2013 from www.financialstabilityboard.org/publications/r_130111a.pdf.

Gower, L.C.B. (1984) *Review of investor protection*. London: Stationery Office Books.

Haldane, A. (2012a) *Tails of the unexpected*. Speech at University of Edinburgh Business School. Edinburgh, 8 June. Bank of England, retrieved on 10 May 2016 from www.bankofengland.co.uk/archive/Documents/historicpubs/news/2012/058.pdf.

Haldane, A. (2012b) *Towards a common financial language*. Speech to Securities Industry and Financial Markets Association (SIFMA) Building a Global Legal Entity Identifier Framework Symposium. New York, 14 March, Bank of International Settlements, retrieved on 10 May 2016 from www.bis.org/review/r120315g.pdf.

HM Treasury. (2011) *A new approach to financial regulation: A blueprint for reform* (June). Consultation Document Cm 8083 June 2011. Retrieved on 10 May 2016 from www.gov.uk/government/uploads/system/uploads/attachment_data/file/81403/consult_finreg__new_approach_blueprint.pdf.

Joint Committee on the draft Financial Services Bill. (2011) *Draft Financial Services Bill*. HL paper 236/HC1447. Stationary Office: London.

Mason, J. and Rosner, J. (2007) *Where did the risk go? How misapplied bond ratings cause mortgage backed securities and collateralized debt obligations market disruptions*. Retrieved on 6 May 2016 from http://papers.ssrn.com/papers.abstract_id=1027475.

National Commission, 2004. *National Commission on Terrorist Attacks Upon the United States*. Final Report. Retrieved on 18 October 2015 from http://govinfo.library.unt.edu/911/report/index.htm.

Office of Financial Research. (2012) *Annual report*. Washington, DC.

O'Malley, P. (2012) *From risk to resilience. Technologies of the self in the age of catastrophes*. Retrieved on 18 October 2015 from www.thecarceral.org/cn7_OMalley.pdf.

Rayner, G. (2012) 'Queen gives bank lesson in economics', 13 December. Retrieved on 10 May 2016 from www.telegraph.co.uk/news/uknews/queen-elizabeth-II/9744153/Queen-gives-the-Bank-a-lesson-in-economics.html.

Singh, D. (2003) 'The role of third parties in banking regulation and supervision', *Journal of International Banking Regulation*, 4(3): 1–18.

Sollis, R. (2009) 'Value at risk: A critical overview', *Journal of Financial Regulation and Compliance* 17(4): 398–414.

Tucker, P. (2009) *The debate on financial system resilience: Macro prudential instruments. Speech to Barclays.* London, 22 October. Retrieved on 10 May 2016 from www.bankofengland.co.uk/archive/Documents/historicpubs/speeches/2009/speech407.pdf.

Tucker, P. (2011) *Macro and microprudential supervision.* Speech to British Bankers' Association Annual International Banking Conference, London, 29 June. Retrieved on 10 May 2016 from www.bankofengland.co.uk/archive/Documents/historicpubs/speeches/2011/speech506.pdf.

Turner Review. (2009) 'A regulatory response to the global market crisis'. London: Financial Services Authority.

19

Shattering Glass–Steagall

The power of financial industries to overcome restraints

Paul M. Hirsch, Jo-Ellen Pozner, and Mary Katherine Stimmler

In the aftermath of the mortgage lending debacle of 2007, which generated a recession for the US and world economies, former US Treasury Secretary Paul Volcker urged the restoration into banking regulations of the Glass–Steagall Act. This Act, initially passed in the aftermath of the Great Depression, prohibited the financial organizations in the US from engaging in both investment and commercial banking. Subsequent to its repeal in 1999, large mergers occurred and major banks in the US, such as J.P. Morgan Chase, and Bank of America (now including what had previously been Merrill Lynch), and Citibank expanded their business portfolios to encompass derivatives, commercial loans, and mortgage and consumer banking. The irony of these banks appearing to spend some of their government's "bailout" money for lobbying against the passage and enforcement of new banking regulations, occurring alongside Volcker's urging that the Glass–Steagall Act and its earlier restrictions on such expansions be reinstituted, has not gone unnoticed.

Our image of institutions, such as the Glass–Steagall Act, as powerful and legitimate fortresses impervious to change, is deceptive; such stability simply does not exist in the vast majority of institutional settings. Lawrence and Suddaby's (2006) challenge to the presumption of their permanence, calling for the examination of the process and dynamics of the creation, maintenance, and disruption of institutions refocused attention on actors' agency and intentionality with respect to institutional change. Instead of the myth of negotiated agreement, the perception that the settlement of earlier conflicts is permanent generally opens a window of opportunity for institutional entrepreneurs, whose primary motivation is to disrupt, often to their own advantage.

In this chapter, we present a case that demonstrates how a new legal and regulatory framework, passed with strong public support, may provide coercive and mimetic legitimacy and yet—despite apparently achieving "taken-for-granted" status—remain vulnerable to contestation, continued resistance, and eventual defeat. We find the settlement of a conflict in the public arena to be like a truce, rather than a permanent reframing that alters the cognitive mapping of those adversely affected by the outcome. That is, apparent settlement through regulation does not necessarily forestall the possibility that the parties that lost out in the conflict might mobilize their structural and symbolic resources to resist and reverse the new status quo. In so tracing the case of Glass–Steagall, we utilize Greenwood, Suddaby, and Hinings' (2002) *theorization framework* for mapping an institutional change, and extend it to incorporate the simultaneous and subsequent efforts by resisters—at each stage from adoption to completion—to "retheorize" the change by developing narratives, discourse, and rhetoric to ultimately reimage and reverse it. In this chapter, we trace the rise and fall of Glass–Steagall, noting how, despite a 60-plus-year history, it was easily dismantled during the Clinton administration, and has little chance of being reinstituted.

The institutional change we trace, the Banking Act of 1933, commonly known as Glass–Steagall after its primary sponsors, mandated the division of commercial and investment banking in the United States after the Great Depression. This bundle of legislation was subject to contestation for over half a century before its de-institutionalization by the US Congress in 1999 through the passage of the Gramm–Leach–Bliley Act. Of particular interest is how, after 60 years of mandating that a "wall" separate securities writing, commercial banking, and insurance sales operations, the law was still subject to successful attack by the bankers that were constrained by its regulations. The repeal of this legal framework, which had appeared to strictly control the actions of bankers and to have attained a taken-for-granted legal standing, suggests that the agency of actors is highly resilient, while the institutions they target are more prone to change than previously considered (Funk and Hirschman, 2015).

The Glass–Steagall Act: Passage and de-institutionalization

The public image and legitimacy of bankers in the United States hit its all time low at the beginning of the Great Depression. "Near-hysterical public rage" was reported towards banks and bankers (Bentson, 1990), who, according to newly elected President Franklin Roosevelt (1933), stood deservedly "rejected by the hearts and minds of men" while "pleading tearfully for restored confidence." This bust had been preceded by the post-First World War "Jazz Age," an era marked by virtually unregulated markets in many domains. In the financial services industry, this period brought sustained economic growth, increasing banks' scope of operations, and leading them to create and market new types of securities. During the late 1920s, the number of banks engaged in underwriting equities and originating bonds doubled and tripled (respectively); between 1892 and 1931, the number of national banks with securities affiliates had risen from ten to 114 (Kroszner and Rajan 1994). This was the age of universal banking, whereby financial institutions could operate almost unfettered in any and all combinations of investment and deposit-taking activities.

After the stock market crash of 1929, the banks' particular combination of deposit-taking and underwriting businesses raised questions about potential conflicts of interest. Of major concern was the easy access commercial banks had to the uninsured savings of a large number of unsophisticated depositors, which raised a question of moral hazard: banks could play with their depositors money and enjoy the upside with minimal downside risk, all of which was borne by the unsuspecting depositor. Argued Senator Robert Bulkley in 1932:

> The banker ought to be regarded as the financial confidant and mentor of his depositors. Obviously, the banker who has nothing to sell his depositors is much better qualified to advise disinterestedly and to regard diligently the safety of depositors than the banker who uses the list of depositors in his savings department to distribute circulars concerning the advantages of this, that or the other investment.
> *(Congressional Record, May 10, 1931, p. 9912, cited in Kroszner and Rajan, 1994)*

To alleviate this potential conflict of interest, the US Congress passed the Glass–Steagall Act in 1933. This legislation bifurcated these two sides of banking, assigning the collection of now federally insured deposits to commercial and thrift banks, while leaving to investment banks the more risky and uninsured businesses of underwriting and selling stocks and bonds. While the banking industry at the time did not have the political wherewithal to prevent the successful enactment of this high-profile legislation, it certainly did not support the Act or its intent. So began a 66-year long campaign to discredit and deinstitutionalize the restrictions imposed by Congress.

In analyzing the rhetoric of both supporters and critics of the Glass–Steagall Act and tracing how the balance of power shifted over time, we investigate the purposive actions of individuals and organizations aimed at retaining or altering support for continuation of this institutionalized regulatory framework. We examine the moves made as well as the ideologies, interests, and histories that agents drew upon to drive their aims forward. We focus on the institutional strategies followed by Glass–Steagall's resisters to dissociate it from its moral foundations (Lawrence and Suddaby, 2006), and otherwise delegitimate it through acts of manipulation, assault, and defiance (Oliver, 1992). In James Thompson's classic terms (1967, p. 24), we trace how the agents of opposition succeeded in converting the regulation from an unwelcome "constraint" to a more manageable "contingency," and finally to a manipulable "variable."

The theorization and retheorization of banking regulation

The separation of the banking industry that resulted from the Glass–Steagall Act evolved in a way that closely models the six stages of institutional change described in Greenwood, Suddaby, and Hinings' (2002) theorization model: *precipitating jolts; deinstitutionalization; preinstitutionalization; theorization; diffusion; and reinstitutionalization*. The jolt that shook up the longstanding institution of universal banking was the stock market collapse on October 24, 1929, a day on which at least 11 well-known bankers committed suicide. The crash triggered a four-year implosion of American financial markets, during which 40 percent of the nation's banks failed or were merged out of existence (Bentson, 1990), and the national unemployment rate hit 25 percent. These jolts shook the foundations of both the financial services industry and public perceptions of its trustworthiness, severely diminishing its social identity.

At the same time that the financial services field became so significantly delegitimated during the Great Depression, the seeds of a new kind of banking system were being planted. The pervasive image of bankers during this period was one of greed, imprudence, and the absence of self-control. President Hoover, who downplayed the consequences of the Great Depression that marked his single term in office, nevertheless saw the country's economic turmoil as the result of the darker aspects of human nature. "The economic system cannot survive unless there are real restraints upon manipulation, greed, and dishonesty," he wrote (Hoover, 1952, p. 24), reflecting a broadly accepted theorization of the roots of the crisis. Greed was to be blamed, and greed needed to be controlled. This change in public perception ultimately led to the *deinstitutionalization* of the institution of universal banking.

During the stages of *preinstitutionalization* and *theorization*, policymakers sought to understand the causes of the Great Depression, as well as potential solutions that might revitalize the American economy. During the hearings held by the Pecora Commission, a congressional inquiry into the causes of the great crash, fallen bankers (and not-quite-yet-fallen bankers) submitted to fierce questioning and constant media ridicule. Ferdinand Pecora worked closely with Senator Carter Glass to identify potential legislative reforms, recognizing a need to separate businesses that could steer the unwitting consumer's deposits into investment securities underwritten, promoted, and sold by the same bank. It was this process of theorization that eventually led to the drafting and passage of Glass–Steagall.

Justifications for Glass–Steagall were drawn from what legislators saw as a need to protect consumers from bankers and bankers from themselves. Neither bankers nor their customers were to be trusted to make responsible decisions, instead the state's role was to create a safe banking system, where neither banks nor their customers were in danger of taking on too much risk. It was this theorization of the causes of the Great Depression, which led Senator Glass, co-author of the Glass–Steagall Act, to state that "I think something should be done to deprive people of the privilege of mortgaging their homes and their futures to buy stocks on margin and to keep blowing up bubbles that are certain to break in their faces" (quoted in Ayres, 2014, p. 94). The goal of depriving individuals of their "privilege" of taking unsound risks, and of banks of profiting by encouraging such risk-taking, was at the heart of the Glass–Steagall Act.

This *theorization* of the causes of the Great Depression as described by Glass, Pecora, and others of like minds resulted in the *diffusion* of a new system of banking, one in which the activities of creating securities and managing loans and deposits were to be conducted in separate firms, thus mitigating the potential for serious conflicts of interest. The legislation brought the process of banking reform to the final step of Greenwood and colleagues' theorization model; the institutional change represented by the Glass–Steagall Act redefined the legitimate and legal framework of the financial services industry, *reinstitutionalizing* it in the form of two distinct organizational forms.

At the *reinstitutionalization* stage, the innovation or reform ought to become objectified by gaining cognitive legitimacy and social consensus around its pragmatic value (Suchman, 1995). Accordingly, the Glass–Steagall Act's legal framework was implemented and became reified through regulatory enforcement for the next half century. Consumers grew accustomed to what became a taken-for-granted system in which they got loans and saved money with one organizations, but bought stocks, bonds, and mutual funds from another.

Deinstitutionalizing Glass–Steagall

> In the financial world, the players think of their business as a never-ending game. Deals can always be renegotiated. They often work to change the circumstances to change the odds.
> (Abolafia, 2010)

If institutions are the result of compromises between actors with divergent interests, then coercive and normative legitimacy can be fleeting, and cognitive legitimacy can be a liability. Once a set of actors takes for granted an institution, there will likely be another set of actors waiting to pounce. Cognitive legitimacy creates vulnerability by reducing vigilance and maintenance by the actors whom an institution benefits; this opens an opportunity for opponents to challenge the institution and catch its defenders off guard. Greenwood *et al.* (2002) recognize this potential for institutional adversaries to create conflict, noting that the appearance of an institution's stability "is probably misleading." Lawrence and Suddaby's (2006) conceptualization of institutional work, with its focus on the agency of actors required to create and maintain institutions, similarly recognizes that such work can create conflict among parties with divergent interests who will "consequently work when possible to disrupt the extant set of institutions" (see also Bourdieu, 1993; Bourdieu and Wacquant, 1992; DiMaggio, 1988; Abbott, 1988).

Because examples of successful attempts at institutional disruption are rare, institutional work often appears straightforward and problematically unconstrained. A closer inspection of institutions, however, would reveal them to be the outcome of long series of compromises among willful, pro-active actors with divergent interests. The balance between the efforts of one set of institutional actors to create institutions on one side and the efforts by another set of actors to disrupt them on the other results in a series of momentary truces or negotiated settlements. When investigating the creation, maintenance, or disruption of institutions, therefore, understanding the conflicts among institutional actors is essential to comprehending the results of their institutional work. While coercive and normative legitimacy may be found as a reinstitutionalized change comes close to becoming taken-for-granted, its cognitive acceptance as legitimate by all parties remains problematic. In the case of the Glass–Steagall Act, its deinstitutionalization was the result of what Lawrence and Suddaby aptly call continuous "backstage" negotiations. Their unfolding also involves parallels with and invite comparisons to the stages of theorization that the Act's passage followed.

The institutionalization and eventual deinstitutionalization of Glass–Steagall serve as a demonstration of the role of compromise in the creation of institutions and the liability of cognitive legitimacy. Commercial bankers, investment bankers, insurance companies, commercial bank customers, corporate investment banking clients, insurance policy holders, and policymakers were all vying to create a legal framework that best represented and promoted their interests above those of competing stakeholder groups. Despite its apparent cognitive legitimacy and taken-for-grantedness, even after a half-century of working under the restrictions of the Act, commercial bankers were still capable of resisting it and, eventually, disrupting it. Understanding why the legal framework remained intact as long as it did, and why it was finally discarded when it was, requires an analysis of both the structural balance of power among the various actors in the financial services field and the effectiveness of their strategies for gaining legitimacy.

Conflicting bankers' agendas delay unified push for repeal

The long life and seemingly abrupt end to the Glass–Steagall Act can be traced to the delicate balance of power among the trio of industries it regulated: investment banks, commercial banks, and insurance brokers. Although each of these industries sought to increase their power and reduce the limitations imposed on their businesses by the legislation, they were each extremely wary of any deregulation that would allow one of the other industries access to their closely guarded domain. A newsletter from the American Banking Association, a lobbyist group for commercial banks, described the struggle this way in 1997:

> For the last two decades, legislation to modernize the banking system has had a Perils-of-Pauline sort of story line, occasionally passing one chamber, only to fail in another, often because of the competing lobbying by the three powerful industries.
>
> *(McConnell, 1997)*

Investment banks feared that allowing commercial banks to sell securities would invite competition for the business of creating and selling securities, while commercial banks feared they could not compete if risk-seeking investment banks were allowed to line their coffers with retail customers' deposits. Consequently, each tried to work around a full repeal of Glass–Steagall, and instead sought one-way deregulation that would allow one side to take advantage of the other.

For example, investment banks often argued that allowing commercial banks the ability to underwrite securities would undermine the safety of the banking system. "The notion that bank securities caused the 1929 stock market crash ... is a myth propagated by the securities industry to assure Glass–Steagall a perpetual life," wrote legal historians (Isaac and Fein, 1988). The major lobbying organization for investment banks told the Federal Reserve Board in 1995 that "perilous underwriting operations and stock speculation" was the cause of the Depression and recommended that Glass–Steagall's ban on universal banking be upheld. Nevertheless, while investment banks, including Merrill Lynch and First Boston, were making such claims to limit the activities of commercial banks, they were also making aggressive efforts to get into the business of commercial banking by acquiring "nonbanks" (an interesting nomenclature), organizations that were permitted to offer deposit-like cash management accounts. Investment banks were relying on Glass–Steagall to keep commercial banks away from their own business, while at the same time siphoning some business from commercial banks through the acquisition of "nonbanks."

The hastening of the proliferation of nonbanks was in part a function of the Federal Reserve's Open Market Committee's (FOMC) reaction to inflationary pressures in the 1970s, spurred by increasing government spending on social welfare programs and the Vietnam War. To manage inflation, the FOMC increased the discount rate to increase the cost of credit, which had the secondary effect of causing savers and investors to pull money out of savings deposits and to invest in federal and commercial bonds. Higher discount rates also encouraged banks to borrow dollars from abroad, which was enabled by the emergence of Eurodollar deposits, or dollar-denominated assets held in foreign countries. Consequently, the Federal Reserve allowed banks to begin borrowing from each other, creating the Federal Funds market by the late 1960s, and deregulated large and long-term CDs in 1974. These reforms in turn enabled practices such as commercial banks meeting funding requirements via brokerage houses, larger investors, and foreign subsidiaries, an unanticipated consequence; commercial banks therefore began to behave more like investment banks (Hammond and Knott, 1988).

In addition to the emergence of nonbanks and other practices, which blurred the long-upheld distinction among different types of financial institution, new technologies in both deposit taking and lending that appeared starting in the 1970s tipped the balance in the political arena from the traditional beneficiaries of geographical restrictions—small banks—towards more expansion-minded large banks. This swung power towards the large banks, which favored deregulation. Consequently, we see stronger efforts towards deregulation in states with fewer small banks, where small banks were financially weak, and with more small and bank-dependent firms (Strahan, 2003). Moreover, the presence of strong insurance lobbyists forestalled deregulation, particularly when it came to injunctions against banks could competing for the sale of insurance products. The relative strength of potential winners (large banks and small firms) and losers (small banks and the rival insurance firms) from deregulation can therefore explain the timing of reform.

Despite the efforts of investment banks to bolster support for Glass–Steagall, by the late 1990s, commercial banks had gained a powerful ally in the United States Office of the Comptroller, which began to allow commercial banks to reach beyond their charters and start offering securities. This prompted investment banking lobbyists to object that such actions were "a one-way street," arguing that the Comptroller's allowances would "allow banks to have a full range of securities activities' but would do "nothing for the securities firms that want to offer banking products" (quoted in Wayne, 1998). After both commercial and investment banks and their regulators had chipped away at Glass–Steagall independently of new legislation in the US Congress, a consensus developed which resulted in their successful joint effort to delegitimate the Glass–Steagall Act more fully. This was hastened when the merger of commercial bank Citicorp and insurance giant Travelers was announced, unchallenged by government regulators, notwithstanding its apparent violation of the Glass–Steagall Act's injunction against merging these particular business segments.

Retheorization: from safety to efficiency

Upon settlement of their internal differences, a new coalition of financial industry participants was formed, overcoming the differences of their ultimately contradictory earlier campaigns against one another to topple the Glass–Steagall Act. Actually, they overturned only parts of the legislation, preserving those elements which best served their interests. Their purposive efforts to retheorize regulation and universal banking closely follow Lawrence and Suddaby's (2006) strategy for disruption by actively dissociating Glass–Steagall from its moral foundation through the suggestion that the issues it addressed were merely technocratic and no longer salient due to improved banking technology. In this way, they relied heavily on a teleological rhetorical strategy (Greenwood et al., 2002) to valorize "modernization" (deregulation) and demonize the old-fashioned Glass–Steagall legal framework.

The rhetoric of surrounding Glass–Steagall shifted from a logic that emphasized protecting individuals from human greed and encouraged restraint to a logic that focused on efficiency, innovation, and flexibility. The mythologies adopted for and against Glass–Steagall were not based on diametrically opposite arguments, but rather on completely different sets of values. For instance, arguments in favor of Glass–Steagall emphasized the need for consumer safety, but arguments against Glass–Steagall rarely discussed safety at all. Instead, they emphasized the need for efficiency in the service of consumers. In this way, proponents of deregulation decoupled the meanings of Glass–Steagall and reattached new meanings through mythologizing, valorization, and demonization of a different set of values (see Table 19.1).

Prior to deregulation, the mythologized history of Glass–Steagall was that the Great Depression was caused by greed that caused bankers to sell consumers investment products that were not in their best interests, and that caused consumers to take on excessive risks. According to this mythology, the result was a superheated economy that spun out of control and eventually imploded. This theorization demonized bankers and portrayed consumers as helpless victims of their manipulation. Thus, the solution to the Great Depression was to put in place restraints that prevented bankers from capitalizing on their avarice. The political bases for altering financial markets were that bankers needed to be protected from their own bad judgments, and consumers were also in need of protection from their imprudent decisions, which Senator Glass articulated as "something should be done to deprive people of their privilege of mortgaging their homes and their futures to buy stocks on margin and to keep blowing up bubbles that are certain to break in their faces" (1927).

The arguments in favor of deregulation turned the argument for protection on its head. Its advocates balked at depriving people of their privilege to take whatever risks they wanted. Where Glass–Steagall promoters argued for restraint and protection, those in favor of deregulation argued instead for freedom and flexibility. The ban on universal banking was depicted as an unnecessary burden. The main argument was that technological advancements in the field of finance had innovative new ways of managing risk precluded any need to protect consumers or bankers.

Table 19.1 Rhetoric dissociating the Glass–Steagall Act from its moral foundations

	Regulation	*Modernization*
Moral argument	Safety	Freedom
Mythologized human nature	Greedy	Creative
Valorization	Protect	Enable
Demonization	Human morals, bankers	Restrictions
Theorization	Need to protect citizens and businesses from their own folly	Need to enable citizens and businesses to find the best solution

This undermining of beliefs and assumptions, noted by Lawrence and Suddaby (2006) as an effective strategy to destabilize an existing institution, was evident in the arguments of high executives in the US government. Commissioner of the Securities and Exchange Commission Evans (1982, p. 7) stated that "whatever the case may have been in 1933, today with modern technology there is no *natural* dividing line between investment and commercial banking," and that continuing to "force an arbitrary division would impose economic costs far in excess of any benefits." The "outdatedness" of the law was also underlined by Alan Greenspan, former Chairman of the Federal Reserve (1995):

> There is, I think, general agreement on the forces shaping our evolving financial system—forces that require that we modernize our statutory framework for financial institutions and markets. The most profound is, of course, technology: the rapid growth of computers and telecommunications. Their spread has lowered the cost and broadened the scope of financial services, making possible new product development that would have been inconceivable a short time ago, and, in the process, challenging the institutional and market boundaries that in an earlier day seemed so well defined.

The ability of both competition to limit avarice—consumers would surely find the least exploitative banks—and financial innovation to improve the quality and equity of financial services was valorized by financial services lobbyists. These voices touted product diversity, innovation, and efficiency, all derived from entrepreneurs' incentives to take on risk, and the ability of competition to ensure a form of self-regulation through restraint and cost-cutting. At the same time that they valorized freedom of choice and convenience for customers, deregulation supporters demonized strict government control as a burdensome nuisance. Bank lobbyists begged Congress to give them "regulatory relief," and regulators began to balk at the idea of enforcing restraint, despite the fact that their power derives from the ability to enact controls. On the one hand, SEC Chairman Arthur Levitt boasted to Congress that his agency had offered firms a "flexible, voluntary regulatory framework" (Levitt, 2000); on the other, an executive from JP Morgan explained that "regulatory diversity has served our industry well" (WayneNightly Business Report, 1998).

The crux of the deregulation argument was a teleological theorization in which, through experimental innovation, bankers would create newer and better financial products and services while removing barriers to competition would ensure that the cost for these improved services would remain as low as possible. Hence, much of the rhetoric surrounding deregulation adopted a strategic vocabulary that emphasized "modernization." The rhetoric around regulation switched from a moralistic stance founded on the need for "protection" to a technologically-driven euphoria for the potential for human invention to overcome moral shortcomings. This rhetoric, combined with the new alliance among financial services firms, worked by shifting the focus of attention from safety to convenience, from moral hazard to technological advancement, and from control to flexibility. It worked by allowing Congress "in the name of modernization to forget the lessons of the past, of safety and of soundness," as explained by Senator Bryon Dorgan, one of the eight who voted against the Financial Services Modernization Act (quoted in Labaton, 1999).

Of course, the teleological rhetoric, to some extent, did reflect real developments within the financial industry. New technologies, such as software that enabled the instantaneous pricing of complex securities, and financial innovations, such money market mutual funds, reshaped the technical environment in which banks operated. The argument that new technologies diminished the need for financial regulation, however, was a rhetorical construction, rather than a foregone conclusion. Take, for example, Evans' (1982, p. 7) acknowledgement that:

> it has been suggested that the one way to deal with [new financial technologies] would be to clarify and strengthen the Glass–Steagall Act in order to establish a clear barrier between investment and commercial banking ... In my opinion, the proper approach is to remove the antiquated anti-competitive prohibitions.

Lobbyists arguing for removal of Glass–Steagall created a teleological argument that made their agenda not only the correct one, but an inevitable one.

The utilization of such teleological rhetoric emphasized how technological innovation served to undermine past assumptions, creating a need for change. It worked by allowing Congress "in the name of modernization to forget the lessons of the past," as explained by Senator Bryon Dorgan (quoted in Labaton, 1999), one of the eight who voted against the Financial Services Modernization Act, the carefully-named legislation which ultimately repealed Glass–Steagall. When the bill passed, Treasury Secretary Lawrence Summers said, "With this bill, the American financial system takes a major step forward toward the 21st Century—one that will benefit American consumers, business, and the national economy" (quoted in *New York Times*, November 13, 1999). The theorization of deregulation as "modern" was so thorough that the irony that this legislation actually brought the financial sector back to a time before the Depression was lost.

The greater convenience for consumers gained by loosening the boundaries separating commercial from investment banks was valorized by the advocates of "modernization," largely ignoring the "regulation" proponents' concern that eliminating these barriers removed the provisions intended to protect consumers. Their rhetoric reframed this moral argument by celebrating the capacity of financial "one-stop shopping" to provide "greater access to the broadest array of financial products" (a bank lobbyist quoted in Jonathan Glater, *Washington Post*, February 28, 1995). This argument was further echoed by policymakers, such as Treasury Secretary Robert Rubin, who said:

> As an individual depositor I don't think I'd react one way or the other [to deregulation]. You still have the federal guarantee. But if I were the bank or brokerage customer, I would be likely to get greater conveniences as a consequence of more competition and efficiency, and probably lower prices.
>
> *(Daniel Kadlec, February 28, 1995,* USA Today*)*

Employing a second type of institutional work, deregulation supporters dissociated the moral foundation position of the law's defenders (Lawrence and Suddaby, 2006) by both ignoring it and emphasizing the "convenience" of their alternative, demonizing strict government control as unnecessary and burdensome. Press headlines across the country cited the new freedom banks would enjoy when Glass–Steagall was finally repealed (e.g. "Law Frees Banks" [*Sun Sentinel*, November 13, 1999, p. A1]; "Unfettered Banking" [*Arizona Daily Star*, November 11, 1999, p. A1]; and "Walls Tumble Down" [*Akron Beacon Journal*, November 13, 1999, p. G1]). "We think banking organizations ought to have the choice of the most effective way to conduct their activities," said the Comptroller of the Currency in 1998 (Wayne, 1998). Similarly, the chairman of the SEC, Arthur Levitt, boasted to Congress that his agency had offered firms a "flexible, voluntary regulatory framework" (Levitt, 2000). As an executive from J.P. Morgan explained, referring to a bank's ability to choose its regulator by rewriting its charter, "regulatory diversity has served our industry well" (Wayne, 1998) Thus, legislation that had been enacted as a means to restrain industries and protect consumers was undermined through rhetoric that moralized the liberties of companies to choose their own regulatory standards.

Disconnecting sanctions and rewards is the third mechanism identified by Lawrence and Suddaby (2006) contributing to the deinstitutionalization of an established and "taken for granted" rule. In the case of the Glass–Steagall Act, the most vivid example of this devolution was the merger of two giant firms, whose combination it barred. This merger, of Citibank with the Travellers Insurance Company in 1998, created the largest financial company in the world, and (once allowed) set off a wave of additional combinations which all crossed the dividing line drawn by the Glass–Steagall Act between commercial and investment banking. To reap the rewards and avoid sanctions specified by this law, the *New York Times* (April 8, 1998) reported "within 24 hours of the deal's announcement, lobbyists for insurers, banks, and Wall Street firms were huddling with Congressional banking committee staff members to fine tune a measure that would update the 1933 Glass–Steagall Act." Rather than moving to discipline the companies for violating rules, politicians acted to change the law to enable the merger. One insurance lobbyist noted that while this legitimated the merger after the fact, it would enable Congress to appear as leading the modernization of the industry, rather than the financial executives leading the charge against Glass–Steagall. The lack of law enforcement was evidence that actors within the industry had successfully disconnected the sanctions for bridging the Glass–Steagall divide. Within seven months, Congress officially repealed the Act.

Consensus and compromise in disruptive institutional work

The long life and eventual end to the Glass–Steagall Act can be traced to the delicate balance of power among the trio of industries it regulated—investment banks, commercial banks, and insurance brokers—and the three government powers that controlled them – Congress, courts, and regulators (especially the Federal Reserve and the Office of the Comptroller of the Currency (OCC)). Although each of the industries sought to increase their power and reduce the limitations on their businesses enforced by the Depression Era institution, they were all extremely wary of any deregulation that would allow one of the other industries onto their closely guarded turf. According to the *Washington Post*, "Lobbyists from the well-heeled banking, securities, and insurance industries have spent an untold number of hours and tens of millions of dollars pushing financial overhaul legislation, but until now were defeated by their own in-fighting, as each sought to enter the other's business while continuing to try to bar entry into their own.' Investment banks feared that allowing commercial banks to sell securities would invite competition for the business of creating and selling securities, while commercial banks feared they could not compete if risk-seeking investment banks were allowed to pad their coffers with retail customers' deposits. As a result, commercial and investment banks and insurance sellers and companies tried to work around a full repeal of Glass–Steagall and instead sought one-way deregulation that would allow their own sides to take advantage of the other.

In the decade prior the 1998 passage of the Financial Modernization Act, which officially repealed Glass–Steagall, there were significant but failed attempts by lobbyists and sympathetic members of Congress to make sweeping deregulatory changes. The first crack in Glass–Steagall appeared in 1988, when the first version of the Financial Modernization Act, which granted broader powers to commercial banks to issue securities, was passed in the Senate but failed in the House. "Something on the order of a quarter-million letters and post cards went to members of Congress from bank employees, officers, and directors," boasted the American Banker Association

(*ABA Journal*, November 1988). The bill's main proponent was Senator William Proxmire who argued that "Technology is rapidly revolutionizing the credit industry.... Instead of promoting safety, Glass–Steagall has promoted a monopoly environment" and noted that "greater competition is the benefit" of the repeal (*Herald Tribune*, February 14, 1988). Despite the rhetorical efforts to reframe the debate, the legislation got caught up in the House of Representatives, where lobbyists for community banks argued that the bill would concentrate power in the hands of a few large banks. Insurance lobbyists wavered; at first they opposed the bill because it enabled banks to sell insurance, but when this new power was restricted to only the home state of a bank holding company, they supported the legislation. Added to the arguments among the finance industry sectors were the bill power disputes between legislative committees (Hendrickson, 2001). In the end, a compromise could not be reached before Congress adjourned for the session.

A second failed attempt at deregulation occurred in 1991, during the fallout from the savings and loans crisis. Investment banks and insurance companies claimed that deregulation would bring greater solvency to the industry, but this argument was again lost to disputes among legislative committees. In particular the "jurisdictional rivalries" (Skidmore, December 23, 1991) between the House Energy and Commerce committee and the House Banking Committee, which had drafted different versions of the bill (Skidmore, December 23, 1991). Some pundits faulted the first Bush Administration's unwillingness to compromise with non-investment banking interests: "I don't know whether they could have done it, but I think they should have tried to cut a deal with some of the forces lined up against them," said William Seidman, former chairman of the FDIC (quoted in Skidmore, December 23, 1991). The Associated Press reported, "With no compromise in advance, each of the financial interests involved—small banks, large banks, securities firms and insurance companies—proved to have enough influence to block legislation they disliked, but not enough to pass what they advocated."

The third attempt at a full repeal happened in 1995 and, unlike the previous efforts, was undertaken by Congress in response to moves made by regulators. The Comptroller of the Currency, Eugene Ludwig, ruled that banks in small towns could offer insurance. Furthermore, the Federal Reserve Bank, under Alan Greenspan, signaled that it would increase the amount of bank holding company business that could be generated through securities affiliates. These moves by regulators demonstrated to Congress that reform needed to be addressed legislatively. Representative Jim Leach, a Republican from Iowa, championed legislation that would create financial services holding companies that would allow firms to control both securities and commercial banks and permit them to provide mutual funds, investment advice, and corporate underwriting, among other services. The bill was strongly supported by large commercial and investment banks, but failed due to resistance by the insurance industry, which feared banks would have an unfair advantage in cross selling insurance and traditional commercial banking products, and small bankers, who feared competing with banking Goliaths that could profit from securities and savings and loans activities. Although insurance agents did not provide the amount of campaign donations that banks provided, they had significant power and influence. As Representative Barney Frank explained:

> They can beat the banks and the securities firms and the insurance companies put together, because everybody has insurance agents in their district, and their corporate culture is, "Hi, how are ya? I'm your friend"—I mean, you know, they're door-to-door salespeople.
> (*quoted in the New York Times, May 5, 1995*)

In a compromise, the House added a barrier that prevented national banks from further entry into insurance sales, but in the end, both commercial banks and insurance brokers balked at the concessions and the attempt at repeal failed. "We need to see industry groups lined up in some kind of accommodation before we can go anywhere," said Representative Bill McCullum, "If there is no agreement reached then, there may be no proposal or only parts" (Bradsher, 1995).

A fourth Congressional attempt to repeal Glass–Steagall happened the next year. The urgency of effort was somewhat lost, however, because of a pending Supreme Court decision on whether banks could sell insurance. Congress took a wait-and-see approach (Hendrickson, 2001) until the Court decided to allow banks' insurance sales in March, 1996. After the decision in the banks favor was announced, insurance agents and companies took a very stanch stance that they would not support any reform that didn't place stronger restrictions on banks' moves into insurance. Once these were added to the bills, the primary industry that had been calling for reform—commercial banks—refused to support them because they threatened to limit the insurance sales that had just been approved by the court. For members of Congress, this meant that a vote either way on the repeal would alienate important industries during an election year (Hendrickson, 2001). Over 75 amendments were proposed to the House bill before its sponsor decided the deadlock could not be broken.

As a result of the congressional stalemate, regulators, who were not responsible to all three industries and therefore could side with one or another, took it upon themselves to further address increased mixing between banks, securities firms, and insurance (Hendrickson, 2001). The Office of the Comptroller of the Currency (O.C.C.), which oversaw about one-third of the US banks, citing the deadlock in Congress (Hershey, 1996), issued a regulation enabling banks under the OCC's jurisdiction to expand into securities, insurance, and other non-banking businesses. The move was met with hostility by insurance and securities lobbyists. The American Council of Life Insurance stated: "At a time when all financial-service providers were ready to make peace, the O.C.C. has decided to renew the war, forcing people into old, entrenched positions" (*New York Times*, June 1996 "Glass–Steagall Over"). The securities industry was quick to point out that this piecemeal approach to deregulation resulted in banks gaining privileges that investment firms did not have.

In 1997 and 1998 Congress again made attempts to repeal Glass–Steagall with no success. Undeterred by previous failures, the Clinton Administration proposed that all sections of the financial industry be regulated by the same federal agency. This caused the commercial banks to balk because they had gotten around much of the Glass–Steagall obstacle with help from their regulator, the OCC. Without the support of the commercial banks, the repeal attempt went nowhere. The reform attempt was reenergized after the Citibank-Travellers merger, but again failed when Treasury Secretary Robert Rubin told President Clinton to veto the bill because it transferred his department's regulatory power over banking to the Federal Reserve.

Deinstitutionalization of the Glass–Steagall Act finally prevailed in 1999. In that year the *New York Times* reported that moves by insurance, commercial banks, and securities firms onto each others' turf had already blurred the line between to the industries to the point that "industries once at odds are now largely in accord on most of the central issues" (July 1, 1999). Similarly, a lobbyist for the American Insurance Association noted that the consensus had formed because "the market has advanced so that everyone has decided it's in their interests to have this bill" (quoted in the *New York Times*, July 1, 1999). "We have become each other," said Mark Brickell, a managing director at J.P. Morgan & Co. "There has been a convergence of our commercial activities and our political interests" (quoted in the *Washington Post*, 1999).

Conclusions

The story of the ups and downs of Glass–Steagall is of theoretical significance. By understanding the conflict that surrounded the institutionalized banking system, it becomes possible to understand both why this system persisted as long as it did in its divided form and why it eventually changed to a universal banking system. Even institutions that have outlived their creators can be vulnerable to disruption, because institutions are always tentative arrangements among actors with divergent interests. This observation could apply to many institutional settings. "Winners" may come to rest on their laurels, while "losers" may benefit from upsetting institutional arrangements. In light of recent financial events, we see that the deregulation which was so highly sought after has lost its appeal when the institutional actors who sought it have again lost their legitimacy.

The void created by financial services' deregulation in the United States has been linked to significantly negative outcomes with far-reaching consequences. Regulations might have helped prevent recent scandals, including that of collusion among banks to systematically misstate their borrowing costs for the purposes of gaining more favorable trading terms in the Libor scandal of 2008, and the global financial crisis of 2008, which has been attributed to excessive risk taking, engagement with complex financial products. The failure to disclose conflicts of interest, and the failure of regulators, credit rating agencies, and the markets to rein in excesses have led to calls for greater supervision, along with continued strong lobbying efforts to prevent it from coming to pass. Even Alan Greenspan, who oversaw the dismantling of Glass–Steagall, noted the failure of this course of action, stating that "Those of us who have looked to the self-interest of lending institutions to protect shareholders' equity, myself included, are in a state of shocked disbelief," in front of the House Committee on Oversight and Government Reform (Andrews, 2008).

Yet, in 2014, the banking lobby succeeded in convincing Congress to weaken the substance of the very legislation designed to help prevent a repeat of the global financial crisis of 2008. Banks' success in this case is typical of the power this industry has to define the terms of its regulation and to have its members appointed to the very governmental positions that are supposed to monitor and rein in their excesses. There are few industries in which a revolving door between regulators and practitioners swings more widely or smoothly; between early 2009 and mid-2010, 148 former employees of financial regulatory agencies registered as lobbyists. Top positions at financial market regulators—and even within Congress—have increasingly become occupied by former big bank executives. As a result of this revolving door, regulators are seen to defer to bankers within their social and professional networks, and with and for whom they may want to work in the future.

Given the nature of the relationships among what are now universal banks and regulators, it is unclear from where the next stakeholders invested in deinstitutionalization and institutional work might emerge. The stakeholders most likely to be negatively impacted by the effects of deregulation and the new institutional order are individual investors and businesses, as well as small financial institutions. These are notoriously difficult groups to mobilize because of their relatively low status and power, the degree to which they are dispersed, and their essential conservatism. What will spur the next wave of institutional contestation in this domain? We can but hope that it is not another serious financial crisis.

References

Abbott, A. (1988) *The System of Professions*. Chicago: University of Chicago Press.
Abolafia, M. (2010) Correspondence with Author.
Andrews, E.L. (2008) 'Greenspan concedes error on regulation'. *New York Times*. Retrieved on May 6, 2016 from www.nytimes.com/2008/10/24/business/economy/24panel.html.
Ayres, R.U. (2014) *The Bubble Economy: Is Sustainable Growth Possible?* Cambridge, MA: The MIT Press.
Bentson, G. (1990) *The Separation of Commercial and Investment Banking*. Oxford: Oxford University Press.
Bourdieu, P. (1993) *Sociology in Question*. London: Sage.

Bourdieu, P. and Wacquant, L. (1992) *An Invitation to Reflexive Sociology*. Chicago: University of Chicago.

Bradsher, K. (1995) 'Bank mergers with insurers are set back', May 4, retrieved on May 16, 2016 from: www.nytimes.com/1995/05/04/business/bank-mergers-with-insurers-are-set-back.html.

DiMaggio, P. (1988) 'Interest and agency in institutional theory'. In Zucker, L. (ed.) *Institutional Patterns and Organizations: Culture and Environment*: 3–22. Cambridge, MA: Ballinger.

Evans, John R. (1982) 'Glass–Steagall in Transition'. Address to Second Annual Southern Securities Institute, Key Biscayne, Florida, February 5, 1982.

Funk, R.J. and Hirschman, D. (2015) 'Rethinking endogenous legal change: How organizations re-shaped Glass–Steagall'. *Administrative Science Quarterly* (in press).

Greenspan, A. (1995) Statement by Alan Greenspan, Chairman, Board of Governors of the Federal Reserve System, before the Committee on Banking and Financial Services, *US House of Representatives*. February 28, 1995.

Greenwood, R., Suddaby R., and Hinings, C.R. (2002) 'Theorizing change: The role of professional associations in the transformation of institutional fields'. *Academy of Management Journal*, 45: 58–80.

Hammond, T.H. and Knott, J.R. (1988) 'The deregulatory snowball: Explaining deregulation in the financial industry'. *The Journal of Politics*, 50.

Hendrickson, Jill M. (2001) 'The long and bumpy road to Glass–Steagall reform: A historical and evolutionary analysis of banking legislation', *American Journal of Economics and Sociology*, 60 (4): 849–79.

Hershey, R. (1996) U.S. to ease banks' way in selling stocks and insurance', November 20, retrieved on May 16, 2016 from www.nytimes.com/1996/11/21/business/us-to-ease-banks-way-in-selling-stocks-and-insurance.html.

Hoover, H. (1952) *The Memoirs of Herbert Hoover: The Great Depression, 1929–1941*. New York: MacMillan.

Isaac W.M. and Fein, M.L. 1988. 'Facing the future—life without Glass–Steagall', *Catholic University Law Review*, 37 (2): 281–322.

Kroszner, R. and Rajan, R. (1994) 'Is the Glass–Steagall Act justified? A study of the US experience with universal banking before 1933', *American Economic Review*, 84: 810–32.

Labaton, S. (1999) 'Congress passes wide-ranging bill easing bank laws', *New York Times*, November 5, retrieved on May 16, 2016 from www.nytimes.com/1999/11/05/business/congress-passes-wide-ranging-bill-easing-bank-laws.html?pagewanted=all.

Lawrence, T. and Suddaby, R. (2006) 'Institutions and institutional work', in Stewart R. Clegg, Cynthia Hardy, Thomas B. Lawrence and Walter R. Nord (eds), *Handbook of Organizational Studies*. Thousand Oaks, CA: Sage Publications.

Levitt, Arthur. (2000) Prepared testimony of Arthur Levitt, Chairman, *US Securities and Exchange Commission*. June 21. Retrieved on May 16, 2016 from www.sec.gov/news/testimony/ts112000.htm.

McConnell, Bill. (1997) 'Congress lags market forces in reshaping finance world', September 26.

Oliver, C. (1992) 'The antecedents of deinstutitonalization', *Organizational Studies*, 13: 563–88.

Roosevelt, F. (1933) Inaugural Address.

Strahan, P.E. (2003) 'The real effects of US banking deregulation'. The Federal Reserve Bank of St. Louis. Retrieved on May 6, 2016 from https://research.stlouisfed.org/publications/review/03/07/Strahan.pdf.

Suchman, M. (1995) 'Managing legitimacy: Strategic and institutional approaches', *Academy of Management Review*, 20: 571–611.

Thompson, J. (1967) *Organizations in Action: Social Science Bases of Administrative Theory*. New York: McGraw-Hill.

Washington Post (1999) October 22, retrieved on May 16, 2016 from www.washingtonpost.com/wp-srv/pmextra/oct99/22/banking.htm.

Wayne, L. (1998) 'Signs of shift in senate stance on bank law', *New York Times*, June 5; Business Day. Retrieved on May 16, 2016 from www.nytimes.com/1998/06/05/business/signs-of-shift-in-senate-stance-on-bank-law.html.

Part VI
Dysfunctional global finance and banking reform

20
How finance globalized
A tale of two cities

Gary A. Dymski and Annina Kaltenbrunner

This chapter argues that the unique historical and economic circumstances of the United Kingdom and of the United States underlie the development of global finance as we have it today. These circumstances, rather than primitives such as technological change and/or the information revolution, explain the current shape of globalized financial institutions and practices. The apparent technological necessity of a super-leveraged, risk-shifting global financial complex is a mirage; this complex, anchored in the cities of London and New York, has emerged due to unique circumstances, most notably, these cities' host nations' sponsorship of gold-based global currency systems, and more recently the 30-years'-long current-account deficit/capital-account surplus that has made the US a global liquidity sink. The chapter presents some empirical evidence suggesting that this turn toward globalized finance has been associated with reduced development-finance capability, in these two nations.

> We had everything before us, we had nothing before us, we were all going direct to Heaven, we were all going direct the other way – in short, the period was so far like the present period, that some of its noisiest authorities insisted on its being received, for good or for evil, in the superlative degree of comparison only.
> (Charles Dickens, *A Tale of Two Cities*, Book the First – Recalled to Life)

> Has anyone bothered to study the cumulative effect of all these things [the new regulations on capital adequacy, mortgage standards, and so on, being considered after the 2008 subprime crisis]? Do you have a fear, like I do, that when we look back and look at them all, that they will be a reason it took so long that our banks, our credit, our businesses and, most importantly, job creation started going again?
> (Jamie Dimon, CEO of J.P. Morgan Chase, questioning Federal Reserve Chair Ben Bernanke at an Atlanta monetary conference on June 7, 2011)

Introduction

Many economic historians and development economists have recognized that a step-change in income and employment growth – that is, successful national or regional development – requires an effective means of financing investment.[1] This means, almost invariably, a functional system of finance. As this chapter is written, Europe (including the UK), the US, and Japan all are suffering through prolonged periods of stagnant growth and recession. Each of these growth slowdowns was triggered by a major collapse in these countries' financial systems. Japan's stagnation commenced with the 1990 collapse of an asset bubble fed by the speculative behavior of its financial institutions, including the largest and most sophisticated. The economies of the US and Europe, on the other hand, were laid low by financial practices that treated the securitization of high-risk mortgages and other credit instruments, as well as unregulated and unrestrained zero-sum derivative bets on these instruments' market valuations, as virtually riskless – until the possibility of revaluation without crisis was already foreclosed.

A profound irony of the current fix is that these national areas' positions of global leadership in per-capita income and wealth stems from periods of extended industrial and commercial development that depended on the capacity to successfully finance large-scale investments in infrastructure and industrial development. So what went wrong? How did once-successful systems of finance become so dysfunctional?

We argue here that this turn to dysfunctionality can be attributed to the deregulation and globalization of financial practices in an era of declining national governmental power. This decline has, in the past century and a quarter, been the most profound for the UK and the US, both of which have laid claim to having the world's strongest economy, and both of which had hegemonic currencies – that is, currencies valued above all others for stability and dependability. Each nation's currency has in this time frame been strong enough to be fixed in value relative to gold. And these nations' periods of global currency dominance had transformative institutional implications – these periods witnessed the growth of firms that could broker deals and arrange payments in different currencies, that could underwrite cross-border risks, store reserves, and so on; and alongside them grew a set of national regulatory agencies whose scope of authority ended with national borders, but whose actions affected the character and volume of financial transactions in many nations.

In effect, global currency hegemony required the creation of the elements of a financial center, or *hub*; these hubs' principal players were well positioned to spread innovative practices and instruments along their global networks, even after those national currencies were no longer as good as gold; and these innovative practices and instruments have sometimes entailed net transfers from the rest of the world to these hubs' principal players. These transfers were enabled by the protections these players enjoyed because of their privileged access to globally-hegemonic currencies.

We not only focus on the US and the UK because they issued the hegemonic currency of their times, but also because the scope and reach of these two centers' activities has shaped financial-system evolution around the world. It is their financial hubs, the City of London and Wall Street, that have been driving globally integrated finance in its purest form. Both have uniquely operated with hegemonic power in global currency markets, for extended periods of time; and both have been progenitors of the deregulation and marketization that have swept much of the global economy.[2]

In some fundamental sense, then, the Great Financial Crisis, as some have called it, was a tale of two cities. Our analysis, like many of Dickens' novels, is a cautionary tale. Our analysis of these two hubs suggests that financial innovations arising in global financial hubs not subject to the same regulator are difficult, if not impossible to control. It follows that these regulatory difficulties will only multiply as the number of global financial hubs under different regulatory regimes expands. But even in the current post-crisis period, new generations of aggressive young bankers are itching to transform their home cities into new hubs which can "insist," as Dickens puts it in the passage cited above, "on its being received, for good or for evil, in the superlative degree of comparison only." The fact that the way to stake out such a claim is to take tail risks that more prudent players have shied away from or overlooked only adds to the challenge.

Finally, we show the overall impact of these two nations' financial evolution on their systems' functionality and on development banking therein. We define development banking as the provision of the finance needed to build and sustain the asset base required for robust industrial and commercial activity, and for secure residential life. A financial system is *functional* when it carries out the textbook functions of finance efficiently, and *also* makes adequate provisions for development banking. This financial function can be performed in different ways, but it must be performed. Bank credit is just one of the possible forms of development banking. It can also be supplied by public authorities, private enterprises, and individuals. In effect, every sustainably growing region or nation needs development banking, as defined here. A system is *dysfunctional* when it systematically creates systemic risk and when its operational failure or collapse generates costs that must be borne, directly or indirectly (through the intermediation of government bailouts) by citizens.

We proceed as follows. The next section describes the growth of globalized finance in the United Kingdom, focusing on the City of London; the following section does the same for the United States and Wall Street. These two sections, which go as far as the crisis of 2007–08, also discuss the implications this growth had for system functionality. The next section then considers whether these two financial hubs' behavior and structures have changed in the post-crisis period. The final section briefly concludes.

Evolving financial practices and structures in the United Kingdom

In recent financial history, only the UK and the US have had currencies that anchored gold-linked global currency systems – the British gold standard (1816–1914) and the US Bretton Woods system (1946–71) – and then became global reserve currencies. Both nations have long traditions of intertwined military and industrial development. And each has hosted one of the two dominant global financial hubs in the twentieth and now twenty-first centuries. It is these hubs that host the megabanks and now shadow banks that are driving the pace of cutting-edge financial innovation in this industry's organizational forms, technologies, and practices.

British economic development, based on the twin pillars of overseas trading/resource-extraction ventures (especially via joint-stock companies, often with Royal charters) and domestic industrialization based on coal and rail, featured the pursuit of public purposes through privately-held enterprises. The Bank of England itself was privately-owned until 1946. Soft-touch regulation among privileged "gentleman" stakeholders prevailed as the preferred behavioral norm in British banking. English high-street banking has been dominated by a small number of institutions – five in 1918, four today – for the past 100 years. For example, whereas US banking was transformed by a series of banking laws in the 1930s, British banking survived those years via a series of publicly-guided mergers and acquisitions of distressed banks, without significant changes in banking laws. Only in 2012 did parliament pass the Financial Services Act, which established the Financial Conduct Authority and the Prudential Regulation Agency as "twin peaks" agencies to look after the safety, soundness, and competitiveness of UK financial institutions.

The international experience and relationships of many of the core institutions in what has become known as the City of London – the nexus of domestic and foreign banking and non-bank financial institutions centered in London – have a long history, rooted in the management of the far-flung British empire (Sutherland, 2013). These commercial and financial linkages were deepened during Britain's century administering its gold standard. Britain's key geopolitical position after the Second World War permitted it to bolster its position as a dominant global financial hub despite the fading importance of British industry and the struggles of the pound sterling. There have been three crucial steps in the contemporary emergence of the City of London. The first was the creation of an active Eurodollar (offshore money) market in the early 1960s. London became the preferred global hub for what Machlup (1970) famously termed "stateless money." And as Coakley and Harris (1983) pointed out, by the late 1960s the City of London had become a supranational enclave managing the Eurocurrency (offshore) financial system, largely independently of domestic industry. The Eurocurrency business, most denominated in dollars, created risk for the banking entities involved and undercut the global competitiveness of British industry.[3]

The second definitive step for the City was the "big bang" deregulation of the London Stock Exchange – including the ending of fixed commission charges and of traditional trading practices – in October 1986. As Lambie puts it:

> the USA became the world's "hegemon" after the Second World War, but London retained its power in finance; well placed to challenge the post-war Keynesian regulatory consensus in favor of globalizing interests, theoretically and politically served by the rise of neo-liberal ideology.
>
> (Lambie, 2013, p. 239)

The combination of the tradition of "soft touch" regulation, experience in managing the exchange-rate and other risks of offshore financial relationships, and the deregulation of activities and roles, proved a boon in the 1970s and 1980s, during which Great Britain (and other European nations) found it impossible to maintain quasi-fixed exchange rates with the chronically strong German economy. As Warsh (2011) recounts, Europeans' continually frustrated efforts to maintain their integrity as an economic bloc without exchange-rate slippage eventually led to two grand ideas: a single market, which would solidify Europe's status as a megamarket; and a single currency, which would require macroeconomic harmonization. In the end, Britain joined the single market – the European Union (EU) – but not the single currency – the European Monetary Union. This was the third element in solidifying the capital of post-hegemonic Britain as a global financial capital. Arnold and Fleming (2014) have reported that more than 250 foreign banks locate their main European subsidiaries there as a base for wholesale (investment and corporate banking) European operations in the EU single market – investment and corporate banking. Indeed, the combination of EU membership and Eurocurrency experience, in the era of deregulation, meant that London could function as an ideal base for offshore and onshore financial activities for large multinational firms and the banks that service them. As Palan (2002) and Palan et al. (2009) document, many small nations commercialized their sovereignty and teamed with City firms to create tax havens that permitted the creation of financial activities that could escape from regulation and taxation even while being conducted within the same physical space.

The special place of Great Britain's banking industry is readily seen when contrasted with global competitors. Figure 20.1 shows that whereas the size of the largest banking firm relative to gross domestic product (GDP), in the six nations shown, grew steadily in every case between 1989 and 2012, a UK bank was consistently at or near the top of this list.[4] Figure 20.2 shows that the UK's export earnings from its financial/insurance industry are far greater as a share of its exports than for other nations. Figure 20.3 makes the same point, in terms of the contribution of financial/insurance exports as a share of British GDP. Figure 20.4 shows that Britain has

How finance globalized

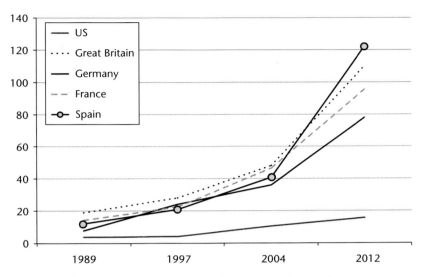

Figure 20.1 Assets of largest bank as % of GDP, selected countries: 1989, 1997, 2004, and 2012

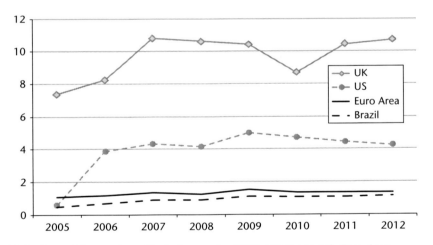

Figure 20.2 Financial exports as % of all exports, 2005–2012: UK, US, Euro Area

a relatively high level of financial/insurance-related imports, illustrating its financial openness; however, the import ratio is far less than is the export ratio.

Whereas the UK's large banks thrived on the global operations facilitated by London's role as leading financial centre, development banking was left at the wayside.[5] Britain's economic soft spot lay in the areas that had formed the basis of its industrial strength in an earlier day – its great Midland and Northern industrial cities, with their mines, mills, and shipyards. Britain had no development bank to steer a renaissance for these areas.[6] What passed for an industrial policy involved Northern relocations of City back-office operations and government bureaucracies, and a housing boom fuelled by the Building Societies Act of 1986, which de-mutualized Britain's building societies and opened the way to deregulated mortgage lending. The subprime lending

355

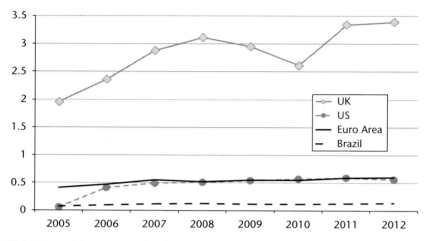

Figure 20.3 Financial exports as % of GDP, 2005–2012: UK, US, Euro Area, Brazil

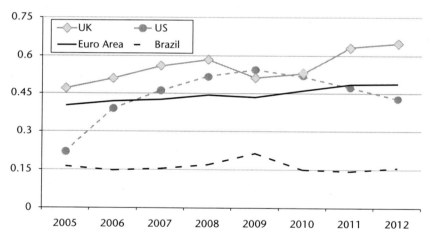

Figure 20.4 Financial and Insurance imports as % of GDP, 2005–2012: UK, US, Euro Area, Brazil

and securitization methods perfected in the United States were adapted and spread throughout the United Kingdom by building societies, in competition with high-street British banks. The special competence of City bankers in using over-the-counter instruments to hedge exchange-rate and other risks came to the fore as subprime securitization instruments spread across borders. City of London firms thrived as the markets for global financial instruments expanded. London grew ever more prosperous (and its real-estate ever more pricey) on the back of its global financial industry, even while the remainder of the British economy stagnated (Chakrabortty 2013). Figure 20.5 shows that British high-tech manufacturing declined substantially as a share of all exports in the 2005–12 period.[7]

While significant numbers of small loan-brokers and funds selling the undercollateralized, unpayable mortgages of the subprime era began failing early in 2007, the subprime crisis proper began with the failure of the Newcastle-based building society, Northern Rock. A significant

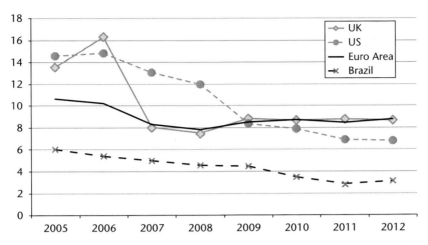

Figure 20.5 High-tech manufacturing exports as % of all exports, 2005–2012: UK, US, Euro area

number of UK building societies failed or were merged. Two of the UK's "big five" banks – the Royal Bank of Scotland and Lloyds – needed huge infusions of public money to avoid insolvency. The Labour government of PM Gordon Brown, which was in power when the Shearson Lehman meltdown occurred, briefly considered nationalizing the problem banks; but instead opted to inject public funds without nationalization.[8] So the central role accorded to megabanks in the UK contributed to the dysfunctionality of the financial system in two ways: first, by creating competition for smaller, regional banks; second, by generating contagion and requiring bailouts in the subprime crisis.

With the election of a Conservative government in 2010, led by PM David Cameron, any discussion of nationalization remained off the table. However, this was not due to the private-sector banks' lively reaction to the crisis. To the contrary: the big banks were not lending. This was due to the fact that they were riddled with bad loan problems, and concerned with recapitalization; initially, in the wake of the crisis, loan demand was low as well; but eventually this condition changed. Vince Cable, an influential politician and advocate for effective financing of business, proposed a business bank. This was eventually passed, but at a very modest scale of £300 million. Justin Welby, the Archbishop of Canterbury, called for establishing a set of regional development banks (Goodley, 2013). Meanwhile, the big banks didn't resume lending, and their monopolistic control of the market – 90 percent of business loans and 85 percent of business current accounts (Fleming, 2014) meant that business expansion was strangled in the UK.

Evolving financial institutions and practices in the United States

As Ha-Joon Chang (2002) has reminded us, during the period of its geographic expansion, the US was a developing nation. Investments from abroad provided much of the financing for its railroads and its canals; and it capitalized on infant-industry protections to build the industries that made it rich, and permitted its growth into a continental giant. No federal development bank was established prior to the 1930s. Instead, however, the continual spatial expansion was undertaken in the context of state supervision of banks: between 1836 – the demise of the

Second Bank of the United States – and 1914 – the Federal Reserve – states governed bank chartering, or in some cases permitted "free banking." The upshot was that financing – including whatever development banking was feasible – was provided through state-chartered, often unstable or unreliable banks. These provided the finance needed to continue the nation's westward push.

The Great Depression brought two significant developments, for our purposes. One was a huge increase in the size and scope of federal expenditure. Among the purposes served by this expanded budget were aims associated above with development banking. In 1932, President Hoover sponsored the creation of the Reconstruction Finance Corporation (RFC), which provided subsidies and loans to distressed state and local governments, and which provided loans and capital to US non-financial businesses and banks threatened with insolvency. Under the New Deal, the RFC focused on bank recapitalization. It functioned until 1957.[9] This entity was joined by a variety of federal vehicles for putting Americans to work and building public buildings, bridges, parks, and other needed infrastructure. Among these were the National Recovery Administration, the Tennessee Valley Authority, the Agricultural Adjustment Administration, and the Works Progress Administration. No one of these took the form of a bank: they were mixed entities that both generated needed aggregate demand, patient finance for businesses and farms, and investment financing for infrastructure projects. The second development stemming from the Great Depression was a new set of banking laws aimed at stabilizing the banks and removing the threat of destabilizing financial dynamics. These laws provided deposit insurance, split investment and commercial banking, restricted commercial banks' geographic and product-line competition, set limits on rates, and so on.[10]

The demise of the New Deal initiatives was not followed by the creation of a US public DFI. Instead, specialized vehicles were used. Development banking support was provided for US housing expansion through federally-subsidized and underwritten financial entities.[11] The Nixon Administration created a modest Small Business Administration financing program, and the Clinton Administration an even more modest Community Development Financial Institutions program. As Mazzucato (2013) and Weiss (2014) have shown, the principal form of development financing support for industrial innovation came indirectly through a massive set of budgetary supports for nuclear laboratories and for research and development, operated by the US's defense, energy, and national securities agencies.

These supports for industrial innovation through the federal-budgetary backdoor grew in significance with the Reagan Administration, just as a decade of high inflation and recession, along with rising interest rates, had put the fragmented, regulated US banking system under severe stress (Dymski 1999). The US entered the 1980s with 14,400 insured commercial banks. Deregulation and permissive regulatory oversight fed a bank merger wave that left the country with just over 6900 banks by September 2009. The largest US banks were heavily involved in consolidation: of the 24 largest US bank holding companies as of 1997, only 10 remained by September 2011. Further, the largest US banks grew at a much faster rate than did even mid-size banks, as restrictions on bank geographic locations and permitted activities fell through a series of deregulation laws in the 1980s and 1990s.

These large banks' growth was fueled by four additional intertwined factors (Dymski, 2009). One was the collapse of the US's thrift-based housing-finance system in the 1980s; it was replaced by a securitization-based system, in which mortgages were originated and then distributed to investors. Second, the expansion of securitization to encompass high-rate, high-risk, and predatory lending (including subprime mortgages), often to households formerly excluded from home ownership or credit extension. The third factor in large banks' growth was the rising competition between Wall Street and London, linked to the changing international monetary order. The fourth factor, in turn, was the US's steady capital-account inflow, a by-product of its persistent current-account deficits throughout the neo-liberal period.

If the current-account deficits of the latter years of the Bretton Woods system foreshadowed the inability of the US to maintain (and reap the benefits from maintaining) an orderly global system, the current-account deficits from the 1980s onward marked a post-hegemonic interregnum. The US's contribution to global economic order was no longer to insure worldwide prosperity, but instead to provide residual aggregate demand for the increasing number of nations trying to export their way to renewed growth, especially after crisis episodes. In effect, the US current-account deficit became an entrenched part of global economic functioning – albeit a largely unacknowledged one, as this contradicted the policy orthodoxies of the IMF and of the increasingly dominant Classical approach to macroeconomics. As a crucial side benefit for the declining US economy, the dollar's role in currency reserves and cross-border transactions was thereby preserved. The Doobie Brothers' phrase, "What were once vices are now habits," could be reworked to capture this situation: "What once undermined policy now reinforces policy."

The broad-based deregulation and large bank holding companies' expansion put them into direct competition with large non-bank Wall Street firms. Given the ocean of reserves seeking investment outlets that was pouring systematically into the US financial markets, this competition focused on the bundling, holding, and sale of subprime paper and of CDOs – and, in turn, on the ancillary derivative and underwriting products that could be created in tandem with securitized credit. Enhancing the demand for these new products was the multiplication of largely unregulated investment funds, including hedge and private equity funds. Wall Street grew stronger by the year, as did the megabanks and shadow banks that dominated it.[12] Not coincidentally, large Wall Street firms moved into the lead in numerous areas of "global financial services," and indeed the Wall Street megaplex became seen as a key source of competitive advantage for the United States (Franko, 2004).

If the City of London's global-hub role was rooted in its cross-border relationships, Wall Street's role was securitization-based. Of course, each global hub competed to create financial products that complemented or competed with the other. Regarding the Eurodollar market, for example, Cassis has observed, "While American banking legislation thus strengthened London's international role to the detriment of New York's, American banks took full advantage of the situation, dominating the Euromarkets and integrating them into their global strategy" (Cassis 2006, p. 227). Wójcik argues that "the degree of commonality, complementarity and connectivity" between the two financial hubs is so profound as to justify the term, "the New York–London axis" (Wójcik, 2013, p. 2736).

Figure 20.2 shows that US exports, like those of the UK, were proportionately very reliant on financial/insurance exports in the 2000s, though this reliance was far less relative to GDP (Figure 20.3). Figures 20.5 and 20.6 show that the US, like the UK, experienced a substantial relative decline in high-tech exports between 2005 and 2012, while domestic credit rose steadily as a share of GDP through 2007.

We defer here any discussion of the details of the subprime episode.[13] We might simply note that the rise of subprime-linked securitization in the decade before the crisis set in cemented the integration of US megabanks, mortgage-brokers, underwriters, funds, and broker-dealers into a financial complex optimized to extract maximum fees from originating, selling, insuring, and taking highly-leveraged bets on an ever-expanding stream of securitized credit. The excessive leverage was especially distinctive; it was accomplished through the inter-mixing of contingent and spot commitments, facilitated by exchanges and multiple uses of the same "safe" assets as collateral. This "rehypothecation" formed just one method by which shadow banking emerged as a fundamental structural element in global financial centers.[14]

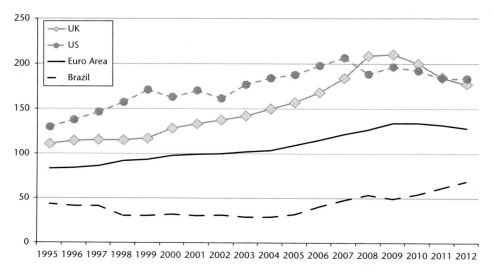

Figure 20.6 Domestic credit to private sector as % of GDP, 1995–2012: UK, US, Euro Area

Once the subprime crisis hit home, the price of the dizzying financial competition of the 2000s was revealed: in 2008, three of the five largest Wall Street non-commercial-bank firms either failed or disappeared through merger (Lehman Brothers, Merrill Lynch, Bear Stearns); the other two were converted into bank holding companies. Federal Reserve and Treasury policy decisions in these weeks of crisis revealed that the Wall Street complex was fragile, and at the same time had to be maintained via any means necessary: its core institutions were too big to save, too intertwined with shadow banks and other global behemoths to untangle, and thus constituted the new reality of modern money and credit markets.

As of December 2009, six megabanks – Bank of America, J.P. Morgan Chase, Citibank, Wells Fargo, Goldman Sachs, and Morgan Stanley – stand alone as the commanding heights of US banking. The 2008 TARP program that preserved these megabanks' existence was fully consistent with the broader design of US banking policy. The US government provided subsidies for large banks to buy failed savings and loan associations after the 1980s "thrift" crisis, and then encouraged their transformation to megabanks through a series of financial deregulation acts. In effect, the emergence of the six largest US megabanks through the eventual intersection of Wall Street and super-sized commercial banks should be understood not as an accidental by-product of the 2007–08 subprime crisis, but as the endpoint of a lengthy period of intentional policy choices regarding the activities and market scope of a reshaped, more efficient US banking industry. What was unintended was that these megabanks' final emergence should have required such huge public interventions to survive crises of their own making.

Also not intended was that the US, after a 30-year bank merger wave, would have two essentially distinct banking sectors: a megabanking sector at the hub of the Wall Street financial complex, and a community banking sector in which more than 9 of every 10 US banks have under $1 billion in assets. The former sector securitizes at least a third (if not all) of what it lends, while the latter does virtually no securitization. And the six dominant megabanks represent an uneven mix of two former investment banks, two former retail banks, and two US versions of universal banks. Figures 20.7–20.9 show the dramatic differences among these six banks' balance sheets, while comparing them with three representative large US regional banks.

How finance globalized

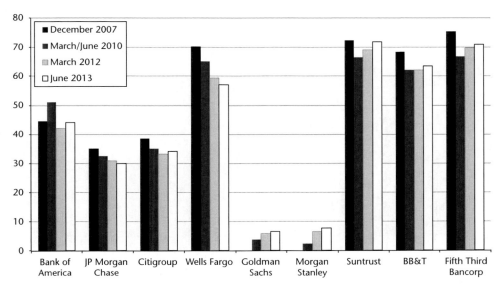

Figure 20.7 Net loans and leases as percentage of assets, selected large U.S. bank holding companies: 2007–2013

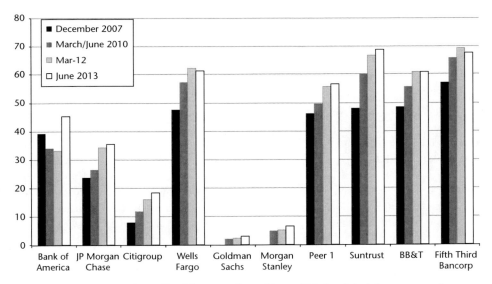

Figure 20.8 Core Deposits as % of Assets, selected large U.S. bank holding companies: 2007–2013

The shift of US banking toward increasing dominance by a megabanking sector affected system functionality in several ways. These megabanks lent less to the non-financial sector, imposed systemic instability on the rest of the financial system and on the economy as a whole, and undercut the provision of productive finance via harmful competition, even while occupying a favored position in the US bank merger wave. The extent of the potential dysfunctionality

361

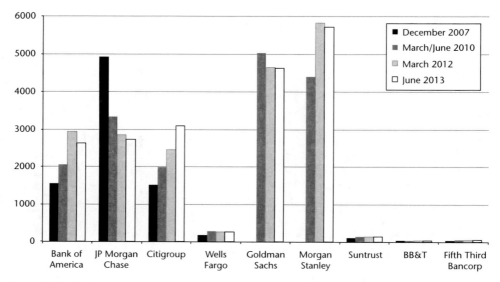

Figure 20.9 Derivatives as % assets, selected large U.S. bank holding companies: 2007–2013

of a megabanking/shadow-banking led financial system would only become clear as the full scope of the subprime crisis became clear.

The New York–London "axis" after the 2007–08 financial crisis

The two previous sections broke off as the Great Financial Crisis of the past several years began and then gathered momentum. There is little doubt that the mixture of deregulation, fragmented regulation, globally mobile finance, and misalignments between risk-origination and risk-bearing, all played their parts. So how much has changed for the New York-London "axis" after the crisis? Has legal or legislative action transformed its behavior?

The effort to identify the causes of the subprime crisis has taken on a "Rashomon"-like quality: different analysts seem to have been witnessing completely different events.[15] Some point the finger at excessively aggressive behaviors within the New York-London "axis": hubris, excessive leveraging and complexity, the fragmentation between risk-creation and risk-bearing, the capacity to take zero-sum bets on real and synthetic securities, the asymmetric knowledge bases of broker-dealers and investors. Others blame government over-regulation, or the lack of adequate regulatory oversight. Still others blame greedy home-buyers whose reach exceeded their grasp. Others (including this author) have emphasized predatory lenders' targeting of minorities and lower-income neighborhoods that had previously been denied access to mortgage credit. It is not important for our purpose to decide shares of blame. It is sufficient here to second the conclusion of Wójcik (2013, p. 2736):

> the global financial crisis 2007–09 originated to a large extent in the [New York–London] axis rather than in an abstract space of financial markets. The dominance of the axis in global finance can be easily underestimated and evidence suggests that, contrary to expectations the axis is not in decline.

The crisis itself was incredibly costly. Estimates of costs vary widely, depending on whether out-of-pocket costs to taxpayers is being considered, or overall impacts on economic growth and financial and non-financial wealth. An IMF report (2009) provided preliminary estimates of the costs of the crisis, reporting "upfront government financing" at the following levels of GDP: United Kingdom, 18.9 percent; Norway, 15.8 percent; Canada, 9.8 percent; Austria, 8.9 percent; United States, 7.5 percent; Netherlands, 6.2 percent; Greece, 5.4 percent; Ireland, 5.4 percent; Sweden, 5.2 percent; Belgium, 4.8 percent; Spain, 4.6 percent; Germany, 3.7 percent; Portugal, 2.4 percent; Russia, 1.7 percent; France, 1.6 percent.[16] Of course, subsequent reports indicated smaller eventual payouts, narrowly considered; for example, at the end of 2010, Her Majesty's Treasury (2010) estimated an eventual out-of-pocket taxpayer cost for the UK of £512 billion, down from a £955 billion estimate made one year earlier. The figures for "all in" estimates are remarkably higher, as they take into account lost GDP momentum, the destruction of equity value, and other factors. The IMF (2009) estimated "all-in" global costs at $11.7 trillion; and two recent estimates for the US economy put overall losses at $10 trillion (General Accountability Office, 2013) and $6 to $14 trillion (Luttrell et al., 2013).

The crisis was thus a demonstration of the dysfunctionality of the megabank-shadow-banking-led financial complex. This might be viewed as an exorbitant cost of transiting from an antiquated hold-to-maturity loan-based system to a modern originate-and-distribute securitization-based system more fully able to exploit the advances in information and communication offered by the technology revolution.[17] In other words, beyond this demonstration of its dysfunctionality, the question is, is the new system providing needed credit – here, our criterion is the provision of credit for development – effectively? We have already alluded to the move in the UK to establish a business bank because Britain's "big five" banks were not able or not willing to lend broadly enough to the small and medium enterprises joining in the country's nascent economic recovery.

Figures 20.10 and 20.11 provide empirical evidence for the US case. Figure 20.10 contrasts GDP growth and credit growth, for several categories of loan, for economic cycles from 1961 to the present.[18] Figure 20.10A includes data from the four full business cycles (measured trough to peak) between 1961 and 1990. Note that average loan growth exceeds GDP growth in every cycle, across all categories of credit (commercial and industrial loans (made to non-financial firms), loans secured by real estate, and loans to individuals) and for overall lending (net loans and leases). Note that average GDP growth declines across these cycles, a pattern reflected in the loan-growth data. Figure 10B shows data for the three subsequent business cycles, beginning respectively in 1991, 2001, and 2008 (as mentioned in note 35, cycles are measuring trough-first to permit the inclusion of the post-crisis period). The pattern is shockingly different. For one thing, GDP growth rates are successively lower, cycle after cycle. But with the exception of loans to individuals, there is no longer any systematic pattern of credit growth amplifying GDP growth. Real-estate loans, predictably, show the excessive lending of the 2000s, followed by the collapse of subsequent years. There is, however, virtually no cyclically-responsive growth of commercial and industrial loans.

Much was said above about the increasing dominance of US megabanks in US financial dynamics. Figure 20.11 isolates loan volumes for the "Big Four" that have emerged from the extended bank-merger period – J.P. Morgan Chase, Bank of America, Citibank, and Wells Fargo – and contrasts this with the loan volumes for all other FDIC-insured banks. The period 2002–13 is depicted.[19] Figure 20.11A shows that Big-Four real-estate-secured loans are almost equal to the total for the remainder of the banking system; and while other banks' real loan volumes have stabilized and even grown slightly in the current recovery, those for Big-Four banks have steadily declined. Figure 20.11B illustrates a very similar pattern for commercial and

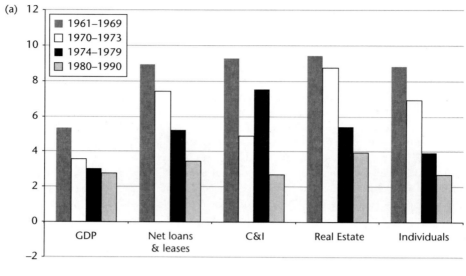

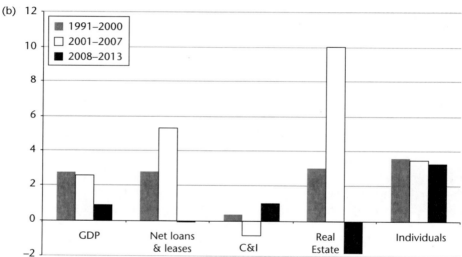

Figure 20.10 (a) Trough-to-peak GDP and Loan Growth, U.S. Commercial Banks, Average annual % change, Five-year time-spans, 1969–1990. (b) Trough-to-peak GDP and Loan Growth, U.S. Commercial Banks, Average annual % change, Five-year time-spans, 1991 to present

industrial loans; in this case, however, other banks' loan volumes are increasing noticeably, but Big-Four loan volumes are not. Figure 20.11C, depicting loans to individuals, shows the same Big-Four/other-bank contrast for the post-crisis years; note that Big-Four banks have accounted for over half this loan market since 2004.

In short, these data provide an empirical correlate to the conclusion that Minister Cable implicitly reached in the UK – the current intermediary structure lacks for something. Specifically, there is no strong commitment shown by the Big Four banks to support for development banking as a means of rekindling industrial and business activity. This sort of initiative at the

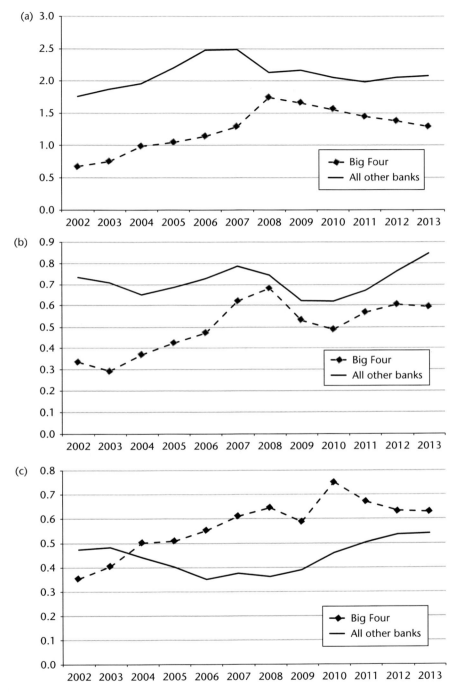

Figure 20.11 (a) Outstanding real-estate-secured loans, at "Big Four" and all other US commercial banks, in trillions of 2005 dollars, 2002–2011. (b) Outstanding commercial and industrial loans at "Big Four" and all other US commercial banks, in trillions of 2010 dollars, 2002–2013. (c) Outstanding loans to individuals at "Big Four" and all other US commercial banks, in trillions of 2005 dollars, 2002–2011

parliamentary or Congressional levels is, further, ruled out the political power of lobbyists for the established banks. Further, there is reason to be skeptical about the possibility that the megabank/shadow-bank complex's tendencies toward dysfunctionality – and toward spreading costs to taxpayers, to the formerly and newly unemployed, and to those dispossessed of homes and businesses – will end soon.

In particular, efforts at financial reform have been stalled, watered down, and largely frustrated. The Big Four UK banks have fought aggressively against efforts by the European Union to strengthen financial regulation. As Arnold (2014) noted in the *Financial Times*:

> The UK has already launched four legal challenges to EU financial services regulation including the power to ban short selling; the requirement that clearing houses handling euro transactions be based in the Eurozone; the financial transaction tax; and the bonus cap.

US megabanks and shadow-banks, in turn, resisted the passage of the Dodd–Frank Act, even after their legal departments shaped many of its sections; they have taken measures to slow its implementation; and they have worked long and hard to limit its scope via the rule-making process (Bair, 2012; Eavis, 2014).[20] In both national capitals, and indeed in Brussels, passing effective reform legislation is rendered nearly impossible by the often definitive influence of lobbyists and experts working for financial interests.

The problem of the New York–London axis' uncontrollability, in short, remains, due to its interconnectedness combined with multiple regulatory jurisdictions—a formula for insuring that whatever reforms are passed will be subject to Goodhart's law.[21] As Pozsar *et al.* (2013, p. 14) demonstrate, shadow banking itself is not external to the megabanks; rather:

> The "internal" shadow banking subsystem refers to the credit intermediation process of a global network of banks, finance companies, broker-dealers, and asset managers and their on- and off-balance-sheet activities—all under the umbrella of financial holding companies. . . . the "external" shadow banking subsystem refers to the credit intermediation process of diversified broker-dealers and a global network of independent, nonbank financial specialists that includes captive and stand-alone finance companies, limited-purpose finance companies, and asset managers.

Consider the evidence of interconnection provided by Wójcik (2012) in his description of the pre-crisis period: AIG originated credit-default swaps that were viewed by their purchasers as providing insurance against the non-performance of securitized credit bundled into CDOs (collateralized debt obligations) created, in part, from mortgages created by Northern Rock in Britain and (say) Countrywide Financial in the US, which in turn were invested in vehicles registered in offshore tax havens by hedge funds. We can extend Wójcik's string of interconnections further: short and long options were created on the basis of these CDOs in New York, leading to options swaps in London, and now to new emergent indices and zero-sum hedging instruments not yet defined in law.

It must be acknowledged that many of these instruments are being forced into trading on exchanges in the wake of post-crisis regulatory reforms. However, the game cannot be considered frozen into place just yet. With so many financial hubs and offshore centers and vehicles involved, Goodhart's Law remains very much in effect – efforts to regulate one financial instrument invite innovations that escape whatever regulatory umbrella was established. To get an idea of how this game is being played, consider this passage from a recent *Financial Times* article. The authors, Alloway and Mackenzie (2014), describe the emergence of two new instruments, total return swaps and "swaptions", as follows:

> A total return swap enables an investor to receive a payment based on the performance of an underlying basket of assets. Such a strategy in this case enables an investor to leverage their exposure to the performance of credit, without owning an actual asset. The downside is that any sharp deterioration in the value of credit means an investor would need to compensate the other party in this transaction, usually a bank that arranged the deal.
>
> "The new TRS product is really, really interesting in that you do now have a number of TRS products referencing credit indices," says Andrew Jackson, chief investment officer at Cairn Capital. "We're even starting to see options on TRS." ...
>
> The use of options tied to CDS indices, known as "swaptions", has grown sharply, buoyed in part because the instruments are not required to be centrally cleared. Such swaptions allow investors to protect their portfolios from large movements in markets, known as "tail risk".
>
> More than $60bn of CDS index options currently exchange hands each week—up from just $2bn traded *per month* back in 2005, according to Citigroup analysts.

A further problem in reining in and regulating the "axis" is the transformation of international law in the neo-liberal years.[22] What Machlup might have called "stateless interests" have increasingly been asserting, establishing, and protecting their legal rights over the disposition of contracts that extend beyond domestic borders.[23] The problem in the case of securitized credit transactions resides in the fact that two contracts are made on the basis of the same cash-flow. Offshore purchasers are increasingly asserting their prior rights over financial promises to pay based on securities they purchased, regardless of the status of payment by the original borrower on the original credit contract.[24] Wójcik notes that these securities take the form of IVs and SPEs that are protected by a phalanx of "financial, legal and accountancy firms" (2012, p. 333) He writes: "the advanced business services hold considerable power, which they exercise by operating legal and financial vehicles designed to escape the control of governmental or intergovernmental organizations through the use of offshore jurisdictions" (2012, p. 330).

The fact that the sovereigns engaged directly (in the case of the US) or indirectly (in the case of the nation-state members of the European Union) are now often treated as unworthy borrowers, to be disciplined by markets, adds to the difficulties of reform efforts. Can an entity that can be disciplined by market forces also shape markets and their forces? Consider, for example, that the not-yet-fully-implemented Dodd–Frank Act was passed in July 2010, four years from the time of this writing. The asymmetric pace of regulation and innovation leads some to despair. For example, Alloway and Mackenzie (2014) quote Janet Tavakoli, president of an eponymous Tavakoli Structured Finance, as follows: "We've reformed nothing. . . . We have more leverage and more derivatives risk than we've ever had." Others hold out hope of using market discipline to rein in excess. For example, Ingo Walter (2012, p. 114) argues:

> Improving the financial architecture in a disciplined, consistent, internationally coordinated and sustained manner with a firm eye to the public interest should ultimately be centered on market discipline. By being forced to pay a significant price for the negative externalities SIFIs generate – in the form of systemic risk – managers and boards will have to draw their own conclusions regarding optimum institutional strategy and structure in the context of

the microeconomics and industrial organization of global financial intermediation. If this fails, constraints on their size, complexity and interconnectedness will be a major part of the policy reaction to the next financial crisis.

The challenge for such an approach is for regulators to keep pace with market participants' creation of innovations that create systemic risk, not to mention anticipating the scope of this risk before its implications have been fully understood. Pozsar et al. (2013, p. 1) argue that, in any case, "increased capital and liquidity standards for depository institutions and insurance companies will likely heighten the returns to shadow banking activity." Therefore, they conclude, "Shadow banking, in some form or another, is therefore expected to be an important part of the financial system for the foreseeable future." These reflections amplify the point made by Wójcik: "if global finance is to change, the New York–London axis has to change" (2013, p. 2736).

Conclusion

This chapter has provided an account of how the unique historical and economic circumstances of the United Kingdom and of the United States and their hegemonic position in the world economy underlie the development of global finance as we have it today. Starting with national economic circumstances, rather than with primitives such as technological change and/or the information revolution, permits us to see that the current shape of globalized financial institutions and practices have evolved from historically specific circumstances. As Thomas Piketty (2014) has emphasized in his opus on income inequality, empirical patterns that appear to be characteristic of long-term trends in capitalist development have political roots. The apparent technological necessity of a super-leveraged, risk-shifting global financial complex is a mirage; this complex has emerged, anchored in the cities of London and New York, due to a series of events, circumstances, and decisions. Opportunities and crises have both played their part. The formation and then dismemberment of gold-based global currency systems played a role, as have the 30-years'-long current-account deficit/capital-account surplus that has made the US a global liquidity sink (Dymski, 2011).

Having highlighted the importance of historical events and institutional developments, including the transformation of the global monetary order, it must immediately be acknowledged that the dynamics of global finance include far more than has been captured in this analysis of two financial hubs. Hubs in France, Germany, Switzerland, Japan, China, and São Paulo, among other global cities, do follow the tail-return possibilities left by the cauldrons of innovation in New York and London; one example is large German banks' purchases of subprime securities from Wall Street houses in the waning days of the US housing boom (Lewis, 2010). But beyond this follower behavior, these financial hubs have independently created – and continue to create – new instruments and practices, triggering further behavioral responses in the New York–London axis.

This last insight makes it all the more clear that acknowledging the historical contingency that brought about the current fix – the world of the 1 percent of the 1 percent, as Piketty (2014) and his numerous co-authors have emphasized – does not mean that this path-dependent path is easily undone. To the contrary; because things are done as they are in this sector – because the politicians now understand they must bail out or make special arrangements for "systematically important institutions," because the megabanks circulate and recirculate short-term securities to support their speculative position-taking, because credit can easily flow only when there are "investors" willing to absorb securitized loans sold by "banks" – then behaviors in virtually every other sector in the economy and society have had to make adjustments. The core question at hand – "what precisely are the economic functions that the banking system performs for the other agents in the economy?" – is out of bounds for any polite policy discussion. Yet if this question is not asked, then policy discourse will be the equivalent of intermission chatter until the audience gathers for the coming of the next systemic, global-economy-threatening crisis. We conclude then by paraphrasing Wójcik's insight: if global finance is to change, the New York–London axis and the governments and non-financial firms and households that have adjusted to the reality of coercive and unproductive global finance has to change. And as Jamie Dimon has suggested, in the quote that begins this essay, the place to start is to ask the right questions.

Notes

1. Among the most insightful works on the relationship between financial development and economic growth are Cameron (1960, 1967), Cassis (1994, 2006), Demirgüç-Kunt and Levine (2004), Gerschenkron (1962), and Goodhart (1988). These works have the added virtue of recounting national banking histories in far more depth than is possible here.
2. These are not the only financial hubs: others include Singapore, Tokyo, Hong Kong, and Frankfurt. However, New York and London are globally dominant: in part, because of the reach of their financial practices Wójcik (2013); and in part, because the integrative global practices they invented or expanded led directly to the global financial crisis of 2007–08.
3. Making financial transactions denominated in dollars in a pound-sterling home-base in an economy that was experiencing chronic current-account deficits put the interests of British industry and international finance into direct conflict. The City had to maintain a high pound-sterling to maintain its margins, exactly the opposite of what industry needed.
4. The banking statistics shown in Figure 20.1 are drawn from various issues of *Business Week* and *Forbes* magazine, featuring lists of the 1000 or 2000 largest business enterprises across the globe; the data for GDP in Figure 20.1, as well as the data shown in Figures 20.2–20.5 are taken from the OECD.
5. More than that, the existence of large systematically important institutions arguably undercut system functionality through creating competition for smaller, local players and exacerbating the risk of systemic contagion – most visible in the subprime crisis.
6. Britain's sole development bank, the Colonial Development Corporation, was established in 1948 to "develop self-sustaining agriculture, industry and trade in the British empire" (*The Economist* 2001). The Blair administration transformed it into a public-private partnership that would raise capital from the private sector for developing-nation projects that could earn market returns. Its paltry budget of £2 billion (in 2002) made it at best an afterthought in financial markets and development planning alike.
7. Whilst manufacturing was in decline, Figure 20.6 shows that domestic credit to the private sector as a share of GDP – the majority of which was directed toward housing – rose until 2009 at a pace even faster than that in the US.
8. The "big five" are HSBC, the Lloyds Banking Group (which includes the Bank of Scotland and TSB Bank), the Royal Bank of Scotland Group (which includes National Westminster Bank and Ulster Bank), Barclays, and Standard Chartered. Lloyds is 25% owned by the UK government, and the RBS Group is 84% owned by the UK government; both however remain active as private-sector entities.
9. For histories of the RFC and the New Deal, see Jones and Angly (1951) and Olson (1988).
10. See Dymski (1999) for a concise history of twentieth-century US banking. These restrictive new rules are viewed by some analysts, even in the wake of the 2008 subprime crisis, as having deleterious effects; for example, Neal and White argue that the Glass–Steagall Act limited small-medium enterprises' access to credit and limited investment banks' capital base.
11. The main entities here were two government-sponsored enterprises – the Federal National Mortgage Association (Fannie Mae) and the Government National Mortgage Association (Ginnie Mae). Fannie Mae was privatized in 1968.
12. Jane D'Arista began warning of the emergence of a "parallel banking system" engaged in speculative loan-making in the late 1980s and early 1990s – a system which "divided intermediation between two separate entities, each of which dealt directly with the public through only one side of the balance sheet" (D'Arista 1994, p. 418) – and thus escaped regulation as banks. The term "parallel banking" is, of course, a precursor to the term "shadow banking" in use today.

13 Sorkin (2010) gives a blow-by-blow insiders' account of the Wall Street crisis as it unfolded between September and November of 2008.
14 Pozsar et al. (2013) define shadow banking as consisting of "financial intermediaries that conduct maturity, credit, and liquidity transformation without explicit access to central bank liquidity or public sector credit guarantees."
15 Dymski (2013) summarizes and provides citations to some of the contrasting views about the causes of the subprime crisis.
16 Smaller percentages are excluded here; for the full list of countries, see Table 2.1 (IMF, 2009).
17 Nobel laureate Robert Shiller expressed at the very commencement of the subprime crisis (Shiller, 2008) and has maintained it in subsequent writings (Shiller, 2012).
18 The bank data depicted in Figures 10A and 10B are drawn from the historical banking series of the Federal Deposit Insurance Corporation (FDIC; see www.fdic.gov); the figures are for all FDIC-insured commercial banks. GDP deflator and GDP data are drawn from the Bureau of Economic Analysis (www.bea.gov). All data are annual. The deflator series is used to convert the nominal FDIC data into real terms. Since cycles include trough and recovery periods, and since there has been no trough since the end of the recession in 2009, cycles are measured from the beginning of a trough to the end of that cycle's recovery. Since cycles vary in length, only the first five years of any given cycle, measured from the trough forward, are used in the figures shown. Including full cycles has little effect on the patterns shown.
19 Since end-of-year figures are used, note that between 2007 and 2008, "Big Four" balance sheets are swelled due to their acquisition of two large depositories that failed in Fall 2008. Washington Mutual, a savings bank with $307 billion in assets as of June 2008, was acquired by JP Morgan Chase. Wachovia's substantial balance sheet (it was the fourth largest US bank holding company in June 2008, with $812 billion in assets) was taken over by Wells Fargo. Washington Mutual's balance sheet is not included in FDIC totals prior to this acquisition; but Wachovia's is, explaining most of the 2007-to-2008 shift in loan totals shown.
20 Legal challenges to provisions of Dodd–Frank, including the consumer finance protection agency it establishes and its orderly liquidation procedure, have also delayed its implementation.
21 Goodhart's formulation of this "law" is as follows: "Any observed statistical regularity will tend to collapse once pressure is placed upon it for control purposes" (Goodhart, 2004, p. 96). Alloway and Mackenzie (2014), in the same recent *Financial Times* article quoted below, inadvertently invoke Goodhart's law in that same article when they observe, "in fighting the vanguard of the last financial crisis, regulators have missed new areas of danger in the system."
22 Glinavos (2008) argues that this effort has been systematic; he points to the "current promotion of law reform by international institutions like the World Bank as the product of neo-liberal economic theory;" in his view, "the use of law reform to impose what neo-liberalism considers "rational" solutions undermines the legitimacy of democratic institutions in developing and transitional countries' (p. 1087). Also see Chiong, Dymski, and Hernandez (2014).
23 Supranational authority over otherwise domestic economic activity, of course, is increasingly being asserted via international treaties. The North American Free Trade Agreement (NAFTA) and the EMU provide the outstanding examples of such action to date. Such treaties, while not the topic of this study, are relevant insofar as they serve to reduce the authority of domestic law over economic transactions.
24 The use of legal action by hedge funds NML and Aurelius Capital Management, in their holdout against accepting a debt write-down on outstanding Argentinian debt, and the New York court's upholding of these funds' claim, provides dramatic evidence of the importance of this new terrain of globalized legal rights.

Bibliography

Alloway, T., and Mackenzie, M. (2014) 'Investors dine on fresh menu of credit derivatives', *Financial Times*, August 19.
Arnold, M. (2014) 'Possibility of 'Brexit' threatens London's prospects', *Financial Times*, August 18.
Arnold, M., and Fleming, S. (2014) 'US banks plan ahead for UK exit from EU', *Financial Times*, August 17.
Bair, S. (2012) *Bull by the Horns: Fighting to Save Main Street from Wall Street and Wall Street from Itself*. New York: Free Press.
Cameron, R. (1960) *Banking and Economic Development*. Oxford: Oxford University Press.

Cameron, R. (1967) *Banking in the Early Stages of Industrialization: A Study in Comparative Economic History*. Oxford: Oxford University Press.
Cassis, Y. (1994) *City Bankers, 1890–1914*. Cambridge: Cambridge University Press.
Cassis, Y. (2006) *Capitals of Capital: A History of International Financial Centres, 1780–2005*. Cambridge: Cambridge University Press.
Chakrabortty, A. (2013) 'London's economic boom leaves rest of Britain behind', *The Guardian*, October 23.
Chang, H.-J. (2002) *Kicking Away the Ladder: Development Strategy in Historical Perspective*. London: Anthem Press.
Chiong, M., Dymski, G.A., and Hernandez, J. (2014) 'Contracting the Commonwealth: John R. Commons in the neoliberal era', *Journal of Economic Issues* 48(4): 927–47.
Coakley, J., and Harris, L. (1983) *The City of Capital*. Oxford: Basil Blackwell.
D'Arista, J.W. (1994) *The Evolution of US Finance, Volume II: Restructuring Institutions and Markets*. Armonk, NY: M.E. Sharpe.
Demirgüç-Kunt, A., and Levine, R. (2004) *Financial Structure and Economic Growth: A Cross-country Comparison of Banks, Markets, and Development*. Cambridge: MIT Press.
Dymski, G.A. (1999) *The Bank Merger Wave*. Armonk, NY: M.E. Sharpe.
Dymski, G.A. (2002) 'The global bank merger wave: Implications for developing countries', *The Developing Economies* 40(4), December: 435–66.
Dymski, G.A. (2009) 'Racial exclusion and the political economy of the subprime crisis', *Historical Materialism* 17(2): 149–79.
Dymski, G.A. (2011) 'Limits of policy intervention in a world of neoliberal mechanism designs: Paradoxes of the global crisis', *Panoeconomicus (πανœconomicus)* 58(3), September: 285–308.
Dymski, G.A. (2013) 'Understanding the subprime crisis: Institutional evolution and theoretical views', Chapter 2 in *Where Credit is Due: Bringing Equity to Credit and Housing After the Market Meltdown*, co-edited by Christy Rogers and John Powell. Lanham, MD: University Press of America, pp. 23–67.
Eavis, P. (2014) 'Fight brews on changes that affect derivatives', *New York Times*, August 14.
Economist, The (2001) 'Two fingers to the poor', June 14.
Fleming, S. (2014) 'George Osborne to reveal shake-up of SME loans', *Financial Times*, August 5.
Franko, L.G. (2004) 'US competitiveness in the global financial services industry', Working Paper 1001. Boston: Financial Services Forum, College of Management, University of Massachusetts Boston.
General Accountability Office (2013) 'Financial regulatory reform: Financial crisis losses and potential impacts of the Dodd–Frank Act', GAO-13-180. Washington, DC: General Accountability Office, January.
Gerschenkron, A. (1962), *Economic Backwardness in Historical Perspective: A Book of Essays*. Cambridge, MA: Harvard University Press.
Glinavos, I. (2008) 'Neoliberal law: Unintended consequences of market-friendly law reforms', *Third World Quarterly* 29(6), pp. 1087–99.
Goodhart, C.A.E. (2004) 'Problems of monetary management: The UK experience', Chapter III in *Monetary Theory and Practice: The UK Experience*, by C.A.E. Goodhart. London: Macmillan, London, pp. 91–116.
Goodhart, C. (1988) *The Evolution of Central Banks*. Cambridge: MIT Press.
Goodley, S. (2013) 'Justin Welby calls for more regional banks to break dominance of London', *The Guardian*, October 24.
Her Majesty's Treasury (2010) 'Maintaining the financial stability of UK banks: Update on the support schemes.' Report by the Comptroller and Auditor General, HC 676 Session 2010–2011. London: House of Commons, December 15.
International Monetary Fund (IMF) (2009) 'Fiscal implications of the global economic and financial crisis', prepared by a Staff Team from the Fiscal Affairs Department. Washington, DC: International Monetary Fund, June 9.
Jones, J.H., and E. Angly (1951) *Fifty Billion Dollars: My Thirteen Years with the RFC (1932–45)*. New York: Macmillan.
Lambie, G. (2013) 'Globalisation before the crash: The City of London and UK economic strategy', *Contemporary Politics* 19(3): 339–60.
Lewis, M. (2010) *The Big Short: Inside the Doomsday Machine*. New York: W.W. Norton.
Luttrell, D., Atkinson, T., and Rosenblum, H. (2013) 'Assessing the costs and consequences of the 2007–09 financial crisis and its aftermath', *Economic Letter* (Federal Reserve Bank of Dallas) 8(7), September: 1–4.
Machlup, F. (1970) 'Euro-dollar creation: A mystery story', *Banca Nazionale del Lavoro Quarterly Review* 23(94): 219–60.
Mazzucato, M. (2013) *The Entrepreneurial State*. London: Anthem Press.

Neal, L., and White, N. (2012) 'The Glass–Steagall Act in historical perspective', *Quarterly Review of Economics and Finance* 52: 104–13.

Olson, J.S. (1988) *Saving Capitalism: The Reconstruction Finance Corporation and the New Deal, 1933–1940*. Princeton, NJ: Princeton University Press.

Palan, R. (2002) 'Tax havens and the commercialization of state sovereignty', *International Organization* 56(1), Winter: 151–76.

Palan, R., Murphy, R., and Chavagneux, C. (2009) *Tax Havens: How Globalization Really Works*. Ithaca, NY: Cornell University Press.

Piketty, T. (2014) *Capital in the Twenty-first Century*. Cambridge, MA: Belknap Press.

Pozsar, Z., Adrian, T., Ashcraft, A., and Boesky, H. (2013) 'Shadow banking', *Economic Policy Review* (Federal Reserve Bank of New York) 19(2), December: 1–16.

Shiller, R. (2008) *The Subprime Solution*. Princeton, NJ: Princeton University Press.

Shiller, R. (2012) *Finance and the Good Society*. Princeton, NJ: Princeton University Press.

Sorkin, A.R. (2010) *Too Big to Fail*. New York: Penguin.

Sutherland, D. (2013) *Financing the Raj: The City of London and Colonial India, 1858–1940*. Rochester: Boydell Press.

Walter, I. (2012) 'Universal banking and financial architecture', *Quarterly Review of Economics and Finance* 52: 114–22.

Warsh, D. (2011) *The Euro: The Battle for the New Global Currency*, Revised Edition. New Haven: Yale University Press.

Weiss, L. (2014) *America Inc.? Innovation and Enterprise in the National Security State*. Ithaca: Cornell University Press.

Wójcik, D. (2012) 'Where governance fails: Advanced business services and the offshore world', *Progress in Human Geography* 37(3): 330–47.

Wójcik, D. (2013) 'The dark side of NY–LON: Financial centres and the global financial crisis', *Urban Studies* 50(13), October: 2736–52.

21

How the American financial meltdown of 2008 caused the global financial crisis

Neil Fligstein and Jacob Habinek

The worldwide financial crisis that began in 2007 was set off by the collapse of the subprime mortgage market in the US, which caused widespread banking failures in the US and forced the federal government to provide a massive bailout to the financial sector. The crisis simultaneously reverberated to banks around the world, and eventually brought about a worldwide recession. This paper documents why other countries, especially in Western Europe, were so susceptible to the housing price downturn. We explore various mechanisms by which the financial crisis might have spread including the existence of similar regulatory schemes, government deficits and current account imbalances, trade linkages, and the presence of a housing bubble. We present a surprising result: European banks went down because they were pursuing the same strategies to make profit as the American banks in the same markets. They had joined the market in the US for mortgage-backed securities and funded them by borrowing in the asset-backed-commercial-paper market. When the housing market turned down, they suffered the same fate as their US counterparts. Our study makes a broader theoretical point suggesting that subsequent studies of global finance and financial markets need to consider the identities and strategies of the banks that structure the main markets for different products. This insight has implications for the literatures on financialization, globalization, and the sociology of finance.

Introduction

Home sales in the United States began to fall in 2006 and defaults on subprime mortgages began to increase. Beginning in 2007, this rising wave of defaults spread to the wider mortgage market. By the spring of 2008, banks in the United States and Western Europe were announcing devastating losses, touching off a financial panic that culminated in a wave of bank failures in the United States and at least ten different European nations during September and October of that year. By one count, 23 countries experienced a systemic bank crisis by the end of 2009 (Laeven and Valencia, 2010). These crises were followed by a deep and long-lasting recession.

There are two unusual features of this financial crisis. First, it started in the US. While the US has not been immune to financial crises in the post-war era (Kauffman, 2009), they have tended to be localized and mostly contained. For example, the savings and loan crisis of the late 1980s destroyed a large part of the savings and loan industry and dramatically affected the economy of the southwestern US.Yet it failed to even cause a recession in the US (Barth, 1991). Second, the crisis was most severe in the advanced industrial societies and in particular Western Europe. Most of the cases of economic contagion in the post-war era have involved less developed countries, but this crisis did not generally spread to the less developed world. Indeed, one of the most stunning features of the worldwide recession precipitated by the collapse of the subprime mortgage market in the US was that for the first time since the Great Depression, many advanced industrial societies went into a deep and sustained recession together. This economic collapse happened in just a little over a year. What theories are useful to explain what happened?

In international economics and political economy, economic contagion and the mechanisms by which financial crises spread are a central concern (Forbes and Rigobon, 2001; Reinhart and Rogoff, 2008, 2009; Claessens, Dornbusch, and Park, 2001; Allen and Gale, 2007; Moser, 2003; Forbes, 2004; for a recent review, see Claessens and Forbes, 2004). This perspective has been applied to the current crisis (Rose and Spiegel, 2010, Claessens et al., 2010). Here, scholars have drawn mostly negative conclusions. Surprisingly, there is little evidence that countries that went into recession in 2008 and 2009 shared fundamental features that may have left them more likely to have a recession or pushed financial investors towards a flight to safety. Rose and Spiegel (2010) note that the thing most of the countries that had a deep recession appear to have shared in common was that they were amongst the richest countries in the world.

Sociologists have tended to focus on how the nature of the linkages between countries has fundamentally changed in recent decades, increasingly exposing countries' economies to shared risks through the global market for financial products. Scholars interested in the globalization of finance have tried to document the origins and spread of new financial markets, financial motives, and financial flows at the national and the international level (Ertürk *et al.*, 2008; Martin, 2002; Krippner, 2011; Stockhammer, 2004; Fligstein, 2001; Davis, 2009; Zorn *et al.*, 2004; see Carruthers and Kim, 2011 and Keister, 2002 for reviews). Others have focused on the role of the various kinds of new financial instruments, particularly the securitization of assets such as mortgages, at the core of this integration of global financial markets (Knorr Cetina and Bruegger, 2004; MacKenzie, 2006; 2011; Aalbers, 2008, 2009; Zaloom, 2006; Leyshon and Thrift, 2007; Carruthers and Stinchcombe, 1999; Bryan and Rafferty, 2006). These authors document the development and global extent of financial flows and financial products, but they tell us little about how those products came to occupy such an important and precarious role at the core of the global economy.

What is missing in these sociological accounts is a way to understand how American mortgage-backed securities became so important to the strategies – and the fates – of so many American and European banks. We argue that this is because the sociology of globalization and financial instruments omit one key factor in their attempts to understand the global financial system: how both US and foreign banks made use of asset securitization and organized the US market for mortgage-backed securities on a world scale. We use Fligstein's "markets as politics" (1996, 2001) conceptual framework to direct attention to the role of non-US banks on the US mortgage-backed-securities market and the tactics they employed to finance those activities. The main theoretical innovation in this paper is our use of the sociology of markets to understand how many of the largest banks in the global financial system came to make their core investment American mortgage-backed securities.

The main empirical contribution of this paper is to demonstrate the connection between the involvement of global banks in US financial products markets and the spread of the global financial crisis. We present descriptive evidence showing that between 2003 and 2007 banks from mostly Western European countries dramatically increased their holdings of US mortgage-backed securities and their activities in the asset-backed-commercial-paper market, the sector of the interbank loan market or "shadow banking system" mostly closely linked to the production of mortgage-backed securities and exotic derivatives such as collateral debt obligations (see Adrian et al. (2011) and Stigum (1989) for an account of how these markets work). We then test the degree to which the level of holding American mortgage-backed securities and asset-backed commercial paper were the direct cause of a banking crisis in particular countries and the recession that ensued. We operationalize the kinds of factors that have been suggested in the economics and political economy literatures as measures of what might have caused that crisis. We reproduce the results presented by Rose and Spiegel (2010) using more elaborated measures and show that the contagion factors have little or no effect on banking crises. We demonstrate that the strongest predictor of a banking crisis in a particular country was the level of holdings of American mortgage-backed securities and their use of asset-backed commercial paper. We also demonstrate that these banking crises were the most important explanation of pushing countries into recession.

This chapter has the following structure. First, we review the literature in economics, political economy, and sociology more extensively and develop some hypotheses about potential factors that may explain the origins of this particular international banking crisis and recession. We do this in two parts, the first focusing on the mechanisms proposed by authors in the economics and political economy literature and the second, based on a reading of the more sociological literature on globalization, the sociology of finance, and the sociology of markets. Next, we discuss our data and methods and provide results. In our conclusion we return to the empirical case and how our theoretical approach might inform subsequent research on financialization, globalization, and the sociology of finance.

Theoretical discussion and hypotheses

At the core of this paper is an attempt to understand how the downturn in US housing prices beginning in late 2006 spread quickly to cause widespread economic devastation in the US and mainly Western European countries. Our purpose is not to explain the rise and fall of the housing market in the US but to treat that event as the catalyst for bank crises in different countries and the subsequent global recession. There is now a small mountain of literature on why the US mortgage market got so overheated. Recently, for example, Lounsbury and Hirsch (2010) have collected two volumes of papers that consider various aspects of that crisis in the US from a sociological perspective. Less clear is how the effects of the collapse of the US housing market were transmitted other banking systems and other countries' economies.

There are literatures that attempt to explain how financial crises spread across countries in economics, sociology, political science, and geography. There is actually quite a bit of agreement across disciplines on the mechanisms by which such contagion is possible. Economists have generally focused on identifying explanatory factors predicting incidents of financial contagion, while sociologists, political scientists, and geographers have tended to study the evolution of global finance and financial instruments. But scholars on all sides agree that fundamental conditions in each country make them more or less susceptible to economic crises. They also agree that the international integration of financial markets plays a role in creating more direct and possibly consequential linkages that can transmit crises from one country to another.

Financial contagion in international economics

In the economics literature, the word "contagion" is often used to describe how crises in one country can spread to other countries (Forbes and Rigobon, 2001; Claessens, Dornbusch, and

Park, 2001; for some formal modeling, see Allen and Gale, 2007). However this term is used in at least three different ways to describe the mechanisms by which economic problems in one society can move to other societies. First, the fate of different countries can be closely linked simply by having similar underlying structures to their economy. Hence when something happens in one economy it quickly occurs in others with similar characteristics because of common fundamentals, rather than any mechanism of transmission. Second, financial crises may spread via links between countries' economies. Countries dependent on trade or remittances may experience spillover effects when their trading partners experience adverse economic conditions. Finally, contagion may occur through the actions of financial intermediaries. In the context of financial crises, financial investors may perceive the risks in one society as high relative to others and therefore they shift their investment strategies by moving funds from one place to another in response to extreme uncertainty. Here, the principal mechanism is that investors disinvest in the local stock, bond, or property markets in order to reinvest in markets where there is less risk. This last form of contagion is more rapid and difficult to predict than the other two, and is closest to our common sense understanding of the term. Each contagion mechanism suggests a different set of factors that might explain the spread of the crisis that began in 2007.

Structural factors: There are two main underlying structural factors that economists have identified as exposing countries to the risk of this particular crisis. The first is deregulation in the financial sector. Economists have generally thought that the financial deregulations of the past 30 years have produced a wider availability of credit for all kinds of borrowers, helped create jobs, and by implication, economic growth. But some have warned that financial deregulation is a two edged sword. Allowing banks to enter into many markets potentially encourages them to take more risks (Schiller, 2003; Minsky, 2008; Nesvetailova, 2011). In the context of the current crisis, some have argued that deregulation allowed banks to take more risks and left them unprepared to take on the challenges of the downturn (Johnson and Kwan, 2009; Kaufman, 2009). This implies that in countries with higher levels of deregulation, we should observe more banking crises and a deeper recession.

> Hypothesis 1: Countries with recent financial deregulation were more susceptible to bank crises and recession because of higher levels of risk and indebtedness in those societies.

The second and most important structural factor that economists have focused on is the housing bubble itself (Reinhart and Rogoff, 2008, 2009). The basic argument is that the financial crisis was caused by house prices rising too quickly. This created a speculative bubble that fed on itself. In this version of the story, as the bubble grew, banks had a booming business loaning as much money to as many people as possible. Borrowers in the housing markets where prices were rising dramatically took out ever larger loans. Many borrowers took out exotic loans that put them in the position of having to re-finance every two or three years or face steadily increasing house payments. They paid for refinancing out of price increases in the underlying value of the house (Davis, 2009). When housing price appreciation started to slow down, this created a wave of defaults on loans. These defaults affected the entire banking structure of the mortgage market from loan originators, to mortgage banks, commercial banks, and investment banks, and other institutional investors. Based on this perspective, we would expect that countries that shared in the rapid appreciation of housing prices would be more susceptible to a bank crisis and the resulting recession.

> Hypothesis 2: Countries that experienced housing price increases between 2000 and 2006 were more at risk of both a bank crisis and a recession because of their exposure to defaults when those prices turned down.

Trade linkages: In economists' discussion of contagion through direct linkages between economies, the dependence of a country on exports for economic growth is commonly seen as the most important factor. One of the main ways in which countries can experience economic downturn is through a slowdown in economic activity of their principle trading partners. If trading partners experience a recession (here induced by the housing bubble bursting followed by a systemic banking crisis), then they will simply import less. To the degree that any given economy is more dependent on export partners for growth, they are likely to suffer a recession themselves. So the most likely countries to be affected by economic recession are those that are highly dependent on exports. One could also argue that a high level of trade with the US would trigger a bank crisis or a recession as well. Given that the US economy entered a steep recession, it follows that countries with lots of exports to the US would experience an economic slowdown.

> Hypothesis 3: Countries with large amounts of exports and exports to the US in particular found themselves more likely to have a recession because as the US economy turned down, their economies turned down as well.

Investor panics: Finally, true contagion may involve true panicked investors punishing countries that exhibit neither similar underlying conditions, nor particularly strong connections, nor higher forms of risk. Not surprisingly, most economists believe that most of the time, contagion is rational, i.e. motivated by actors who experience or surmise similarities in underlying conditions or riskiness (see the reviews by Moser, 2003; Forbes, 2004; Reinhart and Rogoff, 2008, pp. 240–7). Wherever investors in financial markets worry about the ability of a given country to continue to avoid a banking crisis or a recession, the dependence of a country on external creditors will be a crucial factor. One of the main measures of the vulnerability of a particular economy to such crises is the current account deficit (measured as the gap between a country's imports and exports). A second measure of that vulnerability is whether or not a government is running a large and unsustainable government debt. Countries that are running a high current account deficit or have governments that are deep in debt may not be able to raise sufficient funds to keep that debt funded. If debts cannot continue to be paid, then defaults will happen. Defaults on government bonds, commercial paper, and other loans will weaken a national banking system and may even cause a systemic banking crisis. Such a crisis will also precipitate a recession. Investors who are worried that a given country will not be able to continue to service its debts, will liquidate their holdings and flee to what they view as safer investments. It was this kind of contagion that some have argued caused the Asian financial crisis of the late 1990s (Claessens *et al.*, 2004; Halliday and Carruthers, 2009).

> Hypothesis 4: Countries that were running a large budget public debts or current account deficit were more susceptible to financial crisis as investors sold assets to buy safer assets. These deficits thus led to both a financial crisis and a recession as investors sold assets to buy safer assets, raising borrowing costs dramatically and making loans less available.

Sociological and political economy perspectives on financial crisis

Scholars in political science, sociology, and geography have focused less on the factors predicting financial crises and more on how global finance has changed and evolved since the mid-1970s (Block, 1978; Helleiner, 1994; Frieden, 1991; Strange, 1996; Cerny, 1994; Epstein, 2006;

Harvey, 2010; Arrighi, 1994; Montgomerie, 2008). From the perspective of international political economy, the American government in the 1970s gave up on a more coordinated approach to global finance as indexed by the Bretton Woods agreement (Block, 1978). Instead, they encouraged the deregulation of worldwide financial markets and the use of market mechanisms to determine exchange rates and the allocation of capital in general. This American-led transformation of the global financial system dramatically increased the size of such markets and the cross border trade of financial products of all kinds (Montgomerie, 2008; Krippner, 2011). It has also spurred the development of new techniques for converting investments into standardized, apparently reliable financial products (Carruthers and Stinchcombe, 1999; Leyshon and Thrift, 2007).

Over the past 30 years, scholars have amply documented how financial markets, financial motives, financial institutions, and financial elites in the operation of the economy and its governing institutions have become increasingly important at the national and international level (see the papers in Epstein, 2006 and Ertürk et al., 2008). Harvey (2010) has argued that the growth of financial integration in the world economy reflects the fact that after the 1970s, investors in the richest countries could not find good and safe investments in their own countries. As advanced economies matured, the ability to make high returns by investing in domestic manufacturing or new services were limited. This pushed investors to look elsewhere for both riskier forms of investment with higher returns, including currency, credit, and asset markets. Put another way, the breakdown of highly regulated international finance led to a set of new opportunities that allowed financial investors to seek out higher returns in other places. The result was a dramatic expansion of financial flows between rich and poor countries.

In this environment, money also flowed into new activities in domestic economies in advanced industrial countries. For those interested in political economy, the argument was that the "Fordist" form of production had given way to a new set of ways to organize capitalism, what came to be called "financialization" (Boyer, 2000). Sociologists have shown that in the US, an emphasis on financial market and concepts, such as "shareholder value conception of the firm," came to restructure the relationships between boards of directors, top level managers, and financial markets (Davis and Stout, 1992; Davis, 2009; Useem, 1996: Fligstein, 2001; Zorn et al., 2004). Krippner (2011) has shown that the financial sector of the economy increased its prominence by increasing its share of profits over this period. It also pushed managers of nonfinancial firms to increase their use of financial tools to produce profits.

This literature has often viewed what goes on in these markets as speculative and not very economically productive (Schiller, 2003; Lipuma and Lee, 2004; Blackburn, 2006; Bookstaber, 2007). Strange goes so far as to call worldwide financial markets "casino capitalism" implying that they serve no useful economic or political function (Strange, 1998). Schwartz (2009) and Schwartz and Seabrooke (2008) have recently applied the perspective of comparative political economy to housing provision and similarly stress the dangers of speculation concomitant with the liberalization of mortgage markets. While some of these judgments differ from economists' views that mostly see these linkages as a good thing, this literature points to a similar set of factors at the root of financial crises. These authors mostly agree that policies which deregulate the financial sector, create inflation, encourage high indebtedness and current account deficits, and favor consumption over production particularly in the consumption of housing, are likely to result in an increased risk of either a domestic debt crisis or financial investors removing their capital from a particular country, potentially resulting in a downward spiral whereby a banking crisis ensues and the economy tips into recession. Thus, their predictions as to the potential causes of this financial crisis are in line with those in the economics literature (i.e. Hypotheses 1–4).

The sociology of markets and the sociology of finance

Several alternative hypotheses can be derived by drawing together other elements of the sociology of markets and the sociology of finance. Our basic argument is that there emerged a global market for financial instruments linked to US housing prices where banks came to interact with one another and use similar market strategies in order to make money. After 2001 the market for American mortgage-backed securities and collateralized debt obligations (hereafter, CDOs) became populated by not just American banks, but also the developed world's largest banks. Moreover, not only did they come to hold these instruments, but foreign banks used the same tactic as the American banks to fund their purchases of mortgage-backed securities and CDOs. This involved borrowing money in the asset-backed-commercial-paper market, where credit was cheap and short-term, in order to purchase these products, which were long-term investments. As a result, when the market turned down for the American banks, it also turned down for the foreign banks. Because foreign banks were part and parcel of the American market for mortgage-backed securities and CDOs, the financial crisis spread directly to the countries where they were headquartered, and they suffered the same fate as their American counterparts.

The sociology of markets and the sociology of finance both help to unpack this argument. The sociology of markets begins with the idea that a market is made up of a set of players who observe one another and then position themselves in the market in a role structure (White, 2004; Fligstein, 2001). Fligstein argues that it follows from this definition that for a market to be global, that market must contain participants from countries around the world who form a field where they watch one another and are organized around a recognizable set of rules and strategies (Fligstein, 2001, p. 224). Thus if the mortgage-backed-security and CDO markets were truly global markets, then we would expect foreign banks to be heavily present in those markets. In order to understand why foreign banks might have decided to enter the US mortgage-backed-security and CDO markets, it is necessary to consider the sociology of finance. Here we use that literature to suggest how to understand the role of the products that undergird this aspect of the globalization of finance.

Securitization, one of the core strategies in finance, emerged in the US for the first time in 1970 when the American government issued the first mortgage-backed-security (Fligstein and Goldstein, 2010, p. 37).[1] The US mortgage market remained heavily dependent on the government which orchestrated the production of mortgage-backed securities through the so-called government sponsored enterprises, otherwise known as Fannie Mae and Freddie Mac (Carruthers and Stinchcombe, 1999). Carruthers and Stinchcombe (1999) provide a lucid discussion of how mortgages, which are contracts made with individuals who live in different places and have differing abilities to pay back their mortgages, can be turned into standard products like bonds. They argue that turning mortgages into mortgage-backed securities and using bond ratings to describe their riskiness takes messy individual mortgages and turns them into standard products whose riskiness and return can be evaluated "objectively." These products then can be easily bought and sold without buyers having knowledge of individual borrowers thus allowing a large and liquid market in mortgages (Carruthers and Stinchcombe, 1999). It is not just mortgages that can be securitized. Securitization allowed potentially nearly any kind of asset capable of generating revenue to be converted into a standardized financial product with an expected rate of return and risk. By the mid-1980s, the ability to create the tools to engage in securitization were well known in the mortgage market and had spread to credit cards, new car loans, manufactured housing, and industrial loans.

Securitization strategies and products quickly spread across the world. Leyshon and Thrift (2007) view the securitization of assets as one of the key financial innovations underlying the integration of global finance. Banks in most of the advanced industrial countries used securitization to raise money to buy assets, to create securities based on those assets, and to both hold onto those securities and sell those securities to others. Markets for securitized products are amongst the largest financial investments worldwide. ABA Alert.com reported that in 2010, there were over $93.5 trillion in asset-backed securities worldwide.

Aalbers (2008, 2009) argues that the US mortgage market played an important role in the expansion of this form of international finance. US mortgage-backed securities and related financial products became a huge source of investment for banks around the world particularly after 2000.[2] In the period 2000–06, interest rates were low in many countries and therefore investors got low returns for holding government bonds. What they were seeking out was higher return investments that were relatively low risk. What they found was products based on American mortgages.

The main reason these investments were so consequential is because they were quite large and profitable. The mortgage origination market in the US fluctuated between $2–4 trillion a year from 2001 to 2007. About 90 percent of these mortgages were being packaged into securities. This meant there was a tremendous amount of mortgage-backed securities for sale. In 2003, the American banks that were involved in these markets which comprised about 9 percent of GDP and 7 percent of employment in the economy were producing 40 percent of the profits in the economy (Krippner, 2011). If foreign banks saw this opportunity as the sociology of markets suggests they would, then we would expect them to emulate the tactics of American banks in order to try to make such outsized profits for themselves.

The sociology of markets pushes us to ask the question about how banks were making money in these markets. Many banks (especially American banks), were making fees off of originating mortgages and packaging mortgages into securities and selling them. But the bulk of the money they were making came from their holding onto the financial products they were producing. Gorton (2010) and Brunnermeier (2009) document that American banks were making money by borrowing money on short-term loans to buy these securities. Acharya et al. (2013) show that the main place that this money was borrowed was the part of the interbank loan market known as the asset-backed-commercial-paper market.

The asset-backed-commercial-paper market has a long history (Stigum (1989) tells this story). The market was originally created by the Federal Reserve in 1914 in order to provide a market so that banks could borrow or lend money on a very short-term basis (usually 1–90 days) that was backed by collateral. For much of the history of the market, government bonds were the form of collateral that was most frequently put up as assets. The original purpose of the market was to aid exporters who might have to wait for their goods to arrive overseas before payment arrived. They would borrow short term to cover their expenses until payment arrived. But over time, both banks and other large nonfinancial corporations saw the advantage of being able to borrow money to fund their short-term needs as well as to lend money that they did not immediately need. Acharya et al. (2013), Gorton and Metrick (2009) and Adrian et al. (2011) show that during the early 2000s, the market for asset-backed commercial paper became dominated by borrowing money to buy mortgage-backed securities and CDOs. Between 2003 and 2006, for example, Acharya et al. (2013) show that something like 75 percent of the $1.4 trillion asset-backed-commercial-paper market was issued to buy mortgage-backed securities and CDOs. Gorton (2010) describes these investments as "borrowing short to buy long."

The market for mortgage-backed securities and CDOs and the strategy of "borrowing short to buy long" was not just for US banks and financial firms. We hypothesize that foreign banks were drawn into this market and they formed a huge part of it between 2003 and 2007. They recognized that American banks were making record profits by buying "AAA" rated mortgage-backed securities and CDOs with borrowed money. Beginning in 2003, they entered the market with a vengeance. We argue that by 2007, the market for US mortgage-backed securities and CDOs was a global market. It contained players from many countries around the world who held substantial shares of mortgage-backed securities and CDOs and purchased those products by borrowing money in the asset-backed-commercial-paper market. Its main players, both US and foreign banks were pursuing the same strategy: use asset-backed commercial paper to buy mortgage-backed securities and CDOs.

> Hypothesis 5: After 2001, the US mortgage-backed-security and asset-backed-commercial-paper markets witnessed a large influx of foreign banks, particularly those in Western Europe thereby creating a global market for American mortgage-backed-security and the use of asset-backed commercial paper to fund those purchases.

This global market (most of the buying and selling of the products in this market was done in New York and London) was directly connected to the fortunes of the US mortgage market and housing prices. When US housing prices stopped rising and foreclosures begin to occur, many foreign banks found themselves facing the same kind of liquidity crises as American banks. The money they were borrowing short-term came due and many of these banks were unable to find funding for their mortgage-backed securities and CDO holdings. There was little market to buy these bonds as their value was unknown. This proved to be a big problem when banks found themselves in the summer of 2008 with large amounts of mortgage-backed securities that were losing value and had to quickly raise funds to cover their borrowings. It was this crisis that spread across US banks, but also to the financial investors around the world who were also key players in this now global market. To the degree that banks and investors in many countries had purchased such securities, the banking systems in those countries plunged into a systemic banking crisis. That crisis brought that country's economy into recession.

> Hypothesis 6: Countries where banks had large holdings of US mortgage-backed securities and asset-backed commercial paper were more likely to experience a bank crisis because when the underlying value of the mortgage-backed securities began to drop these losses were transmitted through the banking system vie these financial instruments. The crisis made credit difficult to come by in those countries and recession followed.

Who held US mortgage-backed securities?

In this section, we consider what we know about the foreign ownership of US mortgage-backed securities in the period before the crash.[3] There is a dramatic increase in foreign purchase of mortgage-backed securities from 2001 to 2008. Most of the purchases were by banks and investors in the most advanced industrial countries. We also demonstrate that many of these banks were heavily involved in the asset-backed-commercial-paper market. In essence, we show that Hypothesis 5 is correct. We then turn to multivariate analysis to test the various hypotheses about the causes of bank crises and recession across countries.

Figure 21.1 presents data on the largest holders of US mortgage-backed securities from 2001 to 2008. This data was collected by Inside Mortgage Finance (2009), a company that specializes in gathering data on the US mortgage industry. We can see from the graph that during the real estate bubble, large investors increased their holdings of American mortgage-backed securities dramatically. US commercial banks increased their holdings from about $700 billion to almost $1.1 trillion, an increase of over 50 percent. Mutual fund holding more than doubled from about $425 billion to almost $850 billion. But the category that showed the most dramatic increase was foreign holdings of mortgage-backed securities. Holdings grew from about $200 billion to over $1.2 trillion at the peak. In the space of five years, foreigners increased their holdings of US

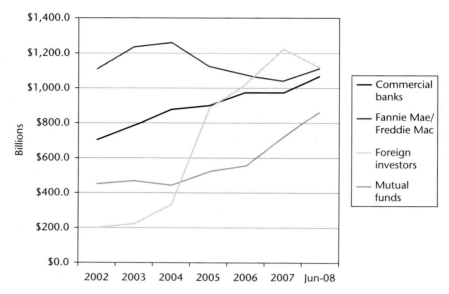

Figure 21.1 Mortgage-related security holdings of four largest investor types
Source: Inside Mortgage Finance (2009).

mortgage-backed securities by $1 trillion, an increase of nearly 600 percent. This is direct evidence that at during the most dramatic growth in the real estate bubble, the main purchasers of mortgage-backed securities, particularly those based on subprime mortgages, were foreign buyers. This figure shows the strong linkage between world financial markets and the American mortgage-backed-security market. This confirms our argument that foreign holders became big players in the market for mortgage-backed securities.

The Inside Mortgage Finance data does not allow one to decompose the holders of those bonds by country. The US Treasury, however, gathers this data on a yearly basis (2007, table 11, p. 15, table 24, pp. 51–5). Table 21.1 provides evidence on the ten largest holders of mortgage-backed securities in 2007. The ten countries who were the largest holders of American mortgage-backed securities in 2008 were the United Kingdom, Belgium, Ireland, Japan, Germany, Iceland, the Netherlands Norway, Switzerland, and France. All of the largest holders of American mortgage-backed securities were advanced industrial societies. Unfortunately, neither Inside Mortgage Finance nor the US Treasury collects information about individual holders of US securities.

There are more indirect ways to figure out who the foreign holders of American mortgage-backed securities were. During the financial crisis the Federal Reserve Bank bought vast amounts of government sponsored enterprise mortgage-backed securities as part of their effort to stabilize the financial markets. The Federal Reserve bought about $1.25 trillion worth of these securities from 14 banks. Bank of America, Citigroup, Goldman Saks, J.P. Morgan, Merrill Lynch, and Morgan Stanley sold about $600 billion to the Federal Reserve in 2008–09. Barclays (UK), BNP Paribas (France), Credit Suisse (Switzerland), Deutsche Bank (Germany), Mizoho (Japan), Normura (Japan), RBS (UK), and UBS (Switzerland) sold almost $625 billion to the Federal Reserve during the same period. This list of banks includes some of the largest banks in the world. Again, of the foreign banks, all were in advanced industrial countries and most were in Europe.

A very similar pattern is apparent in the market for asset backed commercial paper. Table 21.1 also contains information on the 10 largest sponsors of asset-backed commercial paper in January

Table 21.1 Foreign countries with the highest amount of mortgage-backed securities (MBS)/GDP, 2006

Highest MBS/GDP	Highest asset-backed commerical paper (ABCP)/GDP
Ireland	Netherlands
Belgium	Belgium
France	Germany
Germany	United Kingdom
Iceland	France
Netherlands	Canada
Norway	Switzerland
Switzerland	Japan
United Kingdom	Denmark
Japan	Spain

Source: US Treasury Department (2007) and countries with highest amount of ABCP/GDP, Acharya et al. (2013).

of 2007. These include the Netherlands, Belgium, Germany, United Kingdom, France, Canada, Switzerland, Japan, Denmark, and Spain. We note that this list overlaps with the list on mortgage-backed securities for seven of the ten countries. This implies that not all buyers of mortgage-backed securities were borrowing short-term using asset-backed commercial paper and vice versa. Acharya et al. (2013) show that asset-backed commercial paper was used to buy other financial products, particularly CDOs and other derivatives for which aggregate data does not exist. This suggests that the decline in value of US mortgage-backed securities and the liquidity crisis in the short-term funding market are two overlapping but potentially distinct mechanisms by which the shock of the decline in the US mortgage market was transmitted to foreign banks.

We have some information on the identity of the largest players in the asset-backed-commercial-paper market. Table 21.2 presents the 20 largest foreign players in that market and the 8 largest US players. The foreign list confirms that many of the world's largest banks were substantially involved in the asset-backed-commercial-paper market. All of these banks with the exception of Mitsubishi and the Royal Bank of Canada were either substantially reorganized or went bankrupt during the crisis. On the US list, all of the banks were either bailed out by the government or went bankrupt. We note that both Bear Stearns and Lehman Brothers are on the list. Lehman Brothers failure is seen by most observers as the event that caused the crisis to spike (Swedberg, 2010). Here too the Federal Reserve also stepped in to provide emergency support to foreign banks. Beginning in January 2008 the Federal Reserve expanded its short-term loan activities for banks to help them through a "liquidity crisis." During the period 2008–09, the Federal Reserve lent money to 438 banks of which 156 were branches of foreign owned banks. Most of the banks (138) were branches of European banks.

It is clear that the largest banks in the world financial system became players in the American mortgage-backed-securities market during the peak of the housing bubble from 2001 to 2007. They increased their holdings 600 percent in a six-year period and came to own almost $1.2 trillion in American mortgage-backed securities. The bulk of these banks were located in Europe and Japan. It is also clear that many of these banks were funding their purchases of mortgage-backed securities by using the asset-backed-commercial-paper market. US mortgage-backed securities were huge investment vehicles for the largest banks and investors in the developed world. The evidence supports Hypothesis 5 that during this period, the market for these securities became global. Now we turn to considering whether or not their presence on the balance sheets on banks and investors around the world caused bank crises and recessions.

Table 21.2 Largest sponsors of ABCP conduits with country of origin

Foreign	US
ABN Amro (Netherlands)	Citigroup
HBOS (United Kingdom)	Bank of America
HSBC (UK and Hong Kong)	JP Morgan Chase
Deutsche Bank (Germany)	Bear Stearns
Societe Generale (France)	GMAC
Barclays (United Kingdom)	State Street Corporation
Mitsubishi (Japan)	Lehman Brothers
Rabobank (Netherlands)	Countrywide Financial
Westdeutsche Landesbank (Germany)	
ING Groep (Netherlands)	
Dresdner Bank (Germany)	
Fortis (Belgium)	
Bayerische Landesbank (Germany)	
Credit Agriciole (France)	
Lloyds Banking Group (United Kingdom)	
Hypo Real Esate (Germany)	
Royal Bank of Canada (Canada)	
BNP Paribas (France)	
KBC Group (Belgium)	
Bayerische Hypo-und Vereinsbank (Germany)	

Source: Acharya et al., 2013.

Data and methods

It is useful to begin our discussion of our data and methods by discussing our research design. Figure 21.2 portrays our basic underlying model of the process. Our argument has two elements. First, we attempt to predict whether or not a country had a systemic banking crisis. Our argument is that two sorts of underlying conditions might predict why this has occurred. There may be similar regulatory or economic processes in each country that affect the likelihood of a systemic banking crisis, including structural factors, trade linkages and debt conditions that may lead to investor panics. We have also argued that mortgage-backed-securities holdings and the use of asset-backed commercial paper to fund those securities in a country may predict such a crisis. The second element of our argument is to examine how these underlying conditions predicted the depth of a recession in any given country. Here, we use the underlying conditions in the country plus a variable indexing whether or not a country had a systemic banking crisis.

There are several serious data problems in trying to use this model. First, much of our theorizing has been about the conditions under which the crisis would spread. This implies a model whereby we are able to predict the time ordering of banking crises and entry into recession as the crisis spreads from one country to another. Unfortunately, the systemic banking crises and the recession occurred very close in time and it is difficult to untangle exactly the order in which countries entered into each of them sequentially. Macroeconomic data is rarely available at any finer temporal resolution than the quarter, and at that level only for the wealthiest and most developed countries. This problem is compounded by the fact that any date selected for declaring a systemic banking crisis will be somewhat arbitrary. In the US, for example, does the crisis begin

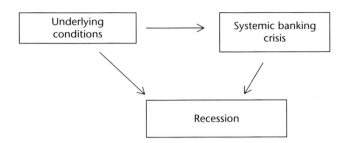

Figure 21.2 Model of process of bank crises and recession

with the collapse of Bear Stearns in the spring of 2008, the government takeover of Fannie Mae and Freddie Mac in September 2008, the collapse of Lehman Brothers a week later, the passage of the Troubled Asset Relief Program (TARP) by the Congress in October 2008, or the government forcing banks to be reorganized and accept TARP money in December 2008? The official definition of a recession as two straight quarters of GDP decline makes it hard to exactly date the beginning of a recession. These events moved very fast and in the space of less than a year many countries experienced both a systemic banking crisis and the onset of a recession.

Thus, we are not able to study how the crisis moved from one country to another directly and have to pursue another strategy in order to assess which of these conditions led to a banking crisis. Much of the economics literature reviewed above argues that the risks of financial contagion can best be explained in terms of similarities and differences in the fundamental conditions of different countries' economies. Therefore, we treat our variables as initial conditions that might be useful to predict whether or not a country had a systemic banking crisis or a recession. This approach is standard in macroeconomics, and implies a cross-sectional data design of events that did or did not occur in a particular time frame. For the sake of avoiding problems of endogeneity in constructing our model of "causation," all of our independent variables refer to measurements that occurred before 2007, the earliest one might date as the beginning of the crisis.

The inclusion of banking crises in our model as an explanatory factor for the onset of recession creates a similar problem. Both the systemic banking crises and countries' entry into recession unfolded over the same time period from 2008 to 2009, meaning that our measure of banking crisis may be an effect of the crisis not its cause. In order to produce the cleanest possible model, we use as a measure of economic performance, the change in GDP in 2009. In coding which countries had banking crises, we chose to focus only on countries where we could clearly identify that the banking crisis had occurred by the end of 2008. This leaves us with a smaller set of cases of banking crises, but gives us a stronger claim that the crisis occurs before the change in GDP. It is a more conservative test of our central hypotheses but also a more compelling test.

Selecting a sample of countries also was difficult. Ideally, we would like to have data on as many countries as we can in order to include as many countries as we can who did and did not have a financial crisis and who did and did not suffer a serious recession. We are highly limited by data availability. We have relatively complete data for 75 countries. These are listed in Table 21.3. They include countries that are both very rich and very poor, and countries from many parts of the world. However, they tend to exclude the very poorest parts of Africa, the Middle East, and Latin America because the legal and institutional infrastructure for collecting the relevant macroeconomic indicators simply does not exist.

One of the biggest problems is missing data on house price appreciation. Using multiple sources, we were still only able to find comparable data on this variable for 44 countries, and these countries were overwhelmingly developed European, North American, or Asian countries with liberalized economies, creating major selection problems. We tried several strategies to deal with this problem, and report three types of models in order to mitigate it. First, we ran models without this variable on the whole sample of 75 cases and models including this variable on the reduced sample of 44 cases. Then, we ran models where we treat the missing data as a variable in the 77 cases and compare it to the results from the 44 cases. We do this first recoding the house price appreciation variable so that it codes the percentage change in house price appreciation from 2000 to 2006 if there is data and is coded "0" if there is no data house price appreciation. Then we created a second variable coded "0" if the data is not present and "1" if it is present. This allows us to examine the effect of having or not having data on whether or not countries are more likely to have a financial crisis. Finally, we estimated models for sample selection and missing data which we do not report here. Models using the Heckman correction for data censoring and Bayesian multiple imputation do not change the substance of the results.

The two dependent variables refer to 2008 and 2009. All of the independent variables refer to conditions that existed in the country in 2006 unless otherwise indicated. Systemic banking crisis is measured with a dichotomous variable coded "1" if there was a systemic banking crisis in 2008 and "0" if there was not such a crisis, following Laeven and Valencia (2010). Laeven and Valencia (2010) use five criteria to determine whether or not a systemic banking crisis has occurred in any given country. These include: (1) banks required extensive injections of

Table 21.3 List of countries in the analysis, by first year negative change in GDP

2008	2009		After 2009 or Never	
Bahamas	Armenia	Lithuania	Albania	South Korea
Denmark	Austria	Macedonia FYR	Argentina	Kyrgyz Republic
Estonia	Belgium	Malaysia	Australia	Mauritius
Ireland	Brazil	Malta	China	Morocco
Italy	Bulgaria	Mexico	Colombia	Panama
Japan	Canada	Netherlands	Dominican Rep.	Peru
Latvia	Chile	Norway	Egypt	Poland
Luxembourg	Costa Rica	Paraguay	Haiti	Sri Lanka
New Zealand	Croatia	Russia	Indonesia	Tunisia
Portugal	Cyprus	Singapore	Israel	Uruguay
Sweden	Czech Rep	Slovakia	Kazakhstan	
	Ecuador	Slovenia		
	El Salvador	South Africa		
	Finland	Spain		
	France	Switzerland		
	Georgia	Thailand		
	Germany	Trinidad/Tobago		
	Greece	Turkey		
	Guyana	Ukraine		
	Hong Kong	United Kingdom		
	Hungary	Venezuela		
	Iceland			

liquidity, (2) banks were required to significantly re-structure their activities, (3) governments engaged in significant asset purchases from banks in order to provide them with liquidity, (4) governments provided significant guarantees on liabilities, and (5) governments nationalized some banks. A systemic banking crisis is said to have occurred if a country meets at least four of these five criteria.

Table 21.4 presents the list of the countries that fit our definition. One can see from the list the predominance of developed countries in general and European countries in particular. We note that the US and Great Britain are both on the list. We also note that Iceland, Ireland, Latvia, and Spain are on the list as well. Less well known is the fact that Germany experienced a systemic banking crisis, and that both France and Switzerland met at least some of the criteria of a banking crisis. Given the events of the past five years, the list suggests a kind of face validity to the measure of systemic banking crisis.

The second dependent variable in the analysis is the percent change in real GDP in 2009. We constructed this measure using real GDP as reported by the Economist Intelligence Unit (2010). This measure can take on both negative and positive values. So, a positive effect of a given independent variable indicates an increase in GDP over the course of the year, while a negative effect of an independent variable indicates a decrease in GDP.

It is also useful to describe the measures of our independent variables. We have created a measure that codes holdings of US non-agency mortgage-backed securities (that is, issued by private lenders and not enjoying guarantees from the US federal government) in each country in 2006 using securities data reported by the US Treasury's International Capital System (2007). Holdings are measured in millions of US dollars and we have standardized this measure by making it a percentage of GDP and logging the result. The importance of scaling for the size of a countries economy is intuitively clear, but we also logged the variable in order to adjust for outliers because small countries that house large banking centers like Bermuda and Luxembourg constituted significant outliers in these data, often with mortgage-backed securities holdings several times the size of GDP. Our measure of asset-backed commercial paper as a percentage of GDP was created in a similar fashion. The source for this data was Acharya et al. (2013).

Table 21.4 Countries that experienced a banking crisis, 2008–09

Systemic Banking Crisis (13 countries)	Borderline Banking Crisis (10 countries)
Austria (late 2009)*	France
Belgium	Greece
Denmark	Hungary
Germany	Kazakhstan
Iceland	Portugal
Ireland	Russia
Latvia	Slovenia
Luxembourg	Spain
Mongolia (late 2009)*	Sweden
Netherlands	Switzerland
Ukraine	
United Kingdom	
United States	

Note: *We treat these cases as non-incidences of systemic banking crises in our models because they did not meet Laeven and Valencia's conditions for a systemic banking crisis before the end of 2008.

Source: Laeven and Valencia (2010).

To obtain a measure of credit market deregulation, we used each country's 2006 Credit Market Freedom Score, from the Fraser Institute's Economic Freedom of the World Index. The score is scaled from one to ten. The higher the score, the more deregulated the country's credit market. This is a score that many scholars who study the effects of financial deregulation on economic growth (e.g. Rose and Spiegel, 2010; Giannone et al., 2010) have found useful as a metric to measure the degree to which societies have taken government regulation and intervention out of their financial sector.

In order to measure the vulnerability of a country to default in the event of an economic downturn, we use a variable measuring the current account balance in 2006 as a percentage of real GDP. The source for this measure was the World Bank's "World Development Indicators" database. We measured trade linkages in terms of export dependence using a measure that reflected exports in 2006 as a percent of real GDP. We also coded up the percentage of exports as a percentage of GDP that were sent to the US in 2006. The source was also the World Bank's Development Indicators.

Our measure of house prices was the percent change in the price of the median residence from 2000 to 2006. To construct this variable we relied primarily on data from the Bank of International Settlements, but supplemented it with information from Claessens et al. (2010) and the European Mortgage Federation (2009). We note that this measure is tricky to interpret because the underlying way in which median house price was determined varied across countries. In compiling housing data, different countries may choose to include or exclude different regions of the country, different types of dwelling, and different vintages of housing stock. In order to deal with this heterogeneity, for each country we chose the maximally inclusive annual measure of median house price available, and computed the percent change in house prices between 2000 and 2006. Therefore this measure is in units of percent change with respect to a baseline of prices in 2000. The means and standard deviations of the variables are in Table 21.5.

We ran two kinds of models. First, we ran a logit model using whether or not a bank crisis occurred during the period 2008. Then, we ran an ordinary least squares regression modeling the percentage change in GDP from 2009. Because our sample is small and the distribution of cases is often quite skewed, we employ robust estimates of the standard errors in all cases. We will discuss the specification of the model in the results section. The correlation coefficients are in Table 21.6.

Results

We begin by considering the causes of systemic banking crises. Table 21.7 presents the results of a logistic regression analysis where the dependent variable is whether or not a country has a systemic banking crisis in 2008. The first column of the table presents results for our sample of 75 countries and the second column adds the variable for house price appreciation. The third column presents the model run only on the 44 cases for which we have data on house price appreciation.

The models provide no support for Hypothesis 1 that credit market deregulation drove the banking crisis. It also provides no support for Hypothesis 2 that countries that experienced housing bubbles were more likely to have a banking crisis than countries that did not experience such house price increases. The housing price appreciation variable's effect on a systemic banking crisis is worth discussing more extensively. This runs counter to many claims in the literature and in the press. But, our result is consistent with the results of other empirical studies.

Table 21.5 Summary statistics

Variable	Obs.	Mean	Std. Dev.	Min	Max
2009 Change in GDP	75	−2.62	4.85	−18.00	8.70
Log 2006 Corp. MBS % GDP	75	0.29	0.64	0	3.98
Log 2006 ABCP % GDP	75	0.21	0.58	0	2.98
Systemic Banking Crisis	75	0.15	0.36	0	1
2006 Credit Market Dereg'n	75	8.55	1.00	5.74	9.98
2006 Current Account % GDP	75	−1.02	10.42	−25.75	39.49
2006 Gov't Debt % GDP	75	47.16	30.02	4.41	191.34
2006 Exports / GDP	75	51.65	38.57	14.30	243.44
2006 % Exports to USA	75	16.75	20.29	0.93	85.97
Housing Price Reported?	75	0.59	0.50	0	1
Real Housing Price App'n '00-'06	44	54.35	55.91	−25.64	228.05

We modeled effect house price appreciation in two different ways. First, for the equation with 75 cases (column 2 in Table 21.5) we created a dummy variable coded "0" if the housing price was not reported and "1" if it was. We then also created a variable equal to the house price appreciation where present and zero where no data was available. This produces a spline function. In column 2 of Table 21.7, one can observe that the change in housing prices has no effect on the 75 cases. But, there is a huge and nearly significant effect such that if a housing price is reported, then the country is likely to have had a systemic banking crisis. When we only include the 44 cases where we have complete data, the results are virtually identical to the results for the 75 cases without the house price variable. Recoding cases of late crises also has no effect on these results.

There is also no support for Hypothesis 3 that countries with large exports or exports to the US experienced crises. Indeed, countries with lots of exports to the US actually were consistently less likely to have a banking crisis than countries with large exports, though the effect is not significant. Finally, government debt and current account deficits (Hypothesis 4) also do not have statistically significant effects. All in all, our results confirm earlier work that the "usual suspects" for causes of the spread of financial crises are simply not factors this time around.

The two strongest predictors of whether or not a country has a systemic banking crisis is the size of US mortgage-backed securities as a percentage of GDP and asset-backed commercial paper as a percentage of GDP. This confirms Hypothesis 6 that the cause of the banking crises around the world was the participation of that country in the US mortgage-backed-security and asset-backed-commercial-paper markets. The fact that both of these variables predict banking crises implies that they exert independent effects on bank crises. Holding lots of mortgage-backed securities that were losing value pushed banks in many countries to the financial brink. But, equally important was the use of short-term asset-backed commercial paper to fund those and similar instruments. Obviously in countries where both of these conditions were present, financial crises were more likely.

Table 21.8 presents the results for the equations predicting GDP change in 2009. The first three columns present specifications that include 75 cases and the last column presents a specification only on the 44 cases with data on the house price appreciation measure. It is useful to review what does and does not predict change in GDP across model specifications and samples.

There is a large statistically significant negative effect of the presence of a banking crisis on change in GDP in both samples. Having a systemic banking crisis in 2008 reduces GDP by 5–7 percent in 2009. This is a very large effect. There are no consistent effects for either the mortgage-backed-security or asset-backed-commercial-paper measures on change in GDP. We

Table 21.6 Correlation matrix

	2009 Change in GDP	Log 2006 Corp. MBS % GDP	Log 2006 ABCP % GDP	Systemic Banking Crisis	2006 Credit Market Dereg'n	2006 Current Account % GDP	2006 Gov't Debt % GDP	2006 Exports/ GDP	2006 % Exports to USA	Real Housing Price App'n '00-'06
2009 Change in GDP	1									
Log 2006 Corp. MBS % GDP	0.101	1								
Log 2006 ABCP % GDP	0.060	0.574	1							
Systemic Banking Crisis	−0.448	0.519	0.446	1						
2006 Credit Market Dereg'n	−0.392	0.039	0.063	0.169	1					
2006 Current Account % GDP	0.422	0.426	0.196	−0.198	−0.195	1				
2006 Gov't Debt % GDP	0.240	0.158	0.219	−0.140	−0.356	0.287	1			
2006 Exports / GDP	−0.049	0.363	−0.079	−0.039	0.201	0.432	−0.039	1		
2006 % Exports to USA	0.282	0.122	0.121	−0.335	−0.099	0.206	0.216	−0.066	1	
Real Housing Price App'n '00-'06	−0.497	−0.169	−0.125	0.197	0.395	−0.453	−0.540	−0.150	−0.158	1

Table 21.7 Logit models of systemic banking crisis

Model	1	2	3
Log 2006 Corp. MBS % GDP	1.766+	2.907*	2.540*
	(0.955)	(1.283)	(1.246)
Log 2006 ABCP % GDP	3.036***	2.240**	2.248**
	(0.883)	(0.717)	(0.696)
2006 Credit Market Dereg'n	−0.649	−1.201	−1.131
	(0.808)	(1.079)	(1.035)
2006 Current Account % GDP	−0.113	−0.128	−0.129
	(0.086)	(0.099)	(0.097)
2006 Gov't Debt % GDP	−0.056+	−0.039	−0.035
	(0.033)	(0.026)	(0.025)
2006 Exports / GDP	0.009	−0.003	−0.004
	(0.013)	(0.015)	(0.017)
2006 % Exports to USA	−0.081	−0.065	−0.041
	(0.065)	(0.052)	(0.038)
Real Housing Price (no misses)		0.010	
		(0.012)	
Housing Price Reported?		4.494+	
		(2.406)	
Real Housing Price App'n '00-'06			0.009
			(0.011)
Constant	4.011	3.877	7.629
	(6.900)	(8.072)	(8.605)
N	75	75	44
Ll	−13.243	−10.830	−10.640
Chi-square	29.891	33.311	24.679
d.f.	7	9	8

Notes: Robust standard errors are in parentheses.

† $p < 0.1$; * $p < 0.05$; ** $p < 0.01$; *** $p < 0.001$.

note that in two of the models (the ones for 75 countries that includes the measure for systemic banking crisis), there is a positive effect of mortgage-backed securities as a percentage of GDP. This effect does not appear in the sample restricted to the 44 cases. Our interpretation of these results is that the effect of mortgage-backed securities and asset-backed commercial paper on economic growth goes entirely through the presence or absence of a systemic banking crisis. This exposure caused larger economic problems by precipitating a systemic banking crisis and that crisis triggered a substantial drop in GDP. Taken together, these results support our sociological version of the story which focuses on the particular way in which mortgage-backed securities became implicated in the global financial system.

There is some evidence for effects of some of the other variables on change in GDP. Countries with high levels of credit market deregulation experience greater decreases in GDP (although this effect disappears in the regression with 44 cases) implying that at least half of Hypothesis 1 is true. One interpretation of this result is that once the banking crisis got going and the economy turned down, countries with highly deregulated credit markets found that years of easy lending had left borrowers vulnerable in the economic downturn. In this case, the banking crisis caused by mortgage-backed securities and asset-backed commercial paper precipitated a cascading economic decline. Similarly, we also found a nearly significant effect of a local housing bubble on negative

Table 21.8 OLS models of 2009 change in GDP

Model	1	2	3	4
Log 2006 Corp. MBS % GDP	0.424	1.657*	1.212+	1.525
	(0.624)	(0.650)	(0.690)	(1.194)
Log 2006 ABCP % GDP	−0.603	1.249	1.278+	0.878
	(0.619)	(0.794)	(0.713)	(0.829)
Systemic Banking Crisis		−6.567**	−5.432**	−4.898*
		(2.244)	(2.005)	(2.240)
2006 Credit Market Dereg'n	−1.879***	−2.067***	−1.593*	−1.498
	(0.532)	(0.524)	(0.665)	(1.139)
2006 Current Account % GDP	0.062	0.017	0.014	0.086
	(0.055)	(0.050)	(0.046)	(0.081)
2006 Gov't Debt % GDP	0.022	0.006	0.001	−0.028
	(0.024)	(0.023)	(0.023)	(0.023)
2006 Exports / GDP	−0.006	−0.003	−0.005	−0.021
	(0.012)	(0.012)	(0.012)	(0.014)
2006 % Exports to USA	0.027	0.018	0.006	0.042
	(0.021)	(0.021)	(0.024)	(0.036)
Real Housing Price (no misses)			−0.020	
			(0.013)	
Housing Price Reported?			−0.686	
			(1.269)	
Real Housing Price App'n '00-'06				−0.026+
				(0.014)
Constant	12.312*	14.777**	12.284*	12.951
	(5.040)	(5.063)	(5.817)	(10.569)
N	75	75	75	44
LI	−211.924	−205.546	−202.872	−115.526
R-square	0.281	0.393	0.435	0.499
d.f.	7	8	10	9

Notes: Robust standard errors are in parentheses.

† $p < 0.1$; * $p < 0.05$; ** $p < 0.01$; *** $p < 0.001$.

GDP growth confirming half of Hypothesis 2, but only in the sample with 44 cases. To the degree that these countries had a housing bubble, their economies were more vulnerable to economic turndown. We interpret this to imply that once the banks went into crisis, lending dried up and the economic growth that had been propelled by house price increases dried up.

Taken all together, our multivariate models provide strong evidence that the banking crises experienced in Western Europe and the US were mainly caused by high levels of participation in the mortgage-backed-security and asset-backed-commercial-paper markets. The bank crises then set off economic downturns. These crises were made worse in countries where credit standards were the most lax and housing prices had increased the most. These results bring together the two stories of the economic crisis in an interesting way (as suggested by Aalbers, 2009). Many countries followed the US lead and deregulated credit markets to stimulate demand in the 2000s. This also led to housing bubbles in some places. What caused the downturn was bank participation in the global market for American mortgage-backed securities. The purchase of those products plus their funding with asset-backed commercial paper was the tinder that started the downturn. When American house prices stopped going up, mortgage-backed securities started heading down. To the degree that these purchases were funded by asset-backed commercial paper, banks in these markets entered a crisis. The bank crisis caused a local recession that was made worse in countries that had emulated America's lax credit system and had produced a housing bubble.

Conclusions

We began by pointing out that the "Great Recession" originated in the US and spread to the more industrialized world. Our empirical results offer a consistent story as to how this worked. The main path to the crisis was through the American housing market. The housing price bubble in the US fueled the production of mortgage-backed securities. These securities were extensively sold and marketed around the world to banks and investors in the richest countries who funded much of these purchases with asset-backed commercial paper. During the run up in the US housing market from 2001 to 2007, foreign investors increased their holdings of these securities by $1 trillion. As those securities began to lose their value in 2007 and 2008, banks in the US and in foreign countries began to fail. It was these failures which spurred systemic banking crises in many countries around the world. These crises forced governments in the rich world to intervene aggressively into their banking systems to stabilize them. But, the damage was so extensive that a deep recession followed. This recession was made worse in countries that had more deregulated systems of finance and had experienced their own housing bubbles. Put colloquially, it was the global character of the American mortgage-backed-security market which sucker punched the world economy and brought it to its knees in the richest countries.

Some caveats are in order. First, we acknowledge that just because in this case the "normal" sort of variables that help explain the spread of these crises do not work, does not mean that in some future crisis they will work. Second, in the years since the financial crisis began in 2008, the market for non-agency American mortgage-backed securities dropped dramatically and the subprime market virtually has disappeared (Inside Mortgage Finance, 2009). The use of asset-backed commercial paper to fund these securities has also disappeared as the contracts supporting those purchases expired and were not renewed (Acharya et al., 2013). From the point of view of the sociology of markets, this particular international financial market no longer exists as most of the big players went bankrupt, were reorganized, or exited the market. Those financial institutions that continue to exist have mainly been the so-called universal banks that had other kinds of businesses to fall back on. This implies that whatever the next financial crisis is, it will not emanate from this particular market and this strategic use of financial instruments.

Our study raises a number of provocative issues for subsequent research. One of the most fascinating issues to explore is the link between the demand for mortgage-backed securities and their funding by asset-backed commercial paper and the housing bubble in the US. In the low interest rate environment of the 2000s, investors in the US and abroad were looking for safe investments that were returning more than 1–2 percent. American mortgage-backed securities became the vehicle that made a lot of sense for those investors. But in 2003, the market for conventional mortgages to package into securities began to dry up. Beginning in 2004, the subprime market began to replace the prime market as the main source of mortgages to be securitized (Fligstein and Goldstein, 2010). Investors generally liked subprime mortgages because they could attain high credit ratings and they tended to have higher returns. This implies that the demand for mortgage-backed securities appears to have outstripped the supply of mortgages that could be used to construct them.

Future research should try and explore the links between the supply of mortgages for securities and the demand for those securities. One way to read what happened is that the demand for mortgage-backed securities from American and foreign investors pushed forward the housing bubble in the US In order to find people to take out new loans, banks needed to entice people to take out large loans with unconventional terms. The whole business of selling mortgage-backed securities was obviously a big part of what banks were doing. But in order to keep that business going, they needed a steady supply of those loans. There is certainly prima facie evidence consistent with the bubble being driven at least partially by the high demand for those securities. Gorton (2010), for example, alludes to this argument. This demand was partially being driven by foreign banks that discovered this market and the tactics to buy mortgage-backed securities.

Our study also has implications for the study of financialization, global financial markets, and the sociology of finance more generally. Overall, our results point to the usefulness of using the sociology of markets to make sense of global financial markets. The literature on global financial markets and the sociology of finance did not do a good job of discovering that American mortgage backed securities were so important to the global financial system. Our study suggests that scholars have made two sorts of errors. First, they have focused too broadly on global financial flows. This has caused them to not work to understand what banks and other financial institutions were actually doing in particular markets and the significance of those markets to the overall fragility or stability of a country's financial system. The other error has been to focus too narrowly on the construction of particular financial products. By watching how traders traded currencies, stocks, futures, or derivatives, scholars have missed how those traders were situated in a larger system of banks and a larger set of coherent tactics. So, our study shows that banks buying mortgage-backed securities and CDOs and using asset-backed commercial paper to do so made countries where such banks were located particularly vulnerable to the housing market downturn.

The theoretical pay-off of our study is that it adds a new conceptual tool for studies of global finance and financial instruments. The sociology of markets causes scholars interested in global finance and financial instruments to consider the embedding of those flows and instruments in the underlying structure of the market. This study has demonstrated the utility of extending our empirical work to the financial organizations that make up these markets. Scholars will get a clearer understanding of what is going on by considering who are the players, what are the main tactics, and how people are making money. While a few scholars did recognize that housing was being used as a securitized asset on the world market (i.e. Aalbers, 2008, 2009; Leyshon and Thrift, 2007; Schwartz and Seabrooke, 2008), few of those involved in the literature on financialization, global finance, or the sociology of finance saw the importance of the US housing market in this period. They missed how important the market had become to some of the world's largest banks and how central American housing prices had become to the world financial order.

This implies a new research agenda for scholars interested in the sociology of finance and its role in globalization. These markets should be dissected by the identities of the market participants, their tactics, what is causing either crisis or growth, and most of all, how these markets are connected to the larger financial systems in which they are embedded. There are many facts to be discovered. First, how many of these markets are really global, i.e. contain banks from many countries including those outside of the US and Western Europe? What is the degree to which many of the global financial markets are actually dominated by a small number of participants? Are these the same participants across markets implying that the 30–40 largest banks might be dominating all of these markets? Finally, and perhaps most importantly, how are these markets connected to one another and to particular national market systems?

Hardly anyone saw that American mortgages were the hottest commodity being traded across this system. The next crisis will certainly not be caused by a housing bubble originating in the US, but it will require some of the same conditions: a hugely large market of underlying assets that can be traded as securities, securities that can be rated for risk, and probably by a relatively few number of players who are pursuing very high returns without regards to those risks (following the insights of Carruthers and Stinchcombe (1999) and Leyshon and Thrift (1997)). Dissecting these markets and their dynamics requires delving not just into the flows and the instruments but the social structure of these markets.

Notes

1. Securitization is the process whereby one takes a given asset that generates a cash flow and one sells the rights on that cash flow to an investor in a standardized product that looks like a bond. The technology of securitization can be applied to a wide variety of financial assets. The riskiness of these assets and the likelihood of default can be rated by credit rating agencies. These ratings can then be turned into prices for bonds. The riskier the investment is the higher rate of return. Securities are commonly backed by large packages of individual loans, but may be backed by insurance policies, court settlements, components of other securities, and even more exotic financial products.
2. Aalbers has also argued that the US mortgage market has further encouraged international financial expansion by providing a model for practices around using securitization to fund mortgages adopted by some countries. For the purposes of the analysis presented here, this kind of influence can be seen as an element of wider changes in the fundamental structural conditions of different countries, rather than the financialization of international linkages in the sense they are discussed here.
3. It is quite difficult to get detailed data on the holdings of foreign banks in any of these markets. There is no central reporting of these statistics nor do national governments generally break this data out. This means that we must rely on fragmented sources of evidence or data painstakingly collected by scholars on a deal by deal or bank by bank basis.

References

Aalbers, M. 2008. 'The finalization of home and the mortgage market crisis', *Competition and Change*: 12: 148–66.
Aalbers, M. 2009. 'The sociology and geography of mortgage markets: Reflections on the financial crisis', *International Journal of Urban and Regional Research* 33: 281–90.
Acharya, V., P. Schnabl, and G. Suarez. 2013. 'Securitization without risk transfer', *Journal of Financial Economics* 107: 515–36.
Adrian, T., B. Begalle, A. Copeland, and A. Martin. 2011. 'Repo and securities lending'. Staff Report no. 529, New York Federal Reserve.
Allen, F. and D. Gale. 2007. *Understanding Financial Crises*. Oxford, UK: Oxford University Press.
Arrighi, G. 1994. *The Long 20th Century*. London: Verso.
Barth, James R. 1991. *The Great Savings and Loan Debacle*. Washington, DC: American Enterprise Institute Press.
Blackburn, R. 2006. 'Finance and the fourth dimension', *New Left Review* 39: 39–70.
Block, F. 1978. *The Origins of International Monetary Disorder: A Study of United States International Monetary Policy from World War II to the Present*. Berkeley, CA: University of California Press.
Bookstaber, R. 2007. *A Demon of Our Own: Markets, Hedge Funds, and the Perils of Financial Innovation*. New York: John Wiley.
Boyer, R. 2000. 'Is finance led growth regime an alternative to Fordism?' *Economy and Society* 29: 111–45.
Brunnermeier, M. 2009. 'Deciphering the liquidity and credit crunch 2007–08', *Journal of Economic Perspectives* 23 (1): 77–100.
Bryan, D. and M. Rafferty. 2009. *Capitalism with Derivatives*. New York: Palgrave.
Carruthers, B. and J.C. Kim. 2011. 'The sociology of finance', *Annual Review of Sociology* 37: 239–59.
Carruthers, B. and A. Stinchcombe. 1999. 'The social structure of liquidity: flexibility, markets, and states', *Theory and Society* 28: 253–82.
Cerny, P. 1994. 'Money and finance in the international political economy', *Review of International Political Economy* 1: 591–612.
Claessens, S. and K. Forbes. 2004. 'International financial contagion: The theory, evidence, and policy implications'. Paper presented at the conference 'IMF's Roles in Emerging Market Economies'. November 18–19, 2004, Amsterdam, Netherlands.

Claessens, S., R. Dornbusch, and Y. Park. 2001. 'Contagion: Why crises spread and how they can be stopped', in S. Claessens and K. Forbes (eds) *International Financial Contagion*: 19–41. Boston, MA: Kluwer.

Claessens, S., G. Dell'Aricia, D. Igan, and L. Laeven. 2010. 'Global linkages and global policies', *Economic Policy*: 267–93.

Davis, G. 2009. *Managed By the Markets: How Finance Reshaped America*. New York: Oxford University Press.

Davis, G. and S. Stout. 1992. 'Organization theory and the market for corporate control', *Administrative Science Quarterly* 37: 605–33.

Epstein, G. 2006. *Financialization of the World Economy*. Cheltenham: Edward Elgar.

Ertürk, I., J. Froud, S. Johal, A. Leaver, and K. Williams. 2008. *Financialization at Work*. New York: Routledge.

European Mortgage Federation. 2009. *Hypostat 2008: A Review of Europe's Mortgage and Housing Markets*. Brussels: European Mortgage Federation.

Fligstein, N. 1996. 'Markets as politics: A political-cultural approach to market institutions', *American Sociological Review* 61: 656–73.

Fligstein, N. 2001. *The Architecture of Markets*. Princeton, NJ: Princeton University Press.

Fligstein, N. and A. Goldstein. 2010. 'The anatomy of the mortgage securitization crisis', in M. Lounsbury and P. Hirsch (eds) *Markets on Trial: The Economic Sociology of the US Financial Crisis*: 29–70. Bingham, UK: Emerald Publishing.

Forbes, K. 2004. 'The Asian flus and the Russian virus: The international transmission of crises in firm level data', *Journal of International Economics* 63: 59–92.

Forbes, K. and R. Rigobon. 2001. 'Measuring contagion,' in S. Claessens and K. Forbes (ed.) *International Financial Contagion*: 43–66. Boston, MA: Kluwer.

Frieden, J. 1991. 'Invested interests: The politics of national economic policies in a world of global finance', *International Organization* 45: 425–51.

Giannone, D., M. Lenza, and L. Reichlin. 2010. 'Market freedom and the global recession'. Paper presented at the conference 'Economic Linkages, Spillovers, and Financial Crises' Paris, Paris School of Economics, January 28–29.

Gorton, G. 2010. *Slapped by the Invisible Hand*. New York: Oxford.

Gorton, G. and A. Metrick. 2009. 'Securitized banking and the run on repos', Cambridge, MA: NBER.

Halliday, T. and B. Carruthers. 2009. *Bankrupt: Global Lawmaking and Financial Crisis*. Stanford, CA: Stanford University Press.

Harvey, D. 2010. *The Enigma of Capital*. Oxford, UK: Blackwell.

Helleiner, E. 1994. *States and the Emergence of Global Finance*. Ithaca, NY: Cornell University Press.

Inside Mortgage Finance. 2009. *The Mortgage Market Statistical Annual*.

Johnson, S. and G. Kwan. 2009. *13 Bankers*. New York: Wiley.

Kaufman, H. 2009. *The Road to Financial Reformation: Warnings, Consequences, Reforms*. New York: Wiley.

Keister, L. 2002. 'Financial markets, money, and banking', *Annual Review of Sociology* 28: 39–61.

Knorr Cetina, K. and U. Bruegger. 2004. 'Traders engagement with markets', in A. Amin and N. Thrift (eds) *The Cultural Economy Reader*: 121–44. Oxford, Eng.: Blackwell.

Krippner, G. 2011. *Capitalizing on Crisis*. Cambridge, MA: Harvard University Press.

Laeven, L. and F. Valencia. 2010. 'Resolution of banking crises: The good, the bad, and the ugly', IMF Working Paper 10/146. Washington, DC: International Monetary Fund.

Leyshon, A. and N. Thrift. 1997. *Money/Space: Geographies of Monetary Transformation*. London: Routledge.

Leyshon, A. and N. Thrift. 2007. 'The capitalization of almost everything', *Theory, Culture, and Society* 24: 97–115.

Lipuma, E. and B. Lee. 2004. *Financial Derivatives and the Globalization of Risk*. Durham, NC: Duke University Press.

Lounsbury, M. and P. Hirsch. 2010. *Markets on Trial: The Economic Sociology of the US Financial Crisis*. Bingley, UK: Emerald Publishing.

Martin, R. 2002. *Financialization of Daily Life*. Philadelphia, PA: Temple University Press.

MacKenzie, D. 2006. *An Engine, not a Camera*. Cambridge, MA: MIT Press.

MacKenzie, D. 2011. 'The credit crisis as a problem in the sociology of knowledge', *American Journal of Sociology* 116: 1778–841.

Minsky, H. 2008. *Stabilizing an Unstable Economy*. New York: McGraw-Hill.

Montgomerie, J. 2008. 'Bridging the critical divide: global finance, financialization, and contemporary capitalism', *Contemporary Politics* 14: 233–52.

Moser, T. 2003. 'What is financial contagion?', *International Finance* 6: 157–78.

Nesvetailova, A. 2011. *Financial Alchemy in Crisis*. New York; Pluto Press.

Reinhart, C. and K. Rogoff. 2008. 'Is the US subprime crises so different?', *American Economic Review* 98: 339–444.
Reinhart, C. and K. Rogoff. 2009. 'The aftermath of the financial crises', *American Economic Review* 99: 466–72.
Rose, A. and M. Spiegel. 2010. 'Cross country causes and consequences of the crisis'. NBER Working Paper 16243. Cambridge, MA: NBER.
Schiller, R. 2003. *The New Financial Order*. Princeton, NJ: Princeton University Press.
Schwartz, H. 2009. *Subprime Nation*. Ithaca, NY: Cornell University Press.
Schwartz, H. and L. Seabrooke. 2008. 'Varieties of residential capitalism in the international political economy: Old welfare states and the new politics of housing', in H. Schwartz and L. Seabrooke (eds) *The Politics of Housing Booms and Busts*: 1–27. London: Palgrave Macmillan.
Stigum, M. 1989. *The Repo and Reverse Markets*. Homewood, IL: Dow Jones-Irwin.
Stockhammer, E. 2004. 'Financialization and the slowdown in accumulation', *Cambridge Journal of Economics* 28: 719–41.
Strange, S. 1996. *The Retreat of the State*. Cambridge, UK: Cambridge University Press.
Strange, S. 1998. *Casino Capitalism*. Manchester, UK: Manchester University Press.
Swedberg, R. 2010. 'The structure of confidence and the collapse of Lehman Brothers', in M. Lounsbury and P. Hirsch (ed.) *Markets on Trial: The Economic Sociology of the US Financial Crisis*: 71–114. Bingley, UK: Emerald.
US Department of the Treasury. 2007. *Annual Report on Foreign Holdings in the US*. Washington, DC: US Government Printing Office.
Useem, M. 1996. *Investor Capitalism: How Money Managers are Changing the Face of the World*. New York: Basic Books.
White, H. 2004. *Markets from Networks*. Princeton, NJ: Princeton University Press.
Zaloom, K. 2006. *Out of the Pits: Traders and Technology from Chicago to London*. Chicago, IL: University of Chicago Press.
Zorn, D., F. Dobbin, J. Dierkes, and M. Kwon. 2004. 'Managing investors: How financial markets reshaped the American firm' in K. Knorr Cetina and A. Preda (eds) *The Sociology of Financial Markets*: 269–89. New York: Oxford University Press.

22
Reforming the culture of banking

Grahame Thompson

Introduction

There have been many recent calls for a reform of the culture of banking, particularly by journalist, banking professionals, and politicians (Augar, 2014; Spicer *et al.*, 2014; Lambert, 2014; Lanchester, 2013b; Parliamentary Commission on Banking Standards, 2013). These mushroomed in the great recession period after the financial crisis of 2007–08—mainly in the US and the UK, the countries at the heart of the financial crisis. The calls for reform arose in the context of a series of financial misdemeanors committed by both retail and investment banks in the early 2010s: mis-selling of payment protection insurance, money-laundering and sanction-breaking activity, Libor rate rigging and forex manipulation scandals, accusations of insider trading, tax avoidance schemes, and much more besides. As a result a number of staggeringly large fines were imposed by the regulators in USA, UK, and Switzerland on the main international banks involved.[1] And as the year 2014 closed the *Financial Times* reported that all in all the total fines paid by major global banks for the financial crisis and its aftermath had by then topped US$178 billion! (*Financial Times* 31 December 2014, p. 7). But that was not the end of the matter since fines continued to mount up in 2015. As of November 2015, fines that year imposed by the UK Financial Conduct Authority on banks operating in London alone were over £840 million (www.fca.org.uk/firms/being-regulated/enforcement/fines: accessed December 1, 2015).

But despite this spate of financial scandals and regulatory crackdowns, improving market conditions and less risk-taking was again being rewarded with higher banker bonuses.[2] The EU had tried to limit these bonuses in the European context but as of the end of 2014, apparently with little success (see below). A toxic culture of contamination was argued to exist between retail and investment banking and the Governor of the Bank of England, Mervyn King (2003–13), commented that the bankers involved were possibly guilty of criminal fraud. As of the end of 2014, however, very few bankers (or others involved)—particularly executives—had been charged with or, convicted of, a criminal offence: the authorities seem to have concentrated on fines, which the banks readily paid, and returned to "business as usual." And in a way the "fines response" approach adopted by the regulatory authorities operates as a "partial legitimation" of the whole culture of banking it is designed to redress. It acts as rebuke but without a proper clampdown on malpractices or clear positive steer on the alternatives (though see below).

The reaction to all of this has basically been twofold. If the banks were institutionally flawed and morally corrupt, the answer was to tackle both of these aspects simultaneously: to institutionally reform matters on the one hand and to correct the moral bankruptcy on the other. Feature films like *Wall Street* (1987—where the Michael Douglas character, Gordon Gekko, utters the famous line "greed is good, greed is great") and *The Wolf of Wall Street* (2013), and Michael Lewis' books *The Big Short* (2010) and *Flash Boys* (2014) brought the practices and attitudes of the bankers to the attention of a wider popular cultural audience. And public attitudes towards bankers plummeted as they came to be seen as untrustworthy, greedy, only interested in their own personal gain, and doing very little for the common good. Banking was supposed to serve a social purpose but it looked as though it was actually socially destructive and dangerous, draining resources away from supporting genuine productive activity, ignoring the genuine interests of needy householders, and not supporting deserving governmental activities that added real social value. The question became how to achieve this, how to reform the "culture of banking" with regulatory reform and improvement in the standards and working practices of the banking business. In a moment we come back to the developments on both these fronts but first it will be useful to outline what has happened to several aspects of banking activity that indicate to the deep-seated nature of these problems, and how matters have evolved since the crisis. As will become clear, little seems to have changed as of the end of 2014.

First we can point to the level of bank lending to key sectors of the UK economy. This collapsed in the wake of the financial crisis (2007–08) and despite huge effort by the Bank of England to ease lending conditions for the banks—ultra low official interest rates, massive quantitative easing, a "funding for lending" program[3]—there was little sign of an improved position by the beginning of 2013 (NEF, 2014, Figure 1, p. 6). And this malaise in respect to bank lending was paralleled in other economies which had been badly affected by the crisis and the subsequent recession. Thus whilst the monetary base (liquidity) had increased dramatically after 2008 in the Eurozone, the USA, and UK (as Central Banks stepped in to rescue the banks and the financial systems more widely), bank lending to the private sectors stagnated in each case (Koo, 2013, figure 10, p. 144). Finally, concentrating on just the USA this time, the extent of "market finance" (comprising money market funds, repurchase agreements, and commercial paper as opposed to financing made available through the issuance of equities), which is often taken as indicating the extent of "shadow banking" activity in an economy (see Chapters 3, 6 and 13) – remained severely depressed in 2013. Whilst the growth in this might have been excessive in the run up to the crisis—and partly a causal factor in triggering that crisis—the sharp downturn after 2007 indicates to a severe lack of access to this kind of funding from the shadow banking sector, which inhibits corporate activity and overall liquidity in these markets, again possibly stunting real growth prospects (Goodman, 2014, Figure 1). It is important to devote some attention to the shadow banking sector whilst discussing the culture of banking reform since many of the practices of the commercial banks are parallel in the shadow banking business as well.

Frameworks for considering the reform of banking culture

Of course not all the responsibility for the trends just outlined can be attributed directly to the culture of banking: there are wider forces at work. It is in respect to the *supply* of funds to households and the productive sector that the culture of banking most readily relates: how banks go about the business of raising funds and allocating these to potential customers. But this does not deal with the *demand* for such funds: it may be that there is no desire to take out loans because of austerity and lack of aggregate demand in the economy. However, the underlying culture of banking is often held responsible for the general malaise in the financial system. It impinges on all aspects of banking and in as much that the practices of the banking sector were at least in large part responsible for the crisis and the banks behaved quite reprehensibly subsequently, it is sensible to concentrate upon those practices and attitudes in the first instance.

The huge fines detailed earlier were the first and foremost attempt to change the culture of banking. They can be viewed as a "reform thyself" policy. We (the authorities) will fine you (the bankers) which will hurt you and your investors or shareholders, and that in turn will put pressure on internal bank management to initiate change so as not to incur the wrath of regulators in the future by flouting the rules once again. Clearly, this is not an adequate response viewed by itself. It could be argued that the banks have just shrugged their shoulders, paid the fines and got on with business very much as usual. So it needs to be—and has been—accompanied by other reform policies which tackle the setting of banking standards, the monitoring of bank practices more closely, the organization of harsher sanctions and penalties, and the establishment of effective regulatory oversight more generally.

In a moment we return to these other policies. But first it is important to register the underlying rationale for them. They rely upon a conception that it is *incentives* that drives behavior: the regulatory arrangements are about changing the incentives for action—indeed this also lies behind the rationale for fines. But is couching this all in terms of incentives a sufficient response? Underlying this approach is one that views behavior as rationally motivated: if agents see that their existing behavior is leading to a perilous outcome they will adapt their future actions accordingly. The difficulty with this approach is that the practices of the financial system and the banking industry in particular are not necessarily "rational" in a traditional sense. As we will see in a moment there are a whole host of reasons why banks (and bankers) might not be quite in complete control of their own behaviors or their organizations in a contemporary analytical and organizational context.

A second preliminary point is to raise the issue of "corporate culture" in a general sense. For a very long time the nature of corporate culture has been at issue in the management literature: involving its status and its consequences. The phrase began to be widely used to describe organizational practices in the 1980s after Geert Hofstede published his pioneering study of the cultural attitudes of IBM employees in the late 1970s (Hofstede, 1980). Hofstede stressed the impact of individual cultural differences for organizational effectiveness and efficiency, where these cultural differences were seen as inherited from people's social and national backgrounds and "imported" into organizations on that basis. A few years earlier another pioneer of the cultural studies approach, Charles Handy (1976), had stressed the importance of organizational structures as a key aspect in the shaping of institutional cultures: business cultures are embedded in an organizational context, so this context becomes a key aspect if the question of change is to be addressed. So we had a classic "structure and agency" ("institutions and behaviors") picture emerging from this early discussion, which has tended to shape the manner in which this matter has been dealt with since. Into this framework has been floated further issues such as leadership, management style, rituals of behavior, cogitative appreciations, goal achievement, patterns of innovation and creativity, and more besides. Business culture is now generally recognized to involve a set of shared mental assumptions that guide interpretation and action in organizations by defining appropriate behavior for various situations: involving the meaning that people attach to those behaviors. It includes the organization's vision: its values, norms, symbols, language, assumptions, beliefs, and habits. And it is now taught assiduously in Business Schools and on executives training programs, recognized to be a crucial component of any informed approach to organizational management.

But "culture" is a rather vague term: think of all those aspects just outlined. Is there any singular meaning to a "corporate culture" for an organization? Might there be very many, competing and perhaps rapidly shifting cultures typifying organizations, existing within quite different aspects of the business (in the case of banks: on the trading floor, in the back office, as viewed differently by product and marketing managers, locked within risk assessment and "financial models" deployed for trading purposes, etc.)? If this is the case, changing a corporate culture might appear as a thankless task—one almost impossible to realize quickly in any meaningful sense. Those opposed to the idea of corporate culture being the key to organizational reform point to the absolute centrality of the institutional context for shaping culture and insist that it is at this level that effort should be focused for initiating reform rather than concentrating on culture as such. In the next section it is this institutional context that is focused upon, while we return to the wider issues later.

The institutional context for culture and its reform

In this section we briefly outline the context and initiatives taken to institutionally reform the culture of banking. There are several levels at which this discussion could be pitched. In a rather more macro setting two key elements would be the separation of retail and investment banking and the "stress testing" of the systemically important banks.

One of the major criticisms of the structure of the banking industry that emerged after the crisis was the way "universal banks" had grown to fuse together the day-to-day routine of ordinary retail banking ("boring banking") with the much more risky and often speculative activity of investment banking. This was deemed responsible for a contamination in the culture of bad banking, moving it mainly from the investment side to the retail side. But a consequence had been that risks to the "innocent" retail customers had risen accordingly, with their deposits put in danger by the activity of investment banking.[4] The answer was to separate these two anew by "ring-fencing" each separate activity. Quite how this was to be done and enforced was the subject of many regulatory initiatives in the post 2007–08 period[5] (see Chapters 15, 16 and 18 in this volume).

In the case of stress testing this involves trying to ensure banks maintain enough quality capital on their balance sheets to ride out any financial crisis without resorting to the public authorities for bailout assistance. Initiatives on this front (see Chapter 17 in this volume) have arisen from the Basel Committee, from the European Banking Authority, the US Fed, and the Bank of England, amongst others.

As well as these overall regulatory moves, there have been attempts to trim the extent of bonuses awarded to bank employees. The EU Parliament and the EU Council led this initiative as new rules came into effect in the second half of 2014 to limit bonuses to between 100 percent and 200 percent of basic salary. The UK government appealed against these moves so the effectiveness of the cap remains uncertain. Prior to this the UK government had initiated ad hoc and time limited tax penalties on banker's bonuses.

All these measures are designed to change the institutional logic of banking culture. They do not tackle that culture directly but serve to frame a set of incentives and penalties that will encourage such a change in culture by the banks. And these kinds of official reforms are backed up by other more directed institutional initiatives that concentrate on micro standard setting practices and close monitoring of bank behaviors, often at the behest of the industry itself.

In the UK this was led with an enquiry conducted by the joint House of Commons and House of Lords Commission on Banking Standards (Parliamentary Commission 2013: see also the responses by the FCA 2013 and the government—HM Treasury 2013). These reports deal with restoring trust in banking by strengthening the individual responsibilities of senior level managers, reforming corporate governance to enhance the soundness of decision taking and standard setting, creating better functioning markets so as to discipline bankers more effectively, and beefing up the regulatory oversight by domestic authorities and governments. In an attempt to head off further full blown interventionary initiatives by government the industry itself responded by creating an "independent" Banking Standards Review Council (Lambert, 2014) which would established a set of new guidelines for the industry and provide an annual update on banks' behavior. Part of the long-tradition of self-policing by the City of London, this body is voluntary but it is unclear quite how many banks will eventually "sign-up" to its charter.

The "persona" of banking and bankers

Returning directly to the issue of banking culture we examine this more closely in this section. One preliminary difficulty is whether companies can be legitimately considered as equivalent to "moral persons." Since culture conjures up a set of attitudes and beliefs comparable to those of "natural persons" who are imparted with a certain moral agency, can this be translated in any meaningful sense to the operations of banks or any other commercial business? Moral beings are subjects of rights which they must administer in the form of intentions, and can be held individually responsible and subject to scrutiny and accountability for their consequence. If banks are increasingly being viewed as ethical entities, undertaking public as well as private duties and paying particular attention to the moral consequences of their actions, corporate rules and procedures specifying organizational behavior in this respect (their "culture") should embody a concept of moral intentionality. Can this be appropriately ascribed to corporations? For many it is surprising how frequently this has become part of corporate culture: articles of association and mission statements abound with such invocations. In that corporate internal decision structures incorporate and impart these objectives into properly considered procedures that are followed through, events are re-described as corporate policy and attributions made accordingly. In effect, these become the "intentionality" of the corporation independently of those of its officers. But in as much that corporate responsibility can become re-described as social responsibility in this way, does this necessarily coincide with them being considered morally culpable? Couching matters in terms of corporate culture pushes any analysis towards considering corporations as necessarily morally constituted, so banks would become morally compromised when flouting the standards or breaking the rules.

In what follows we attempt to cut through the framework of "institutionality *versus* culture" (or more generally "structure versus agency") as the terms for reform by setting up corporate behavior in a different manner: asking the question of the *persona* of the corporation and its operatives (rather than their "cultural or moral attributes and attitudes"). As explored below, the idea of a persona is that this is a deliberately constructed "image" involving a range of determinations that are exercised, enacted, and performed rather than being moral or ethical beliefs or values held as a consequences of an agents subjectivity.

The question to ask in this case is whether banking behavior should be about the public mindedness of these companies? About them recovering a spirit of humanity in an expression of their social virtue? This is what the banks and the authorities are claiming as the key aspects for reforming banking culture. But on the other hand is it more about the possession of certain definite powers and capacities derived from a certain position occupied by banks in the domestic and international sphere? Is the source of their corporate personality to be found in the persona of their modern banking imaginary—its powers and capacities, its attributes imagined and fostered—and not in the form of some "ideal" of cultural agency? Thus to ask the question of the persona of the corporation is to ask the question in a way that avoids issues of direct moral agency. Rather it speaks to a presentation, a performativity and an enactment by banks themselves of a certain set of procedural roles.

A new persona for banking? Suggestions for reform of banking culture

It is clear that a more radical conception of the reform of banking culture should bring some critical reflection to bear along these lines on alternative financial arrangements, ones directed at social and public purposes, with an eye to their democratic accountability in the longer run. In the remaining section of this chapter we outline an alternative framework for considering this. The key category operating in this analysis is that of the artisan. This category stands for a re-engagement with an anti-technocratic conception of financial activity and the persona of those who inhabit it. We concentrate upon the notion of the "artisan of finance" and relate this in the first instance to the rise of high frequency trading (HFT) as an illustration of many of the issues involved. The practical conditions under which these suggestions might be operationalized are not considered here (though see Thompson, 2015a, Chapter 7 for illustrations). The analysis is presented here as more of a thought experiment in the interests of furthering conceptual clarity in these matters.

The particular context for this discussion is the huge surge in high-speed trading—and ultra-high-speed trading (UFT)—in financial markets (Financial Oversight Stability Council, 2013). In 2012 it was estimated high frequency trading (HFT) was responsible for almost 60 percent of all US equity trades, 55 percent of global futures trading, 40 percent of global forex trading, and 20 percent of global fixed income bond trading. HFT involves the automated use of sophisticated computer programs (algorithms) to take advantage of miniscule prices discrepancies, executed in fractions of a second. Although we have known about the use of new technologies in financial trading environments for some time, where anonymous transactions have displaced relationship-based finance in all spheres (with some potentially disquieting consequences—Huault and Ranielli-Weiss, 2013), the development of HFT and UHFT represents another ratcheting up of the technological frontier. It takes the trading environment into another realm of extreme technicality and represents a further move away from considered judgment towards a blind acceptance of what the algorisms determine (Bhidé, 2010; Thompson, 2015b). This can have further downside consequences in terms of unintended systemic risks, and it poses yet more challenges to already harassed regulators (Haldane, 2011; Sornette and von der Becke, 2011).

In this world there are two basic forms of high speed algorithmic trading: "automated" and "speculative" (Gomber et al., 2011; Viliante and Lannoo, 2011). It is claimed that automated trading serves some social purpose as it allows asset managers to "rebalance" their portfolios quickly and efficiently. On the other hand "speculative" trading serves no particular social purpose: it is manly undertaken by hedge funds (shadow banking) and proprietary traders (commercial banks) who make short-term trades in their search for yield on behalf of wealthy investors and the banks. And in as much that traditional asset management bodies are increasingly employing the services of organizations like hedge funds in an attempt to boost their own returns, these are also becoming complicit in the systemically riskier "speculative" form of HFT. Thus the rapid development of HFT and UHFT is threatening to become ubiquitous and the distinction between automated and speculative activity is breaking down. As will be discussed below this bodes ill for the future of a socially functional financial system, something the ideas of the artisan and partisan are designed to confront.

Artisanal craft production embodies some rather attractive ethical qualities: skill, integrity, dignity, honesty, self-reliance, and also a certain fortitude. What is important about the emphasis on skill in connection to craft production, however, is that it does not just involve codified and cognitive knowledge but also tacit knowledge and a necessary inventiveness in respect to its operationalization. You cannot just consult a handbook, template, or manual to read off the method of doing things but you have to have a certain sensitivity to manipulate and mold the materials under construction. It involves an intuitive knowledge as well as a cognitive one. Of course, this comes after a long apprenticeship—the artisanal craft producer goes through a thorough training in the shadow of the master craftsman. But this apprenticeship is not just there to develop reproducible productive skills, it is also there to train the attitude of the apprentice, to instill all those informal characteristics mentioned above associated with the "moral training" of the artisan (what might be more traditionally be termed "culture").

And this element of the informality associated with tacit skill means that there is no set model of how to do things or what to exactly copy. Each new crafted artifact is therefore "unique" at some level: there is a necessary variation built into it, even though reproductions can be continually made. Diversity and difference are embodied in each additional, though similar, product.

On the other hand, artisanship also presents the possibility of expressiveness. It connects to a certain willfulness, playfulness, and excessiveness, even though it also and at the same time embodies modesty and restraint. It engenders a hesitation at each new encounter with the material on which the craftsman works. This "now exactly what am I going to do and how am I going to do it?" moment in artisanal life means that each such act requires a decision: artisanal production is decisionist in character. It is not just a slavish repetition.

Financial sociability rather than financial culture?

A second resource developed here concerns how financial sociality is understood, which is stressed instead of the usual emphasis on culture. How is sociality conceived and constructed? There are four aspects to this, the latter three of which are the ones that seem the most pertinent in the case of financial/banking sociability. These four arrangements are: as a consequence of a contract, in terms of interrelatedness (involving connections, combinations, communications, exchanges, transaction, interactivities, flows, chains, relationality, and entanglements), as the consequence of habit or repetition, and finally as a consequence of will and passion (Thompson 2015a, Chapter 6). These conceptual aspects have an immediate impact on how (financial) subjectivities are thought to be constructed and their consequences for shaping the (financial) world.

Whilst the first three conceptual positions—contracting, interrelatedness, and habit or repetition—remain the most theoretically elaborated approaches, the final one—will and passion—is rather neglected. But this, along with chance, fortune, and determination, speak to a particular conception of that which is involved with sociality/culture. This combination is less associated with rational agreement, more with irrationality, excessive exuberance, blind enthusiasm, momentary feverish drives, etc. It involves the dissipation of a certain psychic energy and the destructiveness or ostentatious display of wealth for its own sake. In respect to the financial system it connects most closely with the ideas of excessive exuberances, cascading, herding, and the like. Indeed, it could be argued that it provides an underlying explanatory figuration for these attitudes and features.

One of the reasons this position is rather neglected is it seems to imply a fatalistic resignation: there is nothing that can be done to prevent the eruption of these emotions since they are written into our psyche or the existential nature of social existence.

However this is the site for an important theoretical clarification. There is a temptation to think of rationality and passion/will as polar opposites: that reason and emotion occupy quite different conceptual and operational spaces. In cultural studies the latter—the emotional terrain of feelings—is often summed up under the notion of *affect*, and there has been a "turn to affect" in cultural studies more generally (e.g. Connolly, 2002; Thrift, 2004, see McFall, Chapter 2 in this volume). Several matters are involved here, which it will be useful to untangle and clarify from the point of view of this chapter.

The first involves the notion of emotion/affect itself and whether this is as distinct from rationality as is often claimed. In part this depends upon exactly what rationality is taken to be. For our purposes we take a fairly loose definition, as in the notion of the "arts of reasoning," or alternatively described as thinking: people make decisions on the basis of thinking about them rather than just as a consequence of a momentary emotional impulse. Temporarily substituting "thinking" for "reason" is a tactical move to distinguish this conception of reasoning from "rationality" understood in the traditional sense of an instrumental means to an end considered via an intention and after attending to individual preferences. It is closer to the idea of different "modes of rationalization": characterizations of why things were done the way they were (Lentzos and Rose 2009, p. 236). So from this point of view passions or emotions and reasons are more closely related than commonly considered: passions and emotions can be considered within terms of reasons and are not necessarily pitched against them.

The second clarification has to do with the relationship between the passions and (self-)interests. Interests are linked to rationality as they are thought to be a consequence of rational thinking conceived in the traditional manner as just described. But we can be more nuanced about "interests" in the same way we were about "rationality." Self-interests, for instance, are not necessarily selfish and individualistic, determining behaviors that are indifferent to the common good and necessarily self-serving. For instance Hirschman (1977) and Holmes (1995) point to how the notion of interests was vital for limiting and controlling the passions in the early stages of capitalist development. Here the self-interests of the emergent commercial class served to establish a relative social peace from which all benefited. It helped to suppress the warring passions of religious strife and its associated murderous impulse.

Thus passions and emotions are not necessarily at odds with reason or rationality. However, under certain conditions (panics, extreme pressure, and bewilderment) passions and emotions can overwhelm rationality and even reason. Given the notion of the way passion and will enter into the construction of financial sociality the next step is to link it to features of the artisan. It speaks to the non-rationalistic character of artisanal activity, to the way intuition and sensibility are a necessary feature of craft practice, and the way a modest deployment of will and passion enter into craft production.

Handing decisions over to a quasi-automatic mechanism driven by a technological fix is a recipe for major problems since it prevents the operation of genuine decision-making. It replaces the technique involved in the art of decision-making with a technology. The artisan is replaced by the computer. Automaticity is substituted for a considered choice.

Organizational implications and consequences for banking reform

The pervious sections elaborated the intellectual resources providing access to thinking about the artisan of finance. But why might such a figure be an attractive one from the point of view of an analysis of the new financial persona and the reform of banking culture? It is around the features that such a persona would bring into the frame that an answer could be given.

First there is the idea of a "long apprenticeship" or training associated with artisanal activity and the ethical context that this brings to the final day-to-day activity of the work situation. It would be useful to think that this could be—indeed, should be—part of the process of formation of a new kind of financial analyst or worker.

Second, the artisan of finance must make decisions. It is not sufficient to rely on automatic, computer driven (non-)decision-making (repetition), which so easily allows—"encourages" even—herding behaviors, following the market, doing what others do, graphology, momentum trading, crowding, index trading, etc. which can so easily create financial bubbles and added systemic risks. The artisan of finance embodies technique and tacit skill and does not just rely on an automating technology or a model. It engenders a "hesitation" before each such decision, allowing for consideration and reflection.

Third, and relatedly, the artisan cannot simply rely upon financial models or algorithms to provide a guide to what should be done as there are no adequate models for artisanal activity. The mode of financial production needs to be recast as a result, to encompass considered judgment on each occasion of a product design, granting a loan or trading decision.

Fourth, the artisanal mode of financial production must embrace all those non-rationalistic features of financial sociability discussed above. This is not to say that conceptions of rationality in decision-making should be abandoned altogether—that would clearly be silly and counter-productive. Rather, this must be considered alongside the recognition of cognitive intuitionism and sensibility, and a commitment to exploring its practical and regulatory consequences (see Thompson, 2015a).

Fifth, the artisan of finance is not a traditional financial entrepreneur. "Entrepreneurialism" is innovatory activity and it is often associated with figures like Warren Buffett and George Soros. But most financial entrepreneurialism is a form of arbitrage, the linking together of already available possibilities in new ways to make small gains possible on differences between the prices of financial products in different markets or different times. Very little of it is really new and innovative. To some extent artisanal activity is like the routine rolling out of financial products which are slight variations on already existing products, which happens in the household orientated financial sector in particular (Lopes, 2013).

Sixth, the artisan would also be a partisan. The re-territorialization of financial activity is an imperative for a properly functioning financial system, and the notion of an artisan provides some of the intellectual resources to help in this task.

Seventh, outlining these contours of an artisanal mode of financial production enables us to appreciate in a quite concrete sense what its ethical qualities might entail. It provides a vivid but practical set of ethically grounded "values" that are not abstractly attached to or floated into the realm of financial behaviors on the back of the notion of culture, but which would arise there "spontaneously" from the day to day practical activity of such a craft-like operations.

Finally, is this invocation just a nostalgic desire for the recreation of an artisanal economy of craft-like production, but now reinvented for the financial sphere? Without being able to do this justice here it is rather to the contrary: artisanal activity in necessarily forward looking. In its hesitations, its inherent decisionism, its relationship to the imaginary (Beckert, 2011), its break with the tyranny of models, artisanal activity promises to provide a way forward for a more stable, productive, and efficient financial system.

What would be the operational characteristic of such a system?

This section discusses a series of organizational and operational features that would inform the kind of artisanal financial structure being argued for here. Obviously, we are not going to jettison the use of computer technologies in the financial system altogether, nor even elaborate algorithmic trading in various contexts (Thompson, 2015b). There would be a place for these in any artisanal system, but one where their characteristics were embedded in a different organizational and operational context. The persona of the artisan discussed above provides the image of an organizational arrangement where its characteristics act as a metaphor for an alternative set of techniques and practices orientated towards locally based, socially useful financial functions. Elsewhere several indicative actual developments in the realm of finance that embody many of the features outlined here (and above) are elaborated (Thompson, 2015a, Chapter 7). Of course, the existence of huge financial institutions with enormous power and influence, and which have a clear vested interest in "more of the same" in terms of financial products and activity, represent a formidable obstacle to any of these developments.

Perhaps one of the most important clarificatory reorientations to be considered in the field of artisanal finance is to re-stress the importance of organizational matters in an attempt to overcome a commitment amongst organizational theorists and practitioners, innovation scholars and knowledge experts, and the like, to celebrate what could be termed a "discombobulated firm" formulation. This is the idea that the firm is best considered as a dislocated agglomeration of relative independent features and functions, little more than a "nexus of contracts" (Jensen and Meckling, 1976, Aoki *et al.*, 1990), or a Mobius strip organization with no clear inside or outside (Sabel, 1991), or an arena for dissonance and differentiation (Stark, 2009, Chapter 4), a loosely configured non-hierarchical quasi-structure of fragmented elements and weak connections, etc. And what is more, this idea has taken such a hold of the popular and scholarly imagination that these features are viewed as the necessary characteristics for any firm to be "fleet of foot," to be entrepreneurial and innovative, to become a "learning organization," etc. This attempted dissipation of the entity that is the firm takes many forms, but it has the effect of undermining and destroying any clear idea of ordered structure and organizational control. Too much autonomy is given to particular agents to make too many isolated decisions (as in the case of financial traders, for instance): the organization—qua its character as an organization—is hollowed out from within so it loses its capacities to make sensible decisions, the consequences of which could be calculated for and assessed, and it expresses a widespread "fear of formalism" that pervades contemporary organizational theory. In fact, of course, it is just such an ordered internal system operating within companies that fosters genuine innovation, skills, and real learning. Those organizations without a seemingly bureaucratic mentality of this kind, where employees do not know exactly where they are placed, what their precise responsibilities are, what they have to do, etc., are the ones who are not innovative and that fail to learn. Confidence for people to act—and to act sometimes beyond their normal mandate—is a consequence of a well ordered and clear structure, not the inhibiter of this (Stinchcome, 2001). And this relates directly to much financial dealing. Financial managers in banks often complain bitterly that they have (or had) no idea what exactly goes on "at the business end" of their company's activities: on the trading floors and in offices where financial deals and transactions are actually conducted. Either this is too complex, or too rapid, or too opaque for managers to appreciate. They complain they have "lost control" over much of this business activity as a consequence, so that the overall exposure and risks positions of the banks are unclear. A technology introduced in part to enable managers to track this and keep them informed in real time has had the exact opposite effect. It has disabled managerial control.

So one should be rather skeptical of the discombobulated company formulation and indeed work against its sentiment. Coherent organizational structure, an attention to resource constraints, clear boundary demarcations, and so on, i.e. proper formality, needs to be re-emphasized. There should be more cognizance and less dissonance, more simplicity less complexity, more organization less differentiation.

A second fairly obvious set of comments relates more to what is actually done in the financial sphere rather than its organizational forms. To try to reduce the "nervous excitement" that often captures the trading floor environment, there needs to be less trading of risk or volatility and more trading in underlying instruments. So this means turning attention to the primary market and away from secondary market activity, away from debt instruments and toward credit instruments, less trading on "news" and more judgment, all designed to try to keep ever present "feral spontaneity" in check.

The consequential issue becomes how to learn the techniques of handling money in an artisanal fashion. This is to master the artistry of money: managing and manipulating money, private credit, and government debt in a way that forsakes technologies that leave the operators *(a)part from* the market to ensure they become *part of* the market. And it obviously implicates the trading of money, financial instruments, and their derivatives: so this is not an argument to entirely turn back financial operations to an era of, say, pit trading, though that obviously had the attraction of direct contact amongst market traders. But those days are gone. How some semblance of financial artistry reconfigured along these lines in today's technologically sophisticated and hyperactive banking environment could be generated is the issue for future elaboration.

Conclusions

In this chapter we have examined what "banking culture" means and how and it might be reformed. In large part this depends upon exactly how both conceptual matters and banking operational characteristics are understood. Banking culture is in desperate need for reform given the multiple misdemeanors associated with the banking business in the lead up to the financial crisis of 2007–08 and developments since. There seems little point in just endlessly fining banks for their socially destructive behavior if they simply react by paying those fines and reverting to business as usual subsequently. But there are real issues associated with how to reform banking culture which is not easily intellectually settled, let alone how this could be operationalized and implemented.

The chapter has responded to these dilemmas by outlining an alternative conceptualization of "culture" based upon the idea of the persona of banking and bankers, and the introduction of the notion of artisanal activity as a key element in any reform agenda. Until we know quite what it is that we are aiming for in terms of serious reform there is little point in changing institutional structures or tackling behavioral shortcomings. The way the idea of an "artisan of finance" might be an attractive persona for thinking around these issues was developed in the final sections of the chapter, which could act as a means for developing an alternative socially responsive banking industry.

Notes

1   In the context of the *Libor scandal*, in 2012 Barclays Bank alone paid £59.5 million in fines to the UK Financial Services Authority (FSA), US$160 million to the US Department of Justice (DoJ), and US$200 million to the US Commodity Futures Trading Commission (CFTC), a round total of about £290 million. UBS agreed to pay US$1.2 billion to the DoJ and the CFTC, £160 million to the FSA, and 59 million in Swiss francs to the regulators in that country. RBS paid US US$325 million to the CFTC, US$150 million to the DoJ, and £87.5 million to the FSA, a total of about £390 million (Lanchester, 2013a). For *money laundering* Standard Chartered Bank paid US$340 million to the New York State Department of Financial Services in settlement, then in December another US$227 million to the DoJ and US$100 million to the US Federal Reserve. In the context of the *forex debacle,* in

November 2014 the UK FCA imposed fines totaling US$1.7 billion on five banks for failing to exercise control over their business practices in the spot foreign exchange markets: Citibank US$358 million, HSBC US$343 million, J.P. Morgan US$352 million, RBS US$344 million, and UBS US$371 million. The FCA claimed that between January 1, 2008 and October 15, 2013 those five banks failed to manage risks around client confidentiality, conflict of interest, and trading conduct. The banks used confidential customer order information to collude with other banks to manipulate G10 foreign exchange rates and profit illegally at the expense of their customers and the market. At the same time, the CFTC in coordination with the FCA imposed collective fines of US$1.4 billion against the same five banks for attempted manipulation of, and for aiding and abetting other banks' attempts to manipulate, global foreign exchange benchmark rates to benefit the positions of certain traders: US$310 million each for Citibank and J.P. Morgan, US$290 million each for RBS and UBS, and US$275 million for HSBC. Collectively, the *Financial Times* estimated that a total of US$4 billion in fines in connection to the forex activity had been imposed by the end of 2014, with more in prospect ("NY regulator probing Barclays and Deutsche over forex algorithms," December 11, 2014—www.ft.com/cms/s/0/863a7b3c-813e-11e4-896c-00144feabdc0.html?siteedition=uk#axzz3NIAmZKtC – accessed December 28, 2014). As a lead in to these events, of course, there was the *mis-selling of mortgage securities*, which in 2014 resulted in Citigoup, for instance, agreeing to pay US$7 billion after an investigation by the US DoJ. J.P. Morgan Chase & Co. (JPM), the biggest US bank, agreed in November of that year to pay US$13 billion to resolve similar federal and state probes—and there were reports that the US government had sought about US$17 billion from Bank of America ("Citigroup Reaches $7 Billion Mortgage-Bond Settlement," www.bloomberg.com/news/2014-07-14/citigroup-reaches-7-billion-mortgage-bond-settlement.html—accessed December 23, 2014). In the UK context, banks have set aside more than £24 billion to settle anticipated *PPI mis-selling* claims.
2 "London financiers expect a 21% bonus boost for 2014 despite banking scandals" (Lianna Brinded, *International Business Times*, December 22, 2014).
3 See Thompson, 2015a, chapter 8 for the characteristics of these policies, and Thompson, 2016 (forthcoming).
4 As indicated above, however, the culture of retail banking seems to have been just as corrupted as that of investment banking in the early 2000s.
5 In the USA it is the Volker Rule—part of the Dodd–Frank Wall Street Reform and Consumer Protection Act of 2012—that governs this aspect of banking practice. This Act, along with the 2002 Sarbanes-Oxley Act, contains the main instruments deployed to legally back the DoJ and the CFTC investigations and fines mentioned in note 1 and above. But the difficulty for the authorities in this regard is indicated by the growing length of these Acts: Sarbanes-Oxley Act, 66 pages; Dodd–Frank Act, 2400 pages. In the UK, the Bank of England and the FCA regulates this and other aspects of banking practice.

References

Aoki, M., Gustafsson, B. and Williamson, O.E. (eds) (1990) *The Firm as a Nexus of Treaties*, London: Sage.
Augar, P. (2014) 'Investment banking: The culture of a casino or of a profession?' New City Agenda, October. Retrieved on December 20, 2014 from http://newcityagenda.co.uk/wp-content/uploads/2014/10/Philip-Augar-transcript-for-website-2.pdf.
Beckert, J. (2011) 'Imagined futures: Fictionality in economic action', *MPIfG Discussion Paper 11/8*, Max Planck Institute for the Study of Societies, Cologne.
Bhidé, A. (2010) *A Call for Judgment: Sensible Finance for a Dynamic Economy*, New York: Oxford University Press.
Connolly, W.E. (2002) *Neuropolitics: Thinking, Culture, Speed*, Minneapolis: Minnesota University Press.
Financial Conduct Authority (2013) *The FCA's Response to the Parliamentary Commission on Banking Standards*, October. Retrieved on December 21, 2014 from www.fca.org.uk/static/documents/pcbs-response.pdf.
Financial Oversight Stability Council (2013) *Annual Report 2012*, US Treasury Department: Washington DC. Retrieved on February 20, 2013 from www.treasury.gov/initiatives/fsoc/studies-reports/Documents/2012%20Annual%20Report.pdf.
Gomber, P., Arndt, B., Lutat, M. and Uhle, T. (2011) *High-Frequency Trading*, Deutsche Börse Group/Gothe Universität: Frankfurt-am-Main, Germany.

Goodman, L. (2014) 'Shriveling shadow banking limits liquidity and damages the economy: CFS money supply statistics' *Center for Financial Stability*, November 19.

Haldane, A. (2011) 'The race to zero', Speech given to the International Economic Association Sixteenth World Congress, Beijing, China, July 8, Bank of England. Retrieved on February 23, 2013 from www.bankofengland.co.uk/publications/Documents/speeches/2011/speech509.pdf.

Handy, C.B. (1976) *Understanding Organizations*, Oxford: Oxford University Press.

Hirschman, A.O. (1977) *The Passions and the Interests: Political Arguments for Capitalism Before its Triumph*, Princeton, NJ: Princeton University Press.

HM Treasury/Department of Business Innovation and Skills (2013) *The Government's Response to the Parliamentary Commission on Banking Standards*, Cm 8661, July.

Hofstede, G. (1980) *Culture's Consequences: International Differences in Work Related Values*, Beverly Hills, CA: Sage Publications.

Holmes, S. (1995) *Passions and Constraint*, Chicago, IL: Chicago University Press.

Huault, I. and Ranielli-Weiss, H. (2013) 'The connexionist nature of modern financial markets: From a domination to a justice order' in du Gay, P. and Morgan, G. (eds) *New Spirits of Capitalism? Crises, Justifications, and Dynamics*, Oxford University Press: Oxford, Chapter 8, pp. 181–205.

Jensen, M. and Meckling, W. (1976) 'Theory of the firm: Managerial behavior, agency costs and ownership structure', *Journal of Financial Economics*, 3: 305–60.

Koo, R. (2013) 'Balance sheet recession as the other half of macroeconomics', *European Journal of Economics and Economic Policies: Intervention*, 10 (2): 136–57.

Lambert, R. (2014) *Banking Standards Review*, May. Retrieved on December 20, 2014 from www.bankingstandardsreview.org.uk/assets/docs/may2014report.pdf.

Lanchester, J. (2013a) 'Are we having fun yet?' *London Review of Books*, July 4, pp. 3–8.

Lanchester, J. (2013b) 'Let's consider Kate', *London Review of Books*, July 18, pp. 3–8.

Lentzos, F. and Rose, K. (2009) 'Governing insecurity: Contingency planning, protection, resilience', *Economy and Society*, 38 (2): 230–54.

Lopes, D.S. (2013) 'Metamorphoses of credit: Pastiche production and the ordering of mass payment behaviour', *Economy and Society*, 42 (1): 26–50.

NEF (2014) *Strategic Quantitative Easing: Stimulating Investment to Rebalance the Economy*, London: New Economics Foundation.

Parliamentary Commission on Banking Standards Final Report (2013) *Changing Banking For Good*, HL Paper 27-1/HC 175-1.

Sabel, C. (1991) 'Moebius-strip organizations and open labor markets: Some consequences of the reintegration of conception and execution in a volatile economy' in Bairdieu, P. and Coleman, J.S. (eds) *Social Theory for a Changing Society*, Boulder, CO: Westview Press, pp. 23–61.

Sornette, D. and von der Becke, S (2011) *Crashes and High Frequency Trading*, Government Office for Science, UK.

Spicer, A., Gond, J.P., Patel, K., Lindley, D., Fleming, P., Mosonyi, S., Benoit C. and Parker, S. (2014) *A report on the culture of British retail banking*, New City Agenda, November.

Stark, D. (2009) *A Sense of Dissonance: Accounts of Worth in Economic Life*, Princeton, NJ: Princeton University Press.

Stinchcome, A. (2001) *When Formality Works: Authority and Abstraction in Law and Organization*, Chicago, IL: University of Chicago Press.

Thompson, G.F. (2015a) *Globalization Revisited*, London: Routledge/Taylor & Francis.

Thompson, G.F. (2015b) 'Time, trading and algorithms in financial sector security' paper delivered to the NordSTEVA Annual Conference 'The Organization of Societal Security in Europe: Technology, Values and Institutional Choices', Stockholm University, September 27–29, 2015 (forthcoming in *New Political Economy*).

Thompson, G.F. (2016) 'Reform from within: Central banks and the reconfiguration on neo-liberal monetary policy?', in Jones, B., O'Donnel, M. and Papadopoulos, T. (eds), *Alternatives to Neo-Liberalism*, Bristol: Policy Press, Chapter 6, forthcoming.

Thrift, N. (2004) 'Intensities of feeling: Towards a spatial politics of affect', *Geografiska Annaler Series B: Human Geography*, 86 (1): 57–78.

Viliante, D. and Lannoo, K. (2011) *MiFID 2.0: Casting New Light on Europe's Capital Markets*, Center for European Policy Studies: Brussels.

23
Consumer finance and the social dimension of banks in a global economy[1]

Toni Williams

Introduction

Beliefs about the efficiency of financial markets and the resilience of giant financial firms, such as banks, exerted a powerful influence before they were disrupted by the crash that started in 2007–08. One belief that was influential on the development of consumer finance markets is that dealings between financial firms and retail consumers of financial products are essentially private and mostly local in scope and purpose (Williams, 2013a; FSB, 2011; Piccioto and Haines, 1999). No matter that financial consumption had become a key element of economic policy in many countries or that financial products were supplied by giant transnational corporations through global brands (Tschoegl, 2005, 1987), the idea persisted that consumption of financial products reflected only the self-defined private goals of individual consumers, producers and retail market intermediaries and did not engage broader public or collective interests. This view influenced national and international policymaking throughout the twentieth century with the result that financial consumer protection regulation was constructed as a matter of local preferences about the distribution of contract power between producers and consumers of financial products and regarded as of little significance to global financial regulation.

The role played by securitization practices in the rampant mis-selling of US consumer finance products that triggered the 2007 crash exposed as anachronistic this view of financial consumption and its regulation as private and domestic. Much of the ensuing debate about reforming global finance focused on the regulatory architecture of the capital and wholesale finance markets that facilitated the production of toxic securitized and derivative products and enabled the destabilizing effects of their circulation to reverberate across the globe. But there also have emerged strands of transnational policy discussion about retail finance markets, the role of financial consumers in global finance, the social responsibilities of financial firms to consumers and the societies in which the firms do business, and the contribution of financial consumer protection reform to the resilience of the global financial system.

This chapter discusses this emerging consumer dimension of transnational policymaking about the regulation of banks and other financial firms and their market practices. It contextualizes and discusses a set of transnational principles on financial consumer protection that in the aftermath of the crash were solicited and endorsed by the G20 leaders, drafted by the OECD and disseminated by the Financial Stability Board (OECD, 2011; FSB, 2011; G20, 2011).

Transnational policymakers envisage consumer financial protection as contributing to global financial stability (G20, 2011; FSB, 2011), but it is unclear whether consumer financial protection regulation will advance that end. Equally unclear – and more important to this chapter – are the implications of pursuit of this financial stability objective for thinking about the responsibilities of banks for their conduct in consumer finance markets. Questions arise as to whether retail-finance markets structured on the basis of the new transnational standards will deliver better at lower prices in a non-discriminatory manner to more financial consumers; and will banks take responsibility to end the predatory practices that have characterized this era of neo-liberal financialization and improve the safety of consumer finance markets (Nottage and Kozuka, 2012; Bar-Gill and Warren, 2008).

Answers to these and similar questions depend in part on the standards set forth in the initiatives and on the ability of national and international regimes to implement and enforce them. More fundamentally, the answers depend on how effectively the reforms envisaged by the new international standards restructure the socio-economic relations of consumer-finance markets and specifically whether the reforms are capable of changing those exploitative aspects of financial firm–consumer relations that triggered the crisis and have since intensified its effects.

This chapter explores the capacity of the G20's model of financial consumer protection to reconfigure relationships between banks and consumers, focusing in particular on the market conduct of financial firms. The second section describes the dominant paradigm of consumer-finance regulation before the crash and then outlines two important aspects of contemporary consumer-finance markets that bear on the relationships between firms and consumers – the increasing importance of household financial products to the revenue streams of many global banks and inequalities in the distribution of consumer debt. The third section outlines the elements of the G20 model of consumer protection in retail-finance markets and critically analyses the capacity of that model to compel banks and other financial firms to protect consumers of their products. The final section concludes.

Domestic policy contexts of the transnational reforms

Neo-liberal policy before the crash

The era of neo-liberal economic policy that preceded the 2007–08 crash treated consumption as a driver of economic growth and consumer-finance products as a crucial enabler of that consumption (Ramsay, 2006). Policymakers and large financial firms promoted product innovations that purportedly expanded access to finance and credit for individuals and households – credit's so-called democratization (Austin, 2003; Kumar, 2005; Helms, 2006; Ertürk *et al.*, 2007). These innovations were coupled with measures to improve the quality of decision-making on the part of both firms and consumers and they led to the replication around the world of institutions and policies to facilitate the expansion of consumer-finance markets. Relevant institutions include credit bureaus to expand firms' access to information about financial consumers, disclosure obligations to increase consumers' access to information about financial products, financial literacy education to improve consumers' confidence, skills and ability to use disclosure effectively, and the establishment of financial ombudsmen to provide low-cost redress for problems (Ramsay and Williams, 2011; World Bank, 2009; Helms, 2006; Kumar, 2005).

Although neo-liberalism is often characterized as deregulatory, regulation was central to its pre-crisis restructuring of consumer-finance markets. In practice, regulators governed firms not by implementing mandatory rules, but rather by indirectly steering them through risk-based regulation constructed in the form of principles, standards and guidance (Black, 2001; Osborne and Gaebler, 1992). Regulators sought to enable and maintain market conditions that would subject firms to competitive discipline, rather than to control the nature, safety, quality, or market price of financial products. Policies that contributed to the neo-liberal project of intensified competitive discipline aimed to change the conduct of financial consumers – not firms – focusing on consumers' abilities to make their purchasing decisions influence the conduct of banks and other financial firms through complaints, comparison, switching and so on. Activation of bank's responsibilities towards consumers thus was indirect and structured to depend on the capacity of financial consumers to hold firms accountable to regulatory standards.

The international campaign to encourage the adoption of financial literacy as a policy priority illustrates this notion of consumer-driven accountability and expresses influential ideas about the socio-economic relations of retail-finance markets that flourished before the crash occurred and persist today (Zokaityte, 2015; Williams 2007). Local financial education schemes led by public and private bodies have a long history, particularly in the United States (Zelizer, 1997; Mitchell, 1912). Financial literacy became a particular focus of international policymaking in 2003 when the OECD launched its Financial Education Project, sponsored by Prudential PLC's Corporate Responsibility Program. This campaign encouraged national governments to treat improved consumer financial literacy as a regulatory priority (OECD, 2005a; 2005b; 2004). To this end, the OECD sponsored national, regional and international conferences, published a steady stream of promotional and evaluative reports, including principles for evaluation of financial education (OECD, 2012), and founded an international network on financial education and a global clearinghouse on financial education as a repository for data, research and other informational resources.[2]

This 'edu-regulatory' project of financial literacy democratization (Zokaityte, 2015) was launched with the overtly market-expansionary objectives of improving the confidence, enthusiasm and skill of financial consumers and increasing their participation in retail-finance markets (OECD, 2005a). Pursuit of these objectives was advocated to improve economic growth, reduce poverty and potentially moderate the volatility of financial markets in emerging economies (OECD, 2005a). An economy populated by financially literate consumers also was expected to alleviate pressure on the public purse, as states sought to impute to individuals and households more financial responsibility for economic security and for the protection that social welfare programs and defined-benefit pension schemes used to provide (Zokaityte, 2015; Ertürk *et al.*, 2007; Williams, 2007).

In addition to these macroeconomic benefits, financial literacy education was conceived as transformative for individual consumers' agency. Considered capable of managing the risks of illness, income loss and other biographical contingencies, the literate consumer is constructed also as serving a market disciplinary role as she proactively demands more and better-quality financial services from financial firms and products that enable her to more effectively smooth income flows and ensure economic security (Zokaityte, 2015; Ertürk *et al.*, 2007; Williams 2007).

Financially literate consumers thus could be expected to understand what information they need to make rational financial decisions, how to search for that information and how to interpret that information. They would take responsibility for their own decisions and have the skills and knowledge to protect themselves against the risks of predatory practices by banks and other financial firms. In the view of the Financial Services Authority (FSA), then the United Kingdom's main financial regulator, the literate financial consumer is able 'to exercise a stronger influence in markets; to take greater responsibility for their own actions; and to protect themselves through less mis-buying and being less susceptible to mis-selling' (FSA, 2005, p. 29). Markets populated by financially literate consumers should require less regulatory 'intervention', which, in turn, should be less burdensome for firms (FSA, 2003). In these ways, financial literacy is conceived as transforming financial consumers into vigilant 'regulatory subjects' (Williams, 2007) whose decisions have beneficial effects on the market conduct of financial firms. Just as consumer demand is supposed to increase price competition and stimulate innovation, so also is consumer vigilance supposed to discipline firms, reducing the need for regulatory action in consumer-finance markets (FSA, 2003; FSA, 2006a).

Changes in banking practice and the growth of household debt: the increasing significance of consumer debt under neo-liberalism

Since the 1980s, neo-liberal regulation of financial markets generally has been associated with an extraordinary expansion in financial sectors – an expansion that has been dubbed the 'financialization' of economic, social, and political life (Dore, 2008; Martin, 2002). A notable indicator of financialization that relates to the uptake of consumer-finance products is the increase in household debt (Brown et al., 2013; Barba and Pivetti, 2009; dos Santos, 2009; Cynamon and Fazzari, 2008; Dynan and Kohn, 2007). During the five years preceding the crisis, household debt-to-income ratios in 'advanced economies' rose by an average of 39 per cent to reach 138 per cent in 2007 (IMF, 2012). These ratios have since declined in the United States and the United Kingdom where the crisis hit the retail-finance sector hard (Bhutta, 2012). But, as Table 23.1 indicates, a trend of declining household debt is not universal. By 2013, household debt-to-net income ratios had increased well beyond the 2007 levels in countries such as Canada (from 143 per cent to 164 per cent) and Sweden (from 154 per cent to 170 per cent), and the 2013 ratios reported for Denmark (313 per cent), Ireland (213 per cent) and the Netherlands (281 per cent) are considerably higher than the peak debt household levels of the United States and the United Kingdom.

Aggregate debt-to-income ratios invite speculation about the reasons for inter-temporal and inter-jurisdictional variation, but these data are crude indicators of the financial health of

Table 23.1 Household debt, total % of net disposable income, 2000–13

Country	2000	2007	2010	2013
Canada	**110.1**	**143.4**	**160.7**	**163.8**
France	**77.5**	**96.7**	**107.5**	**104.15**
Germany	**116.5**	**102.6**	**98.3**	**94.5**
Italy	54.5	80.2	90.4	90.6
Japan	140.7	133.6	131.9	129.1
United Kingdom	118.9	183.3	158.7	152.0
United States	103.5	143.1	127.2	115.1
Denmark	232.8	324.7	325.1	313
Ireland	–	233.3	231.3	213.5
Netherlands	199.1	261.4	293.9	280.9
Norway	135.3	207.9	212.1	221.9
Portugal	106.8	145.7	154.4	139.5
Spain	84.2	154.1	148.6	134.1
Sweden	108.6	154.4	170.7	169.7

Source: OECD (2015).

household or national economies. It is also difficult to base inter-jurisdictional comparisons of household behaviours on these ratios because the numbers do not take into account variations in the incentive and institutional structures of consumer-finance markets that different countries may deploy, such as tax incentives that support high levels of mortgage borrowing[3] (EU, 2012). Even taking into account appropriate cautions and qualifications the data do show that financial firms continued to expand household lending in many countries with economies in various states of disrepair and distress throughout the Great Recession.[4]

Mortgage and consumer credit are among many personal finance products that banks and other financial firms have aggressively peddled to retail consumers during the past thirty years or so. These loans along with pension, insurance, and investment products regularly feature in scandals about the predatory mis-selling of retail-finance products (Hanrahan, 2014; Engel and McCoy, 2011; Black and Nobles, 1998; Calavita, Pontell and Tillman, 1997). The regularity of these exploitative episodes are indicative of a particular structure of relationships between banks and consumers rather than idiopathic regulatory or market failure. They are likely to continue to erupt episodically until there is a change in the structuring of responsibilities in retail banking markets.

Consumer lending products alone now account for a significant portion of revenue generation at large banking groups (Beck et al., 2012; dos Santos, 2009). Paulo dos Santos (2009, p. 181) details how by 2007 'banking had become heavily dependent on lending to individuals and the direct extraction of revenues from ordinary wage-earners'. Data from his survey of the corporate disclosure documents of major global banking groups show that the UK banks in the study almost quadrupled the proportion of their direct-lending activity in retail markets between 1976 and 2006, increasing the share of individual lending from 11.6 per cent to 40.7 per cent of total direct lending (dos Santos 2009, p. 191). These banks also increased lending to the financial intermediaries that serve retail markets from 20 per cent to 32 per cent of total lending – a 50 per cent increase. The study found that by December 2006, individual lending accounted for over 40 per cent of the loan portfolios of Barclays and HSBC, two major UK banking groups, and more than 75 per cent of the total loan portfolios of two US banking groups, Citigroup and Bank of America (ibid.). Unsurprisingly this scale of consumer lending activity had a substantial impact on the firms' balance sheets. By 2006, for example, the consumer-finance divisions of Citigroup and HSBC were generating substantial shares of their groups' profits, 56 per cent in the case of Citigroup, and 43 per cent of total profits at HSBC, where the consumer finance division substantially outperformed the banks commercial (27.3 per cent of total profits) and investment-banking (26.3 per cent of total profits) divisions (ibid.).[5]

This expansion of consumer lending and other personal finance products has been accompanied by the creation of lucrative revenue streams from fees, charges, and ancillary services such as credit insurance (Ertürk and Solari, 2007). According to dos Santos, account service charges amounted to more than 25 per cent of the revenues of some UK and US banks in 2006 and a 2006 US Government Accountability Office (GAO) report found that late-payment penalty fees charged by major credit card issuers in the United States had almost tripled in ten years, rising from an average of $13 in 1995 to $34 in 2005, and that these fees had been levied on 35 per cent of 'active US accounts' in 2005 (US GAO, 2006).

A 2008 market study on current personal accounts, published by the United Kingdom's Office of Fair Trading (OFT), found that bank revenues from those accounts amounted to £8.3 billion in 2006, of which £2.6 billion (just over 30 per cent) consisted of fees levied on insufficient funds and over-limit transactions (OFT, 2008).[6] In 2011 the Treasury Select Committee (para. 95) reported that '£3.6 billion, almost 50 per cent of total bank revenues from current account provision, derive from overdraft, insufficient funds and other charges'.

That report also referred to a 2009 OFT document[7] that cited an additional revenue stream to banks of £9 billion derived from the cost to consumers of foregone interest on current accounts (Treasury Select Committee, 2011, para. 69).

Personal finance products evidently produce substantial revenues for their suppliers in the form of apparently randomly calculated penalties and charges as well as the allegedly risk-based pricing of interest rates.[8] These revenues represent an extraction of household income obtained from sources such as employment, pension, or social security payments (dos Santos, 2009). Expansion of the economy of personal finance under neo-liberalism thus increased financial firms' access to household income during a period of stagnating or declining household incomes (Dynan, Elmendorf and Sichel, 2012; dos Santos, 2009; Barba and Pivetti, 2009). Financial firms then used this revenue stream as a resource that fuelled trading in the lucrative secondary markets, the collapse of which then led to additional loss of income as well as assets for many financial consumers (Crouch, 2012; Gowan, 2009).

This brief account of developments in the role of consumer-finance products in the business models of large financial firms provides insight into their dealings with financial consumers during the period leading up to the crash. Of particular interest to this chapter's focus on financial consumer protection and social dimensions of the conduct of banks are the ways that predatory lending practices, including the levying of excessive fees, charges and penalties increase debt loads and exacerbate inequalities.

The unequal distribution of debt in the UK

Aggregate data are an established tool of economic policymaking and they often usefully inform debates about regulatory frameworks for achieving policy goals. But aggregate data on household debt-to-income ratios may be misleading when analysing economic relations between financial firms and consumers because household or personal debt, like household income and financial assets, is unequally distributed. A comparison of the change in household debt-to-income ratios with recent studies reported in the Bank of England's quarterly bulletins illuminates this point (Waldron and Young, 2006). Table 23.1 shows that the proportion of UK households with some kind of debt increased their debt-to-income ratio by 50 per cent, jumping from 117.1 per cent in 2000 to 183.1 per cent in 2007. But as Table 23.2 indicates, there was almost no overall widening of debt-holding during this period as the proportion of households with debt changed very little, increasing by only two percentage points from 55 per cent to 57 per cent.

These data show variations in how holdings of different types of debt portfolios changed over the six-year period. They show a decline from 18 per cent to 14 per cent in the proportion of households holding secured debt only. As secured debt in the United Kingdom essentially refers to home mortgages, this decrease in debt reflects a rise in outright home ownership over the period (Waldron and Young, 2007). Among households that do hold mortgages, there was no

Table 23.2 The unequal distribution of debt among British households, 2000–06

Distribution of Debt	2000	2004	2005	2006
None	45	42	43	43
Unsecured Only	15	23	20	22
Secured Only	18	13	16	14
Both	21	22	21	21

Source: Waldron and Young (2006).

change between 2000 and 2006 in the proportion also holding unsecured debt, which was 21 per cent. By contrast, there was a sizeable increase of 7 per cent over the same period in the proportion of the households owing unsecured debt only.

Closer scrutiny of the data reveals additional trends and distributional inequalities between indebted households. Mortgaged households as a whole owed 62 per cent of the unsecured debt and 96 per cent of the entire stock of household debt in 2006 (Waldron and Young, 2006). From 2000 to 2007, a period in which the UK housing markets were considerably overheated, there was a corresponding shift from smaller to larger amounts of household secured debt. About 75 per cent of secured-debtor households in 2000 owed less than £60,000 in secured debt (Waldron and Young, 2007). Seven years later, the percentage of secured-debtor households with a mortgage of less than £60,000 had fallen to about 40 per cent, and about 40 per cent of mortgaged households owed more than £90,000 (Waldron and Young, 2007 p. 513). The debt-to-income ratios of some mortgaged householders also changed substantially during this time. Whereas about 10 per cent of mortgaged households owed more than three times their pre-tax annual income in 2000, the proportion of mortgaged households owing more than three years income amounted to about 25 per cent by 2007 (Waldron and Young, 2007, p. 514).

Renter households owed a small proportion (about 3 per cent) of the United Kingdom's total household debt, but debt levels also increased within this group during the first decade of the twenty-first century. Data reported by the Bank of England show that the percentage of indebted-renter households expanded from just above 40 per cent in 2000 to about 50 per cent in 2007 (Waldron and Young, 2007 p. 513). In 2006, about two-thirds of these households owed less than £5000, which is about the same proportion of renters with debts under £5000 as in 2000 (Waldron and Young, 2006 p. 398). But again there are striking inequalities. The Bank of England's report on 2006 data observes that while 'the majority of renters with debt owed small amounts with seemingly affordable repayments ... a small minority (9 percent of renters with debts) had unsecured debts in excess of their annual pre-tax income' (Waldron and Young, 2006 p. 398).

In sum, the burden of the UK's approximately 50 per cent increase in household debt-to-income ratio from 2000 to 2007 fell differentially on UK households. Almost half were unaffected, as they held no debt at all. Debt-holding generally widened among renter households and it may have intensified substantially for about 1 in 10 indebted renter households. Debt-holding deepened significantly among mortgaged households that also held unsecured debt.

These findings about the intensification of retail lending markets are consistent with the point discussed above about financial firms extracting revenues from household incomes that are most accessible to them, for example through the second mortgages and refinancing of households that already hold secured debt. The resulting inequality in the distribution of debt is a significant indicator of social injustice, particularly in so far as debt inequalities exacerbate, compound and interact with other income, asset and social inequalities.

Findings about inequalities in the distribution of household debt highlight the need for critical scrutiny of how firms conduct their business in retail-finance markets. UK regulators attempted to change some unfair practices of financial firms during the crisis, focusing in particular on fees and the mis-selling of credit-related products. But these interventions generally received little support from UK courts, legislatures or economic policymakers and some assess them as ineffective (Ferran, 2012).[9]

A recent study (Bunn et al., 2013) on the effects of high household debt levels on economic growth and stability, suggests a rather different stimulus than inequality and social justice for the further development of financial consumer protection regulation. Through analysis of microdata on household spending and debt, this study found that higher levels of indebtedness may have contributed to faster growth before the crisis but estimated that highly-indebted households substantially reduced their spending after 2007.[10] Reductions in spending by these households were more substantial than those that held less debt. Moreover, the study estimates that the fall in consumption attributable to this drop in (highly-indebted) household spending was larger than the additional growth that could be attributable to their higher spending before the crash and as such it effectively unwound 'the faster growth in spending by highly indebted households, relative to other households, before the financial crisis' (Bunn et al., 2013, p. 304).

These findings are consistent with other studies reporting that high and increasing levels of household debt tend to 'amplify downturns and weaken recoveries' (IMF, 2012, p. 97; Mian and Sufi, 2010) and that this compounding effect does not simply reflect the loss of household wealth associated with significant falls in house prices. Such findings make a robust case for policies to strengthen social safety nets and with respect to private consumption to use financial consumer protection to limit the risks of consumers becoming highly or over-indebted and to facilitate household debt restructuring when excessive debt does occur.

But UK policymakers have instead deployed stringent public spending cuts and austerity programmes and used concerns about the effects of high household debt on financial stability to enlist financial consumer protection regulation in aid of other political goals. For example, in 2014, the Bank of England's Financial Policy Committee recommended a specific affordability stress test for financial firms to employ when assessing mortgage loans and a limit of 15 per cent of high loan-to-value loans in their new mortgage business to be monitored by the UK's financial market regulators (Bank of England, 2014). These direct interventions on responsible lending, ostensibly in support of financial stability, then contributed to Chancellor George Osborne's defence of the government's Help to Buy housing scheme,[11] a private consumption initiative that was roundly criticized for increasing the risk of another house price bubble and helping to fuel high debt levels (IMF, 2013; Osborne, 2013).

In sum, it seems likely that the enlistment of financial consumer protection in support of macroprudential goals such as the management of systemic risk, financial stability and consumption driven growth gives more policy prominence to the responsibilities and conduct of financial firms in retail financial markets. This increased visibility can potentially create opportunities for critics of neo-liberalism and advocates of the consumer interest to expose and challenge the practices of financial firms based on their socio-economic consequences such as over indebtedness. However, the policy interest in financial consumer protection is bidirectional so that financial stability considerations are also intended to influence financial consumer protection regulation (as well as financial stability policy incorporating consumer protection concerns). The chapter turns now to consider how likely it is that financial consumer protection regulation premised on the values and goals of the new global financial stability project will restructure market relations to give substantive content to the social responsibilities of banks towards consumer interests.

The G20 model of reform

In November 2011, the leaders of the G20 nations adopted ten 'High-Level Principles on Financial Consumer Protection' (Principles) prepared by the OECD (OECD 2011; G20, 2011) and endorsed a more general FSB report on policy options for improving financial consumer protection in relation to credit products (FSB, 2011). As they endorsed these principles and committed to their implementation, the G20 leaders asserted that financial consumer protection was a means of advancing their goals of financial stability and economic growth (G20, 2011, para. 33). Thus, the preamble to the Principles opens with the assertion that 'consumer confidence and trust in a well-functioning market for financial services promotes financial stability, growth, efficiency and innovation over the long term' (OECD, 2011, p. 4). Rather than dwelling on established consumer regulation priorities such as the distribution of market and contracting power between firms and financial consumers (Ramsay 1995), the text focuses instead on factors that purport to strengthen competitive dynamics and improve consumer confidence and capacity in a well-functioning market.

Neo-liberal themes feature prominently in the preamble to the Principles text which characterizes the role of financial regulation as enabling market expansion and fostering consumer participation in financial markets. These themes are particularly evident in the construction of developments in consumer finance regulation as responding to the 'increased transfer of opportunities and risks to individuals and households' (OECD, 2011, p. 4) and the 'increased complexity of financial products and rapid technological change' (ibid.). Notably, these stimuli for reform appear in the text as established facts rather than as consequences of neo-liberal political and economic choices that could be changed. Similarly, the assertion that consumer rights 'come with consumer responsibilities' (ibid.) merely reiterates neo-liberal confidence in the ability of rights-bearing financial consumers to exert market discipline. As such it glosses over the complex and contestable political choices about the relative responsibilities of firms, regulators and consumers to protect individuals and safeguard financial markets against the consequences of predatory practices and dangerous financial products.

Within the Principles themselves, there are further examples of the persistence of neo-liberal norms that characterized the pre-crisis era in many jurisdictions. Perhaps the most explicit example is Principle ten's reaffirmation of the power of competition to discipline banks and other financial firms (OECD, 2011, p. 7). Several other principles draw on regulatory practices that were well established in various jurisdictions before the crisis. These include Principle four's focus on disclosure and transparency, Principle five's promotion of financial education and awareness, Principle seven's protection of consumer assets against fraud or misuse, Principle eight's emphasis on data protection and consumer privacy and Principle nine's focus on redress and handling of complaints.

The ideological continuities with neo-liberalism expressed in the Principles referenced above are not unexpected, but the benefit to financial consumers of internationalizing these norms and standards is unclear. G20 countries are relatively rich, with mature economies and all have consumer protection laws providing for at least some of the matters covered by these Principles, such as information disclosure and protection against fraud (FSB, 2011). The Principles may expose gaps in explicit regulatory provision such as the lack of a comprehensive legislative regime of consumer privacy and data protection in the United States (Federal Trade Commission, 2012). But such gaps likely reflect political interests and the dynamics of policymaking in the jurisdiction in question rather than a lack of knowledge or understanding of the particular aspect of consumer protection (Federal Trade Commission, 2012; Langenderfer and Cook, 2004). These local dynamics may not be particularly susceptible to reforms derived from external agencies, no matter how concerted the international pressure.

In addition to the well-known norms of consumer protection outlined above, the Principles include four standards that are less common and potentially could presage change in regulatory architectures and practices in some G20 jurisdictions. Principles one and two concern local institutional frameworks for the development and implementation of financial consumer protection regulation. These Principles respond to the finding of the FSB options that retail-finance market regulation in many jurisdictions had a very low profile (FSB, 2011). General purpose consumer protection agencies, the FSB found, often lacked expertise in the production, marketing and disputing over retail financial products. Conversely, finance authorities typically had little knowledge or understanding of how financial firms conducted their business in consumer finance markets.

Principle one seeks to close this gap in regulatory capacity, which the FSB believed tended to inhibit the proactive development of a comprehensive regime of financial consumer protection. It requires financial consumer protection to become 'an integral part of the legal, regulatory and supervisory framework' of a country's financial sector, and it requires firms and their agents to be 'appropriately regulated and/or supervised' (OECD, 2011, p. 5). Principle two (OECD, 2011, p. 5) adds the institutional dimension to the regulatory scheme by requiring the designation of oversight bodies with explicit responsibility for financial consumer protection and 'the necessary authority to fulfil their mandates'. In addition to their roles in the regulation of particular domestic consumer-finance markets, these oversight bodies should be responsible for coordinating their work internationally so as to maintain 'a level playing field across financial services', especially in international transactions and cross-border sales.

The remaining Principles – three and six – arguably have the potential to reshape economic relations between financial consumers and firms if implemented in a proactive manner. Principle three (p. 5) requires consumers to be 'treated equitably, honestly and fairly at all stages of their relationship with financial service providers' and states that this 'treating customers fairly' principle should be 'integral' to the 'good governance and corporate culture of all financial services providers and authorized agents'. Principle six (p. 7) requires financial firms and their agents to conduct their business responsibly in consumer-finance markets. This norm is elaborated to require firms generally to 'work in the best interest of their customers' and to take responsibility 'for upholding financial consumer protection' (OECD, 2011, p. 7). Principle six also details specific areas of a firm's operations that should be organized to reflect the responsible business conduct standard. These areas include systems of accountability for the conduct of authorized agents; the responsible sale of financial products and services to individual customers; management of conflicts of interests; and staff qualification, training and remuneration (ibid.).

This summary of the High-Level Principles illustrates that the G20's model of financial consumer protection largely relies on, and reproduces, a construct of competitive market relations in which restless sovereign consumers select among standardized products provided by myriad competing suppliers. It imagines that these choices influence and constrain the conduct of financial firms and the contracts they supply to retail markets. That this construct of the vigilant, active and capable consumer persists despite its implausibility illustrates the resilience of neoliberal ideas about regulation facilitating the expansion of consumer-finance markets (Crouch, 2011). These markets are dominated by giant banks and insurance companies that epitomize the late modern corporation, directed by the visible hand of internal planning rather than classical market forces. Such businesses constitute markets for their products rather than respond to them (Crouch, 2011; Galbraith, 1967). While financial firms may point to their market research as responding to, or at least engaging with, the preferences of financial consumers, their investigations may in practice be more about creating demand, marketing products or differentiating products than about meeting the desires and preferences of buyers.

The managerial decisions of global corporate empires may be influenced by many factors including shareholder value, vanity, ambition, fashion, irrational exuberance, fear and the dynamics of their internal bureaucracies. But there is little evidence that the preferences of financial consumers exert significant influence on their conduct. For example, how many individuals wish to expose themselves to the risk of paying fees and charges that were unknown to them when they opened a bank account or responded to a credit card solicitation? How many would choose to be subjected to the aggressive and exploitative sales practices associated with the mis-selling of many consumer-finance products including credit insurance, subprime mortgages and pension funds? What proportion of households intended that their incomes be used to fuel financial trading in secondary markets?

Perhaps there is more potential for change in those principles that aim to modify the conduct of banks and other financial firms and hold them accountable for their decisions. These norms target banks' interactions with financial consumers, and establish a regulatory standard of consumer-focused decision-making that is supposed to govern all aspects of a bank's participation in consumer-finance markets. This aspect of the Principles appears to have greater potential to alter the power relations of financial consumer markets because it challenges traditional ideas about the autonomy of banks and other financial firms over their services, products and operations, and because it affords the regulator a proactive role in securing market discipline. Norms that hold banks accountable for their dealings with financial consumers are likely to be resisted by banks, however, which seems to be anticipated by the G20's explicit addition of sanctioning and surveillance work to the regulator's core role of enabling and encouraging the capable, vigilant consumer.

Improved regulatory surveillance and stronger sanctioning powers potentially will help to expose significant problems in retail-finance markets, especially problems that may otherwise remain masked by the firm's capacity to set the terms of what constitutes routine business practice. But it is not self-evident that these powers will bring about systematic improvement in firms' treatment of their customers. Consider for example the experience of the UK regulator's 'Treating Customers Fairly' (TCF) initiative, a project that sought to alter the organizational cultures and business models of financial firms. The goal of this initiative was for firms to incorporate within all aspects of their business and market practices the same kinds of customer-protection principles that the G20 leaders endorsed. The FSA expected TCF to become embedded in the management of financial firms through leadership, strategic planning, decision-making, management controls, staff recruitment, training and monitoring. A firm was regarded as having satisfied TCF standards only when it was able to demonstrate, not simply assert, that it had fully integrated the fair treatment of customers into its corporate culture (FSA, 2012; Williams, 2010; FSA, 2007a, 2007b, 2007c, 2006b).

In practice, the FSA found that attempts to reform banks and other financial firms fell far short of its aspirations, even in relation to the high-profile payment-protection insurance (PPI) markets, which the FSA and other UK regulators and consumer organizations had targeted as a priority area.[12] Far from taking responsibility to reform their market conduct financial firms more or less ignored the regulatory strictures and TCF principles until UK regulators banned the most predatory – and lucrative – form of PPI, imposed extensive controls on sales, and forced the firms into adopting a comprehensive and expensive redress scheme.[13] In contrast to these mandatory measures that have produced results, the FSA's campaign to change how financial firms conducted their business in the lucrative PPI markets – based on principles that closely resemble the G20 model – did not cause these firms to improve their treatment of financial consumers or prevent the materialization of consumer detriment (FSA, 2011; Williams, 2013a).

But it may be that the FSA's work in this market had some notable effects, such as helping to expose the scale of the firms' exploitation of financial consumers. This work also may have contributed to an understanding of predatory marketing practices that were endemic to the market for PPI products as a systemic problem rather than an aberration attributable to rogue firms or the mistakes of financially illiterate consumers. These may be real achievements, but how much protection do they offer financial consumers? The experience of the FSA, a large, well-funded regulator operating in a rich country, raises significant questions about the capacity of the Principles to reconfigure the economic relations of retail-finance markets and to make financial consumption safer.

Conclusion

This chapter has drawn on an emerging interest in the regulation of consumer finance markets among international policymakers to illustrate the limitations of existing regulatory paradigms in holding banks responsible for social dimensions of their consumer business activity. Under the neo-liberal consumption driven growth paradigm that dominated financial regulation until the 2007–08 crash, this interest in consumer finance markets was manifested mostly in what Zokaityte (2015) terms 'edu-regulatory' policies directed at market expansion through acting on the conduct and capacities of financial consumers. International policymakers paid little attention to how banks and other financial firms conducted their retail businesses. Instead they promoted financial literacy education to make consumers wiser and more vigilant, together with information remedies and the development of information institutions to improve the quality of market decision-making.

The vigilant consumer approach paid little explicit attention the social responsibilities of banks and generally rested on heroic assumptions about relationships between financial firms and consumers. It assumed that capable and vigilant consumers would be able to hold firms accountable for compliance with regulatory standards and reduce the scope for firms to benefit from exploitative conduct. It assumed also that financial consumers are similarly affected by the conduct of financial firms and thus share an interest in changing established business models and retail market practices. Studies discussed in this chapter about expansion of consumer finance markets and the distribution in household debt provides reasons to doubt this latter assumption.

Neo-liberal expansion of consumer finance markets led to a substantial increase in household debt across Western Europe and North America and allowed financial firms to target the incomes of financial consumers as a source of revenue to then plough into the production of securitized and derivative products. Evidence of inequality in the resulting distribution of debt suggests that banks and other large financial firms are able to segment markets for their consumer finance products, using business models based on risk-based pricing and information resources such as credit bureaus. Consequently, financial consumers encounter different levels of exposure to the risks of predatory, exploitative practices depending on factors such as location, wealth and aspects of identity (such as race, gender and age) (Austin, 2003). The resulting fragmentation of the risks experienced by different groups of financial consumers militates against the notion of mass consumer vigilance influencing firms and performing an effective regulatory role.

Many of the principles of the international model of financial consumer protection recently adopted by G20 countries reproduce elements of the vigilant consumer paradigm that so dismally failed to protect individuals and households before the crash occurred. But some G20 principles focus more explicitly on the responsibilities of financial firms and on strengthening the capacity of regulatory institutions to influence market relations between financial consumers and firms. Similar principles on the responsibilization and accountability of firms for their treatment of financial consumers were in operation in the UK for several years before the crash. The experience in that jurisdiction perhaps serves as a reminder of the scale of the problem that regulators face in attempting to responsibilize the retail market operations of financial firms.

Although the FSA's responsibilization principles appeared to have had little impact on how firms treated consumers, the regulators' work may have had the beneficial effects of exposing problems with the conduct of firms and changing the perception of these problems from episodic to systemic. Noting that these effects are real achievements, this chapter nonetheless questioned their capacity to make financial consumption safer or to protect consumers in other ways.

There may be little in the new international model of financial consumer protection to render financial consumption safer or change the socio-economic relations of consumer finance markets. The challenge that remains is for policymakers and regulators to look beyond the vigilant consumer as market disciplinarian and instead confront directly endemic misconduct and systemic corporate irresponsibility in consumer-finance markets.

Notes

1 This chapter draws on work previously published in Williams, T. (2013) 'Continuity, not rupture: the persistence of neo-liberalism in the internationalization of consumer finance regulation' in Wilson, T. (ed.) *International Responses To Issues Of Credit And Over-Indebtedness In The Wake Of Crisis*. London: Ashgate Publishing pp. 15–45 and (2013) 'Who wants to watch? A comment on the new international paradigm of financial consumer market regulation', *Seattle University Law Review*, 36: 1187–211.
2 Online at www.financial-education.org/join_INFE.html and www.financial-education.org/home.html (retrieved 25 October 2015).
3 For example, it has been reported that high household debt is a structural feature of the Danish Economy because of the interplay between mortgages and tax (EU, 2012).
4 Payday lending markets grew in many countries including the UK, after the crash and expansion of predatory mortgage lending has recently been reported in the UK (Jones, 2015).
5 Citigroup continues to rely heavily on its consumer finance business. Its website reports that in 2014 Citigroup's Global Consumer Banking (GCB) business 'generated $10 billion in pretax earnings, more than half of Citicorp's total' for the entire company. Retrieved on 1 November 2015 from www.citigroup.com/citi/about/consumer_businesses.html.
6 The remaining £5.7 billion was largely accounted for by the foregone interest on current accounts. In a 2013 update on the market study, the OFT reported that bank revenues from unauthorized lending charges had declined substantially – by about 23 per cent – between 2007 and 2011 but that revenues from interest and charges for authorized loans rose significantly over the same period (OFT, 2013 Chapter 5). Unauthorized borrowing is so much more expensive than authorized loans that it is not surprising that the OFT estimated a net reduction in costs to consumers of 'between £388 million and £928 million since the 2008 market study' (OFT, 2013, p. 5). While the regulator commented that the reduction in consumer charges was 'significant and welcome', the report notes also that it came about 'largely the result of pressure from OFT and others' (p. 5) and as such provides little evidence of banks embracing and internalizing their responsibilities to consumers. It is interesting to speculate whether the banks' inertia might be partly explained by the support they received from the Supreme Court in the high profile litigation over unauthorized borrowing charges (*OFT v. Abbey National*, 2008, 2009).
7 'Review of barriers to entry, expansion and exit in retail banking', cited at note 77 (Treasury 2011).
8 These characterizations of the penalties, charges and pricing reflect repeated findings about the opacity and complexity of banks practices (see e.g. US, 2006; OFT, 2008; Treasury, 2011).
9 On bank charges see *Office of Fair Trading v Abbey National Plc*, 2009. PPI complaints sometimes obtained redress in county courts but tended to fare poorly in higher courts, e.g. Harrison v Black Horse Ltd (2011). In Plevin v Paragon Finance the Supreme Court essentially overturned Harrison, holding that an undisclosed commission of 71 per cent on an attached PPI transaction rendered the credit relationship unfair under section 140A of the Consumer Credit Act 1974.
10 The reduction is attributed to (a) payment distress; (b) fears of payment distress; and (c) restrictions on credit supply. The study found that 'cuts in spending associated with debt ... reduced the level of aggregate private consumption by around 2% after 2007 (out of a total fall of around 5%)' (Bunn *et al.*, p. 314).
11 www.gov.uk/government/news/bank-of-england-review-confirms-that-help-to-buy-supports-responsible-lending; www.gov.uk/government/news/help-to-buy-mortgage-guarantee-loans-new-lending-limits.
12 The Financial Ombudsman Service also played an active part in the conflict over PPI (FOS, n.d.), as did the Competition Commission Report on the PPI market (Competition Commission, 2009).
13 The FSA's work on PPI included rules on the marketing of PPI and other insurance products, thematic review of PPI sales practices, mystery shopping exercises, incorporation of review of PPI sales files into FSA supervision of individual financial firms and enforcement action against twenty-four firms for PPI sales misconduct, which resulted in fines ranging from £28,000 to £7 million. It also established the complaints-and-redress scheme that required financial firms to pay consumers more than £21 billion in compensation as of August 2015 (FCA, 2015). Key documents from the FSA's work as well as ongoing actions by the Financial Conduct Authority (FCA) are available on the FSA website: www.fca.org.uk. For more extensive discussion of the regulatory response to PPI in the UK see Ferran (2012) and Williams (2013b).

Bibliography

Austin, R. (2003) 'Of predatory lending and the democratization of credit: Preserving the social safety net of informality in small-loan transactions', *American University Law Review*, 53(6): 1217–57.

Bank of England (2014) *Financial Stability Report* 35 (June). Retrieved on 27 October 2015 from www.bankofengland.co.uk/publications/Documents/fsr/2014/fsrfull1406.pdf.

Barba, A. and Pivetti, M. (2009) 'Rising household debt: Its causes and macroeconomic implications – a long-period analysis', *Cambridge Journal of Economics*, 33(1): 113–37.

Bar-Gill, O. and Warren, E. (2008) 'Making credit safer', *University of Pennsylvania Law Review*, 157(1): 1–101.

Beck, T. et al. (2012) 'Who gets the credit? And does it matter? Household vs. firm lending across countries', *The BE Journal of Macroeconomics*, 12(1) Article 2. Retrieved on 1 November 2015 from www2.gsu.edu/~ecofkr/papers/published_version_BEJM.pdf.

Bhutta, N. (2012) *Mortgage Debt and Household Deleveraging: Accounting for the Decline in Mortgage Debt Using Consumer Credit Record Data*. Federal Reserve Board Washington Finance and Economics Discussion Series, Working Paper No. 14, 2012. Retrieved on 8 May 2016 from www.federalreserve.gov/pubs/feds/.

Black, J. (2001) 'Decentring regulation: Understanding the role of regulation and self-regulation in a "post-regulatory" world', *Current Legal Problems*, 54: 103–47.

Black, J. and Nobles, R. (1998) 'Personal pensions mis-selling: The causes and lessons of regulatory failure', *The Modern Law Review*, 61(6): 789–820.

Brown, M., Haughwout, A., Lee, D. and Van der Klaauw, W. (2013) 'The financial crisis at the kitchen table: Trends in household debt and credit', *Current Issues in Economics and Finance*, 19(2) (Online). Retrieved on 31 October 2015 from http://data.newyorkfed.org/research/current_issues/ci19-2.pdf.

Bunn, P. et al. (2013) 'The financial position of British households: Evidence from the 2013 NMG Consulting survey', *Bank of England Quarterly Bulletin*, Q4: 351–60.

Calavita, K., Pontell, H.N. and Tillman, R. (1997) *Big Money Crime: Fraud and Politics in the Savings and Loan Crisis*. Oakland, CA: University of California Press.

Competition Commission (2009) *Report of the Payment Protection Market Investigation*. Retrieved on 30 October 2015 from http://webarchive.nationalarchives.gov.uk/20140402141250 and www.competition-commission.org.uk/our-work/directory-of-all-inquiries/ppi-market-investigation-and-remittal/final-report-and-appendices-glossary.

Crouch, C. (2011) *The Strange Non-death of Neo-liberalism*. London: Polity Press.

Crouch, C. (2012) 'Employment, consumption, debt, and European industrial relations systems', *Industrial Relations: A Journal of Economy and Society*, 51(s1): 389–412.

Cynamon, B.Z. and Fazzari, S.M. (2008) 'Household debt in the consumer age: Source of growth – risk of collapse', *Capitalism and Society*, 3(2) (Online, Berkeley Electronic Press). Retrieved on 1 November 2015 from https://password.nottingham.ac.uk/cfcm/documents/workshops/cynamon-fazzari.pdf.

Dore, R. (2008) 'Financialization of the global economy', *Industrial and Corporate Change*, 17(6), 1097–112.

dos Santos, P.L. (2009) 'On the content of banking in contemporary capitalism', *Historical Materialism*, 17(2): 180–213.

Dynan, K.E. and Kohn, D.L. (2007) *The rise in US household indebtedness: Causes and consequences* (Online, Federal Reserve Board). Retrieved on 1 November 2015 from www.federalreserve.gov/pubs/FEDS/2007/200737/200737pap.pdf.

Dynan, K., Elmendorf, D. and Sichel, D. (2012) 'The evolution of household income volatility', *The BE Journal of Economic Analysis & Policy*, 12(2) (Online). Retrieved on 1 November 2015 from www.degruyter.com/view/j/bejeap.2012.12.issue-2/1935-1682.3347/1935-1682.3347.xml.

Engel, K.C. and McCoy, P.A. (2011) *The Subprime Virus: Reckless Credit, Regulatory Failure, and Next Steps*. New York: Oxford University Press.

Ertürk, I. and Solari, S. (2007) 'Banks as continuous reinvention', *New Political Economy*, 12(3): 369–88.

Ertürk, I., Froud, J., Johal, S., Leaver, A. and Williams, K. (2007) 'The democratization of finance? Promises, outcomes and conditions', *Review of International Political Economy*, 14(4): 553–75.

European Union (EU) (2012) *In-Depth Review for Denmark in Accordance with Article 5 of Regulation No 1176/2011 on the Prevention and Correction of Macroeconomic Imbalances*. Retrieved on 1 November 2015 from http://ec.europa.eu/europe2020/pdf/nd/idr2012_denmark_en.pdf.

Federal Trade Commission. (2012) *Protecting Consumer Privacy in an Era of Rapid Change: Recommendations for Businesses and Policymakers*, March. Retrieved 1 November 2015 from www.ftc.gov/reports/protecting-consumer-privacy-era-rapid-change-recommendations-businesses-policymakers.

Ferran, E. (2012) 'Regulatory lessons from the payment protection insurance mis-selling scandal in the UK', *European Business Organization Law Review*, 13(2): 247–70.
Financial Conduct Authority (FCA). (2015) 'Monthly PPI refunds and compensation'. Retrieved on 29 October 2015 from www.fca.org.uk/consumers/financial-services-products/insurance/payment-protection-insurance/refunds.
Financial Ombudsman Service (FOS). (n.d.) *Online PPI Resource*. Retrieved on 30 October 2015 from www.financial-ombudsman.org.uk/publications/technical_notes/ppi.html.
Financial Services Authority (FSA). (2003) *Towards A National Strategy For Financial Capability*. Retrieved on 1 November 2015 from http://hb.betterregulation.com/external/Towards%20a%20national%20strategy%20for%20financial%20capability.pdf.
FSA. (2005) *Annual Report for the year 2004/05*. London: FSA.
FSA. (2006a) *Financial Capability In The UK: Establishing A Baseline*. Retrieved on 31 October 2015 from www.fsa.gov.uk/pubs/other/fincap_baseline.pdf.
FSA. (2006b) *Treating Customers Fairly—Towards Fair Outcomes For Consumers*. London: FSA.
FSA. (2007a) *Treating Customers Fairly: Measuring Outcomes*. London: FSA.
FSA. (2007b) *Treating Customers Fairly: Guide to Management Information*. London: FSA.
FSA. (2007c) *Treating Customers Fairly: Culture*. London: FSA.
FSA. (2011) *The Financial Conduct Authority: Approach to regulation*. London: FSA.
FSA. (2012) *FSA Handbook (now FCA Handbook)*. London: FSA. Retrieved on 8 May 2016 from www.handbook.fca.org.uk/handbook/.
Financial Stability Board (FSB). (2011) *Consumer Finance Protection with Particular Focus on Credit* (October). Retrieved on 12 October 2015 from www.financialstabilityboard.org/wp-content/uploads/r_111026a.pdf?page_moved=1.
G20. (2011) *Cannes Summit Final Declaration—Building our common future: Renewed collective action for the benefit of all*, G20 (4 November). Retrieved on 1 November 2015 from www.g20.utoronto.ca/2011/2011-cannes-declaration-111104-en.html.
Galbraith J.K. (1967) *The New Industrial State*. New York: New American Library.
Gowan, P. (2009) 'Crisis in the heartland', *New Left Review* 55(2): 5–29.
Hanrahan, P.F. (2014) 'Should the FSI revisit the philosophy of financial services regulation?', *Law and Financial Markets Review*, 8(3): 199–203.
International Gateway For Financial Education. (n.d.) Retrieved on 28 October 2015 from www.financial-education.org/.
International Monetary Fund (IMF). (2012) *World Economic Outlook: Growth Resuming, Dangers Remain* IMF: Washington. Retrieved on 1 November 2015 from www.imf.org/external/pubs/ft/weo/2012/01/pdf/text.pdf.
IMF. (2013) *Transcript of the UK Article IV Mission Concluding Press Conference with David Lipton*. Retrieved on 31 October 2015 from www.imf.org/external/np/tr/2013/tr052213.htm.
Jones, R. (2015) 'Sub-prime mortgages make surprise comeback in the UK', *The Guardian* 30 October, online. Retrieved on 30 October 2015 from www.theguardian.com/money/2015/oct/30/sub-prime-mortgages-make-surprise-comeback-in-the-uk?CMP=EMCNEWEML6619I2.
Harrison v Black Horse Ltd [2011] EWCA Civ 1128 (12 October 2011).
Helms, B. (2006) *Access For All: Building Inclusive Financial Systems*. Washington, DC: World Bank.
Kumar, A. (2005) *Access to Financial Services-Brazil*. Washington, DC: World Bank.
Langenderfer, J. and Cook, D.L. (2004) 'Oh, what a tangled web we weave: the state of privacy protection in the information economy and recommendations for governance', *Journal of Business Research*, 57(7): 734–47.
Martin, R. (2002). *Financialization of Daily Life*. Philadelphia, PA: Temple University Press.
Mian, A. and Sufi, A. (2010) 'Household leverage and the recession of 2007–09', *IMF Economic Review*, 58(1): 74–117.
Mitchell, W.C. (1912) 'The backward art of spending money', *American Economic Review*, 2(2): 269–81.
Nottage, L. and Kozuka, S. (2012) 'Lessons from product safety regulation for reforming consumer credit markets in Japan and beyond', *Sydney Law Review*, 34: 129–61.
Office Of Fair Trading (OFT). (2008) *Personal Current Accounts In The UK*. London: OFT. Retrieved on 1 November 2015 from http://webarchive.nationalarchives.gov.uk/20140402142426/http:/oft.gov.uk/OFTwork/markets-work/personal/.
Office of Fair Trading v. Abbey National Plc (2009) UKSC 6. Retrieved on 25 October 2015 from www.bailii.org/uk/cases/UKSC/2009/6.html.
Office of Fair Trading v. Abbey National Plc (2008) EWHC 875. Retrieved on 25 October 2015 from www.bailii.org/ew/cases/EWHC/Comm/2008/875.html.

Office of Fair Trading. (2013) *Review of the Personal Current Account Market*. London: OFT.

Organisation for Economic Cooperation and Development (OECD). (2004) 'OECD's Financial Education Project', 87 *Financial Market Trends* 223.

OECD. (2005a) *Improving Financial Literacy: Analysis of Issues and Policy*, Paris: OECD. Retrieved on 15 October 2015 from www.oecd.org/daf/fin/financial-education/improvingfinancialliteracyanalysisofissuesandpolicies.htm.

OECD. (2005b) *Recommendation on Principles and Good Practices for Financial Education and Awareness*, Paris: OECD. Retrieved on 30 November 2015 from www.oecd.org/finance/financial-education/35108560.pdf.

OECD. (2011) *G20 High-level Principles on Financial Consumer Protection*. Retrieved on 26 October 2015 from www.oecd.org/daf/fin/financial-markets/48892010.pdf.

OECD. (2012) *INFE High-Level Principles for the Evaluation of Financial Education Programmes*. Retrieved on 8 May 2016 from www.oecd.org/daf/fin/financial-education/49373959.pdf.

OECD. (2015) *Household Debt*. Retrieved on 15 October 2015 from https://data.oecd.org/hha/household-debt.htm#indicator-chart.

Orhangazi, Ö. (2008) *Financialization and the US Economy*. Cheltenham: Edward Elgar Publishing.

Osborne, D. and Gaebler, T. (1992) *Reinventing Government: How The Entrepreneurial Spirit Is Transforming The Public Sector*. Reading MA: Addison-Wesley.

Osborne, H. (2013) 'Rising household debt is cause for alarm, warns thinktank IPPR', *The Guardian*, 28 December Online. Retrieved on 10 October 2015 from www.theguardian.com/politics/2013/dec/28/rising-household-debt-cause-for-alarm.

Piccioto, S. and Haines, J. (1999) 'Regulating global financial markets', *Journal of Law and Society*, 26: 351–68.

Plevin v Paragon Finance [2014] UKSC 61.

Ramsay, I. (1995) 'Consumer credit law, distributive justice and the welfare state', *Oxford Journal of Legal Studies*, 15(2): 177–97.

Ramsay, I. (2006) 'Consumer law, regulatory capitalism and the new learning in regulation', *Sydney Law Review*, 28: 9–36.

Ramsay, I. and Williams, T. (2011) 'The crash that launched a thousand fixes: Regulation of consumer credit after the lending revolution and the credit crunch' in Alexander, K. and Moloney, N. (eds) *Law Reform & Financial Markets: Institutions and Financial Governance*. Cheltenham: Edward Elgar, pp. 221–49.

Treasury Select Committee (UK). (2011) *Competition and Choice in Retail Banking*. Retrieved on 8 May 2016 from www.publications.parliament.uk/pa/cm201011/cmselect/cmtreasy/612/61205.htm#n77.

Tschoegl, A.E. (1987) 'International retail banking as a strategy: An assessment', *Journal of International Business Studies*, 18(2): 67–88.

Tschoegl, A.E. (2005) 'The world's local bank': HSBC's expansion in the US, Canada and Mexico', *Latin American Business Review*, 5(4): 45–68.

US Government Accountability Office (US GAO). (2006) *Credit Cards: Increased Complexity In Rates And Fees Heightens Need For More Effective Disclosures To Consumers*. GAO-06-929. Retrieved on 1 November 2015 from www.gao.gov/assets/260/251427.pdf.

Waldron, M. and Young, G. (2006) 'The state of British household finances: Results from the 2006 NMG Research survey', *Bank of England Quarterly Bulletin*, Q4: 397–402.

Waldron, M. and Young, G. (2007) 'Household debt and spending: Results from the 2007 NMG Research survey', *Bank of England. Quarterly Bulletin*, 47(4): 512–21.

Williams, T. (2007) 'Empowerment of whom and for what? Financial literacy education and the new regulation of consumer financial services', *Law and Policy*, 29(2): 226–56.

Williams, T. (2010) 'Open the box: An exploration of the Financial Services Authority's model of fairness in consumer financial transactions', in Kenny M., Devenney, J. and Fox O'Mahony, L. (eds) *Unconscionability in European Private Financial Transactions*. Cambridge: Cambridge University Press, pp. 227–45.

Williams, T. (2013a) 'Continuity, not rupture: the persistence of neoliberalism in the internationalization of consumer finance regulation' in Wilson, T. (ed.) *International Responses To Issues Of Credit And Over-Indebtedness In The Wake Of Crisis*. London: Ashgate Publishing, pp. 15–45.

Williams, T. (2013b) 'Who wants to watch? A comment on the new international paradigm of financial consumer market regulation', *Seattle University Law Review*, 36: 1187–211.

World Bank (2009) *Good Practices for Consumer Protection and Financial Literacy in Europe and Central Asia: A Diagnostic Tool* (September). New York: World Bank.

Zelizer, V.A. (1997) *The Social Meaning Of Money*. Princeton, NJ: Princeton University Press: Princeton.

Zokaityte (2015) *The Financial Capability Project: Edu-Regulating Consumer Financial Markets Through The Democratisation of Financial Knowledge* (Unpublished PhD thesis. University of Kent).

Index

ABN Amro 243
ACA Management LLC 243
algorithmic trading 403
Ambac 35
American International Group (AIG) 2, 35, 85, 89, 90–2, 94–102, 366
amoral calculator hypothesis 41, 42
Anglo-Saxon banking model 177–8, 194, 276
arbitrage 14, 24, 26, 29–33, 37, 121–2
Argentina 243
artisan of finance 5, 404–8
asset-backed commercial paper market (ABCP) 380–4, 392–4
asset-backed securities (ABSs) 9–16, 20, 22, 27–8, 38, 90
asset-backed securities' collateralised debt obligations (ABS CDOs): causes of credit crisis 34–43; evaluation practices 9–16; evolution 28–34
auditors and auditing 98, 326–7
austerity 101, 135–6, 145, 175–6
Austria *140*, *143*, 256, 363
automated trading 242, 403
automatic information exchange (AIE) 262–3
A.W. Jones and Co 240

Bahamas 255
Bahrain 257
Bank for International Settlements (BIS) 81, 112–13, 235
Bank of America 18, 35, 335, 360, 363, 382, 415
Bank of England: ease of lending conditions 399; and financial innovation 112; financial market regulation 290–1, 295; Financial Policy Committee (FPC) 317–18, 322, 326, 418; location 152; monetary policy 256; and private ownership 353; rising interest rates 313; securitisation 199
Bank of Italy 215
Bank of Scotland 285
bank-based systems, non-financial companies finance 192–5
Bankers Trust 25, 26–7, 212

Banking Act (1933) (US) (Glass-Steagall): deinstitutionalisation 338–9; delay in repeal 339–40; passage and de-institutionalisation 336–7; repeal 93, 95, 344–6; re-theorisation 340–4; rise and fall 335–6; significance of rise and fall 4, 346–7
Banking Acts *see* United Kingdom: Banking Acts
banking crisis (1973–74) 68–9
banking crisis (2007–09) *see* financial crisis (2007–09)
banking culture: calls for reform 398–9; financial sociability 404–5; frameworks for reform 399–401; institutional context 401–2; need for reform 408; operational characteristics of reform 406–8; organisational implications for reform 405–6; persona of banking 5, 402–3; suggestions for reform 403–4
banking regulation: consensus and compromise 344–6; credit risk practices 2; deinstitutionalisation 338–9, 346–7; Eurozone 3, 176–7; internal models 303, 307–9; post banking crisis 1–6, 69–70, 273–5, 286–7, 315; power of industry 347; regulatory capital 304–7; re-theorisation 340–4; rising interest rates 312–15; risk 2, 279; securitisation 307–9; stress testing models 4, 308–11, 315; theorisation and re-theorisation 4, 337–8; vulnerability of institutions 335–6 *see also* financial market regulation; regulation
Banking Standards Review Council (UK) 402
banking supervision 4, 175–80, 184–8, 318–20, 326–7
banks and banking: account service charges 415; assets *195*, 196–200, 354, *355*; balance sheets 304–7; business models 5, 137, 177–9, 194, 275–80, 286, 303, 307–9; changes 137, 193–5; customer funding 201–3; domestic debt 143; education and training 2, 5, 154–6; ethnographic studies 170; Eurozone government debt 140; fines 398, 400; funding 138–9; holding companies *361*, *362*; internal models 303, 307–9; lending 175, 192–3, 399; liabilities 201–3; misconduct 3; power of industry 347; Provident

Index

(C&S) 65–71; re-capitalisation 274; rising interest rates 312–15; secrecy 256, 258, 259; varieties in EU 192–5 *see also* banking culture; banking regulation; commercial banks; development banking; investment banking; shadow banking
Barclays Bank 67, 233–4, 277, 280–2, 382, 415
Barings 325
Basel Accords 273–4, 279, 295, 304–8, 309, 314
Bear Stearns 35, 360, 383
Belgium *140*, *143*, 229, 363, 382, 383
Bermuda 255
'Big Bang' (UK) 85, 92, 354
Bishopsgate International Investment Management plc 320
Black-Scholes-Merton option model 25, 226
BNP Paribas 382
Bourdieu, Pierre 74, 75–6, 81
Bretton Woods system (1946–71) 353
bricolage 2, 126–9
British Bankers Association 226, 227
British gold standard (1816–1914) 353, 354
British Virgin Islands 257, 258
building societies 355–7
Building Societies Act (1986) (UK) 355
Bundesbank banking model 177–8, 179
business models for banks 5, 137, 177–9, 194, 275–80, 286, 303, 307–9

C12 280
Cable, Vince 357, 364
Canada 363, 383, 414
canonical-mechanism markets 10, 27–8
Capital Ideas (Bernstein) 116
capitalism 117, 123, 192–5
capital-labour nexus 161, 163–4, 166–7, 169
Cassano, Joe 95, 97, 100
Cattle's (Holdings) Ltd 68
Cayman Islands 255, 257
central banks 144, 177–81
check trading *see* documentary check trading
Chicago Board of Trade (CBOT) 210
Chicago Mercantile Exchange 225, 226
Church of England 247
Citibank 335, 344, 346, 360, 363
Citicorp 340
Citigroup 35, 39, 233, 275, 382, 415
City of London *see* London
collateral damage, euro crisis 141–2
collateral motive, in the Eurozone 137–45
collateralised debt obligations (CDOs): corporate 23–8, 40, 41; credit rating 93–4; evaluation practices 2, 10–11, 12–16, 23–8; explanation *19*, 106, *106*; and falling house prices 90–1; global markets 380–1; growth 84–5, 100; and hedge funds 245–6; history 15–16; losses 9–10; securitisation 89*b*; subprime crisis 245–6; trading 10

commercial banks 140, 336–7, 339–40, 344, 345–6, 358, 401
community banking 360
Conservative party (UK), hedge fund donations 247
consumer finance 5, 56, 284–6, 411–18, 422
Consumer Financial Protection Bureau (US) 286
consumer protection 5, 411–12, 418–21
continental banking model 177–8, 194
Cooperative, credit club system 58
corporate culture 400–1
corporate governance 2, 84–8, 94–8
corporate loans 25, 33
correlation: ABS CDOs 30–3, 40; ABSs 29–30; and evaluation of CDOs 12, 24–7, 89*b*; and vulnerability of mortgages 20–1
correspondent banks 259
credit: derivatives 25; development 161–2; domestic to private sector 359, *360*; growth in the US 363–6; regulation 60–1, 67; regulation of risk 2; and shadow banking 78
credit cards 415
credit crisis (2007–09) *see* financial crisis (2007–09)
credit default swaps (CDSs): and ABSs 28, 37; and AIG 35, 85, 89, 95–9, 366; cause of insurers' losses 39; and CDOs 26–7, 90–2; growth 89*b*; not classed as insurance 42
credit rating: ABS CDOs 29–34, 41; ABSs 28; CDOs 24, 25, 28, 34, 89–90; and evaluation practices 12–14; mortgage-backed securities 19–20, 35–6; Provident (C&S) 63; risk 80; standards 35–6; subprime mortgage lending *31*
Credit Suisse 382
credit support annexes (CDAs) 97
Crisis without End? The Unravelling of Western Prosperity (Gamble) 290
Crowther Committee Report on Consumer Credit 67
currencies 242, 244, 352, 353, 359
customer funding gap, banks 201–3

data challenges: judgement based supervision 325–8; and Legal Entity Identifiers (LEIs) 328–9
Davenport, Richard 67
De Larosière group 181
default: ABS CDOs 29–30, 33–4; mortgages 35, 37–8; subprime mortgage lending 22–3
defined contribution pension plans (401k) 161–2, 166
deinstitutionalisation: Banking Act (1933) (US) (Glass-Steagall) 338–9, 346; universal banking 337
Deloitte & Touche 258
democracies, financial market regulation 295–8
Democratic Republic of Congo 243
Denmark *143*, 383, 414
Depfa Bank (Germany) 255

Index

deregulation: attempts 344–6; favoured by large banks 340; fear of competition 344; financial contagion 375; measure 388; negative outcomes 347; pressure on firms and states 159; re-theorisation 340–4; subprime mortgage lending 84–5; unevenness 121–2

derivatives: credit 25; definition and types 208–12; and evaluation of CDOs 25; expansion 86; function of risk management 210, 216–17; Italian local authorities 212–16; mainstream financial theory 216–17; markets 209–10; over-the-counter (OTC) 208

Des Moines Investments Ltd 243

Deutsche Bank 1, 38, 40, 119, 120–1, 275–7, 382

development banking 353, 355–8

Diamond, Bob 280

Dimon, Jamie 280, 282

documentary check trading 55, 56–8, 60–3, 70

domestic banks 140, 142–3, 144

Drexel, Burnham, Lambert 23

economics: British development 353–7; and consumer finance 412–13; contagion 374–7; finance as a subdiscipline 117, 122–3; geographies 154, 156; impact of financial crisis 363; and offshore finance research 254–5; UK development 368; US development 359, 368

education, City of London 154–5

education and training 2, 5, 88, 154–6, 413

efficient market hypothesis, City of London 168–9

Elliot Associates 243

emotions, and financial sociability 404–5

entrepreneurialism 406

Ernst & Young 258

ethical concerns, and hedge funds 243

ethnographic studies, banking activities 170

Euribor (Euro Interbank Offered Rate): bets 232; generic information *229*; history 225–7; list of main pubic consultations *231*, 235; multi-referential benchmark 227–9, 237–8; normal banking practice 229–33; rate manipulation 3, 234–5; reaction to manipulation and reform 235–7

Euribor-EBF *see* European Money Markets Institute (previously Euribor-EBF)

Eurocurrency (offshore) financial system 354

Eurodollar market 225–6, 256, 354, 359

Europe 134–5, 137, 138–9, 175, 352

European Banking Authority (EBA) 81, 235, 311

European Banking Federation 225, 228

European Central Bank (ECB): European Systemic Risk Board (ESRB) 81, 176, 181–7, 311; financial supervision 184–8; gain of supervisory powers 3, 175–81, 188; inclusion of banking stress-test results 310; Outright Monetary Transactions 144; rising interest rates 313; Single Supervisory Mechanism (SSM) 1, 177, 185–8; sovereign debt 139, 142, 143, 145; support for securitisation markets 199

European Commission: Common Consolidated Corporate Tax Base (CCCTB) 264; De Larosière group 181; European Systemic Risk Board (ESRB) 181; financial benchmarks reviews 235; financial market regulation 297; regulatory reforms in sovereign debt 138–9; Single Resolution Mechanism 177

European Exchange Rate Mechanism, and sterling 242, 244

European Money Markets Institute (previously Euribor-EBF) 227, 236

European Parliament 235

European Securities and Markets Authority (ESMA) 235, 246

European System of Financial Supervision 176

European Union: Bank Recovery and Resolution Directive 274; Banking Union 177, 186, 187–8, 299; and beneficial ownership 263; Capital Markets Union (CMU) 293, 299–300; Capital Requirement Directive (2015) 264; changing nature of bank assets 196–200; changing nature of bank liabilities 201–3; changing nature of loan markets 199–200; Credit Requirement Directive IV (CRD IV) 274; Credit Requirement Regulation 274; European Directive 2002/47/EC 137; Financial Collateral Arrangements directive 2002/47/EC 138; financial market regulation 299; financial regulation 366; hedge funds regulation 246; High-Level Group on Financial Supervision 245; implications of market-based banking 203–4; joining of by Britain 354; Liikanen Review 273–5, 280; Market Abuse Directive 235; Saving Tax Directive 262; shadow banking 195–6; Stability and Growth Pact (SGP) 212–13; tackling of tax evasion 262; tax loss 260; varieties of capitalism and banking 192–5

Eurozone: bank regulation 3, 176–7; central banking 177–81; collateral motive 137–45; collateral motive and investor loyalty 140–5; crisis 141–2, 175, 183; Member States 178–84, 187–8; shadow banking 196; sovereign debt crisis 140, 144, 145

evaluation practices: ABS CDOs 16, 40–3; ABSs 16–23; beliefs 41; CDOs 23–8; clusters 11–16; credit crisis 40–3; financial markets 11–16; and historical shaping of for mortgage-backed securities 16–23; importance 10; in scientific practice 11

excess spread safety mechanism 21

exchanges: futures 210–12; organised for derivatives 209–10

expected loss, banks 304

exports: financial 354, *355*, *356*, 359; high-tech manufacturing 356, *357*, 359

429

Index

Fair and Effective Markets Review (UK) 293
Federal Deposit Insurance Corp 234
federal funds rate *107*
Federal Home Loan Mortgage Corporation (Freddie Mac) 17
Federal Housing Administration (FHA) 16–17
Federal National Mortgage Association (Fannie Mae) 17
Federal Reserve Bank: deregulation 345; financial benchmarks 236; financial market regulation 292; Open Market Committee (FOMC) 340; purchase of mortgage-backed securities 382; rising interest rates 312, 313; short-term loan activities 383; stress testing models 310–11; supervision 358; support for securitisation markets 199
FICO (Fair, Isaac and Company) scores, use of for mortgage-backed securities 20
films, highlighting attitudes of bankers 399
finance: attempt to 'dis-essentialize' 161; boundaries 3, 159–62, 169–71; as an economic subdiscipline 117, 122–3; expansion 160; geographies of 149–50, 156; link with innovation 114–15; market-based 2; relationships with states 160; social studies 116–17; sociology 379–81; theory 114–18
Financial Conduct Authority (FCA) 284, 286, 293, 317–18, 353, 398
financial contagion 375–7
financial crisis (2007–09): ABS CDOs 16, 34–40; anatomy 88–92; asset-backed commercial paper market (ABCP) 392–4; banking regulation since 1–6, 69–70, 273–5, 286–7, 315; causes 362, 373; CDOs 40–3, 245–6; context 85–8; costs 363; countries that experienced *387*; evaluation practices 40–3; failure of corporate governance to prevent 84–5; features 373–5; financial innovation 112; as a 'global' crisis 149; and global finance 393–5; and hedge funds 245–6; and house prices *389*, *392*; institutional analysis 169–70; losses 9; meltdown of risk 91; mortgage-backed securities 374–5, 384–95; negative change in GDP *386*; New York-London axis after the 362–8; product of a 'perfect storm' 100–2; and recession model *385*; and securitisation 88–90; sociology 9–16, 378; subprime mortgage lending 245–6, 356–7, 362, 393; theoretical discussion and hypotheses 375–81
financial engineering 115
financial innovation: bricolage 126–9; conjuncture 123–6; crisis 112; critical perspectives 2; current concepts 114–18; hedge funds 244; macro-framing 121–3; reconceptualisation 111–14, 118–21, 129–30; and technological innovation 122

financial literacy 413–14
financial market regulation 289–90, 298–300; and democracies 295–8; detachment from politics 290–4; history 294 *see also* banking regulation; regulation
financial products, mis-selling 280, 284–6
financial secrecy index 252
Financial Services Authority and others v. Amro International and Goodman Jones LLP (interested party) 326
Financial Services Authority (FSA): approach to financial supervision 319; ARROW supervisory framework 319, 323; and consumer finance 421; creation 317–18; financial innovation 112; and HBOS 327; and Libor manipulation 233; and Northern Rock 321, 327; and Royal Bank of Scotland 327; rules and guidance 322; third parties 326
financial sociability, rather than financial culture 404–5
financial stability: and regulatory havens 261–2; and secrecy jurisdictions 260–1, 264
Financial Stability Board (FSB) 144, 196, 197, 295, 328–9
financial working cultures 149–50, 152–3, 156
financialisation: connectedness through 170; consumer products 414–16; government bond markets 134–9; literature 117–18, 159–61; local governments 208–17
financialised bank business models 275–80, 286
first-loss pieces 18
Fitch 12, *13*, 20, 25, 26, 30
floating-rate loans 21
Fool's Gold (Tett) 129
forwards 209, 210, 211
France 140, *143*, 170, 187, 363, 382, 383
Fraser Institute, Economic Freedom of the World Index 388
free banking, in US 358
futures 209–12

G20: automatic information exchange (AIE) 262; consumer protection 412, 418–21; Global LEI System Regulatory Oversight Committee (ROC) 329; High-Level Principles on Financial Consumer Protection 418–21; secrecy jurisdictions 261
Gaussian copula models 25–7, 32
Gen Re 95–6
gender in London financial centre 152
'gentlemanly capitalism' 152–4
geographies of finance 149–50, 156
Germany: accounting rules 169–70; bank funding 203; costs of the financial crisis 363; Eurozone banking union 187–8; Eurozone government debt 140; Frankfurt 151; mortgage-backed securities 382; 'safe' sovereign debt 138–9, 142;

secrecy jurisdictions 257; sovereign bond markets *140*; sovereign debt *143*, 145; sponsor of ABCP 383
Glass-Steagal Act *see* Banking Act (1933) (US) (Glass-Steagall)
global financial crisis (GFC) (2007–09) *see* financial crisis (2007–09)
Global LEI System Regulatory Oversight Committee (ROC) 329
Global Rate Set Systems Ltd 227–8
globalisation 351–3, 374
gold-based monetary systems 5, 351, 352, 353–4, 368
Goldman Sachs 37, 38, 42, 97, 243, 360, 382
Goodhart's Law 366
government bond markets: austerity and financialisation 2, 135–6; collateral damage in the euro crisis 141–2; collateral motive and financialisation 137–9; collateral motive and investor loyalty 140–1; Europe 134–5; and hedge funds 247; limits of loyalty 142–5
Government National Mortgage Association (Ginne Mae) 17
Great Depression 16, 337, 341, 358
Greece: costs of the financial crisis 363; and hedge funds 245; sovereign bond markets *140*; sovereign debt 139, 142, *143*, 175; and vulture fund 243
Greenberg, Hank 94, 95–6, 101–2
Greenspan, Alan 245

hazard rate models, for credit rating of mortgages 20
hedge funds: benefits and costs 243–5; connection with pension funds 170–1; development 240–1; function and features 240; reasons for existence 248; regulation 246–7; resurgence 247; role in the subprime crisis 245–6; strategies 3, 241–3; volumes 122
Hester, Stephen 276
High Frequency Trading 242
hire purchase schemes 61, 67
HM Treasury (UK), and financial market regulation 290
'hold-up' strategy of hedge funds 243–4
Home Owner's Loan Corporation 16
home ownership, and normalising subprime 92–4
Hong Kong 255, 256, 257
House of Commons and House of Lords Commission on Banking Standards 401–2
house prices 375, 388, *389*, *392*
household debt 414–18
households 122, 161–2
HSBC 415
human resources, for judgement based supervision 323–5, 326–7

IBM 400
ICE Benchmark Administration Ltd 227
Iceland 382
IKB 243
Imperial Savings Association 23
imports, financial 354–5, *356*
incentives, driving behaviour 400
inflation, as threat to 'new growth model' 86
information and communication technologies (ICTs) 122, 127
information exchange: automatic (AIE) 262–3; international regulation 295–6; prevention of tax evasion 262–3; sabotage of for tax evasion 259
innovation *see* financial innovation
insurance 19, 42, 340, 345–6
interbank money markets 121, 225–6
interest rate swaps 213–15
interest rates 124, 209, 225–7, 312–15
international financial centres (IFCs) 149–52, 257
International Monetary Fund (IMF) 101, 113, 250, 308, 363
International Organization of Securities Commissions (IOSCO) 235
international political economy (IPE) discipline 252–4, 377–8
International Standards Organisation 328
International Swaps and Derivatives Association (ISDA) 28, 210
internationalisation: City of London 153, 154; financial market regulation 295, 419
investment banking: acquisition of nonbanks 340; business practices 153; competing with commercial banks 339–40, 344; deregulation 345–6; division from commercial banking 336–7; education and training 2, 5, 154–5, 156; failures in risk management 280; leverage 87; separated from retail banking 273, 286; separation from commercial banks 401; working practices 153–4, 156
Investment Management Regulatory Organisation 320
Ireland: bailout 142; costs of the financial crisis 363; household debt-to-net income 414; Irish Financial Centre 256; mortgage-backed securities 382; and offshore finance 256; sovereign bond markets *140*; sovereign debt 139, 142, *143*
Italy: bank funding 203; local authorities and derivatives 3, 212–16; sovereign bond markets *140*; sovereign debt 139, 140, 142, 143, *143*

Japan 352, 382, 383
Jones, Alfred 240, 248
J.P. Morgan 25–6, 95, 119–21, 382
J.P. Morgan Chase 280, 282–4, 335, 360, 363

Index

judgement based supervision: challenges to success 4, 331; components 320–3; contestability 330–1; data challenges 325–8; evolution 318; human resources 323–5, 326–7; LEIs 328–9; links between micro and macro 318–19; obstacles 323–31; origins 319–20
junk bonds 23, 124
jurisprudence, pension funds 168–9

Kaupthing Singer & Friedlander (KSF) 330
knowledge: expert 151; generation 10; importance in IFCs 151, 152–3; sociology 9–16
KPMG 258

labour 124–5, 154–5, 159
Lamfalussy structure 176, 181
law, New York-London axis and international 367
law firms, judgement based supervision 326–7
LCH Clearnet 142
Lebanon 256, 257
Legal Entity Identifiers (LEIs), judgement based supervision 328–9
Lehman Brothers 91–2, 329, 357, 360, 383
leverage, and conjuncture 124
leveraged buy-outs 124
Lévi-Strauss, C. 126–8
Libor (London Interbank Offered Rate): bets 232, 232*b*; generic information *229*; history 225–7; list of main pubic consultations *231*, 235; multi-referential benchmark 227–9, 237–8; normal banking practice 229–33; rate manipulation 3, 233–5; reaction to manipulation and reform 235–7
Liechtenstein 256
liquidity, and hedge funds 244
litigation, judgement based supervision 330–1
Lloyds Banking Group 284–6, 357
Lloyds TSB 285
loan markets 193, 195, 196–7, 199–200
local governments 208–17
logic-of-interpretation claim 179
logic-of-position claim 178–9
logistic regression models, for credit rating of mortgages 20
London: autonomy 294–5; dominance 151; education and training 154–5, 156; emergence 5, 353–4; evolution of financial practices and structures 353–7; financialised working culture 153–5; and global finance 368–9; importance of EU 354; secrecy jurisdictions 257; working culture 149–50, 152–3, 156
London Stock Exchange 354
Long-Term Capital Management hedge fund 18, 244–5
loyalty: and collateral motive in the Eurozone 140–5; government bond markets 135–6; limits in the collateral markets 142–5

Lucas, Charles M. 95
Luxembourg 256, 257

market-based systems: and bank assets 196–200; and non-financial companies finance 192–5; and varieties of capitalism 203–4
market-neutral hedge funds 241–2
markets, sociology of 379–81
Marshall Island 257
MBA degrees 155
media 113, 124
megabanks 360–2, 363–6
Meriwether, John 244
Merrill Lynch 35, 39, 40, 360, 382
mezzanine tranche of securitisation 18–19, 22–3, 36, 89–90
Milken, Michael 23
Mirror Group Newspapers 319–20
misconduct in banking 3
Mitsubishi 383
Mizuho Financial Group 40, 382
monolines 19
Moody's: credit rating 12, *13*; credit rating of ABSs correlation 30; credit rating of CDOs 24, 25, 28; credit rating of mortgage-backed securities 19–21; use of Gaussian copula models 26
Morgan Guarantee Trust 120
Morgan Stanley 35, 39–40, 360, 382
mortgage-backed securities: and banking crisis 384–95; evaluation practices 11, 16–23; explanation *106*; explosion 86–7; foreign ownership 381–4; and the global financial crisis 374–5; and global markets 379–81; losses 9; and shadow banking 79; showing failing to make payments 90; subprime 22 *see also* asset-backed securities (ABSs); collateralised debt obligations (CDOs)
mortgages 16–23, 35, 37–8, 42
multinational companies (MNCs) 256, 259–60, 263–4
mutual funds, volumes 122

National Clothing and Supply (NCS) 59, 60
National Westminster Bank 23
nationalisation, as possibility for UK banks 357
neo-liberal policy 92, 412–14
Netherlands: costs of the financial crisis 363; household debt-to-net income 414; mortgage-backed securities 382; non-bank financial intermediation 197; and offshore finance 256; sovereign bond markets *140*; sovereign debt *143*; sponsor of ABCP 383
networks 151
'new growth model' 85–6, 99, 100–1
New York 5, 149–50, 368–9
New York-London axis 151, 362–8
Nomura 382

Index

non-bank financial institutions 192–7, 340
Northern Rock 92, 201, 278, *278*, 321, 327, 356
Norway 363, 382
NY-LON (New York London) 151, 362–8

off-balance credit intermediation 78–9
offshore financial centres (OFCs): dimensions and effects 259–61; evolution 255–7; growth 250; lack of regulation 3–4, 250–1; lack of research 264; numbers and extent 257–8; regulation 261–5; research 251–5; and tax evasion in banking 250; techniques of avoidance 258–9; users 258
Offshore World, The (Palan) 253
options 25, 209, 226
Organisation for Economic Corporation and Development (OECD) 112, 250, 254, 262, 263–4, 413
organisational procedures: and evaluation practices 12; and vulnerability of mortgages 20–1
organisational structure, and arbitrage 41
organised exchanges: for derivatives 209–10; futures 210–12
'Our Towns' (Women's Group on Public Welfare) 60
overcollateralization safety mechanism 21
over-the-counter (OTC) derivatives 208, 209, 210
ownership 259, 263

Panama 256, 258
Panama papers 82
Parliamentary Commission on Banking Standards 324
pass-through certificates 18
Paulson, John 37, 38, 243, 245
Paybonds Ltd 66
payment protection insurance (PPI) 284–6, 421
Pecora Commission (US) 337
pension funds: connection with hedge funds 170–1; emergence 162–4, 169–70; governance 165–6; investment policies and standard of prudence 166–9; re-allocation of risk to workers and households 161; theoretical and methodological considerations 164–5; volumes 122
People's Bank 2, 67–71
performativity, concept 117
personal accounts, in UK banks 415
personal finance products 416
political parties, hedge fund donations 247
politics, detachment from financial market regulation 290–4
portfolio theory, and standard of prudence 167–9
Portugal: bailout 142; costs of the financial crisis 363; sovereign debt 139, *143*; use of Libor and Euribor *228*, 229–30, 231, 234–5
power, and capitalism 117
practitioners 118–19

prepayment of mortgage-backed securities 17–18, 21–2, 24
PricewaterhouseCoopers 98, 258
private equity: and financial market regulation 297–8; fund volumes 122
Private Equity and Venture Capital Association 297–8
product identifiers 329
professional intermediaries 258
profits, shifting for tax avoidance 263–4
protection, purchases 37–9
Protium Finance LP 280–2
Provident Financial (formerly Provident Clothing and Supply, Provident (C&S)): 1880–1950 56–60; 1950s–1950s 60–5; competitors 59–60; and documentary check trading 55–8; identity 55–6; introduction of vouchers 61; lack of change of system 58–9; marketing sample *66*; as 'the people's banker' 2, 65–71; rapid growth 57; and regulation 2, 56, 60; regulatory flexibility 70; restructuring and listing 61–5; shopping guides *58*, *59*, *65*
prudence: and internal models for banks 307–9; standard for pension fund investment 163–4, 166–9
Prudential Regulatory Authority (PRA): and contestability of judgements 330–1; data challenges 325–8; formation 317–18, 353; human resources 323–5, 326–7; judgement based supervision 318–19, 322–3; key 'bite points' for 320–1; micro supervision 322–3; Proactive Intervention Framework (PIF) 322
Prudential Securities 28–9

Quantitative Easing 247
Quantum Fund 242, 244

ratings-spread nexus, in evaluation practices 13–14
rationality, and financial sociability 405
recession: and ABS CDOs 29; definition 385; model of process for bank crises *385*; and subprime mortgage lending 21
Reconstruction Finance Corporation (RFC) 358
recruitment, into financial services in the City 154–5
reflexivity of shadow banking 74–82
regulation: consumer finance markets 412–13; credit 60–1, 67; differences between supervision and 320; documentary check trading 60–3; financial markets *see* financial market regulation hedge funds 246–7; hire purchase schemes 67; local government use of derivatives 215–16; offshore financial centres (OFCs) 3–4, 250–1, 261–5; prior to financial crisis 317–18; secrecy jurisdictions 261–4; securitisation 81; shadow banking 76, 77, 78–82; stress testing

433

models 401 *see also* banking regulation; deregulation; financial market regulation
'regulatory arbitrage' 121–2
regulatory capital 304–7
regulatory havens 251, 261–2 *see also* offshore financial centres (OFCs)
reinstitutionalisation, of banking activities 338
relationships: banking 153–4; international financial centres (IFCs) 151–2; state and finance 160
relative exposure 136, 140
repo (repurchase agreement) markets 137–8, 142, 176, 201–2
Republican party, hedge fund donations 247
retail banking 273, 280, 284–6
re-theorisation, and deregulation 340–4
return on equity measure, banks 276–7, 279
risk: base of approach to regulatory capital 304–7; calculating 80–1; financial innovation and marketisation 115–16; hedge funds and systemic 244–5; judgement based supervision 321–2; management by derivatives 210, 216–17; meltdown of financial crisis 91; model-based approaches to evaluating 307–9; reallocation to unregulated areas 280–6; regulation 2, 279; shadow banking 78–82; sovereign 142; strategic management at AIG 94–5; stress testing models for evaluation 308–9; systemic 244–5, 318–19, 328–9; valuation 282–4
Rose Funding 23
Royal Bank of Canada 383
Royal Bank of Scotland (RBS) 86, *120*, 243, 245, 276, 277, 357, 382
Russia 363

'safe assets' 137–8, 142
Salamon Brothers 18
Satsuma loan company 70
Sawyer, Andrew J. 211–12
Second Bank of the United States 358
secondary debt market 124
secrecy jurisdictions: dimensions and effects 259–61; and financial stability 260–1, 264; identified by Tax Justice Network (TJN) 257–8; and offshore finance 251; ranking 252; regulation 261–5; research 254–5; and shadow banking 264; users 258
Securities and Exchange Commission 240
Securities and Investments Board (SIB) 320
securitisation: and bank regulation 307–9; boom 124; by building societies 355–7; and conjuncture 124; Europe 199–200; and global finance 379–81; and global financial crisis 88–90; regulation 81; and role of Wall Street 359; United States 199; wonders 107
senior tranche of securitisation 89–90

shadow banking: and banking culture 399; and credit 2, 78; emergence 359; external 366; and financial stability 260–1; growth 137–8; importance 74–5; internal 366; and the New York-London axis 368; as non-bank intermediation 78; notion 75; offshore financial centres (OFCs) 251, 258; reflexivity of 74–82; regulation 76, 77, 78–82, 261–4; rise 195–6; and secrecy jurisdictions 255, 260–1, 264; size of assets 258
shareholder-value oriented corporate governance: banks 275–6, 280, 286–7; case studies of banks 280–6; and cheap credit 85–6; and financial instability 84, 88, 101–2
Singapore 256, 257
Singer, Paul 243
skilled persons reporting in judgement based supervision 326
small and medium-sized businesses (SMEs) 279
social studies of finance 5, 116–17
sociology: and global finance 374; and global financial crisis 15, 378; knowledge 9–16; markets and finance 379–81; offshore finance research 253–4
Soros, George 242, 243, 244, 297
sovereign debt 138–45, 176
sovereign risk 142–5
sovereign wealth funds 122
Spain 139, *140*, 143, *143*, 170, 363, 383
special-purpose vehicles 18, 23, 255
speculative trading 212, 403
Spitzer, Eliot 96
spreads-rating nexus 13–14
Standard & Poors (S&P) 12, *13*, 19–20, 24, 25, 26, 30, 32
standard of prudence, pension fund investment 163–4, 166–9
states: and offshore finance 252–3; relationships with finance 160
sterling, attack on rate from hedge funds 242, 244, 297
stock market crash (1929) 337
stress testing models: bank regulation 4, 315, 401; credit rating of mortgages 20; evaluation of risk 308–9; Federal Reserve Bank 311; post-crisis enhancements 309–11; and rising interest rates 312
subprime mortgage lending: building societies 355–7; collapse 373; concern over default 22–3; credit rating 20–1, *31*; crisis 245–6, 356–7, 362, 393; deregulation and relaxation of restrictions 84–5; and integration of US financial industry 359–60; limitations of corporate governance 85; and mild recession 21; normalising 92–4; and prepayment 21–2; probability assumptions versus realized default rate *34*; role of hedge funds 245–6; showing

failing to make payments 90; shutdown 38; structure of a security 22
Sullivan, Martin 96, 97, 100, 101–2
swaps 209, 212, 213–15, 367 *see also* credit default swaps (CDSs)
swaptions 367
Sweden *143*, 363, 414
Switzerland 256, 257–8, 382, 383
systemic risk: and data challenges 328–9; and hedge funds 244–5; PRA judgements about 318–19 *see also* judgement based supervision

tax avoidance 260–1
tax evasion 259, 260–1, 262–3
tax havens 250–1, 255, 259–60, 354 *see also* offshore financial centres (OFCs)
Tax Justice Network (TJN) 251, 252, 257
tax losses 260–1
technological innovation 122, 341–3, 345
telecommunications 124
Themis Capital 243
theorisation, and bank regulation 4, 337–8
Theory of Economic Development, The (Schumpeter) 114, 124, 129
Thomson/Reuters/Intercontinental Exchange (ICE) 227–8, 231
'too big to fail' 91, 101, 188, 277
total return swaps 367
'Towards Better Reference Rate Practices: A Central Bank Perspective' (BIS) 235
tradable credit indices 37, 38
tranched credit indices 27–8
Trans-European Automated Real-Time Gross Settlement Express Transfer System (TARGET2) 227
transnational companies (TNCs) 252–3, 255, 259
Travellers Insurance Company 340, 344, 346
treasury management firms 254–5
trusts 163, 165–6, 169, 256, 259
Turner Review (UK) 319

UBS 35, 40, 382
unemployment rates 337
unexpected loss 304
United Arab Emirates 257
United Dominions Trust 66
United Kingdom: bailout of banks 91; Banking Acts 69, 320, 330; banking industry 353–7; Banking Standards Review Council 402; banks' customer funding gap 202; 'Big Bang' 85, 92, 354; costs of the financial crisis 363; direct-lending in retail markets 415; economic development 352, 353; evolution of financial practices and structures 353–7; Fair and Effective Markets Review 293; financial centre 352; Financial Services Acts 273, 274, 280, 320, 325, 353; Financial Services Bill (2011) 323, 325–7, 331; and global finance 351–3, 368–9; hegemonic currency 352; high-tech manufacturing 356, *357*; Hire Purchase Acts 60, 61; home ownership 92; House of Commons and House of Lords Commission on Banking Standards 401–2; industrial policy 355–6; mis-selling of PPI 284–6; Moneylenders Acts 60; ownership of US mortgage-backed securities 382; Parliamentary Commission on Banking Standards 324; retail banking 280; sovereign bond markets *140*; sponsor of ABCP 383; taxation 255; university education debt 88; Vickers Report 1, 273–4 *see also* London
United Nations 243
United States: bailout of banks 91; bank holding companies *361*, *362*; banking industry 357–62; commercial banks 358; community banking 360; Community Re-investment Act (CRA) (1977) 85, 92–3, 100; Comptroller of the Currency 345; corporate law 255; corporations with subsidiaries in tax havens 260; costs of the financial crisis (2007–08) 363; credit rating 12; current-account deficit 359; Department of Labor 167; discount rates 340; Dodd-Frank Wall Street Reform and Consumer Protection Act (2010) 1, 246, 273–4, 311, 366, 367; economy 352; Employee Retirement Income Security Act (ERISA) (1974) 165–6, 168–9; evolution of financial practices and structures 357–62; falling house prices 37; federal funds rate *107*; financial centre 4, 352; financial crises 373–4; Financial Modernization Acts 93; Financial Services Modernization Acts 336, 342–3; Financial Stability Oversight Council 273; 'flash crash' (2010) 244; Foreign Account Tax Compliance Act (FATCA) 262–3; GDP and loan growth 363–6; Glass-Steagal Act *see* Banking Act (1933) (US) (Glass-Steagall) and global finance 351–3, 368–9; Gramm-Leach-Bliley Act (Financial Services Modernization Act 1999) 93, 336, 342–3; growth of Wall Street 359; hedge funds regulation 246; hegemonic currency 352; high-tech manufacturing 359; home equity bubble 87; home ownership 87, 92–3; home sales 373; house prices 33, 90–1, 93; housing finance 358; industrial innovation 358; investment banking 87; loan growth 363–6; loan trading 199; megabanks 360–2, 363–6; mortgage defaults 35; mortgage lending 16–23; Office of the Comptroller of the Currency 340, 345; and offshore finance 257; pension funds 162–9; Reconstruction Finance Corporation (RFC) 358; secrecy jurisdiction 257; stock market crash (1929) 337; taxation 255; unemployment rates 337 *see also* New York
universal banking 188, 336–7, 339, 341, 347, 401

Index

value-at-risk (VAR) technique 308–9
Vanquis Bank credit card business 70
Vasicek, Oldrich, model for evaluation of corporate loans 25, 33
venture capital 297
Virgin Islands 257
vouchers 61–3, 70
vulture funds 243

Waddilove, Joshua 56, 57
Warren Report 99
wealth concentration 245, 247, 248, 260
Welby, Justin 357
Wells Fargo 360, 363
Willumstad, Robert 97–8, 102
women, as check trading agents 62, 63–4
workers, exposure to financial markets 161–2
World Bank, World Development Indicators 388